# Supply-Side Economics: A Critical Appraisal

# Supply-Side Economics: A Critical Appraisal

EDITED BY

## RICHARD H. FINK

Director, Center for the Study of Market Processes
Economics Department
GEORGE MASON UNIVERSITY

ALETHEIA BOOKS
UNIVERSITY PUBLICATIONS OF AMERICA

© 1982 by University Publications of America, Inc.
Frederick, Maryland
ISBN: 0-89093-460-6.
Library of Congress Catalog Card Number: 82-051294

Printed in the United States of America

# Table of Contents

# Acknowledgments

The editor expresses his thanks to the following for their generous cooperation:

Paul Craig Roberts's "The Breakdown of the Keynesian Model" is reprinted with the permission of the publisher from *The Public Interest*, no. 52 (Summer 1978), pp. 20-33.

George Gilder's "The Supply Side" is reprinted with the permission of the publisher from *Wealth and Poverty* (New York: Basic Books, Inc., 1981, chapter 4).

Robert L. Heilbroner's "The Demand for the Supply-Side" is reprinted with the permission of the author and publisher from *The New York Review of Books*, vol. 28 (June 11, 1981), pp. 37-41.

Robert E. Keleher's and William P. Orzechowski's "Supply-Side Fiscal Policy: An Historical Analysis of a Rejuvenated Idea" represents the views of the authors, and not necessarily those of the Federal Reserve Bank of Atlanta.

Arthur B. Laffer's "Government Exactions and Revenue Deficiencies" is reprinted with the permission of the publisher from *The Cato Journal*, vol. 1 (Spring 1981), pp. 1-21.

Max Moszer's "A Comment on the Laffer Model" is reprinted with the permission of the publisher from *The Cato Journal*, vol. 1 (Spring 1981), pp. 23-44.

David Henderson's "Limitations of the Laffer Curve as a Justification for Tax Cuts" is reprinted with the permission of the author and publisher from *The Cato Journal,* vol. 1 (Spring 1981), pp. 45-52.

Bruce R. Bartlett's "The Kennedy Tax Cuts" is reprinted with the permission of the publisher from *Reaganomics: Supply-Side Economics in Action* (Westport, CT: Arlington House, 1981, chapter 10).

John Burton's "The Thatcher Experiment: A Requiem?" is reprinted with the permission of the publisher from *The Journal of Labor Research* (1981).

James Tobin's "The Reagan Economic Plan: Supply Side, Budget, and Inflation" is reprinted with the permission of the author and publisher from the *Economic Review* (April 1981).

Robert Hall's "The Reagan Economic Plan: A Discussion" is reprinted with the permission of the author and publisher from the *Economic Review* (April 1981).

Lester C. Thurow's "Slow Economic Growth" is reprinted with the permission of the author and publisher from *The Zero-Sum Society* (New York: Basic Books, Inc., 1980, chapter 4).

James C. Roberts's "The Case for a Return to the Gold Standard: An Interview with Lewis Lehrman" is reprinted with the permission of the publisher from *Human Events*. May 23, 1981.

I would also like to thank all the authors for their contributions and for waiting patiently for the book to appear.

On a more personal level, I would like to thank Randolph Boehm of University Publications of America for his near heroic assistance in helping to make the introduction more readable, tracing down footnotes, proofreading, and a thousand other things. Bruce Bartlett of the Joint Economic Committee was particularly helpful in terms of suggestions for articles to include in this volume. Tyler Cowen and Patti Flynn were able research assistants and Sandy Lore and Jane Williamson steadfastly kept the project organized. I would also like to thank the personnel at Fenwick Library at George Mason University for making work space available for this project.

# Contributors

**Bruce R. Bartlett** is deputy director of the Joint Economic Committee, U.S. Senate, and author of *Reaganomics: Supply-Side Economics in Action.*

**John Burton** is a lecturer in industrial economics and business studies at the University of Birmingham, England. He is the author of, among other works, *The Trojan Horse: Union Power in British Politics.*

**Tyler Cowen** is a research assistant at the Center for the Study of Market Processes, George Mason University, Fairfax, Va.

**Otto Eckstein** is Warburg Professor of Economics at Harvard University and president of Data Resources, Inc. He is the author of, among other works, *Public Finance* and *The Great Recession* and was a member of President Lyndon B. Johnson's Council of Economic Advisors.

**Michael K. Evans** is president of Evans Economics, Inc. and the author of *Macroeconomic Activity: Theory, Forecasting, and Control.*

**Richard H. Fink** is an assistant professor of economics and the director of the Center for the Study of Market Processes, George Mason University, Fairfax, Va.

**George Gilder** is the author of several books on social philosophy, including *Wealth and Poverty* and *Sexual Suicide.* Mr. Gilder is also the program director of the Manhattan Institute.

**Robert Hall** is a professor of economics at Stanford University and a research fellow at the Hoover Institution and was a member of the Reagan administration transition team in 1980.

**Thomas W. Hazlett** is a lecturer in economics at California State University, Fullerton. He has been published in popular periodicals and serves as commentator for "Perspectives on the Economy," a radio program syndicated by the Manhattan Institute.

**Robert L. Heilbroner** is a Norman Thomas Professor of Economics at the New School for Social Research and the author of more than a dozen books, including *The Worldly Philosophers, The Limits of American Capitalism,* and *Marxism, For and Against.*

**Walter W. Heller** is Regents' Professor of Economics at the University of Minnesota and the author of *New Dimensions of Political Economy* and *The Economy: Old Myths and New Realities,* among other works. Professor Heller was chairman of the

President's Council of Economic Advisors, 1961-1964.

**David C. Henderson** is a senior staff economist for the Council of Economic Advisors.

**Manuel H. Johnson** was associate professor of economics at George Mason University and is at present assistant secretary designate for economic policy, U.S. Treasury. He is coauthor of *The Political Economy of Federal Government Growth* and *Deregulating Labor Relations.*

**Stanley Kaish** is chairman of the Department of Economics, Rutgers University, New Brunswick, N.J., and research associate for the Center for International Business Cycle Research. He is the author of *Microeconomics: Logic, Tools, and Analysis.*

**Robert E. Keleher** is senior financial economist for the Federal Reserve Bank of Atlanta and coauthor with William P. Orzechowski of *Supply-Side Economics and the Reagan Experience* (forthcoming).

**Lawrence Klein,** Nobel laureate, is university professor of economics at the University of Pennsylvania and chairman of the board of Wharton Econometric Forecasting Associates. Professor Klein is the author of *The Keynesian Revolution*, and he served as coordinator of President Carter's Economic Task Force.

**Arthur B. Laffer** is the Charles B. Thornton Professor of Business Economics at the University of Southern California. He is the author of *Private Short-Term Capital Flows* and coauthor of *The Economics of the Tax Revolt.*

**Lewis Lehrman** is chairman of the board of Rite-Aid Corporation and president of the Lehrman Institute.

**Max Moszer** is a professor of economics at Virginia Commonwealth University, Richmond, Va.

**William P. Orzechowski** is an assistant professor of economics at George Mason University, Fairfax, Va., and coauthor with Robert E. Keleher of *Supply-Side Economics and the Reagan Experience* (forthcoming).

**Paul Craig Roberts** holds the William E. Simon Chair of Political Economy at Georgetown University's Center for Strategic and International Studies. He was assistant secretary of the treasury for economic policy during the first year of the Reagan administraton and was the chief architect of the original Kemp-Roth tax-cut bill as a Senate staff economist. He is the author of *Alienation and the Soviet Economy* and *Marx's Theory of Exchange, Alienation, and Crisis.*

**Joseph Salerno** is an assistant professor of economics at Rutgers University, New Brunswick, N.J.

**Lester C. Thurow** is a professor of economics and management at the Massachusetts Institute of Technology and the author of *Investing in Human Capital, Generating Inequality*, and *The Zero-Sum Society*, among other works. He is also a popular columnist for the *Los Angeles Times* and *Newsweek.*

**James Tobin,** Nobel laureate, is the Sterling Professor of Economics at Yale University and the author of *Asset Accumulation and Economic Activity* and *The New Economics, One Decade Older.* Professor Tobin served on President Kennedy's Council of Economic Advisors, 1961-62.

**Norman B. Ture** is a former undersecretary of the treasury for tax and economic affairs. He was president of the Institute for Research on the Economics of Taxation, staff economist to the Congressional Joint Economic Committee, 1955-61, and a member of President Nixon's Task Force on Taxation.

# Introduction

Richard H. Fink

Discussions on economic policies often show a tendency to get carried far afield from fundamental issues. Participants in the debate, both consciously and unconsciously, lapse into polemics which both intensify the dispute and serve to obscure the essence of the issues at hand. This tendency, no doubt, springs from anxieties over the potentially significant redistribution of wealth inherent in much economic policymaking. Also prevalent is a certain ideological hubris, particularly when there appears to be a wide divergence in the approaches to as well as results of economic policy alternatives. Given such stakes, both material and mental, perhaps it should not be surprising for economic policy debate to sometimes degenerate into attacks upon the motives or character of the contending parties. The cluster of economic policy proposals introduced by the Reagan administration over the past year (to mention nothing of its congressional and academic antecedents) is clearly of such a nature as to prick the material anxieties and intellectual hubris of both policy makers and citizens alike. The stakes in both areas *are* significant. The debate has shown a tendency toward posturing, emotional excess, and obscurity from many quarters.

This volume is designed to help readers cut through much of the polemics. While not utterly devoid of polemical outbursts itself (they are, after all, useful when kept in a proper perspective), the focus here is to examine the most important issues in economic theory that converge on "supply-side economics." For it is on the level of ideas and not on the level of emotion that the policy should in fact be judged. In deference to the actual stakes, the editor feels that it is absolutely crucial at least to clear the theoretical ground—if not to settle all of the issues—before hardening our positions one way or the other.

In deference also to the fact that there is a considerable ideological dimension to the debate—even when carried on to its more abstract theoretical reaches—this selection presents a fairly full array of perspectives from the different schools of economic thought. Although it was not possible to strike anything like a perfect balance in each of the chapters or the volume as a whole, it should not be difficult for a reader of the text to come away with a fairly good impression of the wide range of perspectives challenging the efficacy of supply-side economic policies and vying to institute their own remedies. Despite the wide range of alternatives, the vital tension in the book is not so much among the critics of supply-side economics, but between those critics (from whatever perspective) and supply-side economics itself. How well do the theoretical underpinnings of America's now-official national economic policy hold up under the onslaught?

Chapter 1 presents three of the finest expositions in favor of supply-side economics that have yet been written. There could probably be no more fitting article to lead off a volume such as this than Paul Craig Roberts's "The Breakdown of the Keynesian Model," for it is clear that this piece has become the modern supply-sider's opening salvo upon the mainstream of contemporary macroeconomic theory. That Roberts was the principal architect of the Kemp-Roth tax-cut plan as a U.S. Senate staff economist reinforces the significance of this essay. This is probably the most important single essay in the supply-side corpus.

Roberts's major point is that the level of aggregation employed in Keynesian economics ignores the critical role of individual decision making in response to government economic policies that affect the self-interest of economic actors. Furthermore, he argues, the present tax structure is a particularly notorious example of the way Keynesian fiscal policy overlooks impacts upon individual decision making, particularly as regards the decisions to work, save, and invest. Thus emerges the policy paradox that, Roberts believes, has been responsible for hobbling American productivity over the past decade: since Keynesian policymakers, see tax cuts or tax rises only in light of their impact upon aggregate demand, they have often stressed the perceived inflationary elements of tax-cut proposals, and ignored the unrelieved and climbing burden of taxation that discourages individuals and firms from saving, investing, and augmenting aggregate supply. Rather than relying on aggregates, Roberts suggests examining the effects of high marginal tax rates in light of microeconomic price theory. Far from eliciting a mere outburst of increased inflation, he argues that, from the point of view of the individual if not from the Keynesian macroeconomist, cuts in marginal tax rates permanently enhance the incentives for Americans to produce their way out of stagflation.

Continuing along these lines is George Gilder. In an extract from his best-selling *Wealth and Poverty*, Gilder focuses upon the role of the individual entrepreneur and also presents a case for a resurrection of the classical supply-side notion embodied in Say's Law—a notion that runs directly counter to the assumptions of the demand-management theories of Keynesian policymakers. He insists that the evidence of modern capitalism makes it clear that it is the producers, the entrepreneurs, in short, "the suppliers" who are the wellspring of economic development. By implication, the demand-orientation of mainstream economics redirects attention from those policy options which are the most hospitable to economic growth.

Norman Ture, until recently President Reagan's under secretary for tax and economic affairs at the U.S. Treasury, provides a more detailed, theoretical analysis in support of supply-side assertions. He builds on the points made by Roberts that Keynesian theory has been at a loss to explain—and has been partly responsible for the poor performance of the economy, and that individuals are more sensitive to policy changes than those with an eye toward aggregate impacts are ever aware. Standard Keynesian tax analysis couches its discussions around the concept of aggregate income effects. Ture suggests applying a neoclassical framework where the impact of tax policies are analyzed in terms of price theory—that is how marginal tax rates affect the relative prices of such things as saving, work, and investment in the eyes of individuals who might be disposed or discouraged to save, work, or invest on the basis of the marginal costs imposed by taxes. He suggests that in light of supply-side price effects, tax policy could be used to deal with an array of economic policy problems conventionally thought neutral in regards to taxation.

Although many of the issues, both explicit and unsaid, that run through the supply-side position presented in the first chapter are discussed in depth throughout all of the succeeding chapters, Chapter 2 offers a broad spectrum of possible points of departure. Walter Heller broaches the subject from the Keynesian perspective; Robert Heilbroner crystalizes a number of fundamental Marxist objections; and Thomas Hazlett responds to Gilder's position in *Wealth and Poverty* from an ardently free market position based on insights of the Austrian school. Heller's admonition that supply-side tax policies of the Reagan administration are on a collision course with their monetarist inclinations regarding money growth is an issue that receives more detailed attention in later chapters as well.

From Robert Heilbroner's point of view, even if the supply-side invention were to work precisely as hoped, inducing a surge of economic "growth," Americans would have done little but jumped from the frying pan into the fire. The assumption common to supply-siders is that once the capitalist engine is well tuned and running to capacity, the passengers seated throughout the whole economy will enjoy a relatively smooth ride of prosperity. Freed from the impediments of government intervention and control, supply-siders feel that the market system is an inherently stable social structure. Indeed, a controversial element of Gilder's thesis is that capitalism is inextricably linked to social cooperation and even to altruistic morality. For Heilbroner, explicitly drawing upon a tradition that he sees stretching from Adam Smith, through Marx, Weber, and Schumpeter, the unencumbered market economy is an inherently unstable and crisis-prone social structure. Government intervention, a crippling factor in

the supply-sider's view, is, for Heilbroner, the delicate bind that alone
keeps the modern capitalist system from unravelling altogether. Given
this rather forbidding chasm between the premises of their respective
positions, Heilbroner suggests that the Marxist debate with supply-
siders must remain on a more fundamental philosophical level than
policy analysis or contemporary economic theory is likely to permit.

Coming from just the other end of the spectrum as defined by
Heilbroner is Thomas Hazlett, who charges that supply-siders do not
go nearly far enough in respecting the "spontaneous order" of the
market process as envisioned by Austrian thinkers such as Menger,
Mises, and Hayek. Unlike Heilbroner, however, Hazlett finds sufficient common ground between Austrian and supply-side analysis to
focus on some of the technical economic implications of supply-side
theory. He argues that supply-siders, especially as represented by
Gilder, confuse demand-management theory with demand theory
(which must indeed be "prior" to supply) and ultimately wind up
defending a version of the cost theory of value. He continues that the
misguided emphasis on supply exhibits a tendency toward govern-
ment-forced "reindustrialization" and expresses an uneasiness that
supply-side goals, as typified by Laffer Curve analysis, are more aimed
at enhancing government revenues than in unleashing the potential of
the market economy.

Chapter 3 examines the link of supply-side thinking to the past.
Robert Keleher and William Orzechowski offer a lengthy argument to
the effect that supply-side economic insights were commonplace for
over a century and a half of Western economic thought. Beginning
with the physiocratic revolt against the high taxes and general economic stagnation throughout France in the eighteenth century, they show
that a sensitivity toward the potentially depressing effects of taxation
has been a major theme running through classical fiscal policy from
Adam Smith through J. B. Say, the Mills, and well on into the
twentieth century, only to be cast into desuetude during the depression
of the 1930s. Far from being an exotic and groundless fad, the authors
argue that supply-side economics rests on coherent classical principles
of public finance, both as regards its claims on economic growth and
on increasing government revenues.

Tyler Cowen focuses on the meaning of Say's Law in the mind of
classical economists (an issue shrouded in considerable controversy)
and to the relevance of Say's Law to the Keynesian revolution of the
1930s. Whether supply-siders are correct in claiming descent from Say
at all is an issue probed in this selection as well.

Probably no single aspect of the supply-side movement has received
more popular attention than the Laffer Curve, which is the subject of
our fourth chapter. The first selection is by Professor Laffer himself,
and offers a theoretical defense of the economic reasoning underlying
his analysis. He claims little originality for the insights depicted by the

curve and like Keleher and Orzechowski in the previous chapter, he traces such insights back to a host of illustrious predecessors. The major question is to decide where the U.S. economy presently stands on the curve. Laffer points to the response of the economy to the federal tax cuts in 1962 and 1964 as evidence that supply-side tax-cut policies are presently appropriate. He argues that the Reagan tax cuts are quite modest but should still evoke supply-side effects.

Max Moszer concedes some of the theoretical relationships portrayed by the Laffer Curve but disputes whether Laffer's analysis is indeed appropriate for the present—that tax receipts could be increased with reductions in tax rates. He claims that the effects of tax cuts claimed by Laffer are contrary to the results of the major econometric models used over the past twenty-five years and suggests that the curve itself may not be the simple parabola which Laffer depicts. In conclusion, Moszer argues that deregulation offers more hope in the areas of economic growth and tax returns than marginal tax cuts.

Like Moszer, David Henderson also argues that the Laffer Curve is overly simplistic, noting the possibility that varying elasticities might enter the picture and warp the curve beyond popular recognition. Indeed, he presents a scenario that runs directly opposite to supply-side claims when the curve does take on a more complex shape. Henderson also casts suspicion on the claim that tax cuts in the early 1960s afford support for supply-side predictions of rapid growth through Reagan tax cuts. There were other factors prevalent throughout the 1960s, such as tariff reductions and the aggregate demand attendant to the coming of age of the postwar baby boom, that need to be worked into any comprehensive model explaining the rapid growth of the decade. Henderson concludes that the best arguments for tax reduction do not follow from supply-side theory at all. Indeed, if the latter were proven spurious, the case for tax relief would not be jeopardized.

One of the major points in Roberts's essay in Chapter 1 is that the aggregate-demand orientation of Keynesian economics has biased econometric models against the supply-side impacts of alternative government policies. He argues that this is particularly true in regard to the disincentive effects of taxes upon work, saving, and investment. Such criticism stirred a running debate among policymaking economists as to whether the traditional large-scale econometric models relied upon by such institutions as the Congressional Budget Office for their evaluations of major legislative policies were in fact suffering from a severe bias themselves. This debate was aired openly (if not conclusively) in 1980 in hearings before the Congressional Joint Economic Committee. The prepared statements submitted to the committee by Otto Eckstein, Lawrence Klein, and Michael K. Evans weigh in on the debate with considerable experience and prestige.

Eckstein, president of Data Resources, Inc., one of America's most prominent economic forecasters, agrees with the charge and points to possible supply-side factors to be included in future models. On the basis of early Data Resources, Inc. analysis, Eckstein feels the overall impact of supply-side policies on economic growth are likely to be significant and he concludes by advocating a moderate supply-side policy.

Lawrence R. Klein, a recent Nobel laureate and chief architect of the Wharton econometric model, disagrees that there has been a bias against supply-side factors in contemporary models. He argues that his Wharton model has accounted for supply-side factors for years and yields results that warrant no special enthusiasm for the likely impact of supply-side policies on economic growth. He warns that while substitution effects may present themselves as a result of supply-side policies, so may income effects. And it is by no means clear what will result from the interplay of the two.

Michael Evans, on the other hand, displays confidence that supply-side policies can make a significant impact on overall economic growth. He outlines his evidence for this position on the basis of his model, which is designed to account fully for supply-side econometric factors, and which is frequently cited by leading supply-siders.

Robert Keleher offers a survey of the empirical evidence relating to the efficacy of supply-side tax policy. He stakes out a position in favor of supply-side policies by integrating the findings of Eckstein and Evans with some more recent empirical studies that show a significant effect on saving and investment from marginal tax cuts. Keleher claims that despite their protests to the contrary, macromodels fail to provide acccurate simulations of supply-side tax cuts because of their aggregate-demand bias, the measurement problems inherent in statistical proxies, and the notorious unreliability of the models in accounting for long-run effects of policy changes (while supply-side effects would appear to be more manifest in a longer-run framework). Instead of relying on econometric models, Keleher suggests that it might be fruitful to focus on historical case studies of supply-side policies and he offers some casual evidence (developed in more depth in Chapter 3) on the Gladstone, Mellon, and Kennedy policies.

To the consternation of many Democratic policymakers, contemporary supply-siders continually point to the experience of the Kennedy tax-cut program as the prototype of what they hope to accomplish. In Chapter 6 Bruce Bartlett and Walter Heller offer conflicting claims over just how close the similarities really are. Bartlett reconstructs the climate in the battle over the Kennedy program, showing that the opponents balked at the tax cuts for fear of diminished revenues and rising deficits, while the administration, including the President himself, stressed the need to stimulate private-sector growth as the real key to fiscal health.

Heller, then chairman of Kennedy's Council of Economic Advisors, offers a personal recollection. Viewing the Kennedy program as consistently Keynesian rather than supply-side, he argues that the immediate result was the stimulation of aggregate demand, and that any supply-side considerations were secondary. He recants his 1963 testimony (cited by Bartlett) claiming that the tax cut would be self-financing, and warns that the Kennedy program should not be lifted out of context. He provides details of the policy implementation that only an insider could, and reiterates that any supply-side effects of the program must be seen in conjunction with aggegrate-demand stimulation.

Another case study of an attempt to revive a slumping economy is Margaret Thatcher's Britain. It is a subject that causes supply-siders nearly as much unease as their own references to Kennedy bring to American liberals. This is the subject of an essay by British economist John Burton. While Thatcher campaigned as an ardent free market advocate, Burton shows that she never embraced the tax-cut program at the heart of supply-side theory. What she did was lower selected taxes in an effort to stimulate investment while raising consumption-oriented taxes in an effort to hedge against budget deficits. On both counts, the results have been dismal. But Burton feels that tax policy is really a minor theme in the Thatcher experiment. Instead he suggest that it can stand as an object lesson to market-oriented policymakers on the perils of attempting to implement free market policies in a society dominated by special interests with a large stake in the status quo; and it also serves as a warning to economists of a monetarist persuasion of just how complex control of the money supply can be.

Both contributors to Chapter 7, America's recent Nobel laureate James Tobin and former Reagan Transition Team advisor Robert Hall, express different kinds of doubts about the monetarist leanings of the Reagan administration. Both fear that a determined effort to crimp money growth will clash head-on with supply-side progrowth aims. Tobin downplays the likely effect of supply-side policies irrespective of monetary policy. He argues that increased taxes do not seem to discourage work effort, so lower tax rates will probably not summon a creative burst of productivity from individual employees. In regards to supply-side effects on saving, Tobin provides his own Laffer Curve analysis to rebut the charge that present tax levels impair aggregate saving.

As if waving a red flag at supply-side's very point of departure from mainstream economics, Tobin asserts that the "aggregate" impact of across-the-board tax cuts will be virtually neutral if tax cuts are followed with cuts in government spending. The impact of the one will tend to cancel out the other. He favors instead a more precisely targeted pattern of tax relief, such as tax inducements for noninflationary wage settlements and pricing policies and tax-cut stimuli for nonresidential fixed capital investment. Targeted tax relief, in his view, holds much more promise in the battle against inflation and sluggish growth than stubborn monetarist strictures on money growth and across-the-board personal tax cuts. In the final analysis, Tobin fears that the Reagan program will accomplish little in reducing inflation and unemployment, but will go far indeed toward regressively redistributing income and in jeopardizing public-sector commitments to protecting the environment.

Robert Hall defends the Reagan administration's attempted deep cuts in domestic budget programs as well as the desirability of the tax cuts (regardless of the validity of the Laffer Curve), but maintains serious reservations with the adminstration's support of the monetarist prescription of a constant rate of growth of the money supply. He argues that except for a safety net of social programs, many domestic programs have become financial "rat holes," being both ineffective and increasingly unpopular. But more than the fiscal drag of these cumulative inefficiencies, Hall fears that excessive government control over economic resources, energy development, and foreign trade seriously impairs economic growth. Yet Hall feels that large defense expenditures are not inconsistent with the other elements of the Reagan program. Like Tobin, he argues that the total size of the public sector relative to the private sector is not the major factor impinging on economic growth. Foreign nations with a larger relative public sector than the U.S. have performed much better economically in recent decades. The key, in Hall's view, is that the American public sector tends to distort and discourage rather than facilitate economic growth.

The problem of growth in the American economy is the subject of closer analysis in Chapter 8. While none of the contributors would classify themselves as supply-siders, each does endorse an element of the supply-side agenda. But in each case, the supply-side prescriptions are enveloped in frameworks quite distinct from the archetypal supply-side argument presented in Chapter 1.

While Lester Thurow feels that the corporate income tax has become an unreasonable double tax upon investment and recommends its abolition, the major thrust of this excerpt from his best-selling *Zero-Sum Society* is that greater government involvement is ultimately necessary to keep pace with rival industrial nations. Thurow argues that the real American growth problem is not merely the need to increase saving and investment but rather to accommodate "disinvestment" from obsolete and unproductive enterprises. Because disinvestment from obsolescent industries entails painful side effects such as unemployment, bankruptcies, and stock losses, economic change tends to be resisted. The American government has responded to this problem by throwing obstacles in the way of disinvestment, when, in Thurow's view, it should be involved in easing the necessary transition of capital and labor to more productive enterprises. Thus, he advocates establishing a national investment board—an organization where government and big business together decide how to redirect resources from "sunset" industries to "sunrise" industries.

My own contribution offers an alternative view of America's growth problems, one whose conclusions diverge sharply from Thurow's. I trace America's growth problems to the misdirection of resources caused by a host of government policies imposing themselves on a market process which is anything but a zero-sum game. From this perspective, the strategy for growth is to remove government obstacles not only from inhibiting "disinvestment" but from allowing the market to perform its coordinating functions among economic plans. I suggest that there is a mistaken tendency to merely juxtapose the American economy with that of Germany or Japan as the grounds for debate on economic growth remedies for America. This sort of analysis confuses correlation with causation. One can find any number of differences between two systems and added together they do not guarantee to be anything more than random impressions, perhaps suggestive as far as they go, but ultimately arbitrary selections of what "count" as the really vital differences. Furthermore, not all the differences would seem to point to the usual conclusion that the U.S. should adopt more elements of the Japanese system—such as creating an America, Inc. along the lines of the much heralded Japan, Inc. For a perhaps vital difference between the nations is that a much larger share of the Japanese economy is oriented to the more competitive international market; while the U.S. economy is largely national—dependent on frequently controlled American markets that inhibit the rigors of competition. If this distinction were to "count" as vital, the implication would be to free the domestic American economy of government regulations to the largest extent possible.

We could go on suggesting vital differences almost without end. The only way, in this author's view, to settle the question of what factors are relevant to economic growth is to turn from the grab bag of sociological generalities and subject explanations to the rigorous tests offered by economic theory. I therefore present the rudiments of a theoretically consistent model of growth as the backdrop against which to evaluate the effect of government policies on sustained economic growth. Finally, this model focuses on factors which tend to be ignored by supply-siders as well as by Keynesian and neoclassical economists, namely the need to take full account of uncertainty and the diffusion of knowledge in the process of coordinated economic growth.

Stanley Kaish both casts suspicion on the claim that supply-side tax cuts will augment savings (which he agrees with supply-siders is the key to sustained economic growth) and advances a proposal to redirect the Reagan tax cut to the Social Security trust fund, saving the fund and bolstering aggregate investment in the process. Kaish argues that there is no sound evidence to suggest that much of the individual tax cuts would find their way into savings. In the aggregate, however, the personal tax cuts represent a significant sum which could be diverted to a new social security fund chartered to invest its proceeds in the economy and eventually supplant the massive transfer obligations of the present system. In time, the self-financing social security system could reduce and eventually eliminate payroll taxes as interest earnings on the fund compound.

Monetary policy tended to receive rather scant attention from supply-side advocates during the late 1970s as well as in the immediate postelection vision of many Reagan administration supply-siders. But the neglect was amply compensated during the summer of 1981 with interest rates soaring and dire predictions of the failure of supply-side policy despite the fact that the policy had hardly been tested. Nevertheless, as growth remained sluggish, unemployment climbed, and the deficit widened, supply-siders increasingly began airing their concerns over the need to link supply-side tax stimulation with monetary policy. Some blamed the limpid supply-side response to the Reagan tax cut on monetarist stringincies on money supply growth. Others advocated a return to some form of the gold standard. Others still defended monetarism as a long-run strategy that will eventually vindicate itself.

Chapter 9 displays a fairly complete range of supply-side positions on monetary policy and concludes with an essay by a non-supply-sider which nevertheless serves in part as a summary of contending monetary policy prescriptions. Manuel Johnson, assistant secretary designate for economic policy of the U.S. Treasury, is one of the supply-siders who subscribe to monetarism as well. As such, he presents the case for the compatibility of these two strains of theory. Indeed, Johnson goes beyond the matter of compatibility to argue that monetarism and supply-side tax relief are mutually dependent. Far from the claims of James Tobin and Robert Hall, Johnson insists the Reagan economic program is consciously coherent. He discusses the general areas of agreement between monetarists and supply-siders, especially their reaction against Keynesian-inspired stagflation. Johnson locates the nub of their disagreement over the issue of the flexibility of the velocity of money. He takes pains to add that the gold-standard advocates among supply-siders are unrepresentative of supply-siders within the Reagan administration.

William Orzechowski suggests that the compatibility between monetarism and supply-side economics is appealing in the long run but runs into potentially insurmountable obstacles in the short run. This is especially so in the case of the more bold supply-side formulations that suggest deep revenue cuts can be made without corresponding cuts in government expenditures—if supply-side effects are not almost immediate, a gaping deficit appears almost inevitable. This in turn brings pressure on the administration to either abandon the tax-cut (supply-side) policy or monetize the difference, thus abandoning monetarist policy. In either case, the supply-side/monetarist combination is ruined. A third alternative is to ignore the deficit altogether. And this is what many supply-siders argue. But that raises the specter of government borrowing having a "crowding out" effect on private enterprise in the capital market, bidding up the interest rate to levels that make it unprofitable for many firms to summon the capital with which to take advantage of the supply-side incentives. Orzechowski suggest that in the short run, it may be necessary to accompany the supply-side/monetarist mix with substantial revenue reductions.

Lewis Lehrman is one of the most outspoken advocates of the gold standard in high level Republican policy circles. An admirer of the late French Finance Minister Jacques Rueff, who twice this century rescued the failing French currency by restoring convertibility of the franc to gold, Lehrman believes convertibility is also a key to rescuing the American economy. In Lehrman's view, interest rates are high, not only because of the "crowding out" impact of budget deficits upon the private capital markets, but because both lenders and savers do not trust the value of money which can be depreciated by a mere change of heart in any federal administration. They thus exact an inflationary premium which will not subside until confidence in the value of the dollar is restored against the inflationary tendencies of the federal government. In Lehrman's view, gold backing is not a panacea, but is historically the only workable solution to shore up the erosion of confidence in money.

Joseph Salerno overviews the debate on the revival of the gold standard with admirable concision and also analyzes Keynesian and monetarist policies. He advances the case for a 100 percent gold standard—a position fundamentally different from Lehrman's fractional reserve requirement proposal—under the belief that any link between the money supply and government exposes society to the likelihood of disastrous inflation as governments eventually abuse their control. In addressing objections to the gold standard itself, Salerno argues that the critics usually fail to consider the ability of the price mechanism to clear supply and demand for money just as it does for other economic goods and services. He traces most of the alleged clumsiness of the system not to anything inherent in a true 100 percent gold standard but to the fact that historical gold-based currency systems have themselves been abused through government interference. To the degree that governments have maintained any control over the gold-based monetary system, and especially when they intentionally abuse it, the natural price-clearing mechanism has been thwarted. It is this, in Salerno's view, that has given the gold standard an undeserved reputation as an impractical system. And it is this that Salerno claims constitutes the major flaw in Lehrman's proposal.

Having ranged from Roberts's challenge to Keynesian macromodels, to Lehrman's and Salerno's arguments for comprehensive monetary reform; from Heilbroner's apprehensions that supply-siders are plodding down the primrose path to social disruption to Thomas Hazlett's suspicion that they do not truly respect the spontaneous order of the unhampered market; from case studies of alleged supply-side policies to historical assessments of supply-side's intellectual heritage; from macromodels to Laffer Curves—it becomes obvious that there is a rather large constellation of issues emerging with the dawn of supply-side economics. This is so whether supply-side is viewed primarily at the theoretical level or at the level of policy implementation. What is supply-side economics really all about? Has the Reagan administration adopted too much of the doctrine or not enough? It is the editor's hope that the contributions which follow help to sharpen the issues in what promises to be a long and robust debate.

# Chapter 1:
# The Supply-Side Argument

## The Breakdown of the Keynesian Model

### Paul Craig Roberts

There is much talk these days about "the crisis in Keynesian economics." That some such crisis exists is evident from the bewilderment and impotence our economic policymakers are displaying in their confrontation with economic reality. But what exactly is the nature of this crisis? What went wrong and what can put it right?

The answer, I would suggest, is almost embarrassingly simple. Today in the United States, public economic policy is formulated in bland disregard of the human incentives upon which the economy relies. Instead it is based on the Keynesian assumption that the gross national product (GNP) and employment are determined only by the level of aggregate demand or total spending in the economy. Unemployment and low rates of economic growth are seen as evidence of insufficient spending. The standard remedy is for government to increase total spending by incurring a deficit in its budget. GNP, it is believed, will then rise by some multiple of the increase in spending. Keynesian economics focuses on estimating the "spending gap" and the "multiplier" so that the necessary deficit can be calculated.

This view of economic policy is enshrined in the large-scale econometric forecasting models upon which both Congress and the executive branch rely for simulations of economic policy alternatives. It is a view that is extraordinary in its emphasis on spending. True, it is obvious that if people did not buy, no one would produce for market. It also seems obvious that the more people buy, the more will be produced and, therefore, that the use of government fiscal policy to increase total demand will increase total production or GNP. All this is so obvious to Keynesians that they believe any fiscal policy that produces an increase in government spending, even a spending increase matched by a tax increase, will produce an increase in GNP.

The concept of the "balanced-budget multiplier" illustrates the primacy that Keynesians give to spending as the determinant of production. According to this concept, government can increase total spending and, thereby, GNP by raising taxes and spending the revenues. The reasoning is as follows. People do not pay the higher taxes only by reducing their spending (consumption); they also reduce their savings. Therefore, when taxes are raised, the decrease in private spending is less than the increase in government spending. Conversely, a cut in tax rates, matched by a decrease in government spending, would result in a reduction in total spending (i.e., saving would increase), a fall in GNP, and a rise in unemployment.

For years after the 1964 presidential election, college students were asked a standard question on economic exams: What would happen if Barry Goldwater's prescriptions for a tax cut, matched with a spending cut, were implemented? They missed the answer if they did not reply that there would be a reduction in aggregate demand and, therefore, a fall in GNP and employment. Alas, for too many policymakers that is still the answer.

Since the "balanced-budget multiplier" implies that the greater the increase in taxes and in government spending, the greater the increase in GNP, it is a wonder no one ever asked what happens to production as tax rates rise. This question confronts economic policy with the incentive effects it has disregarded. It should be obvious even to Keynesians that when marginal tax rates are high, people will prefer additional leisure to additional current income and additional current consumption to additional future income. As work effort and investment decline, production will fall, regardless of how great an increase there might be in aggregate demand. Such a recognition of disincentives implies a recognition of incentives, and Keynesians are gradually having to rethink the answer to their standard question about Barry Goldwater. Once one recognizes that people produce and invest for income, and that income depends on tax rates, one has reached the realization that *fiscal policy causes changes not just in demand but also in supply.*

## The economics of supply

The economics of spending has thoroughly neglected the economics of supply. On the supply side there are two important relative prices governing production. One price determines the choice between additional current income and leisure; the other determines the choice between additional future income (investment) and current consumption. Both prices are affected by the marginal tax rates. The higher the tax rates on earnings, the lower the cost of leisure and current consumption, in terms of foregone after-tax income.

As an illustration, consider the decision to produce. There are two uses of time—work and leisure. Each use has a price relative to the other. The price of additional leisure is the amount of income foregone by not working, and it is influenced by the tax rates. The higher the tax rates, the smaller the amount of after-tax income foregone by enjoying additional leisure. In other words, the higher the tax rates, the lower the relative price of leisure. When the marginal tax rate reaches 100 percent, the relative price of additional leisure becomes zero. At that point, additional leisure becomes a free good, because nothing has to be sacrificed in order to acquire it.

We often hear that a person works the first five months of the year for the government, and then starts working for himself. But that is not the way it goes. The first part of the year, he works for himself; he only begins working for the government when his income reaches taxable levels. The more he earns, the more he works for the government, until rising marginal rates discourage him from further work.

Take the case of a physician who encounters the 50 percent rate after six, eight, or ten months of work. He is faced with working another six, four, or two months for only 50 percent of his earnings. Such a low after-tax return on their efforts encourages doctors to share practices, to reduce their working hours, and to take longer vacations. The high tax rates thus shrink the tax base by discouraging them from earning additional amounts of taxable income. They also drive up the cost of medical care by reducing the supply of medical services. A tax rate reduction would raise the relative price of leisure and result in more taxable income earned and also in a greater supply of medical services.

The effect of tax rates on the decision to earn additional taxable income is not limited to physicians or to the top tax bracket; it operates across the spectrum of tax brackets. Studies by Martin Feldstein show that the tax rates on the average worker practically eliminate the gap between his after-tax take-home pay and the level of untaxed unemployment compensation he could be receiving if he did not work. In this case, a marginal tax rate of 30 percent (including state and federal income taxes and Social Security taxes) reduces the relative price of leisure so much that, by making unemployment competitive with work, it has raised the measured rate of unemployment by 1.25 percent and shrunk GNP and the tax base by the lost production of one million workers.[1]

It is useful to give another example to illustrate that it is not just the top marginal rate that causes losses to GNP, employment, and tax revenues by discouraging people from earning additional taxable income. Blue-collar workers do not yet encounter the top marginal tax rate (although if inflation continues to push up money incomes, and the tax rate structure remains unadjusted for inflation, it will not be many years before they do). Nevertheless, the marginal tax rates that many blue-collar workers already face are high enough to discourage them from earning additional taxable income. Take the case of a carpenter facing only a 25 percent marginal tax rate. For every additional $100 he earns before income tax, he gets to keep $75. Suppose that his house needs painting and that he can hire a painter for $80 a day and hire himself out for $100 a day. However, since his after-tax earnings are only $75, he saves $5 by painting his own house, so it pays him to choose not to earn the additional $100. In this case, the tax base shrinks by $180—of which $100 is the foregone earnings of the carpenter, and $80 is the lost earnings of the painter who is not hired. (Also, the productive efficiency associated with the division of labor vanishes.)

Suppose, instead, that the marginal tax rate on additional earnings by the carpenter was reduced to 15 percent. In this case, his after-tax earnings would be $85, and it would pay him to hire the painter. The reduction in the marginal tax rate would thus expand the tax base upon which revenues are collected by $180.

Studies by Gary Becker have made it clear that capital and labor are employed by households to produce utility through nonmarket activities (e.g., a carpenter painting his own house).[2] Utility produced in this way is not purchased with income subject to taxation. Therefore, the amount of household-owned capital and labor supplied in the market will be influenced by marginal tax rates. The lower the after-tax income earned by supplying additional labor and capital in the market, the less the utility that the additional income can provide, and the more likely it is that households can increase their utility by allocating their productive resources to nonmarket activities. A clear implication of the new household economics is that *the amount of labor and capital supplied in the market is influenced by the marginal tax rates.*

Now consider how relative prices affect the choice concerning the use of income. There are two uses of income, consumption and saving (investment), and each has a price in terms of the other. The price of additional current consumption is the amount of future income foregone by enjoying additional current consumption. The higher the tax rates, the smaller the amount of after-tax future income foregone by enjoying additional current consumption. In other words, the higher the tax rates, the lower the relative price of current consumption.

Take the case of an Englishman facing the 98 percent marginal tax rate on investment income. He has the choice of saving $50,000 at a 17 percent rate of return, which would bring him $8,500 per year before taxes, or purchasing a Rolls Royce. Since the after-tax value of that $8,500 additional income is only $170 per year, the price of additional consumption is very low: He can enjoy having a fine motor car by giving up only $170 per year of additional income. This is why so many Rolls Royces are seen in England today. They are mistaken for signs of prosperity, whereas, in fact, they are signs of high tax rates on investment income.

A tax-rate reduction would raise the price of current consumption relative to future income, and thus result in more savings, making possible a growth in real investment. A rate reduction not only increases disposable income and total spending, *it also changes the composition of total spending toward more investment.* Thus, labor productivity, employment, and real GNP are raised above the levels that would result from the same amount of total spending more heavily weighted toward current consumption.

## Tax cuts and rebates

The econometric models upon which the government relies for simulations of policy alternatives do not take into account these supply-side effects on GNP of these relative price changes. Consider the alternatives faced by the Keynesian policymaker who wants "to get the economy moving again." His goal is to increase aggregate demand or total spending. How can he do this? He has the choice between the balanced-budget multiplier (i.e., increasing both taxes and government spending) or a deficit. He will discard the balanced-budget multiplier, because it is relatively weak and deficits are more politically acceptable than legislating higher tax rates. Having settled on a deficit, he has to choose how to produce it. He can hold tax revenues constant and increase government spending, or he can hold government spending constant and cut tax revenues. In the latter case, he has a choice between rebates and permanent reductions in tax rates. Wanting the most stimulus for his deficit dollar, he will ask for econometric simulations of his three policy alternatives: a tax rebate, a tax rate reduction, or an increase in government spending programs.

The simulations, all based on Keynesian assumptions, will show that a revenue reduction of a given amount, whether in the form of a rebate of personal income taxes or a reduction in personal income tax rates, will raise disposable income—and thereby spending and GNP — by the same amount. The policymaker may prefer the rebate for reasons of "flexibility." The spending stimulus may not be required in the following year, and, if it is, he has the option of providing it either by another rebate or by an increase in government spending programs. But on the basis of the econometric simulation, he will be indifferent as to the choice between rebates or rate reductions. As for his third option, an increase in government spending programs, the simulation may report that, dollar for dollar, an increase in government purchases (as contrasted with transfers) will have a more powerful impact on GNP because the government spends all the money, whereas if it is returned to consumers they will save part of it. Based on the econometric simulation of his alternatives, he will conclude that there is no compelling economic reason in favor of any of the three, and he will make his choice on a political basis.

But the econometric models have misled the policymaker. Unlike a reduction in personal income tax rates, a rebate affects no individual choice at the margin. It does not change the relative prices governing the choices between additional current income and leisure or between additional future income and current consumption. It does not raise the relative prices of leisure and current consumption. Therefore, a rebate directly stimulates neither work nor investment. For any given revenue reduction, a rebate cannot cause as great an increase in GNP as a rate reduction, because it does not affect the choices that would cause people to allocate more time and more income to increasing production for the market.

An increase in government spending fares no better by comparison, and may fare even worse. It too fails to raise the after-tax rewards for work and investment. Furthermore, it increases the percentage of total resources used in the government sector. If the government sector uses resources less efficiently than the private sector, as seems to be the case, the result is a decline in the efficiency with which resources are used—which means GNP would be less than it otherwise would be. Yet the econometric simulations of the policymaker's alternatives will pick up none of the incentive and disincentive effects of these relative price changes. Instead, they focus on the effects of these alternatives on disposable income and on spending.

There are a number of adverse consequences of this extraordinary preoccupation with spending. One is that *the models exaggerate the net tax-revenue losses that result from cutting tax rates.* The only "feedback effect" on the tax base and tax revenues that they provide for is the expansion of GNP in response to an increase in demand. They do not provide for the expansion in GNP that results from higher after-tax rewards for work and investment. The supply-side "feedback effects" are ignored. Similarly, revenue gains from tax rate increases will be overestimated, because the disincentive effects are left out.

A second consequence follows from the popular misidentification of a tax rebate as a tax cut, and from a similar tendency on the part of most policymakers to see rebates and rate cuts as variations of the same policy instrument. If Milton Friedman is correct that personal consumption is a function of *permanent* income, a temporary rebate has little impact even on spending.[3] Thus, on the basis of experience with rebates, tax cuts per se might come to be seen as relatively ineffectual, leaving the field open to proponents of government spending programs.

A third consequence is that the true effects of large tax increases (such as the proposed energy taxes, or the $227 billion increase in the Social Security tax over the next decade) will not be accurately calculated. Policymakers see these tax increases as withdrawals from disposable income and spending, and their only concern is "to put money back" into spending so that aggregate demand does not fall. However, these tax increases change the *relative* prices and incentives of leisure and work, consumption and investment. They produce resource reallocations that have adverse implications for employment and the rate of economic growth. Yet the econometric models, as now constructed, flash no warning lights.

Consider what Arthur Laffer, in the *Wall Street Journal*, has called the "tax wedge." The Social Security tax increase provides a good example of this phenomenon. It is a tax on employment, and, as economists should know, a tax on employment will reduce employment. The employer's decision to hire is based on the gross cost to him of an employee. The employee's decision to work is based on his after-tax pay. We know that the higher the price, the less the quantity demanded, and the lower the price, the less the quantity supplied. The Social Security tax both raises the price to the demander and lowers it to the supplier. By increasing the Social Security tax, policymakers reduced both job opportunities and the inclination to work.[4] They raised the cost of labor relative to capital for the employer, and they narrowed the gap between unemployment compensation and after-tax take-home pay for a wider range of workers. Since the revenues available for paying Social Security benefits depend on both the tax rates and the number of people paying into the system, the increase in rates will be offset to some degree by a decrease in the number of people paying into the system. It is hard to see how the Social Security system can be saved by decreasing employment, or how increasing the demand for unemployment compensation is likely to free general revenues for Social Security benefits.

### "Crowding out" investment

There are at least two other important points on which economic policy is misinformed by the neglect of incentives and of choices made at the margin. One is the impact on GNP of reductions in the corporate income tax rate, and the other is the controversy over whether government fiscal policy "crowds out" private investment.

Simulations run by the Congressional Budget Office and the House Budget Committee on two of the three large-scale commercial econometric models show *declines* in GNP as a result of reductions in corporate tax rates.[5] In one of the models, corporate investment did not depend on after-tax profits in a very strong way, but was very sensitive to changes in interest rates. Since interest rates rise as the Treasury increases its borrowing to finance the deficit resulting from the tax cut, investment falls, and *the model predicted a decline in GNP as the result of a tax rate reduction that increased the profitability of investment.*[6]

The other model predicted that a corporate tax rate reduction would slightly raise real GNP after a lag of a couple of quarters, but it predicted a lower nominal GNP for two years. Nominal GNP declined because the corporate tax rate reduction reduced the user cost of capital, the price mark-up, and thereby the inflation rate, thus lowering the nominal price level.

To the extent that Keynesians think about the "crowding out" of private investment by fiscal policy, it is in terms of upward pressure on interest rates as a result of government borrowing to finance budget deficits. They do not realize that *investment is crowded out by taxation, regardless of whether the budget is in balance.* To understand how, consider the following example. Suppose that a 10 percent rate of return must be earned if an investment is to be undertaken. In the event that government imposes a 50 percent tax rate on investment income, investments earning 10 percent will no longer be undertaken. Only investments earning 20 percent before tax will return 10 percent after tax. Taxation crowds out investment by reducing the number of profitable investments. When tax rates are reduced, after-tax rates of return rise, and the number of profitable investments increases.

So "crowding out" cannot be correctly analyzed merely in terms of events in the financial markets: "Crowding out" occurs in terms of real output. It is the preempting of production capacity by government outlays, regardless of whether these outlays are financed by taxing, borrowing, or money creation.

## Responding to incentives

A concern with the supply-side effects of fiscal policy is incompatible with the concept of economic policy that currently reigns in the Congress and in the executive branch. Members of the House Budget Committee asked Alice Rivlin, director of the Congressional Budget Office, and Bert Lance, then director of the Office of Management and Budget, about the neglect of the incentive effects of tax rate changes on supply and also about the econometric predictions that GNP would fall in response to a reduction in corporate tax rates.

Dr. Rivlin said that she and her staff had been "particularly troubled" by model findings that GNP declines if corporate tax rates are reduced. However, she went on to say:

> Studies have generally found that tax-rate changes are less important than changes in the cost of capital and changes in levels of national output in influencing the level of investment. It follows that an investment tax credit or liberalized depreciation will increase investment more than a corporate tax rate reduction of equivalent revenue loss. While we do not believe that corporate tax rate cuts reduce investment, it would not be surprising to find that tax cuts had only a minor expansionary effect.[7]

The OMB staff reply to this question was ambiguous.

Both CBO and OMB realized that the question about incentive effects most fundamentally challenged their concept of economic policy. The comments of Rivlin, Lance, and the OMB staff all unequivocally acknowledged that the econometric models upon which they rely for guidance in the choice of economic policy alternatives do not include any relative price effects of changes in personal income tax rates. However, since they believe that the performance of the economy is a function of spending levels, not of production incentives, they expressed no concern over this neglect. They said that economic theory and empirical studies leave it unclear whether the neglected supply-side effects are important; regardless of how the issue is resolved, they questioned the practical importance of supply incentives for short-run policy analysis.

There are two parts to this argument. One is that it is unclear whether lowering personal income tax rates will increase or reduce work effort. The other is that it is unclear whether any incentive effects on work effort and investment would show up as quantitatively important in a short-run policy framework. The first proposition questions the existence of the incentive effects; the second questions whether they would be effective in time to deal with an immediate problem of economic stabilization.

It is easy to dispose of the latter point. The long run consists of a series of short runs. If policies that are effective over a longer period are neglected because they do not have an immediate impact, and if policies that are damaging over the longer period are adopted because they initially have beneficial results, then policymakers will inevitably come to experience, sometime in the future, a period when they will have no solution for the crisis they have provoked. In the United States, that future might be now.

As for the first point, Rivlin acknowledged that a personal income tax rate reduction raises the relative price of leisure, and that work effort will increase as people substitute income for leisure. This is known in economics as the "substitution effect," and it works to increase supply. However, Rivlin also said:

> It is also theoretically arguable that when a tax cut provides people with more after-tax income, many of them will *reduce* effort through what is called the income effect. For most people, leisure has some positive value, and it may even be a "luxury" good; these people could respond to a tax reduction by reducing their working hours, benefiting from more leisure time and still maintaining their after-tax income. For other people who like their work, there may be little or no labor supply response to the income *or* the substitution effect. In much of the United States economy, work weeks are fixed, leaving little possibility for individuals to make marginal adjustments in hours of work.[8]

In other words, CBO believes that the "income effect" works to decrease supply.

Rivlin then went on to say that it was an empirical question whether the "income effect" offset the "substitution effect," referred to a narrow range of studies that left the question unresolved, and concluded: "In the range of policy options that we have been dealing with, I think the assumption that changes in marginal tax rates have no quantitatively significant effect on labor supply is quite plausible."

But the concept of a targeted or desired level of income unaffected by the cost of acquiring such income is foreign to the price-theoretical perspective of economic science. Rivlin's idea that people respond to a cut in income tax rates by maintaining their existing income levels while enjoying more leisure implies that, if their tax rates went up, they would work harder in order to maintain their desired income level. Lester Thurow has actually employed this reasoning to argue for a wealth tax.[9] According to Thurow, a wealth tax is a costless way to raise revenues because the "income effect" runs counter to and dominates the "substitution effect." He assumes that people have a targeted level of wealth, irrespective of the cost of acquiring it. Therefore, he says, a tax on wealth will cause people to work harder in order to maintain, after tax, their desired wealth level.

Note the perverse ways in which people respond to incentives and disincentives according to the Rivlin-Thurow line of argument: When tax rates go down and the relative price of leisure rises, people demand more leisure; when tax rates go up and the relative price of leisure falls, people demand less leisure. In economics, any time the "income effect" works counter to the "substitution effect," we have the relatively rare case of what is called an "inferior good" (i.e., people purchase less of it as their income rises). Since income is command over all goods, Rivlin's argument implies that *all* goods are inferior goods: A tax cut will cause people to purchase only more leisure, not more income (i.e., goods). What kind of people are these? Well, the only kind of people who fit this kind of economic analysis are people who respond to a monetary incentive in perverse ways.

Perhaps Rivlin merely meant to say that lower tax rates would allow people to have a *little* more income for a *little* less work. Even so, as long as she maintains that the "income effect" works counter to the "substitution effect," her argument carries the implication that goods in general are inferior.

## A perverse logic

Whatever the weight one assigns this point, there is a more fundamental defect in her argument. Notice the stunning inconsistency: People respond to a tax rate reduction "by reducing their working hours . . . and still maintaining their after-tax income." But it is impossible for people *in the aggregate* to reduce their work effort and maintain the same level of *aggregate* real income! If people respond to tax cuts by working less, real GNP would fall, and it would be impossible to increase real disposable income, spending, and demand in the aggregate. Rivlin's argument is directed against the effectiveness of incentives in raising aggregate output, but if she were correct, it would mean that Keynesian fiscal policy also is ineffective!

The fatal error in the Rivlin-Thurow argument can be put this way:

It derives from trying to aggregate a series of partial equilibrium analyses (individual responses to a change in relative prices) and, in the aggregate, ignoring the *general* equilibrium effects.

There are various ways a noneconomist can grasp this point. Assume that the government cuts taxes and maintains a balanced budget by reducing spending. In this case, the higher income accorded the taxpayers whose rates are reduced must be matched by a negative impact on the incomes of recipients of government spending. Some or all of these may be the same people. Assume, for example, that both the tax burden and government spending are evenly distributed. In this case the "income effect" (the substitution of leisure for work) "nets out" for each individual. Since the aggregate income effect is zero, it cannot offset the "substitution effect" (the substitution of work for leisure).

If taxes are cut and government spending is unchanged (resulting in a budget deficit), the nominal disposable income of taxpayers as a group will rise relative to the nominal disposable income of the recipients of government spending as a group. The former will be able to bid real resources away from the latter. The real income gains of the former will be matched by the real income losses of the latter. Since the bidding will raise prices, the real income loss might be suffered by individuals who hold money. Regardless of who loses and who gains, the individual income effects "net out," leaving only the "substitution effects," which unambiguously increase work effort.

There can be no aggregate "income effect" unless the impact of incentives is to raise real aggregate income. Economic theory makes it perfectly clear that a tax rate reduction will increase work effort and total output.

In the final analysis, Rivlin's argument is not that the supply-side incentive effects are unimportant, but the equally false argument that their impact is perverse—that is, only a tax rate *increase* can produce a rise in real national income! She may not actually believe any such thing, of course—but that is where her reasoning leads her.

### From economics to politics

An economist might see the flaw in the Rivlin-Thurow argument, but it is not obvious to politicians. Take something simple, like Rivlin's assertion that a fixed work week precludes adjustment of the labor supply to tax rate changes. To an economist her assertion is obviously false, but to the politician it sounds reasonable enough. He will not realize that the "adjustments" will be reflected in absenteeism rates, turnover rates, the average duration of unemployment, labor negotiations for shorter work weeks and more paid vacation rather than higher wages, and in the quality and intensity of work. Nor will he think of the entrepreneur who, because of high tax rates, loses his incentive to innovate—to make the economy itself (all of us) more productive.

Besides, one has to have an idealistic view of government to believe that politicians even want to know. The Keynesian concept of the economy is that of an unstable private sector that must be stabilized by fiscal and monetary policies of the government. This view has served as a ramp for the expansion of the interests of government. It has also served the interests of economists by transforming them from ivory-tower denizens to public-spirited social activists, a transformation which has much increased their power and enlivened their lifestyles. Unemployment can always be said to be too high. And the rate of economic growth can always be found to be below "potential." This means that there is always a "scientific" economic reason for expand-ing government spending programs that enlarge the constituencies of the Congress and of the federal bureaucracy. From the standpoint of the private interests of policymakers, Keynesian economic policy will always be judged a success.

To write about all of the problems of econometrics and economic policy would require a book, not an article, but one other important problem must be mentioned in closing. Professor Robert Lucas has demonstrated that the standard econometric models assume that the structure of the economy remains invariant under wide variations in policy paths.[10] What this means is that the models assume that people do not learn. But people do learn, and their expectations change as they experience various policies: They may not repeat the same behavior in response to the same policy at different times. Therefore, the policy simulation may always misinform the policymakers. This is not an optimistic note on which to end an article about public policy in a country that believes we need a great deal of it. But our faith in public policy has exceeded our knowledge, and we will find out that, in this area, there is no such thing as free faith.

# Notes

1. Martin Feldstein, "Unemployment Compensation: Its Effect on Unemploy-ment," *Monthly Labor Review* 99 (March 1976): 39-41; idem, "The Effect of Temporary Unemployment Insurance on Temporary Layoff Unemployment," *American Economic Review* 68 (December 1978): 834.

2. Gary S. Becker, *Human Capital: A Theoretical and Empirical Analysis*, 2d ed. (University of Chicago Press, 1975).

3. Milton Friedman, *A Theory of the Consumption Function* (Princeton University Press, 1957).

4. Theoretically, the effect on work effort depends on the present value of the Social Security benefits and taxes. If the increased tax means increased future benefits, the employee's work decision will take into account his increased future income, as well as his reduced current income. However, the recent changes in the Social Security law raised taxes and reduced benefits as a proportion of pay before retirement. As the *Wall Street Journal* put it, "The extra money will go to pay people now or soon to be on the retirement rolls, not to finance your own high living in the 21st century" (February 6, 1978).

5. *See Congressional Record*, House of Representatives, February 22, 1977, p. 81308, Mr. Rousselot.

6. According to staff in the Office of Management and Budget, there have recently been changes in the model, but one can still get the perverse result because a reduction in the tax rate directly and substantially reduces multi-unit housing starts.

7. Letter from Alice Rivlin to Reps. John Rousselot and Del Latta, March 11, 1977, cited in *Congressional Record*, House of Representatives, July 11, 1978, p. 20134-20135, Mr. Rousselot.

8. Ibid.

9. Lester C. Thurow, "Tax Wealth, Not Income," *New York Times Magazine*, April 11, 1976, p. 32.

10. Robert E. Lucas, "Econometric Policy Evaluation," in Karl Brunner and Allan H. Meltzer eds., *The Phillips Curve and Labor Markets* (New York: American Elsevier Pub. Co., 1976).

# The Supply-Side

George Gilder

The source of the gifts of capitalism is the supply-side of the economy. In the capitalist economies of the West, this simple recognition is the core of all successful economic policy. It is a principle sometimes as obscure to conservatives, with their often excessive preoccupation with the statistics of money and deficit spending, as it is to liberals, with their obsession for aggregate demand and consumer spending. Wisdom on the subject can sometimes be found in strange places. Even Karl Marx knew enough not to stress, as the crux and keystone of capitalism, control over the means of *consumption*! Or even of the supply of money.

Marx, however, erroneously located the means of production in the material arrangements of the society rather than in the metaphysical capital of human freedom and creativity. The problem of contemporary capitalism lies not chiefly in a deterioration of physical capital, but in a persistent subversion of the psychological means of production—the morale and inspiration of economic man—undermining the very conscience of capitalism: the awareness that one must give in order to get, supply in order to demand.

The trend seems to have begun in politics. In fact, our current situation recalls the world in which economic science gained its first triumphs. This was the age of mercantilism, a time of a similar hypertrophy of politics, when Adam Smith reproached the governments of Europe for believing that the power of demand, in the form of accumulated gold, constituted the source of wealth. In *The Wealth of Nations* Smith argued that the real riches came from the power of production and supply, not bullion collected through a trade surplus.

But during the two centuries since Smith won this initial victory for supply-side economics, the demand side has all too often triumphed. The problem begins in political philosophy: in the theory of politics and public opinion.

Democratic politics are founded on a group of formal equalities—legal and electoral—ultimately deriving from a religious belief in the equality of men before God. Nonetheless, these equalities, in a more immediate sense, are largely mythological. One man may be restricted to one vote, but some men by their energy and eloquence, or their command of the media, may sway the opinions of millions. An elected leader may be expected to represent the views and interests of his constituency. But he may also, during the course of campaigning and in the conduct of his office, deeply affect the beliefs and decisively interpret the interests of his public. A realistic analysis will show that leaders, to the extent that they bear real authority, tend to create the views of their larger constituencies more than they follow them, particularly on technical or complex matters.

The public—as Walter Lippmann demonstrated, one should have thought for all time, in his magisterial work *Public Opinion*—is largely a phantom. On many issues, public opinion, as the term is commonly used, does not exist. Polls, it might be plausibly said, often create their own opinion. Out of the shifting and shadowy shapes of largely amorphous sentiment, they contrive spuriously discreet and definite sums—aggregates of air. Political leaders, in a deeper way, forge their own majorities. In their campaigns, speeches, and consultations, in all the performance of their official duties, successful politicians are engaged not in passive response to public demand, but in the active supply and marketing of ideas. Supply can create its own demand, even in the political realm.

By analogy, leadership is supply and public opinion is demand. In a democratic system, a reversal of the appropriate direction of influence allows impressionable figments of mass sentiment to dictate to the powerful and permanent mechanisms of representative leadership. The result is a restive and alienated electorate, a failure of political authority, a sluggish and uncreative government, and a tendency toward national decline—many of the disorders of inverted hierarchy described by Ortega y Gasset in *Revolt of the Masses*. In economics, when demand is permitted to displace supply in the order of priorities, the result is a sluggish and uncreative economy, inflation, and a decline in productivity. Such disorders afflict both our politics and our economics today.

The problem is that demand, like public opinion, does not exist in any very definite and identifiable way; it is a flux of hungers and sentiments which assume particular forms chiefly in response to the flow of supplies. Because there is no demand for new and unknown goods, no demand for the unforeseeable fruits of innovation and genius, preoccupation with demand fosters stagnation. Egalitarianism in the economy tends to promote greed over giving. It downplays the various and specific sources of supply to favor the diffuse and sterile clamor of demand. To the ordinary mind, there is no reason for an assumption of equal importance for the two concepts. Demand attained parity only in our economic texts, and it achieved its deceptive supremacy only through our deluded politics.

In our texts its initial breakthrough was the theory of value: the determination of price by the intersection of supply and demand curves. These graphs and equations are the central images of economic learning, and they seemingly assert an equivalence of potency between demand and supply.

But the impression betrays two fallacious modes of reasoning. One is what philosophers call misplaced concreteness or reification (from the Latin word res meaning "thing"). In reification, objective substance, "thingness," is ascribed to an abstraction, such as public opinion, or to a subjective concept such as value (for example, in such contentions as "the real value of money lies in gold"). Psychologist Wilhelm Reich reached a famous extreme of reification when he decided that sexual energy was a real collectible substance, called it orgone, and created orgone collection boxes. The other mistake of the economic texts is nearly the opposite of reification—namely, false abstraction, turning things into concepts and manipulating them as such. Much utopian thought consists of such spurious abstraction, assuming that human beings are simply mutable bundles of ideas rather than specific and partly unchangeable biological and social creatures.

In the computations of classical or "laissez faire" economists—with their models of perfect competition—demand tends to be reified and supply to be ideated. The elusive and subjective impulses of consumer demand are treated as definite and specific sums, while the definite and specific objects of supply, produced over long periods of time, are sometimes treated as instantly changeable ideas and numbers. Demand curves signifying the purely mental reactions of consumers to particular goods and prices are assigned the same weight and priority as supply curves registering the real efforts, sacrifices, and intentions of producers (which determined what and how much they were already producing). In the equations, moreover, these processes are assumed to occur simultaneously. Conceptions of cause and effect are continually jumbled.

The notion of perfect competition—a prime image of classical theory—is extremely useful in depicting the behavior of particular markets for existing goods. But it has little to do with the central activity of capitalism, which is the turbulent process of launching new enterprise. As has been often observed in academic analyses, perfect competition actually comes to mean no competition at all: an equilibrium in which all participants have perfect information and in which companies can change neither prices nor products and can essentially affect neither supply nor demand.

Perfect competition thus excludes most supply-side behavior: all the acquisition and manipulation of knowledge that is the main activity of real entrepreneurs. Free men and creative enterprise—all the secrets and surprises of actual competition—are banished in favor of a mechanism by which savings are automatically invested, supplies and demands are simultaneously reconciled, and the entrepreneurial role could be best performed by modern computers.

Despite its elegance and insights, moreover, the classical model is less useful to conservatives than their commitment to it would suggest. Though it seems to provide an argument for limited government, it, in fact, gives endless pretexts for state intervention to remedy the inevitable imperfections. Indeed, the perfectionist view has often served more as a way to discredit the messy dynamics of real capitalism than to illuminate its workings.

Demand, however, was not to reach its supreme triumph until the development of macroeconomics as a separate discipline and the ascendancy of the Keynesian school, largely misinterpreting the works of Keynes. Keynes began his *General Theory of Employment, Interest, and Money*, with an apparent refutation of Say's Law.[1] Then he proceeded with a complex and abstruse argument, which was interpreted as meaning that the level of output and employment responds chiefly to the rate of consumer demand.

The chief role of government in the economy, according to the followers of Keynes, was to maintain suitable levels of aggregate or total demand by fiscal and monetary policies. Since governments in capitalist countries could seemingly control the supply of money—the instrument of demand—politicians came to suppose they could thereby influence the supply of everything else. Demand, as manipulated by government, came to preoccupy bureaucrats and economists. In their computations and analyses, supply gradually became a derivative. Say's Law was not only refuted, it was implicitly reversed, with cause and effect hopelessly confused in the proposition that demand creates its own supply—"take and you will be given unto."

It may be said that the alleged refutation of Say's Law by Keynes was the crucial event of modern economics since it affirmed emphatically in the economics of the whole society (macroeconomics) the more insidious triumphs of demand in the economics of the individual and the firm (microeconomics). Yet the actual works of Keynes, even in relation to Say's Law and the role of supply, are far more favorable to supply-side economic policy than current Keynesians comprehend.

As Thomas Sowell has explained in two books (*Say's Law: An Historical Analysis* and *Classical Economics Reconsidered*), the theorem, associated with the name of French economist Jean Baptiste Say, essentially maintains that the sum of the wages, profits, and rents paid in manufacturing a good is sufficient to buy it. This does not mean that the same people who make a thing will necessarily buy it, but that they could. The sum of money paid to the factors of production, chiefly in rents, wages, salaries, and profits, for the making and marketing of an automobile, for example, is precisely enough to purchase it. Therefore, across an entire system, purchasing power and producing power can always balance: there will always be enough wealth in an economy to buy its products. There cannot be a glut of goods caused by inadequate total demand. Producers, collectively, in the course of production, create demand for their goods. This idea is obviously simplistic in many ways, but it bears a number of key economic truths and implications never refuted by Keynes or anyone else. These truths are the foundation of contemporary supply-side theory.

Keynes saw the essential theory as a truism, but he stressed the problems that arise when some of the money earned in the course of production is *saved*. If these funds are then borrowed and invested, as the classical economists believed, the money would go to wages, profits, and other incomes in the capital goods industries, and the balance would be maintained. If, in the example, the savings of the auto workers were not borrowed by their bosses to purchase machinery for the auto plant, those funds might be loaned to U.S. Steel to acquire equipment for steel workers; and the makers of blast furnaces would receive enough income to make a down payment on a house, and the home builders would be paid enough to buy a new motorboat, and so on until some recipient of the funds decided to buy an automobile and Say's circle was closed. Keynes, however, argued that savings very well might not be borrowed or invested at all; the money might just sit there, in the bank or elsewhere.

According to Keynes there are many reasons why businessmen may not choose to invest the savings of the public. For example, the same kind of economic crisis that would prompt consumers to buy less and save more might also frighten businessmen into borrowing less and making fewer investments. Goods would pile up in shops and warehouses while savings accumulated in banks and mattresses and workers lost their jobs. This situation, surrounding Keynes at every hand as he wrote *The General Theory* in the England of the early 1930s, seemed to him a sure refutation of Say's Law. Demand had apparently evaporated despite the presence everywhere of unsold supplies.

According to Keynes, whether savings are in fact requited by investment depends on the fickle intentions and "animal spirits" of the businessman and financier. Knowing Say's Law and its mathematical assurance of buying power, perhaps the businessman should invest. But, Keynes contended:

> Enterprise only pretends to itself to be mainly actuated by the statements in its own prospectus, however candid and sincere. Only a little more than an expedition to the South Pole is it based on an exact calculation of benefits to come. Thus, if the animal spirits are dimmed and the spontaneous optimism falters, leaving us to depend on nothing but a mathematical expectation, enterprise will falter and die.[2]

Even in the absence of depression, said Keynes, there are many reasons for a faltering of the animal spirits.[3] Perhaps the key Keynesian argument is the paradox of thrift: one person can provide more for his future by saving more—that is, by foregoing consumption. But if most people decide to buy less goods and save more money, incomes will collapse because of a lack of consumer demand and a resulting decline in investment. In the end, people will have less money to save than they had in the first place. In Keynes's world of volatile business leaders, an act of saving or foregone consumption in no way assures a corresponding purchase of capital goods.

Keynes, in fact, sometimes leaves one wondering why there is *ever* enough investment to defray savings—why economies do not stall endlessly, as they did for much of human history, in a slough of depression caused by insufficient buying power, stagnant savings, and hoarded funds, all untapped by the magic wand of entrepreneurship. And so indeed it appeared to many in the wearied world of the thirties. Keynes and others did not fully understand that investment collapsed during this period not merely because of a decline of spirit, but because of a collapse of the international trading system as a result of the Smoot-Hawley Tariff Act, a severe contraction of the money supply as a result of bank failures and central bank errors, a sharp rise in real interest rates (that is, nominal rates adjusted for expected deflation), and a series of crippling tax rate increases.

Nonetheless, Keynes had to acknowledge that investment does happen sometimes, and he attributed it to two considerations beyond mere animal spirits. One he called the *"marginal efficiency of capital,"* and the other *"effective demand."* Eschewing a lot of needless Bloomsbury complexities, these two concepts reduce to an affirmation of Say's Law in yet another sense, a firm assertion of the primacy of supply.

Both effective demand and the marginal efficiency of capital depend on *anticipated* profits, on "the proceeds that entrepreneurs *expect* to receive."[5] Demand, we discover, even in the works of Keynes, is mostly in the mind of the supplier. He does not invest in a productive plant because he is assured of buyers for his goods; he cannot be certain that new inventions or changing tastes will not make his factory worthless. If his product is new, it may create demand, perhaps over time. But the demand does not already exist, except in the imagination of the entrepreneur.

Today Keynes is known as an advocate of expanded spending—of enlarged aggregate demand—as the answer to all economic distress. But, in fact, he believed that income earners would spend and save their money in relatively fixed proportions and that what mattered was assuring enough investment. With enough investment, the problems of income, consumption, and savings would take care of themselves. In this belief, he broke, in a rightward direction, from the classical assumption that if savings were suffcient, investment would take care of itself. As the key act of capitalism, he replaced the measurable and passive setting aside of money with the active and aggressive investment of it.

Keynes thus restored to a position of appropriate centrality in economic thought the vital role and activity of the individual capitalist. It is free men rather than abstract forces or mechanisms that impel the Keynesian economy. In his view, the key to material progress lies not in the workings of automatic accumulation or in passive thrift and savings or in a benign tendency toward general equilibrium, but in "skilled investment" designed "to defeat the dark forces of time and ignorance which envelop our future."[6] Because the Keynesian world is not rational and predictable, the true message of Keynes cannot be reduced to mathematics or a scheme of reliable planning.

As George Shackle, the leader of the British school of "epistemic" critics of modern Keynesianism, has written:

> In *The General Theory*, the analysis of business life as a steady application of reason to changeable, but knowable and coherent circumstances, the analysis of business conduct as an informed, collected and undismayed response to a stream of understandable and largely foreseen events, was destroyed, rejected, overthrown in ruin and contempt.[7]

Keynes knew the limits of social science and predictable rationality[8] and saw that beyond all systems was the originative force of the human mind responding to a flow of frequent surprises. Economics is possible because human beings are reasonable and seek rationally to pursue their interests. But the ark of reason sails in turbulent and fogbound seas.

When Keynes made the individual investor the central figure in economics, he overthrew not only the more simplistic classical models, but indeed all the systems and sciences upon which totalitarian schemes are founded. Investment is dependent on "changing views about the future," and "the outstanding fact," wrote Keynes, "is the extreme precariousness of the basis of knowledge on which our estimates of prospective yield have to be made. . . . The actual results of an investment over a long period of years very seldom agree with the initial expectation."[9]

In these circumstances,

> The *state of confidence* [Keynes's italics] is a matter to which practical men always pay the closest and most anxious attention . . . .Businessmen play a mixed game of skill and chance. . . . If human nature felt no temptation to take a chance, no satisfaction (profit apart) in constructing a factory, a railway, a mine, or a farm, there might not be as much investment merely as a result of cold calculation.[10]

The cold calculations of mathematical economics left out what for Keynes—and all realistic observers of economic life—are the most vital matters. This is the conservative germ of truth in Keynes's too negative view of saving: the inert piling up of liquid funds does not provide for the future without daring acts of entrepreneurship that cannot be taken for granted.

As disdainful of Marxism as of laissez faire, Keynes rejected all systems that saw the economy as a mechanism, whether of dialectics or markets. He offered for the economy a hierarchical ideal. The creative center of the system was the skilled entrepreneur and the goal of policy was to cultivate his skills and ensure his inducement to invest. This today is the theme of the editorial page of the *Wall Street Journal* and the rhetoric, at least, of the Republican party in America.

An essential appreciation of the centrality of supply, ironically, also explains the plausibility and appeal to America's leading socialist intellectual, John Kenneth Galbraith. In his trilogy on the U.S. economy—*The Affluent Society, The New Industrial State,* and *Economics and the Public Purpose*—Galbraith's theme is actually an interesting though deeply flawed reformulation of Say's Law. Like Keynes, Galbraith dismisses Say's Law itself ("It would be hard, though not yet impossible, to find an American economist who still subscribes to the historic dictum.")[11] But in a broader sense Galbraith refurbishes it and names it first the *dependence effect,* and then in a later work *the revised sequence* (which merely puts supply before demand). "As a society becomes increasingly affluent," he writes, "wants are increasingly created by the process by which they are satisfied. . . . Or producers may proceed actively to create wants through advertising and salesmanship." He sums up: "*Wants thus come to depend on output.*"[12]

Supply creates its own demand may be a more felicitous way of putting it. But the essential point is fruitless to deny. Producers play a leading and initiatory role in eliciting, shaping, and creating demand. Investment decisions will be crucial in determining both the quantity and the essential pattern of consumer purchases.

Perhaps impeded by a little known streak of modesty, though, Galbraith fails to tell the full range and implication of his discovery. He seems to believe that this proposition reflects a revolutionary change in the structure of modern industry and applies only to large corporations committed to long and technologically intensive modes of production. Such businesses must plan so far in advance, invest so heavily, and depend so much on intermediate suppliers that management is virtually forced to shape and manipulate its market, create its demands. But the dependence effect applies to small businesses as well. They also forge their own demands. The differing patterns of commerce in various communities reflect not only the existing patterns of consumer wants, but also the configuration of entrepreneurial skills and ideas. Great Barrington, Massachusetts, contains a Somali restaurant, a baroque music school, and an Outward Bound Youth Center not because of spontaneous need for these ventures, but because of the presence of men who chose to start them and succeeded in creating a demand for them. There are many obvious differences between large and small businesses, but Galbraith's dependence effect applies to both.

Nor are the passage of long periods of time and commitments of large amounts of capital novel characteristics of modern enterprise. Modern corporations are indeed far more complex than earlier firms. But contemporary businesses may often have less need to plan ahead. They benefit from far more elaborate and flexible capital markets, from more readily responsive consumers, from far more effective advertising and marketing, and from prodigiously more efficient modes of transport and communication. It is difficult to imagine contemporary businesses with greater requirements for early investment and planning or for complementary government aid than the worldwide trading companies of sixteenth-century England or the canal and railroad firms of the early industrial United States. The dependence effect is no mere peculiarity of modern corporations.

Galbraith maintains that businesses, far from giving without predetermined returns, actually seek to control their markets, often with the aid of government, to "administer" prices and quantities of production and exclude all rivals. This revelation is sometimes offered in the spirit of a child discovering that his parents indulge in sexual intercourse. But we must grant that the child is right. For all their ideological commitment to free enterprise, businesses are primarily devoted to successful enterprise, pursue it any way they can, and are delighted to benefit when government blocks the competition. In precisely the same way that many "liberal" economists can profess egalitarian socialism while waxing rich on the capitalist system, corporations can feed off of government while celebrating free markets.

Neither the profit-making socialists nor the business leaders are really hypocritical. Both honestly believe in their ideals but succumb to immediate temptations and demands, from stockholders, wives and children, or their own needs. But as was taught by Adam Smith, what is good for particular merchants is not, despite their nationalistic appeals, necessarily good for the country. The merchants, with their claim that every tariff is a patriotic duty, said Smith, "were by no means such fools as they who believed it."[13] Government officials who succumb to the demands of businesses for protection or subsidy have only themselves to blame. The responsibility for equal application of the laws rests on the public sector, not the private.

What Galbraith and his followers see as the revolutionary new powers of business are, in fact, the inevitable workings of capitalist supply. Few measures would so deflate the rhetoric of the Left as the simple acknowledgment that the very essence of capitalism is the competitive pursuit of transitory positions of monopoly. To the extent that the equilibrium theory has crystalized as a religion of the Right, such an acknowledgment might seem radical and disruptive. But no supply-side ideas are as disruptive to the classical vision as the dynamics of capitalism itself.

Capitalist creativity is guided not by any invisible hand, but by the quite visible and aggressive hand of management and entrepreneurship. Businesses continually differentiate their products, their marketing techniques, their advertising, and their retailing strategies in order to find some unique niche in the system from which they can reap, as long as possible, monopoly profits. Without the aid of government, protecting patents or otherwise excluding competitors, these monopoly positions tend to be short-lived. But they are the goal of business strategy, the focus of creative entrepreneurship, the motivation of original research and development.

The monoply positions, moreover, are not all unlimited, because they are always held—unless government intercedes to enforce them —under the threat of potential competitors and substitutes at home or abroad. To the question of how many companies an industry needs in order to be competitive, economist Arthur Laffer answers: one. It will compete against the threat of future rivals. Its monopoly can be maintained only as long as the price is kept low enough to exclude others. In this sense, monopolies are good. The more dynamic and inventive an economy, the more monopolies it will engender. The ideal of perfect competition, like the ideal of an economy without business power, translates into an economy without innovations. A rapidly developing system will be full of monopolies as new industries repeatedly crop up and have a lucrative run before the competition can emerge and catch up, benefiting from the advantages of imitation. Every now and then a company like IBM or Polaroid will get such a lead and exploit it so efficiently that it retains dominance for decades, to the great benefit of the country.

This form of "monopoly capitalism" does not readily or automatically result in the fulfillment of the preexisting desires of consumers, for consumers do not know what they desire until they have tried a sample at a specified price. Consumers respond to the creative experiments of business. Demand, as Galbraith points out, "does not arise in spontaneous consumer need. Rather the dependence effect means that it grows out of (depends on) the process of production itself. If production is to increase, the wants must be effectively contrived."[14] Exactly. The quality of capitalist society depends not on automatic mechanisms, but on the quality, creativity, and leadership of the capitalists.

The contemporary Left prefers economic leadership from government. But Say's Law, in general terms, is a rule of all organized human behavior. The will of the people is often no more "spontaneous" or free of elite initiative and manipulation in politics than in economics. Democratic masses cannot be generative or creative; they can merely react and ratify. They affirm or reject the creative offerings of entrepreneurs in both business and politics. Howard Jarvis was no less an enterpriser in launching the Proposition 13 tax cut movement in California than was Ray Kroc in launching McDonald's. Both gave specific form to the previously amorphous though finally sovereign wishes of the public.

An economy can be democratic chiefly in proportion to its diversity of choices—the proliferation of monopoly experiments—corresponding to the huge multiplicity of individual tastes and desires. In its cornucopia of choice the capitalist marketplace contrasts vividly with even the most democratic political marketplace with its near monopoly of power vested at every election and with the requirement that voters select a whole cluster of policies in order to get the one desired. Representative democracy is a better system than any other, chiefly because it evokes the experimental competition of elites. There is little evidence, moreover, that capitalism corrupts democracy and much evidence that capitalism is essential to it. The widespread belief that capitalist societies, perverted by corporate power, show a persistent bias in favor of business goods and against public services has not stood up well under recent experience. Government has been growing faster than business in most democratic countries.

Nonetheless, the crucial source of creativity and initiative in any economic system is the individual investor. Economies do not grow of their own accord or by dint of government influence. They grow in response to the enterprise of men willing to take risks, to transform ideas into monopolies, and monopolies into industries, and to give before they know what they will get in return.

The essential thesis of Say's Law remains true: supply creates demand. There can be no such thing as a general glut of goods. There can be a glut of "bads," but in the world of necessary scarcity in which the very science of economics finds its meaning, an apparent glut of all goods merely signifies a dearth of creative production, a lack of new supplies and fresh demands. Private savings, moreover, in the current inflationary period, *are* invested. Saving, in fact, signifies a commitment to the future, a psychology of production and growth. Since World War II the countries that have saved most, preeminently Japan and other Asian capitalist lands, have grown fastest. The apparent gluts of goods have emerged chiefly in countries that fail to save.

This situation illuminates a central fallacy of demand-oriented economics. Like the politician in the thrall of "public opinion," who lives always in the past, demand-oriented businesses rarely create new goods, for there is no measurable demand for what is not already familiar. The market surveys are mute on most innovations. Without a flow of new products, the marketplace can be filled with stale items, produced with ever greater efficiency, continually redesigned in trivial ways, repackaged in brighter colors, and marketed with a more expensive and harder sell. *Jaws III* will be followed by IV and V; Cheerios become Sugar Cheerios; and corporations grow chiefly by purchasing proven firms. New businesses that provide new products, new hierarchies, new opportunities, new patterns of jobs and skills, more rarely emerge and acquire the resources for rapid growth. The employment market becomes more stratified, bureaucratized, and alienating; the consumer market seems less diverse and savory; advertising appeals grow more strident and clamorous. The public becomes jaded and pressures mount on government for further expansion of demand. It is a vicious circle that steadily erodes the creative forces of capitalism.

Originating in a liberal effort to respond to the popular will and relieve the pressures of poverty, demand-oriented politics ends in promoting unemployment and dependency and creating a less open and accessible economy and a more stratified and hierarchical political order. Government bureaucracies proliferate to furnish the services that overtaxed businesses no longer can provide and to subsidize the favored private interests of a depleted capitalism. As bureaucracy grows, moreover, industrial progress declines. For progress is always dependent on the creativity of suppliers.

Say's Law, in all its variations, is the essential enactment of supply-side theory. But its value does not reside in its mathematical workings. In economics, mathematical models, however elegant, must always defer to the behavior and psychology of persons with free will, who often act, and interact, in unexpected ways. The importance of Say's Law is its focus on supply, on the catalytic gifts or investments of capital. It leads economists to concern themselves first with the motives and incentives of individual producers, to return from a preoccupation with distribution and demand, and concentrate again on the means of production.

This return is crucial to understanding the current predicament of capitalism. But it will be difficult for economists. Reversion to the supply-side means leaving the comfort of rigorous models and computations and again entering the fray of history and psychology, business and technology. Economists should again focus on the multifarious mysteries of human social behavior and creativity which Adam Smith luminously addressed in *The Wealth of Nations*, which Marx stuffed into the maw of his theory, which Keynes treated in most of his writings, and which even Galbraith, in his often perverse way, delights in describing.

The mathematical dazzle of the theory of general equilibrium, launched by Leon Walras, and the scintillating novelties arrayed by his modern followers, should not distract the economics profession from the continuing sagas of cabbages and kings, bombs and beanstalks, silicon chips and business psychology. In this effort, it may be useful to return to Keynes, both because of his massive role in modern economics and because he is known as the leading apostle of the primacy of demand.

In Keynes's paradox of thrift, he showed that intentions and declarations of individuals may be a quite unreliable guide to the effects of their behavior (one man may intend to save, but if too many do, the result may be less savings). This is the aggregative fallacy, and it can be found in many of the key issues of contemporary political economics, from the effects of taxes to the role of the state.

Paul Craig Roberts, the brilliant young pioneer of supply-side economics, long an editorial writer for the *Wall Street Journal*, used this Keynesian mode of thought to great advantage in an article entitled "The Breakdown of the Keynesian Model."[15] Roberts was responding to the thesis of liberal economists that tax cuts can reduce work effort and tax hikes can increase it. Such theorists believe that people have a target income, or a target level of savings. If a tax cut gives them more take-home pay, they will not have to work as long to reach their targets. Therefore, so these advocates of high taxes maintain, people may tend to take their tax cuts in the form of more leisure, working less rather than spending and saving more. Alice Rivlin, head of the Congressional Budget Office, made this argument against the Kemp-Roth tax cut bill, as did Walter Heller and most of its other opponents.

Making an exemplary Keynesian argument, Roberts pointed out that one person could respond to a tax cut by working less and taking more leisure (less overtime, more vacations, and less extra work in seeking promotions). But if many people responded that way, the total income and production of the economy would fall and each person would tend to have less real income than he started with.[16]

Leisure is uncommited time, foregone work. It is, in a sense, liquid time, time that can be converted to any purpose as the opportunity arises. The desire for leisure in that way resembles the desire for liquidity, which Keynes associates with hoarding or saving without investing. In all these cases, men hang loose; they refuse to commit themselves to productive activity or investment—or even to particular consumption goods—in order to be open to opportunities to consume or use time in an unspecified way in the future. They wish to retain the power to decide later. But if too few decide what to produce now, there will be little to buy later. If most people take extra income in leisure rather than in purchasing power, there will be no extra income. If most people keep their income liquid rather than investing or spending it, the money will eventually become nearly worthless. In all cases, the prolonged refusal to commit oneself to particular work, investment, or even consumption deprives the community of demand or productivity and thus reduces total income. A few people can do it, but an aggregate cannot do it without defeating its original goals. The unflagging initiatives of suppliers are indispensable to the system.

Living at a time when government and taxes were seen as a relatively minor force in capitalist economies, Keynes did not apply his mode of thinking to governmental activity. But Keynes's paradox of savings applies just as much to forced savings by taxation as to consumption voluntarily foregone by private citizens. Like any group of individuals, the government may *intend* to save, but if it cannot generate real investments, the result will be merely a decline in total incomes and a tendency toward stagnation.

Through the progressive tax structure, government revenue tends to come from funds that might otherwise have been invested. But Washington itself does relatively little productive investment. As the federal budget grows, much of it goes to transfer payments that are spent heavily on the bundle of goods in the rapidly rising consumer price index, from gasoline to hamburgers, and to federal pay and contracts that go to bid up the price of real estate in the District of Columbia. Some money does go to "investments" in public works of various kinds and in education, but many appropriations are motivated less by their economic and social benefits than by political pressures.

Furthermore, from Keynes's theory of the sources of poverty arise vital new reasons for concern about the nature of government growth. Throughout human history, he wrote,

> The weakness of the inducement to invest has been at all times the key to the economic problem. . . . The desire of the individual to augment his personal wealth by abstaining from consumption has usually been stronger than the inducement to the entrepreneur to augment the national wealth by employing labor on the construction of durable assets.[17]

One reason for this gap, according to Keynes, has been the continual existence of *sumps* of wealth, *sinks of purchasing power*, which divert money from productive use. Like Henry George, the eloquent author of economics' leading best seller, *Progress and Poverty*, Keynes believed that during many historic periods land played this role. Since mortgage rates were often higher than the yield of the land in farming, it often could be purchased only by people inexpert in using it, chiefly urban speculators. Other important sinks of purchasing power have been gold, jewelry, art, and collectibles, such as stamps and coins.

The purchase of such goods—the sinking of money into these sumps of wealth—does not itself directly reduce investment, production, or purchasing power. If I have an ounce of gold and you give me $600 for it, you have simply transferred your investing or buying power to me; no wealth is lost. The problem arises when throughout an entire economy an ever-increasing number of people choose to spend their money or gold on other sumps of wealth. Then the price of gold will continually rise, absorbing more and more purchasing power. A rising price means that there is a steady increase of buyers or demands over sellers or supplies. The problem becomes worse when the sellers (in this instance, me with my $600) spend it on other relatively nonreproducible objects—land, works of art, historic buildings, or durable consumer luxuries such as Rolls Royces, and jewelry—and then the men who profit from these transactions, also tend to refrain from creative investment and instead themselves bid up the price of gold and van Goghs, antiques and old autos, Rembrandts and real estate. The result is a decline in the returns to productive capital and a rise in the profits of collection and speculation. The economy is reoriented away from productive enterprise and toward nonproductive activities, away from inventions and risks and toward Caribbean resorts and early retirements. The land, the precious metals, the works of art just sit there, growing more valuable for a while, but for the most part contributing little to the welfare of the people or the productive capital of the economy.

All these sumps benefit from a belief in their ultimate liquidity. Supplies of land and gold are inelastic; they cannot be easily enlarged. But they will always be highly prized. Their scarcity assures their value as population grows. Therefore, seeking safety and salability, people have often put far too much of their wealth into these unproductive forms; and kings and nobles down through the centuries have lived what today would seem impoverished lives amid their stores of gold and jewels and on their vast demesnes.

To Keynes, however, in the period in which he wrote, the greatest sink of purchasing power had been money—liquidity itself. Within stable modern economies, so Keynes believed, the desire to hoard has been directed more frequently to holdings of cash than to land or gold. It is *liquidity preference*—the desire to hoard for speculation or security, by corporations as well as by individuals, through excessive funds for "depreciation" as well as through excessive stores of ready cash from profits—that kept interest rates at a level often well above the expected yield of capital goods. Throughout *The General Theory*, Keynes stresses the insidious role of excessive interest rates in deterring investment—an impact always greater, he maintained, than their effect in expanding savings. Keynes even urged policies to assure that interest rates would be lowered every year to sustain the level of capital spending during recessionary years.

In the seventies, however, the interest rate may have declined as a deterrent to investors. Although it seems high, the rate actually consists largely of an *inflation premium* to compensate the lender for the declining value of his unrepaid principal. In addition, interest is tax deductible, and as taxes and inflation premiums rise with inflation, the interest rate does tend to become lower, in real terms, each year. In fact, in the late 1970s, interest rates, adjusted for inflation and taxes, were consistently negative. If the purpose of lowering interest is to enhance the inducement to invest, an appropriate Keynesian policy now is not to cut interest rates annually, but to cut taxes. High tax rates on income and capital presently play a greater role in deterring investment than did interest rates in the past, when government and taxation were often relatively small.

Inflation steadily erodes the attractions of money as a store of value and liquidity. Keynes's flirtation with a system by which all cash would have to be validated from one period to another by the purchase of stamps—government interest on its issues of cash—is now virtual reality. Inflation exacts a penalty on the hoarder just as regular and sure as any stamping system.

As a result, the hoarders are once again turning to real estate, gold, and jewelry. But the most important sump of investment and purchasing power—the new Keynesian sink toward the end of the seventies—was manifestly government: federal, state, and local, in the United States and throughout the West. It was government, not land or gold or money, that was providing profits well above the interest rate and the private yield of investments.

The government reward went to the displaced enterprise of bureaucrats. In the hands of the state, the return on capital seemed deceptively higher and surer than in the hands of authentic entrepreneurs, because it was guaranteed by the power of progressive taxation.

Over the decade, government steadily acquired most of the characteristics that Keynes listed as signs of a "limitless sink" of wealth. There is no obvious limit on governmental expansion or forced profitability through taxes, few supply-side constraints on its size, no tendency for demand for government to slop over onto other products, and little short-run tendency for government to decline when the economy fails. When people want the Keynesian "moon," which he described as liquidity but which is now better seen as security, they turn to Washington and its outland satellites.

During the seventies, these enterprising bureaucrats gathered, bringing all their human capital and entrepreneurial aggressiveness to the ventures of the state. Many of them were lawyers, because governmental expansion is best achieved through exploiting the fertile chinks and fissures in the tomes of federal regulation. They joined with congressmen in mobilizing constituencies of private interests that could be profitably served. The programs multiplied, the money supply grew, inflation raised taxes, and the spurious yield of federal programs—which often gave no valuable service—and of government bonds—which often financed waste—remained as high or higher than the real profits of private capital. In fact, one could say that the yield of government from inflation has risen to 60 percent, since each percent of increase in the price level results in a 1.6 percent jump in federal revenues.[18] As government expanded, in a vicious circle, it also enlarged its tax receipts.

This is the new Keynesian source of stagnation and poverty in the nations of the West. What politicians are essentially selling—the new liquidity—is tenure and security, and there seems to be no end to the demand for these services. Yet security, too, like thrift, liquidity, and leisure, has its own paradox of aggregation. Some people can gain exemption from risk, and safety from inflation, by turning to the state. But when a majority does, the security and stability of the nation declines. In a perilous and changing world, the best defense against risk is innovation and creativity, research and discovery, competition and enterprise, "skilled investment . . . to defeat the dark forces of time and ignorance which envelop our future."[19]

As the enterprising spirit is channeled increasingly into law and other professional schools, and thence into government, its lobbies, consultant groups, and organized clientele—as great tycoons arise more readily selling "security" in HEW than in selling securities in private firms, or selling real products to the public—the crucial inducement to invest once again sinks below the attractions of other wealth. People without access to the state buy gold and yachts, government bonds and foreign money, or parlay private housing—with its special government protections—into a trillion-dollar sump exceeding in nominal value all the assets of American corporations.

What has happened is emergence of a final corollary of Say's Law: subsidized supply destroys demand. Production without a willing market is a form of disguised consumption, and despite first appearances it does not stimulate an economy.[20] Nonproductive government spending, even when designed to spur demand, actually soon reduces it, regardless of any statistical increase in "purchasing power." The artificial stimulus, like an addiction, requires even greater injections to sustain the initial effect.

When government gives welfare, unemployment payments, and public-service jobs in quantities that deter productive work, and when it raises taxes on profitable enterprise to pay for them, demand declines. In fact, nearly all the programs that are advocated by economists to promote equality and combat poverty—and are often rationalized in terms of stimulating consumption—in actuality reduce demand by undermining the production from which all real demand derives. Buying power does not essentially "trickle down" as wages or "flow up" and away as profits and savings. It originates with productive work at any level. This is the simple and homely first truth about wealth and poverty. "Give and you will be given unto." This is the secret not only of riches but also of growth.

This is also the essential insight of supply-side economics. Government cannot significantly affect real aggregate demand through policies of taxing and spending—taking money from one man and giving it to another, whether in government or out. All this shifting of wealth is a zero-sum game and the net effect on incomes is usually zero, or even negative.

Even a tax cut does not work by a direct impact on total disposable incomes, since every dollar of resulting deficit must be financed by a dollar of government debt, paid by the purchaser of federal securities out of his own disposable income. Even in the short run, real aggregate demand is an effect of production, not of government policy. The only way tax policy can reliably influence real incomes is by changing the incentives of suppliers. By altering the pattern of rewards to favor work over leisure, investment over consumption, the sources of production over the sumps of wealth, taxable over untaxable activity, government can directly and powerfully foster the expansion of real demand and income. This is the supply-side mandate.

# Notes

1. John Maynard Keynes, *The General Theory of Employment, Interest, and Money*, Harbinger ed. (New York: Harcourt, Brace & World, 1964), pp. 18-22 and passim.

2. Ibid., pp. 161-162.

3. Among the reasons for low investment levels stressed by Keynes were: (1) artificially high interest rates caused by speculation and profit-taking in bonds whenever their prices rose very high (that is, interest rates dropped); (2) low profits caused by excessive saving by consumers; (3) low demand caused by wage levels that drop as population grows; (4) financial markets that discourage risk-taking by compounding it. (In a particular venture both lender—the bank—and borrower—the business—may lose the entire amount invested, but only the business has the possibility of huge gains; thus bankers are afflicted with undue caution and may not be willing to lend despite the existence of opportunities attractive to enterpreneurs.) Except for this last item, these arguments are among Keynes's weakest and have been little confirmed by subsequent events. Even his observations on the natural caution of lenders seem somewhat overblown in view of the banking trends of the 1970s. However, the bleak Keynesian vision of bond and other loan markets would seem to enhance the importance of stock markets and of private wealth in supporting risky but potentially lucrative projects. Yet Keynes denounced the stock market in fiery language.

4. *See* Alan Reynolds, "50 Years Later: What Do We Know About the Great Crash?" *National Review* 31 (November 9, 1979): 1416-1421; Milton Friedman and Anna Schwartz, *A Monetary History of the United States, 1867-1960* (Princeton, N.J.: Princeton University Press, 1963), pp. 299-419; and for a detailed rendition of the case that in 1929 the market simply anticipated the passage of Smoot-Hawley, *see* Jude Wanniski, *The Way the World Works* (New York: Basic Books, 1978), pp. 116-148.

5. Keynes, *General Theory*, p. 29 and passim. *See also* ibid., chapter 5 (pp. 46-51) and chapter 11 (pp. 135-140, especially p. 141).

6. Keynes, *General Theory*, p. 155.

7. G. L. S. Shackle, *Epistemics and Economics: A Critique of Economic Doctrines* (London: Cambridge University Press, 1972), p. 429. This view of the central meaning of Keynes's thought is shared by Lord Richard Kahn, perhaps Keynes's closest friend and associate at Cambridge. In an essay responding to an attack on Keynesianism by Walter Eltis of Oxford ("Mr. Eltis and the Keynesians," *Lloyds Bank Review*, no. 124. (April 1977), pp. 1-13), Kahn wrote that Keynes was much less

concerned with hiking government spending to increase employment than with lowering interest rates to stimulate private investment. Kahn derided as "vulgar Keynesianism" the conventional formula that consumption, investment, and government spending together can be managed to achieve full employment. "There is no such thing as a definite level of full employment," he wrote.

8. Keynes, *General Theory*, p. 155.

9. Keynes (in *General Theory*, pp. 297-298) writes, with explicit reference to *his own* mathematical models included in *The General Theory*: "It is a great fault of symbolic pseudomathematical methods . . . that they expressly assume strict independence between the factors involved and lose all their cogency and authority if this hypothesis is disallowed; whereas in ordinary discourse, where we are not blindly manipulating but know all the time what we are doing and what the words mean, we can keep 'at the back of our heads' the necessary reserves and qualifications and the adjustments we shall have to make later on, in a way in which we cannot keep complicated partial differentials 'at the back' of several pages of algebra which assume that they all vanish. Too large a portion of recent 'mathematical' economics are mere concoctions, as imprecise as the initial assumptions they rest on, which allow the author to lose sight of the complexities and interdependencies of the real world in a maze of pretentions and unhelpful symbols." Most of Keynes's present-day followers lack the master's modesty, but their mathematical models make the even greater error of assuming that all the variables and interdependencies can themselves be plotted. The most intricate and prestigious models have consistently predicted national output losses as a result of tax cuts.

10. Keynes, *General Theory*, pp. 148-150.

11. John Kenneth Galbraith, "The American Economy: Its Substance and Myth," in *Years of the Modern: An American Appraisal*, John W. Chase, ed. (New York: Longman, Green & Co., 1949), pp. 151-174. Reprinted in *The Galbraith Reader* (Ipswich, Mass.: Gambit, 1977), p. 86.

12. John Kenneth Galbraith, *The Affluent Society* (Boston: Houghton Mifflin Company, 1958), p. 158. *The Revised Sequence*, which is merely *The Dependence Effect* in new packaging, was introduced in John Kenneth Galbraith's *The New Industrial State* (Boston: Houghton Mifflin Company, 1967), p. 212. I owe this insight to Simon Lazarus.

13. Adam Smith, *The Wealth of Nations*, Edwin Cannan, ed. (New York: G.P. Putnam's Sons, 1904). Quoted from Pelican Classics, rev. ed., 1974.

14. Galbraith, *The Affluent Society*, p. 160.

15. Paul Craig Roberts, "The Breakdown of the Keynesian Model," *The Public Interest*, no. 52 (Summer 1978), pp. 20-33.

16. Roberts did not say that the target income theory was necessarily untrue in all circumstances. People with free will can clearly respond to tax cuts any way they like. Roberts showed, however, that the target-income approach would soon tend to nullify the demand-side effects of tax cuts as well as the supply-side effects, thus leaving no explanation for the repeated history of revenue gains in the aftermath of reductions in tax rates.

17. Keynes, *General Theory*, pp. 347-348.

18. Lacy H. Hunt, chief economist for the Fidelity Bank of Philadelphia, quoted by Alfred L. Malabre, Jr., in "As Salaries Climb with Prices, People Pay More of Income Despite Rate Cuts," *Wall Street Journal*, November 28, 1979, p. 48. The Hunt estimate compares with a U.S. Treasury Department figure of 1.67 as the increase in federal revenues resulting from a 1 percent growth in nominal GNP.

19. Keynes, *General Theory*, p. 155.

20. W. H. Hutt, *A Rehabilitation of Say's Law* (Athens, Ohio: Ohio University Press, 1974), pp. 34, 35, and passim. Hutt's interesting argument defines away the problem of possible gluts by classifying them as "unintentional consumption." To supply, in his glossary, is "to offer inputs or outputs at prices or values which induce their sale." The key point, however, is not the definitions, but the appropriate policies. In case of widespread unintentional consumption, such as government often causes in the name of investment, the solution is to relieve the supply-side of government inhibitions to commerce.

# The Economic Effects of Tax Changes: A Neoclassical Analysis

Norman B. Ture

## I. Introduction: The "Supply-Side" Versus Aggregate Demand Approach to Fiscal Policy

Since the late 1930s, fiscal policy in much of the noncommunist world has been strongly influenced by a set of theories developed from *The General Theory of Employment, Interest, and Money,* by John Maynard Keynes. Keynes's views represented major shifts in many respects from the then prevailing neoclassical way of looking at the determinants of the total economy's performance. His analysis ascribed an extremely important role, quite different from that following from the neoclassical analysis, to public policy. No place was this difference more dramatic than in the case of fiscal policy.

The signal attribute of the Keynesian theory as addressed to fiscal policy is its emphasis on aggregate demand as the determinant of the economy's performance, and the influence of tax and expenditure policies on aggregate demand. A collateral view, quickly perceived and implemented by Keynes's disciples, is that if one or more of the private sector components of aggregate demand is a stable function of variables subject to government control, government policies can dictate the aggregate performance of the economy. A third major proposition is that consumption is a highly stable function of disposable—after tax—income; no matter how volatile other components of aggregate demand might be, government can assure a relatively smooth growth path for the economy by adding to or subtracting from disposable income, hence consumption, through tax and spending actions. In this conceptual framework, the conditions of supply of factors of production are treated as determined by long-term autonomous influences. For the most part, therefore, aggregate supply is taken as given and is not seen as an appropriate or feasible fiscal policy target—indeed, not significantly subject to fiscal influence. As a corollary, the possible effects of aggregate demand management policies on the conditions of factor supply, hence on the change in production capacity, are largely ignored. With supply conditions unaffected by fiscal actions, changes in output and employment are treated as responses to changes in demand, which are subject to fiscal influences.

Given this conceptual context, the emphasis in fiscal policy on tax and spending aggregates as the keys to control of disposable income, consumption, aggregate demand, and employment is quite understandable. The focus in tax policy on the structure of the tax system has been primarily on equity and income distribution criteria, not on the likely consequences of structural changes for the total level and composition of economic activity. To be sure, on occasion, tax policy has stressed promoting or curbing private capital formation; but, as often as not, this has been a concern with an allegedly unruly element of aggregate demand rather than with the contribution of capital-stock growth to the expansion of the economy's production potential.

The fiscal policies embodying the Keynesian ideas have continued to prevail even as aggregate economic outcomes have repeatedly failed to conform with the results forecast by econometric models built in the Keynesian image. The persistence of serious problems of unemployment, slowing productivity growth rates giving way to decreases, and accelerating inflation has led many of these designers of the conceptual content of fiscal policy to conclude that the economic world has changed its shape and that it is the mutation of the structure of the economy which accounts for the failures of contemporary fiscal policy; not any inadequacy of that policy's theoretical foundations.

Until a few centuries ago, the conventional wisdom held that the world was flat. With the technology of those times, this perception was acceptable; within the spatial limits of travel for most people, there was little likelihood of mischance in assuming that the earth was a plane surface. At a later point, it became clear that it was much more nearly accurate to describe the world as a sphere. As this conviction spread and become the conventional wisdom, no one asserted that the earth had once been flat but had, in some mysterious way, suddenly become globular. Surely we would treat as fatuous any assertion that the earlier theories about the world being flat had been right and would still be useful if the shape of the world had not changed.

By the same token, we should dismiss as inane the notion that the shape of the economic world has changed. In fact, no sudden or major structural change in the economy has occurred. The basic technical relations which govern output have not abruptly altered, no drastic or abrupt shift in consumers' tastes and preferences have been noted, there is no observable overnight transformations of the basic institutional arrangements of the economy, and the fundamental laws of production have not been repealed—nor have the basic principles of optimizing behavior for households and businesses been eliminated. To be sure, the economy and its institutions have not been static, and there is much to be learned about the economy's current conditions and prospects in examining these changes. For example, it surely seems reasonable to associate the enormous growth in public regulation, which has limited the efficient exercise of property rights and reduced incentives and rewards for innovation, with an apparent blunting of the entrepreneurial drive. Inflationary monetary policies have taken their toll on saving and investment and have accentuated the biases in the existing tax system against productive personal effort and capital formation. The growth in the scope and composition of government, similarly, has increasingly preempted production resources and increased the costs of their use in the private sector. In these institutional changes and their economic consequences we can find many insights concerning the slowdown in the growth of—indeed, decreases in—labor's productivity, the shift toward services and away from manufacturing, the deterioration of our trade relations with the rest of the world, and the many other stresses on our economy. These unhappy developments do not, however, reflect a change in the shape of the economy; they are, instead, a measure of the extent to which public policies have been misguided.

Recently, there has been an increasing awareness and acceptance of this proposition by many public policymakers. The Joint Economic Committee, which many times in the past has taken the lead in signaling the need for new public economic policies, in its 1979 and 1980 annual reports, pointed to the requirement for refocusing policy —away from concerns with the level of aggregate demand and toward concerns with the adequacy of incentives for production. To many observers, this change in focus appears to be impelled by a "new economics." In fact, the turn to "supply-side" fiscalism is properly perceived as a return to basics, not as a daring venture into hitherto unexplored intellectual territory. Effective implementation of this shift in focus will entail major changes in the content of all public policies; these changes will be particularly dramatic in tax policy. Whether the policy changes which will be made will be appropriate to the change in focus will depend on a clear understanding of the differences in concepts underlying "supply-side" fiscalism and those on which aggregate demand fiscal policies have been based.

At first blush, the distinction seems clear. Aggregate demand policies presumably have been based on analysis of how tax and government spending actions affect households' and businesses' demands for goods and services; in parallel fashion, the supply-side approach presumably should focus on how the fiscal action affects the supplies of goods and services. In fact, however, far more fundamental distinctions are involved and their implications for public policy concern not merely the identified objective of fiscal actions—control of aggregate supply or of aggregate demand—but, far more importantly, how any fiscal action affects either or both supply and demand conditions.

In the Keynesian aggregate demand analysis, tax changes (and changes in government expenditures) are identified in terms of their effects on the amount of income available to the affected persons or businesses. In the "supply-side" analysis, the initial effect of any tax or government spending change is identified as a change in the actual or implied price of something(s) relative to that of others. In the technical terminology, the distinction is between first-order income effects or first-order relative price effects, respectively. This distinction transcends that of supply or demand effects, although in tracing out of the adjustments of fiscal changes, the Keynesian approach emphasizes demand consequences while the neoclassical analysis simply follows the lead of the relative price change to a demand and/or supply adjustment.

There is an enormously important implication of this distinction for the basic strategy of fiscal policy. The Keynesian approach, for the most part, calls for changes in aggregate tax collections relative to aggregate government expenditures—i.e., for changes in the budget totals—in order to generate changes in aggregate economic activity. The neoclassical analysis, on the other hand, demonstrates that changes in the tax structure, even those entailing no initial net change in tax liabilities, may nevertheless have substantial effects on the magnitude as well as the composition of total economic activity.

The reliance on first-order income effects in the Keynesian approach explains much of its concern with average or "effective" rates of tax. The neoclassical analysis, on the other hand, incorporates the well-known, generally accepted, but widely neglected principle that taxes enter into household and business decision making at the margin— that it is the amount of tax to be extracted from (or offset by) the incremental dollar of income (or expense) which affects the price or cost of alternatives and therefore is the relevant decision-making tax variable. Since structural tax changes may entail increases or decreases in marginal tax rates—without changes in total tax liabilities (hence in average tax rates)—pursuit of aggregative policy objectives need not be confined to changing budget totals. While the neoclassical approach thereby enlarges opportunities for constructive tax policy concerned with the total economy's performance, it also imposes the requirement for great care in making structural tax changes ostensibly aimed at serving other objectives. Tax changes aimed at improving fairness or at easing administrative or compliance burdens, for example, may well have significant effects on the allocation of production resources and on the total amount of resources employed (hence on total output and income) even if these tax changes result in no changes in total tax revenues.

The distinction between first-order income and first-order price effects (which will be elaborated in Part II of this study) is highly significant with respect to the appropriate tax strategies for dealing with a wide range of policy problems. For example, consider the contribution of fiscal policy to efforts to curb inflation (recognizing that the fundamental approach must be to slow the growth in the stock of money). The Keynesian fiscal strategy focuses on attempts to reduce or slow the rate of growth in aggregate demand by reducing or slowing the increase in disposable income, either by raising taxes, reducing government outlays, or both, relative to the amounts that would otherwise prevail. But in the Keynesian analysis, decreases in demand are virtually the same as reductions in output. In effect, therefore, this strategy calls for reducing output, a prescription which puzzles those who believe that inflation results from "too much money chasing too few goods."

In the Keynesian approach, moreover, the form of the tax increase intended to reduce aggregate demand is of secondary significance, at best, for this purpose. Thus, whether the tax increase is effected by raising marginal rates or by any other device is deemed to be of little consequence; the criterion, instead, is the change in tax liability relative to income; that is, the increase in the effective tax rate.

In contrast, a fiscal policy embodying the neoclassical analytics would concentrate on reducing marginal tax rates in order to reduce the costs of effort and of saving, thereby increasing the amount of labor and capital services supplied and employed, resulting in increases in real output. It would also seek to reduce government spending, particularly those outlays which tend to raise the cost of labor and capital services to the private sector. The neoclassical approach, in other words, focuses on increasing the supply of goods and services by reducing the costs of production services, with any given stock of money. Any such increase in real output will reduce upward pressure on the price level.

Note that it is the marginal tax rate on which the neoclassical analysis is focused. As indicated, it is the tax on the marginal dollar of income which affects one or more relative prices and which, therefore, enters into individual and household discussions about the amount and composition of economic activity. A tax reduction which reduces tax liability without reducing marginal tax rates, accordingly, is ineffectual.

For public policymakers, the relevance of the distinction between the Keynesian and neoclassical approach is far more complex a matter than whether the focus of policy should be on demand or supply. If policy is to continue to be based on the Keynesian analysis, the principal criteria will continue to be the effects of tax changes on the income level distribution of tax liabilities, horizontal equity, and compliance and administration concerns. These are, to be sure, important concerns of tax policy, but tax changes designed with only these criteria in mind should not be seen as having no allocational or aggregative economic effects. On the other hand, if the neoclassical approach is to be implemented in policy formulation, policymakers will confront both with a far greater range of opportunities in designing and enacting tax changes and substantially greater problems of analysis in doing so.

To illustrate, a current pressing concern of public economic policy is to identify the obstructions to growth in labor's productivity and, if feasible, to reduce these impediments. While a large number of factors may well be adversely influencing productivity, surely the observable and measurable declaration of the growth in the capital: labor ratio in recent years must be an important contributing factor.[1] Relying on the neoclassical price analytic approach, policymakers will discover that a large number of existing public policies discourage savings relative to consumption, and therefore discourage capital formation. Such policies impede a rate of capital formation adequate to sustain the growth in productivity at acceptable rates.[2] Dealing effectively with these public policy barriers to capital formation will require policymakers to change sharply the focus of their concerns and priorities.

## II. Basic Features of the Neoclassical Fiscal Theory

The principal distinction between the neoclassical and Keynesian analyses of how tax changes affect the economy concerns the identification of the attribute of a tax to which affected households or businesses respond. As indicated in Part I, the Keynesian approach perceives a tax acting principally to reduce the income available to the taxpayer and seeks to identify how that disposable income change affects behavior. In the neoclassical approach, on the other hand, the aspect of a tax which results in changes in economic behavior is its effects on the cost to the affected household or business of one good relative to another.

### A. First-Order Income Effects in the Keynesian Approach

The basic deficiency in the Keynesian approach is its assumption of and heavy dependence on first-order income effects of a tax or tax change. The view that a decrease in the income tax liability on one's given income increases one's command over goods and services is intuitively appealing; it is also correct from the perspective of any one person. It is wrong, however, when applied to the economy as a whole. In the aggregate, a tax reduction cannot itself increase the command over goods and services at any given pretax income level; it can merely redistribute the potential effective exercise of those claims. This is true, moreover, whether the tax reduction is selective or applicable to all taxpayers.

Reducing taxes in and of itself cannot and does not instantaneously increase the total real output of goods and services which, by definition, equals the aggregate real income of the economy. Real output increases only as a result of using more production inputs, or of using a given amount more efficiently. A tax reduction alone does not increase the amount of real productivity of production inputs or enhance the efficiency of their use. Change in aggregate output and income, therefore, is not an inherent attribute of a tax change.

In the Keynesian exposition, the question of the first-order income effect on which the analysis relies is finessed by delineating the response rather than its cause. A tax reduction, for example, is deemed to result in an increase in spending, which generates an increase in demand for output, in turn increasing the demand for production input, hence an increase in their employment, leading to an increase in output and in real income which validates the increase in spending— that is, provides the real income which affords the real command over goods and services. The fatal and obvious flaw is in the sequence of those responses: no increase in total real spending can ensue from the tax reduction itself without a coincident increase in total output and real income. By assuming that a tax reduction results in an increase in aggregate effective demand, which then generates the necessary increase in output and real income, the Keynesian approach relies on an analytical sleight-of-hand.

To be sure, the Keynesian exposition focuses on the consequence of a tax change for disposable income rather than aggregate real income. This distinction, however, is without substance. A tax reduction for everyone, unless accompanied by an equal reduction in government purchases, cannot increase the amount of production inputs used to produce goods and services which households and businesses can buy; it cannot, in and of itself, increase the total output for which the private sector can exercise income claims.

Efforts by the private sector to increase the total amount of their claims on output could be effectuated only if private sector entities more rapidly turned over the stock of money and/or if the stock of money available to the private sector increased. But, in either case, the increase in monetary claims on the unchanged amount of output could result only in an increase in the average price of the output which the private sector buys. If the tax reduction is not accompanied by a discretionary increase in the stock of money and if the velocity of money is relatively stable, not even the nominal increase in private sector claims on output would occur.

If government were to reduce its purchases, production inputs would thereby be released for use in the private sector to meet private sector demands. This would change the composition of total output but not, in and of itself, increase the amount thereof.[3,4]

## B. First-Order Price Effects in the Neoclassical Analysis

The neoclassical analysis, in contrast with the Keynesian approach, treats changes in income as a second-level consequence of a tax or tax change. The first-order effect, to repeat, is a change in one or more of the relative costs which private sector entities confront.

Every tax has this attribute of altering relative costs. This proposition is obvious in the case of selective excises. An excise tax on, say, mink coats is seen by virtually everyone as an increase in the price the buyer must pay for the coat compared with the price he must pay for other things. This price or cost effect, however, is not limited to levies we identify as excises. Every tax, to repeat, increases the price or cost of one good relative to another. Indeed, it is appropriate to think of every tax as having some "excise effect."

A truly neutral tax, were it possible to design one, would not alter any of the relative prices or costs confronting any entity in the private sector; it would increase the cost of effort in the same proportion as the cost of leisure, the cost of consumption in the same proportion as the cost of saving, the cost of any one consumption good or service in the same proportion as the cost of capital services and of any one kind of labor or capital service in the same proportion as any other, etc. On the other hand, even a perfectly neutral tax would have to increase the cost to the private sector of using production inputs to produce output for the private sector—relative to the public sector's use of production inputs or of the private sector's use to produce output for the public sector. If it were not to have this effect in increasing private sector costs relative to public sector costs, the tax would not, in fact, act as a tax.

No perfectly neutral tax or tax system has yet been devised, nor is its attainment a realistic objective of public policy. As a practical matter, the objective of tax policy in this connection is to reduce to the greatest extent possible the excise effects of existing taxes and to rely to the greatest feasible extent on taxes which least alter the relative costs confronting households and businesses.

Effective pursuit of any such policy objective requires identification of the excise or differential cost effects of existing taxes. The number and variety of these excise effects in the existing tax system is so great that trying to delineate any substantial number of them would greatly exceed the compass of this paper. The type of analysis that is called for, however, may be illustrated in a number of the existing tax system's features which contribute to raising the relative cost of effort and of saving.

## 1. Effect of an Income Tax on the Relative Cost of Effort

To begin with, consider some of the principal elements in the existing tax system which distort the cost of effort relative to leisure. "Effort" is an expositional shorthand for those uses of one's time, energy, skills, tools, and other resources to produce goods and services exchanged in market transactions; these activities give rise to income flows which are measured by the market mechanism. "Leisure" refers to nonmarket uses of one's time and resources. This type of activity may be just as productive of satisfactions, but for the most part, there is no explicit measure of the income it affords because it is not directed through the market and ordinarily does not entail a market transaction.

Insofar as the income generated by effort is subject to a tax whereas that produced in leisure activities is not, the tax must raise the cost of the former relative to the cost of the latter. The concept of cost that is relevant for this purpose, as in the case of most economic analysis, is that of opportunity cost—the value of that which must be foregone in using production resources in a particular way. The concept derives its pertinence from the rudimentary facts of economic life that production resources are scarce relative to the wants they are used to satisfy and that, with few exceptions, the use of given quantities of given resources to produce particular outputs excludes production of other outputs in that same time period.

In the case of effort and leisure, with twenty-four hours per day, it is clear that for each hour in which one uses one's resources for effort there is an hour less leisure available. The cost of a marginal hour of effort, then, is the value of the hour of leisure which must be foregone. For example, suppose a person were to earn $10 an hour in a particular job. Each hour the person could spend on the job but chooses instead to spend in leisure costs him or her $10. To optimize, the person would allocate time between the two alternatives such that the value of the rewards for the last hour of leisure was just equal to $10.[5] Then one might say that the marginal cost of the effort is $10 (the value of the foregone leisure): similarly, the marginal cost of leisure is $10 (the foregone reward for effort). The cost-ratio of effort relative to the cost of leisure is 1:1.

An income tax which is levied on the explicit rewards for effort but not on the imputed returns for leisure uses of one's time clearly increases the cost of the former relative to the latter. For example, suppose an income tax is imposed and that the marginal tax rate the person in the preceding example faces is 25 percent. With the 25 percent marginal tax rate, the net reward for an hour's effort is $7.50— the amount of hourly wage left after paying the tax. The marginal cost of an hour's leisure falls, therefore, from $10 to $7.50, while the marginal cost of an hour's effort—the value of the foregone leisure— remains at $10, in absolute terms. The cost of leisure relative to the cost of effort becomes $7.50/10 = .75$, and the cost of effort relative to the cost of leisure becomes $10/7.50 = 1.33$. In other words, the marginal cost of effort increases by a third relative to leisure; equivalently, the marginal cost of leisure falls by 25 percent relative to effort.

This excise effect on effort in the income tax is greater the higher the marginal rate of tax. A 50 percent marginal tax rate, for example, doubles the cost of effort relative to leisure; a 70 percent marginal rate increases the cost of effort by 233 1/3 percent.

A graduated or progressive income tax enhances this excise effect. On the appealing assumption that, for the most part, the higher the rate of compensation for effort the more productive the effort is, a graduated income tax increases the cost of effort relative to leisure the more productive the effort.

There is an even more severely adverse, though perhaps more complex, aspect of this excise effect of progression. In the general case, achieving a higher level of productivity is not costless but entails investment, in one form or another. It appears fair to posit a positive relationship between the extent of the productivity advance and the amount of cost which must be incurred to attain it. A graduated income tax adds to the cost of advancing productivity; moreover, the higher the attained level of productivity, the greater is the tax-induced increase in the cost of achieving any given dollar amount of additional productivity gain. Graduation of income tax rates may be usefully perceived as a surcharge on activities to advance productivity.

There are numerous other elements in the fiscal system which contribute to increasing the cost of effort relative to leisure. The second largest revenue producer in the federal tax structure is the payroll tax which is an excise on labor. Given the present and projected upper limits on taxable wages and salaries and the rates at which the tax is and will be imposed, the payroll tax in itself substantially increases the cost of effort relative to leisure.[6] With the income tax taken into account, the excise on effort is substantial even at quite low levels of compensation.

Less familiar, because it is more difficult to identify, is the excise effect in welfare and similar programs. For the most part, whatever their stated purposes, these programs may be appropriately perceived as imposing negative taxes on leisure, hence as subsidizing leisure relative to effort. Most obvious in this respect is unemployment compensation, but virtually any transfer program which affords payments to recipients on a means basis contains a substantial element of this negative excise on leisure.[7] For example, the earnings test in the Social Security retirement system creates an explicit and very high excise on effort after a given amount of wages and salaries have been earned in the year.

## 2. Effects of Taxes on the Relative Cost of Saving

In the same vein, but perhaps not so obviously, the income tax raises the cost of saving relative to the cost of current consumption. Just as effort and leisure exhaust one's available time, saving and consumption exhaust one's available income. The cost of saving a part of one's income, then, is the amount of current consumption that one must forego. Similarly, the cost of using part of one's income for current consumption is the amount of saving given up. Since saving is the purchase of a future income stream, the cost of any given amount of consumption is the future income which one must forego.

For example, suppose that with no tax one might use a marginal $1,000 of income to buy $1,000 worth of consumption goods and services now or buy an asset, say a bond, which, at an interest rate of 10 percent, will produce $100 a year forever. Clearly, the marginal cost of $1,000 of current consumption is the foregone $100 per year; by the same token, the marginal cost of an additional $100 of income every year is $1,000 of foregone current consumption.

If an income tax of the sort levied in the United States is imposed, the terms of this trade-off between current consumption and future income are altered. Again suppose one's marginal tax rate is 25 percent. Then one's marginal $1,000 of income is reduced by the tax to $750, with which one can buy $750 of consumption goods and services now or a future income stream of $75 per year, assuming the interest rate remains at 10 percent. But the $75 of future income will also be subject to income tax, let us assume at the same marginal rate of 25 percent. Then the net-of-tax future income is $56.25. Before the tax was imposed, one had to give up $1,000 of current consumption to obtain $100 per year of additional income; the marginal cost per dollar of future income was $10. With the tax, one must forego $750 of current consumption to obtain $56.25 additional income per year; the marginal cost with the tax is $13.33 per dollar of future income. The 25 percent income tax increases the cost of future income relative to current consumption by 33 1/3 percent.[8]

With graduation of income tax rates, the tax increases the cost of future income relative to consumption more than in proportion to the amount and/or productivity of saving. At a 50 percent marginal tax rate, for example, a marginal $1,000 of current income will buy $500 of current consumption but only $25 per year of additional future income. The marginal cost per dollar of future income becomes $20, twice its cost in the absence of the tax. At a marginal tax rate of 70 percent, the relative cost of savings is 3 1/3 times the no-tax cost. Since the marginal tax rate depends in large part on the amount of one's income, and since the amount of one's current income is likely to reflect in some part the amount one has saved in the past, the excise effect of the tax on saving is likely to be greater the greater the amount one saves. Similarly, the greater the return per dollar of saving (i.e., the more productive one's saving), the higher the marginal tax rate is likely to be and, therefore, the greater the cost of additional saving relative to additional consumption.

To an even greater extent than in the case of the effort-leisure trade-off, the existing tax system is biased against saving and in favor of consumption. The basic bias, as shown, derives from the fact that the individual income tax is levied both on the amount saved and on the future income generated by the saving. But severe as this tax penalty it-self may be, it is only the base of a pyramid of taxes resting on the same income stream. In the federal tax system, the corporation income tax constitutes another major tier of taxes on the returns to individuals' saving. The amount an individual saves is taxed as part of his current income as shown above. If the saving takes the form of purchase of cor-porate stocks, the returns on the saving will be taxed initially under the corporate income tax at marginal rates as high as 46 percent. Insofar as the corporation pays dividends to the individual saver-shareholder, the individual pays tax again, further reducing the return to him per dollar of saving. For a 25 percent bracket individual, for example, $1,000 of current income shrinks to $750 after tax which, when invested in a corporation with a pretax yield of 10 percent, affords a pretax return of $75. If the corporation pays tax at a marginal rate of 46 percent, this return shrinks to $40.50 in the corporation. If the after-tax earnings were paid to the shareholder, the individual tax at 25 percent would apply, reducing the available return to $30.37. Then to obtain $30.37 per year in additional income, the individual must forego $750 in current consumption; the marginal cost per dollar of the additional future income in $24.69, not quite 2 1/2 times the cost in the absence of the tax. For a 70 percent bracket taxpayer, the individual and corporate taxes raise the marginal cost per dollar of future income to $61.73, more than six times the cost absent the taxes.

Another layer of tax on the returns to savings is provided by the tax on capital gains. A capital gain is the market's capitalization of an increase in the expected future income attributable to an asset. Suppose that the corporation in the previous example were to pay out as dividends only half of its after-tax earnings, instead of the full amount, investing the retained earnings in assets which also produced returns to 10 percent a year, before tax. Then the shareholder's equity grows at a rate of 2.7 percent a year (given the assumptions in this ex-ample), representing the annual rate of increase in the market's capitalization of the increase in the future income resulting from the corporation's retention and investment of part of each year's earnings. At the end of ten years, the shareholder's initial investment will have increased by 30.53 percent. If he decides to liquidate this investment, a capital gains tax will be imposed, at a maximum rate of 28 percent. This is an additional "one-shot" tax on the same stream of future income which the shareholder bought with the initial investment. It is the equivalent of a capital levy of 8.55 percent on the original saving or of an additional tax of 4.6 percent per year, in the case of the 70 percent bracket taxpayer and of 1.8 percent per year for the person with a 25 percent bracket, on the returns to that saving over the ten years the in-vestor holds the shares.

The source of the capital gain is the amount of earning retained after the corporate tax was paid. At the time the gain is realized, it is the capitalized value of the expected increase in future earnings, which will, in turn, be taxed as they accrue. The tax on capital gains, thus, is an additional levy on an income stream subject to several layers of tax in any event.

The same returns on saving are also subject to the income taxes imposed by all but a few of the states. And insofar as the saving takes the form of real property, the same income stream is likely to be subject to state and local government property taxes, which though levied on the assessed value of the assets may be usefully perceived as imposts on the explicit or imputed income they generate.

Federal and state taxes on property transfers by gift or at death are akin to capital gains taxes with respect to their effects on the cost of future income compared with present consumption. The base of such taxes is the market value of the transferred property, which in turn equals the present value of the future income the property is expected to produce. That future income will, in the ordinary course of events, be taxed as it materializes over time. Taxing its capitalized amount on the occasion of the property transfer is an additional levy on the same income stream.

Moreover, the property may also be perceived as the accumulated amount of past income which had been reserved from consumption: Again, in the ordinary course of events, that past income had been taxed as it was received. Taxes on the value of the property on the occasion of its transfer are a further layer of tax on the same income stream.

The extra burden of these transfer taxes on saving is mitigated by the various tax provisions which reduce the amount of the taxable property. It is also moderated by the fact that for many individuals the tax liability lies in the relatively remote future; the present value of the tax liability as it enters saving-consumption choices is relatively low except for the elderly or those contemplating inter-vivos transfers in the relatively near future. Notwithstanding, these taxes must be seen as incremental burdens on the returns to saving, hence as increasing the cost of saving relative to current consumption.

The tax laws, particularly the income taxes, contain numerous provisions which somewhat ameliorate the effects of the multiple layers of tax on the rewards for saving. For example, if saving takes the form of depreciable property used in a trade or business, depreciation deductions and the investment tax credit mitigate the additional income tax burden entailed in taxing both the amount saved and the subsequent income generated by the saving. But unless the present value of the depreciation deduction and investment credit equals the present value of the costs incurred to acquire the depreciable property (i.e., the amount saved), at least some of the additional costs of saving, imposed by the income tax, remains. To satisfy this condition, the amount saved (equivalently, capital outlays) would have to be expensed—that is, deducted in full in the year in which the saving occurs—while the gross returns on the saving are included in taxable income as they are realized.[9]

Apart from capital recovery deductions, a wide array of special provisions are generally noted as reducing the aggregate burden of the income taxes. These so-called tax expenditures are often characterized as subsidies, but are more appropriately seen as mitigations of the effects of the income tax in increasing the cost of saving and of effort relative to the cost of consumption and of leisure, respectively. According to a recent estimate, after allowing for all of these tax expenditures, the tax-induced extra cost of saving relative to current consumption is about 66 2/3 percent.[10] Applying the neoclassical analysis, one finds that whatever the case that may be made for eliminating or reducing these "tax expenditures" on equity grounds, doing so will in all likelihood raise the relative cost of effort and of saving.

## C. Comparison of the Neoclassical and Keynesian Analyses of Tax Changes

The neoclassical analysis begins with identification of the initial impact of a tax on relative costs and seeks to describe and explain how affected persons alter their behavior in response to tax-induced changes in relative costs. The adjustments people make in their behavior, in response to the initial relative cost changes resulting from the tax, comprise the tax-shifting process. When this process has been completed, there is a new equilibrium state of affairs. The differences between this state of affairs and that which would have existed if the tax had not been levied, with respect to the volume and composition of economic activity and the amount of distribution of income and wealth, delineate the incidence of the tax.

While the neoclassical analysis posits that it is the relative price effect of a tax or tax change which initiates the adjustment process, it by no means excludes or deprecates the consequent changes in income as influences on the nature and magnitude of the adjustment. Indeed, the adjustment process far more likely than not will result in income changes, and these changes in income will, in turn, affect economic behavior, hence influence further adjustments. But the tax change in and of itself does not alter income; the change in income is one of the consequences of the responses of households and businesses to the change in some relative price which the tax change does, in and of itself, produce. A tax or tax change, in other words, has a first-order price effect; its effects on income are second order.

To compare and contrast the Keynesian and neoclassical analyses, consider some specific, although hypothetical, tax changes.

Suppose the Congress were considering as alternative tax reduction measures a $50 per capita rebate or an across-the-board individual income tax marginal rate reduction of equal effect, initially, on federal tax revenues. In the Keynesian system, these two tax reductions would be perceived as having essentially the same aggregative economic effects. Each would be seen as reducing the effective income tax rate to the same extent. Each would be seen as increasing households' disposable incomes by the same amount, leading to essentially the same increase in aggregate consumption outlays, which would be determined by the marginal propensity to consume—a presumably stable relationship between changes in consumption and changes in disposable income. The expansion of consumption would result in an expansion of nominal disposable incomes of the producers of consumption goods, leading to a further increase in consumption outlays.[11] If resources were less than "fully" employed at the time of the tax reduction, this increase in consumption spending would result in increases in real output, which would entail increases in the demands by business for labor and capital. Hence, employment would increase as would capital formation. The increase in capital formation would generate further increases in disposable income, leading to further increases in consumption outlays.[12] If "full" employment were reached in the process of this multiple expansion of private sector demands, any further expansion of consumption of investment outlays would generate increases in the price level—inflation.

This is, to be sure, a much simplified and reduced explanation of the Keynesian analysis, but it does capture the relevant major elements of the analytical apparatus. Note that in the Keynesian analysis, either tax reduction does lead to an expansion of supply—total real output increases except where "full" employment exists or after it is attained in the course of the adjustment. But neither of these tax reductions results in an increase in the amount of production inputs which will be supplied at any given market (pretax) price. Neither tax cut, in other words, is treated as directly affecting the conditions of supply. The output adjustment is, essentially, a passive response to the change in demand. Note, further, that in terms of the magnitude of the effects on employment, output, price levels, etc., the analysis makes no distinction between these tax reductions.

This is not to say that those employing the Keynesian analysis would be indifferent between these (or any other) tax changes. But their choice would be determined by considerations other than the magnitude of the aggregate economic effects they would attribute to each. For example, the rebate might be preferred on the grounds that more of the tax reduction might go to lower-and middle-income individuals than in the case of the across-the-board rate cut. Other considerations, trading on refinements of the Keynesian analytics (e.g., the likely speed of response to one or another tax cut), might also be addressed in favor of one or the other tax proposal, but no basic distinction between the two with respect to effectiveness in expanding aggregate demand would be drawn.

This limitation on the discriminating power of the Keynesian analysis stems from its dependence on first-order income effects as the attribute of a tax or tax change which affects economic behavior. The consequence is that with this approach "a dollar of tax (or tax cut) is a dollar of tax (or tax cut)," irrespective of the form it takes.

The neoclassical analysis, by virtue of its reliance on first-order price effects, would treat the two tax proposals as very different, indeed, with respect to their relevant economic effects. The across-the-board rate cut, because it reduces marginal tax rates, would be identified as a reduction in the cost of using one's time and capabilities in market-oriented activities compared with their use in household or leisure activities. It would also be identified as cutting the cost of saving relative to consumption. The response to the tax rate reduction, therefore, depends on how people behave when these relative prices change. Assume that when market-oriented effort becomes less costly relative to leisure and saving becomes less costly relative to consumption, given the level of income, people work and save more. More precisely, for any given number of hours of labor services, the required price per hour is lower than before the tax cut. Equivalently, at any given pretax wage rate, more hours of labor services will be offered when the tax rate is cut. Similarly, for any given amount of saving, the required pretax rate of return will be lower after the tax rate reduction, and at any given pretax rate of return, more dollars will be saved when the tax is lower.

On the basis of these assumptions, the income tax rate reduction results in an increase in the amount of labor services offered at any pretax wage rate and in the amount of saving at any pretax rate of return. With (initially) unchanged conditions of demand for labor services, there will be an increase in employment. Similarly, with initially unchanged conditions of demand for capital services, the reduction in the cost of capital entailed in the increase in the amount saved will result in an increase in investment. Both labor and capital inputs, therefore, increase, although not necessarily in the same proportions. The proportionate amounts of the increase depend on: (1) the respective percentage reductions in the relative cost of market-oriented effort and of saving; and (2) the elasticities of the respective supply and demand conditions. With the existing tax structure, for any given across-the-board rate reduction, the reduction in the cost of saving is likely to be proportionately greater than that in the cost of effort. The consequence may well be a proportionately greater increase in the amount of capital services than in the amount of labor services employed. If this is indeed the result, this increase in the capital:labor ratio will result in an increase in labor's marginal productivity and, therefore, in the real wage rate. This, in turn, implies a further increase in both the quantity of labor services supplied and demanded.

These increases in employment of labor and capital services consequent to the tax rate reduction necessarily result in increases in total real output. It is this expansion of real output which is the source of an increase in real income, and this increase in real income will, in turn, affect both the amount of saving and of labor services offered in the market.

As just stated, saving responds positively to an increase in income, according to the neoclassical analysis. That is, given the cost—the amount of current consumption which must be foregone to acquire a source of future income, the desired or optimum stock of such sources —the desired or optimum stock of capital—will grow through time with the growth of total income. With a decrease in this cost, resulting in this example from the reduction in marginal income tax rates, there is an increase in the desired stock of capital at each income level, hence a new growth path for the stock of capital through time. Proceeding from the existing to the new growth path in response to a change in the cost of capital, however, is not likely to be achieved instantaneously; as this adjustment occurs, the rate of investment—the share of total output allocated to adding to the stock of capital—will increase. When the new growth path is achieved, annual net investment will reflect the year-to-year change in the desired stock of capital along with new equilibrium growth path.

As the additional capital is brought into use, aggregate income will increase above the levels that it would otherwise reach. On this higher growth path of income there is at any point a larger stock of desired capital. Thus, even with no further change in the relative cost of capital, the expansion of income generates a further increase in the optimum capital stock. The ultimate change in the growth path of the optimum stock of capital, therefore, will reflect the change in both the relative cost of saving and the increase in income which results as people adjust to the relative price change.

In the case of effort, on the other hand, the increase in income which emerges as a second-order effect of the marginal income tax rate reduction is generally deemed to have a negative effect on the supply of labor services. At the higher than otherwise levels of income, that is, less labor services will be offered at any given wage rate. At issue is which of these effects predominates; the empirical evidence pertaining to the relative strength of these income and price effects is subject to conflicting interpretation. It seems more likely than not, however, that there will be some increase in the supply of effort compared to that which would otherwise be forthcoming in response to a reduction in the cost of effort relative to the cost of leisure.[13]

The neoclassical approach, it is clear, does not ignore income effects; on the contrary, these are important determinants of the ultimate outcome of a tax change. In contrast to the Keynesian approach, however, the effect of the tax change on income is a second-order effect in the neoclassical analysis.

The adjustment of the supply of labor to the tax-induced change in the relative cost of effort and to the subsequent changes in income is likely to be relatively prompt. On the other hand, as indicated, the adjustment in the stock of capital is likely to be an extended, time-consuming process. The adjustment process comes to an end, in the ordinary case, when the new equilibrium growth path of the stock of capital and of total income is achieved. On this new growth path, the amount of investment is larger than it otherwise would be, although the share of the aggregate output allocated to capital formation is likely to be much the same as before. As indicated, the equilibrium growth path of total output and income is also higher than otherwise; the amount of consumption, therefore, is also greater than it would have been had the tax rates not been reduced.

Note that the neoclassical approach does not ignore demand nor assign a secondary role in the analysis to the effects of tax changes on demand. The change in saving out of a given level of income in response to the tax change clearly is the complement to an equal change in consumption of opposite sign. Indeed, there is no impediment in theory to specifying a consumption instead of a saving function through which to trace the initial response to a change in the relative cost of saving, hence of consumption, resulting from the tax change. Similarly, the analysis assigns a significant role to the change in investment in response to the tax change. But in both cases, these changes in demand components occur initially in response to changes in relative prices, rather than to changes in income.

The higher level of the equilibrium growth path of total output and income means that most tax bases will be larger than before the marginal income tax rate reductions. This does not mean, however, that total tax revenues will be greater than if the tax rates had not been reduced. If individual income tax revenues were to be greater than they otherwise would have been, the percentage increase in the income tax base would have to be substantially greater than the percentage reduction in tax rates. For example, if the reduction in marginal tax rates averaged, say, 20 percent, the increase in individual income subject to tax would have to increase by close to 25 percent merely to obtain the same tax revenue that would be provided without the tax cut.[14] In the general case, this implies that the stock of capital and the number of employed persons would have to be about 25 percent more in each year than if the tax rates had not been reduced. In turn, such gains in employment and in the stock of capital imply extraordinarily high degrees of responsiveness in the supply of labor services and in the optimum stock of capital with respect to the reductions in the relative costs of effort and of future income, respectively.[15]

The "feedback" effect of increases in output and income on tax revenues offsets some part of the revenue loss resulting from the reduction in tax rates. In some cases, the feedback effect may be sufficiently large to generate larger revenues than would otherwise be realized; this is likely to be the case when taxpayers may confidently anticipate the reduction in the cost of effort and/or of saving resulting from the tax change in advance of the actual reduction in tax liability. For the most part, however, feedback will offset something less than the full effect of the tax reduction on tax revenues.

Applying the neoclassical analysis to the alternative tax reduction, the $50 tax rebate, the first problem is to identify the relative price which is altered by any such tax device. As a flat per capita sum, the rebate obviously has no effect on any marginal tax rate; accordingly, it cannot affect the price of effort relative to leisure nor of consumption relative to saving. If perceived to be a continuing rather than one-shot disbursement, the rebate is the equivalent of a negative poll tax. As such, it would very modestly reduce the cost of raising children and might conceivably, over time, have some effect on average family size. Other than that, however, the neoclassical analysis would conclude that the rebate has no systematic effect on economic behavior. Its likeliest application is to finance the marginal government deficit (the reduction in tax revenues relative to government expenditures) which it generates.

Comparisons of the neoclassical and Keynesian approaches might be extended with a very long list of tax changes. The neoclassical analysis would identify a reduction in the capital gains tax rate, for example, as a decrease in the relative cost of saving, leading to a shift in the use of existing income from consumption to saving and in the allocation of existing production inputs from production for consumption to capital formation. The resulting additions to the stock of capital would enrich the capital/labor ratio, increase the real wage rate, and lead to an increase in employment. Total output and income would expand above the levels that would otherwise be attained by virtue of the increases in both labor and capital inputs. Moreover, these expansionary effects do not derive from the actual reductions in tax payments but from the change in the tax liability contingent upon realization of gains. As a consequence, the total tax base might well increase sufficiently to provide net gains in tax revenues.

In the Keynesian approach, on the other hand, the initial effect of the reduction on the capital gains tax rate would be identified and measured as a decrease in tax liabilities, hence an increase in the disposable income of the taxpayers currently realizing capital gains. This increase in disposable income would be treated as resulting primarily in an increase in consumption, not in saving. The increase in consumption would, presumably, have some multiple effect on total income, entailing increases in employment and investment. But this tax cut would be deemed to have substantially the same aggregate economic effects as virtually any other tax reduction of equal effect on existing tax liabilities.

One of the conclusions which emerges very forcefully from all such comparisons is that the neoclassical analysis not only provides a sounder theoretical basis for determining the effects of taxes and tax changes, it also affords a vastly greater capacity than is available in the Keynesian approach to distinguish among taxes and tax changes with respect to these effects. The explanation, of course, is that the first-order price effects of tax changes which are their distinguishing attributes in the neoclassical system are more varied in character and magnitude than the alleged first-order income effects upon which the Keynesian approach relies. The neoclassical approach, accordingly, provides a greatly expanded capacity to analyze and differentiate among tax alternatives. It affords the basis for tax policy formulation far better informed with respect to the effects of the policy on the allocation of the economy's production resources and the expansion of economic potential over time.

## III. Taxes, Effort, and Saving

There can be little argument that most taxes—particularly income taxes—affect the cost of effort relative to leisure and of saving relative to consumption. There are, on the other hand, widely differing views about how people respond to these changes in relative costs. Will a person want to work more hours or less if a tax cut increases his after-tax wage rate? Will one want to save more or less of one's current income if the after-tax return on one's saving increases? The answers to these questions have obvious implications for tax policy. For example, if, as is often assumed, people want to work less when their take-home pay increases, reducing taxes on labor income will be a counterproductive strategy for increasing employment and output. And if people save less when the after-tax return on their saving increases—presumably because they can obtain some targeted amount of future income and consume more currently—reducing taxes on capital returns at the same time will be counterproductive in a policy aimed at accelerating the growth in production potential. Important as these questions are in theory, they are also of great consequence for shaping public economic policy.

At issue are the fundamental determinants of an individual's trade-offs between market-directed effort (labor) and leisure and between saving and consumption. A close examination of these determinants would entail a substantially more extensive excursion into economic theory than is warranted in this discussion, which will, instead, briefly summarize the basic analytical propositions, point up their policy implications, and show how they are incorporated in the neoclassical analysis of aggregate economic performance.

## A. The Labor-Leisure Choice

As presented earlier in this discussion, an individual's allocation of his time and resources between labor and leisure depends on the opportunity costs of these alternatives. The individual is perceived to optimize in this allocation when the return for the marginal amount of labor service he provides equals the marginal cost of that amount in terms of the value of the marginal amount of foregone leisure. By the same token, when he optimizes, the marginal return on leisure just equals its marginal cost—the compensation for the marginal amount of foregone labor service. While the rewards for labor are usually explicitly stated—e.g., so many dollars per hour, the importance the individual attaches to these rewards is not generally known. These rewards comprise the person's command over current consumption and future income. Presumably, the greater the amount of current consumption, with any given amount of future income, the less the satisfaction to be obtained from an additional unit of this consumption. And the greater the amount of future income, with any given amount of current consumption, the less the importance attached to an additional amount of future income. The larger the amount of current income, then, the less the additional satisfaction to be obtained from an additional amount of current income.

Presumably, the same sort of thing is true with respect to leisure. Some of the leisure uses of one's time and resources take the form of particular kinds of consumption, and some leisure activities are directed toward expanding one's capacity to obtain income in the future—or to obtain greater satisfaction from any given amount of income. The greater the amount of the rewards for leisure, then, the less the additional satisfaction to be obtained from an additional amount of leisure.

Both labor and leisure, therefore, are perceived to entail diminishing marginal returns. For this reason, both involve incurring increasing marginal costs. To repeat, the individual optimizes when the marginal returns and marginal costs of each are the same.[16]

Given these attributes of labor and leisure, two conclusions about the supply of labor services follow. First, with any given, fixed amount of income, an individual requires an increasing reward per unit of labor service the greater the amount of labor he provides; he has a positively sloping labor supply curve; the *price* elasticity of this supply of labor is positive. Second, the greater the amount of an individual's income, the less labor service he will provide at any reward per unit of labor or, equivalently, the greater must be the reward per unit for any given amount of such service. The income elasticity of labor supply is negative.[17]

In pure theory, there is no basis for determining whether price or income effects are stronger—whether the response to a higher rate of reward for labor services most often is more or less labor services supplied. It does seem clear that a higher reward is required to induce a person to work additional hours a day or additional days per week or weeks per year or to work more intensively in any given hour. On the other hand, if a person receives a higher rate of pay for any given amount of labor, it is not certain whether this will induce more or less hours of labor or more or less intensive effort per hour. On the one hand, the person can obtain the same amount of income as before while working less than before or more income than before working the same amount as before. On this score, it may be difficult to perceive any impetus for the person to work more at the higher than at the lower rate. On the other hand, the increase in the reward for any hour of work means that the cost of leisure is greater than before which should induce one to economize on it—to allocate less time to leisure and, accordingly, more to work. Then the question remains whether the negative income or positive price effect is stronger.

The empirical evidence, unfortunately, is not sufficiently clear-cut to resolve the theoretical issue. On the one hand, it certainly is true that over quite long periods of time, the average hours per year in which a person is employed in market-oriented work has decreased as real per capita income has increased. There can be little doubt that this historical record provides solid evidence of strong income effects. On the other hand, in itself this record does not argue that these income effects are more powerful than the price effects. Income gains have been generally derived from sources other than labor rewards along with the increases in the real wage rate. Predominance of income over price effect depends on demonstrating that the percentage decrease in average labor hours with respect to the percentage increase in real labor income per unit of labor—the income elasticity—is numerically greater than the percentage increase in units of labor service which are forthcoming, for a given percentage increase in the real wage rate, holding income constant—the price elasticity.

Part of the ambiguity in interpretation of the record stems from changes in the composition of employment along with differences in the institutional arrangements of various lines of work and from demographic trends. The post-World-War-II period affords an instructive illustration. Since 1947, average hours of work per week for the U.S. private nonagricultural labor force have decreased quite substantially and steadily—from 40.3 hours in 1947 to 35.8 hours in 1978. In the same period, the average real wage rate increased at an overall trend rate of about 1.75 percent per year. This record is frequently cited as persuasive evidence of the dominance of income effects. But these overall averages conceal important variances from one employment sector to another. For example, the data reveal no downward trend in average weekly hours in manufacturing, a slight decline in construction, and a sharp drop in trade. If these changes in hours were to reflect the relative strength of income and price effects, one would expect to find that real hourly earnings had increased slightly less in manufacturing than in construction and substantially less than in trade. In fact, the rates of increase in hourly earning rates were substantially the same for manufacturing and trade and significantly less than in construction; measured on a weekly basis, gross earnings increased only slightly more rapidly in construction than in manufacturing, and in both manufacturing and construction, the increase was far more rapid than in trade.

These disparate relationships between rates of compensation and hours of work reflect, among other things, the increasing prevalence of part-time employment in trade, occurring to a far lesser extent in manufacturing and construction. And the fact that less than full-time employment schedules have become increasingly commonplace in trade results in part from the increasing labor-force participation by students and housewives seeking part-time jobs for which no extensive training is necessary. The sharp decline in average weekly hours of work in trade, therefore, more reflects the increasing use of part-time employees than the response of workers in trade to changes in the real wage rate. And with the increasing shift from manufacturing to nonmanufacturing employment, the change in the institutional arrangements for employment in trade has depressed the overall average weekly hours of work throughout the private, nonagricultural sector.

The inconclusiveness of both abstract reasoning and of empirical analysis regarding the way in which any one person responds to changes in the rate of compensation for labor services does not pertain in examining the effects of tax changes on the aggregate supply of labor. As shown in Part II, a payroll or income tax raises the cost of labor relative to that of leisure. In and of itself, this relative price effect will tend to reduce the amount of labor services supplied compared to the amounts that would be forthcoming at the same pretax wage rate if there were no tax. For example, if a person with a given amount of total income were to require a take-home hourly wage of, say, $10 if he is to provide, say, eight hours of labor service per day in a five-day-a-week, forty-eight-weeks-a-year work schedule, then the imposition of a, say, 25 percent tax on his wages will result in his requiring $13.33 per hour if he is to provide the same amount of labor service. At a lower pretax wage, hence a lower after-tax wage, the cost of leisure to him is less than in the absence of the tax and, other things being equal, he will allocate a larger fraction of his time and resources to it.

But does not the reduction in his income induce him to work more in order to maintain his former income level? Possibly so. As already indicated, theory provides no firm conclusion as to whether the person's total amount of effort will be greater or less than if there were no tax. But as shown in Part II, the imposition of the tax, in and of itself, does not alter the aggregate amount of production resources in the economy or their utilization. It does not, therefore, change the amount of total income produced. To the extent that the income of taxpayers is reduced by the tax, some other persons must have more income than if the tax had not been levied. For those who receive the additional income, the income effect, of course, is opposite to that of those who pay the tax. At least to a first approximation, therefore, *these* income effects cancel out. On the other hand, insofar as people reduce their supply of labor services in response to the price effect of the tax, aggregate income will be less than if the tax had not been levied. Then any income effect of the tax on the aggregate quantity of labor services materializes only after the initial response to the price effect of the tax. The tax has a first-order price effect on the aggregate supply of labor which may be offset in some part by the second-order income effects.

One of the principal deficiencies in the Keynesian aggregate demand approach is its disregard of the price effects of tax changes on the condition of labor supply. In this approach, the supply of labor is treated, essentially, as given and not significantly affected by changes in the way in which the rewards for labor services are taxed. Indeed, those relying on the aggregate demand approach generally reject the utility of tax changes aimed at reducing the relative cost of effort as a means of expanding employment, arguing that the income effects of the tax change are likely at least to offset its price effects so that no change, possibly even a decrease, in the supply of labor will result. Given the Keynesian reliance on first-order income effects of tax changes, the distinction between marginal and average tax rate changes in terms of how each affects economic behavior is at best secondary to the effects of each in altering disposable income.

If there were a first-order negative income effect on the aggregate supply of labor, this would be as damaging for the conventional aggregate demand policies as it would be for supply-oriented policies. In essence it would mean that income tax reductions aimed at boosting aggregate demand would have no effect on employment or would reduce the amount of labor service offered at any wage rate. By the same token, there would either be no gain in real output or an actual decrease. But then, if the tax reduction in fact were to result in an increase in aggregate demand, the consequence would necessarily be an increase in the overall level of prices. The Keynesian approach, no less than the neoclassical, must rest on the assumption that the positive price effects of changes in net-of-tax rates of reward for labor services are greater than the negative income effects.

## B. The Saving-Consumption Choice

The discussion in Part II was at pains to show how various attributes of the existing tax system serve to raise the cost of saving relative to that of consumption. The question is whether this price effect of taxation is consequential with respect to the amount people save out of any given aggregate income.

In neoclassical theory, the impetus for saving is to acquire sources of future income streams in order to have a greater command over resources at a future time than one would otherwise have. The greater the amount of future income to which one has claim, the less is likely to be the gain in satisfaction from acquiring any additional amount of future income. The marginal utility of future income decreases, in other words, with increases in its amount.

As pointed out in Part III, acquiring sources of future income entails foregoing current consumption uses of one's current income. The real cost of any amount of such future income sources is the amount of satisfaction from current consumption which must be foregone by using some of one's income to acquire those sources. Presumably the marginal utility of current consumption also decreases the greater the amount of this use of income. Thus, with any given income, the real cost of any incremental amount of future income increases as the amount of saving—foregone consumption—increases. Similarly, the real cost of any increment of consumption is the additional satisfaction which would have been obtained from the future income which must be sacrificed. The real marginal cost of consumption increases, therefore, as the amount of consumption increases.

To optimize, an individual will allocate his available current income between consumption and future income in such a way that the marginal cost and marginal utility of each is the same. If something changes the amount of current consumption one can obtain with a stipulated amount of current income, i.e., the explicit price of consumption, the allocation between consumption and saving will change, given no change in the person's preference system. Similarly, if the amount of current income one must forego to obtain any given amount of future income (i.e., the explicit price of future income) changes, this will impel the person to change the division of available income between saving and consumption. For example, a reduction in the cost of future income relative to current consumption will increase the amount of future income desired. With real income held constant, this entails an increase in the proportion of current income which is saved, (i.e., used to acquire sources of future income) and a reduction in the amount of consumption. Allowing for an increase in real income, both saving and consumption will increase.

These relationships may be depicted as the conditions of supply of capital. At each given level of real income, an individual requires a greater amount of future income per dollar of foregone current consumption, the larger the amount of current consumption he foregoes. Expressing the amount of future income per dollar of foregone current consumption as the rate of return on his saving, the amount of saving out of any given current income is described as positively elastic with respect to the rate of return. At higher levels of income, a greater amount of saving will be undertaken at any given rate of return; that is, saving is also positively elastic with respect to income.

The amount of return that can be obtained (in contrast with the amount of return desired) per dollar of foregone consumption used to acquire capital depends on how much capital is used in production with given amounts of other production inputs. Given the technical conditions of production and the demand for the output of the production process in which the capital is used, the greater the amount of capital in relation to the other production inputs, the less will be the incremental total revenue obtained from any given additional amount of capital. The marginal value productivity of capital, in other words, decreases with increases in the amount of capital, given the quantity of other production inputs.

The equilibrium amount of capital is such that its marginal value product equals the rate of return that people require to willingly hold that quantity, i.e., to forego that amount of current consumption.

With taxes levied both on the current income which is saved and on the future income acquired with the saving (as in the present U.S. tax structure) the relative cost of saving—the amount of current consumption which must be foregone to obtain any given net-of-tax future income—increases. Unless the imposition of the taxes per se decreases people's preferences for future income compared with current consumption, the pretax rate of return required to elicit any given amount of saving will be higher than that required in the absence of the taxes. But with no change in the basic determinants of capital's productivity, the higher pretax return is obtained only with a smaller amount of capital in relation to labor services and other production inputs. A tax structure of this sort, therefore, results in a smaller stock of capital than would otherwise exist.[18]

Since the productivity of labor, hence real wages, depends in significant part on the amount of capital with which labor is employed, this tax-induced shortfall in the stock of capital also results in lower rewards for labor services than would be provided in the absence of the tax. And as shown in the preceding discussion, this is likely to entail less employment than otherwise.

In turn, the lesser amounts of capital and labor services employed mean that total output and real income are less than would be forthcoming in the absence of the tax bias against saving and capital formation. And at the lower level of income, aggregate saving will be less than otherwise.

Analogous to the case of the labor-leisure choice, the initial effects of taxes on the saving-consumption choice are responses to the tax-caused distortion of the cost of saving relative to the cost of consumption. These responses to this relative price change lead to lower levels of productivity and of total production inputs, hence to lower income than would otherwise be realized. In turn, this reduced level of income, the second-order income effect of the taxes, further reduces saving and capital formation.

In the aggregate demand approach, as indicated earlier, consumption is deemed to be determined primarily by disposable income; so, too, is saving. The relative costs of saving and consumption are either completely ignored or given little weight as determinants of the allocation of income between these alternative uses. Saving, hence consumption, is described as completely "interest inelastic." By the same token, the effects of taxes on these relative costs are generally dismissed as inconsequential in the determination of individuals' saving-consumption choice. Instead, taxes are treated as having first-order income effects on consumption and saving, by virtue of their effects on disposable incomes.

This treatment should pose an interesting paradox to those relying on the aggregate demand approach. Consider a tax structure which is heavily biased against saving in the sense that it raises the cost of saving relative to current consumption. Whether or not one believes that saving and consumption are influenced by these relative costs, there is some division—presumably a functionally stable allocation — of income between current consumption and saving. Now suppose the tax structure is drastically altered so as to reduce, if not completely to eliminate, the bias against saving, i.e., the tax structure becomes more nearly neutral, in the sense defined in Part II, between saving and consumption. Suppose, for example, that the existing income taxes were replaced by a uniform value added tax.[19] And suppose, further, that initially the tax change involves no change in total tax liabilities. Then the cost of consumption has been significantly increased and the cost of saving has been dramatically reduced. But since disposable income has not been changed, the aggregate demand approach would hold that there would be no change in consumption or in saving. If this were in fact the result, not only must saving be characterized as completely "interest inelastic," consumption must be treated as completely inelastic with respect to its price as well. But if this is so, there clearly is no basis for the assertion that a value added tax or a sales tax is in any meaningful sense a burden on consumption.

A second paradox in the aggregate demand approach lies in its treatment of the response by business organizations to tax changes which are deemed to affect the net rate of return on business-owned capital. A reduction in the corporation income tax, more accelerated depreciation allowances, an increase in the investment tax credit, and similar tax changes are perceived as increasing both business cash flow (the sum of after-tax profits plus capital consumption allowances) and the net-of-tax rate of return. Both the income and price effects are deemed to lead to increases in business demands for capital facilities —to greater capital outlays by business. "Businesses," in other words, are deemed to have interest elastic demands for capital.[20] Individuals, the ultimate owners of businesses, on the other hand, are deemed to have completely interest inelastic saving behavior. This suggests that the proprietor of an unincorporated business closes his eyes to the after-tax rate of return when, as the owner, he considers how much capital to keep in the business rather than withdraw and consume, while as the manager of the business he is keenly responsive to the effects of tax changes on the net rate of return obtainable on the business capital.[21] The notion of any such split view is highly implausible and if one believes that sooner or later corporate business executives and managers must come to realize, if only when facing a collapse in equity values or bankruptcy, that they are merely the stewards for the company owners, it is just as implausible to attribute to them the same split personalities.

## C. Policy Implications

A major distinction between the neoclassical and Keynesian treatment of the effects of taxes on the saving-consumption choice derives from identifying taxes in terms of first-order price effects (neoclassical) or first-order income effects (Keynesian). This is, of course, the same distinction that was identified with respect to the neoclassical and Keynesian treatment of the labor-leisure choice. As a corollary to this distinction, the neoclassical analysis identifies taxes and tax changes in terms of their effects on marginal tax rates and treats these effects as the operational mechanism of tax policy; the aggregate demand approach, on the other hand, focuses on changes in average tax rates as the means by which taxes affect economic activity.

There are important implications for public policy in this difference in analytical approach. The failure to distinguish between price and income effects and their sequence accounts for much of the misdirection of tax policy in the past. By the same token, appreciation of these differences and of their priorities will contribute to the design of a tax system which less significantly burdens saving, effort, and productivity-advancing economic activity.

One of the most broadly applicable as well as important of these implications is that tax changes should operate to change marginal rather than average or effective tax rates if tax policy is to be efficiently used in the pursuit of economic objectives. For example, if the aim is to make more intensive use of the labor force, it is necessary to reduce the cost of labor relative to leisure; the focus of the tax policy to this end should be on reducing marginal income tax and payroll tax rates. Reducing effective tax rates, for example, by providing a per capita tax credit or rebate while leaving marginal tax rates intact, will not alter the cost of effort relative to leisure and will not, therefore, expand the supply of labor and employment.

Similarly, in order to offset the adverse effects of inflation on the supply of labor, the focus should be on reducing marginal tax rates.

The argument frequently advanced by the Treasury Department that by virtue of discretionary tax reductions effective income tax rates have not advanced with inflation is not really an answer to those urging indexing or some alternative income tax adjustment to offset the tax-bracket creep inflation produces. Only if the Treasury could demonstrate that these discretionary adjustments had also held constant the incremental tax per dollar of incremental real income could they show that tax policy had effectively offset the adverse thrust of inflation with respect to the conditions of labor supply.

In the same vein, a higher overall saving rate in the interests of achieving a larger stock of capital, a higher capital-labor ratio, hence greater advances in productivity, real wage rates, and employment calls for reducing the amount of tax on the marginal returns to saving rather than the overall effective tax rate on these returns. As shown in Part II, this can be accomplished by reducing marginal individual income tax rates. Highly effective would be reductions in corporate income tax rates. Increasing the width of income tax brackets is a useful device for this purpose. Indeed, a wide variety of tax provisions, not merely reductions in statutory tax rates, may be used to this end. For example, more generous capital recovery provisions, e.g., the proposed "10-5-3 capital cost recovery system," the investment tax credit, ADR, etc., serve to reduce the marginal tax rate on the returns to capital, hence to reduce the marginal cost of saving.

To be sure, many such tax features do not, initially, impact with equal weight on all of the alternative channels for saving. Insofar as they reduce the marginal tax rate on the returns on one or more types of capital relative to others, these tax provisions impel a shift in the composition of saving and investing toward the tax-favored and away from the less-favored saving outlets. Other production inputs also shift, in varying proportion, with this shift in saving and capital allocation. As this shift occurs, the pretax rate of return on the types of capital favored by the tax provision tends to fall while that on the unfavored capital rises. This adjustment process continues until the after-tax rates of return on capital in all uses are once again equal. When the shift is completed, the allocation of the total amount of capital among all alternative uses is likely to differ, possibly substantially from its composition if all taxes equally altered, initially, the cost of saving in all uses.

Unless marginal tax rates on the returns to capital in the nonfavored uses are increased so as to offset precisely the reduction in marginal tax rates effected by the tax differentials on the favored uses, the overall marginal rate of tax on all capital returns will decline. So, too, therefore, will the overall cost of saving. The aggregate volume of saving, hence the size of the total stock of capital, will increase.

Tax provisions which differentially reduce the marginal rates of tax on the returns to particular types of capital, therefore, not only change the allocation of capital but increase its total volume as well.

There may well be a loss of efficiency resulting from the change in the allocation of capital, and it is to this efficiency loss, seldom if ever measured, that the attention of policymakers is generally directed. A tax structure which is more nearly neutral with respect to its effects on the cost of capital in alternative use is certainly highly desirable. It does not follow, however, that there would be any gain for the economy in merely eliminating tax differentials. The real question is whether the efficiency losses resulting from tax differentials are as great as the efficiency gain which results from the reduction, overall, in the tax bias against saving and the consequently larger stock of capital. In general, the efficiency losses in the misallocation of the stock of capital are likely to be of secondary importance compared with those resulting from the shortfall of capital from the amount which would be forthcoming if the tax system were less severely biased against saving. By the same token, eliminating these tax differentials without offsetting tax changes—i.e., those which equivalently reduced marginal tax rates on the returns to saving—would entail a net efficiency loss to the economy.

This further emphasizes the point that evaluation of the effectiveness of any proposed tax change in achieving economic policy objectives must rely on identifying how the tax change affects relative prices, and for this purpose it is the effect of the tax change on marginal tax rates, not tax liabilities, per se, which matters.

This is not to say that there is no policy objective reflected in concern over effective tax rates. Insofar as equity criteria can be rigorously and meaningfully delineated in terms of the amount of tax per dollar of income borne by persons in differing economic circumstances, clearly the average rate of tax is a useful measure. But for purposes of understanding how taxes enter into decisions to work and to save rather than to use one's resources in nonmarket-oriented pursuits and to consume, respectively, the focus should be on marginal tax rates.

## IV. Summary and Conclusions

The ineffectual application of tax policy to the pursuit of economic policy objectives during the last decade has sometimes been ascribed to an explicable change in the nature and structure of the economy. Others have concluded that taxes, per se, are ineffectual policy instruments and that, accordingly, taxes should be used solely to raise revenues.

Neither conclusion is warranted. The fact that the economic results sought in the use of tax policy have not been achieved does not mean that the world used to be flat and just suddenly became a sphere, nor does it mean that taxes are impotent devices for influencing economic outcomes. The inference that is properly drawn, rather, is that policy has been formulated on the basis of misapprehension as to how taxes affect economic behavior. In the popular view, correcting the tax policy mistakes of the past calls for shifting the focus from control of aggregate demand to expansion of aggregate supply. What is really called for, however, is reliance on a different analytical approach in identifying the attributes of taxes that affect economic behavior and, therefore, the development of a better, more accurate understanding of how people react to taxes and tax changes.

For the past several decades, tax policy has been largely guided by a set of views about how taxes affect behavior derived from the work of John Maynard Keynes. In this approach, the operational attribute of taxes is their effect on disposable income. Changes in disposable income are perceived to result in changes in consumption and, to a substantial extent, in investment which, in turn, leads to changes in total output and income. The conditions of supply of production inputs are deemed to be little influenced by taxes and their effects on disposable income. Hence the focus in this approach on aggregate demand.

There is a growing awareness that this aggregate demand approach relies on a misspecification of the attribute of taxes which affect economic behavior. The neoclassical analysis demonstrates that taxes and tax changes can have no initial impact on the aggregate income of the economy and cannot accordingly influence economic outcomes by way of first-order income effects. Instead, taxes initially affect the behavior of households and businesses by altering the relative prices, explicit or implicit, of the economic alternatives they confront. Thus, to understand how tax policy will affect the aggregate economic performance of the economy, it is necessary first to identify the relative prices which are altered by taxes and to specify how individuals respond thereto.

At the highest level of aggregation, the initial effect of a tax change is identifiable in terms of a change in the price of saving relative to consumption and/or of effort relative to leisure. This identification tends to focus the analysis initially on the conditions of supply, since tax-induced changes in these relative prices lead to changes in saving, hence in the stock of capital and the flow of capital services in production, and in the amount of labor services offered at any given pretax wage rate. But changes in the conditions of supply of capital and labor services obviously entail changes in total output and income, and these second-order changes in income themselves influence the willingness of individuals to work and to save at given rates of reward for effort and saving. In turn, therefore, these second-order effects of tax changes alter the volume of consumption and investment—the private sector components of aggregate demand. The relevant distinction between the neoclassical and Keynesian analyses, therefore, is not that one is concerned with the supply effects and the other with the demand effects of taxation, but that one perceives taxes as first altering relative prices leading to changes in income while the other identifies taxes as primarily changing income, with effects on relative prices treated as of secondary importance, if any.

The neoclassical analysis does not discard analysis of the effects of taxation on aggregate demand and its components; instead, it joins to that concern an explicit analysis of the effects of tax changes on the conditions of factor supply. The "supply-side" characterization of this analysis is warranted only by contrast with the aggregate demand approach which, for the most part, does not explicitly consider factor supply responses to tax changes.

Relying on the neoclassical analysis has major implications for tax policy. For one thing, insofar as tax policy is concerned with economic policy objectives, the neoclassical analysis urges de-emphasis of average rates of tax and a focus, instead, on marginal tax rates, since marginal, rather than average, tax rates affect relevant relative prices. As corollary, changing the aggregate amount of taxes relative to income is not the effective way to use tax policy to achieve desired changes in economic aggregates: devices such as per capita income tax credits or rebates should not be relied upon to affect aggregate levels of output or employment. By the same token, to implement the current policy concern for more rapidly increasing the stock of private business capital, in the interests of raising productivity, real wage rates, and total output potential, the focus should be on reducing the existing excessive tax cost of saving relative to consumption. This calls for reducing marginal income tax rates, rather than for reducing average tax rates.

This is not to say that there is no occasion for concern with effective tax rates. If equity objectives can be meaningfully specified in terms of the amount of tax per dollar of income paid by persons in differing economic circumstances, the average or effective rate of tax becomes an important and useful measure. But policymakers should be alert to the likelihood that pursuit of equity objectives, guided by changes in effective tax rates, may seriously conflict with pursuit of economic objectives for which changes in marginal tax rates are the operational instrument.

The application of neoclassical, price-theoretic analysis to tax policy offers enormous promise for greatly expanding our understanding of how taxes affect economic behavior. It greatly enriches the potential of tax policy for dealing constructively with a far larger array of economic problems than have been effectively dealt with in the past. The path to a more constructive tax system, one which is more congenial to productive effort, to advancing productivity, to innovation, and to economic self-reliance is made far clearer by the application of this sort of analytical approach. In the last analysis, however, the progress on that path will depend on policymakers' willingness to shift their intellectual gears. Hopefully, this study will facilitate the transmission.

# Notes

1. Other things being equal, maintaining a given rate of advance in labor's productivity requires maintaining a given rate of increase in the capital:labor rate. A slower rate of increase in that ratio may well result in a reduction, not merely a slower rate of increase in labor's productivity. Cf. Norman B. Ture and B. Kenneth Sanden. "The Effects of Tax Policy on Capital Formation," Financial Executives Research Foundation (New York, 1977), pp. 16-23.

2. Several of the features of the existing tax system which increase the cost of saving relative to consumption are discussed in Part II.

3. An increase in total output might ensue if production inputs were more productively employed in meeting private sector than public sector demands.

4. In some analyses, instead of an income effect, a tax change is represented as having a wealth effect. But wealth is, by definition, the capitalized amount of expected continuing or permanent income. A change in taxes, therefore, can no more *initially* change aggregate wealth than it can change aggregate income.

5. This assumes the person is substantially free to determine hours of work and of leisure. The popular view is that there are severe institutional limitations on one's ability to determine the allocation of one's time between leisure and effort. This view, however, grossly exaggerates the constraints; through an array of devices, people can and do respond to changes in the relative cost of effort and leisure by changing their allocation of time between the two.

6. A contrary view holds that the payroll tax is best perceived as a fee paid by workers for their postretirement maintenance and security. This view may be challenged on the basis that there is no precise functional relationship in the system between the amount of such fees one pays and the amount of annuities and other benefits one receives, as well as on the basis of the involuntary character of the "fees."

7. The excise effect on effort is often most severe on low income individuals. Welfare programs with means tests impose an earnings barrier to effort; when earnings exceed some maximum the welfare recipient not only is subject to payroll and income taxes but also loses part of the welfare benefits. The real marginal tax rate, which enters into determination of the cost of effort relative to leisure, may exceed 100 percent.

8. An equivalent way of looking at this effect is that prior to the tax, with an interest rate of 10 percent, the capitalized value of the $100 per year of additional income is $1,000 (=$100/.10). With the income tax, the capitalized value of the after-tax additional income per year is $562.50 (=$56.25/.10). Before the tax, the ratio of the marginal outlay on consumption to the present worth of the future income is $1,000:$1,000=1; with the tax, the ratio becomes $750:$562.50=1.333. The cost of future income relative to the cost of consumption increases by one-third; equivalently, the cost of consumption relative to saving falls by 25 percent.

9. Cf. Ture and Sanden, "Effects of Tax Policy," pp. 93-94.

10. Cf. Norman B. Ture, "The Tax Bias Against Saving." Proceedings of the Sixty-Ninth Annual Conference, 1976. National Tax Association-Tax Institute of America, p. 23.

11. The limit on the expansion in a static analysis would be $(\alpha 1-\alpha)(\Delta t)$, where $\alpha$ is the marginal propensity to consume and $\Delta t$ is the initial change in tax liabilities. The term $\alpha 1-\alpha$ is the tax change multiplier.

12. If investment is specified as some function of disposable income, there emerges the concept of the marginal propensity (of the private sector) to spend (on both consumption and investment). Then the limit on the expansion is $\lambda 1-\lambda \, \Delta t$, where $\lambda$ is the marginal propensity to spend, the sum of the marginal propensity to consume and the marginal propensity to invest.

13. The issue of the relative importance of income and price effects in the determina-

tion of the supply of labor and some of the empirical evidence pertaining thereto are examined in Part III.

14. If all of the revenue loss were to be made up by expansion of the individual income tax base, that expansion would have to be 25 percent. Since other tax bases will also increase, something slightly less than 25 percent gain in the individual tax base would be needed to break even.

15. In the case of labor services, the implied elasticity—the percentage change in the amount of labor services supplied in response to the percentage change in the cost of effort—would be somewhere in the neighborhood of 5. For capital, the implied elasticity is something like 2. Neither elasticity is realistic.

16. The costs of labor often include items in addition to the value of the foregone leisure. One's job may entail risks of injury, emotional stresses, and other nonpecuniary costs as well as monetary costs for clothing, commuting, meals, etc. Similarly, the costs of leisure often include more than the foregone rewards for labor.

17. For a theoretical discussion of this point, see appendix A.

18. For a theoretical elaboration of this point, see appendix B.

19. For a demonstration of the proposition that a value added tax of the so-called "consumption" variety in fact equally increases the cost of consumption and saving, see Norman B. Ture, "The Value Added Tax: Facts and Fancies," The Heritage Foundation and Institute for Research on the Economics of Taxation, Washington, D.C., 1979.

20. All too familiar is the Keynesian litany that "tight" money drives up interest rates which reduces business's capital outlays.

21. The cure for this schizophrenia, if in fact it afflicted proprietors, would be to get them to kick the Keynesian habit and take up the old-time religion of neoclassical economics.

22. There is some discussion in the profession over how to measure the use of capital in this type of graph. Some would put capital on the horizontal axis. Others would put capital services on the axis, noting that capital can be used more or less intensively as circumstances dictate, at least in the short run. However, in a long-run stock adjustment picture, and adjusting for changes in technology, services of capital move in rough proportion to the capital stock. Thus, a tax on either capital or the services of capital will reduce the quantity of both capital and the services of capital supplied to and used by the market.

## Appendix A

### *Income as a Parameter of the Supply of Labor Curve*

The relationships among the amount of labor services offered and the income and price effects of alternative wage rates are illustrated in Figure I, in which the amount of labor service is shown on the horizontal axis and the wage rate is shown on the vertical axis. Each of the lines $S_1$, $S_2$, $S_3$, etc., represents the various amounts of labor service the individual will offer at each alternative wage rate, given a fixed amount of total income. The supply curve $S_2$ represents the conditions of labor supply when the individual has some greater total income than the amount for which the curve $S_1$ is drawn; $S_3$ represents greater total income than $S_2$, etc.

It is obvious, of course, that other things being equal, an increase in the amount of labor services provided with an increase in the reward per unit of labor service results in an increase in total income. But then the individual's conditions of labor supply are no longer correctly represented by the original labor supply line but by a new line drawn with respect to the greater amount of income. For example, suppose to begin with an individual were supplying $L_1$ hours of labor serviced at a wage rate of $W_1$ on supply curve $S_1$. At wage rate $W_2$, the individual

*FIGURE 1*

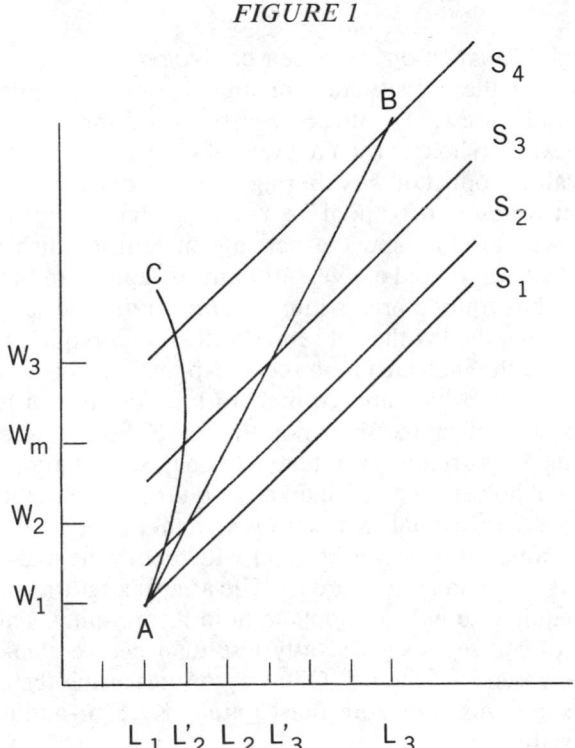

would provide $L_2$ of labor *if his total income were unchanged.* But taking into account the gain in his income, he will provide $L'_2$ of labor at wage rate $W'_2$—he'll now be on supply curve $S_2$. At wage rate $W_3$, the amount of labor he would offer would be $L_3$ if his income remained the same amount as that for which $S_1$ is drawn. But at the higher income level, the amount of labor offered at $W_3$ is $L'_3$ and this point lies on labor supply curve $S_3$. And so on. Connecting the points $W'_1L'_1$, $W_2L'_2$, $W_3L'_3$, etc., which allow for the effect of the income changes on the individual's willingness to offer labor services at any given wage rate, i.e., which recognize the negative income effect, there emerges the supply of labor curve AB. This curve, it should be noted, depicts increasing amounts of labor with increasing wage rates; the positive price effect is greater than the negative income effect.

Curve AC, in contrast, shows much less responsiveness of the amount of labor service offered to increases in the wage rate and much more negative response to the implied increase in income. At a wage rate $W_m$, halfway between $W_2$ and $W_3$, the amount of labor supplied is a maximum. At higher wage rates, for example at $W_3$, less labor is supplied than at $W_m$. This labor supply curve bends backward. At a wage rate greater than $W_m$, the negative income effect of a wage increase exceeds the positive price effect.

## Appendix B
### The Effect of Taxation on the Stock of Capital

The effect of the tax structure on the size of the capital stock is illustrated in Figure II. The line S represents the amount of capital—K—people want to hold at each net rate of return—r. The line D is the marginal value product of the differing amounts of K. With no tax, the equilibrium amount of capital is $K_{nt}$, the amount for which the marginal value product and the net rate of return which individals require if they are to hold a given amount of capital are the same—r. With a tax, the required pretax rate of return must rise sufficiently so that after paying the tax the net return will be that required to induce people to hold the indicated amount of capital. The line S' delineates the pretax returns which are required to provide the net returns for various amounts of capital shown on the line S. For $K_{nt}$ of capital, for example, the pretax return would have to be $r'_1$, so that after paying the tax the capital holders would obtain a net return of r. But the marginal product of $K_{nt}$ of capital is r, for less than $r'_1$. With the tax, the equilibrium amount of capital is $K_t$, at which both the marginal value product and the pretax return are $r'_1$. The after-tax return is $r_1$, the rate of return required to induce people to hold $K_t$ of capital. This amount of capital, of course, is significantly less than people would want to have in the absence of the tax. One way of measuring the cost of the tax, thus, is in terms of the foregone capital—$K_t$, $K_{nt}$—and the income it would produce.[22]

*FIGURE 2*

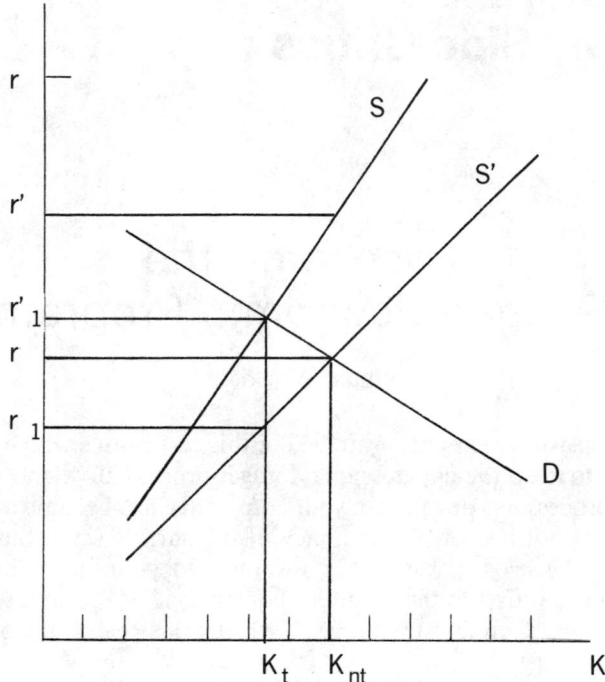

# Chapter 2:
# Supply-Side Critics

# Assessing the
# Reagan Economic Program

### Walter W. Heller

It is a pleasure to appear again before this committee which has done so much to keep the congressional budget process alive and vigorous. As that process has developed, your committee has become a powerful instrument not just of budget policy in the narrow sense but of fiscal policy in the broadest sense. In response to your invitation, I will address myself first to the broad economic logic of President Reagan's proposals and then take up more specifically the Reagan tax policy and proposals.

The Reagan program represents a sharp reordering of priorities and burdens. Although the *economic* impact of this reordering has received top billing, it is important to recognize that the dominant thrust of the Reagan scenario is a sea change in *political* philosophy. It expresses itself in a four-ply shift of priorities and burdens: a shift of priorities from the public to the private sector and from civilian to defense spending; and a shift of burdens from federal to state and local governments and from upper to lower income groups. This is not to say that the Reagan economic program is a mere byproduct of this quadruple shift. But it is clear that its economic content had to be tailored to fit the broad political shifts, not vice-versa. Given this forced interweaving of a political warp with an economic woof, it is hardly surprising that the resulting pattern of economic plans and projections is seriously flawed.

### The Reagan Economic Program As a Whole

The Reagan economic scenario is not the "old-time religion," putting the economy through the wringer in order to squeeze out inflation before resuming expansion (as the Thatcher government's program).[1] Rather, it is the "new faith," opting for prompt and vigorous expansion and relying on supply-side effects plus revised expectations to subdue inflation along the way. Unfortunately, economic experience tells us that this approach is both overoptimistic and internally inconsistent. With any direct attack on the price-wage spiral ruled out by an uncompromising free-market philosophy, one cannot expect inflation and interest rates to recede once brisk recovery replaces the current softness in the economy. At that point, a fiscal policy devoted to promoting expansion will collide with a monetary policy devoted to curbing inflation.

## Fiscal Policy

When one examines the demand-stimulating and demand-dampening features of the Reagan fiscal program, as is done in the accompanying table, it becomes apparent that while the fiscal shifts are large and bold, they add up to a fairly conventional demand-stimulus program: (1) Without exception, the combination of defense spending boosts and tax cuts that take money out of people's hands exceeds the combined budget cuts and user fees that put money into people's hands. This excess grows steadily throughout the period, to reach nearly $100 billion by 1985. The fiscal stimulus will largely offset the normal fiscal drag from the trend increase in revenues generated by economic growth and inflation. (2) Surprisingly, the Reagan budget's demand effects in 1981-1985 are more stimulative than those that were implicit in the Carter budget. Much like Kennedy's budget in the early 1960s and Nixon's ten years later, it is a budget geared to promoting a brisk cyclical expansion to high employment. (3) If the full three-year 30 percent tax cut is put on the books this year, the Reagan program could turn out to be a lot more expansionary than projected. Taxpayers might well treat their guaranteed tax cuts as "money in the bank" that could support more spending now, expecially for durable goods on which installment payments could be met out of future tax-cut monies. (4) Also, in spite of persistent administration promises of a second stage of tax cuts—including such candidates as tuition tax credits, easing of the "marriage penalty" on two-earner couples, estate tax relief, capital gains easing, and so on—no allowance is made in the Reagan budget for the resulting revenue losses. (5) Coupling these omissions with the optimistic assumptions spelled out in the note in the following table suggests that the projected budget balance by 1984-85 cannot be realized. Indeed, the recent projections by the Congressional Budget Office make clear that with less rosy—and in my view, more realistic—assumptions, the 1984 budget will not be in balance but will still be nearly $50 billion in deficit.[2]

As both the staff of this committee and of the Congressional Budget Office have pointed out, economic assumptions that are more in line with the consensus of private economists—the great majority of whom project higher inflation, interest rates, and unemployment rates than those underlying the Reagan budget—would expand the 1982 deficit from the $45 billion White House figure to $67 billion. These private projections reflect in part the likelihood of an expansionary fiscal policy clashing with a contractionary monetary policy. Mr. Reagan seems to be relying on fiscal policy to boost demand and speed recovery, monetary policy to curb inflation, and supply-side policy to promote long-run economic growth.

## Anatomy of the Reagan Fiscal Program
## 1981-1985 (billions of dollars)

|  | 1981 | 1982 | 1983 | 1984 | 1985 |
|---|---|---|---|---|---|
| Baseline budget deficit or surplus before Reagan Program* | −49 | −34 | − 1 | +48 | +103 |
| Fiscal stimulus: |  |  |  |  |  |
| Defense spending | 2 | 6 | 21 | 27 | 50 |
| Personal tax cuts | 6 | 44 | 81 | 118 | 142 |
| Business tax cuts | 3 | 10 | 19 | 30 | 44 |
| Total | 11 | 60 | 121 | 175 | 236 |
| Fiscal restriction: |  |  |  |  |  |
| Specified budget cuts | 5 | 47 | 66 | 80 | 91 |
| Unspecified budget cuts | — | — | 30 | 44 | 44 |
| Increased user fees | — | 2 | 3 | 3 | 4 |
| Total | 5 | 49 | 99 | 127 | 139 |
| Budget deficit or surplus after Reagan program | −55 | −45 | −23 | 0 | +6 |

Note: Underlying the tax and spending numbers in this table are the optimistic Reagan economic assumptions: (1) real GNP growth averaging 4.5% a year from 1982 through 1985; (2) inflation (CPI) steadily receding from 11.1% this year to 4.7% in 1985; (3) unemployment shrinking from 7.8% in 1981 to 6.0% in 1985 and (4) interest rates declining steadily, for example, Treasury bill rates dropping from about 14% to 6% in 1985.

Source: Office of Management and Budget *Fiscal 1982 Budget Revisions* (Washington D.C.: OMB) March 10, 1981.

*This baseline represents the Carter budget as modified by sizable "technical adjustments" made by Reagan officials.

But experience demonstrates that the economic world does not work in this neatly compartmentalized way. Fiscal stimulus will expand jobs and output, but it will also tend to prop up prices and wages. Tighter money will tend to slow down inflation, but its main impact will be to cut into jobs and output, raise interest rates, and discourage investment. And as for supply-side responses, they will be far too weak and too slow to lead the economy out of this dilemma.

## Monetary Policy

The Reagan policy of stimulating demand through fiscal policy is pitted against the Federal Reserve policy of restraining demand through monetary policy. There is no reasonable way to reconcile the White House GNP growth projections with the Fed's monetary growth projection, namely, a halving of monetary growth rates by 1986. The Reagan scenario projects the growth rate of nominal GNP (real growth plus inflation) at an average of 11-½ percent per year from 1981 through 1984. Yet, the implicit target for average money supply growth in 1981-84 is only 4 percent a year for M1B (currency plus demand and other checkable deposits) and 6-¼ percent for M2 (M1B plus, in the main, savings and small-time deposits—and money market funds). To bridge the big gap between the GNP and money growth rates would require money turnover to grow far faster than it has at any time in the past two decades. The most rapid increase in the turnover or velocity rate (the ratio of nominal GNP to M1B or M2) for any four-year period was 4.2 percent a year for M1B and 1.2 percent a year for M2. Yet, the Reagan scenario would require the effective turnover or velocity rate to grow 7.5 percent a year for M1B and 5.2 percent a year for M2. Even if financial innovations permit the growth in money velocity to reach these unprecedented rates and thereby threaten to thwart monetary restraint, one could confidently expect the Fed to cut its money targets in order to maintain such restraint.

Thus, if Fed policy holds to its indicated policy of containing nominal GNP growth, the Reagan economic plan just won't work. Neither nominal nor real GNP will be allowed to grow as fast as that plan projects. And both deficits and interest rates will be higher than projected. The conflict is fundamental: until inflation is substantially lower, monetary policy as currently targeted will frustrate Mr. Reagan's "new faith" policy for economic expansion.

## Expectations and Supply Effects

Since the Reagan program uses neither fiscal policy to restrain demand pressures nor any form of wage-price policy to cut cost pressures, any antiinflation impacts would have to come as indirect effects of changing expectations, expanding supply, or enhancing productivity. How do these measure up?

*Expectational Effects.* If inflationary expectations could be reduced, this could lead to some moderation in actual price and wage setting. How much is hard to say, because so much of the price-wage spiral is based on catching up rather than looking ahead. But as the British experience suggests, and as the recent declines in the bond market and in indexes of business and consumer confidence attest, expectations are not swayed by rhetoric alone. They tend to follow, not precede, positive action. And unlike an "old-time religion" program that might bring on a massive recession as in Britain (heaven forbid), there is little in the "new faith" Reagan package to generate expectations of progressive disinflation. Only monetary policy is playing that role, and it is doing so in a gradual way.

*Supply Effects.* Fortunately, in spite of much talk about huge supply-side responses to tax cuts, the projected responses built into the Reagan program are merely optimistic, not overblown. The rise in real potential GNP is pitched at 11.5 percent for the 1982-84 period. As compared with either recent history or the Carter projections for the same period, this represents a substantial speedup of 0.5 percent per year in the average growth of U.S. supply capacity. Even this optimistic supply-side response is overtaken by the projected rise of 15 percent in real demand over the period. In other words, the gap between total demand and potential output (supply) that is exerting some downward pressure on inflation today will be eliminated under the President's plan. When it is, inflationary pressures will rise again.

*Productivity Effects.* The strong projected rise in business investment—11 percent a year after correcting for inflation, according to Treasury Secretary Regan—is the main hope for accelerating productivity under the White House program. Productivity may also improve as regulatory burdens are lightened and red tape eliminated. But it may be impaired by cutbacks in public-sector investments and in support for health, research, and education. On balance, the Reagan scenario must be counting on some step up in productivity growth. That would be welcome in and of itself. But a one-half percent per year acceleration in GNP potential is hardly a cure for an inflation rate twenty times that large.

### The Net Outcome

Drawing these threads together, one can draw the following conclusions about the economic consequences of the Reagan package: (1) Its projected cutback of the inflation rate to 5 percent in 1984 might be realized if both fiscal and monetary policy severely restrained demand, keeping unemployment high and output stagnant for an extended period. (2) Its 15 percent real growth during 1982-84 could be realized if monetary policy accommodated expansion rather than restraining it. But we would then have to expect 1984's inflation to be as high or higher than today's. (3) The most likely outcome lies between these extremes, with expansion repeatedly checked by high interest rates and with neither the inflation nor the unemployment goals fully realized. (4) The current lull in the upsurge of food and fuel prices and interest rates should bring the inflation rate out of the double-digit range in the next few months. But a hard core of perhaps 8 percent to 9 percent inflation will remain to frustrate Mr. Reagan's economic hopes.

## Congress to the Rescue?

Will Congress step in to save the Reagan administration from itself by going slow on big tax cuts while moving ahead on big budget cuts? Conventional wisdom might see Congress doing just the reverse: (1) balking at big budget cuts, especially the $44 billion of future unspecified cuts shown in the table and (2) adding to general rate reductions and depreciation reform a second-stage tax cut embracing such items as personal exemption boosts, easing of the marriage penalty, corporate rate cuts, and special savings credits. The result would be bigger deficits and a more stimulative budget.

A second and more plausible outcome is that Congress will (1) put through a large part of the Reagan budget cuts and (2) restructure and then enact in 1981 only the first stage of Reagan's tax-cut program, though with less revenue loss than he projects the composition of tax and budget cuts would change, but the overall demand-side effects would be similar to those in the table.

A third possibility, by no means ruled out, is that Congress will (1) accept a high proportion of the Reagan budget cut targets, (2) use the "reconciliation process" under the Congressional budget procedures to translate those targets into committee-by-committee spending limits, and (3) make the size and timing of personal tax cuts contingent on budget-cut action and progress in curbing inflation. Questions of social policy aside, this could remove much of the contradiction between fiscal and monetary targets in the Reagan package and thus make for more rational economic policy.

## Tax Policy

To redeem an early and repeated campaign pledge, President Reagan called upon Congress to enact this year—under the Stockman threat of a veto—a 30 percent across-the-board cut in personal income tax rates, to be phased in over a three-year period. This proposal is a prime example of "for every problem there is a solution, simple, neat, and wrong." Or, perhaps more to the point, too simple, too big, and too soon. Let me examine those charges in reverse order.

*Too Soon.* To enact a $142 billion personal income tax cut all at once—from a fiscal 1982 cost of $44 billion, the cost zooms to $142 billion a year when fully effective in fiscal 1985—involves unnecessary risks. The administration is banking on this huge cut to bolster savings and lubricate investment. But there are two major risks or flaws in this do-it-now approach. First, putting the whole three-year cut on the books now would be an open invitation to consumers to make a lot of purchases on the cuff. They could count on tax-cut boosts in take-home pay to meet their installment payments. This would thwart the administration's hopes for a prompt increase in personal saving. Second, it puts the cart before the horse. The path of fiscal prudence would be *not* to put the whole three-year personal tax cut on the books at once, but rather to fit the pace and size of tax cuts more closely to budget cuts and inflation prospects. This is not to argue against a significant personal tax cut to take effect later this year. Taxpayers deserve it as an offset to tax increases, and a soft economy has enough slack to absorb it. But a step-by-step approach, putting further personal tax cuts in place only after they have been "earned" by further budget cuts and/or clear evidence of subdued inflation, would be the fiscally responsible course to take.

*Too Big.* Given the current slack in the economy, given the automatic increases in tax liabilities as the economy expands and inflation continues, given unprecedented budget cuts, and given good luck on the inflation front (absence of external shocks from oil, food prices, and interest rates), given all these things, one cannot say that the overall dimensions of the Reagan tax cuts are too big. But that's a lot of "givens." Not all of them are likely to materialize, which again underscores the case for taking one step at a time.

But beyond this, it seems particularly ironic that an administration dedicated to furthering capital formation and curbing inflation should come forward with massive personal tax cuts and only modest business tax cuts.

Strangely enough, this reverses the approach taken in the Kennedy tax cuts, which supply-siders tell us they are emulating. The Kennedy supply-side initiatives came primarily in a series of sharply focused measures to stimulate investment and curb costs in 1961-62: (1) the investment tax credit, to this day the backbone of business tax incentives for growth; (2) liberalized depreciation guidelines; (3) reduction of long-term interest rates, and (4) the wage-price guideposts to help ensure that stimulative measures would not run off into price and wage inflation.

Once these supply-side measures (we called them "incentives for capital formation and economic growth without inflation") were in place, and the economy was still operating well below par, we followed through with the great tax cut of 1964. Good as it was for incentives, there were not then, and should not be now, any illusions about its primary purpose: It was designed to boost demand and make use of the existing (and expanding) supply capacity. That's precisely what it did.

If the current tax-cutters want to draw the right lesson from the Kennedy tax-cut experience, it would be this: Utilize the existing margin for tax cuts first and foremost for carefully crafted and sharply focused incentives to capital formation and cost-cutting. Then, after these are firmly in place and budget-cutting has moved from rhetoric to reality, use the further elbow room for broad-gauged personal tax cuts.

*Too Simple.* Huge across-the-board cuts of the Roth-Kemp type would use up all of our elbow room for tax cuts and thus crowd out other measures that might have a far worthier claim for tax relief. For example, a reduction of the so-called "marriage penalty"—perhaps by allowing 10 to 20 percent of the earnings of the spouse with lower earnings to be deducted—would be more effective than across-the-board tax cuts in two ways: (1) It would provide relief for an obvious case of over-taxation; (2) it would have a bigger payoff in stimulating additional work effort—careful studies show that while tax cuts on existing earners don't have much net effect on work effort, second earners in a family do respond to lower tax rates. Accelerated depreciation is another obvious case in point: it would be better for the economy to phase in accelerated depreciation more rapidly and thus avoid the postponement of investment to get the benefit of progressively more favorable tax treatment.

Although it does not seem to be high on today's tax agenda, the lifting of some of the burden of increased payroll taxes off the backs of employers and employees merits serious consideration. Part of the increase in hard-core inflation traces to the big boost in payroll taxes this year. Shifting the costs of hospital insurance to the general revenues, where they belong, and cutting back the payroll tax rates would ease business costs and price increases. Doing the same thing for employees would increase take-home pay without wage increases. Both moves would be helpful in removing some of the cost-push pressure on inflation.

Other examples abound: In adjusting taxes for inflation, any reasonable concept of fairness would call for an upward adjustment of personal exemptions and standard deductions to compensate for the erosion by inflation. Other candidates for a list of carefully tailored tax cuts (not necessarily my list) would include reduction of the top rate on unearned income from 70 percent to 50 percent, reduction in capital gains taxes, and special tax stimulants for personal saving.

Insofar as personal income tax cuts are designed to counteract the impact of inflation in pumping taxpayers into higher brackets, the Congress should be aware that the 30 percent across-the-board cuts overcompensate those in the high brackets and undercompensate those in the bottom brackets for this "inflation creep." If brackets were simply widened to offset bracket creep, taxpayers with incomes over $100,000 would get a 7.8 percent share of the tax cut; the Reagan plan gives them a 17.9 percent share of the cut. For taxpayers in the $10,000 to $20,000 bracket, bracket-widening to offset bracket-creep would provide an 18.1 percent share; the Reagan plan provides an 8.7 percent share. In the $0-$10,000 bracket, bracket-widening would provide 5.4 percent of the total relief, while the Reagan cut provides only 3.3 percent.

With respect to tax actions to stimulate saving, it is worth making several points about such special tax incentives: (1) While there is some room for argument as to whether, say, 10 percent or 17 percent or

20 percent of an across-the-board personal tax cut goes into savings, there is very little argument about the fact that roughly 50 percent of a corporate tax cut goes into saving. (2) Further tax preferences for individual saving may well go into the housing sector, where there are large tax advantages, rather than the business sector. And given the fear of both inflation and recession, uncertainties about the payoff on investments may be a greater drag on capital formation than any lack of saving. This suggests a "stop, look and listen" approach to special tax incentives for savings, which are highly costly in revenue terms. (3) Advocates of huge personal tax cuts should also be aware of their potential adverse impact on saving as the economy climbs back to high levels of operation: they may well prolong and enlarge deficits, that is, dissaving by government, thereby undermining the flow of savings in the economy as a whole. Or to put it the other way around, increasingly as the economy recovers, a reduction in the government deficit offers greater assurance than special tax preferences that savings will in-crease. Seen in this light, excessive tax cuts could be the enemy rather than the friend of higher saving.

*Accelerated Depreciation.* As already implied, accelerated depreciation and more liberal investment tax credits—both with a proven track record of stimulating investment—should be the first order of tax business. But 10-5-3, even as now modified in the Reagan plan, has some very serious drawbacks: (1) Its gradual phase-in (to be completed by 1986 when it will cost $60 billion a year), will cause delay in many projects in order to qualify for progressively more generous tax treatment. (2) The 10-5-3 plan is heavily tilted towards construction and against most equipment, toward capital-intensive and against labor-intensive industry, toward investment in physical things and against investment in research and development. (3) Even in the equipment area, it is the long-lived heavy equipment that benefits most richly from the 10-5-3 formula. In particular, oil refineries, which have a writeoff period of at least 13 years, would get great benefits from a five-year writeoff. Given the existing benefits to the oil industry from full price decontrol, percentage depletion, and so on—and given also the current excess of refining capacity—this aspect of 10-5-3 would seem to be the wrong incentive at the wrong place and the wrong time. (4) The very fast writeoffs for structures will also create what *Business Week* has called "the best shelter opportunity to come along in years— a tax bonanza for real estate speculators." I cite these defects and dangers of 10-5-3 not to propose an alternative formula (though I can think of many better alternatives), but rather to suggest once more that the process of tax-cutting should be a responsible and deliberate one. It should seek out "the biggest bang for a buck" of tax cut and follow a prudent schedule of tax cuts that will give us the best chance for a fiscal policy that will be both stimulative and noninflationary and that will avoid putting fiscal policy on a collision course with monetary policy.

In concluding, let me add a final word or two on the noneconomic aspects of taxation. We should never lose sight of the fact that democracy depends on the consent of the governed. In cutting spending and taxes, you are carrying out what you—I believe, properly—regard as a mandate, or at least the perceived preferences of the electorate. Well and good. But nothing in that mandate calls for suspending the rules—the rules of equity and fairness in taxation.

I say "equity" advisedly, rather than "equality." Why? Because I am not making a plea for a particular distribution of the tax burden, but rather that in our emphasis on economic objectives, we do not generate a deep sense of unfairness among taxpayers. If in flaunting incentives, we flout equity, we run a grave risk of undermining the democratic basis for confidence in the tax system.

## Notes

1. This section is adapted in part from Walter W. Heller and George L. Perry, *U.S. Economic Policy and Outlook* (Minneapolis: National City Bank of Minneapolis, 1981).

2. Summary Table 5 of the March 1981 Congressional Budget Office Staff Working Paper, *An Analysis of President Reagan's Budget Revisions for Fiscal Year 1982*.

# The Demand for the Supply-Side

Robert L. Heilbroner

Supply-side economics has taken Washington by storm. Both a diagnosis and a prescription, supply-side economics comprises ideas about what is wrong with the economy and remedies to put it right. As its name would indicate, both diagnosis and prescription emphasize the actual production of goods and services rather than the buying of them. From this vantage point, supply-siders see our fundamental difficulties as constraints, mainly caused by taxes that deter productive effort, rather than as problems deriving from a lack of purchasing power. We catch a vision of the economy as a coiled spring held down by the weight of government. Remove the weight, and the spring will reveal its inherent force.

Most of the heated discussions about supply-side economics are concerned with how much tension the spring really has and how vigorously it will respond to the removal of various tax disincentives. I shall come back to these matters later. But it seems foolish to begin an appraisal of supply-side economics with debates about how far we must cut income taxes to achieve renewed growth, or how quickly inflation will be overcome by increased output. At the root of all supply-side remedies lie profoundly held if sometimes implicit convictions about the nature of the capitalist system itself. Since I am convinced that these views are wrong, I cannot get much exercised about the particular prescription on supply-side medicines. The task, rather, is to examine the patient.

I do not know of any formal definition or description of capitalism that has been provided by supply-side economics. But a coherent image of the system arises nonetheless from the writings of its proponents. I would sum it up as follows:

1. Capitalism is a "natural" economic system, in that it accords in some deep way with human nature. It is the manner of organizing the production and distribution to which mankind will spontaneously drift, once impediments of various kinds (including ignorance) are taken away.

2. Capitalism is an evolutionary system. Its evolutionary tendencies are described by the term *growth*. Growth means an increase in real per

capita income. This increase in real income, reasonably distributed among the population, is perceived as bringing welcome social and political consequences: higher individual morale, less political disaffection.

3. Growth arises naturally within capitalism from the interplay of two elemental constituents of the system. One of these is the profit motive, embodied in both individual and institutional agencies, acting as a force for innovative and expansionary economic activity. The other is the restraining mechanism of competition. The two forces together comprise the thrust and feedback of the market.

4. The capitalist economy contains two sectors, one public, one private. The private sector is mainly responsible for growth. The public sector's main responsibility is the provision of defense, law and order, and necessary public goods. Beyond these functions, whose boundaries are admittedly not always clear-cut, government is deemed to weigh on, and to diminish the vigor of, the private sector.

5. Capitalism is an international system, in that its constituent nation-states are bound together by market forces. There is therefore a world economy which exerts a restraining, and ultimately commanding, influence over the movements of its national capitalist members.

This is certainly not a complete list of the identifying elements of capitalism as seen from the supply side, but I think the vision that emerges is not untrue to its intentions. At any rate, it should serve as a contrast with my own view, which I outline below. I shall make no attempt to compare the two positions point by point or to refute the supply-side view. No such attempt is possible because the two conceptions are so fundamentally different as to be beyond comparison.[1]

1. Capitalism, in my view, is quintessentially a means of organizing labor to produce a social surplus. By a surplus I mean the production of material wealth over and above whatever is needed to maintain ordinary life at its existing level. The line between surplus and mere replenishment is always blurred, as are most social distinctions, but in the large there is no difficulty in distinguishing the form and extent of surplus in all surplus-producing systems.

2. Capitalism is not the only such system. Indeed, all social orders above the most primitive produce surpluses. This is true of ancient Egypt, European feudalism, and the contemporary USSR. What is distinctive about capitalism is the form that its surplus takes. Other social orders use surplus for war, public adornment, religious observances, and for the maintenance of privileged classes. Capitalism also uses its surplus in part for these purposes, and indeed distributes increments in consumption more widely than any previous system. But its distinctive use is something else: *surplus is employed to create the means to gather additional surplus.* That is, "wealth" under capitalism takes the form of machines, equipment, plants, factories. No such systematic use of surplus existed in any prior society. Its

persistence in the USSR and in other industrial socialist societies testifies to their incomplete separation from capitalism.

3. A second distinguishing characteristic of capitalism is the manner in which surplus is gathered. Unlike other systems, it is not extracted by naked force, or by tradition backed by latent force. Surplus under capitalism accumulates as a consequence of the institution of wage labor as the arrangement by which production is carried on. Wage labor has the historically unique attribute of legally denying the worker the ownership of his labor-product, which belongs instead to the owner of the physical equipment with which he works.

In this regard it is always enlightening to reflect on who owns the cars that roll off GM's assembly line. The workers? No. The technicians? The management? No. The stockholders? No. (Try going into a GM factory and claiming a car, waving your stock certificate as justification.) Who, then? The company, the fictional person who owns the assembly line itself and the products that emerge from it. This is the unique capitalist wage-labor relation to which John Locke referred when he wrote, "The grass that my horse has bit, *the turfs my servant has cut*, and the ore I have digged in any place . . . become my property without the assignation of consent of anybody." What a host of assumptions and mystifications lie in that italicized phrase, which goes to the core of the surplus-gathering process in its wage-labor form!

Peasants, for example, own what they produce, however much of it they must hand over to landlords. Even feudal serfs owned the output from their own strips of land, although not from the lord's strips that they were forced to cultivate. Only the slave could be said not to own his product. Hence the expression: "wage slavery."

4. The separation of work from the right to claim the product of work establishes the rationale for the organization of the work process typical of capitalism. This is an organization in which the volume of output per hour takes precedence over most other considerations, such as fatigue, interest, creativity, etc. The hallmark of this mode of organization is the "division" of labor not just by occupational variety but by fragmentation of physical and mental tasks into their simplest components. This division of labor is not a "natural" tendency of mankind, and is not found in other societies to anything like the degree we find it in capitalism. The division of labor endows capitalism with its immense superiority with respect to productivity, but also saddles it with the need to maintain the strictest supervision over, and discipline within, the labor process.

5. The productive activities of capitalism are coordinated by market exchange among individuals and firms. This is its vaunted market mechanism, the source of its remarkable adaptability and its self-regulating properties. There are, however, two vital areas into which the buying and selling mechanism does not enter. The first is the allocation of work within the office or factory. Although the hand of

the manager is restrained by union bargaining and government regulation, essentially he is a commander of troops, a boss, not a buyer of labor services. Employees in a plant or office do not offer the amount of work that they happen to feel like at that moment, nor are they free to dicker on the spot, the way a butcher can take advantage of an opportune situation. The market relations that regulate the economy outside the factory or office do not penetrate within.

Second, the market does not make crucial macro allocations. Government often determines the direction in which the economy will go, as well as braking or accelerating it. For example, the government builds the road network without which the auto industry could not function. So, too, government provides the research and development on which the agricultural sector depends, the schools from which its trained work force emerges. In these ways government provides an indispensable, although usually overlooked, foundation for the accumulation process.

6. The wage labor system in which workers are hired for a given length of time and then released from their "servant" status effectively creates an "economy" distinct from a "society." This separation of an economic sphere from its social matrix creates two pathologies for capitalism. The first is the generation of problems that arise because we systematically exclude consideration of the social consequences of economic behavior. Thus the agricultural enclosures of the peasant "commons," undertaken for economic reasons, bring unanticipated social distress; the creation of the factory brings the undesired mill town; the free workings of competition plunge regions into social decline or thrust them into the disorders of sudden affluence; the extension of the wage labor system destroys the extended family; the development of advertising corrodes moral virtue (on which, more later). It is characteristic of capitalism that it perceives no connection between these "problems" and its underlying mode of production.

The second, more familiar pathology is the continuing difficulty in accumulating surplus successfully. There are potential disruptions and mismatches at every stage of the process, from engaging a labor force, through assuring its disciplined performance, to selling its output. These difficulties are also recognized by conventional economists, but a radical view stresses the self-generated nature of these problems, largely rooted in the wage-labor relationship. Capital is thus seen as the source of its own economic crises, rather than as the victim of crises thrust upon it from outside forces, such as government "intrusions."

7. Finally, capitalism, as I see it, is a world system, but not merely because it is linked by market forces. The unifying process of the world system of capitalism is the extension of the wage-labor system from the developed center to the "underdeveloped" periphery, for the purpose of gathering surplus on a global scale. On the whole, this international surplus is gathered as "naturally" as is the case within national

systems, although resort may be had to military intervention from time to time, as has also been the case within national capitalism when troops have been used to put down strikes or to maintain vital services.

The existence of a world system does not preclude tensions, even wars, among "center" countries, just as national systems often suffer severe conflicts among factions of the nation, all of whom benefit from the surplus. The systemic unity of capitalism, on a national or global scale, is not perceived within, but only from without. This mystifying aspect of capitalism was first noticed by Adam Smith, who used the term the Invisible Hand to describe the coordination of individuals, unbeknownst to themselves. The equivalent of the Invisible Hand imposes a system of accumulation on a world scale over the appearance of international capitalist rivalry and discord.

This is of course not a complete list of the characteristics of capitalism. My purpose, as I have stated, is only to project a vision that can be contrasted with that of supply-side economics. Of course some characteristics overlap, but it must be plain that a point-by-point comparison would be irrelevant. They are simply two different views of the world. To my mind, the essential difference between them is the absence of a historical dimension in the supply-sider's view. To this criticism it will no doubt be retorted that they see history, but not *my* history.

Two important conclusions follow from these opposing visions. Even if we cannot establish which is true and which is a shadow, it should be useful to make these conclusions explicit.

First, the role of government is entirely different in the two visions. I have already suggested that government is regarded from the supply side as an encroaching force, an intruder into the private sphere, a weight on the system. Its necessity is not denied, but its virtues are held to be minimal.

In the radical view this demarcation becomes ambiguous. The designation "private" refers to functions that are directly connected with the generation of surplus, whereas "public" refers to functions indirectly connected with it. *Both public and private functions, however, are seen as actively supporting the process itself.*

From this viewpoint, the fact that there is often conflict, even bitter conflict, between those who directly work with the surplus-generating process and those who work at a remove from it is not surprising: the Roman imperium fought bitterly against senatorial privileges to maintain the empire; monarchs warred against barons in order to preserve an aristocratic social order; Parliament acted against the immediate interests of English factory owners to secure the future of the capitalist system; Roosevelt curbed the prerogatives of bankers and industrialists to ward off a feared social revolution. Governing elements within all social systems must often curb the activities of particular privileged groups within that system.

Second, supply-side economics sees the capitalist order as tending "naturally"—that is, in the absence of the artificial impediments and distortions introduced by government—toward equilibrium and harmony. By equilibrium I mean they see no obstacles in the way of more or less steady growth, with reasonably smooth microadjustments, and well-limited departures from full employment. If there are such impediments, supply-siders attribute them to government intervention into the flux of the market process. By harmony I mean that supply-siders see the successful achievement of economic growth bringing social morale and political stability. In a word, they see no economic or social contradictions in the system, in the sense of dysfunctions brought about by the *success*—not the failure—of capitalist processes.

The opposing, radical, view sees things upside down. The system tends naturally toward economic disequilibrium and toward social and political tension. Economic strains or crises are the unavoidable, "natural" consequences of matters I have already mentioned, namely the difficulties of pursuing the accumulation process without constantly overreaching it.[2]

The radical view also sees change militating against harmony. In politics it sees an intrinsic conflict between the "horizontal" tendencies of a democratic and egalitarian view and the "vertical" tendencies of a hierarchical and inegalitarian structure. In social life it sees strains that result from the continuous restructuring of daily life as the side effect of economic "growth." Indeed, in place of the conventional assumption of a tendency toward stability and harmony, the radical view asks how it is possible to maintain social continuity in the face of continuous economic fluctuation, social insecurity, and political strain. The answer is essentially by the use of government as a sustaining and restraining force.

To turn to more strictly economic matters: supply-side economics puts forward two policy prescriptions. First, it advocates a substantial reduction in marginal tax rates, in order to create a burst of response. A response of what? The supply-siders are convinced that more hours will be worked, that less effort will be diverted into the underground economy, that more risks will be taken. In a word, we will produce more, giving rise to more employment, and ultimately to a diminution of inflationary pressure.

Here everything hinges on the crucial matter of how individuals or firms respond to tax cuts. The fact of the matter is that we do not know very much about this problem. Worse, it is possible to construct two quite opposing, but equally convincing predictions. The supply-siders see individuals using their tax bonanzas, such as the Kemp-Roth proposed reduction of taxes by 10 percent a year for three years, to add to their savings, or as a spur to more effort because more income will be kept. Skeptics see an entirely different picture. They see families reacting to a tax bonanza the way they react to all income increases: they will spend about 95 percent of it. They also see an increase in their after-tax incomes permitting a lot of people to give up moonlighting, overtime, or other distasteful tasks to which high taxes have driven them. Thus the skeptics see the impact of supply-side policies as boosting inflation far more than production. I number myself among the skeptics.

And what about the stimulus to production that firms will experience, as taxes are rolled back and onerous regulations repealed? In all likelihood there will be some response: the crucial question is how much. Again two views are plausible. One of them, exemplified by George Gilder's stress on the creative efforts of individual entrepreneurs, sees a great burst of small business formation, not only creating jobs but providing the innovative zest needed to restore economic vitality. The other, more skeptical view looks to the great corporations that dominate so much of economic life and asks whether tax reductions or milder regulation will suffice to turn the automobile industry around, to reinvigorate the steel industry, to strengthen the transportation system, to solve the energy problem, and the like. Once again, I number myself among the skeptics.

Second, supply-siders want to roll back government, not merely to get it off our backs, but also because government is perceived as essentially a wasteful, not a productive, use of resources. This last is a very interesting contention. I would be the last to deny the presence of government waste: the MX missile system, the space shuttle, the tax subsidies to various upper-income groups, not to mention the petty cadging and occasional grand larceny among welfare clients. However, I want to call attention to a curious aspect of the question of waste. It is that there is no waste in the private sector. This is the case because all "wasteful" activites are eliminated by the market, like the famous Edsel. On the other hand, whatever survives the test of the market is not waste. The five giant buildings that will be erected between 53rd and 57th Streets along Madison Avenue are not waste, whatever chaos they create, unless they cannot be rented. The $100,000 Rolls Royce is not waste, assuming that it sells. There is not waste in the production of *anything* that sells, because the very act of purchase provides the justification for whatever resources have been used.

Clearly there are entirely different criteria for waste in the public and private domains. Suppose that the scrutiny usually directed at government were brought to bear on private output, and that each act of private production had to justify itself by the *noneconomic* criteria we apply to public output. Would we not find a great deal of waste in the private sphere? And suppose that the government limited its production to those things it could sell—pocket-sized missiles and saleable services of all kinds. Would not all waste disappear from the public sphere? This leads one to think about the meaning of the "waste" perceived from the supply side.

It leads one also to reflect on the ideological element within supply-side thinking. To be sure, all social orders have ideologies, and none could exist without them. Therefore societies never think of their prevailing views as being "ideological," but rather as expressing self-evident or natural truths. As Immanuel Wallerstein has acutely remarked, during most periods of history there is effectively only one class that is conscious of itself, and this dominant class sincerely expresses its own views as representing those of the entire society. Thus the senators of Rome, the lords of the manor, the monarchs of France and England, and the members of the Soviet elite all speak with unself-conscious assurance in the name of their societies. None feels itself to be a "privileged" class or thinks its views to be other than universal.

The upper class in capitalism also speaks with a universal voice—as witness the degree to which it speaks for the working man. Nonetheless, the view of the upper class under capitalism is more clouded than under other dispensations. This is the consequence of the rise of democratic, egalitarian, and even revolutionary ideas at the same time as, and indeed as part of, the bourgeois struggle for ascendancy. These ideas remain to haunt the bourgeois serenity of spirit: as Schumpeter wrote, "Capitalism creates a critical frame of mind which, after having destroyed the moral authority of so many other institutions, in the end turns against its own."

As a result, bourgeois ideology at its most refined assumes a defensive position unlike that of any other social order. It recognizes the stormy historic origins of capitalism, the arbitrary foundations of its property rights, the shortcomings of its philosophy. Against these deficiencies it ranges the very great achievements of its economic system and the unparalleled political and intellectual accomplishments of bourgeois culture. Here we find the defense of capitalism offered by Schumpeter, Weber, and in a manner of speaking even by Marx himself. Among modern-day expositors of this sophisticated view I would place S.M. Lipset, Nathan Glazer, Daniel Bell, Irving Kristol, and others.

There is, however, another view of ideology—one that marshalls arguments that cannot withstand the examination of history, philosophy, or social science in general. Here, for example, we find the most vulgar materialist reductionism, in which capitalism is presented as embodying a primordial and unchanging "economic man." For instance, Jude Wanniski writes in *The Way the World Works*, "In mother and father . . . the child has a diversified portfolio," a point of view that pervades his book. Such a materialistic crudity, which puts to shame the most blatant "economism" of the left, would be treated with the scorn it deserves if it were adduced as a defense of, say, the

Marxian view of history. Yet it is treated with respect, even by so sophisticated a critic as Irving Kristol. Or George Gilder tells us in *Wealth and Poverty* that love and altruism are the true essence of capitalism (they used to be trotted out as the soul of monarchy), and this equally strange statement—which recalls the analysis of Bruce Barton, who wrote in the 1920s that Jesus was the most successful businessman who ever lived—is also treated as a "serious" pronouncement.[3]

The question to be pondered is why supply-side economics has attracted the worst ideology, and why it has dulled the sensibilities of the best ideologists. I am ashamed to say the one convincing reason that occurs to me: supply-side economics has as its immediate objective the improvement of the conditions of the rich. What bonanzas will result from the lowering of the high marginal rate on property income and on the reduction of the capital gains tax! I too rub my hands at the prospect. To be sure, like all policies, the *ultimate* objective of supply-side economics is the improvement of the condition of everyone. Just the same, I do not think supply-side economics would adduce quite the same fervor, or quite the same dulling of critical sensibilities, if its *immediate* aim were the improvement of the poor and its ultimate aim the bettering of the rich. Self-interest has extraordinary powers of persuasion.

Two further matters must also be considered. One is morality. The supply-siders are high on morality. They deplore the fallen moral state of the nation. And they are right. It is badly fallen and the consequences are potentially graver even than a prolonged recession.

There are many reasons for the decline in the levels of public behavior. I wish to point out only one. It is the displacement of traditional values by commercial ones. A Gresham's law seems to operate as effectively in the world of moral values as in that of economic values; and the bad currency here strikes me as the steady insinuation of advertising mush into the vocabulary and communication of our society. "Have a nice day" and "We're Am-*mer*-ican *Air*lines, doing what we do best!" are more than trivial irritants. They are instances of a process that empties communication of its content, that substitutes reflex for creative spontaneity, that destroys credence in the written or spoken word.

If I were asked to name the deadliest subversive force within capitalism—the single greatest source of its waning morality—I should without hesitation name advertising. How else should one identify a force that debases language, drains thought, and undoes dignity? If the barrage of advertising, unchanged in its tone and texture, were devoted to some other purpose—say the exaltation of the public sector—it would be recognized in a moment for the corrosive element that it is. But as the voice of the private sector it escapes this startled notice. I mention it only to point out that a deep source of moral decay for capitalism arises from its own doings, not from that of its governing institutions.

Second, I want to say something about the relation of capitalism to freedom. There are many kinds of freedom, some more easily espoused by capitalism than others. But I do not think there is any doubt that bourgeois society—the social order that has created the capitalist system—has gone further than any other, including that of the ancient Greeks, in establishing and tolerating political, social, and intellectual liberty. From my point of view, and I daresay that of the readers of this review, that is its chief glory.

I have always felt that there was a powerful argument to be made for the mutual support among various freedoms, including the very important support offered to political or social liberties by economic freedom. When we look to the Gulag we appreciate how precious is the property of the working class in owning its own labor power, which it is entitled to withhold from arbitrary seizure. So I am far from blind to the virtues of bourgeois property concepts, which have been the intellectual support of capitalism.

What must be pointed out, however, is that political and intellectual freedom, the freedoms that are most immediately in jeopardy in bourgeois societies, have seldom been actively supported by the "private," i.e., the business, institutions of the capitalist order. Intellectual and political freedoms are only indirectly connected with the institution of wage labor on which the capitalist economic system rests. Indeed, to the elements of the upper class immediately engaged in production, these liberties are likely to seem inimical to the stability of the capitalist order, the province of trouble-makers and agitators. These freedoms, it must be recognized, have for the most part been the concern of those political, cultural, and professional elites who oversee, not those who themselves directly carry on, the capitalist process of accumulation. That is something to think about for those who wish to tilt the balance of power in the direction of the agents, not the guides, of the economic process.

What is likely to happen over the next decade? Nothing. I say so from a profound skepticism about the efficacy of supply-side stimuli. But from a more history-laden point of view, I mean something different by "nothing." I mean that the slow, almost invisible trends of the past will continue to have their way, not because these trends have a life of their own but because they express the inner motions, the self-created dynamic of the system. I will mention only two of these trends:

1. *State-owned or state-dependent organizations will emerge as the leading agents of accumulation.* We are all familiar with the slow drift in the texture of the representative firm, from a single-product, single-plant, single-family enterprise to a multi-product, multi-plant, multinational managerial bureaucracy. This has been the consequence of the continuing division of labor and of technologies of control which have

brought concentration and centralization in virtually every field of human endeavor.

This trend now seems likely to move to a new level of organizational size and strength by combining the capital-mobilizing and competition-buffering abilities of the state with the independence and drive of private management. Most capitalist nations today have public-private firms in airlines or airframes, in steel, automobiles, chemicals, and the like.

Many of these public-private firms have been formed to prevent private bankruptcies. That in no way weakens my argument. But the Japanese present a more interesting case. Japan is evidently now preparing to enter the semiconductor industry on a public-private basis with one or two huge firms. That industry today is still dominated by the United States, where numerous businesses compete vigorously for market shares. The result, as Lester Thurow has written, is that in the U.S. the market is likely to eliminate the losers, and the Japanese will thereafter eliminate the winners.

Whether or not the Japanese "model" of public-private coordination can be exported, I would think that statist enterprise of some sort is very likely to be the form in which the accumulation of capital is carried on in the coming years.

2. As part of this statist movement, I would also expect to see the emergence of an ever more explicit reliance on national planning. This will assume two forms. One will be macroplanning for adequate employment, probably through government work programs, for acceptable price behavior through a network of controls and mandatory incomes policies, and for international buffers through protectionism. The other form of planning will be microplanning aimed at channeling labor and capital into socially advantageous uses and at coping with disruptive problems such as energy, urban decay, etc.

It may be objected that planning does not "work," that we are now in retreat from it—a retreat led by supply-side economics. That depends on what one means by "work." As I see it, *no organizational system can smoothly combine the explosive technology, restless polity, and deadening work experience of contemporary industrial society.* This is as true for self-styled socialist societies as for capitalist ones. Hence I do not expect state capitalism to "work" particularly well, but I expect it to survive and to continue the function that is the driving force of capitalism—the accumulation of capital by means of wage labor.

It is possible, of course, that ideological opposition may reverse this two-century-long trend toward centralization. Social orders sometimes refuse to adopt changes which, to outsiders, would preserve their regimes: one thinks of the refusal of the Roman senators to undertake land reform, or of the opposition of the French aristocracy to tax reform. To identify historical trends is not to deny social orders the right to commit suicide.

These considerations lead inescapably to the question of how long capitalism is likely to survive. I would think for quite a long while. No one can project an "indefinite" life span for capitalism. It is by its nature dynamic, and is constantly changing. Today it is pressing against the absorptive limits of the environment and thereby threatening the pace and scope of accumulation. Its moral cement, as I have remarked, is dissolving in its commercial ethic. It faces the contradictions of its antagonistic policy and economy, and the Laocoön-like struggles of its accumulation mechanics. Its broad movement today seems toward a bureaucratic statist regime. After that, who can tell?

Nonetheless, I do not see any immediate "end" of capitalism. Much of the world remains to be penetrated by its formidable mode of labor organization, its seductive technology, its intellectual brilliance. However decadent at its center, capitalism is today without a serious rival as an economic system, dangerous though the Soviet Union may be as a military rival.

This expectation of continued life seems all the more likely because, as I have just said, there is really nothing yet visible beyond capitalism. As an imaginable institutional arrangement, socialism has become a word almost without content. If it means the nationalization of industry or private-public planning, it can be seen—at least, so I suggest—as the extension of capitalism. As a deindustrialization of society it holds forth the specter of a catastrophic decline in living standards. As a vast extension of worker participation, it suffers from a complete lack of any economic and political institutions—or conception of such institutions—within which workers' autonomy could be expressed. In the underdeveloped world it is all too likely that socialist revolutions will usher in narrow, inefficient, and xenophobic regimes.

Hence there is little enthusiasm for socialism today, always excepting the burning desire of oppressed peoples or abused workers to throw off cruel or simply sclerotic regimes. After that, the realities of the industrial process, the impatient expectations of the masses, the contagion of Western ideas and goods must somehow be accommodated. The next stage of economic history, whatever its label, will not be a pleasant one. That supply-side economics, the darling and fad of conservative thought, imagines itself to be the vehicle of this next stage strikes me as an extraordinary fantasy. It is to confuse a small eddy, located in a few board rooms and academic centers, with the Gulf Stream of history.

# Notes

1. A word about pedigrees. The supply-side vision (which is only marginally different from that of conventional neoclassical economics) derives from Marshall, via Hayek and Friedman. My own vision comes from Adam Smith, Marx, Weber, Schumpeter. I am aware that mine has a "radical" flavor. If that word means a penetration to the roots I welcome it. If it means "extreme," I reject it, maintaining that the supply-side vision is far more skewed than my own. Certainly its most

influential recent popular statements, such as Jude Wanniski's *The Way the World Works* and George Gilder's *Wealth and Poverty* seem to me far more remote from Adam Smith, the great tutelary figure of conservative thought, than my own.

2. This is a matter than cannot be argued here. It rests on the long history of the theory of instability whose roots are to be found in Marx.

3. Gilder's romantic vision of capitalists is the counterpart of the rosy visions of the proletariat entertained by the left. Perhaps each side can better assess its opponents than its allies.

# The Supply-Side's Weak Side: an Austrian's Critique

Thomas W. Hazlett

It is not without mixed emotions that a so-called Austrian economist sets out to critique the so-called supply-side economics. In a remarkably rapid period, the supply-siders have enthusiastically helped to: (a) put tax-cutting at the very head of our list of national priorities; (b) rearrange the public debate such that stimulation of *private* activity is taken as the catalyst to economic recovery and the longer-term solution to unemployment.

While from the Austrian perspective there is more than a kernel of truth in the supply-side theories, possibly even an entire cob, one is hard-pressed to announce a whole husk of good theory. As one dives deeper into the supply-side idea box—in fact as soon as one submerges beneath the newspaper clippings and public speech transcripts—they cannot help but be struck by the appropriateness of Henry Hazlitt's reaction to Lord Keynes's *General Theory*: "What is original in the book is not true; and what is true is not original."[1]

For any theory which has come to rest so close to where public policy is imposed, this is a nervous state of affairs. The encouraging headlines generated by a theory's rough, first approximation do not obviate the need for the painstaking process of refining details and rechecking conclusions. On the contrary, refinement becomes all the more important as a theory storms the gates of national policy. A policy speculation toasted on the outskirts of power need fear little from an analytical contradiction of even great proportion: What damage can it do? But a framework which erroneously arranges society's resources as a matter of public policy can achieve capital catastrophes.

What is, then, the Austrian criticism of supply-side theory, and does it carry over into supply-side policy? The answer to the latter is: Yes. The answer to the former may be divided into six broad areas of contention: a theory of value, Say's Law, inflation and monetary policy, the optimality of political institutions, the "Laffer Curve," and the theory of spontaneous order. This essay will deal with but four of these topics, leaving a discussion of inflation and politcal institutions for another forum. We shall conclude with a comment on the implications for policy as a result of these theoretical qualms.

A final introductory note. The question of whom to address when confronting supply-siders looms large in any debate on this topic. The supply-side argument is unique: its "theoretical" works have been written by journalists, and its economists claim that there is no new theory. To the extent that Professor Laffer, who is certainly the best known supply-side economist, becomes involved, it is to deny that he is saying anything at all outside the well-established boundaries of the Walrasian general-equilibrium model. To attack Dr. Laffer would be to attack the whole of neoclassical price theory; and that would be to write quite a different paper. Professors Boskin and Feldstein have joined Laffer in conducting some empirical tests on the precise shape and texture of the Laffer Curve; to attack these would also be to write a different paper.

The most complete and distinctive theory of supply-side economics that we are left with comes from George Gilder's *Wealth and Poverty*.[2] Supply-side theory is just not to be found anywhere else. Bruce Bartlett's *Reaganomics*[3] provides only a fleeting attempt at theorizing and in the main serves only as a useful supply-side workbook which winds its way through illustrative historical examples. Jude Wanniski's *The Way the World Works*[4] was unshyly patronized upon its publication in 1978, Professor Laffer commenting generously, "In all honesty, I believe it is the best book on economics ever written." But this seems somewhat mysterious because vast portions of the book are directly contradicted by Gilder's book, which received an equally uproarious reception among supply-siders. I have chosen, charitably I think, to concentrate on the more recent and better known *Wealth and Poverty*.

If it is curious that the supply-side economists have spent no time theorizing while the supply-side journalists have been breaking their backs with the heavy chore of model-building, it is equally odd that so little feedback has been traded publicly between disagreeing compatriots. Should not the economists seek to lend their precious expertise to their hard-working friends embarked on a mission of such great import? While the political implications of this division of labor appear curious, let us simply say that we would welcome a chance to analyze a supply-side *economist's* economic theory.

## A THEORY OF VALUE

Any buyer, whether of a coconut, a haircut, or a steel guitar, pays not ultimately in the currency of demand that can be expanded or restricted by government, but in his own provision of goods and services. His demand arises and is more vitally expressed not in the market where he performs the perfunctory act of purchase, but in the factory or office where he takes risks and suffers hardships in his vital creation of supply. He values his money because his expenditure of funds is psychologically rooted in his earlier expenditure of effort.

—George Gilder
*Wealth and Poverty*

Directors and managers providing income for thousands of people sometimes think of their corporation merely as a great money-making machine. In their eyes, its one purpose is to earn money dividends for the stockholders, money interest for the bondholders, money wages and money salaries for the employees. What happens after these payments are made seems too private a matter to concern them. Yet this is the nub of the whole arrangement. It is only what we carry out of the market place into our homes and private lives which really counts. Money is no use to us until it is spent. The ultimate wages are not paid in terms of money but in the enjoyment it buys. The dividend check becomes income in the ultimate sense only when we eat the food, wear the clothes, or ride in the automobile which are bought with the check.

—Irving Fisher
*The Theory of Interest*

The most boisterous supply-side claim is that they have created a whole new mode of analysis to supercede 100 years of miseconomics. Their theory will replace the fallacies of "demand-oriented economics"[5] with "the centrality of supply"[6] and with the axiom: "supply creates its own demand." Thus, in claiming that "Say's Law in all its variations is the essential enactment of supply-side theory,"[7] Gilder believes that he is able to stake out a position for "the primacy of supply."[8] His central disagreement with neoclassical theory is over the fundamental explanatory nature of consumer demand, an error which he believes was planted by the neoclassical microtheorists and reached full bloom in the flowering of Keynesianism: Keynes, he writes, "affirmed emphatically in the economics of the whole society (macroconomics) [sic] the more *insidious triumphs of demand* in the economics of the individual and the firm (microeconomics)."[9] For Gilder, the Keynesian revolution seems to have been no revolt at all, but a mere extention of "insidious" demand theories. This conclusion would appear rather odd to Lord Keynes, *all* of Lord Keynes's eager followers, *all* of Lord Keynes's professional opponents, and *all* economists who have come to watch these parties spar. But it is Gilder's misconceived supply-side theory—and not three generations of economists—that erroneously arranges the parameters of neoclassical price theory and of Keynes macroeconomics.

No Austrian critic could here fail to see—or fail to take credit for—the primary culpability of Carl Menger in this rising tide of demand analysis. It was Menger's great contribution in *Principles of Economics* (1871)[10] to solve the numerous errors of classical price theory by directing all eyes to the principle of marginal evaluations made subjectively by consumers. The older approach employed an objective theory of value based on finding the sum of all relevant costs to deduce the price of a commodity. In thoroughly rejecting this line, and placing subjective consumer demands at the center of the economic machine, Menger helped (with Jevons and Walras) touch off the so-called marginalist revolution. Joseph Schumpeter explained the essence of Menger's discovery this way:

> The critics of Menger's theory have always maintained that no one could ever have been unaware of the fact of subjective valuation, and that nothing could be more unfair than to put forward such a triviality as an objection to the Classics. But the answer is very simple: it can be demonstrated that almost every one of the classical economists tried to start with this recognition and then threw it away because he could make no progress with it. What matters, therefore, is not the discovery that people buy, sell, or produce goods because and insofar as they value them from the point of view of satisfaction of needs, but a discovery of quite a different kind: the discovery that this simple fact and its sources in the laws of human needs are wholly sufficient to explain the basic facts about all the complex phenomena of the modern exchange economy, and that in spite of striking appearances to the contrary, human needs are the driving force of the economic mechanism.[11]

In its crudest and most often stated form, supply-side value theory suffers from the premarginalist cost-sets-price fallacy. While brandishing the motto of Jean Baptiste Say, "supply creates its own demand," the supply-siders understand little of the rule's complexities and nothing of its application. What is never appreciated is that the simple "supply creates its own demand" tells us nothing of what we truly wish to know: what is the *value* of the supply that is creating its own demand. It is not incidental that this question is left unasked, for the only way questions of "value" may be answered is in the illuminating spotlight of consumer *demand*. Not since 1871 have economists attempted to settle questions of value any other way. Until now.

The supply-side argument proceeds rapidly from Say's Law to "the primacy of supply" (quite distinct, as we shall see, from Say's Law) to a theory of demand-is-determined-by-supply. It is from this theoretical precipice that the supply-side argument leaps to the policy conclusion that our only hope for economic revival is to promote the incentives of producers.

So rash is the attack on theories which allow consumer choice to occupy center stage that we are afforded the opportunity to witness glaring defects in supply-side thinking. Hence, Gilder attempts to criticize price theory on these grounds: "Demand curves signifying the purely mental reactions of consumers to particular goods and prices are assigned the same weight and priority as supply curves registering the real efforts, sacrifices, and intentions of producers."[12]

This particular misunderstanding throws Gilder's confusion in stark relief. The supply-side position on exhibit here is exactly the reverse of the facts: it is only the *demand* curve which determines the price-quantity equilibrium point for all goods and which therefore dominates the analytic importance of the so-called supply curve. This supply curve, after all, represents no more than the marginal opportunity costs required for various output levels of a particular good. For this reason, supply curves are often labeled (correctly) as marginal cost or opportunity cost curves.

We are left with the realization that there are *only* demand curves, as Wicksteed pointed out nearly seventy years ago.[13] The conditions of supply are wholly determined by the demand for scarce resources in competing uses. The supply of any one good will be controlled by the consumer demands that would have to be sacrificed to obtain it. The reason that an apple "costs" 19¢ is that if Consumer A is unwilling to pay 19¢ for the apple, Consumer B would; i.e., the value of the opportunity foregone by A's consumption of the apple is not a fact of "supply" but of demand—B's demand to use the same resource in an alternative use.

The dependency of supply upon demand can be shown quite simply in a model of a world where only two final consumer products are available. If we hypothesize that many inputs are used to create these outputs, call them Burgers and Fries, and that money is used to pay for these two goods, then we are ready to see how the demand curves for the products are dominant. For simplicity, we also assume that the same bundle of resources are required to create one unit of either output.

The procedure is begun by drawing a demand curve for either output; let us do so for Burgers. This is all the information we require to establish the supply of Fries. To do so, we merely chart the opportunity cost of the Fries, and the costs will be set by the demand for an equal quantity of Burgers (this equality is a consequence of our simplifying assumption that any bundle of resources could produce the *same* number of Burgers or Fries; normally there will exist a proportionality rather than an equality, which does not change the analytics). The principle is that the "cost" of any bundle of Fries is set by the value consumers place on the Burgers that would be thereby lost. This result may be generalized so as to find the Burger supply curve from the Fries demand curve, and the assumptions relaxed so as to derive all real world supply curves from the sum of the demand curves for the resources that can be used to produce the final product in question. There is nothing concrete (or even wooden) in the supply curve, despite Mr. Gilder's preference to think of it as vastly more muscular than the demand curve—"signifying the purely mental reactions of consumers." Supply curves *are* demand curves—read backwards.

While Gilder is led, in his pursuit of the heroic supplier, to belittle consumer demands and trumpet the tough, no-nonsense achievements of production, he misses the very protein of the entrepreneurial

## FIGURE 1
### DEMAND CURVES CREATE SUPPLY CURVES

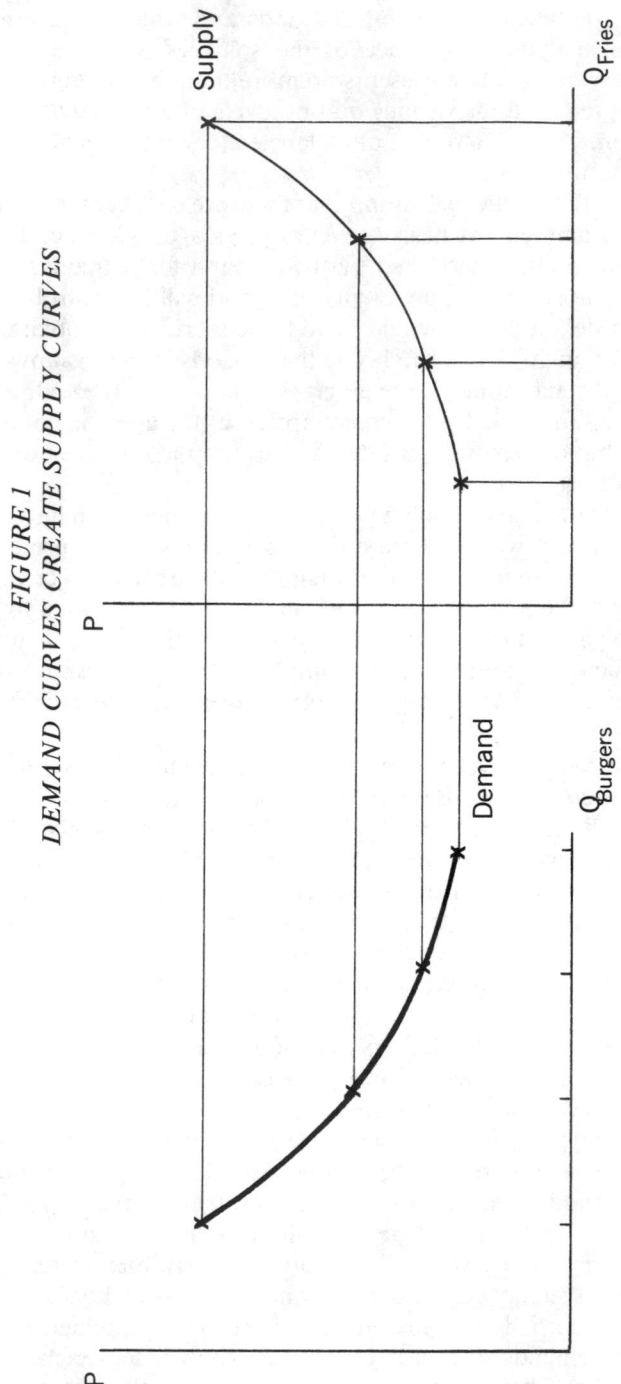

function. It is the entrepreneur's unique ability to *discover* the parameters of consumer demand for resources in their limitless permutations, an abilty capable of satisfying countless desires of unmeasured intensity, while foregoing an unbounded matrix of alternative employments of unknown (or completely subjective and diffused) potential. Buying low and selling high is "simply" the entrepreneur identifying where one set of physical resources, once used to assuage a relatively low-valued want of consumers, is diverted to satisfying a relatively highly valued want. In the strictest sense, it is not the entrepreneur's task to create new supplies; it is his task to increase the consumer demand for a *given* supply. Since the value attached by consumers to the same physical quantity increases, we take this increase in demand to be *itself* an increase in supply. (If we didn't measure our output this way, but attempted to physically measure it, we would find that our "supply" of goods never changes, except on those chance moments when meteors find their way into our atmosphere.) So fundamental is demand that we measure supply not by its "quantity" (i.e., physical size) but always by its demand-created value.

For both the Austrians and the more traditional neoclassical versions of price theory there is little dispute on the centrality of consumer demand in any framework for determining "values," and hence, the society's allocation of resources. There is a confusion, however, when one artificially separates demanders from suppliers. The suppliers are themselves demanders and vice-versa. Every act of supply is equally an act of demand (on the same principle as Say's Law); it is also true that all (effective) demands are equally "supplies"—what you would pay (supply) to obtain a particular good.

The crucial point, however, is that the supply of any good requires a producer to outbid competing consumers for the resources involved to make it; thus the supply is determined by opportunity cost which is in turn determined by consumer demand. Demands of rivalrous purchasers in the auction process of the market set all prices—and these prices become opportunity costs.

Once the anchor of consumer demand is cast away from supply-side theory it soon finds itself drifting into previously forsaken waters. Without the mainspring of consumer choice to set priorities and direct resources the supply-sider must resort to gimmicks to avoid even the most obvious traps. Not even does the diamond-water paradox appear soluble in this muddled state. Moreover, if supply creates (valuable) demands, what is to distinguish one set of supplies from another? Are we to be left to the judgments and manipulations of producers? Have consumers no active role?

Almost incredibly, the answer is: Precisely. According to Gilder, the value of any commodity can be derived just the way Adam Smith or Karl Marx would have proposed—by adding up all the supplier's (sunk) "costs" that went into it. So he writes: "Before the interplay of supply and demand, the basic price of each marketable good is a tip of a pyramid of production, consisting of all the intermediate contributors or claimants to its value. It is the sum of its own intermediate costs plus a share of other costs passed on in its price."[14]

No student of the history of economic thought will have trouble pinpointing this thought as the cost-sets-price fallacy of the premarginalist epoch. Yet, such a disastrous return to the mistakes of another century are the inevitable cul-de-sac awaiting the traveler speeding along the supply-side highway, hurling litter and refuse at the advocates of consumer demand at every turn.

There is but one well-known American economist who could ever come to pick up these scattered tidbits. It is the Galbraithian vision that suppliers determine demands through a combination of monopoly power and irresistable marketing tricks. Gilder, in essence, concurs, as he certainly must for the sake of consistency if supply is the only relevant variable. He applauds Galbraith for "an essential appreciation of the centrality of supply."[15]

Gilder goes on to praise Galbraith's "Dependence Effect" and mistakenly takes it for a replica of Say's Law. "Galbraith refurbishes it [Say's Law] and names it first the Dependence Effect, and then in a later work *The Revised Sequence* (which merely puts supply before demand). 'As society becomes increasingly affluent,' he [Galbraith] writes, 'wants are increasingly created by the process by which they are satisfied . . . or producers may proceed actively to create wants through advertising and salesmanship.' He sums up: '*Wants thus come to depend on output*.'"[16]

Gilder tips his hand by instantly drawing the conclusion: "Supply creates its own demand may be a more felicitous way of putting it. But the essential point is fruitless to deny. Producers play a leading and initiatory role in eliciting, shaping and creating demand."[17] At least it can be said, in Galbraith's defense, that *he* doesn't confuse the Dependence Effect for Say's Law.[18]

## SAY'S LAW

Say's Law, the idea that supply creates its own demand, can best be understood by division into halves. For a barter economy, the law reduces to an identity: the cow that a farmer supplies to market is itself the (effective) demand he makes for other goods. Without money, goods are traded one for another, and each commodity is, consequently, simultaneously a supply and demand of equal value.

When goods trade for money, Say's Law is no longer an identity, but an equality. Simply stated, the aggregate value of the goods supplied equals the aggregate value of the goods demanded. The reason is that goods are sold for money only to the extent that the seller demands to purchase other goods with the money. It is evident that the supply-side confusion is to substitute for this equality of aggregate supply and aggregate demand the very different notion that each specific supply will equal its own demand—*at some specified value.*

This latter qualification is the implication of the Gilder-Galbraith argument. The argument that suppliers produce commodities which are then evaluated by consumers and given a price in the market (a price set by auctioning the product to the highest bidding consumers) is something quite different from their contention. Specifically, they maintain that values—demands—are *fixed* at preordained levels by powerful producers who then impose these values (prices) upon a passive consuming public. To this, Galbraith deplores the unconstrained multinationals; Gilder idolizes the dynamic abilities of such bold productive giants.

Neither have so much as a toehold on the manner in which producers seek profits in the real world. Central to their respective errors is their methodology of attempting to understand the outcome of a process by analyzing the purposeful behavior of the individual participants. Do producers attempt to push their products on the submissive consuming public? To look at the individual members of this process in isolation from the complex web of interactions which form the market in which they operate, it certainly would appear so. Yet, this is but one instance of the "animistic fallacy" which will be discussed below. Suffice it to say that no theory of "administered prices" has convinced great numbers of those who have dared to ask why producers would choose to force relatively poor products on helpless consumers if better products could make greater profits at no greater cost; why the great profits in such exploitative behavior would not attract so little competition from firms, capitalists and entrepreneurs making smaller rates of return; and why, failing business competition, worker and consumer organizations show no enthusiasm for incorporating themselves into such competition.

To return to the value questions at the root of the market structure debate, it is no mystery to see the strange Gilder-Galbraith alliance. Rejecting consumer evaluations as "insidious" economists' propaganda, Gilder touts the supplier as the root of all good, ignoring the "minor detail" that a producer may only succeed on the basis of satisfied *customers* who *consume* his product. It is not our goal to maximize output in some way independent of demand, but to maximize output as *defined* by demanders. Failing to recognize the key role of prices, which fluctuate in response to the bids of consumers for scarce resources which may be used to satisfy competing wants, Gilder easily plops into the waiting arms of Galbraith. While Gilder grins coquettishly at having found such a strange bedfellow stealing his covers, he mistakenly concludes that their supply-creates-demand affinity is a product of their unique understanding from opposite poles of the central importance of great entrepreneurs. But Galbraith's conclusions derive from systematic mistrust of the ability of consumers to make "proper" or "intelligent" choices and thus to be manipulated by a few select megacorporations, which are apparently chosen at random. (That is to say, in failing to explain how the *process* which operates gives us these results, he ends up attacking only *consumer choices themselves*.)

But Galbraith is able to perceive the basic ingredient in this crude supply-creates-demand view: price fixing. It is not sufficient to continually toss Say's Law about while referring only to "supplies" and "demands" as though they were fixed physical quantities. They must be thought of as "values." It is the *value* of what is supplied that will create a corresponding demand, and it is this *value* we seek to understand. Galbraith's claim is that the value of goods is manipulated by large companies which administer monopoly prices. Gilder seems to have missed the point entirely by devoutly sticking to the litany of "supply creates its own demand" and the "primacy of supply"— without acknowledging that the only way suppliers can be superior to demanders is either in the Galbraithian price-fixing sense or in Gilder's own morality play.

Keynes, it should be noted briefly, was aware of the essential role of price adjustments at the bottom of Say's Law, and derived his model of equilibrium unemployment by describing the price-adjustment processes themselves as particularly cumbersome and politically inadequate during certain periods within a money-based (as opposed to barter) economy.

Increasing "supply" will only increase "demand" if, in fact, consumer demand is being satisfied. Gilder is not unaware that not all supply is "good" supply, and takes an entire chapter to divide wealth into "real" and imagined. But where is this line to be drawn? If supply-creates-its-own-demand is the *whole* story, how is it that we may come back, after a supply is produced and label parts of the output "good" and other parts "bad?" Should Chrysler (a *supplier*) be bailed out? Not if you're trying to maximize consumer welfare, for the opportunity cost of Chrysler production exceeds the consumer value derived from its output as attested by record-setting negative profits. Yet, how is a supply-sider to answer this question? While Gilder has made it clear on various occasions that he personally opposes the subsidy, his answer does not seem to rest on anything like a well-developed theory. We should thus be less than surprised to see his close supply-side colleague Jude Wanniski arguing forcefully in favor of the bail-out.[19] The policy question becomes a matter of personal preference.

The false bottom in Gilder's construction of a supply-side value theory becomes painfully evident in his discussion of the alleged lack of real wealth in the Middle East. Setting sail on the "supply-side" principle, Gilder desperately pokes around for *some* qualifying constraint on the supplier's desires. To say that *all* supply is equally valued (because it creates its own demand) or valued at whatever level the owner-seller so desires would be to remove one from any theoretical judgments or policy recommendations whatsoever. One "quantity supplied" is as good as another.

The opportunity to say nothing whatever on this score is unsuitable for Mr. Gilder, and he reaches out in search of some rule of value. What does Mr. Gilder find of value? He states:

> The flows of oil money do not become an enduring asset of the nation until they can be converted into a stock of remunerative capital—industries, ports, roads, schools, and working skills—that offer a future flow of support when the oil runs out. . . .
> At present, individual Saudi Arabians can buy stock in productive facilities in other countries, and they can purchase gold, yachts, Rolls Royces, jewels, art, and other presumptive stores of value. The government can buy guns and planes and port facilities. But Saudi Arabia itself can only become a truly rich nation if it can transform the transitory streams of income from oil into capital goods at home, with a yield for the future. Material resources become durable wealth only when mixed with other resources in profitable combinations.[20]

It is here that the mechanical understanding of economic values demonstrated by the supply-side school rings most metallic. The value of the oil in Saudi Arabia happens to be just whatever the Saudis can get passive consumers to pay for it, that price being partly a function of the level of production the government of Saudi Arabia chooses. But to criticize the oil as a source of "transitory" wealth is to recognize the transitory nature universal to *all* sources of wealth. While Gilder portrays "industries, ports, roads, schools and working skills" as commendable investments, he fails to consider the very alert observations of these "stupid" investors themselves—they make extensive investments abroad (as well as at home) in the very rational (and profitable) effort to diversify and preclude just the fate for themselves that Gilder points out in reference to other once-wealthy civilizations. As for his denunciation of "gold, yachts, Rolls Royces, jewels, art, and other presumptive stores of value," Gilder merely expresses his own personal distaste for what others apparently enjoy. One wonders what is so abhorrent about the prospect of wealthy people purchasing expensive cars, if not the sort of egalitarian sentimentalities that supply-siders so uniformly detest.

The deepest misconception in the Gilder appraisal of "real" wealth versus those things of "transitory" value is the idea contained in the last sentence of the foregoing passage. The implication appears to be that "material resources" are necessary, but not sufficient, for economic prosperity. You must create something more "durable" than this. In point of fact, there are *no* "material resources" in an economic sense, and the claim that there is only one more crafty presentation of the physical-or objective-value school. What is a canvas with a van Gogh worth? A million dollars—today. It was worth nothing—the same physical element—while the great but unfortunate van Gogh lived. As Thomas Sowell writes on a germane subject:

> Perhaps the most widespread misunderstanding of economics is that it applies solely to financial transactions. Frequently this leads to statements that 'there are noneconomic values' to consider. There are, of course, noneconomic values. Indeed, there are *only* noneconomic values. Economics is not a value itself but merely a method of trading off one value against another.[21]

How can the Saudis maximize the value they derive from possessing their array of oil and other goods for which they trade? Gilder seems to want to answer that question *for* them; this is entirely consistent with his theory and entirely at odds with economics.

Rather than attack Keynesianism for its focus on "demand," a far more telling critique would be to question the single-minded pursuit of "aggregate demand." It was Keynes's great contribution to isolate the aggregate demand variable as the one to be watched in the event of business cycle depressions. In lumping all demands together under this one all-inclusive variable, and casting aside the microeconomics concerning just how these demands were individually generated, Keynes eliminated any distinctions between the quality of one set of "demands" and another. It was only the "aggregate" quantity of demand that mattered. Consequently, when private investment opportunities lagged due to population stagnation, the maturity of society, and an exhaustion of new productive ideas, public spending projects could be called upon to remedy the shortfall. The increase in aggregate demand would be effective *even* if the public works were all work and no fun; that is, if they were only for the purpose of putting laborers to "work" and not to satisfy any particular *consumer* demand. Thus, Keynes was ready to have the government pay workers to dig ditches, and then pay them to fill them up.[22] (Does *this* supply create its own demand?)

In this way, Keynes eliminated the individual consumer from his macroeconomic calculus, replacing him with all-important aggregate variables $C + I + G$. To achieve the equilibrium, full employment output, these variables could be manipulated by the fiscal and monetary authorities. Once the full employment level of output was achieved, the story reached its happy ending, but only by abstracting from the actual results of the system: what was the value of the equilibrium output? Suppose that this had been achieved by paying the entire work force to dig and fill these crummy ditches? How would this aggregate demand reflect the true consumer values placed upon the final national product?

It is precisely here that the Keynesian vision is so sadly, and necessarily, silent. The entire notion of aggregate demand is a subversion of the essence of consumer demand, in that it allows the individual preferences of economic actors to be wiped out of the system while the fiscal authorities pursue the proper aggregate demand. It is no surprise, then, that this Keynesian model was hatched by an observer who postulated that by the 1930s the consumers were reaching the saturation point and were having trouble coming up with any bright ideas for new wants, new products, new opportunities, and new demands.[23]

It is no less than a world class irony that the supply-side school follows directly on the heels of the Keynesian aggregate demand theorists. As soon as individual demanders attempting to trade their way to preferred points are eliminated as simply subordinate to "the primacy of supply," what difference is there between the supply-side stimulation of tax-cuts and the supply-side stimulation of public works? Excepting the consumer as referee, how are we to judge which supply is to be the superior? Gilder (who obviously enjoys strange bedfellows, but often fails to realize just how intimate he has gotten with them) lauds Lord Keynes's *un*spontaneous view of the economy. Keynes described a nonautomatic economic fountainhead. From Gilder: "The creative center [of Keynes's system] was the skilled entrepreneur and the goal of policy was to cultivate his skills and ensure his inducement to invest."[24] Neither Keynes nor Gilder seem overly concerned with the skill of producers to please individual consumers, for both advocate theories which ignore the market test, and end up with policies that positively seek to overrule it.[25]

## THE "LAFFER CURVE"

The "Laffer Curve" occupies the most curious spot in supply-side economics. In terms of visibility, the Laffer Curve *is* supply-side economics. No news magazine will feature the supply-siders without a diagram of the curve, a word with the author, and a shot of Dr. Laffer's ever-popular macaw bird. Almost the whole of Bruce Bartlett's *Reaganomics* is devoted to historical examples demonstrating the Laffer Curve in practice, and major portions of Gilder's *Wealth and Poverty* and Wanniski's *The Way the World Works* cover the same turf. But for all its usefulness in *explaining* supply-side economics, it has had very little to do with the *application* of supply-side economics.

Just how little may be gathered from the straightforward agenda of the supply-siders themselves? Bartlett sums up the supply-side policy: "A radical reduction in tax rates, government spending and regulation."[26] The interesting conclusion of the Laffer Curve, of course, is that high tax rates can decrease tax receipts. If lowering tax rates will then increase these receipts, the goal of lowering spending would not be necessary—unless the reduction of tax rates is so marked as to take one from, say, point A to point D on the Laffer Curve. See Figure 2. (But this is just what the supply-siders do *not* suggest we do.) When David Stockman, once an eager supply-sider, takes his budget-cutting pen to the office, he offers blatant testimony that the supply-siders have not found sufficient tax receipts to make the Laffer Curve analysis important to the controversy at hand. As President Reagan found after he cut taxes, reducing expenditures is central to the task of balancing the budget.

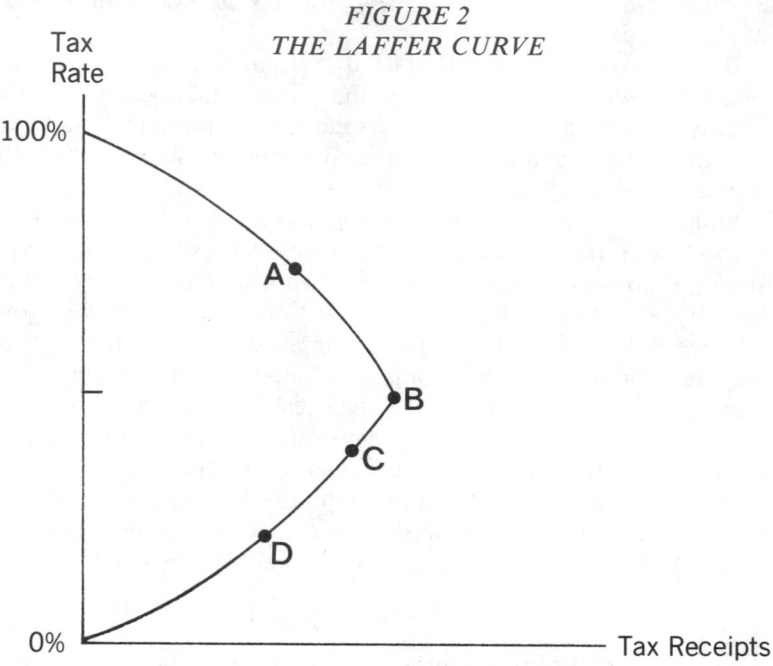

FIGURE 2
THE LAFFER CURVE

Allow us to retreat for just a moment. One "Austrian" attack upon the supply-side theory addressed by Bartlett is the criticism that "supply-side economics (i.e., the Laffer Curve) seeks to cut tax rates so that government revenue can be increased."[27] In response, Bartlett dismisses the Laffer Curve as "merely an analytical device which demonstrates that tax rates can be too high in an economic sense."[28] As for the initial contention, Bartlett is quite correct to downplay the conclusions of any such framework, expository devices themselves being neutral. He then betrays his thought before the sentence is even finished; the Laffer Curve is *not* needed to deduce that "tax rates can be too high in an economic sense"[29]—not unless government spending is the *sole* goal of the economy.

When one considers that all marginal taxes change the pattern of trade from what would occur had consumers been free to express their preferences without such interferences, taxes on economic transactions reduce the optimal allocation of goods at any level. Why is there no supply-side analytic device that details the loss in opportunities to *private* transactors as a result of marginal tax rates? Let us posit the following:

FIGURE 3

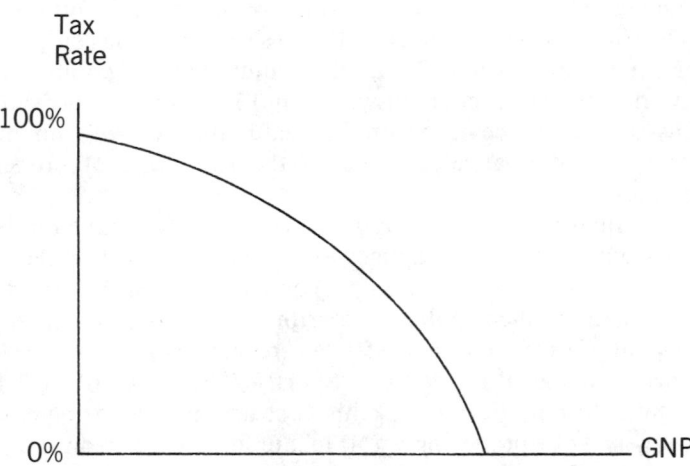

Figure 3 accepts the incentive effects of taxation as described by the Laffer Curve (the second derivative is positive where the first derivative is positive; the second derivative is negative where the first derivative is negative) but measures these effects against a different economic base—the entire economy. This shows us that taxes reduce real income whenever we abstract from the problem of externalities. The Laffer Curve does not.[30]

Neither of these curves, however, look at the allegedly noneconomic effects of taxation. That is, we here look only at the substitution effects of tax rates, and not at the wealth effects. One use of the Laffer Curve, as an "analytical device," would be to point out that there would be no "economic effects" from taxation that redistributed 100 percent of society's resources from citizens to the state. If tax payments were levied such that every citizen were to pay, under the threat of severe penalty, the sum $T^i$ = GNP/n (n = taxpaying population), this would cause no resource misallocation and not only put us on the bottom slope of the Laffer Curve but at the maximum income on Figure 3 (which is derived from the Laffer Curve) for the marginal tax rate would be 0 percent.

Apparently, this scheme would satisfy all the output-maximizing supply-side criteria. As Bartlett writes, "It should be emphasized that it is the tax or tariff *rate* which is critical, not its overall burden."[31] It is just this sort of reasoning which is so alarming, particularly when one considers the long-term implications. In the long run, everything is on the margin, and the overall burden will be the effective tax rate. When referring to marginal incentives, therefore, one actually refers to short-run marginal incentives. No economic resource can be off the margin forever (including us humans, as Keynes's most famous quip about the "long run" reminds us). Dr. Laffer is quite fond of pointing out this very idea with respect to Proposition 13, a property tax cut which many accused of being a simple wealth transfer with no marginal effects in that it affected (mostly) the sunk cost of property tax liabilities.[32]

The extent to which the supply-siders miss the distinction between (short-run) marginal tax changes (which are claimed to directly affect incentives and, hence, total output) and simple wealth redistributions is revealed in their policy prescriptions. Bartlett comments that President Carter's ill-fated $50 tax rebate program exemplified a change in marginal incentives. "Shortly after taking office," Bartlett explains, "Jimmy Carter took his first action toward increasing tax progressively by proposing a $50 rebate for every person in America. Tax credits, by definition, do more to help those with lower incomes than those with upper incomes. (A $50 tax credit would be equal to 0.5 percent of income for someone earning $10,000, but only 0.1 percent of income for someone earning $50,000.)[33] This misses the boat entirely, of course, for the rebate is a perfect example of just the contrary: a lump sum transfer with no (short-run) marginal incentive effects. (The poorer person gains more as a percentage of income, but that is irrelevant. The poorer person gains nothing from being the poorer person; his rebate is still only $50, and he will not lose the rebate by making himself un-poor.)

Again Bartlett stumbles in his claim that "Proposition 13 . . . proved to be almost a textbook example of the Laffer Curve in action." Curiously, this statement is followed on the very next page by the thought that "one might say that Prop. 13 was not a true supply-side tax cut" in that "reducing property tax rates only creates a wealth effect, giving people more money without encouraging them to work, invest, or produce more."[34] (Note: In this passage, Bartlett claims to be extrapolating from the comments of Dr. Laffer.)

In point of fact, lowering California's property taxes changed what was a sunk expenditure (or commitment) for the great majority of landowners. The marginal incentives were changed for those who were considering building a home, office, factory, or apartment building—but by a much reduced ratio. By freezing existing property owners to their 1975-76 assessment levels and permitting only a 2 percent nominal increase in such tax bills annually (provided the property does not change hands), but assessing *new* home (or other property) purchasers at the price they pay for their home in 1979, or 1982, or whenever, most all of the fiscal impact of the Jarvis-Gann amendment is represented by a straight wealth transfer from government to property owners established as of June, 1978.

If the California economy has responded robustly to the tax cut, then, the Laffer Curve fails to provide us with the reason why. Far from being proof of the Laffer Curve's great explanatory powers, the Proposition 13 experience emerges as the Laffer Curve-ball, exposing the supply-side theory's failure to touch all the bases. We are pointed directly towards a theory which may explain why wealth transfers from the state to the citizens increase economic activity.

The Austrian approach can illuminate a great deal about the economics of government allocation, even if the means by which government acquires the funds involves no disincentives (i.e., ignoring the fact that all methods of taxation involve long-run disincentives). From the standpoint of attempting to satisfy the highest consumer preferences from a given set of physical inputs, private transactors operate with far superior information for finding the ways in which to increase utility than do bureaucratic organizations distributing scarce resources which will neither reward nor penalize any of the decision makers involved should they be directed to the highest-valued or lowest-valued uses. Moreover, private market outcomes have the advantage of forcing all decision makers to enlist the truly voluntary cooperation of all parties directly affected by each decision undertaken. If serious information efficiencies are lost when the state allocates the same physical output under different rules, then lump-sum wealth transfers to the state will have serious economic consequences—even in the *short* run. Income effects must join substitution effects in the consideration of a reasonable tax policy.

As a simple analytical tool, then, the Laffer Curve would be wholly unobjectionable if, (a) the supply-siders would consider other variables not covered in this two-dimensional presentation, and (b) the supply-siders did not so often succumb to erroneous application of the Laffer Curve; namely, the single-minded pursuit of maximizing the government revenue variable. While it may be that the simple observation that tax rate reductions will increase tax receipts is a harmless policy statement (and, quite often, a persuasive selling point for tax rate reduction), this does not translate into the normative assertion: Tax rates should be cut *so that* tax revenues may increase. This would preclude the preponderance of tax-cutting opportunities (which do not slide us out and around the Laffer Curve hump) and rule out no tax increase that imposed itself in a lump-sum manner.

Despite strong pleas of denial, the supply-siders have continually used this line in public debate, ostensibly for its political market value: Cut taxes to raise government revenues. As Jude Wanniski states it: "Political leaders must forever strive to find that [tax] rate which maximizes income growth while permitting a distribution of income consistent with welfare."[35]

In a recent statement to the editor of the *New Republic*, Wanniski clarified his position this way:

> We have no interest in cutting taxes but rather we believe that in current circumstances taxes can be raised with lower rates. We don't believe in lower spending, except where economies can be had by the elimination of waste and fraud. Indeed, we believe correct supply-side monetary and fiscal policies would yield greater national output, with an *increased share* going to the public sector for goods and services.[36]

In much the same vein, Bartlett writes: "Considering the magnitude of the tax increase that has taken place over the last fifteen years, it would seem quite in order to have a reduction in tax rates which would put everyone back into the same relative tax position they were in following the Kennedy tax cut."[37] Further, he dubs the tax levels of the early 1960s "tolerable," and offers that "Hong Kong is an almost perfect example of the Laffer Curve in action—low tax rates generate high rates of real economic growth, leading to increased revenues which can be used for social welfare while maintaining low rates."[38] And George Gilder starkly declares, "The purpose of the (tax) cuts, it must be continually stressed, is to expand the tax base—to make the rich pay more taxes by inducing them to consume less and to work and invest more."[39]

The supply-siders appear to have a very tough time remembering that the Laffer Curve is simply an expository aid which leads to no policy conclusions on its own. Implicit in all the supply-side prescriptions is a positive view of government spending such that the goal is not to maximize consumer welfare but to allow some negotiated increase in private welfare as a cost of improved tax receipts. Without any formal analysis, or even quiet mention, we are quickly rushed to accept the entire underside of the Laffer Curve as "tolerable." Where is the theory that allows a mere "pedagogic device"[40] to tell us this?

## THE SPONTANEOUS ORDER

The supply-side view of the economy is a portrait of purposeful action, with the big moves provided by the entrepreneurs, who are in turn discouraged by high marginal tax brackets. Gilder boldly postulates: "Throughout history, from Venice to Hong Kong, the fastest growing countries have been the lands best endowed not with things but with free minds and private rights to property. Two of the most thriving of the world's economies lost nearly all their material capital during World War II and surged back by emancipating entrepreneurs."[41]

Ironically, the poignant insight expressed in this statement appears to be lost on its author. For, to Gilder, the copious riches which flow from the "emancipation of entrepreneurs" somehow depend more on the entrepreneurs than they do on the emancipation. He fails to see the spontaneous order of economic progress, Adam Smith's famous "invisible hand," building the goods of consumer demand. Gilder is only on the lookout for the "visible hand," for the almighty supplier who is just on the edge of his indifference curve between work and leisure. In an approving citation of Keynes, Gilder slaps at the spontaneous theories of society advanced by both Smith and Marx: "As disdainful of Marxism as of laissez faire, Keynes rejected all systems that saw the economy as a mechanism whether of dialectics or markets."[42]

In romanticizing the admittedly formidable achievements of industrial entrepreneurs (Gilder is conspicuously silent in his praise of rock 'n roll entrepreneurs, baseball magnates, fashion jean designers, and housing developers, all of whom produce products which consumers, consumers *other* that Gilder, find highly valuable), Gilder carelessly falls into what F.A. Hayek defines as the "animistic fallacy": the attribution of a particular outcome to the intentional behavior of certain individuals rather than to the conclusion of the *process*. It is not necessary—nor is it advisable—that the structure of a capitalistic economy be purposely designed by any specific human agents. Smith and Marx concurred on the methodology of describing the economy as a *process*:

> Smith had no faith whatever in the intentions of businessmen, whom he characterized as mean and rapacious, but argued that the characteristics of a market economic system would lead to beneficial results which were no part of the intention of those acting within the system. Karl Marx, of course, had a far less benign view of the results of a capitalist system, but he—like Smith—analyzed the results in terms of the presumed characteristics of the system, not the apparent intentions of individual capitalists. In the preface to the first volume of *Capital*, Marx dismissed any idea of explaining the capitalist system by capitalists' intentions. Engels sweepingly rejected that approach with respect to social phenomena in general, "for what each individual wills is obstructed by everyone else, and what emerges is something that no one willed."[43]

Further, Sowell spots strains of animistic thinking in both sides of the current political spectrum. "The animistic fallacy," he writes, "is not the exclusive property of either the political left or right. Conservative economists of an animistic bent explain rational behavior in a timeless context, sometimes with the moral conclusion that the wise are rewarded for their foresight and the unwise penalized for their lack of it—that 'supernormal brains' explain large profits, for example. On the left, social planners eager to save the world from 'chaos' engage in another form of the animistic fallacy."[44]

That Gilder should succumb to this trap, attaching human virtues to the outcome of a process which, to quote Hume, is "the result of human action but not the execution of human design,"[45] is the logical conclusion of his long walk on the supply-side. Demeaning the role of consumer demand while trumpeting the merits of those who manufacture the microchips and other Gilder-approved products can only result in a theory which sees the purposeful behavior of *selected* capitalists as crucial to the society's wealth. This is a radical departure from the classical view of the virtue of free market competition—the idea, concocted by Hume and Smith and further developed by Austrians such as Mises, Hayek, and Schumpeter—that capitalism depends upon freedom of action and self-interest, not upon capitalists. It is the *interaction* of producers and consumers that creates the opportunities for all. Under this view it is nonsensical to isolate Henry Ford as a key to economic progress. It was only within the parameters of market competition that Ford was discovered as successful, let alone fabulously successful. It was only in satisfying consumer demand via impersonal market forces (buying inputs and selling outputs voluntarily to and from people he did not know and wouldn't have cared for if he did) that he was able to satisfy his own desires; at no time was it the foresighted design of any human being that cars be produced and marketed the way they actually turned out, the auto industry evolving over a battlefield of trials and errors sometimes referred to as a "discovery process" or "natural selection."

It is the system that produces Henry Fords, not Henry Fords who produce the system. Take Gilder's much touted microprocessor wizards to the Soviet Union, provide them with one million underlings and a budget to match. What will drop from the factory's spout? What drops now?

If simplicity is the supply-side vice, let us borrow the bad habit to note that the one difference between the socialist and capitalist economies is the greater degree of consumer sovereignty in the latter. To toss out the pull of consumer demand as the system's gravitational force and to look only at maximizing "supply" on some value-free scale apart from the input of consumers is to pave the road to . . . socialism. The Soviet Union is an ardent practitioner of work incentives. They have long, long since abandoned Marx's Golden Rule and replaced it with their own: From each according to his ability, to each according to his work load. Their supplies have no trouble in creating their own demand. Their rulers don't waste their valuable time on the "insidious" theories of consumer demand. The Soviet Union is the quintessential supply-side economy.

No one in the supply-side camp champions socialism in practice. It is that the supply-side misunderstanding of market processes has permeated so far, that is so alarming. Gilder stumbles very far afield, indeed, with the following:

> If the American government could make itself more productive than the private sector throughout the spectrum of needed economic activity, the public would gladly surrender its earnings to the state. At present, however, government is disastrously unproductive even in its most limited roles of keeping order, national defense, and public education. Far more than private services, government must be made to become productive.[46]

No student of the socialist calculation debate can survive that view of government allocation without a shudder.

Even if the socialist organizers have not attempted to harvest a healthy group of supply-sider supporters, it remains significant that the theory of supply-side economics allows for such a vast margin of error. In viewing the economy as the designed outcome of designated entrepreneurial he-men, the supply-side theory logically leads to policy prescriptions aimed specifically at rescuing, or succoring, these key actors. And, if the economic machine does in fact depend on the efforts of these very special performers, it would be illogical not to steer public policy towards the alleviation of their specific sorrows. But here is where the ax falls: any policy to construct some specific, predesignated, salubrious economic effect is doomed to clash with the private wishes of consumers and the outcomes that would have prevailed had a system of spontaneous order preceded without interference.

The supply-side movement, as a consequence, continually finds itself haunted by the specter of "reindustrialization." While interventionist "friends" attempt to use the supply-side criteria to advance Felix Rohatyn-type schemes, "free market" critics wag an accusing finger whenever such measures are contemplated. While the supply-side movement's leading champions should be credited for resisting the most blatant "reindustrialization" programs by a virtually unanimous margin (the one notable exception being Wanniski's affection for Chrysler), the deeper underlying program of supply-side economics is *by its own admission* of the interventionist, central planning variety.

Bruce Bartlett offers a closing chapter to convince us that it's not so, arguing that, "the greatest challenge of the 1980s will be to prevent supply-side economics from being perverted into an industrial policy, which would substitute government subsidies and tariffs for tax reduction or regulatory reform. . . ." First, it must be said, after reviewing supply-side theory, that it is clearly true: keeping the supply-side movement free of the "reindustrialists" will indeed be a keen task. But second, it is remarkable that Bartlett so soon forgets his warning and immediately switches to his own brand of reindustrialization in serving up a version of the supply-side solution: "To get the economy moving again we must increase the incentive to work, save, and invest."[47]

Who would deny the merits of such a program? Only the bravest champion of consumer sovereignty! An Austrian recommendation for a program of economic rehabilitation would be to eliminate the impediments to consumer choice which have been constructed by legislation. This approach does not presume to know the pattern of preferences that would emerge under a wider latitude of freedom. Most importantly, it is not to promote working, or saving, or investing that these measures (tax cuts, deregulation, etc.) be taken, but so that the true patterns of consumer demand may reassert themselves. Should

Americans work more? Or create new jobs? Or save a higher percentage of their incomes? Or increase the capital stock? Any answer which
attempts to prejudice consumer choice should be clearly labeled:
"reindustrialization."

To the extent that current policies punish workers for working,
savers for saving, and investors for investing, deregulation of the
economy would predictably lead to an increase in these categories of
behavior. This accounts for the often close political association
between many free market economists and supply-siders. But if these
parties are to remain good neighbors, the theory of supply-side
economics will have to be dragged, kicking and poetizing, into the
confines of price theory. If it is to insist on being the spoiled child who
refuses to admit to the centrality of consumer sovereignty, and elevates
all-knowing, nay, exogenous industrial entrepreneurs to the caste of a
ruling economic elite, crooners of central planning cannot be far off-
stage. How should one deal with a supply-determined economy? Tax
cuts and deregulation for *consumers*.

The Austrian approach would be just that, of course. Only by
breaking down elements of coercion, which block the effective communication of consumer demand across economic agents, can the real
output of the economy be lifted. It is neither a stimulation of the
supply side nor the demand side which shall bring salvation; it is a
liberation of the progressive elements of spontaneous order. That this
is so often misunderstood is not surprising. The trouble with the
invisible hand is that it is very hard to see.

## A WORD ABOUT POLICY

In a recent call to his fellow supply-siders, Bruce Bartlett had this
suggestion, regarding what he no doubt regards as the pesky, theoretical qualms emitting from Austrian economists concerning his supply-
side program:

> The reality is that cutting back the size of government is a tough
> job. Conservatives have tried to hack away at it for 40 years, and
> the only blood left on the floor was theirs. It was only when the
> supply-siders came along, saying it is just as good to reduce the
> relative size of government by stimulating growth of the private
> sector, that we began to make progress. This is reason enough to
> ignore our [Austrian] critics.[48]

> The purpose of my foregoing Austrian criticism however is
> assuredy the pursuit of a *better* theory than what can be found
> among supply-siders up to now. (And honest labor deserves never
> to be ignored, particularly by a supply-sider.)

When all is said and done the supply-side boast as evinced by
Bartlett is refreshingly simple: Our policy wins. This is a hearty selling
point to all "men of affairs," and shall not be taken lightly. There is
room for caution in this self-congratulation, however, for: (a) we have
seen the recent electoral success of antigovernment parties in other

Western nations with no supply-side camp in a position of influence; (b) the supply-siders strong appeal to the business community may—while accounting for its political success initially—spell its political demise by degenerating the movement into a panoply of pleas for special-interest legislation; (c) their battle is far, far from over.

This should not prevent us from applauding those tax, spending, and regulatory cuts that have been made. Beyond doubt, the most welcome supply-side contribution to policy has been its positive political strategy for de-inflating America. For it is the supply-side promise of private sector stimulation, of a tremendous release of market energies, that makes the painful yet necessary remedy of a tight monetary policy *potentially* acceptable.

By contrast, the shortcoming of Hayek's Austrian business cycle theory in the eyes of supply-siders and, to be honest, all those concerned with practical policies, is its sheer political impossibility. What politician seeking reelection would embrace an avowedly pro-depression (as it appears in the headlines, at any rate) policy? When apprised of his choice between a moderate depression now, or a much larger depression in just a few years, no politician has to check in with his headquarters to choose option B. If there is one thing we have learned about interest rates, it is that our political system induces the politician the highest rate of time-preference for our elected officials to be found anywhere this side of an operating room.

In regards to this business cycle dilemma, most clearly posed by F. A. Hayek, Irving Kristol has written:

> There are two points to be made about Prof. Hayek's prescription. First, it is politically impossible. It may make economic sense, but it is nonsense in terms of the political economy of a modern democracy. In such a political economy, time is of the essence. . . . Rather than placidly "going through the wringer" at the behest of orthodox economists, they will opt for wage and price controls, a vast expansion of "public service" jobs, the nationalization of major corporations to guarantee employment, etc. . . .
>
> Second, it is not even clear that, under conditions of a welfare state, this orthodox prescription makes economic sense. For as that "steep recession" gathers strength, all sorts of government expenditures will be automatically triggered—e.g., unemployment insurance, welfare, food stamps, Medicaid, etc. At the same time, the government's tax revenues will decline as business activity slumps. So it is altogether possible—and Mrs. Thatcher's experience in Britain emphasizes this possibility—that today you simply cannot swap a recession for a balanced budget. On the contrary, it is becoming ever more plausible to think, if you are going to balance the budget, it will have to be through a renewal of economic growth and not a steep recession.[49]

The supply-side strategy is to mitigate the devastating effects of a de-inflation program in the short run—which by nature must be of the high interest rate, low growth variety—with a countermeasure: stimulatory tax cuts. If the economy is down and out under the burden of high tax rates, slashing those may in fact produce an economic boom to offset, or at least partially offset the recessionary monetary course. Unfortunately, this attractive strategy has proven extremely difficult to implement.

In a recent article, John Kenneth Galbraith described the offsetting policies thus:

> On the one hand is the supply-side economics, the commitment to a vigorous expansion in economic output and income that among other things is to bring the increased public revenues that will offset the tax reductions that encourage this same economic expansion. Expansion will also be encouraged by relief from regulation and by reducing the social expenditures, thus putting the malingerers back to work. The companion piece is control of inflation, the most persistent disorder of the last decade and more, by a rigorous control of the money supply. . . . A recession must be engineered. Modern recessions are not wavelike movements inherent in the capitalist system; they are what monetarists induce and must induce to control inflation.[50]

Curiously, all Galbraith can diagnose from this is a terminal case of economic schizophrenia: "What the supply-siders give in taxes, the monetarists take away in tight money and high interest rates." If inflation could be ended by policies which produce a net wash in terms of economic activity for a couple of years, and Dr. Galbraith feels cheated by this, one wonders what sort of alternative program the eminent professor is withholding from us.

Sadly, President Reagan is already finding out how difficult it still is to slay a rampant inflation beast. The supply-siders may well be legitimately faulted for overselling their product. The Reagan deficits have gone South at the crack of the tax-cut bat, despite the way the curve looks on Laffer's cocktail napkin. This moral is understood by a surprisingly wide segment of the government-watching public. Concludes the *Los Angeles Times* in its lead editorial of October 18, 1981:

> The White House now knows, for example, that there is no magic in supply-side economics . . . Thus, all the energy and great-communicating invested in the Administration's new economics have produced a sense of disarray in Washington and of bewilderment elsewhere. The White House itself yielded, in dismay, to a temptation it swore it would resist. It asked the Federal Reserve Board to print a little more money so that a recession would be a little less embarrassing for Republican candidates. Fortunately, the Federal Reserve Board said nothing doing. And the White House now must sit back, as other Administrations have done, and let hard times and high unemployment do the job that the new economics was supposed to do—drag down prices and interest rates. The Reagan Administration inherited inflation and high interest rates, but it made its own life more difficult by raising hopes with talk of turning the economy around quickly with tax cuts . . . No matter how hard the White House begs for more

money and faster growth, the Federal Reserve should resist. Over
the long run, the country will be better off absorbing the punish-
ment of a brief recession than it would be trying to live indefinitely
with high inflation rates.[51]

And it can be no less than alarming when as prominent a supply-side
analyst as Alan Reynolds resorts to the sort of end-run escape found in
this recent report in the *Wall Street Journal*: "Without a gold standard,
Mr. Reynolds says, the economy will experience 'a sharp decline in the
fourth quarter, possibly extending into the first, with some major
bankruptcies and insolvencies.' With a gold standard, he predicts,
'we're off to the races.'"[52]

Still, the basic strategy of combining tax, spending and regulatory
cuts with restrictive Fed policies makes economic sense and offers
political hope. This Austrian's response would be to welcome this
approach, and improve upon it. If an American Renaissance will
flower from the seeds of tax cuts alone, then what miracles will sprout
when a far more aggressive and comprehensive strategy of decontrol is
pursued? The political need for vast efficiency reforms (i.e., dismantling the regulatory apparatus) cries out as the supply-siders learn that
modest tax and spending reductions are not sufficient to provide the
sort of robust private sector expansion which can sustain the economy,
and the perpetrators of such a policy, past the pain of restrictive
Federal Reserve monetary policies.

Beyond the popular goal of tax rate reductions, however, the supply-
side newsmakers have been strangely silent. With the notable exception of David Stockman, who marches to the beat of a different cutter,
the 1981-82 federal budget has drawn little criticism while sustaining
only "cuts" from the level of spending proposed in President Carter's
wish-list going-out-of-business budget, and not from the original
Carter budget projection of early 1980 (adjusted for inflation). Such a
prominent supply-sider as Congressman Jack Kemp has openly opposed further federal spending cuts, apparently relying on the new
improved tax schedules to churn enough money for the Treasury as to
slip right down and around the midfield stripe on the Laffer Curve.
This may be a striking illustration of the principle that a good theory *is*
important for good policy. Now, just when taxes have been cut and
high deficit-inspired interest rates threaten to wreck economic recovery, is the perfect time to cut other social and defense outlays, to move
to a balanced budget. It is not the time to wait for Laffer Curve
acrobatics.

What is most startling is that many supply-siders appear to be
vacationing in the glow of self-perceived unconditional victory. Bartlett opened a recent article, for example, with a relieved, "Now that the
political fight is behind us. . . ."[53] One would think that it had just begun. (Are they really going to leave the FDA just like it is?) Will the
supply-siders be satisfied with a 25 percent tax rate reduction spread

over three years, with "projected increases in income taxes and legislated Social Security tax increases transformed . . . into a form of indexing that served only to keep taxes from rising above 1981 levels."[54]

Have we abolished energy synfuel subsidies, agricultural price supports, import restrictions, Interstate Commerce Commission licensing? In each of these areas the current administration has disappointingly moved towards *greater* intervention. They may be trying to make a prophet out of George Stigler, who predicted that "Reaganomics" would go slower on deregulation where regulation was pro-business than did the Carter Administration.

A consistent market-oriented policy would spare no vitamin capsule in attacking such anticonsumer, output-restricting business programs. It would do so as a corollary to its theoretical commitment to consumer sovereignty and its appreciation of the gains from voluntary trade. This perspective is rooted solidly in the analytics of consumer welfare and has a consistency and sophistication which recommend it highly.

The supply-side policy makers could do well to take their task seriously. Seriously enough to examine, rather than ignore, their critics. Political success should breed a renewed intensity of introspection rather than a desire to dismiss the pesky questioners as mere obstructionists. The arrogance of power is great fun while it infects; it provides its own embarassing sentence when it has decayed both the source of that power and the opportunity it once carried with it to make a change for the better.

Should the response of the supply-siders be to evade the critical issues involved, in favor of shaping whatever policies and arguments meet with the slimmest and least-informed resistance, could we accuse them of something ghastly and terrible? Quite so: they would be guilty of looking only to their demand curve. (And it would be a very short-run demand curve, they would soon find, at that.)

# Notes

1. Henry Hazlitt, *The Failure of the "New Economics"* (New Rochelle, N.Y.: Arlington House, 1959), p.6.
2. George Gilder, *Wealth and Poverty* (New York: Basic Books, 1981).
3. Bruce R. Bartlett, *Reaganomics: Supply-Side Economics in Action* (New Rochelle, N.Y.: Arlington House, 1981).
4. Jude Wanniski, *The Way the World Works* (New York: Basic Books, 1978).
5. Gilder, *Wealth and Poverty*, p. 39.
6. Ibid., p. 35.
7. Ibid., p. 40.
8. Ibid., p. 34.
9. Ibid., p. 32 (emphasis added).
10. Trans. and ed. by James Dingwell and Bert F. Hoselitz (Glencoe, Ill.: The Free Press, 1950).
11. Joseph A. Schumpeter, *Ten Great Economists* (New York: Oxford University Press, 1951), pp. 83-84.

12. Gilder, *Wealth and Poverty*, p. 30.
13. Phillip H. Wicksteed, "The Scope and Method of Political Economy in the Light of the 'Marginal' Theory," *Economic Journal* 24 (March 1914): 1-23.
14. Gilder, *Wealth and Poverty*, p. 202.
15. Ibid., p. 35.
16. Ibid., pp. 35-36 (emphasis in original).
17. Ibid., p. 36.
18. Assar Lindbeck notes this same fallacy in New Left writings and points to an interesting paradox:

> In the context of the terminology of economic theory, we might say that the stronger version of this position is a new form of the celebrated Say's Law, according to which "supply creates its own demand." However, whereas Say's Law is alleged to hold for the economy as a whole, the New Left seems, according to this "strong" interpretation, to apply Say's Law to individual products and individual firms: firms are said to be able quite easily (that is, at low cost) to create markets for whatever products they decide to produce. It is not clear, then, how a number of New Left authors or those who have inspired them (for example, Baran and Sweezy) can at the same time believe that there is a permanent tendency in capitalist societies for aggregate demand to rise more slowly than does supply, causing permanent tendencies to unemployment and stagnation—this in spite of the assumed ability of individual firms to "create" the necessary demand for their products. The "inconsistency" would be lessened, however, by claiming that only *some* industries and firms have this ability to create the necessary demand. But then, why do not these firms drive all the others out of the market?

Assar Lindbeck, *The Political Economy of the New Left* (New York: Harper and Row, 1971), p. 41 n. (emphasis in original).
19. Wanniski's comments were made during an interview with the author in August of 1980.
20. Gilder, *Wealth and Poverty*, p. 48.
21. Thomas Sowell, *Knowledge and Decisions* (New York: Basic Books, 1980), p. 79 (emphasis in original).
22. John Maynard Keynes, *The General Theory of Employment, Interest and Money* (New York: Harcourt, Brace and World, 1964), pp. 128-130.
23. Ibid., p. 106.
24. Gilder *Wealth and Poverty*, p. 35.
25. Gilder's pleas for the "market process" abound in *Wealth and Poverty* (*see* pp. 232, 236). Keynes, however, had to make a special point of not being misunderstood in the *General Theory*:

> But there will still remain a wide field for the exercise of private initiative and responsibilty. Within this field the traditional advantages of individualism will still hold good.
> Let us stop for a moment to remind ourselves what these advantages are. They are partly advantages of efficiency—the advantages of decentralization and of the play of self-interest. The advantage to efficiency of the decentralization of decisions and of individual responsibility is even greater, perhaps, than the nineteenth century supposed; and the reaction against the appeal to self-interest may have gone too far. But, above all, individualism, if it can be purged of its defects and its abuses, is the best safeguard of personal liberty in the sense that, compared with any other system, it greatly widens the field for the exercise of life, which emerges precisely from this extended field of personal choice, and the loss of which is the greatest of all the losses of the homogeneous or totalitarian state.

(*General Theory*, p. 380.)
26. Bruce R. Bartlett, "In Defense of Supply-Side Economics," *The Manhattan Report*, International Center for Economic Policy Studies, New York (October 1981).
27. Ibid.

28. Ibid.
29. Ibid.
30. Writing along these lines was Tyler Cowen, when he noted:

> If the supply-siders are seriously concerned about productivity rather than government revenue, let us issue the following challenge: re-draw the Laffer Curve by replacing "government revenue" on the horizontal axis with "private-sector productivity." Draw a new curve representing the trade-off between the rate of taxation and productivity. This curve will have a negative slope, showing productivity at its maximum when the tax rate is zero. Now choose the appropriate rate of taxation.

Tyler Cowen, "Supply-Side Economics: Another View," *Policy Report*, The Cato Institute, San Francisco (August 1980).
31. Bartlett, *Reaganomics*, p. 15 (emphasis in original).
32. See Thomas W. Hazlett, "An Interview with Arthur Laffer," *Reason* 12 (April 1981): 45.
33. Bartlett, *Reaganomics*, pp. 167-168.
34. Ibid., pp. 144, 145.
35. Wanniski, *The Way the World Works*, p. xii.
36. Jude Wanniski, letter to the editor, *The New Republic* (December 14, 1981), p.6.
37. Bartlett, *Reaganomics*, p. 121.
38. Ibid., pp. 195-196.
39. Gilder, *Wealth and Poverty*, p. 225.
40. See Laffer's comment in Hazlett, "Interview with Laffer."
41. Gilder, *Wealth and Poverty*, p. 232.
42. Ibid., p. 35.
43. Sowell, *Knowledge and Decisions*, p. 99.
44. Ibid., p. 98.
45. As quoted in F.A. Hayek, *The Constitution of Liberty* (Chicago: Regnery, 1960), p. 57.
46. Gilder, *Wealth and Poverty*, p. 216.
47. Bartlett, *Reaganomics*, pp. 204, 209.
48. Bartlett, "In Defense of Supply-Side Economics."
49. Irving Kristol, "A Guide to Political Economy," *Wall Street Journal*, October 19, 1980.
50. John Kenneth Galbraith, "The Market and Mr. Reagan," *The New Republic* (September 23, 1981).
51. Editorial, *Los Angeles Times*, October 18, 1981.
52. As quoted in "What's in Demand? Supply-Siders Are, For Economic Ideas," *Wall Street Journal*, October 12, 1981.
53. Bartlett, "In Defense of Supply-Side Economics."
54. Michael E. Granfield, "Naked Truth About the Supply Side," *Los Angeles Times*, November 13, 1981.

# Chapter 3:
# The Genealogy of
# Supply-Side Thought

## Supply-Side Fiscal Policy:
## An Historical Analysis
## of a Rejuvenated Idea

Robert E. Keleher and William P. Orzechowski

### I. Introduction

Recently, economists are coming to recognize the important effects that changes in fiscal policy—and especially changes in tax rates—can have upon incentives, aggregate supply, and, ultimately economic growth. Several economists, for example, have established the fact that high marginal tax rates can have adverse effects on the supply of factors of production and, hence, on aggregate supply. The view that stresses these effects has come to be known as "supply-side" economics and has had its most popular expression in the so-called Laffer Curve.[1]

Conventional—Keynesian and monetarist—macroeconomic analysis of the effects of changes in fiscal policy has focused almost entirely on impact of such changes on aggregate demand.[2] The effects that changes in fiscal policy might have on relative prices and aggregate supply were not emphasized or were completely ignored. Because of the subordination of aggregate supply, some very important effects of changes in fiscal policy have gone unrecognized, however, and those economists preoccupied with aggregate demand have been unable to make some critical distinctions essential to the understanding of the macroeconomy. For example, conventional economists are unable to distinguish between the different effects of tax cuts and government spending increases, since both were seen to have roughly equivalent effects on aggregate demand.[3] Moreover, they are unable to recognize the possibility that under certain conditions, decreases in tax rates might stimulate aggregate supply and, hence, lead to increases in tax revenues. Finally, they are unable to recognize that because of these supply-stimulating effects, tax rate cuts could contribute to reducing the rate of inflation. Proponents of the supply-side view, on the other hand, emphasize all of these effects.

In light of this, many economists view supply-side economics as a completely novel approach to analyzing the effects of fiscal policy on the macroeconomy. Others yet consider the supply-side approach a mere fad which eventually will be discarded.

A major purpose of our survey is to demonstrate that the supply-side approach is neither novel nor is it a fad—that the entire approach is well-rooted in classical macroeconomic analysis. Indeed, we hope to show that the supply-side view constitutes a return to the orthodox strain of macro-public-finance theory which originated with the attacks of the Physiocrats, Hume, Smith, and others on the doctrines of mercantilism. The classical economists, while recognizing equity, justice, and redistribution, as legitimate elements of tax policy placed most of their emphasis on the effects of taxation on aggregate supply and, hence, economic growth. For these economists, then, the growth aspects of taxation were always the dominant principle of public finance. The supply-side view, moreover, has been more than an academic curiosity. Supply-side policies have actually been implemented by public officials such as William Gladstone and Andrew Mellon on the basis of arguments identical to those endorsed by "modern" supply-side economists.

Indeed, the dominance of the supply-side view continued uninterrupted until the interwar period of the present century when contrary to the orientation of the classical economists, policy concerns such as income redistribution and trade cycle stabilization began to receive more emphasis than did the growth implications of taxation.[4] Thereafter, taxation came to be viewed by most "modern" economists primarily as a redistributive or stabilization tool. It was during this period that the demand-oriented view gained prominence. The recent recognition of the effects of taxation on aggregate supply, then, constitutes a return to the earlier views. Supply-side economics is neither novel nor a fad but instead amounts to a reemergence of classical principles of public finance.

In what follows we will first identify the fundamental propositions of supply-side economics. We will then trace the historical evolution, eclipse, and reemergence of these propositions from the revolt against mercantilism to the revolt against modern-day demand management.

## II. Some Fundamental Propositions of Supply-Side Economics

In contrast to demand-oriented view, proponents of the supply-side economics focus on the effect that tax rates have on relative prices, aggregate supply, and, hence, economic growth. They emphasize that tax rate changes *are relative price changes* and, consequently, will always affect choice, the allocation of resources, and real economic activity.[5] Thus, in their view, changes in tax rates will have important repercussions on the incentives of individuals to supply labor and capital to the market. It has been demonstrated, for example, that tax-induced relative price changes affect choices between (1) work and leisure, (2) consumption and savings (investment), and (3) market activity and nonmarket activity.[6] Consequently, reductions in tax rates —by inducing shifts from leisure to work, from consumption to savings and investment, and from nonmarket activity to market activity have important implications for changes in aggregate supply and economic growth.

## A. The Relationship Between Tax Rates and Aggregate Supply

These general propositions are in turn the basis of more specific relationships that have been postulated by contemporary supply-siders. Supply-side advocates, for example, posit a relationship between tax rates and aggregate (taxable) market output, as illustrated in Figure 1.[7]

*Figure 1*

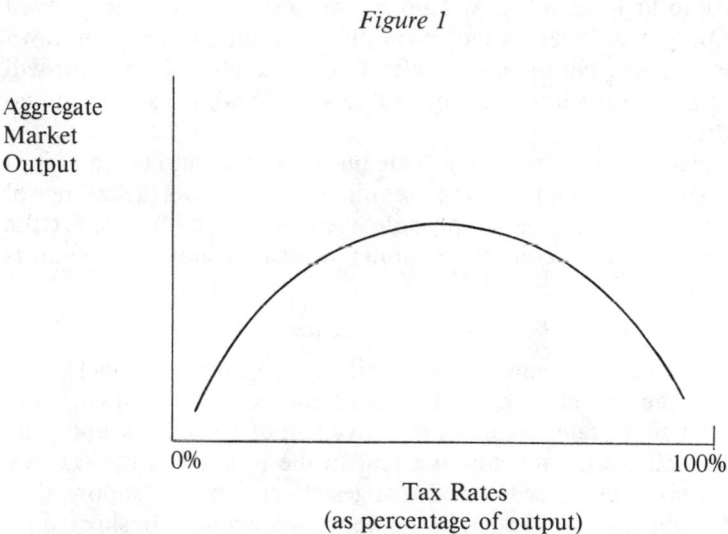

Aggregate
Market
Output

0%                                                                 100%

Tax Rates
(as percentage of output)

On this assumption, the entire tax rate structure of the economy is imbedded in the given tax rates.[8] When tax rates are near zero, output is low because certain public goods which are essential for markets to operate are not being provided. Examples of such goods might include justice (a conducive legal framework), defense, police authorities, the maintenance of roads, and primary education. As tax rates rise, these essential public goods and services are provided and economic activity expands.[9] That is, the provision of these public goods contributes to rapid increases in the productive efficiency of capital and labor and, consequently, in total output. At this initial stage, the effects of increases in productive efficiency outweigh (or increase faster than) any disincentive effects of higher tax rates (i.e., efficiency gains due to government expenditures are greater at initial stages than efficiency losses due to increased tax rates). However, as tax rates increase,

disincentives and inefficiencies become more pronounced. Specifically, increased tax rates alter relative prices and cause a decline in the
after-tax rewards to saving, investing, and working. Consequently,
people shift out of these activities into leisure, consumption, tax
shelters, and working for nontaxable income. As a result, the market
supply of goods and services—i.e., aggregate supply—is less than
would otherwise be the case.[10,11]

At the same time, improvements in the productive efficiency
induced by public goods such as roads and schools increase at a *slower*
rate (because less essential public goods are provided).[12] Consequently,
output gains become smaller and smaller. Eventually, output peaks
and begins to decline as the efficiency gains due to government
expenditures are completely offset by efficiency losses and disincentives due to high tax rates. Additional tax rate increases lead to even
further output declines as factor supplies continue to be withdrawn
from production. Ultimately, an effective tax rate of 100 percent will
result in no factor supply to the taxable sector and, consequently, no
production.[13]

This relationship between aggregate market output and tax rates is of
primary concern to supply-side economists. It represents the essence of
the basic concern of the supply-side view, which is to support the
public policies and conditions under which economic growth is
maximized.

### B. The Relationships Between Tax Rates and Tax Revenue

To show that tax rate changes affect the supply of factors of
production and, hence, aggregate supply and economic growth, is to
imply that these rate changes also have important effects upon tax
revenues because tax revenue is equal to the product of the tax rate
times the tax base. Since tax rate changes affect aggregate supply, they
also affect the tax base—often in the opposite direction. In short, once
it is recognized that tax rate changes affect aggregate supply and,

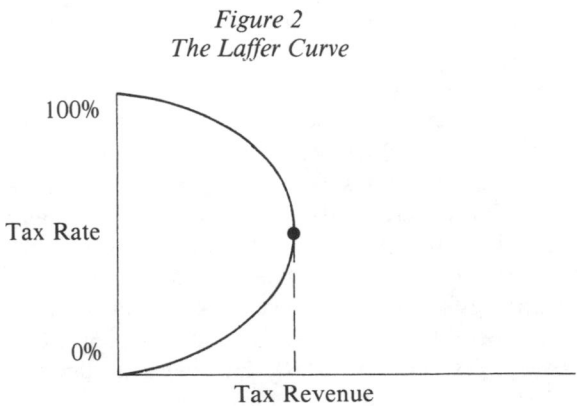

*Figure 2*
*The Laffer Curve*

therefore, the tax base, it becomes apparent that changes in tax revenues are never totally distinct from (and sometimes negatively related to) changes in tax rates. This relationship is popularly illustrated by the "Laffer Curve."

The curve—depicted in Figure 2—is essentially a byproduct of the supply-side effects discussed above.[14] As tax rates increase from zero, revenues begin to increase. Additional tax rate increases begin to erode the incentives of labor and capital (as described above), and, consequently, output and the tax base begin to decrease. Tax revenues will still increase, however, as long as the revenue effect of tax rate increases is larger in magnitude than the revenue effect of tax base decreases. At some point, the loss in revenue due to the reduction in incentives, as well as the increase in tax avoidance, overwhelms the increases in tax rates, and, consequently, tax revenues peak and begin to decline.[15] Eventually, when tax rates reach 100 percent, production ceases in the market economy, since factors will not offer their services if all of their returns are confiscated by government. At this point, the tax base as well as tax revenues fall to zero.[16]

The output/tax and Laffer Curve relationships are two of the most fundamental propositions of the supply-side view. As suggested above, however, these propositions are not new but have considerable precedent in the history of economic thought.

### III. Historical Origins of the Supply-Side View

The prevailing economic worldview in the early and mid-eighteenth century was mercantilism. Although mercantilism is not a homogeneous or easily characterized body of thought, mercantilist writers nonetheless are often associated with a loosely held set of economic beliefs.

A principal objective of the mercantilists was to foster the strength of the national economy, their motive being the maintenance of a strong nation state. Since mercantilists often equated precious metals with wealth, they argued for the accumulation of "treasure" as a source of wealth in the national economy. To this end, they supported policies which increased the nation's stock of precious metals. A high level of economic activity was another factor they felt strengthened the nation state. Toward the maintenance of such activity, mercantilists concerned themselves with promoting both aggregate national purchasing power and adequate markets for their nation's products. Thus, they emphasized the importance of aggregate expenditure or aggregate demand as a major determinant of economic activity and endorsed certain demand-stimulating policies.

Policies designed to foster a favorable balance of trade were viewed as particularly conducive to the goals of amassing precious metals and spurring economic activity. That is, such policies would not only encourage an inflow of precious metals but would also stimulate aggregate demand which would sustain a high level of economic activity. In order to create a favorable balance of trade, mercantilist writers prescribed specific tax and wage policies. Tax policies, for example, were designed to encourage a trade surplus by subsidizing exports while taxing imports. Thus, mercantilist trade policies were highly protectionist; imports were prohibited or highly taxed. In mercantilist view, taxes were not perceived as a tool to maximize either aggregate output, growth, or tax revenue but rather to channel or direct productive effort toward specific ends—to effect a trade surplus. Accordingly, mercantilists believed that taxation could be "carried to a very great extent without injuring national prosperity."[17]

The wage policies endorsed by mercantilist writers were also intended to bring about a trade surplus. Since lower costs of production were seen as beneficial to exports and, hence, the balance of trade, policies were prescribed which promoted and maintained low costs of production, including wages (which were the largest component of these costs). Low wages, according to mercantilist writers, would not only contribute to low (export) production costs and, hence, to a favorable balance of trade but were also viewed as a stimulus to productive work effort. According to this "low wage doctrine," work effort was related to negative (but not positive) incentives. That is, workers would increase their effort only out of necessity; if the existing structure of low wages fell, workers would increase their efforts, whereas high wages led to idleness. Necessity, according to the mercantilists, was the mother of both industry and invention.

Obviously, mercantilists did not recognize the essentials of the supply-side view. They recognized neither the importance of positive incentives to work effort nor the adverse effects taxation might have on these incentives.[19] Moreover, mercantilists gave greater emphasis to aggregate demand and expenditure than to aggregate supply and growth. Indeed, their views on growth were skewed because they held a "static conception of economic activity as a zero-sum game, [so that] . . . one country's gain was another's loss."[20] Or, as put by Thomas Sowell:

> Wealth, to the mercantilists, was something obtained, at the expense of someone else—a differential gain, like winning a race. A whole society could advance its economic interest only "at the expense of other societies."[21]

This view of wealth, of course, was related to their association of precious metals with wealth. But it precluded the mercantilists from sharing in the supply-side view of potentially unlimited growth, given certain incentives for aggregate supply.

## B. The Physiocrats

Mercantilist thought mirrored the conditions and policies in many countries of the world in the mid-eighteenth century. A high degree of regulation and taxation, existed in France during this period in particular. The concurrent economic stagnation there led to the rise of a new school of economic writers known as the Physiocrats.[22] These writers were among the first to react to the theories and policies of mercantilism and to prescribe alternatives consistent with modern-day supply-side views. Although they were the first economists to begin to dismantle mercantilist philosophy, they did not completely extricate themselves from the intellectual tenants of mercantilism.

Their reaction began in rejecting the mercantilist preoccupation with accumulating precious metals. Instead, the Physiocrats emphasized the level of economic activity or the annual flow of goods and services (i.e., net product)—particularly for the agricultural sector. In so doing, their analysis stressed the circular nature of flows of commodities and money in the exchange process—called the spending or income stream—and, hence, the general equilibrium nature of economic activity at the macroeconomic level. The Physiocrats argued that in order to maintain the circular flow of economic activity at high levels, money received had to be restored promptly to the income stream. Anything that prevented money from quickly reentering the stream would cause a slowdown of economic activity. Minus obstructions to the circular flow, increases in output would always lead to increases in incomes and spending. That is, demand would keep pace with an expansion of output. As Blaug puts it:

> The central lesson of [Quesnay's] Tableau is . . . that the creation of output automatically generates the income whose disbursement makes it possible to enter upon another cycle of production.[23]

Thus the Physiocrats anticipated Say's inference that "an increase in output always generates an increase in demand."[24] Physiocratic views, then, were in part consistent with supply-side propositions.

However, the emphasis on the circular expenditure flow model led the Physiocrats to endorse other positions similar to those of the mercantilists. For example, they felt that saving and frugality were hindrances to aggregate economic activity because they believed that such behavior would prevent money from returning quickly to the income stream. Consequently, they tended to discourage or adopt a negative attitude toward saving (and, hence, investment and capital formation). Because of their preoccupation with the continuity of the circular flow, they instead emphasized the importance of maintaining a high level of consumption and spending. In other words, they stressed the primacy of aggregate demand and indicated that spending was preferable to frugality in order to maintain high levels of economic activity.[25]

Yet, the Physiocrats did stress the importance of positive incentives in fostering the supply of labor. Unlike the mercantilists, high wages were viewed as enhancing rather than inhibiting innovative activity and productive work effort. As Spengler points out:

> The Physiocrats—especially Quesnay and Mirabeau—urged that the common man be provided with the opportunity to . . . augment his consuming power. It was barbarous to suppose, as many did, that poverty was the enemy of sloth. . . . The peasant would work the harder by virture of his opportunity to win more than a bare subsistence.[26]

A major impediment to the circular flow of spending and the level of economic activity in the Physiocrats' view was exorbitant taxation. High rates of taxation reduced the rewards to produce and, hence, adversely affected aggregate supply which, in turn, brought about a reduction in aggregate demand and in the circular flow of spending.[27] Circumstances existing in France at the time formed the basis of these contentions. French tax rates during this period were exorbitant. In some sectors, for example, the tax rate was estimated to be as high as 80 percent.[28] As a result, the French economy fell into stagnation, with output and production well below capacity.[29]

As the Physiocrats were aware of the adverse effects these tax rates were having on the French economy, they insisted that tax rates be lowered in order to increase the economy's output and production.[30] According to Joseph Spengler, they argued that "the aggregate amount of revenues collected from the proprietors for the support of the state and church functions (should) not exceed a determined fraction of the income of the landed proprietors. . . . The Physiocrats declared that only about one-third of the net product may be appropriated by the state for the support of functions properly performable by state or church. . . . Were the state to appropriate more than one-third of the net product . . . annual reproduction and net product would decline."[31] The Physiocrats, then, clearly recognized an important relationship between tax rates and output.

In addition the Physiocrats also grasped the tax rate/tax revenue relationship. They maintained that exorbitant tax rates would not produce high tax revenues; indeed, such rates would reduce the income of the people and the revenue of the sovereign.[32] Moreover, they argued that the increasingly higher tax rates which the government had imposed to reduce the public deficit more likely had the effect of increasing it.[33] On the other hand, they contended that lower tax rates would increase tax revenues. As explained by Gide and Rist, "The Physiocrats pointed out that the mere application of their fiscal system [i.e., reduced tax rates] would result in such an increase in net product that the yield from the tax would progressively grow."[34] The Physiocrats, then, supported several elements of the supply-side approach outlined above. They recognized the importance of positive incentives to encourage work effort and acknowledged the relationship between tax rates and output as well as the relationship between tax rates and tax revenues. But on other positions they were inconsistent with the supply-side view, as for example, when they stressed the primacy of consumption and aggregate demand and discouraged saving and, hence, investment. Therefore, although the Physiocrats made a substantial contribution in presenting alternatives to mercantilism, they had not fully removed themselves from the earlier current of thought. Yet they introduced many of the ideas which, when further developed by later economists, lead to the construction of a fully consistent supply-side philosophy.

## C. David Hume

Like the Physiocrats, Hume challenged several mercantilist views on taxes. Indeed, many of the positions Hume took were fully in accord with the modern supply-side view. Yet despite the fact that he was one of the first English writers to dissent from mercantilist theories, like the Physiocrats Hume also failed to break completely from these views. He believed that at least one element of these earlier theories could not be altogether denied.

That one element bore on the relationship between taxes and work incentives. He felt that, under certain conditions, taxpayers might counteract the effect of a tax increase by increasing ingenuity and work effort:

> There is a prevailing maxim, among some reasoners, *that every new tax creates a new ability in the subject to bear it, and that each increase of public burdens increases proportionably the industry of the people.* This maxim is of such a nature as is most likely to be abused; and is so much the more dangerous, as its truth cannot be altogether denied; but it must be owned when kept within certain bonds to have foundation in reason and experience.[35]

This view was similar to the negative incentive notion held by mercantilist writers. Hume, however, acknowledged clear limits to this effect. He held that increased work effort would only occur where (1) the level of taxation was moderate, (2) tax increases were imposed gradually, and (3) taxes did not affect necessities. He stated, for example, that:

> Where taxes are moderate, are laid on gradually, and affect not the necessaries of life, this consequence [i.e., increased work effort] naturally follows; and it is certain, that such difficulties often serve to excite the industry of a people, and render them more opulent and laborous, than others, who enjoy the greatest advantages.[36]

Hume clearly recognized, however, that under different circumstances, tax rate increases could destroy work effort and cause output and aggregate supply to wither. Specifically, he believed that exorbitant tax rates (and sharp increases in tax rates) would destroy industry and productive work effort. Indeed, he believed that this was occurring in Europe at the time he wrote:

> *Exorbitant taxes, like extreme necessity, destroys industry, by producing despair;* and even before they reach this pitch, they raise the wages of the laborer and manufacturer, and heighten the price

of all commodities. *An attentive disinterested legislature, will observe the point when the emolument ceases, and the prejudice begins*: But as the contrary character is much more common, 'tis to be feared that *taxes, all over Europe, are multiplying to such a degree, as will entirely crush all art and industry*; though, perhaps, their first increase, together with other circumstances, might have contributed to the growth of these advantages.[37]

Thus, Hume recognized that taxation had profound effects on production, output, and growth and that these effects are potentially adverse.[38] Consequently, his work suggests that government should support tax policies tending to enhance and encourage productive effort, aggregate supply, and, hence, economic growth.

Contrary to mercantilist notions, Hume also recognized the significance of *positive* incentives to productive work effort. (Mercantilists, it will be remembered, believed that such incentives would lead to idleness, indolence, and sloth). Hume believed that under certain conditions positive direction therefore could enhance output and growth. Such contentions are fully in accord with the modern supply-side view.

Hume also recognized the relationship between tax rates and tax revenues. He indicated that in certain circumstances, tax rate increases may lead to tax revenue decreases—under certain conditions, tax rates and tax revenues were negatively related. He argues in his essay "Of Taxes," for example, that, " . . . a duty upon commodities checks itself; and a prince will soon find, that an increase of the impost is no increase of his revenue."[40]

Moreover, in his essay, "Of the Balance of Trade," Hume points out that exorbitant tax rates on foreign commodities can be counterproductive with respect to government revenues:

> As it is necessary, that imposts should be levied, for the support of government, it may be thought more convenient to lay them on foreign commodities, which can easily be interpreted at the port, and subjected to the impost. We ought, however, always to remember the maxim of Dr. Swift, that, in the arithmetic of the customs, two and two make not four, but often make only one. It can scarcely be doubted, but if the duties on wine were lowered to a third, they would yield much more to the government than at present. . . .[44]

Because he recognized this counterproductive effect of high tax rates on particular commodities, Hume argued that governments should pursue those tax strategies which provide for numerous sources of revenue and maintain a wide tax base.[42]

In sum, although Hume's position with respect to tax issues was not completely divorced from earlier thinking, he was one of the first English economists to endorse many essentials of the supply-side view. He recognized the adverse effects of high taxation on aggregate supply and growth, the importance of positive incentives to productive work effort, and the essence of the tax rate/tax revenue relationship (or the Laffer Curve). As Hume was an eminent Enlightenment figure, his views influenced many later writers, including his good friend, Adam Smith.

## D. Adam Smith

In considering tax-related issues, Adam Smith restated and developed many positions consistent with the supply-side view as it evolved under the Physiocrats and Hume. Among intellectual historians, there is no doubt that these writers had a strong influence on Smith's thinking.[43] However, Smith moved much further from the mercantilist residue, still apparent in Hume and the Physiocrats. As a result, his views on taxes were fully consistent with and supportive of the supply-side view outlined above.

Part of the reason for this arises from his conception of the nature of wealth. He felt that mercantilist views were premised on outright misconceptions of wealth. As Sowell points out, "mercantilistic concepts of the wealth of a nation tended to amount to the power of the national government in general"[44] as well as to its stock of precious metals. Smith's view (which was similar to that of the Physiocrats) was quite different. Wealth, according to Smith, was neither state power nor precious metals but rather the supply of useful goods and services being produced and made available to the people in the marketplace.[45] Following Sowell, "To Smith, wealth consisted of real goods and services, and a nation was rich or poor according to its annual production in proportion to its population."[46] This concept of wealth is both basic to the supply-side philosophy and to Smith's major contribution to economic thought—the growth of aggregate supply is the very nature and cause of wealth.

Smith stressed aggregate supply rather than demand because he believed that the demand for most products was "indefinitely extensible." He found no limit to the expansion of consumption "in civilized commercial societies, where societal pressures made for the expansion and multiplication of wants, and self-interest prompted receivers of money income to spend or invest it promptly."[47] He, therefore, held views which, although rudimentary at the time, would become known as Say's Law when developed by J. B. Say and James Mill.

In order to enhance production and aggregate supply, Smith always emphasized the importance of positive incentives for both labor and capital. He believed such incentives were necessary conditions for increased factor supplies and, hence, growth. Unlike the mercantilists and his close friend Hume, Smith argued that high wages would not reduce the incentive to work. He strongly condemned the mercantilist notion that the short-run labor supply curve is backward-sloping and contended that an increase in wages would always induce an increase in the supply of labor services. Smith asserted, for example that:

The liberal reward for labour . . . increases the industry of the common people. The wages of labour are the encouragement of industry, which, like every other human quality, improves in proportion to the encouragement it receives. . . . The comfortable hope of bettering his condition . . . animates [the laborer] to exert [bodily] strength to the utmost. Where wages are high, accordingly, we shall *always* find the workers more active, diligent, and expeditious, than where they are slow. . . .[48]

Smith, then, always emphasized the importance of positive wage incentives in order to encourage the supply of productive work effort and, hence, the growth of aggregate supply.

In addition to the supply of labor, savings also played a major role in the growth process as envisioned by Smith. Capital accumulation served to "make possible extension of division of labour [and] thus served to increase both output per worker and total output."[49] It was one of Smith's basic preconditions for economic growth:

Wherever capital predominates, industry prevails. . . . Every increase or diminution of capital, therefore, naturally tends to increase or diminish the real quantity of industry, the number of productive hands, and consequently the exchangeable value of the annual produce of the land and labour of the country, the real wealth and revenue of all its inhabitants. . . . The annual produce of the land and labour of any nation can be increased in its value by no other means . . . but in consequence of an increase in capital.[50]

As a consequence, he also emphasized positive incentives to savings and investment,—taking exception to the physiocratic depreciation of "parsimony"—and commended frugality, saving, and investment.[51]

In accordance with these views on the relation of taxes to aggregate output, Smith supported various tax-related fiscal policies by which to enhance the supply of both labor and capital. Building on the writings of the Physiocrats, Smith made some important contributions to the principles of public finance. His four maxims of taxation—equality, certainty, convenience of payment, and economy in collection— showed a real sensitivity to the relationship between taxes and output.[52] His concern on this issue is apparent in the fourth maxim:

Every tax ought to be so contrived as both to take out and to keep out of the pockets of the people as little as possible, over and above what it brings into the public treasury of the state. A tax may either take out or keep out of the pockets of the people a great deal more than it brings into the public treasurys in the . . . following ways. . . . [I]t may obstruct the industry of the people, and discourage them from applying to certain branches of business which might give maintenance and employment to great multitudes. While it obliges the people to pay, it may thus diminish, or perhaps destroy, some of the funds which might enable them more easily to do so. . . . [Moreover] an injudicious tax offers a great temptation to smuggling.[53]

Direct taxes on the wages of labor were "absurd and destructive," in his view, since they led to decreased employment as well as to a "diminution of the annual produce of the land and labour of the country."[54] Moreover, taxes on capital and profits would have disincentive effects on saving and investment, might induce an out-migration of capital, and, hence, would adversely affect growth.[55] Thus, Smith specifically argued that high tax rates—as had existed in the mercantilist era—were neither favorable to the incomes of the masses nor to aggregate supply and production.[56] He cited Holland as an example of a country in which many of the adverse effects of high tax rates were manifest.[57]

While emphasizing the disincentive effects of taxation, Smith stressed the importance of providing a limited set of government services which he viewed as essential for markets to function. While he endorsed such public services as justice, defense, public education, and the maintenance of highways, canals, harbors, etc., he always emphasized that public expenditures should be held to a necessary minimum.[58] The thrust of Smith's message, then, suggests that he recognized that as tax rates rise from low levels, output initially increases because efficiency gains from these public goods outweigh the disincentive effects of higher tax rates and not because higher tax rates induce increases in factor supplies. Continued increases in tax rates, however, lead to decreases in output as disincentive effects of high tax rates overwhelm efficiency gains stemming from the provision of public goods.

In addition to recognizing the relationship between tax rates and output, Smith also clearly recognized the relationship between tax rates and tax revenues along lines similar to contemporary supply-side theory. In several passages, for example, Smith clearly indicates that tax rates and tax revenues were often negatively rather than positively related. The following could hardly be more explicit: "High taxes, sometimes by diminishing the consumption of the taxed commodities, and sometimes by encouraging smuggling, frequently afford a smaller revenue to government than what might be drawn from more moderate taxes."[59]

The recognition of this relationship is particularly evident in another passage where Smith discusses the high tax rates of the mercantilist system. In this passage, he argues that not only do high (mercantilistic) tax rates adversely affect aggregate supply but also that they adversely affect the revenue of the sovereign.[60] This insight is also apparent in Smith's analyses of tariffs, customs duties, and excise taxes. (At the time, it should be noted, a large proportion of governmental revenue —two-thirds, according to Musgrave—came from customs duties and excises.)[61] Smith repeatedly emphasized that because high tariffs discouraged import consumption and promoted smuggling, they worked to diminish government revenues—in some cases entirely annihilating these revenues.[62] He argued if tariffs were used for revenue instead of for prohibition and monopoly, government revenues could be increased substantially.[63]

Smith, therefore, pieced together the first scheme fully consistent with the major points of the supply-side view outlined above. Specifically, he recognized the primacy of aggregate supply for economic growth and always emphasized the importance of positive incentives to enhance the supply of factors of production. Moreover, he recognized the relationship between tax rates and output as well as between tax rates and tax revenues along much the same lines as modern supply-siders.

## E. J. B. Say, James Mill, and Say's Law

Many of Adam Smith's insights proved to be fecund concepts, especially when subject to the refinements of later thinkers. This was particularly true of Smith's thought regarding the primacy of aggregate supply over aggregate demand. It was Jean Baptiste Say and James Mill who refined the theory of the primacy of supply into what has come to be known as "Say's Law." This law in turn became the cornerstone of classical supply-side thought and indeed "dominated economic thinking until the period of World War I."[64]

Building on the Physiocrats, Smith, and others, Say focused on the relationship between aggregate production and income or purchasing power.[65] In doing so, he is credited with establishing "Say's Law." A precise definition of this law is elusive because the traditional formulation offers many implications. Consequently, it has been the subject of numerous interpretations over the years. Nonetheless, the central theme is unmistakable: It is production and aggregate supply that create wealth and economic growth. Real income cannot be expanded without increasing aggregate supply and output; the growth of real income is entirely dependent on the growth of real output. This occurs because the production of a good leaves the producer with purchasing power. The good can be traded for other goods. As this purchasing power is wielded—as producers express their desire to trade their produce—demand becomes manifest. Clearly, then, demand is dependent upon and created by acts of production. In some cases, such as wage labor, produce (or its equivalent, money) will be traded for future produce. But it is nonetheless apparent that it is the availability of produce at the outset that enables exchange to occur, and hence demand to register, at all. Thus, increases in supply or production bring about an increase in purchasing power and creates demand.[66]

There are some important implications of Say's Law that merit further attention. For example, the law implies that aggregate consumption is an effect and not a cause of production.[67] If emphasis is placed on production and supply, demand (and consumption) will automatically follow—hence, demand will take care of itself, making it unneccessary for governments to concentrate on maintaining demand or consumption. These observations lead in turn to the implied proposition that "production can never be too rapid for demand."[68] That is, "too much of all products can not be produced."[69]

As distinct from certain *specific* goods, which can be oversupplied in relation to specific demands, aggregate supply cannot possibly be overstimulated for the production of goods creates the very means of effective demand. Thus, a central feature of Say's Law is the emphasis it places not on demand or consumption but on aggregate supply, production, and, hence, on the encouragement of factor supplies. This emphasis on aggregate supply, according to Say's Law, is the fundamental ingredient to the creation of wealth and, consequently, economic growth.

These principles were also developed by James Mill, as he polished and fortified Say's arguments. Indeed, several authors contend that Say's Law was more forcefully and lucidly stated by Mill than by Say himself. Hutt, for example, says: "James Mill's astonishing *Commerce Defended* (1808) . . . is a better exposition of Say's Law than Say's original enunciation of it."[70] That Mill lucidly presented these arguments is evidenced in these remarks made in 1808:

> Every country will infallibly consume to the full amount of its production. . . . The production of commodities creates, and is the one and universal cause which creates a market for the commodities produced. . . . The collective means of payment of the whole nation . . . consist in its annual produce. . . . A nation can never be naturally overstocked either with capital or with commodities; as the very operation of capital makes a vent for its produce. . . . The demand of a nation is exactly its power of purchasing. But what is its power of purchasing? The extent undoubtedly of its annual produce. . . . How great soever the annual produce may be it always creates a market to itself. . . .[71]
>
> Consumption in the necessary order of things is the effect of production, not production the effect of consumption. . . . The true conception of a nation's wealth is that of her powers of annual production. A nation is poor or is rich according as the quantity of property which she annually creates, in proportion to the number of her people, is great or is small.[72]

David Ricardo also endorsed Say's Law and its implications,[73] but his exposition was merely a restatement and will only receive fleeting attention here.

In emphasizing the primacy of aggregate supply, supporters of Say's Law always stressed the importance of encouraging supplies of factors of production. Accordingly, they underscored the importance of positive incentives in fostering these supplies. Both Say and Mill, for example, held a positive theory of labor incentives. They rejected the view that wages be held down to encourage productive work effort. Like Adam Smith, they contended that an increase in wages would always induce an increase in the supply of labor services and endorsed wage inducements to foster the aggregate supply of labor.[74]

Both Say and Mill also argued along with Smith that capital formation was a critical factor in the growth process. They insisted that saving and investment, rather than consumption, promotes growth and the formation of wealth. Accordingly, a nation could not have too much capital, "nor (was) it likely to have a supply even approximately sufficient in view of man's propensity to multiply and his avidity for pleasure."[75] Thus, neither Say nor Mill feared the underexpenditure or underconsumption that was so heavily emphasized by the Physiocrats and other writers such as Spence and Lauderdale.

Some of the most significant implications of Say's Law relate to fiscal and tax policy. Granted that the assumption that it is production and aggregate supply rather than demand and expenditure that create growth and wealth, those tax (and expenditure) policies most in harmony with the law are those which foster aggregate supply. Say himself stated that:

> The encouragement of mere consumption is no benefit to commerce; for the difficulty lies in supplying the means, not in stimulating the desire of consumption; and we have seen, that production alone, furnishes those means. *Thus it is the aim of good government to stimulate production, of bad government to encourage consumption.* . . . It is impossible to deny the conclusion, that the best taxes, or rather those that are least bad, are . . . such as are least injurious to reproduction.[76]

Regarding the deleterious impact of taxes upon labor supply, Say argued that higher tax rates would *not* "impel the productive class to redouble their exertions."[77] The proposition that taxes tend to stimulate industry and thrift, Say continued, did not contain "the least kernel of truth."[78] Furthermore, high tax rates could also cause the moral fiber of society to decay by promoting "fraud, falsehood, and perjury" among otherwise honest and well-meaning citizens.[79]

Advocates of Say's Law also argued that taxes on capital would adversely affect its supply and, hence, be inimical to economic growth. Ricardo underscored this contention, as illustrated in his remark that, "It should be the policy of governments . . . never to lay such taxes as will inevitably fall on capital; since by so doing, they impair the funds for the maintenance of labor, and thereby diminish the future production of the country."[80]

Although stressing that increases in tax rates do not cause increases in output, Say clearly indicated that such tax rate increases in certain circumstances can be associated with output increases if the proceeds of this taxation are spent on productive projects. That is, taxation may be "productive of good when the sums it absorbs are properly applied."[81] Say contended that such projects might include "improving the internal communications, constructing harbours, or other works of utility."[82]

Advocates of Say's Law recognized the limits of this relationship however. Say himself argued that when taxes reached exorbitant levels they could raise the price level by reducing aggregate supply in relation to the money stock.[83] And, James Mill suggested that the larger the share of government in the economy, the less saving, investment, and economic growth in general, because the "disposition (of government) is not to save but to expend."[84]

These writers also recognized the supply-side relationship between tax rates and tax revenues. Say, for example, wrote that "the best taxes, or rather those that are the least bad, are such as are the most moderate in their ratio" and that, "Taxation, pushed to the extreme, has the lamentable effect of impoverishing the individual *without enriching the state.*"[85]

In other words, exorbitant tax rates would not yield bountiful revenues because of the adverse economic effects on the growth of the tax base. These adverse effects, Say explained, " . . . (were) the reason, why a tax is not productive to the public exchequer, in proportion to its ratio; and why it has become a sort of apophthegm, that two and two do not make four in the arithmetic of finance. Excessive taxation is a kind of suicide. . . ."[86]

Say documents his assertion with several examples of situations where tax rates were lowered (raised) and tax revenues increased (decreased).[87]

Both Say and Mill, therefore, recognized all of the essential features of the supply-side view as presented in Section II: the primacy of aggregate supply, the importance of (positive) incentives, and the relationship between tax rates and output as well as between tax rates and tax revenues. In addition, these writers refined some of the ideas which had been developed by Smith in only rudimentary forms. Hence, the fundamental tenets of supply-side economics were well established with the development and elaboration of Say's Law and its implications. Later contributions consisted largely of more lucid clarifications or more elegant restatements of these basic principles.

## F. Some Contributions of Other Economists

One writer who made a significant restatement of Say's Law was James Mill's son, John Stuart Mill. It is not surprising that John Stuart Mill endorsed many of the same ideas as his father. For as W. J. Ashley points out, James Mill had a strong influence on the economic opinions of his son. This influence, contends Ashley, "was deep and indelible. . . . John (Stuart) Mill's economics remained those of his father down to the end of his life."[88]

One of the younger Mill's major contributions was his elegant restatement of Say's Law. As Sowell has emphasized, Mill's "treatment of (Say's Law) in his *Essays on Some Unsettled Questions of Political*

*Economy* was perhaps the clearest and most advanced presentation in classical economics."[89] Mill argued that one of the most pernicious mistakes made by preclassical writers was the "immense importance (they) attached to consumption. The great end of legislation in matters of national wealth, according to (these writers), was to create consumers. . . . This object . . . was conceived to be the great condition of prosperity." He continues:

> In opposition to these palpable absurdities, it was triumphantly established by political economists, that consumption never needs encouragement. . . . Consumption, therefore, already takes place to the greatest extent which the amount of production admits of. . . . The usual effect of the attempts of government to encourage consumption, is merely to prevent saving . . . and diminish the national wealth by the very means which was intended to increase it.
> What a country wants to make it richer [*sic*], is never consumption, but production. Where there is the latter, we may be sure that there is no want of the former. To produce, implies that the producer desires to consume. . . . There will never, therefore, be a greater quantity produced, of commodities in general, than there are consumers for. . . . Nothing can be more chimerical than the fear that the accumulation of capital should produce poverty and not wealth, or that it will ever take place too fast for its own end . . . .There cannot be permanent excess of production or of accumulation . . . . The legislator, therefore, needs not give himself any concern about consumption. There will always be consumption for everything which can be produced. . . . The legislator has to look solely to two points: that no obstacle shall exist to prevent those who have the means of producing, from employing those means . . . and that those who have not at present the means of producing . . . shall have every facility afforded to their acquiring the means. . . . These general principles are now well understood by almost all who profess to have studied the subject. . . .[90]

Like his father, John Stuart Mill endorsed the full implications of Say's Law. He stressed the importance of encouraging supplies of factors of production, and lauded frugality, saving, and investment, as well as inducements to the supply of labor. He also expressed concern that high tax rates would "discourage industry by insufficiency of reward", and would diminish the motive to save, causing both capital and labor to migrate.[91] Another well-known economist of the period, J. R. McCulloch, forcefully and repeatedly argued that heavy taxation would discourage saving and cause the emigration of labor and capital and, by so doing, would "be a fruitful source of pauperism."[92]

Both Mill and McCulloch also stressed the dire effect of high tax rates on aggregate output and economic growth. Mill reemphasized that "over-taxation, carried to a sufficient extent, is quite capable of ruining the most industrious community."[93] McCulloch continually argued that the goal of taxation should be the maximization of

economic growth.[94] Although he recognized other desirable characteristics of taxation—that taxation should be convenient, certain, and
economical—the overriding consideration was whether it facilitated
(or interfered with) the growth of output. McCulloch's growth orientation is explained by D. P. O'Brien:

> The role of the economist was seen firmly and specifically by
> McCulloch as being to discover the way to keep the economy on
> the path of maximum growth. On this he laid a heavier emphasis
> than any of his contemporaries. Growth he asserted had been the
> economic problem since the *Wealth of Nations*.[95]

Like Mill, McCulloch feared high taxes as a detriment to growth.[96]
Yet he recognized that "light taxation could be a stimulus to growth"
and that "the best taxes . . . may, in general, be said to be the lightest, or
those of which the pressure is least felt."[97] This point was also made by
another influential writer, Sir Henry Parnell. (As shown by O'Brien,
Parnell's book, *On Financing Reform*, "was highly influential; indeed
it (was) probably a major source of the Gladstonian financial orthodoxy.")[98] Parnell, who "devised plans for an overhaul of the tax system
in the light of Smith's four maxims,"[99] argued that:

> The principle [of tax reform] that will be held in view in suggesting
> each [tax] alteration will be that of levying the revenue which is
> wanted for public service in such a manner as to occasion . . . [t]he
> least possible impediment to the progress of national industry and
> national wealth. . . .[100]

Clearly, one of the major contributions made by the successors of
Say and the elder Mill was to focus attention on efforts at tax
circumvention as a result of high tax rates. Not only, they argued, do
high tax rules crimp aggregate production by inducing labor to shift
from work to idleness, but they encourage shifts from taxable activity
in general to nontaxed (and often nonproductive) activities, both legal
(migration of labor and relocation of capital) and illegal (smuggling,
fraud, and tax evasion). Indeed McCulloch felt that evidence of the
tax-evading activities could serve as a sign to public officials "that the
limits of productive taxation have been exceeded."[101]

The tax rate/tax revenue relationship posited by modern supply-side
economics was also recognized by these writers. Both McCulloch and
Parnell, for example, repeatedly argue that when tax rates were
"confined to moderate limits," they were more productive of tax
revenue than when they become excessive.[102] When tax rates increased
beyond moderate levels, tax revenues would decrease because of
decreased production and shifts into nontaxable activities such as
smuggling. Conversely, lowering the tax rates from exorbitant levels
would increase rather than decrease tax revenues. McCulloch states:

> Dr. Swift has shrewdly remarked that, in the arithmetic of the
> customs, two and two do not always make four, but sometimes
> only one. An individual who might be able and disposed to pay a

duty of 1s a bottle on wine might neither have the means nor the inclination to pay 2s or 3s; and, instead of being augmented, the revenue might be diminished by such increase of duty. And hence whenever the duties on commodities are raised beyond certain limits. . . . Their effect is to depress consumption to such an extent as to render them less productive than if they were lower. . . . Besides diminishing the revenue by diminishing consumption, too high duties diminish it by originating and encouraging the practice of smuggling.[103]

Sir Henry Parnell held a similar view with respect to duties:

As the effect of [the] very high duties is in some cases to diminish the revenue, and in all to create smuggling . . . [t]hese duties are exceedingly injurious, and ought to be reduced. . . . There is an absolute limit to every duty, beyond which an increase of it necessarily occasions a loss of revenue. In no instance is an increase of duty followed by an equal increase of revenue; but, on the contrary, the progress of the increase of revenue will be less and less, according as the duty advances, until there is no increase of revenue, but a falling off.[104]

Both McCulloch and Parnell provided historical examples in which tax rate increases (decreases) were followed by tax revenue decreases (increases).[105]

Both Parnell and McCulloch formed very definite conclusions on this relationship. Parnell, for example, asserted that, "These different facts place it beyond all doubt, that when a tax has been carried to an excessively high point, the reducing of it is not necessarily followed by a reduction in revenue, but may lead to an increase."[106] So confident was McCulloch on this issue that on one occasion he advocated a tax cut in the face of a fiscal deficit.[107]

In sum, by mid-nineteenth century, Say's Law and the supply-side approach in economics had undergone a number of fruitful advances, both by way of yielding more refined positions and in attracting adherents. The endorsement of the eminent John Stuart Mill was in itself almost enough to insure complete academic deference to the supply-side view. For it is well known that "all through the second half of the nineteenth century Mill's *Principles of Political Economy* was the undisputed bible of economists. . . . As late as 1900, Mill's work was still the basic textbook in elementary courses in both British and American universities."[108] And indeed the supply-side approach remained largely unchallenged until well into the twentieth century.[109]

*G. Policy Implementation of Supply-Side Propositions: William Gladstone*

While the supply-side view had become the recognized "orthodoxy" in academic economics by the mid-nineteenth century, it was more than just an academic curiosity. Supply-side principles were a significant component of the fiscal (and especially tax) policies of William Gladstone in Great Britain during the period from the 1840s to the

1890s. His administration constitutes one of the first examples of the formal application of these economic principles.[110] Gladstone himself was particularly influenced by the writings of Adam Smith and Sir Henry Parnell. Indeed, he once claimed that he had "carried out for the first time in fiscal and commercial history, the famous fourth maxim, or canon, of taxation laid down by Adam Smith in his *Wealth of Nations* . . . [and accomplished] in 20 years what Adam Smith had deemed well-nigh hopeless."[111]

In the years prior to the Gladstone era, stagnation had plagued the British economy. Trade depression and prolonged periods of high unemployment were commonplace. Moreover, the British suffered chronic budget deficits together with high and rising rates of (indirect) taxation. (Indirect taxation in the form of customs duties and excise taxes constituted the major source of tax revenue for Britain during this period.) Commercial policy was still directed along mercantilist lines as policymakers advocated increased rates of (indirect) taxation in order to reduce the public deficit and to appease protectionist interests. But these policies both failed to balance the budget and contributed to a rapid decline in foreign trade.[112]

Gladstone's program proposed to reverse the economic stagnation, foster economic growth, and balance the national budget by *reducing* the high rates of indirect taxation.[113] The rationale for cutting tax rates was derived from the supply-side orientation of the classical economists who viewed taxation as injurious to economic incentives, the supply of factors of production, and, hence, economic growth.[114] Lowering rates of taxation, it was argued, would work to increase trade and commercial activity to such an extent that these tax cuts would effect increases rather than decreases in tax revenues.

Gladstone's views concerning the relationship between tax rates, output, tax revenues, and governmental expenditures correspond almost identically to those of the modern-day supply-sider. With regard to the tax rate/output relationship, for example, he argued that increases in government expenditures, up to a point, would enhance economic growth and advocated the use of tax revenue for essential public goods and on capital infrastructure, particularly transportation.[115] He realized however that public spending over and above disbursements for these items would have diminishing effectiveness in augmenting national wealth as the disincentive effects of rising taxes upon labor and capital set in.[116]

Of the various supply-side principles endorsed by Gladstone, perhaps the most significant was the relationship between tax rates and tax revenues. His awareness of this relationship is evidenced in his explicit statements justifying his tax policies. He repeatedly argued that whereas increased tax rates would yield increased tax revenues when tax rates were low, tax rate increases (decreases) would decrease (increase) tax revenue when tax rates were high—not only because of disincentives to produce but because of various circumvention activities as well.[117]

Gladstone's notion of the tax rate/tax revenue relationship, together with his ability to sense when tax rates were indeed exorbitant, enabled him to pursue policies of tax reduction with great success. Excluding war years, he was responsible for some of the largest reductions in tax rates in British commercial history. During the same period, Great Britain experienced both rapid economic growth and an elimination of budget deficits.[118] In his own words, the enormous reductions in (indirect) taxes "left [British] revenue from customs and excises actually larger than it was when [he] began the process of abolition and reduction (of taxation)."[119] As Francis Hirst put it:

> It was far harder to raise fifty millions in the middle of the nineteenth century from a population of twenty-seven millions than to raise double that sum at the end of Gladstone's life from a population only one-third larger. A general lightening of taxation had not only made the remaining taxes far more productive, but had diffused such prosperity throughout the nation that every class in the community was enjoying an enormously higher standard of comfort.[120]

Thus, the Gladstone era provided the first and one of the most ambitious experiments in implementing supply-side principles of public finance as developed by classical economists. Gladstone's awareness of these principles, as well as his willingness to apply them, was in large part the reason for his success.

## H. Endorsement of the Supply-Side View: Textbook Writers of the Late Nineteenth and Early Twentieth Centuries

By the turn of the twentieth century supply-side fiscal theory was regarded as the dominant view of fiscal policy within the academic community. A brief review of some representative treatises and textbooks in public finance published in the late nineteenth and early twentieth centuries leaves no doubt on this point.

In their analyses of the economic effects of taxation, most academic economists in this period relied on Smith's four maxims. The equality, convenience, certainty, and economy of taxation were the standards of analysis. As stated by C. J. Bastable, "The maxims associated with (Smith) were in his own day accepted by theorists and statesmen and have by constant repetition become an indispensible part of any exposition of finance."[121] It is revealing, however, to take note of the relative importance they placed on each of Smith's maxims. Most attached greatest importance to Smith's fourth maxim—economy of taxation, the maxim indicating that the best tax system was the one which interfered least with economic growth. Although Smith's fourth maxim on taxation consists of four parts, most authors concentrated their discussion on the (revenue) productivity of taxation and taxation's effect on economic growth.[122] The amount of revenue produced by a tax was seen as intrinsically related to the growth of the economy. A tax system designed for maximum economic growth would produce high levels of tax revenues. One author argues that:

> Next to [revenue] productiveness . . . the most important principle is that taxation should be economical, i.e., inexpensive in collection and at the same time retarding the growth of industry as little as possible. Both [revenue] productivity and economy, although separated by [some authors] have a much closer connection than is at first discernable. Today productivity and economy would be probably regarded as one by the practical financier.[123]

Another author maintained that:

> The public economy depends ultimately on the national economy; anything that reduces the economic power of the individual citizens is an injury to the State. A system of taxation that diminishes the revenue of the subjects without a corresponding return to the public treasury is certain before long to show its effect in reduced receipts from taxation. From a purely national point of view the 'canon' of economy is probably the most important in fiscal science and no efforts should be spared to secure the closest observance of it that existing conditions permit.[124]

The priority given Smith's fourth maxim by writers of this period reflects the strong supply-side orientation of their views. Although equity and justice were important elements of taxation, to these economists they were always subordinate to economic growth.

Given their basic supply-side orientation, it should hardly be surprising that these economists grasped all of the supply-side implications for fiscal policy. In particular, they recognized the disincentive effects of high tax rates on factor supplies, as well as the tax rate/output and tax rate/tax revenue relationships. Like their classical predecessors, for example, they support the theory of positive incentives as the motive force for both labor and capital. They insisted that high tax rates had important disincentive effects and *always* adversely affected the supplies of factors of production.[125]

This view toward the disincentive effects of taxation naturally led these writers to subscribe to the tax rate/output relationship of the modern supply-side view. Indeed their elucidation of this relationship was among the most forceful in the historical literature. They recognized that in spite of the adverse (disincentive) effects of taxation, some governmental spending and, hence, some level of taxation to support this spending were essential to maximize economic growth. Among those public goods frequently commended were primary education and public works involving transportation or capital infrastructure.[126] Leroy-Beaulieu, for example, stated that:

> We can say that taxes are good when their yield is devoted to productive expenditure, such as work which the state is better able to perform than are individuals. . . . We do not, then, consider taxation as an evil. We do not conceal that in our view taxation may be a good. The thesis that the best tax is always the smallest

one seems to us an exaggeration; it is an undue reaction against past and present waste.[127]

This same argument echoed throughout textbooks of the era.[128]

Since they recognized strong disincentive effects with rising taxation, however, all of these economists saw definite limits to government spending and the taxation needed to support it. They indicated that government spending over and above an optimum level would entail high rates of taxation and that the disincentive effects upon economic growth would soon outweigh the benefits from the additional public spending.[129] One of the most comprehensive statements of this position was made by Leroy-Beaulieu:

> It is beyond doubt that very high taxes have considerable drawbacks. . . . They nearly always encourage fraud and concealment, that is to say immoral behavior. They place the country where they are in force at a disadvantage with respect to the other industrious countries of the world. They tend to cause capital and even people to migrate. . . . Some authors have spoken of a lower and an upper limit of taxation, the lower limit being the amount necessary to provide for the indispensable public services, and the upper limit being given by all the useful services which the state is more competent or better able to perform than individuals or associations. . . . We believe that it is possible to fix an empirical lower and upper limit to taxation. The limits are not inflexible, they are only approximate. *We consider that taxation is very moderate when the sum of national, provincial, and municipal taxes does not exceed five or six percent of private incomes.* . . . Taxation is still bearable, though heavy, up to ten or twelve percent of the citizens' income. *Beyond twelve or thirteen percent the rate of taxation is exorbitant.* The country may be able to bear such a rate, but it is beyond doubt that it slows down the growth of public wealth. . . .[130]

Economists of this period were also well aware that there existed a tax rate which would maximize tax revenue—that is, they recognized the tax rate/tax revenue relationship of the supply-side view. This is clearly evident in the following passage where Lutz makes an analogy between the productive power of the soil and of the economy:

> The wise application of the test of fiscal adequacy may be compared, in certain respects, to the wise use of land by the farmer. His aim is, year by year, to get a certain return from the land, and yet to maintain or even increase the productive power of the soil in order that his future return shall not be imperiled. That tax system is a failure, from the viewpoint of fiscal adequacy, which encroaches severely upon the social income, and which tends in consequence to dry up the stream of public revenue. He would be a very improvident farmer who plundered his land so far that his crops were greatly diminished after a few years. It would be quite as improvident for a state to apply a system of taxation that would tend to diminish the flow of private income, and to discourage industry, thrift and initiative, the wellsprings of this flow. . . . Fiscal adequacy must be so construed and applied as always to safeguard, and wherever possible, to increase the ultimate resources of the state and of its citizens.[131]

Additional evidence that this view was fully recognized is provided by Wells:

> It is . . . a matter of the first importance for every government, in framing laws for the assessment and collection of taxes, to endeavor to determine, not only for fiscal but for moral purposes, where the maximum revenue point in the case of each tax is reached and to recognize that in going beyond that point the government "overreaches" or cheats itself.[132]

In sum, the public finance economists of the late nineteenth and early twentieth centuries fully endorsed the supply-side principles that have reemerged in the present day. Building on Smith's maxims they recognized and spelled out the relationships between tax rates and incentives, factor supplies, output, and tax revenues. Indeed, the consensus on these matters became the dominant view in macroeconomic public finance. Lending obvious support for this concensus was Say's Law itself, which dominanted macroeconomics so thoroughly that it was "virtually never challenged."[133] The supply-side orthodoxy was the culmination of an evolutionary process which had continued for more than a century, beginning with the physiocratic critique of mercantilism.

*I. Additional Policy Implementation of Supply-Side Propositions: Andrew Mellon*

Understandably, the orthodox suppy-side position made a considerable impression on government policymakers at the time. This was particularly so in the United States. It has been documented, for example, that President Wilson, Treasury Secretaries Glass and Houston, as well as others during the 1920s, were ever conscious of supply-side strictures.[134] Perhaps the most forceful statements along these lines were presented by members of the Coolidge administration. Treasury Secretary Andrew Mellon not only presented these arguments with remarkable force but was instrumental in the implementation of the ambitious supply-side tax cuts of the 1920s.

Upon entering public service, Mellon—like Gladstone before him—focused upon the adverse economic effects of the prevailing high tax rates. These extraordinarily high rates had been imposed to finance U.S. involvement in World War I. When the war ended, however, they were not entirely removed.[135] Recognizing that they were remnants of war-finance, Mellon argued that these high tax rates were holding U.S. economic growth well below its potential.[136] In effect, Mellon contended that this tax structure placed the postwar peacetime economy in the prohibitive (or negative sloped) portion of both the tax rate/output and tax rate/tax revenue curves. As a consequence, he recommended tax cuts which he believed would result in *both* increased output and growth as well as in increased tax revenues.

In presenting his arguments, like Gladstone, he indicated that much of his position was based on Smith's fourth maxim, that the best tax system was one which minimized its adverse effect on aggregate supply and economic growth. Mellon maintained, for example, that:

> The . . . experience of one hundred and fifty years since [Smith's *Wealth of Nations*] has emphasized the truth of [Smith's] maxims, but those who argue against a reduction of [war time] surtaxes to more nearly peace-time figures cite only the first maxim, and ignore the fourth. . . . When, as a result of an excessive or unsound basis of taxation, it becomes evident that the source of taxation is drying up and wealth is being diverted into unproductive channels, yielding neither revenue to the Government nor profit to the people, then it is time to readjust our basis of taxation upon [such] sound principles [as the fourth maxim].[137]

Mellon also advocated a positive theory of incentives for factors of production, viewing rewards as essential in order to encourage additional factor supplies and foster economic growth.[138] He wrote in this vein that, "Just as labor cannot be forced to work against its will, so it can be taken for granted that capital will not work unless the return is worthwhile."[139] He felt that high rates of taxation on capital would severely reduce the rewards for risk taking and, hence, the supply of that venture capital necessary for economic growth. In response to heavy taxes capital would either migrate or be allocated toward tax-exempt (and often unproductive) investments such as municipal bonds, resulting in a slowdown of economic growth.[140] Recognizing this self-defeating process, he wrote:

> The history of taxation shows that taxes which are inherently excessive are not paid. The high rates inevitably put pressure on the taxpayer to withdraw capital from productive business and invest it in tax exempt securities or to find other lawful methods of avoiding the realization of taxable income. The result is that the sources of taxation are drying up; wealth is failing to carry its share of the burden, and capital is being directed into channels which yield neither revenue to the government nor profit to the people.[141]

Mellon also continually stressed the effects of excessive taxation on output and growth. In discussing the tax rate/output relationship, he directed his attention to the adverse effects of high tax rates and said little about any beneficial effects of public expenditure on infrastructure. This is, of course, understandable given the high tax climate of the early 1920s. His prescription for the U.S. economy in these circumstances was to lower tax rates in order to stimulate output and growth.[142]

In addition to his concern over the relationship between tax rates and output, Mellon was well aware of the tax rate/tax revenue relationship. While aware that in certain (low tax rate) circumstances tax rates and tax revenues are positively related, Mellon contended that in the circumstances prevailing during the early 1920s, a cut in tax rates would work to raise tax revenues. And so, as Secretary of Treasury, he engineered a tax rate reduction in 1923 under the explicit assumption that it would increase tax revenues as well as output:

> It seems difficult for some to understand that high rates of taxation do not necessarily mean large revenues to the Government, and that more revenue may often be obtained by lower rates. . . . [When rates are high as in the 1920's], a decrease in taxes causes an inspiration to trade and commerce which increases the prosperity of the country so that revenues of the government, even on a lower basis of tax are increased.[143]

Virtually indentical views were expressed by President Coolidge in a speech delivered in 1924.[144]

In advocating tax rate reductions, Mellon stressed that such cuts would benefit *all* members of society, not just the higher income groups. And analysts agree that the ambitious tax cuts implemented by Mellon in the 1920s did contribute to the rapid economic growth of the U.S. during that period.[145]

## J. The Demise of the Supply-Side View

The 1920s were to represent the twilight of supply-side principles in public finance. The demise of supply-side propositions is painstakingly clear in textbooks and treatises written on public finance in the 1930s and 1940s. The specific factors and events that culminated in the downfall of supply-side principles are complex and difficult to indentify fully. Those factors suggested below should be considered as conjectural and nothing more.

Crucial to the demise of the supply-side view was the widespread rejection of Say's Law, which was suddenly considered obsolete and yet was superseded by positions which classical economists would have labeled mercantilist. The primary emphasis of fiscal policy shifted to the relationship between government spending and aggregate demand in the short run rather than on aggregate supply in the long run. Economists came to view the effects of taxation on factor supplies as complex and ambiguous. According to the "modern" view, high tax rates were not necessarily inimical to incentives and, hence, not necessarily incompatible with increases in factor supplies, output, and growth. Finally, objectives such as income distribution and trade cycle stabilization displaced the classical emphasis on growth as principal concerns of fiscal policy.

Much of the reason for this dramatic shift seems to lie in circumstances of the period. The virtual collapse of aggregate demand during the 1930s had several very important ramifications. First, the deficiency of aggregate demand and the attendant problems of vast idle capacity and unemployed factors of production understandably brought many economists to reject a view which seemed to insist that such conditions were impossible. As a result of being misinterpreted along these lines,[146] Says Law and the derivative growth-orientation of fiscal policy were cast by the wayside. Similarly, since many economists equated the economic disruptions of the 1930s with a failure of the market system, they were very receptive to calls for an increased governmental role in economic affairs in general, exalting stabilization via government activity over market production and growth.

Secondly, the large deficiency of aggregate demand encouraged a dramatic shift of emphasis from policies encouraging production and supply to aggregate demand-stimulating policies. Increases in output were divorced from increasing supply of factors of production, and rather linked to increases in aggregate demand. Supply constraints were simply not deemed relevant under the circumstances and, hence, did not play a role in the formulation of policy. Supply, then, was no longer viewed as the cause or wherewithal of income or purchasing power. Instead, it was felt that income was dependent on demand. This view is exemplified in the following remark quoted from a typical textbook of the period:

> It is a fallacy to believe that a depression can be overcome by stimulating production and that production then creates demand, in accordance with J. B. Say's Law of the market. In reality the causal nexus proceeds for the most part in the other direction: demand must be activated first and production will follow.[147]

This shift of emphasis was especially relevant to fiscal policy. During this period, it was thought that the money supply could not be increased through traditional bank channels because of a crisis of confidence related to bank failures in the U.S. (and because of international balance of payments constraints during the fixed exchange rate regime in the U.K.). Consequently, monetary policy was viewed as utterly impotent. Because of the supposed inability to stimulate demand via traditional monetary policy, economists thought that the stimulation of aggregate demand had to work through fiscal policy.[148] Hence, the primary emphasis of fiscal policy shifted from encouraging aggregate supply to that of stimulating aggregate demand —a movement away from classical principles of public finance to views consistent with earlier demand-oriented mercantilist views. This shift of emphasis constituted a shift from supply policies related to long-run economic growth to short-run demand policies concerned with stabilizing the business cycle—a shift in orientation from *growth* to *stabilization*.

According to this new view—often referred to as the "New Economics"—government could stabilize the economy in the wake of business cycle fluctuations controlling aggregate demand. Fiscal policy was seen as the fundamental policy tool in managing the economy. Aggregate demand could be increased (decreased) by cutting (raising) taxes. Since excess capacity and idle resources were assumed to be readily available, the stimulation of supply was not a relevant concern of policy. Any effects that changes in tax rates might have on aggregate supply, therefore, were generally ignored, and taxation was no longer viewed in the context of Smith's fourth maxim. This interpretation is epitomized in the following remark by Nicholas Kaldor, "The Keynesian Revolution has meant in the field of public finance that taxation is no longer looked upon as a means of 'funding the money' for expenditure of government, but as one of the primary weapons in the government's armory for ensuring general economic and monetary stability."[149]

Alongside the emergence of the new stabilization role for fiscal policy was a call to use taxes to correct supposed "market failures." For example, certain economists advocated the use of progressive taxation to bring about a "more equitable" distribution of income. This was, of course, nothing really new in tax theory. Classical economists accepted and formally treated such considerations. But, for the classicals, redistribution was always seen as subordinate to other goals such as economic growth. By the 1930s, however, the redistributive function of taxation was assuming an ever more important role in fiscal policy deliberations. According to Schumpeter:

> . . . a new spirit began to assert itself in political practice, and this new spirit did not fail to show in the writings of economists. It is not that only leading academic authorities, such as Marshall, began to approve of what was then considered high direct taxation . . . but also that they began to espouse what was a mortal sin against the spirit of Gladstonian finance, namely, a policy that went beyond taxing for revenue and aimed at taxing in order to change ['correct'] income distribution. Adolf Wagner for Germany and A. C. Pigou for England may serve as examples.[150]

These concerns continued to assume a more important role in the public finance literature during and after the 1930s and eventually supplanted the growth (or supply-side) orientation of fiscal policy, as is particularly evident in public finance textbooks and treatises written since then.[151]

In addition to this dramatic shift in the focus of professional scholarship, the actual increase in the size of the public sector vis-à-vis the growth in the private sector of the economy during and after the 1930s proved to be a powerful impetus for the rejection of the classical supply-side view. These increased public expenditures necessarily brought with them a higher set of tax rates. And so long as the political consensus inclined toward rising public expenditure, policymakers tended to ignore the classical insights regarding high taxes and economic growth.

In this, they received intellectual support in the "new economics," where higher tax rates were considered relatively harmless or at least not necessarily harmful. The relationship between tax rates and output was either downplayed or viewed in a quite different light by the new economics. It operated within an income-expenditure framework and was therefore oriented toward the stimulation of aggregate demand on the one hand, and not much concerned with aggregate supply on the other. Thus, these economists ignored or at least underestimated the relationships between tax rates and (a) incentives, (b) factor supplies, and (c) output (or growth). Most important though, they insisted that high tax rates were not necessarily inimical to aggregate supply or economic growth. An illustration of this is provided by the remark from a typical public finance textbook of the period:

> That taxes affect production adversely is noisily if not always convincingly asserted, by taxpayers protesting against "repressive," "ruinous," and "crushing" taxation. . . . There may be a modicum of truth in their vociferations. . . . On the other hand, taxation may be, not only harmless, but positively beneficial to production.[152]

An important corollary of this new attitude toward the impact of taxation on economic growth was a dramatic shift of emphasis in the analysis of the effects of taxation on incentives and factor supplies. With respect to the effects of taxation on the supply of labor, for example, "modern" economists contended that increased taxation had little if any adverse effects on the supply. Like the mercantilists, some of these economists even argued that increased taxation would actually increase work effort. One particularly successful textbook argued that:

> Incentives are probably much more resistant to tax impairment than might be supposed. . . . Once a standard of living has been established, the taxpayer will fight to preserve it. He may under some circumstances even intensify his economic effort because of the tax.[153]

The subordination of supply-side principles of public finance is even more dramatic in "modern" discussions on saving. Of course, the classical position always viewed saving as beneficial to capital formation and therefore beneficial to aggregate supply and economic growth. Taxes on saving, investment, and, hence, capital were considered harmful in their effect on aggregate supply and economic growth. In contrast, the framework of the "new economics" is premised on circumstances of deficient aggregate demand. Since saving was considered a leakage from the income-expenditure flow, proponents of this position—like the mercantilists centuries earlier—came to view savings as detrimental to the level of economic activity. They referred often to the "paradox of thrift" whereby an increase in aggregate savings was considered harmful to the macroeconomy.[154] Within this framework, then, increasing taxes on saving could actually increase production and output by rechanneling surplus savings into governmental expenditures and back into the spending stream. This is clearly put in the following remark from a typical public finance textbook written in 1960:

> On the assumption that all accumulation is creative, any diminu-
> tion of it will necessarily diminish all economic growth. That, as
> we know, is the traditional [classical] assumption. But we also
> know that it is false. Indeed, it is precisely because the accumula-
> tion of funds for investment [saving] does not necessarily result in
> actual investment but on the contrary does reduce the volume of
> mass consumer purchasing power, and so the market for the
> product of industry, and so industrial expansion and actual
> investment, that we now find it necessary to reduce the volume of
> aggregate saving by such instruments as personal income taxation.
> That ideological attitudes nevertheless persist is understandable.
> But the assumption that a reduction of the rate of saving [resulting
> from income taxation] "must" reduce the rate of economic growth
> is without merit.[155]

With an orthodoxy so self-assured, and with its positions on savings, on factor incentives, on the tax rate/output relationship, and indeed its most fundamental premise on the wellspring of economic activity (aggregate demand)—all at complete variance with the views of the classicals—it is small wonder that the classical supply-side insights remained buried for decades under a mass of "new economic" assumptions. However, the supply-side principles did not give up the ghost. With the self-contradictory (for the new economics) condition of stagflation, the present orthodoxy is on the defensive. And economists are again turning to the supply-side.

### III.  A Rejuvenation of Supply-Side Principles

Today, we live in an economy that is becoming as different from that of the post World War II decades as the depression of the '30s was from the booming '20s. And it is likewise becoming obvious to economists that current economic circumstances do not square with the assumptions of the income-expenditure framework. Simultaneous high rates of inflation and unemployment together with relatively low rates of output growth combining to form what we now call "stagfla-tion"—is spurring economists to question the soundness of the "new economics." The new economics may have provided valuable insights in the context of a severe depression, but it is becoming evident that it is not necessarily applicable in any and all circumstances. On the other hand, the American economy in the 1970s had begun to mirror conditions of the mercantilist era when high taxes and stagnant economics led the classical economists to reject the demand-oriented framework of mercantilist writers. High tax rates, increasing govern-ment regulation and intervention in the economy, a growing under-ground economy, and low rates of productivity and growth have become commonplace. Part of the reason for this surely lies in the fact that economists and policymakers have focused their attention on the manipulation of aggregate demand and on piecemeal interventions to "correct" one or another alleged defect of the market—and all but ignoring the cumulative onus they were laying on aggregate supply.

Amid the disillusion with the present orthodoxy, some economists have come to recognize the adverse effects that high tax rates can have on incentives, factor supplies, and, hence, economic growth. This has led to a reemergence of classical supply-side principles in the field of finance. Modern supply-siders, like their classical predecessors, argue that in order to foster growth, work, savings, investment, and honesty must be rewarded instead of leisure, consumption, and tax-avoidance. Moreover, they have come to recognize that the fiscal system must place priority on incentives and long-run growth rather than short-run stabilization and income distribution. In light of the foregoing analysis, it should be apparent that there is nothing really new in any of the basic supply-side contentions. And because it seems particularly relevant in explaining and correcting the economic doldrums of the present day it is unlikely to pass as a mere fad.

## Notes

1. For fuller descriptions of the supply-side viewpoint, *see* Robert E. Keleher, "Supply-side Effects of Fiscal Policy: Some Preliminary Hypotheses," *Research Paper Series*, Research Paper no. 9, Federal Reserve Bank of Atlanta, June 1979; and James D. Gwartney and Richard Stroup, *Macroeconomics: Private and Public Choice*, 2nd ed., (New York: Academic Press, 1980), pp. 275-83.

2. If aggregate supply (or an aggregate production function) were included in macroeconomic models of the income-expenditure (IS-LM) variety, it was added in the form of a constraint rather than as a well-developed construct of the analysis. Aggregate supply and production functions, however, have always played a more important role in growth models, particularly of the neoclassical variety. Part of the reason for the emphasis given to aggregate demand by conventional analysis is that this analysis took root in the depression era. At that time, the existence of large amounts of idle labor and capital, together with a deficiency of aggregate demand, directed attention away from aggregate supply and toward methods of stimulating aggregate demand. For an analysis of the Keynesian-monetarist aggregate demand orientation in relation to the supply-side view, *see* Keleher, ibid.

3. Assuming they are financed in the same way. Keleher, ibid.

4. Some economists have referred to this shift in emphasis as a "fiscal revolution." For a description of the growing emphasis on stabilization policy, *see* Herbert Stein, *The Fiscal Revolution in America* (Chicago: University of Chicago Press, 1969).

5. Proponents of the supply-side view argue that fiscal policy always affects relative prices and, hence, real economic activity. Among other writers, Paul Craig Roberts forcefully emphasizes these effects. *See* Paul Craig Roberts, "The Breakdown of the Keynesian Model," *The Public Interest*, no. 52 (Summer 1978): 20-33; and idem, "The Economic Case for Kemp-Roth," *The Wall Street Journal*, August 1, 1978.

6. Since tax rate changes affect relative prices and choice, so will government subsidies (negative taxes).

7. *See*, for example, Neil J. McMullen, "Appendix A: Conceptualizing Welfare-Efficiency Relationships," in Theodore Geiger, *Welfare and Efficiency: Their Interactions in Western Europe and Implications for International Economic Relations* (Washington, D.C.: National Planning Association, 1978).

8. That is, the tax rates given include the effects of all taxes—income taxes, sales and excise taxes, tariffs, property taxes, etc.

9. The output/tax rate curve shows the "real output that will be supplied at various rates of taxation given the government's spending pattern and the society's preferences for public and private goods and for leisure." (McMullen, "Welfare-Efficiency Relationships.") The curve assumes a balanced budget.

10. Roberts, "The Economic Case for Kemp-Roth."

11. Shifts out of taxable market activities into nonmarket activities which are not

taxable cause the economy to lose efficiencies from division of labor, specialization, and economies of scale (efficiencies made possible by market exchange).

12. At some point, government expenditures instead of improving productive efficiency may actually diminish it, as welfare payments provide disincentives to labor supply.

13. The shape of this output/tax rate curve and the point at which output peaks depend on the elasticity of factor supplies with respect to changes in tax rates. This elasticity, in turn, depends on several factors, including, for example, the openness of the economy, the uses to which tax revenues are put, the intensity of the work and savings ethics of the society, and the time frame over which the output/tax rate relationships are considered. The elasticities will be larger, the more open the economy and the longer the time frame over which the relationships are considered, for example.

14. As demonstrated by McMullen, "Welfare-Efficiency Relationships," the tax rate/tax revenue curve can be derived from the output/tax rate curve—Figure 1—by multiplying the tax rate times the output to yield tax revenues generated at each tax rate.

15. "Taxes: Can You Have Your Cake and Eat It?" *Monthly Economic Letter* (New York: Citibank, September 1978), p. 8.

16. At this point, the economy is functioning entirely through barter as well as through underground economic activity.

17. James Mill, *Commerce Defended*, 1808 ed., (New York: Augustus M. Kelley, 1965), p. 94.

18. E. A. J. Johnson, *Predecessors of Adam Smith: The Growth of British Economic Thought* (New York: Prentice Hall, 1937), p. 251.

19. Mill, *Commerce Defended*, p. 94.

20. Mark Blaug, *Economic Theory in Retrospect*, rev. ed., (Homewood, Ill.: Richard D. Irwin, 1968), p. 18.

21. Thomas Sowell, "Adam Smith in Theory and Practice," in Gerald P. O'Driscoll, ed., *Adam Smith and Modern Policitcal Economy* (Ames, Iowa: Iowa State University Press, 1979), p. 4.

22. Some estimates indicate that France was functioning three-quarters below capacity. *See also* Henry Higgs, *The Physiocrats* (New York: Langland Press, 1952), pp. 5, 30.

23. Blaug, *Economic Theory in Retrospect*, p. 30.

24. Joseph J. Spengler, "The Physiocrats and Say's Law of Markets," in Joseph J. Spengler and W. R. Allen, eds., *Essays in Economic Theory: Aristotle to Marshall* (Chicago: Rand McNally, 1960), p. 180; and Thomas Sowell, *Say's Law* (Princeton, N.J.: Princeton University Press, 1972), p. 219.

25. Spengler, "The Physiocrats and Say's Law," pp. 170, 175, 177, 181, 190-94. It should be noted that both the amount and the pattern of spending were important to the Physiocrats. In particular, they maintained that spending on agricultural production was especially beneficial to the economy (Ibid., p. 177).

26. Ibid., pp. 176-177.

27. Ibid., pp. 177-178.

28. Henry Higgs, *The Physiocrats*, p. 10. Higgs argues that some estimates of the tax rate on small proprietors were as high as 82 percent of net produce. Moreover, E.G. West shows that upon Adam Smith's visit to France in 1766, "his friend Turgot . . . found that in his district the proportion of net income of the peasant proprietors taken by the government was about 80 percent." (E.G. West, "Adam Smith's Economics in Politics," in O'Driscoll, *Adam Smith*, p. 149). Indirect tax rates were so high according to David Wells, that is was "not an infrequent occurrence that prior to the Revolution of 1789, a duty was levied 27 times on a barrell of wine in the course of its transportation from the place it was grown to that where it is sold; so that is was said to be cheaper to send wine from China to France than from one of the departments of France to Paris." (David Ames Wells, *The Theory and Practice of Taxation* [New York: D. Appleton and Co., 1900], p. 76).

29. Higgs, *The Physiocrats*, p. 5.

30. Spengler, "The Physiocrats and Say's Law," p. 173; and Charles Gide and Charles Rist, *A History of Economic Doctrines from the Time of the Physiocrats to the Present Day* (New York: D.C. Heath and Co., n.d.) p. 43 (Reprint of the 1915 London ed.)

31. Spengler, "The Physiocrats and Say's Law," pp. 173-174.
32. Ibid., pp. 177-178.
33. Ronald Meek, *The Economics of Physiocracy* (Cambridge, Mass.: Harvard University Press, 1963), p. 25.
34. Gide and Rist, *History of Economic Doctrines*, p. 43.
35. David Hume, "Of Taxes," in idem, *Writings on Economics*, ed. Eugene Rotwein, (Freeport, New York: Books for Libraries Press, 1955), p. 83.
36. Ibid., p. 83.
37. Humes "Of Taxes," p. 85 (footnote). Emphasis added.
38. *See* Johnson, *Predecessors of Adam Smith*, pp. 175-177.
39. Ibid., pp. 170, 296.
40. Hume, "Of Taxes," p. 86.
41. David Hume, "Of the Balance of Trade," in *Writings on Economics*, p. 70.
42. Johnson, *Predecessors of Adam Smith*, p. 175.
43. It is well documented that Smith was a close friend of Hume's and that he thought well of the physiocratic writings. It is known, for example, that "Smith was intimately acquainted with Hume and his works," (W. L. Taylor, *Francis Hutcheson and David Hume as Predecessors of Adam Smith* [Durham, N.C.: Duke University Press, 1965] p. 131). Hume and Smith, it will be recalled, were often in correspondence with one another, and as shown by Taylor, "mutually influenced each other's thinking." (Ibid., p. 35)
In addition, as shown by Spengler, "Adam Smith thought well of the physiocratic system. . . . Of this we have evidence in his characterizing it as 'the nearest approximation to the truth . . . yet . . . published . . . upon political economy.'" (Spengler, "The Physiocrats and Say's Law," pp. 182-183.)
44. Sowell, "Adam Smith in Theory and Practice," p. 5.
45. Overton H. Taylor, *A History of Economic Thought* (New York: McGraw-Hill, 1960), p. 183. Spengler argues that Smith "singled out for praise [the Physiocrats' position] representing wealth 'as consisting . . . in the consumable goods annually reproduced by the labor of society.'" (Spengler, "The Physiocrats and Say's Law," p. 183.)
46. Sowell, "Adam Smith in Theory and Practice," p. 5. Following Sowell, "whereas mercantilism concentrated on the *transfer* of wealth . . . Smith and classical economists in general concentrated on the *production* of wealth." (Ibid., p. 6.)
47. Joseph J. Spengler, "Adam Smith's Theory of Economic Growth—Part II," *Southern Economic Journal* 26 (July 1959): 10; *see also* idem, "Adam Smith's Theory of Economic Growth—Part I, *Southern Economic Journal* 25 (April 1959): 403.
48. Adam Smith, *An Inquiry into the Nature and Causes of the Wealth of Nations*, ed. Edwin Cannan (Chicago: University of Chicago Press, 1976): bk. 1, p. 91 (emphasis added). *See* ibid., bk 1., p. 92 for Smith's rejection of the notion that low wages stimulate work effort. *See also* Blaug, *Economic Theory in Retrospect*, p. 48.
49. Spengler, "Adam Smith's Theory—Part I," p. 405.
50. Smith, *Wealth of Nations*, bk. 1, pp. 358, 364.
51. Spengler, "The Physiocrats and Say's Law," p. 183.
52. These maxims were derived in part from the Physiocrats. *See also* Higgs, *The Physiocrats*, p. 41; and Meek, *The Economics of Physiocracy* p. 231.
It may be noted that little is said about the redistributive aspects of taxation in the *Wealth of Nations*. *See also* Richard Musgrave, "Adam Smith on Public Finance and Distribution," in Thomas Wilson and Andrew S. Skinner, eds., *The Market and the State: Essays in Honor of Adam Smith* (Oxford: The Clarendon Press, 1976), p. 296.
53. Smith, *Wealth of Nations*, bk. 2, pp. 351-352.
54. Ibid., bk.2, p. 394; Musgrave, "Adam Smith on Public Finance," p. 307; and Eugene Rotwein, "Introduction to Hume," *Writings on Economics*, p. lxxxiii.
55. Smith, *Wealth of Nations*, bk. 2, p. 376; Musgrave, "Adam Smith on Public Finance," p. 308.
56. Smith, *Wealth of Nations*, bk. 2, p. 411.
57. Ibid., bk. 2, pp. 438, 465. Also, Paul Leroy-Beaulieu, "On Taxation in General," in Richard Musgrave and Alan T. Peacock, eds., *Classics in the Theory of Public Finance* (London: MacMillan, 1964), p. 162.
58. Smith, *Wealth of Nations* bk. 5; Musgrave, "Adam Smith on Public Finance," p. 296; and Spengler, "Adam Smith's Theory—Part I," pp. 412, 414-415.

59. Smith, *Wealth of Nations*, bk. 2, p. 414; and Don Fullerton, "On the Possibility of an Inverse Relationship Between Tax Rates and Government Revenues," National Bureau of Economic Research, *Working Papers Series*, no. 467, (April 1980), p. 3.
    60. Smith, *Wealth of Nations*, bk. 2, p. 411. The specific passage is as follows:

> That the mercantile system [and its high tax rates] has not been very favorable to the revenue of the great body of the people, to the annual produce of the land and labor of the country, I have endeavored to show in the fourth book of this Inquiry. It seems not to have been more favorable to the revenue of the sovereign, so far at least as that revenue depends upon the duties or customs.

61. Musgrave, "Adam Smith's Theory of Public Finance," p. 309.
62. Smith, *Wealth of Nations*, bk 2., pp. 404, 411-412, 429.
63. Smith, *Wealth of Nations*, states that:

> . . . if every duty is occasionally either heightened or lowered according as it was most likely, either the one way or the other, to afford the greatest revenue to the state; taxation being always employed as an instrument of revenue and never of monopoly; it seems not improbable that a revenue, at least equal to the present net revenue of the customs, might be drawn from duties upon the importation of a few sorts of goods of the most general use and consumption. . . , (bk. 2, p. 415).

*See also* D. P. O'Brien, *The Classical Economists* (Oxford: The Clarendon Press, 1975).
    64. Spengler, "The Physiocrats and Say's Law," p. 183.
    65. In developing his thesis, Say used ideas that had been presented by the Physiocrats, Smith, Hume, and possibly Mill. *See also* W. H. Hutt, *A Rehabilitation of Say's Law* (Athens, Ohio: University of Ohio Press, 1974). pp. 4, 6, 7.
    66. Sowell, *Say's Law*, pp. 4, 19-20, 32-33; also Spengler, "The Physiocrats and Say's Law," p. 191; and Hutt, *A Rehabilitation of Say's Law*, pp. 6, 7, 27.
    67. Spengler, "The Physiocrats and Say's Law," p. 192.
    68. James Mill; *Elements of Political Economy*, 3rd rev. ed. (1844) (New York: Augustus M. Kelley, 1965) p. 237.
    69. Spengler, "The Physiocrats and Say's Law," p. 192. Note also, David Ricardo, *Principles of Political Economy and Taxation* (London: John Murray, 1821), Ch. 21.
    70. Hutt, *A Rehabilitation of Say's Law*, p. 25. Sowell offers a similar evaluation, "The ideal that output necessarily equals purchasing power was made plainer and more insistent in *Commerce Defended* than in Say's *Traite*." (Sowell, *Say's Law*," p. 23.)
    71. James Mill, in the *Edinburgh Review* 11 (January 1808): 434-435, quoted in Spengler, "The Physiocrats and Say's Law," p. 190.
    72. James Mill, *Commerce Defended*, pp. 79, 104-105.
    73. "Say's teaching—wheat and chaff—was accepted by Ricardo. . . ." (Joseph Schumpeter, *History of Economic Analysis* [New York: Oxford University Press, 1954], p. 621); *see also* Ricardo, *Principles*, Ch. 21.
    74. Spengler, "The Physiocrats and Say's Law," p. 193. Mill argued that, " . . . where wages are excessively low, as in Ireland, there is no industry; where excessively high, as in the American United States, there is the greatest." (James Mill, *Elements of Political Economy*, p. 245.)
    75. Spengler, "The Physiocrats and Say's Law," p. 192. Say himself "dismissed as unfounded the fear that frugality might lead to a diminution in expenditure and output, because he took it for granted that, as a rule, what was saved was not hoarded but was promptly consumed productively." (Ibid., p. 192.) And Mill insisted that "saving eventuates promptly in investment." (Ibid., p. 190.)
    76. Jean Baptiste Say, *A Treatise on Political Economy or the Production, Distribution, and Consumption of Wealth*, trans. Clement C. Biddle (Boston: Wells and Lilly, 1924), bk. 3, pp. 92, 196 (emphasis added).
    77. Ibid., p. 194.
    78. Charles J. Bullock, *Selected Readings in Public Finance* (Boston: Ginn and Company, 1924), p. 227.
    79. Say, *Treatise on Political Economy*, p. 208.

80. Ricardo, Principles, p. 166. See also Say, Treatise on Political Economy, p. 203.

81. Bullock, Selected Readings, p. 228.

82. Say, Treatise on Political Economy, p. 206.

83. Ibid., p. 223. See also O'Brien, The Classical Economists, p. 256.

84. James Mill, Commerce Defended, p. 89, see also p. 92; and idem, Elements of Political Economy, p. 247.

85. Say, Treatise on Political Economy p. 196 (emphasis added).

86. Ibid., p. 197.

87. Ibid., 197-199.

88. W. J. Ashley, "Introduction" to John Stuart Mill, Principles of Political Economy, 9th ed. (New York: Longmans, Green and Co., 1926), p. viii.

89. Sowell, Say's Law, p. 143.

90. John Stuart Mill, Essays on Some Unsettled Questions of Political Economy (London: John Park, 1844) p. 47, see also pp. 48-49, 49-50, 73-74.

91. John Stuart Mill, Principles of Political Economy, p. 884.

92. For example, J. R. McCulloch, A Treatise on the Principles and Practical Influence of Taxation and Funding System [1863] (New York: Burt Franklin, 1968), bk. 1, p. 6 and bk. 2, p. 41. See also O'Brien, The Classical Economists, p. 243; and D. P. O'Brien, J. R. McCulloch: A Study in Classical Economics (New York: Barnes and Noble, 1970) pp. 236-237.
It should be noted that one aspect of McCulloch's position on tax rates and factors of production was inconsistent with the supply-side approach. He held that when tax rates on labor are moderate and gradually increased, labor will respond by increasing its effort and ingenuity (McCulloch, Treatise, bk. 1, p. 10, p. 327). He felt, however, that the beneficial effects of tax increases have limits, beyond which they will discourage labor input. And indeed he felt that these adverse effects would begin to set in at tax rates which are rather low by modern standards—at "10, 12, or 15 percent." (Ibid., bk. 1, pp. 6, 7, 10; and bk. 2, p. 116.)

93. John Stuart Mill, Principles of Political Economy, p. 821.

94. O'Brien, J. R. McCulloch, pp. 229, 233.

95. Ibid., p. 272.

96. McCulloch, Treatise, bk. 1, p. 414.

97. O'Brien, J. R. McCulloch, p. 281; McCulloch, Treatise, bk. 1, p. 5.

98. O'Brien, The Classical Economists, p. 270.

99. O'Brien, J. R. McCulloch, p. 244.

100. Sir Henry Parnell, On Financial Reform, 3rd ed. (1831) (New York: Augustus M. Kelley, 1968), p. 17.

101. McCulloch, Treatise, bk. 1, pp. 340, 345; bk. 2, pp. 108, 161. O'Brien, J.R. McCulloch, p. 245. McCulloch, moreover, felt that exorbitant income taxes were in effect taxes on honesty and "a bounty on perjury and fraud." (Treatise, bk. 1, p. 116).

102. McCulloch, Treatise, bk. 1, pp. 354, 364; bk. 2, pp. 161-162; and Parnell, On Financial Reform, pp. 93-95.

103. McCulloch, Treatise, bk. 1, pp. 338-340.

104. Parnell, On Financial Reform, pp. 38-39. Jules Dupuit (1844) held similar views with respect to internal taxes: "By . . . gradually increasing the tax it will reach a level at which the yield is at a maxim. . . Beyond, the yield of tax diminishes. . . Lastly a tax [which is prohibitive] will yield nothing. (Quoted in Don Fullerton, "On the Possibility of an Inverse Relationship Between Tax Rates and Governmental Revenues," Working Paper No. 467, National Bureau of Economic Research [New York] April 1980, p. 3.)

105. For example, McCulloch, Treatise, bk. 1., pp. 354-355, 364, 383; and Parnell, On Financial Reform, pp. 39-47.

106. Parnell, On Financial Reform, p. 47 (emphasis added); and McCulloch, Treatise bk. 1, pp. 354-355.

107. See O'Brien, J.R. McCulloch, p. 263.

108. Blaug, Economic Theory in Retrospect, p. 180.

109. See Sowell, Say's Law, p. 142.

110. Although Gladstone's policies were the first to be explicitly developed from a systematic supply-side corpus of theory, there have been other events throughout history where governments or states adopted random elements of the supply-side

approach. These earlier occasions were less systematic because they were unable to draw upon the classical tradition of western economics. *See also* Jude Wanniski, *The Way the World Works* (New York: Basic Books, 1978); and David Ames Wells, *Theory and Practice of Taxation* (New York: D. Appleton and Co, 1900).

111. Francis W. Hirst, *Gladstone As Financier and Economist* (London: Ernest Benn, Ltd., 1931), pp. 196, 281.

112. For example, ibid., p. ix.

113. For example, the Revenue Act of 1842 affected almost every item of trade, with reductions in duties from 5 to 20 percent. Ibid., p. 78.

114. *See* Schumpeter, *History of Economic Analysis*, p. 404.

115. *See* Hirst, *Gladstone As Financier and Economist*, pp. xxii, 89.

116. Ibid., pp. xxii, 139, 140, 229.

117. *See* ibid., pp. 53, 65, 73, 78, 139, 216.

118. *See* ibid., pp. 73, 78, 80, 139, 206, 208, 209, 216.

119. Ibid., p. 215. Gladstone's philosophy on reducing tax rates was well put in his financial statement of 1861:

> There cannot be a grosser delusion than the supposition that the work of Parliament, during [this period] has been to destroy indirect taxation. The hand with which Parliament has wrought has been a pruning hand; its thought all along has been not to destroy the tree, but to strengthen the stock; the aim of the consequence is that at this moment, when indirect taxation has been "destroyed," as the fashionable phrase is, not once, but four or five times over, indirect taxation is larger and more productive—I do not mean in this particular year, but in any ordinary year, and upon the average of the last two or three years—than at any former period in our history. (Ibid., p. 209.)

120. Ibid., p. 73.

121. C. J. Bastable, *Public Finance* (New York: MacMillan and Co., 1903), p. 413.

122. The four components of this maxim are: collection costs, evasion, growth of industry, and productivity of taxation. For a forceful statement that taxation should focus on economic growth, *see also* Harley Leist Lutz, *Public Finance* (New York: D. Appleton and Co., 1929), p. 279.

123. G. Findlay Shirras, *The Science of Public Finance* (New York: MacMillan and Co., 1924), p. 128; Bastable, *Public Finance*, pp. 287-288.

124. Bastable, *Public Finance*, pp. 287-288, also pp. 417-418; and Lutz, *Public Finance*, pp. 278-279.

125. *See*, for example, the comments on the supply of labor and profits made by Bastable, *Public Finance*, pp. 284-287; and Harold Merlin Hunter, *Outlines of Public Finance* (New York: Harper and Bros., 1926), p. 130.

126. Paul Leroy-Beaulieu, "On Taxation in General," in Richard A. Musgrave and Alan T. Peacock, *Classics in the Theory of Public Finance* (London: MacMillan and Co., 1964), p. 162; *see also* Shirras, *The Science of Public Finance*, p. 105.

127. Leroy-Beaulieu, "On Taxation in General," pp. 157, 163.

128. Shirras, for example, states that:

> When taxes are very moderate, the revenue appropriated by the state is small, and individuals, especially in a rich country, may spend far less wisely then if the State imposed taxation for social services such as education. It is sometimes an unwise policy to allow money to fructify in the pockets of the people unnecessarily, but the reactions on production have to be considered by the state in extending taxation beyond a certain limit. (Shirras, *The Science of Public Finance*, p. 130. *See also* Hunter, *Outlines of Public Finance*, p. 130.)

129. Hunter, *Outlines of Public Finance*, p. 129.

130. Leroy-Beaulieu, "On Taxation in General," pp. 162-164.

131. Lutz, *Public Finance*, p. 277. Lutz goes on to say:

> From the standpoint of this test, therefore, many of the proposals to support the state by extremely heavy taxation of the larger incomes, or

the larger accumulations of wealth must be condemned. Such a program of taxation might be temporarily very productive, and for a short time it might be very attractive to the mass of the citizens. If this policy were carried to the extreme it is safe to assert that the large accumulations would rapidly diminish, both in number and size. They could easily enough be broken up by drastic taxation, but the total taxpaying power of the country would be greatly reduced thereby. (Ibid., p. 277.)

132. Wells, *Theory and Practice of Taxation*, p. 214.
133. Hutt, *Rehabilitation of Say's Law*, p. 2.
134. Andrew Mellon, *Taxation: The People's Business* (New York: MacMillan and Co., 1924), pp. 128-131.
135. Mellon notes that before the war, in 1916, the maximum surtax rate was 13 percent, but it had increased to 65 percent by 1921.
136. Mellon, *Taxation*, pp. 71-74.
137. Ibid., pp. 14-15.
138. Ibid., p. 222.
139. Ibid., p. 79.
140. Ibid., pp. 200, 222-223.
141. Ibid., p. 13.
142. Ibid., p. 20.
143. Ibid., pp 16, 20.
144. The speech may be found in Appendix E of ibid., pp. 216-227. Coolidge states in part:

> The first object of taxation is to secure revenue. . . . Experience does not show that the higher rate produces the larger revenue. Experience is all the other way. . . . There is no escaping the fact that when the taxation of large incomes is excessive, they tend to disappear. . . .
> I agree perfectly with those who wish to relieve the small taxpayer by getting the largest possible contribution from the people with large incomes. But if the rates on large incomes are so high that they disappear, the small taxpayer will be left to bear the entire burden. If, on the other hand, the rates are placed where they will produce the most revenue from large incomes, then the small taxpayer will be relieved. . . .
> Taken altogether, I think it is easy enough to see that I wish to include in the program a reduction in the high surtax rates, not that small incomes may be required to pay more and large incomes be required to pay less, but that more revenue may be secured from large incomes and taxes on small incomes may be reduced; not because I wish to relieve the wealthy, but because I wish to relieve the country. (Ibid., pp. 220-221, 224.)

145. *See* Wanniski, *The Way The World Works*.
146. *See* Hutt, *A Rehabilitation of Say's Law*.
147. Gerhard Colm, *Essay in Public Finance and Fiscal Policy* (New York: Oxford University Press, 1955), p. 80.
148. In the view of some economists, fiscal policy was necessary as an alternative mechanism for expanding the money supply.
149. Nicholas Kaldor, "Taxation and Economic Progress," in Joseph Scherer and James Papke, eds., *Public Finance and Fiscal Policy* (Boston: Houghton Mifflin, 1966), p. 273. *See also* Herbert E. Newman, *Introduction to Public Finance* (New York: John Wiley and Sons, 1968), pp. 15-16, where he states:

> As long as the economy is viewed as basically self-regulating in a satisfactory manner, public finance [and government expenditures in general] must remain essentially adjunctive in nature. When one concedes, however, that high levels of income, production, and employment are not automatically built into the working of the enterprise economy, that their attainment and maintenance require a certain amount of management, then there is a different role for the fiscal function of government. . . . Economists began to see in public expenditure, taxation, and borrowing instruments for promoting a

healthier economy. The old precepts of public finance such as . . . skepticism at all times toward increased government outlay, dropped away from newer treatments on the subject.

150. Schumpeter, *History of Economic Analysis*, p. 945.
151. This is amply documented by the treatment of taxation in any of the following textbooks: C. V. Brown and P. M. Jackson, *Public Sector Economics* (New York: Martin Robertson, 1978); Troy Cauley, *Public Finance and the General Welfare* (Columbus, Ohio: Charles Merrill Books, Inc., 1960); Colm, *Essays in Public Finance and Fiscal Policy*; Harold M. Groves, *Financing Government*, 4th ed. (New York; Henry Holt and Co., 1954); Jens Jensen, *Government Finance* (New York: Thomas Crowell and Co., 1937); Norman F. Keiser, *Macroeconomics: Fiscal Policy and Economic Growth* (New York: John Wiley and Sons, 1964); Slade Kendrick, *Public Finance* (New York: Houghton Mifflin, 1951); Newman, *Introduction to Public Finance*; Earl R. Rolph and George F. Break, *Public Finance* (New York: Ronald Press, 1961); Scherer and Papke, *Public Finance and Fiscal Policy*; Philip E. Taylor, *The Economics of Public Finance* (New York: MacMillan and Co., 1948).
152. Jensen, *Government Finance*, p. 215.
153. Groves, *Financing Government*, p. 30.
154. According to the "new economics," saving is an effect rather than a cause of increases in income. In this view, if the flow of spending is maintained, saving will take care of itself. *See,* for example, Keiser, *Macroeconomics*, pp. 229-230.
155. Cauley, *Public Finance and the General Welfare*, pp. 146-147.

# Say's Law and Keynesian Economics

## Tyler Cowen

The extent to which a new paradigm can color and influence succeeding economic thought for decades (sometimes even centuries) to come should not be underestimated. New, although not necessarily fruitful approaches to economic theory and policy often succeed in capturing the minds and the hearts of a whole generation of economists. For instance, even though over forty-five years have passed since the publication of John Maynard Keynes's *General Theory of Employment, Interest, and Money,* a cursory glance at any macroeconomic textbook will show that Keynesian economics is still the dominant macroeconomic paradigm of our day and has been so ever since 1936. Despite the fact that a number of older economists gave the *General Theory* hostile, and sometimes even scathing reviews,[1] (just as Keynes predicted they would), Keynes was able to win the loyalties of the younger generation of economists. Particularly important to Keynes's appeal was the commonly shared view that he was replacing the tottering edifice of classical and neoclassical economics with a new and exciting doctrine and that the *General Theory* was an iconoclastic challenge to the prevailing authorities.

The first and most important attack which Keynes made upon these authorities ("classical" economics) was a denial of the validity of "Say's Law", a proposition usually crudely expressed as "supply creates its own demand."[2] Keynes felt that Say's Law was so important that it "underlies the whole classical theory, which would collapse without it."[3] Once we accept Say's Law, Keynes felt we were bound to accede to all sorts of other classical propositions such as the advantage of saving, the equilibrating role of the rate of interest, the classical theory of unemployment, the quantity theory of money, and even the doctrine of laissez faire.[4] On the other hand, once we deny Say's Law we have opened the door for Keynesian economics.

Keynes was fairly accurate in assessing the importance of Say's Law for classical economics, for, along with the quantity theory of money, Say's Law formed the cornerstone of classical monetary theory. Even more important, Say's Law was the basis for the classical view that the strength of an economy was rooted in its ability to produce goods and services. Therefore, the validity (or nonvalidity) of Say's Law should have important consequences for economic theory and policy.

Although we are still living in an academic environment that was predominantly shaped by the Keynesian revolution, today's scene may best be described as one where we are experiencing a series of post-Keynesian counterrevolutions. One of the most recent manifestations of this counterrevolution is known as "supply-side economics," a doctrine which consists of a reaffirmation of both Say's Law and many of the other tenets of classical economics. The thrust of supply-side criticism of Keynesian economic policy is that several decades of demand management by the federal government through the use of monetary and fiscal policy have resulted in high rates of inflation, high rates of unemployment and huge budget deficits.[5] The reason for this failure is that the Keynesian theoretical apparatus behind these policies tends to ignore (or at least underemphasize) the importance of the "supply-side" of the economy. Therefore, Keynesian policies have concentrated only on stimulating aggregate demand and have ignored the more fundamental considerations of productivity and growth. The constant stimulation of demand has led only to inflation and has failed to create a healthy economy.

In contrast to Keynesianism, supply-side economics represents a policy shift away from demand management techniques and towards measures which will stimulate economic growth. Supply-side economics strongly upholds Say's Law since it asserts that only through an increase in the supply of goods and services can we truly increase demand in a noninflationary manner. An increase in demand not generated by an increase in supply cannot improve economic welfare. Many supply-siders quite consciously claim that they are nothing but a continuation of the heritage of nineteenth-century classical economics.

The points made previously illustrate the importance of Say's Law for classical economics, Keynesian economics, and supply-side economics. Although classical economics is now basically a dead body of thought, Keynesian and supply-side economics are both generating their respective research programs. What is particularly ironic is that although classical economics has perished, the writings of the classical economists on Say's Law are extremely relevant for the current supply-side/Keynesian debate. Hopefully, an examination of such writings will allow us to answer several questions: (1) were the classical economists supply-siders?, (2) is Say's Law valid?, (3) who is right about the meaning of Say's Law—the Keynesians, the supply-siders, or neither?, and (4) if Say's Law is valid, is it an effective criticism of the Keynesian system?

In order to facilitate our discussion of Say's Law, it is necessary to first lay out and define the three different versions of Say's Law that are current in modern economic literature.[6] The first version is an identity, usually called "Walras's Law," which asserts that there is a logical impossibility of an oversupply of all goods in either a barter economy or an economy where money is used only as a numeraire. Even though money may exist in a physical sense, trade has all the characteristics of barter, for money is only an abstract unit of account that is never held for its own sake. Since the numeraire is an arbitrarily chosen commodity, Walras's Law asserts the truism that the total value of all goods (including "money") demanded will be equal to the total value of all goods supplied. General overproduction is impossible.

The second interpretation of Say's Law, known as "Say's Identity," holds that the money market of an economy is always in equilibrium, meaning that there is never an excess demand or supply of money. When people supply commodities for money they will immediately use this money to demand other commodities. Under such circumstances money may rightfully be said to be a "veil," since it exerts no influence over relative prices. However, the lack of a demand for money to hold also implies that the absolute level of prices is indeterminate—thereby generating Lange and Patinkin's famous charge that the classical and neoclassical economists "dichotomized" the pricing process. The conditions described by Say's Identity imply that relative prices are determined by the supply and demand for commodities. The dichotomy arises because the "relative price of money" (i.e., the absolute price level) is determined only by the supply of money, since there is no demand to hold money.

Neither can there be a general overproduction under Say's Identity for, again, the total value of goods demanded must equal the total value of goods supplied if all cash balances are immediately spent. The impossibility of a general oversupply of commodities follows directly from the assumptions of the model. Since money does not function as a store of value the model is effectively identical to a barter economy —a situation where aggregate supply must equal aggregate demand by definition. The difference between Walras's Law and Say's Identity is that Walras's Law gives us the implications of a hypothetical money whose only function is a numeraire, while Say's Identity actually asserts that money actually only has a use as a numeraire.

The third and most sophisticated form of Say's Law is known as "Say's Equality," which asserts that the problems generated by an excess supply of goods or an excess demand for money tend to be self-correcting. If there is not a sufficient demand to sell all the goods that have been produced then the goods have been priced too high. When prices fall to their market clearing levels then any accumulated surpluses of goods (as distinguished from inventories) will be eliminated. Say's Equality does not assert the impossibility of depressions, but only says that under conditions of price flexibility the market will *tend* towards an equilibrium. If prices are at the right levels, then the income generated from the supply of goods will be sufficient to purchase these goods. However, Say's Equality, unlike Say's Identity, does not always claim that we are facing an equilibrium configuration of prices. Neither does Say's Equality rule out the use of money as a store of value or the possibility of an excess demand for cash balances. This may be one of the most important forms of disequilibrium that the market is bound to face—at least according to much of the historical debate over Say's Law.

Although our interpretation of Say's Law does not exactly coincide with any of these three interpretations, they are useful for classification purposes. Not only are they current in modern monetary theory but they also provide us with a spectrum upon which to classify both the positions of the classical economists themselves and other economists' portrayals of the classical position. On one end of the spectrum we have the extremely naive position ascribed to the classicals by Keynes and Lange—a position similar to Say's Identity. On the other end of the spectrum we have John Stuart Mill, whose famous essay "Of the Influence of Consumption on Production" both develops the notion of Say's Equality and satisfactorily integrates the holding of money into the Say's Law debate.

Although Say himself was the first writer ever to explicitly formulate Say's Law, the conception of the law is rooted in Physiocratic thought. On one hand, Say's Law is an affirmation of the Physiocratic tradition, while on the other hand it is intended as a denial of this tradition. A major segment of Physiocratic thought which is maintained by Say is the vision of the economy as a circular flow of goods and services. In such a scheme money is relegated to a secondary role, a role similar to that which is expressed in the familiar classical proposition that "money oils the wheels of trade." This notion of the circular flow is perhaps best illustrated by Quesnay's *Tableau Economique* which explicitly outlines a model showing both the flow of the "produit net" generated by agriculture and the distribution of the social product among different classes. The *Tableau Economique* also implies that production is the source of demand—although this is not a conclusion that the Physiocrats themselves drew from their model. It is only through the "produit net" generated by the agricultural class that allows them, in turn, to demand products, thereby continuing the circular flow of goods and services. The Tableau itself is essentially a barter model where goods are traded for other goods and money ultimately affects neither the end result of such a process nor the operation of the process itself. As we shall see, Say moved somewhat beyond the naive Physiocrats conception of money.

Physiocratic economics is a denial of Say's Law insofar as it asserts the primacy of consumption over production. Specifically, the Physiocrats concentrated on the importance of the consumption of agricultural produce. Such an emphasis was completely foreign to Say, who not only focused his attention upon production, but also denied the distinction which the Physiocrats drew between the agricultural and the nonagricultural sectors of the economy. Joseph Spengler attributes the Physiocratic emphasis upon consumption to the economic conditions of Bourbon France at the time.[7] The Physiocrats felt that the French monarchy's oppressive fiscal policies were depriving the agricultural sector of loan capital, thereby decreasing the demand for both agricultural and nonagricultural products and interrupting the circular flow of the economy. Say's different approach to France's economic difficulties may be due partially to the fact that Say wrote in the atmosphere of a much healthier economy. Also not to be underestimated is the influence upon Say of such radical figures of the French Enlightenment as Condorcet. The unbounded optimism of Condorcet may have much to do with Say's idea that a free economy is always in a basically healthy and growing state. The idea that production, not consumption, is the source of demand is also consistent with the doctrine of the "harmony of rightfully understood interests" which was being developed at the time. One man's wealth (i.e., production) would help all men as it would provide one individual with the power to demand other men's products.

Another important influence upon Say to be noted here is that of his primary intellectual forefather, Adam Smith. The Physiocrats had developed a model of the economy illustrating the circular flow of the spending stream, but prompt and sufficient consumption was necessary for this stream to be maintained. Unless a definite fraction of national income was spent on agricultural products, disaster was likely to befall the economy. In contrast, Smith argued that saving was a far greater virtue than spending because saving was capable of augmenting a nation's capital stock and its productive powers. Like most classical economists, Smith emphasized the existence of circulating, rather than fixed or durable capital. As a result, any money that was saved would generally be used to hire laborers to support a production process. Smith was thus able to have his cake and eat it too when he declared that ". . . what is annually saved is as regularly consumed as what is annually spent. . . ."[8] Any advance that was made to laborers out of savings could then be spent by the laborer on consumption goods. Physiocratic fears that savings would lead to underconsumption were therefore unfounded. Instead, savings were almost automatically converted to investment, which found its way into the hands of laborers to be spent on consumption.

It is likely that Smith's argument helped Say to further visualize the operation of Say's Law. It is because the workers in Smith's example are engaged in *production* that they are able to earn the power of demanding goods and services. Furthermore, Smith's maxim can be read to imply that there are no inherent secular limits on savings and capital accumulation resulting from any problems of underconsumption. As will be argued later, the question of economic growth was foremost in the minds of both Say and many other classical economists during their discussions of Say's Law.

Most likely, when Say originally developed the law of markets he did not think he was being particularly innovative. Instead, he was simply expressing an obvious truth that was already accepted by a fair percentage of the writers on economics of his time. Nowhere in the first edition of the *Treatise* during Say's discussion of the law of markets does he indicate any pretense of uniqueness or originality for his doctrine. Say probably thought that Say's Law was just a logical implication of what could be found both in Smith and in earlier writers. He saw his advocacy of the law of markets as just another step —a step he took with Smith—in moving away from Physiocratic notions about the importance of consumption.

There are several references in the economic literature before Say that may properly be regarded as precursors of the law of markets;[9] however, the first explicit statement of Say's Law by its progenitor does not appear until the untranslated first edition of Say's *Treatise on Political Economy* (1803) in a small chapter entitled "*Des Debouches.*" Although this phrase is usually translated as "on markets," William Baumol points out that in this context the word "markets" actually refers to "making a market" rather than the institution of a market place. Baumol has suggested that perhaps a more accurate translation of "des debouches" would be "on outlets for goods."[10] Note that the title of this chapter has nothing to do with either the possibility or impossibility of a general glut of commodities or the question of cyclical fluctuations. Neither of these topics is mentioned even once in this chapter. Instead, Say's main point was that effective demand is the result of previous output. It is only *production* that is capable of providing the means with which other products may be purchased. Any conclusions that Say later drew about the impossibility of a general overproduction of goods and services should properly be regarded *corollaries* of Say's Law. The original law of markets simply says that *production is the source of demand*.

Say's main point is well illustrated by the opening paragraph of his chapter:

> Every producer produces a quantity of a particular good that considerably exceeds his own consumption. The farmer harvests more grain than is required to feed him and his household; the hatter makes substantially more hats than he produces for his use; the wholesale grocer handles more sugar than he can consume. Each of them needs many other products to live comfortably. The exchanges they carry out of their own products for those of others, constitute what are called the *markets* for those products.[11]

It is Say's attempt to sum up this reasoning in a single sentence that gives us his first formulation of the law of markets: "I trust this shows that it is not the abundance of money but the abundance of other products in general that facilitates sales. This is one of the most important truths of political economy."[12]

It is only at a later point in the first edition of Say's *Treatise* that he discusses the question of gluts. Say starts off by reiterating his proposition that one can only make purchases with what one has produced and then goes on to discuss Garnier's theory[13] that many European nations are on the verge of suffering from a general overproduction of goods because these nations have accumulated so much capital over the last several centuries. In response, Say points out that although a nation may suffer from an overabundance of certain commodities this is due to excessive malinvestment in these lines of production. This problem will quickly be remedied by producing less of those goods which are in abundant supply and producing more of those goods which are lacking. Although Say admits, and indeed emphasizes, the possibility of a partial glut of commodities, he is careful to point out that:

> I cannot conceive that the products of the labour of an entire nation can ever be overabundant since one good provides the means to purchase the other. The sum of its outputs composes the total wealth of a nation, and wealth is no more of an embarrassment to nations than it is to individuals.[14]

This principle—the impossibility of a general overproduction— perhaps should more aptly be entitled "Say's Corollary," while reserving Say's Law for the more basic proposition that production is the source of demand. Immediately after stating Say's Corollary, Say goes on to remind us of Say's Law, which is the underlying truth behind what he is saying:

> This point [concerning a general glut] having been thoroughly cleared up, it provides us an answer to the question with which we are concerned and which I repeat: *upon what elements does the demand for factors of production in general depend?* It depends on the volume of production. . . . [15]

It is important to realize that when Say refers to the question of a general glut he is not considering the question of business cycles or any other short-run fluctuations in economic activity. Rather, in Garnier's example, and in other instances, the alleged general overproduction is always related to the questions of capital accumulation and economic growth. The defenders of Say's Corollary usually saw themselves as heralding the virtues of economic growth and as asserting the impossibility of secular stagnation by their advocacy of the corollary.

By the time of the fourth edition of the *Treatise*[16] Say had fleshed out the implications of his law of markets somewhat more clearly. Once again, Say begins by asserting that " . . . it is production which opens a demand for products."[17] It is only through this fact that we can explain:

> How could it be possible that there should now be bought and sold in France five or six times as many commodities, as in the

> miserable reign of Charles VI? Is it not obvious, that five or six as
> many commodities must have been produced, and that they must
> have served to purchase one or the other?[18]

Of course, the answer is to be found in the fact that the production of
one good furnishes a demand for the other goods that have been
produced. There is no inherent check on the ability of a market
economy to expand through a continuing increase in productivity
since it is the products themselves that will supply the purchasing
power to buy other products.

In the fourth edition, Say is even more willing to admit the
possibility of a partial glut in certain lines of production. However, this
is not due to any sort of general overproduction. It is the result of an
undersupply of other commodities. An excess of any particular commodity may arise from an insufficient demand for that commodity.
Since other products are the source of this demand, we can conclude
that these other products are in short supply. Only a general augmentation of production can cure a problem of partial oversupply.[19]

At the end of Say's chapter on the law of markets in the fourth
edition, he outlines a number of implications of his law which enable
us to see how the law of markets is tied to his broader views on
economic and social philosophy. The first conclusion that Say deduces
is that the more productive a community is, the more profitable such
production will be. Additional production will create additional demand, thereby raising prices and profit margins. The second conclusion is somewhat similar to the first, as both relate to Say's idea that
both production and exchange benefit all members of a community.
Say writes: "Each individual is interested in the general prosperity of
all, and the success of one branch of industry promotes that of all the
others."[20]

Say then goes on to expand this principle to include relations among
nations, as well as relations among individuals within a nation.[21] From
this, Say deduces his third conclusion that nations ought to place no
prohibitions upon the import or export of commodities to other
nations. Not only does Say argue that a policy of free trade will increase
our neighbor's opulence, thereby enriching ourselves, but also that it
will directly increase the scope and productivity of native industry.

Say's fourth and final conclusion is that spending is not the source of
a nation's prosperity:

> [M]ere consumption is no benefit to commerce; for the difficulty
> lies in supplying the means, not in stimulating the desire of
> consumption; and we have seen that production alone, furnishes
> those means. Thus, it is the aim of good government to stimulate
> production, of bad government to encourage consumption.[22]

Say desires to be so explicit about these conclusions that not only
does he spend several pages outlining them, but he also numbered
them from one to four. The conclusions demonstrate that Say's law of

markets was not conceived as an isolated economic principle, but was rather part of the base of the entire edifice of Say's liberal philosophy. The concomitant emphasis on production, saving, free trade, and the mutually beneficial nature of exchange were all an important part of the nineteenth-century brand of French liberalism to which Say subscribed. The law of markets was an important building block of that philosophy.

Perhaps the aspect of Say's Law that has come under the most criticism is his treatment of the question of money holdings. It is possible to find numerous statements in his work (as well as in most other classical economists) to the effect that money is merely a veil and that all exchange is ultimately barter. In some places Say even asserts that any money that is received for productive services will be almost immediately spent.[23] While it is important to realize that Say did underemphasize the importance of monetary factors, we are not concerned with cataloguing his statements to this effect, for this problem in classical monetary theory is quite well-known. It is equally important to understand that there is a difference between making a statement and endorsing all of the implications (often unforeseen) of that statement. There is even a further distinction to be drawn between realizing the implications of a statement and then utilizing these implications in one's analysis. What is being argued here is that although Say may have made statements about money that were both careless and incorrect, he was often capable of simultaneously realizing the insights that such statements would seem to deny. By the time of the fourth edition of the *Treatise*, Say had at least partially integrated money into his analysis.

Although it occasionally appears that Say is denying the utility of money, it is by no means likely that he would have been willing to accept such a charge. The *Treatise* contains a quite explicit discussion of how money originates from a commodity which is commonly valued. Say writes: "I have . . . pointed out the various utility of gold and silver as articles of commerce, wherein originates their value; and considered their fitness to act as money as part of that utility."[24]

The value that money possesses is not only a value for purposes of circulation, but may also be a value to hold. Cash balances represent a stream of utility to their owners and should be considered part of the national wealth. Although Say did not apply this insight consistently, it is so contrary to the usual interpretation of his work that is is worth quoting him at length:

> [I]t would be wrong to subscribe to the opinion of Garnier, who lays it down as a maxim that "so long as silver remains in the shape of money, it is not an item of actual wealth in the strict sense of the word; for it does not directly and immediately satisfy a want or procure an enjoyment." There are an abundance of values incapable of satisfying a want, or procuring an enjoyment, in their

present existing shape. A merchant may have his warehouse full of indigo, which is of no use in it actual state, either as food or as clothing; yet it is nevertheless an item of wealth, and one that can be converted, at will, into another value fit for immediate use. Silver, in the shape of crown pieces, is, therefore, equally an article of wealth with indigo in chests. Besides, is not the utility of money an object of desire in civilized society?

Indeed, the same writer elsewhere admits that "specie in the coffers of an individual is real wealth, an integral part of his substance, which he may immediately devote to his personal enjoyment; although, in the eye of political economy, this same coin is mere instrument of exchange, essentially differing from the wealth it helps to circulate." I hope what I have said is quite sufficient to show the complete analogy of specie to all other items of wealth. . . .[25]

While it is not true that money is completely analogous to all other forms of wealth, the previous passage should help to dispel the popular notion that Say had nothing but a naive conception of money as a "veil."

The question of hoarding is even considered in the chapter on the law of markets. Say points out that money is always desired ultimately for the purpose of spending it, either for consumption or investment. Yet, in a footnote Say adds that, "Even when money is obtained with a view to hoard or bury it, the ultimate object is always to employ it in a purchase of some kind."[26] Lest anyone think that Say is only considering short-term hoarding, he even goes on to give an example of a miser who never intends to spend his money. Even in this case, Say points out, the money will eventually be spent by the miser's heir.

Say goes so far as to consider the possibility of a general excess demand for money. Instead of referring to an excess demand for money, Say instead visualizes it as a shortage of money—the logically equivalent proposition. Say argues that such a scarcity will not create ill effects for an economy:

Sales cannot be said to be dull because money is scarce, but because other products are so. There is always money enough to conduct the circulation and mutual interchange of other values, when those values really exist. Should the increase of traffic require more money to facilitate it, the want is easily supplied, and is a strong indication of prosperity—a proof that a great abundance of values has been created, which it is wished to exchange for other values. In such cases, merchants know well enough how to find substitutes for the product serving as the medium of exchange or money: and money itself naturally pours in, for this reason, that all produce naturally gravitates to that place where it is most in demand.[27]

This is not a completely satisfactory description of the equilibrating forces which will correct an excess demand for money, but it does show that Say was aware of the problem and was working towards a solution. As the above quote indicates, Say saw two different ways that the market could deal with a scarcity of money. Either merchants could resort to "bills at sight . . . bank notes, running credits, [and] write-offs . . ." as money substitutes to facilitate commerce, or the community's supply of money will increase to relieve the shortage. It is not clear from the above passage whether Say is referring to an inflow of money from other nations, an increase in quantity of the money commodity, or both. Nonetheless, one thing is obvious—Say had considered the implications of disequilibrium in the money market and had attempted to work out an answer to this problem.

It should be clear from our discussion that Say did not subscribe to anything even remotely resembling "Say's Identity." Not only does Say discuss at length examples of disequilibrium in the different branches of production, but he also discusses the existence of disequilibrium in money markets. Furthermore, Say explicitly allows for the possibility of both short-term and long-term hoarding. "Say's Equality," however, is a fairly accurate description of Say's actual position. Perhaps the closest Say comes to stating Say's Equality is during his discussion of the causes of partial shortages and partial gluts. Most of these are attributed to either political of natural convulsions. Say concludes by noting that:

> No sooner is the cause of this political disease removed, than the means of production feel a natural impulse towards the vacant channels, the replenishment of which restores activity to all the others. One kind of production would seldom outstrip every other, and its products be disproportionately cheapened, were production left entirely free.[29]

Although it had previously been suggested that James Mill was the originator of Say's Law, this claim has finally been laid to rest by Donald Winch.[30] Joseph Spengler has also credited Say with priority over Mill, but Winch's work must be considered the final word on the subject. Winch effectively argues that not only had Mill read the *Treatise* and cited it in his *Commerce Defended*,[32] but also that Mill had explicitly credited Say with the idea. Nonetheless, as early as 1808, Mill had developed the second fleshed-out statement of Say's law of markets in his *Commerce Defended*.

Mill's pamphlet was written to answer the claim of William Spence, who argued that commerce was not a source of national wealth, and that therefore, the Napoleonic blockade would not injure British prosperity.[33] Also part of Spence's general thesis is that it is spending, not saving, that is capable of advancing national wealth. Mill combats the latter proposition by invoking the most elementary form of Say's Law—production is the source of demand. As a result, a community should be less worried about spending and more concerned with production. Mill writes:

> The production of commodities creates, and is the one and universal cause, which creates a market for the commodities

> produced . . . but if a nation's power of purchasing is exactly
> measured by its annual produce, as it undoubtedly is; the more
> you increase the annual produce, the more by that very act you
> extend the national market, the power of purchasing and the actual
> purchases of the nation. . . .[34]

Therefore, as long as a nation is maintaining an adequate level of production we need not worry about a lack of sufficient spending, for spending will take care of itself. Neither will an increase in saving create any economic problems through underconsumption. Mill reiterated Smith's familiar proposition that what is saved will be as regularly consumed as what is spent.[35] Not only will savings ultimately be spent on consumption anyway, but they also furnish employment for workers in the meanwhile.

We can see that with Mill, just as with Say, the law of markets is not an isolated proposition of economic theory but is integrated into a consistent philosophy of economic and political liberalism. Mill's use of Say's Law is intimately connected with his defense of production and exchange as important components of a nation's well-being. For Mill also counters Spence with a strong defense of free trade and with an attack on Britain's national debt, two important aspects of liberal philosophy. Savings are applauded while spending, especially military spending, is deprecated.[36] The idea of production as the source of demand is just one piece in this entire framework—yet it is a piece that enables the liberal philosophy to cohere.

Another important part of the classical philosophy is its captivation with capital accumulation and economic growth. Mill notes that there is at least one group of economists, the Physiocrats, who deny the beneficial effects of large quantities of capital accumulation:

> The Economistes [the Physiocrats] and their disciples express
> great apprehensions lest capital should increase too fast, lest the
> production of commodities should be too rapid. There is only, say
> they, a market for a given quantity of commodities, and if you
> increase the supply beyond that quantity you will be unable to
> dispose of the surplus.[37]

Mill invoked what we have labeled "Say's Corollary" to dispose of this objection. A general overproduction of commodities is impossible because the production of one commodity creates a market for another. The more production is increased the more we extend the nation's purchasing power. Aggregate demand is quite capable of keeping pace with aggregate supply provided that the commodities produced are correctly proportioned to consumer's desires for them.[38] Even if goods and services are not produced in the proper quantities this can only lead to a partial glut, not a general glut. The solution is then to produce more of other commodities in order to increase the demand for the commodity that was previously in excess supply.

Let us quote Mill's first restatement of Say's Corollary:

> Whatever be the additional quantity of goods therefore which is at any time created in any country, an additional power of purchasing, exactly equivalent, is at the same instant created; so that a nation can never be naturally overstocked either with capital or with commodities; as the very operation of capital makes a vent for its produce. . . . When money is laid out of the question, is it not in reality the different commodities of the country, that is to say, the different articles of the annual produce, which are annually exchanged against one another? Whether these commodities are in great quantities or in small, that is to say, whether the country is rich or poor, will not one half of them always balance the other?[39]

We can see from this quote that Mill's rendition of the law of markets is basically faithful to Say, although it is inferior in two respects. The first problem in Mill's exposition is that he comes much closer to Say's Identity than Say did. Such statements as "will not one half of them (commodities) *always* balance the other" (see previous quote, emphasis added) tend to imply Say's Identity—the proposition that there is no demand for money to hold and that, even *ex ante*, aggregate demand will always equal aggregate supply. While it is true that Mill also admitted the possibility of disequilibrium, he was certainly less insistent about this point than was Say. The second problem is Mill's treatment of money, which is also inferior to that of Say.

Mill conducted his analysis of Say's Law and Say's Corollary under explicit conditions of barter.[40] His only mention of the holding of money in *Commerce Defended* comes in an extremely ambiguous passage where it is not clear whether Mill is expressing his own views or merely citing Spence. In any case, if Mill is citing Spence he does so with seeming acceptance of Spence's point, which is that misers are now too wise to lock up their money at home but will instead lend it out for interest.[41] In spite of Mill's grammatical implication of this point to Spence, it is more likely that he was referring to his own views on hoarding, since Spence himself had casually suggested the possibility of deliberate *ex ante* hoarding,[42] although he was later to deny the importance of such hoarding.[43]

Another of the leading advocates of Say's Law in the nineteenth century was David Ricardo, who became acquainted with the principle from Say's *Treatise* and Mill's *Commerce Defended*. There are many similarities between Ricardo's exposition of the law of markets and the writings of Say and Mill, but there are differences in emphasis worth noting. Ricardo is especially concerned about the implications of Say's Law for economic growth, capital accumulation, and the rate of profit. One important indication of this emphasis can be found in his *Principles of Political Economy and Taxation* where Say's Law is discussed in the chapter entitled "Effects of Accumulation on Profits and Interests."

What Ricardo attempts to argue here is not only that there are no limits placed on expansion of capacity due to problems of aggregate demand but also that any increase in output can be absorbed at the going profit rate. Ricardo wishes to show that the only cause of a falling profit rate is an increase in the real cost of producing wage goods, and, hence, an increase in wages, due to a community's forced recourse to the cultivation of more inferior soils. Ricardo wrote in the *Principles* that "if the necessaries of the workman could be constantly increased with the same facility, there could be no permanent alteration in the rate of profit or wages, to whatever amount capital might be accumulated."[44] In such a context Say's Law was conceived as an answer to the problem of secular stagnation. Even if such stagnation were to arrive, it would come in the way that Ricardo had described and no other. Ricardo explicitly dealt with Smith's position on the declining rate of profit, claiming it had been answered by Say who had shown that "there is no amount of capital which may not be employed in a country, because demand is only limited by production."[45]

Another point of interest to be found in Ricardo's writings is that, like Say, he briefly considered the possibility of an excess demand for money. Such a passage can be found in a letter to James Mill:

> [R]eductions in the amount of the circulating medium should speedily operate on prices, but the resistance which is offered—the unwillingness that every man feels to sell his goods at a reduced price—induces him to borrow at a high interest and to have recourse to other shifts to postpone the necessity of selling. The effect is however certain at last, but the duration of the resistance depends on the degree of information, or the strength of the prejudices of those who offer it. . . .[46]

This passage clearly indentifies Ricardo as an advocate of Say's Equality, not Say's Identity. Not only does Ricardo examine the possibility and the consequences of a shortage of money supply relative to money demand but he also avoids assuming the full and immediate flexibility of all prices—a position commonly misascribed to the classical economists.

It is worth noting in passing that Ricardo and Say were not the only two advocates of the law of markets who introduced the question of money into their analysis. John Ramsey McCulloch, who is usually considered to be at the same time one of the most Ricardian and least sophisticated of the classical economists, also provides us with a discussion of the problems arising from a shortage of money. During McCulloch's discussion of Say's Law he argues that surpluses can only arise from a misdirection of production. However, he cautions his reader that this is only a long-run equilibrium statement which assumes that the value of money has reached its equilibrium level:

> It must, however, be borne in mind, that in the previous statements we have taken for granted that the value of money . . . has

> been invariable, or that, at all events, it has not been sensibly affected by sudden changes in its quantity and value. These changes may, as already stated, exert a powerful influence; and have frequently, indeed, occasioned the most extensive derangement in the ordinary channels of commercial intercourse . . . any sudden diminution of the quantity, and consequent rise in the value of money . . . may be such materially to abridge the power of the society to make their accustomed purchases, and thus occasion a glut of the market.[47]

As will later become evident, McCulloch was anticipating John Stuart Mill's position that a belief in Say's Corollary does not constitute a denial of a "general glut" *if* this glut is nothing more than a shortage of money relative to the supply of commodities.[48]

It was not long before Say's Corollary came under strong attack. A number of "dissenters" from the Ricardian tradition, including Sismondi, Lauderdale, Chalmers, and Malthus, were all quick to assert the possibility of a general glut. Since Malthus is the most important of these dissenters, it is his analysis which we shall examine here.

Like Ricardo and Say, Malthus saw the question of a general glut being ultimately related to capital accumulation. General gluts were neither the result nor the cause of cyclical fluctuations in economic activity, but rather were due to increases in savings as an economy progressed. The chapter in Malthus's *Principles of Political Economy*[49] where he discusses the possibility of a general overproduction is even entitled "On the Progress of Wealth."

The primary reason that Malthus even wrote *Principles of Political Economy* (1820) was to answer Ricardo's *Principles*. Prior to the publication of Ricardo's work, Malthus felt that Adam Smith was the reigning king of political economy and that the British Isles did not need another treatise on economics. It is obvious that both Ricardo and Say felt that Malthus had issued a very important challenge to their work. Such a concern is evidenced by Ricardo's extensive correspondence with Malthus and the publication of Say's *Letters to Mr. Malthus* (1821), a short volume devoted solely to answering the Malthusian arguments for a general glut.

What Malthus meant by a general glut had little or nothing to do with either an excess demand for money or the Keynesian proposition that general overproduction results from an excess of planned saving over planned investment.[51] A general glut occurs when the conversion of revenue into capital sufficiently diminishes aggregate demand so as to create a falling rate of profit that stifles the incentive for further capital accumulation. Such a crisis is brought about by an increase in savings which has the dual effect of increasing investment (and ultimately output) and decreasing consumption. The diminished consumption is unable to absorb the increased output at profitable prices. Malthus aptly summed up his entire point when he wrote that:

> [I]t is impossible that the increased quantity of commodities, obtained by the increased number of productive labourers, should find purchasers, without such a fall of price as would probably sink their value below that of the outlay, or, at least, so reduce profits very greatly to diminish both the power and the will to save.[52]

Such an argument does not necessarily deny Say's Law proper—that production is the source of demand—but only denies Say's Corollary, that a general oversupply of commodities is impossible. This distinction has not usually been made by those commenting on the debate. Since Malthus's basic loyalties were with Adam Smith, he had no wish to say that production was not necessary to maintain demand. What Malthus claimed was that production would not be *sufficient* to maintain demand in the face of falling prices and a falling rate of profit. Although it has been argued that "sticky wages"[53] and "satiation of demand"[54] played an important part of Malthus's discussion of gluts, we shall ignore these points as they are not central to Malthus's case. Malthus often does bring these two additional factors into his analysis, but if his main point was valid, it could stand without the benefit of assumptions of either sticky wages or a satiated demand. It is likely that Malthus realized this point for he would often repeat his argument without invoking either assumption.

Only occasionally in *Letters to Mr. Malthus* does Say truly address the crux of Malthus's case. One of Say's more important preliminary points is that even when individuals save money, that money will ultimately be spent on consumption because savings become part of the wage fund paid to laborers. However, even if it were admitted that savings did not lead to a decrease in consumption, we may still be faced with a falling rate of profit since output is still increasing and prices are still falling. Even if Say's point is well-taken it would not prevent the fall in prices of consumption goods—it would only affect the magnitude of such a fall.

Say's best defense of Say's corollary comes when he counters Malthus's assertion that "cheapness [of products] is always at the expense of profits,"[55] for this assumption is the linchpin of Malthus's argument. Say admits that the difficulty "is to create productions which shall be worth the costs of production."[56] There is no problem with this proposition from the demand side since the increase of other products will furnish a sufficient demand for any other single product that is produced in the right proportion. Neither is there any problem from the supply-side since if prices are falling then costs of production will fall proportionately. Herein lies Say's strongest answer to Malthus, yet he relegates this point to a mere footnote. Say points out that costs of production "are diminished in proportion to the increase of [production]."[57] In the text Say refers us to his *Treatise*, which contains a slight elaboration of this argument:

> [S]avings generally operate in a very short time to the benefit of the community at large; they reduce the charges of production; and in proportion as the economical process becomes better understood, and more generally practised, the competition of producers brings the product gradually to a level with the charges of production.[58]

The Say-Malthus debate centers around the question of whether it is possible to sustain a growing economy with falling prices. The previous passages suggest that Say won this debate, for he demonstrated how falling prices and falling costs can, due to increasing productivity, increase national wealth without occasioning any of the deleterious effects predicted by Malthus. Apparently, Malthus did not feel that such progress was as easy as it seemed to many other classical economists. It is interesting to examine Malthus's social philosophy in light of our previous remarks about the connection between Say's Law and liberalism. Not only is it true that Malthus did not share Say's faith in progress and economic growth but Malthus was also considered to be an opponent of laissez faire and free trade. It is no accident that Malthus was also Say's opponent on the question of gluts.

An additional point of interest which can be found in Say's *Letters to Mr. Malthus* is a discussion of the problem of hoarding. At one point Say briefly repeats the analysis which he presented in the *Treatise*,[59] yet later on we also encounter a footnote in which Say sounds more like John Maynard Keynes than a classical economist. Say starts off by attacking Ricardo's proposition that everything which is saved is invested because individuals will desire to earn interest on their fund. Say argued that many savings are not invested and that:

> Mr. Ricardo is completely refuted, not only by what happened to us in 1813, when the errors of Government ruined all commerce, and when the interest of money fell very low, for want of good opportunities of employing it; but by our present circumstances, when capitals are quietly sleeping in the coffers of their proprietors. The bank of France alone possesses 223 millions of specie (about nine millions of pounds sterling) in its chests, which is more than double the amount of its notes in circulation, and six times what prudence would consider necessary to reserve for the ordinary course of its payments.[60]

Although many classical economists espoused Say's Law and Say's Corollary, the culmination of this entire tradition can be found in John Stuart Mill's classic essay "Of the Influence of Consumption on Production."[61] It is only in this essay that we find a full treatment of the role of monetary factors in Say's Corollary. Most of Mill's essay is concerned with Say's Law, but near the end of the essay Mill brings up Say's Corollary. Mill notes that at first it may seem like Say's Corollary is founded upon the supposition of barter, since each person is both a seller and a buyer. However, once we assume that money is being used, this identity of supply and demand ceases to be immediately true. Mill says that:

> [T]he effect of the employment of money, and even the utility of it, is, that it enables this one act of interchange [barter] to be divided into two separate acts or operations; one of which may be performed now, and the other a year hence, or whenever it shall be most convenient. Although he who sells, really sells only to buy, he needs not buy at the same moment when he sells; and he does not therefore necessarily add to the *immediate* demand for one commodity when he adds to the supply of another.[52]

No one can deny that we may have a temporary general glut of commodities *relative* to money if there is an excess demand for money, but such a situation does not constitute a true refutation of Say's Corollary. Money itself should be recognized as a commodity so we still have only a relative overproduction of certain goods and services according to Mill's terminology. The only sense in which an excess of all commodities is possible is when there has been a temporary fall in their value relative to money. Mill proclaims his belief in Say's Equality when he notes that "an overstocked state of the market is always temporary, and is generally followed by a more than common briskness of demand."[63]

Nowhere is this essay does Mill pretend to be saying anything new —he only claims he is clarifying the notions of previous economists. He is careful to point out that Say's Corollary

> appears a paradox, because it has usually been expressed as apparently to contradict these well-known facts [an excess of nonmoney commodities to money]; which, however, were equally known to the authors of the doctrine, who, therefore, can only have adopted from inadvertence any form of expression which could to a candid person appear inconsistent with it.[64]

Mill's comment indicates that earlier classical economists had considered monetary factors in their analysis—a claim that is supported by our current investigation. Nearly every major classical economist, including Say, Ricardo, and McCulloch, had examined the problems of either hoarding or a shortage of money.

After our brief survey of Say's Law in classical economics we may draw several conclusions: (1) Say's Law was not an isolated principle of economic theory. Rather it was integrated with an entire classical liberal world-view which emphasized the beneficient nature of production and exchange, progress, economic growth, falling prices, saving, capital accumulation, free trade, and international liberalism. Say's Law formed an important theoretical pillar for these views, as even Keynes had pointed out. (2) A useful distinction may be drawn between Say's Law and Say's Corollary. Say's Law, which asserts that production is the source of demand, is the primary proposition which Say had in mind. Say's Corollary, which asserts the impossibility of a general glut, is a secondary proposition which was derived from Say's

Law. It is possible to accept Say's Law while denying Say's Corollary, as did Malthus. (3) Most classical economists accepted what is known as Say's Equality. There is little evidence of any widespread advocacy of Say's Identity. (4) Many classical economists *did* incorporate monetary factors into their analysis of Say's Law and Say's Corollary. Say and John Stuart Mill are the two most notable examples. While it is possible to find statements in nearly every classical economist which imply a denial of the importance of money, it should be remembered that the classicals' treatment of money was far more sophisticated than such statements would imply.

After having briefly examined several of the classical economists on Say's Law, we are now ready to answer our first question: Were the classical economists supply-siders? It would be a mistake to ask whether supply-siders are the new classical economists since the former conception is so narrow and relatively undeveloped compared to the latter. There are entire aspects of classical economics that have neither been asserted nor denied by the supply-siders. However, the insights of supply-side economics are present in classical economics. Not only are the policy conclusions often fairly similar, but each group subscribes to the hallmark of supply-side economics—the idea that demand is a function of supply. It is an economy's ability to produce goods and services that determines how much will be consumed. Also, just as the supply-siders argue, we see that the classical economists tied Say's Law quite closely to the problems of capital accumulation and economic growth.

The publication of John Maynard Keynes's *The General Theory of Employment, Interest, and Money* in 1936 gave a tremendous impetus to another brand of economc thinking—demand-side economics. Instead of supply giving rise to demand, Keynes argues that demand creates supplies. This does not mean that production is directed by consumer demand (an unobjectionable statement) but rather that an increase in aggregate demand will call forth an increase in aggregate supply, a proposition which we shall call "Keynes's Law." Unlike the view common to economists, this increase in demand is not itself occasioned by an increase in supply, however. Aggregate demand in the Keynesian system is instead basically a function of expectations which are imbedded in people's essentially stable consumption habits. In order to further explicate the meaning of Keynes's Law, let us first examine Keynes's attack on Say's Law.

Keynes represents Say's Law as claiming that "the aggregate demand price is equal to the aggregate supply price for all levels of output and employment."[66] Such a statement is clearly a misrepresentation of Say's Law. It is Say's Identity, not Say's Equality, that Keynes is putting into the mouths of the classical economists.[67] No classical economist, with the possible exception of James Mill, could possibly be interpreted as an advocate of Say's Identity. Rather than asserting that aggregate demand is always equal to aggregate supply, what the classicals did say was that through price and quantity adjustments unhampered markets would *tend* towards an equilibrium. If one represents Say's Law as Say's Identity then the "law" is quite easy to refute. All one need do—as Keynes did—is to point to the existence of unemployed resources in order to disprove Say's Identity. However, Keynes never dealt with Say's Equality.

Another problem with Keynes's interpretation is that his use of the terms *aggregate* demand and *aggregate* supply ignore the emphasis that the classicals placed upon the possibility of disequilibrium in various individual branches of production. Only if such partial gluts were allowed to clear up could the entire system function smoothly, a consideration which is ignored by Keynes's aggregate concepts. Finally, even if Keynes was right in his interpretation, he is still only dealing with Say's Corollary, not with Say's Law. As we shall see, it is the latter, not the former, that constitutes the stronger criticism of Keynesian economics.

One reason that a market economy will run into trouble, according to the Keynesian world view, is that production does not always generate a demand for other products. This is so because of the existence of money which creates an intercession between savings and investment, destroying the *ex ante* equality which these two magnitudes enjoyed under barter. Because of Keynes's monetary theory of interest, the interest rate is inherently unable to equilibrate savings and investment *ex ante*. However, Keynes's very definitions of savings and investment require that they be equal *ex post*. Therefore, if there is an increase in planned saving, the interest rate will be unable to perform the function that it does in classical economics—to fall and allow for a corresponding increase in investment. The only way the Keynesian model can accomplish the savings-investment identity is for national income to fall, thus extinguishing the once-planned increase in savings ("the paradox of thrift"). Under such a scenario, production itself is not a source of demand since the income resulting from production may be saved instead of spent. If it is saved it will occasion no increase in demand but only a fall in output.

In classical economics it is production that is the driving force behind an economy's ability to grow and expand. In Keynesian economics production is not considered to be a problem at all because the resources are assumed to be already there. Since Keynes postulates an initial unemployment of resources in all lines of economic activity, there is already more production than can be used. The only problem is to make sure that there is a sufficient aggregate demand to "lure" these resources out of unemployment and direct them towards contributing to aggregate national income.

Keynes's contention of unemployed resources in all lines of production is misguided, both empirically and methodologically. Hayek points out that such assumptions practically constitute a denial of scarcity and ignore the function of the price mechanism.[68] If such conditions are continually present then prices are really performing no function at all. Once we consider pricing to be a meaningful phenomenon, then we must allow for at least a partial fall in prices and a clearing of some of the surpluses. Either these unemployed resources are in danger of soon being exhausted or they are not. To the extent that the unemployed resources are still relatively scarce then Keynes's assumption begins to lose its validity. If the supply of unemployed resources does *not* approach exhaustion then there is virtually no scarcity and prices are not even needed.

A further point against Keynes is that once we assume unemployment of resources as an initial condition we are unable to explain how it is that this unemployment came about. At best, the Keynesian theory can only explain *changes* in the level of unemployment. If we have unemployment to begin with, the theory may tell us what will increase or decrease this unemployment but it cannot explain the very existence of unemployment.[69] By contrast of course, the classical economists did have a coherent explanation of unemployment in general. Unemployment was seen solely as a problem of properly pricing both inputs and outputs.

Since Keynes assumed away any economic growth on the supply-side of the economy, he had a theory of economic output and employment that depends almost solely on monetary demand. Such a theory gives us Keynes's Law—"demand creates supply," or perhaps more appropriately, "demand activates its own supply." The Keynesian system is basically built around three demand schedules, the combination of which determines national income. These three schedules are the consumption function, the marginal efficiency of capital, and the speculative demand for money ("liquidity preference"). The most succinct statement of Keynes's Law in the *General Theory* comes when Keynes declares that "The decisions to consume and the decisions to invest between them determine incomes."[70] Notice how there is absolutely no mention made of either savings or, even more importantly, production. Again, it is important to emphasize that Keynes did not mean that spending determines income by directing production which *generates* income. Although this latter statement is the truth of the matter, what Keynes meant is that spending itself is responsible for the generation of both income and supply.

It is often argued that the great advance made by Keynes over the classicals was that he recognized and outlined the problems created by monetary factors in an economy. However, we have seen that the classical economists were well aware of monetary problems. When we consider the early date at which the classicals wrote, many of their insights into monetary theory are truly remarkable. The difference between Keynes and the classical economists is not that one considered monetary factors while the other did not, but rather that Keynes asserts that monetary factors will necessarily prevent the interest rate from equilibrating savings and investment. Keynes is even quite explicit in saying that "They [the classical economists] are fallaciously supposing that there is a nexus which unites decisions to abstain from present consumption with decisions to provide for future consumption. . . ."[71]

Without actually delving into the Keynesian-classical debate over interest rates, let us at least note that the classical economists had a "real" (as opposed to monetary) theory of the interest rate and felt that at least in principle the interest rate was capable of equilibrating savings and investment. When there was disequilibrium on an unhampered market it was always a problem of pricing, for the rate of interest is a price just like any other price (albeit, an extremely important price).

In the contest between Say's Law and Keynes's Law it is Say's Law which must prevail. Keynes was unable to refute Say's Law. What he attacked was actually Say's Identity, a position which was never commonly held. Neither does the existence of a sophisticated monetary theory invalidate Say's Law, for, as we have seen, the classicals were well on their way towards developing such theory and had even begun to integrate it into their analysis of the law of markets.

Although Keynes did not refute Say's Law, Say's Law and its modern-day advocates (i.e., the supply-siders) are able to score some notable points against Keynes. Keynes's misguided assumptions about unemployed resources led to an analytical neglect of the supply-side from which Keynesian economics has yet to recover. Both Keynesian theory and policy virtually ignore the problem of producing goods and services. However, Say's Law, in turn, does not ignore the problem of demand. Whereas for Keynes external stimulation is needed to insure an effective level of aggregate demand, Say's Law implies that *the problem of demand is essentially a problem of pricing and of coordinating different outputs both with each other and with consumer preferences.*

This point became clear at least as early as the Say-Malthus debate. An advocate of Say's Law may still be a "demand-sider" inasmuch as he admits that it is consumer demand that directs production and that the ultimate purpose of all production is to satisfy such demand. However, Say's Law is still "supply-side" in the sense that it claims that production, not consumption, generates income and that there can be no consumption without production.

A grafting on of supply-side considerations to the Keynesian model would not shore up the model—it would destroy it. Once it is realized that it is production that generates income, not only does it reveal the entire Keynesian apparatus to have reversed causation, but it also shows the usual Keynesian policy prescriptions to be merely inflationary. One must accept either Say's Law or Keynes's Law, for the two are not compatible.

It should be noted in passing that unlike Say's Law, Say's Corollary does not constitute a valid criticism of the Keynesian system. The sort of overproduction that Keynes is referring to is merely an overproduction of goods relative to money[72]—a phenomenon that Say's Corollary (when accurately expressed) does not deny. It is true that the logic which Keynes uses to establish his case of overproduction may be criticized with Say's Law, but Say's Corollary, by itself, does not constitute a contradiction of Keynes's argument. Therefore, we can see that at least in one respect Keynes is the exact opposite of Malthus. Malthus attacks Say's Corollary but accepts Say's Law, while Keynes never really criticizes Say's Corollary but denies Say's Law. However, in another important aspect, Keynes and Malthus are quite similar. Say's Law formed an integral part of nineteenth-century liberalism. Both Keynes and Malthus reject the law of markets[73] *and* the philosophy of liberalism which surrounded it. What is not yet clear is whether the supply-siders, the modern-day advocates of Say's Law, will also become as firmly attached to classical liberalism as was Jean Baptiste Say.

# Notes

1. *See* Dennis Robertson, "Mr. Keynes and the Rate of Interest," reprinted in *Readings in the Theory of Income Distribution* (Philadelphia: The Blakiston Co., 1946); Jacob Viner, "Mr. Keynes on the Causes of Unemployment," *Quarterly Journal of Economics* 51 (1936-1937): 147; and Frank Knight, "Unemployment and Mr. Keynes's Revolution in Economic Theory," *The Canadian Journal of Economics and Political Science* 3 (February, 1937): 100.
2. As will later be shown, Keynes had his own interpretation of Say's Law.
3. John Maynard Keynes, *The General Theory of Employment, Interest and Money* (New York: Harcourt Brace Jovanovich, 1964), p. 19.
4. Ibid., p. 21.
5. The validity of this criticism should be admitted whether or not one is a modern supply-sider. The present author is not, despite his agreement with much of the supply-side criticism of Keynesian economics. *See also* Tyler Cowen, "Supply-side Economics: Another View," *Policy Report* (Washington, D.C.: Cato Institute, August 1980).
6. The distinction to be outlined originates with Gary Becker and William Baumol, "The Classical Monetary Theory: The Outcome of the Discussion," *Economica* 19 (November 1952): 355.
7. Joseph Spengler, "The Physiocrats and Say's Law of Markets—Part II," *Journal of Political Economy* 53 (December 1945): 345.
8. Adam Smith, *An Inquiry into the Nature and Causes of the Wealth of Nations*, ed. Edwin Cannan (Chicago: University of Chicago Press, 1976), p. 359.
9. *See* Paul Lambert, "The Law of Markets prior to J. B. Say and the Say-Malthus Debate," *International Economic Papers* 6 (1956).
10. William Baumol, "Say's (at Least) Eight Laws, or What Say and James Mill May Really Have Meant," *Economica* 44 (May 1977): 147.
11. Jean Baptiste Say, *Traite d' economie politique*, 1st ed., (Paris: Deterville), p. 152. Translation and reference from Baumol, "Say's . . . Eight Laws," p. 147.
12. Ibid., from Baumol, p. 148.
13. Garnier de Saintes, the French translator of *Wealth of Nations*.

14. Say, *Traite*, pp. 175-180. Translation and reference from Baumol, "Say's . . . Eight Laws," p. 156.
15. Ibid. (Emphasis in original).
16. Jean Baptiste Say, *A Treatise on Political Economy*, 4th ed., (New York: Augustus M. Kelley, 1971). The fourth edition was originally published in 1819.
17. Ibid., p. 133.
18. Ibid.
19. Ibid., p. 135.
20. Ibid., p. 137.
21. On the connection between Say's views on economics and his views on foreign policy and war, *see* Edmund Silberner, *The Problem of War in Nineteenth Century Economic Thought* (Princeton, N.J.: Princeton University Press, 1946).
22. Say, *Treatise*, p. 139.
23. Ibid., p. 134.
24. Ibid., p. 228.
25. Ibid., p. 228.
26. Ibid., p. 133.
27. Ibid., p. 134.
28. Ibid.
29. Ibid., p. 135.
30. Donald Winch, ed. *James Mill: Selected Economic Writings* (Chicago: University of Chicago Press, 1966), p. 34.
31. Spengler, "The Physiocrats and Say's Law", p. 338.
32. James Mill, *Commerce Defended* (New York: Augustus M. Kelley, 1965).
33. *See* William Spence, *Britain Independent of Commerce* (London, 1807).
34. Mill, *Commerce Defended*, pp. 81, 84-85.
35. Ibid., pp. 76-78.
36. Ibid., p. 74. *See also* Silberner, *The Problem of Wars*, pp. 37-50.
37. Mill, *Commerce Defended*, p. 80.
38. This proviso is added in ibid., pp. 82-83, 85.
39. Ibid., pp. 81-82.
40. Ibid., p. 82.
41. Ibid., p. 75.
42. William Spence, *Tracts on Political Economy* (New York: Privately Printed, 1933), p. 78n.
43. Ibid., p. 153. For these references to Spence I am indebted to Thomas Sowell's *Say's Law* (Princeton, N.J.: Princeton University Press, 1972).
44. David Ricardo, *Principles of Political Economy and Taxation* (London: J.M. Dent and Sons, 1973), p. 289.
45. Ibid., pp. 290-291.
46. David Ricardo, Letter to James Mill, 8 Sept. 1816, *The Works and Correspondence of David Ricardo*, ed. Piero Sraffa, Vol. VII (Cambridge: Cambridge University Press), p. 67.
47. John R. McCulloch, *Principles of Political Economy* (New York: Augustus M. Kelley, 1965), pp. 216-217.
48. The same point is made forcefully by G. P. Scrope in *Principles of Political Economy* (New York: Augustus M. Kelley, 1969), pp. 212-216. The original edition of Scrope's work is 1833.
49. Thomas Robert Malthus, *Principles of Political Economy*, 2nd ed. (Clifton, N.J.: Augustus M. Kelley, 1974). The original edition of *Principles* was 1820.
50. Jean Baptiste Say, *Letters to Mr. Malthus* (New York: Augustus M. Kelley, 1967).
51. *See* Malthus's *Principles*, pp. 322-323 where Malthus assumes all savings are converted into investment.
52. Ibid., p. 361 (emphasis added).
53. Louis A. Dow, "Malthus on Sticky Wages, the Upper Turning Point, and General Glut," *History of Political Economy* 9 (Fall 1977): 303-321.
54. Salim Rashid, "Malthus's Model of General Gluts," *History of Political Economy* 9 (Fall 1977): 366-383.
55. Malthus is being quoted by Say in *Letters*, p. 29.
56. Say, *Letters*, p. 31.
57. Ibid., p. 29n.

58. Say, *Treatise*, p. 395.

59. Say, *Letters*, pp. 37-38.

60. Ibid., pp. 49-50.

61. "Of the Influence of Consumption on Production" was originally published in 1844; reprinted in Henry Hazlitt, ed. *The Critics of Keynesian Economics* (New Rochelle, NY: Arlington House, 1977).

62. J. S. Mill, "Of the Influence," pp. 41-42.

63. Ibid., p. 42.

64. Ibid., pp. 44-45.

65. It is this emphasis upon expectations that has led such thinkers as Ludwig Lachmann and G. L. S. Shackle to label Keynes a "subjectivist."

66. Keynes, *General Theory*, p. 22.

67. Of course, Keynes's definition of "classical" economics included such "neoclassicals" as Marshall and Pigou.

68. Friedrich A. Hayek, *The Pure Theory of Capital* (Chicago: University of Chicago Press, 1941), pp. 373-376.

69. I am indebted to Roger Garrison of Auburn University for this insight.

70. Keynes, *General Theory*, p. 64.

71. Ibid., p. 21.

72. This is synonymous with a lack of effective aggregate demand.

73. This does not constitute a repudiation of our previous point. Both Keynes and Malthus rejected the law of markets as they saw it.

# Chapter 4:
# The Laffer Curve

## Government Exactions and
## Revenue Deficiencies

### Arthur B. Laffer

The proposition that increases in tax rates discourage market-sector production and may therefore, beyond a certain level, be counterproductive in raising tax revenue is an old issue in the economic literature. Its recent revival has generated considerable controversy and interest among both economists and policymakers. The resolution of this controversy depends on identifying the empirical relationship between the changes in tax rates and changes in economic activity and, hence, in tax revenue. As yet, however, this relationship has been the subject of little systematic empirical analysis.

In the first section of this paper, a simple model of tax rates, output, and revenue is presented. Then we trace some of the historical antecedents of what is now commonly known as the "Laffer Curve." Finally, in the third section, we review the evidence of the 1962 and 1964 federal income tax cuts in order to determine their effects on revenue.

### Tax Rates, Output, and Revenue: A Simple Model

In any serious examination of the influence of taxation on economic activity, it is of paramount importance to distinguish between tax revenue and tax rates. Tax revenue may influence economic activity through an income effect, while tax rates operate through a substitution effect by altering the relative rewards to market and nonmarket activity.

It has long been recognized that within a closed general equilibrium system, a change in relative prices will not ordinarily entail any aggregate income effect.[1] Whether a tax-induced change in relative prices entails an income effect (before economic agents have modified their behavior in response to the tax rate change) depends on how the government diposes of the resulting incremental revenue. If the proceeds from taxation or their equivalent in public services are disbursed in a manner independent of how the taxes are collected, then the *individual* income effects will generally, in the absence of collection costs or distribution effects, cancel out, leaving only the substitution effects. If the government uses the tax revenue to produce public services that are neither more nor less valuable than the lost private consumption, then a tax rate change will entail a zero aggregate income effect.

These ideas may be illustrated with a simple static model of tax rates, output, and revenue.[2] The model assumes that the supply of factors of production to the market sector is determined in part by the net-of-tax factor rewards; the factor supply functions are therefore assumed to be upward-sloping. The demand for factors of production depends on their marginal products; given competition and factor mobility, the factor marginal products will be equal to the gross-of-tax factor rewards. Thus the optimal factor mix used in the production process will depend on relative factor rewards. Only two factors of production are assumed, say labor and capital, and market-sector production is assumed to consist of a simple good that we call market output.

Within this framework, people do not work to pay taxes. Corporate executives do not relocate business facilities as a matter of social conscience. People work in part for after-tax income. Business location decisions are predicated partially on after-tax profit considerations.

A reduction in tax rates on an activity necessarily increases that activity's after-tax profitability. When the after-tax rate of return on an activity is increased, more of the activity will be done and the tax base will expand. Applied to market production, these arguments suggest that the level of market output will be inversely related to the tax rate on market products. Since two factors are used in the production process, the market-product tax rate must be a weighted average of the tax rates on the factors of production. Thus it is apparent that there are numerous combinations of tax rates on each of the factors of production that yield the same product tax rate. That is, there are numerous combinations of factor tax rates that yield the same level of output.

In Figure 1, a family of the iso-output curve is given. Within this two-factor model containing both capital and labor as well as one market output, the effect on total tax receipts of an increase in the tax on either factor of production has conflicting influences. For example, an increase in the tax rate on labor will elicit the following responses:

1. A scale effect—the increase in labor tax rates will increse unambiguously the effective tax rate on the final product, leading to a reduction in the output of market goods. This in turn will lead to a reduction in the employment of both factors of production.

2. A substitution effect—the tax rate will increase the relative cost of labor services. This induces a substitution effect away from labor into capital services.

It is fairly obvious that in the case of an increase in labor tax rates, the scale and substitution effects reinforce each other, leading to an

## FIGURE 1
## THE ISO-OUTPUT LOCUS

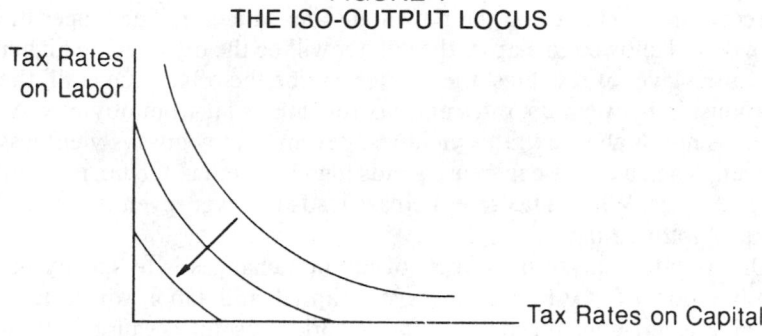

NOTE: The arrow denotes the output direction; that is, the further an iso-output curve is upward and to the right of the origin (where both tax rates are zero), the higher the respective tax rates on capital and labor and the lower the level of output. Notice that the iso-output locus intersects the axes with a positive output (i.e., there is a positive amount produced even if there is no tax levied on one of the factors of production). Finally, the concavity from above the isoquants reflects the implicit assumption of a diminishing marginal rate of substitution between factor tax rates.

unambiguous reduction in the employment of labor services. In the case of capital, on the other hand, the scale and substitution effects tend to offset each other. Whether employment of capital services increases or not depends on the relative strength of the two effects. In what follows, the scale effect is assumed to dominate, in which case the employment of capital services will unambiguously decline.

The increase in the tax wedge on labor will have the following effects:

1. More revenue will be collected per worker; this will tend to increase revenue. Some people call this effect the naive treasury estimate. However, we prefer to call it the arithmetic effect.

2. Fewer workers will be employed; this will tend to lower revenue. We label this effect the direct feedback effect.

3. Less capital will be employed; this will tend to lower revenue. This effect we label the indirect feedback effect.

Under certain circumstances, the additional revenue collected per worker (the arithmetic effect) will predominate, and an increase in the tax wedge on labor will raise revenue. Sometimes the second two effects (the feedback effects) will predominate, and less revenue will be forthcoming. The same set of conditions pertains to changes in the tax wedge on capital.

In actual practice, of course, a number of additional influences are felt. With higher tax rates, there will be more tax avoidance and evasion, which will aggravate the offsetting revenue impact accompanying tax rate increases. Where possible, factor substitution will reduce the economy's reliance on the now higher-taxed factor. The longer the time period allowed to elapse, the greater will be the offsets. The higher the initial level of tax rates, the greater will be the offsets. Overall, the relationship between tax rates and tax revenue is far from obvious. As often as not, higher tax rates yield less revenue; they always yield less output. When a tax rate increase yields higher revenue, the tax is in the normal range. When a tax rate increase leads to lower revenues, it is in the prohibitive range.

One way to analyze the effects of tax rate changes is to specify the combination of tax rate changes on capital and labor where total revenue is left unchanged. This framework is useful because it separates the issues of total spending from those of total tax policies. Thus, if the tax on labor and the tax on capital are both in the normal range, a tax rate reduction on labor will be accompanied by a tax rate increase on capital, or vice versa. On the other hand, if the tax rate on labor is in the prohibitive range while the tax rate on capital is in the normal range, then a tax rate reduction on labor, which by definition would lead to higher revenue, would require a tax rate reduction on capital as well.

A representative pairing of such tax rates on labor and capital can be depicted on a two-axis graph. The horizontal axis is the tax on capital, $t_k$, and the vertical axis is the tax on labor, $t_l$. The locus of points describing the different pairings of tax rates that yield the same amount of tax revenue is named the iso-revenue curve. One such curve is drawn in Figure 2 in the form of an ellipse. The location and angle of the ellipse are purely arbitrary, the diagram being for illustrative purposes only. Four distinct regions can be identified on the iso-revenue line. In the region from $P$ to $S$, both tax rates are in their "normal" range; an increase in the tax rate on capital alone, or the tax rate on labor alone, will raise net revenue. Therefore, if revenue is to stay the same in the $PS$ region of the iso-revenue line, an increase in either tax rate must be accompanied by a reduction in the other tax rate.

In the $PQ$ region, the tax on labor is in its prohibitive range, while the tax on capital is in its normal range: An increase in the tax rate on labor lowers net revenue, while an increase in the tax on capital raises net revenue. Thus an increase in the tax rate on labor (moving up the vertical axis) must be accompanied by an increase in the tax rate on capital (moving to the right on the horizontal axis) to maintain the same level of revenue. Hence, the iso-revenue line in this region is upward-sloping to the right. Holding revenue constant, the higher the tax rate on labor, the higher must be the tax on capital.

$QR$ is the region where both taxes are in the prohibitive range. In this region, an increase in either tax rate lowers revenue. Thus if the tax on capital is increased (movement to the right), the tax rate on labor must

## FIGURE 2
## THE ISO-REVENUE CURVE

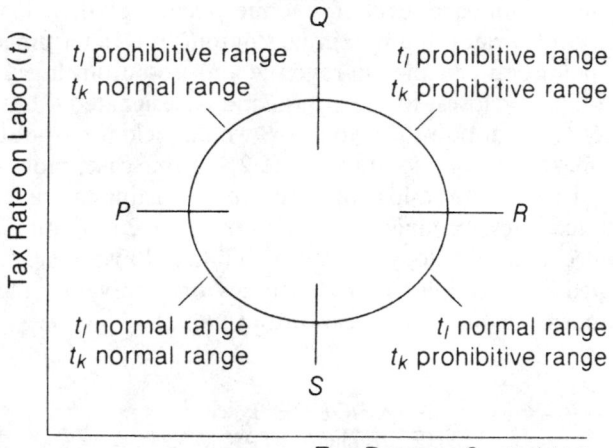

Tax Rate on Capital ($t_k$)

be reduced (movement down) to keep total revenue constant. The iso-revenue line here is downward-sloping to the right.

Finally, in the region *RS*, the tax on labor is in the normal range and the tax on capital is in the prohibitive range. Here a rise in the tax rate on labor, which increases revenue, must be accompanied by an increase in the tax rate on capital, which lowers revenue, in order to keep total revenue constant.

In each of the three regions, *PQ*, *QR*, and *RS*, at least one tax rate is in the prohibitive range. That is, an increase in the tax rate lowers net revenue. In the region *QR*, both tax rates are in the prohibitive range. Only in one region, *PS*, are both tax rates in the normal range, where an increase in either rate raises net revenue.

From the relationship postulated in this tax ellipse, we see that in any region other than *PS* a lowering of at least one tax rate can be accompanied by a lowering of the other tax rate without reducing total revenue or spending. Only in the *PS* range does a lowering of one tax rate necessitate a raising of the other rate in order to maintain the same total revenue.

A higher level of tax revenue can be represented by a new tax ellipse inside the one just described; the larger ellipse, then, represents the lower level of revenue. In all cases, four regions would exist. A maximum point of revenue exists beyond which revenue cannot be increased. Whether tax rates are raised or lowered, less revenue will be forthcoming. In sum then, a whole family of iso-revenue lines or ellipses exists, one for each level of revenue or spending. The existence of these ellipses allows for separation of the effects of tax rates per se and total tax revenue or spending.

Combining both the families of iso-revenue and iso-output lines (see Figure 3), a number of general propositions and derivations emerge. It is apparent that, for each level of revenue (spending), there exists only one pairing of tax rates that maximizes output. It is determined by the tangency point between the iso-revenue and iso-output lines, i.e., the intersection point closest to the origin, and is designated $O^*$. A pairing of tax rates either at point $A$ or point $B$ would yield an iso-output line farther from the origin (iso-output line 2). In this case, more revenue could be raised without a loss in output by adjusting tax rates so that the paired tax rates are tangent to iso-output line 2 at point $C$. Such a pairing, of course, would yield a smaller tax ellipse inside the one diagrammed. The smaller ellipse implies more revenue (spending) while output is held constant (iso-output line 2).

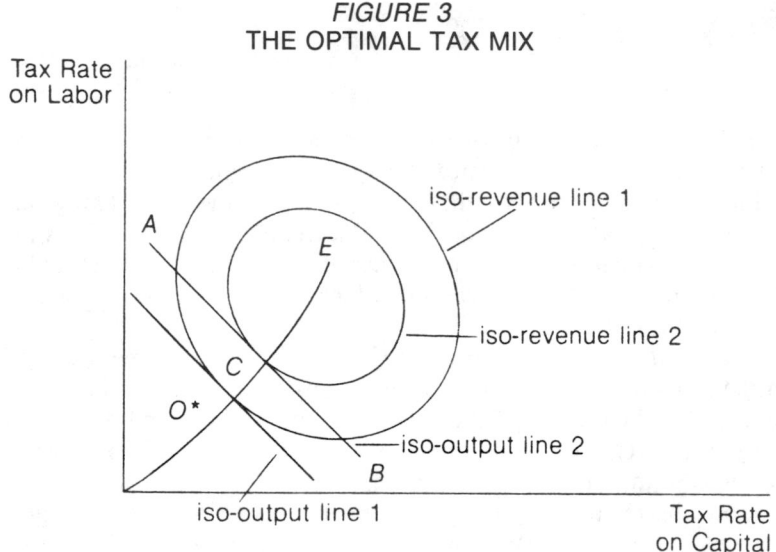

FIGURE 3
THE OPTIMAL TAX MIX

Alternatively, output could be expanded, while revenue is held constant, by a shift in the paired tax rates to point $O^*$ on the higher (in output) iso-output line 1. Taking the tax rate pairings that maximized output for a given level of revenue yields the output efficiency line of $EL$. This output efficiency line designates that precise pairing of tax rates for any level of government spending whereby output is least diminished. This output efficiency line traverses points $O^*$ and $C$, ending where tax rates equal zero, $L$, and also where tax rates yield the maximum possible amount of revenue, $E$.[3]

The tax ellipse also may be used to explore the conceptually ultimate effects of different tax pairings on the net wages received and net yields received for each factor of production. Again, the use of the iso-revenue curve allows revenue, and therefore government spending, to be held constant. The tax rate on each factor of production individually is the incidence of the tax. It is depicted explicitly on the tax pairings. The burden of the tax, though, is the actual change in the net wages received and net yields received caused by the tax change.

The incidence of the tax structure is very different from the burden of the tax structure. The person on whom a tax is levied may well experience no loss in net income if he passes the tax forward on to consumers or backward on to suppliers. Likewise, a person upon whom no tax has been levied may well suffer large net-income losses (the burden) as a consequence of taxes levied on others.

Within the *PS* region, an increase in the tax on capital must be accompanied by a reduction in the tax on labor; this is the condition that holds revenue constant. The increase in the tax on capital will reduce the amount of capital employed. This reduction in demand for capital also shifts back the demand for labor. Labor pays less tax, but the reduction in demand for labor services reduces the wages paid. The overall effect of a lower pretax wage and lower taxes on net wages received is ambiguous. In more intuitive terms, as often as not, taxing capital to upgrade labor will damage labor. Similarly, taxing the rich is sometimes a good way to further impoverish the poor.

To summarize: We have five basic points:

1. Changes in tax rates affect output in a direct fashion. Lower tax rates correspond to higher output.
2. Changes in tax rates directly affect the employment of both factors of production. Lower tax rates on either factor increase employment for both factors.
3. With government spending held constant, the constellation of tax rates affects output. How taxes are collected is important, as is the total amount of taxation and spending.
4. Lowered tax rates on any factor may or may not lower total revenue.
5. With revenue held constant, changes in the pairing of tax rates may shape the distribution of after-tax spending power, but only indirectly. As often as not, when one factor's tax rate is raised and the other's is lowered, the second factor will end up in worse economic shape.

The theoretical model developed in this section suggests that if the tax rate and the factor supply and demand elasticities could be measured, the determination of whether a tax rate is in the normal or prohibitive range would be straightforward. For the United States economy, such an analysis would employ estimates of the tax rate and of the factor demand and supply elasticities from existing studies to determine the value of the output elasticity with respect to tax rates. One careful study conducted along these general lines is reported in a paper by Don Fullerton of Princeton University. Fullerton's basic conclusion is that while "the U.S. economy could conceivably be operating in the 'prohibitive range' for a national tax on labor income, reasonable estimates of an aggregate, economy-wide labor supply elasticity and labor income tax rate are low enough to suggest that a broad-based cut in labor income tax rates would probably lead to lower revenues."[4]

There are several difficulties with this general approach, however. The first is that labor is not homogeneous, though we assumed it is in our simple model. In reality, both the labor supply elasticity and the marginal income tax rate vary across workers. As Fullerton recognizes, it might be possible that certain groups have such high labor supply elasticities or marginal tax rates that they are currently being taxed at prohibitive levels, even though this would not necessarily show up in a highly aggregated analysis. For example, while most studies show that married males typically have low labor supply elasticities, recent work seems to indicate that females may have quite high supply elasticities. Thus, the "'marriage penalty' which places a secondary worker in the higher marginal tax bracket of his or her spouse may represent a high rate of tax on an elastically supplied factor" and may well indicate that married women are being taxed at prohibitive rates.[5] Also, recent evidence indicates that proprietors of small businesses, who have more control over hours worked than do most employees, may have a considerably higher supply elasticity than do males in general.[6] Finally, marginal tax rates can be quite high for those in upper income brackets and can be even higher for the poorest workers and those receiving social security, who stand to lose benefit payments as their earnings increase.[7]

Finally, it is not true, as we've assumed up to now, that the tax base is equal to market-sector output. Taxes can be avoided by acquiring tax shelters. This generally involves some cost in inconvenience, lawyers' and accountants' fees, and lower before-tax income. But the higher that tax rates are, the more affordable these costs become, and the more tax avoidance and outright evasion people will engage in. It is thus possible that an increase in tax rates may lower revenue even if the elasticity of output with respect to the tax rate is less than unity. For all of these reasons, the approach of examining estimated labor supply elasticities can shed important but only limited light on the issue of whether the United States is currently operating at a prohibitive level of taxation.[8]

## Some Historical Antecedents

Although the empirical relationship among tax rates, economic activity, and tax revenues is presently a matter of some controversy, the idea that excessive tax rates may be counterproductive in raising revenues was explicitly recognized in the early economic literature.

The potential for an inverse relationship between tax rates and total revenue was perceived at least as early as the fourteenth century. The Moslem philosopher Ibn Khaldun observed that

> at the beginning of the dynasty, taxation yields a large revenue from small assessments. At the end of the dynasty, taxation yields a small revenue from large assessments. . . .[9]

The early economists were also aware that high tax rates may lead to an erosion of the tax base as economic agents switch from the market sector to the underground or subterranean (untaxed) economy. According to Adam Smith,

> High taxes, sometimes by diminishing the consumption of taxed commodities, and sometimes by encouraging smuggling, frequently afford a smaller revenue than what may be drawn from more moderate taxes.[10]

Similarly, J.B. Say stated that

> taxation, pushed to the extreme, has the lamentable effect of impoverishing the individual, without enriching the state. . . . [T]hus the taxpayer is abridged of his employment, the producer his profits, and the public exchequer of his receipts.[11]

Smith and Say were thus aware of the substitution effect through which increases in the tax rate reduce the tax base. Furthermore, Say explicitly recognized that the elasticity of revenue with respect to tax rates, even when positive, is less than unity. The resultant decrease in economic activity, he wrote, "is the reason why a tax is not productive to the public exchequer in proportion to its rates, and why it has become a sort of apophthegm, that two and two do not make four in the arithmetic of finance. Excessive taxation . . . extinguishes both production and consumption, and the taxpayer in the bargain."[12] It was apparent to Say that the full effect of taxation goes beyond the mere transfer of resources from the private sector to the public sector: "A tax that robs the individual, without benefit to the exchequer, substitutes no public consumption whatever, in the place of the private consumption it extinguishes."[13]

Later economists also recognized the importance of the particular constellation of tax rates, and of the indirect effects of taxation on the tax revenues collected by other taxes. The nineteenth-century American economist Henry George, in *Progress and Poverty*, wrote that

> the mode of taxation is, in fact, quite as important as the amount. As a small burden badly placed may distress a horse that could carry with ease a much larger one properly adjusted, so a people may be impoverished and their power of producing wealth destroyed by taxation, which if levied another way, could be borne with ease. . . .[14]

Finally, regarding the indirect feedback effect of a tax, twentieth-century economist Martin Bronfenbrenner states:

> A direct form limits attention to the specific levy under consideration. As applied in direct form, the argument applied to the tax on

beer states simply that an increased rate would increase revenues from the tax on beer, and vice versa. An indirect form applies to the general . . . tax system. As applied to the beer tax, it states that even though an increased rate may increase receipts from beer, it will decrease receipts from other taxes by more than enough to offset the gross increases. . . .[15]

This brief survey of economic doctrine has shown that earlier economists, too, recognized the salient features of the model discussed in the first section of this paper.

### The Example of the "Kennedy" Tax Cuts

Although the theoretical proposition that increases in tax rates above a certain level may actually reduce revenue is by now widely accepted,[16] there is considerable disagreement over whether any real-world governments have been observed to operate in the prohibitive range of the "Laffer Curve." The remarks cited above indicate that at least some writers regarded prohibitive tax rates not merely as a theoretical possibility, but as an empirical reality. This might not be too surprising when one considers that government in the eighteenth century relied much more heavily on import duties as a source of revenue than do governments today, and that the prohibitive tariff has long been regarded as something more than a theoretical curiosity. Modern governments rely for revenue primarily on broad-based taxes on economic activity, however, and the notion that such governments may be operating in the prohibitive range of the "Laffer Curve" meets with considerable resistance.[17] The issue is essentially an empirical one, and the comments of the eighteenth- and nineteenth-century economists can provide scant evidence on this point.

One approach is to examine past instances of substantial tax rate changes to determine their effects on revenue, although it leaves the final conclusion of whether or not the current tax system is in the prohibitive range a matter of inference and judgment. Controlled experiments are not possible, but the more closely a past experience with tax reduction resembles the current situation, the clearer the implication for current policy.

One such experience was the "Kennedy" tax cuts of 1962 and 1964. There are some obvious differences between the economic environment of the mid-1960s and that of the early 1980s. Inflation and the budget deficit today are at least ten times higher. Unemployment is significantly greater. In addition, the makeup of government spending has shifted away from expenditures related to national defense and the purchase of goods and services to the maintenance of an extensive welfare system. Defense spending in 1979 was 21.3 percent of total federal government expenditures, compared to 46.2 percent in 1962, while transfer payments have risen to 41.2 percent of federal government expenditures, from 25.1 percent in 1962.

These differences, however, detract very little from the appropriateness of the comparison between the two periods. The size of the budget deficit is an important consideration when deciding whether or not to reduce tax rates, if revenue is expected to decline. But the size of the deficit has little to do with the issue of whether or not a certain tax is in the prohibitive range. And today's higher rate of inflation will cause any reduction in tax rates to be partially offset as individuals move into higher tax brackets through "bracket creep," reducing the absolute magnitude of any positive or negative change in revenue.

Moreover, there are important similarities between the two time periods. The fundamental institutional framework underlying the economy remains intact: The U.S. economy today has more in common with itself fifteen years ago than it does with, say, Japan or Brazil today. The economy before 1963, as now, was characterized by lackluster performance. Capacity utilization as measured by the Federal Reserve Board then was 83.3 percent; in the first quarter of 1980, it was 83.7 percent. Unemployment in 1962 was 6.7 percent.

In addition, there is good evidence that effective tax rates today are higher than they were before the Kennedy tax cuts, thereby increasing the chance that tax rates today are in the prohibitive range. The higher the tax rate, the greater the likelihood that rate cuts will increase revenue. Joines estimates that by the early 1970s the weighted average tax rate on income from capital had risen to roughly the same level as before the Kennedy tax cuts, where it has more or less remained into the present period.[18] By the mid-1970s, the weighted average tax rate on labor income was substantially higher than in 1963 (see Figure 4).

Three principal factors are behind these increases:

1. Inflation-induced increases in real personal income tax rates, referred to as "bracket creep";
2. The inflation-induced understatement of true economic depreciation and overstatement of real capital gains;[19]
3. Increases in the social security tax rate and wage base.

All of these factors continued after the mid-1970s, until, by 1979, federal, state, and local personal income tax receipts took 15.6 percent of private personal income (i.e., personal income exclusive of transfer payments to persons) as compared with 11.4 percent in 1963. In 1979 total government receipts constituted 36 percent of the GNP, compared with 28.3 percent in 1963.

These percentages are projected to rise even further in fiscal year 1981 because of continued inflation, further increases in social security taxes, and the enactment of the "windfall profits" tax on domestic oil production. Thus an analysis of the economic and revenue effects of the Kennedy tax cuts would be useful in anticipating the effects of an across-the-board tax cut today.[20]

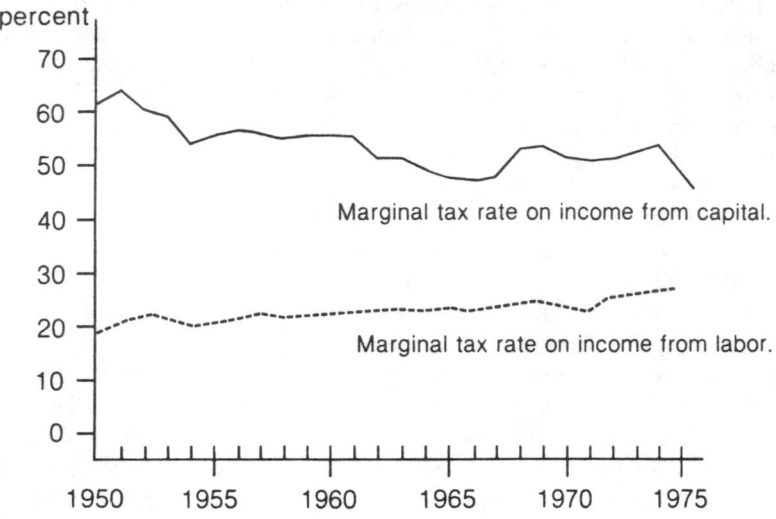

*FIGURE 4*
MARGINAL TAX RATES ON CAPITAL AND LABOR INCOME

Source: Douglas H. Joines, "Estimates of Effective Marginal Tax Rates on Factor Incomes," *The Journal of Business,* in press.

## The Tax Cuts

The first reduction in effective tax rates during the Kennedy/Johnson administration was in 1962, when Congress passed an investment tax credit and existing depreciation schedules were liberalized. The tax credit was equal to 7 percent of a firm's investment in producers' durable equipment with a useful life of eight years, and no credit was given for equipment with a useful life of less than four years. The tax credit applicable to utilities was 3 percent, rather than 7 percent. No credit was given for structures. In addition, guidelines published by the Internal Revenue Service for depreciation were revised, substituting classes of assets for an item-by-item delineation. The new guidelines reduced depreciable lives approximately 30 to 40 percent.

In 1964, income tax rate cuts for both corporations and individuals were enacted. The corporate income tax rate was reduced to 48 percent from 52 percent, and personal income tax rates were reduced across-the-board, declining to 14 percent from 20 percent at the bottom and to 70 percent from 91 percent at the top (see Table 1). In addition, a minimum standard deduction of $200 plus $100 per exemption was introduced. This had the effect of removing from the tax rolls a substantial number of individuals. Thus the effective tax cut was somewhat larger than the reduction in the tax rates alone suggests. The 1964 tax cuts became law in midyear, with about half of the reductions in tax rates retroactive to the beginning of the calendar year. The full reduction in tax rates became effective in calendar year 1965.[21]

*TABLE 1*
THE 1964 REDUCTIONS
IN FEDERAL PERSONAL INCOME TAX RATES

| Income Level (dollars) | Calendar Years 1954-1963 | Calendar Years 1965-1967 | Percent Reduction in Tax Rate |
|---|---|---|---|
| $0-500 | 20% | 14% | -30.0% |
| 500-1,000 | 20 | 15 | -25.0 |
| 1,000-1,500 | 20 | 16 | -20.0 |
| 1,500-2,000 | 20 | 17 | -15.0 |
| 2,000-4,000 | 22 | 19 | -13.6 |
| 4,000-6,000 | 26 | 22 | -15.4 |
| 6,000-8,000 | 30 | 25 | -16.7 |
| 8,000-10,000 | 34 | 28 | -17.6 |
| 10,000-12,000 | 38 | 32 | -15.8 |
| 12,000-14,000 | 43 | 36 | -16.3 |
| 14,000-16,000 | 47 | 39 | -17.0 |
| 16,000-18,000 | 50 | 42 | -16.0 |
| 18,000-20,000 | 53 | 45 | -15.1 |
| 20,000-22,000 | 56 | 48 | -14.3 |
| 22,000-26,000 | 59 | 50 | -15.3 |
| 26,000-32,000 | 62 | 53 | -14.5 |
| 32,000-38,000 | 65 | 55 | -15.4 |
| 38,000-44,000 | 69 | 58 | -15.9 |
| 44,000-50,000 | 72 | 60 | -16.7 |
| 50,000-60,000 | 75 | 62 | -17.3 |
| 60,000-70,000 | 78 | 64 | -17.9 |
| 70,000-100,000 | 87 | 69 | -20.7 |
| 100,000-150,000 | 89 | 70 | -21.3 |
| 150,000-200,000 | 90 | 70 | -22.2 |
| 200,000 & over | 91 | 70 | -23.1 |

Source: Joseph Pechman, "The Individual Income Tax Provisions of the Revenue Act of 1964," *Journal of Finance* 20 (May 1965): 247-72.

## The Economic Effect

There is general agreement that the Kennedy tax cuts did contribute significantly to the economic expansion of the mid-1960s. Unemployment declined to 3.8 percent in 1966 from 5.6 percent in 1963; capacity utilization increased more than 8 percentage points to 91.9 percent in 1966, while real GNP between 1963 and 1966 grew at a compound annual rate of 5.7 percent, compared to just 4.1 percent during the previous three years. Between 1963 and 1966, GNP grew slightly faster than government spending, though government spending had expanded 5 percent more than GNP between 1960 and 1963. And between 1962 and 1966 the ratio of government expenditures to GNP actually fell. It thus seems unlikely that the increase in economic activity can be attributed entirely to the stimulus of increased government spending.

## The Revenue Effect

Whether the economy was operating in the prohibitive range, that is, whether this expansion in economic activity and the general tax base associated with the tax cuts was sufficiently large to offset the tax rate reduction's negative revenue effects, is subject to considerable debate. There is substantial anecdotal evidence that high-income individuals were in the prohibitive range. Michael K. Evans's examination of revenue data for the first half of the 1960s indicates that revenue from individuals with taxable incomes in excess of $100,000 increased from $2.3 billion in 1962 to $2.5 billion in 1963, $3 billion in 1964, and $3.8 billion in 1965.[22]

Viewed in isolation, however, the overall personal income tax schedule appears not to have been in the prohibitive range. With the tax cuts, total personal income tax revenue declined between 1963 and 1964. This suggests that the weighted average of the individual personal income tax rates was in the normal range. The loss in tax revenue from individuals at low income levels exceeded the gain in tax revenue from individuals at high income levels.[23]

A set of revenue loss estimates that allows for any actual feedback of tax rates on economic activity would be useful in anticipating the revenue effects of an income tax cut today similar to the cuts enacted in 1962 and 1964. Such estimates would not be based on any prescribed level of economic activity. First, estimates of what revenue would have been in the absence of tax cuts have to be made. These estimates then must be compared with the actual revenue figures. The difference between the two numbers constitutes an estimate of the revenue change resulting from the tax cuts.

One study conducted along these lines was done by Victor A. Canto, Douglas H. Joines, and Robert I. Webb.[24] Forecasts of various revenue series for the years immediately following the Kennedy tax cuts were obtained using a statistical analysis of the revenues from the personal income and corporate income taxes at the federal level, and income tax receipts at the state and local level, for the period prior to the tax rate reductions. A univariate time-series model, sometimes referred to as a Box-Jenkins or ARIMA model, was used. A study by Charles Nelson shows that such a technique, despite its simplicity, can be used to forecast a time series using only knowledge of its own past history.[25] Generally, such an approach will yield forecasts as accurate as, and frequently more accurate than, those obtained from large and complicated econometric models.

In the first step, the time-series models were fit to the two federal revenue series—real personal income tax receipts and real corporate income tax receipts. Fortunately for the purposes of this analysis, there were no major changes in federal tax rates between 1950 and the Kennedy cuts. The variations in revenue collections during those years, therefore, can be attributed to the normal workings of the economy, rather than to changes in tax rates. Furthermore, this period contains a sufficient number of quarterly observations to make identification and estimation of univariate time-series models feasible. Consequently, the time-series models can be used to forecast what revenues would have been if the economy had continued to evolve along its normal path and the Kennedy tax cuts had not been enacted.

Next, Canto, Joines, and Webb compared their results with the estimates made by Pechman and the Treasury Department.[26] The analysis proceeds through fiscal year 1966, after which Vietnam spending increased markedly, adding a significant fiscal policy change that, in a Keynesian model, would have stimulated economic activity and revenue. The same methodology, a univariate time series, was used to estimate what state and local tax revenues would have been without the change in federal tax policies (i.e., the indirect feedback effects).

Canto, Joines, and Webb concluded that

> the combined revenue effect of the Kennedy tax cuts on federal personal income, federal corporate income, and state and local income tax receipts according to the time series analysis is a loss of $2.5 billion (constant 1963: 4 [i.e., the fourth quarter of 1963] dollars) through 1966 [see Figure 5]. Given the statistical uncertainty attached to this estimate, it is virtually indistinguishable from zero. Furthermore, it contrasts sharply with the Treasury's estimate of the federal revenue loss of $32 billion (constant 1963: 4 dollars); it is quite likely that the static revenue estimates used by the Treasury back in the mid-1960s, as well as now, greatly overstate the negative revenue effects of federal tax reductions. These results, on a cumulative basis through 1966, suggest that it is as likely that the federal tax cuts in 1962 and 1964 increased revenues as that they reduced them. Moreover, the relative gain in federal personal income tax receipts during the first half of 1966 suggests that in about two years, personal income tax revenues were running ahead of what they would have been without the 1964 tax cut. Furthermore, by 1966, federal corporate profits tax receipts and state and local income tax receipts appear to have been running ahead of what they otherwise would have been by ever larger amounts. This suggests that if the net effect of the tax cuts could be calculated on a present value basis, with the net changes in the revenue streams extended indefinitely into the future, it would be even more likely to find that the Kennedy tax cuts had been self-financing.[27]

While increased defense spending associated with escalation of the Vietnam War precludes further empirical extrapolation, the trend in revenues is clear: Beginning in fiscal year 1967, the Kennedy tax cuts were paying handsome dividends in the form of higher tax receipts. There is a substantial range of uncertainty in these estimates; nevertheless, the point estimates provided by this study are exceptionally conservative for the overall budgetary effect of the Kennedy tax cuts.

## FIGURE 5
### THE CUMULATIVE REVENUE EFFECTS
### OF THE KENNEDY TAX CUTS

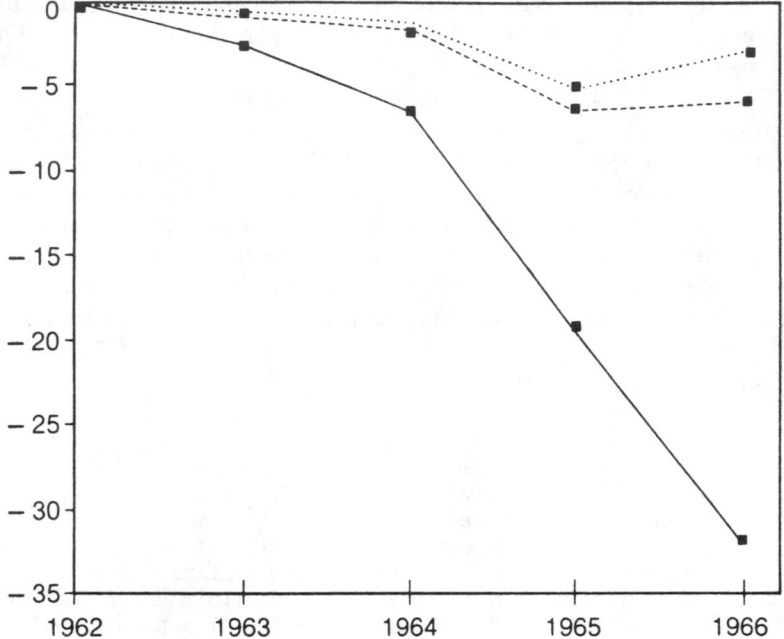

Billions of 1963:4 dollars

Treasury estimate for cumulative change in federal personal and corporate income tax revenues.

Time series estimate for cumulative change in federal personal and corporate income tax revenues.

Time series estimated for aggregate cumulative change in federal, state, and local personal and corporate income tax revenues.

Source: Victor A. Canto, Douglas H. Joines, and Robert I. Webb, "Empirical Evidence on the Effects on Tax Rates on Economic Activity," *Proceedings of the Business and Economic Statistics Section: 1979* [Washington, D.C.: American Statistical Association, 1979].

Many other tax sources, including state and local property and sales taxes, were not included in the analysis. They, too, would be expected to generate more revenue as the economy expanded. Changes in government spending, if included, also would have led to more sanguine estimates of the net budgetary impact of these tax cuts.

In comparison to the Kennedy tax cuts, the tax rate cut proposed by the Reagan administration (30 percent across-the-board, to be phased in over three years), is modest. Personal income tax rate reductions equivalent (based on GNP) to those passed in 1964 would show a static revenue loss of about $40 billion. Equivalent reductions in corporate taxes would show another $10 billion reduction in static revenue losses.

By contrast, the first installment of Reagan's personal income tax cut is less than $20 billion on a static basis. Moreover, the Kennedy tax cut, which was passed in the spring of 1964, was phased in over two years. The first half was retroactive to the beginning of calendar year 1964, with the full tax cuts being effected on January 1, 1965. The Reagan tax cut would be phased in over three years. The expansion of the economy that would occur in anticipation of the additional reductions in tax rates would reduce further the actual revenue losses relative to those experienced in the mid-1950s. Finally, effective marginal tax rates on both capital and labor are now as high or higher than they were at the time of the Kennedy cuts. Higher effective tax rates, per se, increase the likelihood that a tax is in the prohibitive range. Thus the revenue feedback effects from across-the-board tax rate reductions are likely to be greater than those experienced fifteen years ago.

It is reasonable to conclude that each of the proposed 10 percent reductions in tax rates would, in terms of overall tax revenues, be self-financing in less than two years. Thereafter, each installment would provide a positive contribution to overall tax receipts. By the third year of the tax reduction program, it is likely that the net revenue gains from the plan's first installment would offset completely the revenue reductions attributable to the final 10 percent tax rate cut. It should be noted that a signficant portion of these revenues would accrue to state and local governments, relieving much, if not all of the fiscal distress evident in these governmental units as well.

As in the 1960s, spending as a percentage of GNP would be expected to decline. The substantially larger portion of the federal budget devoted today to income-maintenance programs makes the expenditure implications of higher-than-expected economic growth an important part of the overall fiscal analysis. Thus the proposed Reagan tax cut has a far better chance of balancing the budget while restoring vitality to the American economy than programs attempted by the Carter administration.

# Notes

1. John R. Hicks, *Value and Capital*, 2nd ed. (Oxford University Press, 1946), p. 64.
2. For a formal derivation of the model, *see* Victor A. Canto, Douglas H. Joines, and Arthur B. Laffer, "Taxation, GNP, and Potential GNP," *Proceedings of the Business and Economic Statistics Section: 1978* (Washington, D.C.: American Statistical Association, 1978).

3. Again, it is important to remember that in the framework used up to this point, all spending is in the form of lump-sum transfers that do not, in and of themselves, enhance output.

4. Donald Fullerton, "On the Possibility of an Inverse Relationship between Tax Rates and Government Revenues," Working Paper no. 467, National Bureau of Economic Research (New York), April 1980.

5. Ibid., p. 20.

6. Terrance Wales, "Estimation of a Labor Supply Curve for Self-Employed Business Proprietors," *International Economic Review* 14 (February 1973): 69-80.

7. *See* Arthur B. Laffer, *Prohibitive Tax Rates and the Inner-City: A Rational Explanation of the Poverty Trap* (Boston: H.C. Wainwright & Co. Economics, June 27, 1978).

8. Since labor mobility means that the elasiticity of factor supply to a locality is likely to be much higher than to a country as a whole, it is possible that some localities might be operating in the prohibitive range. For evidence that this is the case, *see* Ronald E. Grieson, William Hamovitch, Albert M. Levenson, and R. Dale Morgenstern, "The Effect of Business Taxation on the Location of Industry," *Journal of Urban Economics* 4 (April 1977); and Ronald E. Grieson, "Theoretical Analysis and Empirical Measurements of the Effects of the Philadelphia Income Tax," *Journal of Urban Economics*, in press. For evidence that tax rates in Sweden exceed those that would maximize revenue, *see* Charles Stuart, "Swedish Tax Rates in Revenues," mimeographed (University of Lund, Sweden, 1979).

9. Ibn Khaldun, The *Muqaddimah*; quoted in "Taxation and the Reason for High and Low Tax Revenues," *Wall Street Journal*, September 30, 1978.

10. Adam Smith, *An Inquiry into the Nature and Causes of the Wealth of Nations*, ed. E. Canaan (Chicago: University of Chicago Press, 1976).

11. J. B. Say, *A Treatise on Political Economy*, trans. C. R. Prinsep (New York: Kelley, 1971), p. 449.

12. Ibid., p. 450.

13. Ibid.

14. Henry George, *Progress and Poverty* (New York: Robert Schalkenbach Foundation, 1979), p. 409.

15. Martin Bronfenbrenner, "Diminishing Returns in Federal Taxation?" *Journal of Political Economy* 52 (October 1942): 699-717.

16. Seymour Zucker, alternating quotes from a series of economists, reflects the mainstream of current thought: "To Harvard's Martin Feldstein, the theoretical principle that at some point reducing rate actually increases tax revenues is something we teach in the first week of the course in Public Finance" ("Commentary/Economics," *Business Week*, August 7, 1978, pp. 62-64).

17. The following quotation clearly illustrates the sentiments of many economists on a broad-based tax rate cut. Herbert Stein, in "The Real Reasons for a Tax Cut" (*Wall Street Journal*, July 18, 1978), stated that "economists cannot say that they know with certainty that the Kemp-Roth tax cut would not raise the revenue. They can, or should, only say that the available evidence makes that outcome extremely improbable. It may turn out that such a tax cut would raise the revenue, just as it may turn out that there is human life on Mars. But I would not invest much in a McDonald's franchise on that planet, and I wouldn't bet the nations' economic policy on the assumption that the tax cut will increase the revenue."
Similarly, in a letter to then House Ways and Means Committee chairman Al Ullman (D-Utah), John Kenneth Galbraith referred with his customary moderation to the Kemp-Roth bill and its revenue-raising potential in these terms: "The notion that the revenue can be recouped from the added output is, of course, egregious and irresponsible nonsense" (*Tax Reduction, Economists Comment on H.R. 8333 and S. 1860* [Washington, D.C.: U.S. Congress, House Ways and Means Committee, 1978], p. 42.

18. Douglas H. Joines, "Estimates of Effective Marginal Tax Rates on Factor Incomes," *Journal of Business*, in press.

19. See Arthur B. Laffer and R. David Ranson, *Inflation, Taxes and Equity Values* (Boston: H.C. Wainwright & Co., Economics, September 20, 1979).

20. If the economy were more nearly "fully employed" than in 1963, tax rates might have a smaller expansionary effect now than then. Although it is not clear that these

numbers are reliable indicators of full employment of available resources, it is worth noting that the total unemployment rate was 5.6 percent in 1963, 6.2 percent in January 1980, and 7.7 percent in June 1980. Similarly, the Federal Reserve Board's index of manufacturing capacity utilization was 83.3 percent in 1963, 83.8 percent in January 1980, and 78.4 percent in June 1980.

21. *See* Nicholas J. Gonedes, "Evidence on the Tax Effects on Inflation under Historical Cost Accounting Methods" (unpublished paper, University of Pennsylvania, May 1980).

22. Michael K. Evans, "Taxes, Inflation, and the Rich," *Wall Street Journal*, August 7, 1978. Reprinted in Arthur B. Laffer and Jan P. Seymour, eds., *The Economics of the Tax Revolt* (New York: Harcourt Brace Jovanovich, 1979).

23. Ibid.

24. Victor A. Canto, Douglas H. Joines, and Robert I. Webb, "Empirical Evidence on the Effects of Tax Rates on Economic Activity," *Proceedings of the Business and Economic Statistics Section: 1979* (Washington, D.C.: American Statistical Association, 1979).

25. Charles R. Nelson, *Applied Time Series Analysis for Managerial Forecasting* (San Francisco: Holden Day, 1973); and "The Predictive Performance of the FRB-MIT-PENN Model of the U.S. Economy," *American Economic Review* 62 (October 1972): 902-17.

26. Joseph Pechman, "The Individual Income Tax Provisions of the Revenue Act of 1964," *Journal of Finance* 20 (May 1965): 247-72. *See also* idem, *Federal Tax Policy*, 3rd ed. (Washington, D.C.: Brookings Institution, 1977).

27. Canto, Joines, and Webb, "Empirical Evidence."

# A Comment on the Laffer Model

Max Moszer

One feels constrained to step lightly in an examination of the Laffer Curve. Laffer contends that higher tax rates, by removing incentive, will discourage work, lead to less output, and thereby reduce government's total tax revenue. Surely the contention that lower tax rates will yield greater tax revenue is appealing. It should come as no surprise that it is as popular as apple pie and as holy as motherhood. I am painfully aware that, entering the arena with Professor Laffer, I can only lose—if not directly at his hands, and because of the power of his theories, then because winning the debate would be just a Pyrrhic victory. Even the man on the anti-Laffer side still must continue to pay the present, unacceptably high, taxes; the reward of his position will be no further hope for, nor progress toward, tax relief. But the validity of the Laffer Curve is indeed open to question, as I hope to demonstrate.

Professor Laffer is both the creator and the catalyst of the taxpayers' revolt that is sweeping America. The rapidly accelerating burden of taxation and the growth of the government sector that it has supported have generated a reaction that is still swelling. Doctor Laffer is in the forefront of this movement; he is its intellectual leader. He has provided the theoretical framework, by an accepted, orthodox application of economic theory, to support the demand for lower tax rates. No serious examination of America's current economic problems, and no significant proposal for tax cuts or tax reform, can fail to include an analysis of the Laffer Curve. The Kemp-Roth tax bill is the most persuasive evidence of the public acceptance, the political influence, and the power of this doctrine.

The Laffer Curve is just an upside-down or sidewise U. It shows that increases in the tax rate cannot increase government tax receipts indefinitely and without limits. After a critical point, the rising tax rates will yield lower tax collections. These results are based on a simple but fundamental human response to higher tax rates. Yet this is the same reaction economists predict to any higher price. The Laffer Curve generalizes this behavior to the demand for work. As the tax rate, the government's price for work, increases, the quantity of work desired falls. This is illustrated in the demand curve of Figure 1a. From

## FIGURE 1A
## DEMAND FOR WORK DEPENDS ON THE TAX RATE.

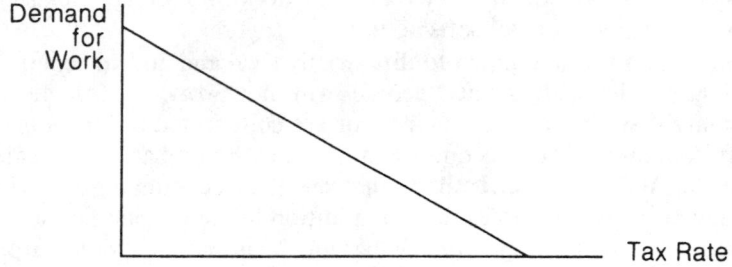

this the Laffer Curve is derived. The curve itself is found in all elementary texts on economics. It demonstrates how a firm with constant unit costs and a linear demand curve can maximize its profits. This is shown in Figure 1b. As price increases, the quantity demanded declines. At first, the higher price applied to the fewer units results in greater total revenue. However, before too long, quantity falls in greater proportion than the rise in price. Therefore, the revenues, or the tax receipts, also fall, despite, or because of, the higher price.

It is immaterial whether this process works through the demand mechanism (whereby higher tax rates for the privilege of working reduce the quantity demanded of work) or through the incentive mechanism (whereby higher tax rates require a greater remuneration to bring forth the same amount of effort). The result is similar: Higher tax rates reduce the desire for work; this reduces total output, and total tax collections decline, since taxes are based on output.

### The Underground Economy

This supply-side approach to fiscal policy is based on the reasonable proposition that the higher the marginal tax rate the greater is the inducement to substitute leisure for work. The high tax rate reduces the rewards of work, and at the same time it cuts the cost of leisure.

## FIGURE 1B
## GOVERNMENT REVENUES DEPEND ON THE TAX RATE.

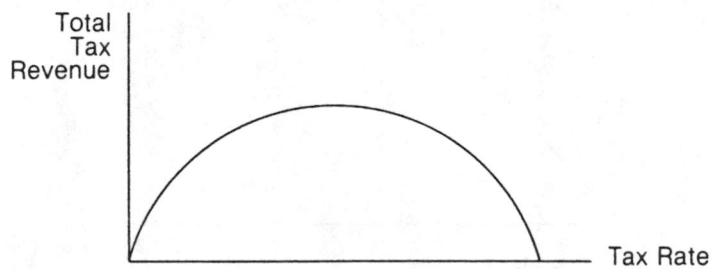

Moreover, the progressive structure of income taxes accelerates this disincentive effect. This becomes especially significant when it is considered in light of the fact that each net-of-tax dollar yields the taxpayer less incremental satisfaction.

Jude Wanniski[1] has added to this strictly legal and ethical economic motivation the claim that "people will not work in the money economy if all the fruits of their labor are confiscated by the government." An underground economy, built on cash and barter, is created instead as individuals attempt to increase their economic gains without paying taxes. High rates thus, in addition to their explicit undesirability, also encourage criminal behavior. This reduces *total* output, since productivity is not as great in the covert market because the optimal specialization and market exchange activities will not be attained. Peter M. Gutmann[2] even introduces the Gutmann Curve, as his contribution to the growing belief that the subterranean economy, flourishing as inflation increases the effective real tax rate, is siphoning off an increasing share of the nation's output. Gutmann believes that the pure incentive effect alone—his interpretation of the Laffer Curve —is not sufficiently large to replace the revenues lost from rate cuts. Only if the Gutmann effect—the shift from the underground to the legal economy as tax rates are reduced—is combined with the Laffer effect will increased market transactions and legal national output yield an increment in the tax base large enough to more than offset the cut in the tax rate. "The Gutmann Curve is very similar to the Laffer Curve but purposely skewed to the right [see Figure 2] to indicate my belief that government revenues are maximized at tax rates higher than 50 percent."

Once it is recognized that these illegal economic activities go on, it becomes necessary to distinguish between the tax effect (1) on government revenue and (2) on total output. The switch to the underground market suggests that the impact of higher tax rates is greater on

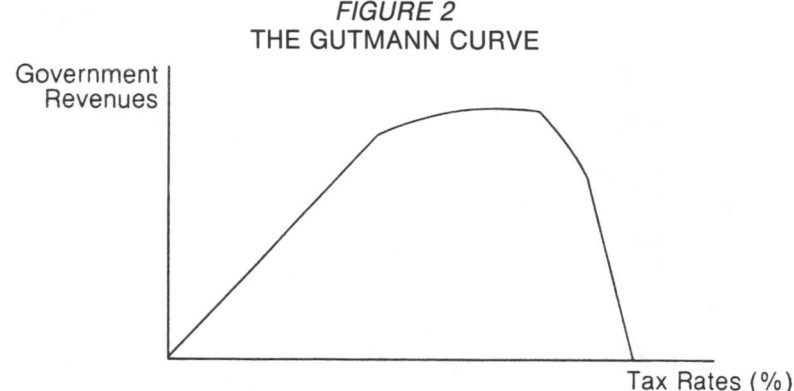

FIGURE 2
THE GUTMANN CURVE

Government Revenues

Tax Rates (%)

government revenue collections than it is on total output. At first it might seem that the total output effect would be close to zero. Yet it is more reasonable to assume that some, if not most, people's ethics prevent them from participating in an illegal market. Even when they engage in illegal activity, moreover, they find their ability to specialize and to exchange is more limited than in the open, and legal, marketplace. This immediately entails a less than optimum allocation, and a less efficient use, of society's resources. Also, costs are incurred in hiding economic activity and income from the tax collector. These costs necessarily exceed those of legal business—or there would be little incentive to report one's income.

It would be unrealistic to assume that people, in response to higher tax rates, move from the open to the covert economy without a significant transition phase. The intermediate stage is tax avoidance and tax shelter—devices familiar to most of us. There is a shift of resources and demand fulfillment as tax-deductible goods become operationally cheaper relative to non-tax-deductible goods. This means that prices paid by the users—after tax savings are deducted— are less than the cost to society of producing these tax-deductible commodities and services. This greatly encourages tax-deductible consumption. Excessive consumption, greater than it would be if the price were equal to the incremental cost to society, yields a less than optimal allocation of resources. This is reflected in a smaller bundle of total output. In addition, it must be recognized that the entire tax shelter industry is a distortion from, and results in a reduction of, the output that could be achieved with lower tax rates. Cattle feed programs and tax-avoidance commodity straddles are just some of the schemes that would have no counterpart in a tax-free world.

In summary, higher tax rates initially reduce output less than tax revenues. After a point, tax avoidance and tax evasion increase, so output decreases. However, there is not a smooth transition to zero output as the tax rate increases to 1.0. Some economic activities will be carried on aboveboard regardless of the tax rate. Government services, and the income derived therefrom, are just the most obvious examples. These will be abandoned completely when the tax rate hits unity, but they will never go underground. (To be sure, they too will decline as the tax rate increases; however, this is the result of the disincentive effect on the workers rather that the subterranean-economy effect of higher tax rates.)

The final output function, with the tax rate as the argument, would have three phases. The first segment would have legal output and some minimum illegal output occurring regardless of the tax rate. In phase two, total output declines. Illegal activity is less efficient than open market transactions, and, also in this stage, tax avoidance increases. As the tax rates rise here, illegal activity increases and the total output achieved by society decreases. The total output, however, declines only slightly. Eventually, the limit of underground activity is reached: Increases in the tax rate cannot shift more production into the illegal sphere. This is shown in Figure 3a.

### FIGURE 3a
### OUTPUT REACTIONS TO CHANGES IN THE TAX RATE

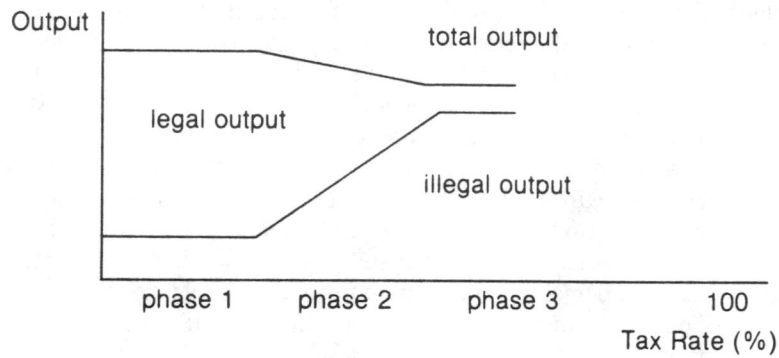

The government tax receipt function, however, is not the same as the total output function. As is shown in Figure 3b, during phase 1, as output stays constant with rising tax rates, total tax receipts rise. During phase 2, with output declining and tax rates increasing, tax receipts initially increase, but after a point they decline. Once illegal output reaches a maximum, and economic activity in total reaches its minimum level, tax receipts *rise*. The last phase is not described in this section, because it does not depend on the shift into illegal activities.

Gutmann, in the cited quotation, expresses the often stated belief that the Laffer Curve peaks at the 50 percent tax rate. Furthermore, he feels that current tax rates in the United States are not high enough to make the Laffer Curve effect operational. Since the horizontal axis

### FIGURE 3b
### TAX RECEIPTS AS OUTPUT SHIFTS WITH TAX RATES

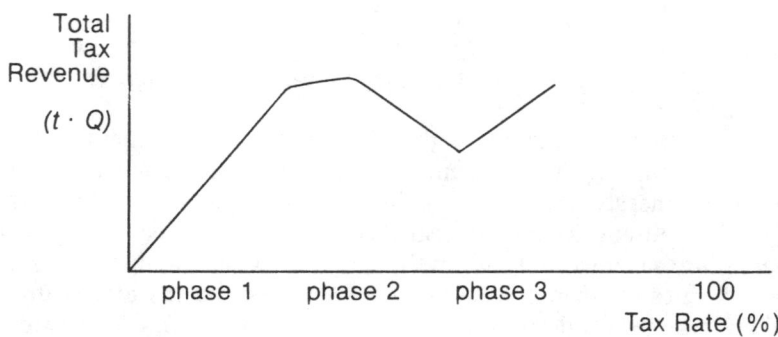

measures *average* tax rates, and a 50 percent average tax indicates a significantly steeper marginal tax on the highest income bracket, this comment is puzzling. Exactly how high need tax rates be for the total receipts function to turn down?

The average federal income tax rate, as a proportion of personal income, was only 13 percent in 1978; state and local income taxes were about 2.5 percent of personal income. Moreover, only 20 percent of income was taxed at marginal rates of 28 percent and higher in 1978. Thus the 50 percent tax rate, the rate at which higher tax rates become self-defeating, is still quite far away.

The maximum point on the tax collection function, however, need not occur at the 50 percent average tax rate point. Referring to Figure 1, it is only when the demand curve is linear that the inflection point of the revenue function is located halfway between the maximum price and the zero mark. There is no logical nor economic reason for the Laffer Curve, just because it is drawn symmetrical to the two end-points, to have its maximum located at the 50 percent tax rate. In fact, the relationship between tax rates and tax receipts, the relationship summarized by the Laffer Curve, is not exactly the same as the demand and total revenue curves of Figure 1. There, the revenue function is

$$R = PQ \tag{1}$$

where
$$Q = f(P);$$

thus
$$R = Pf(P)$$

and
$$O = Pf'(P) + f(P). \tag{2a}$$

Or
$$O = 1 + [P/f(P)]f'(P), \tag{2b}$$

which is the necessary condition for a maximum. This means that the elasticity of demand, the second term in equation (2b), must equal one to reach the revenue maximum. By contrast, the tax revenue formulation, in its simplest form, is

$$T = twL \tag{3}$$

where
$T =$ total tax receipts,

$t =$ the average tax rate,

$w =$ the rate of factor remuneration, and

$L =$ the quantity of the factor.

In this case,
$$w = h(t),$$
$$L = g(w),$$

and thus
$$T = t[h(t)\cdot g(w)].\tag{4}$$

The first order condition for the maximum is

$$O = 1 + E_{w\cdot t} + E_{L\cdot t}.\tag{5}$$

This inflection point depends on the elasticity of remuneration relative to the tax rate, $E_{w\cdot t}$, and the elasticity of factor supply, $E_{L\cdot t}$, responding to the tax rate which, in turn, causes a change in the remuneration rate. Even the stripped-down form of the tax function in equation (3) yields a complex relationship. Moreover, at least two constraints on the maximizing process are required. First, it is necessary that $wL$, the total family income, not be permitted to fall below a minimum subsistence level. Secondly, the factor supply function, especially when it refers to the bulk of income that is earned from providing labor services, is subject to arbitrary, institutional restraints on both the maximum and the minimum number of hours and/or days that can, or need, be marketed.

Furthermore, the revenue function requires disaggregation. It becomes

$$T = \Sigma_j \, \Sigma_i t_j W_{ji} L_{ji}.\tag{6}$$

The elasticities of remuneration differ since market conditions in professions and occupations permit participants various degrees of latitude in passing forward cost increases, such as the change in the rate of taxation. Similar considerations are also valid for the elasiticities of resource supply. Finally, several tax rates must be introduced: ordinary labor income, dividend income, capital gains income, and corporate income.

These complicating factors demonstrate that, at the very least, the Laffer Curve does not have its maximum at the 50 percent average tax rate. In fact, it is likely that it may not be a smooth, well-behaved function at all. Thus, while it is appropriate to claim that tax rates are excessive if government revenues are to be maximized, it is an oversimplification to expect to find this point of no return by examining the Laffer Curve.

## The Micro Market Aspects

Laffer[3] considers the income tax as a wedge between the price received by the factor owner and the cost paid by the firm. The wedge is the amount of the tax; it shifts the supply curve upward, or to the left if prices are plotted vertically. After the tax is imposed, resource owners will reduce the amount of work they are willing to supply— unless their response is completely inelastic to price. The wedge, then, also represents the additional amount needed by the resource to offer the identical level of services as before the tax. The actual effect of the tax depends on the elasticity of the supply curve.

Since this income tax is just another cost of working, it could be treated just like an indirect business tax imposed on a seller. The tax shifts up the supply curve; it is simply added to the offering price. Surely the supplier would like to recoup the entire tax payment. Yet this does not mean that the post-tax price will be greater by the full amount of the tax. The impact of the tax depends also on the elasticity of demand. As is shown in Figure 4, for a given supply curve, the tax has both a price effect and a quantity effect. Only when the demand is completely inelastic, and then regardless of the elasticity of the supply curve, is the tax in its entirety passed on to the buyer. Obviously when the quantity demanded is not at all responsive to price, the amount offered, produced, and exchanged is unaltered by the tax.

## FIGURE 4
## THE IMPACT OF DEMAND ELASTICITIES ON THE SUPPLY OF RESOURCES

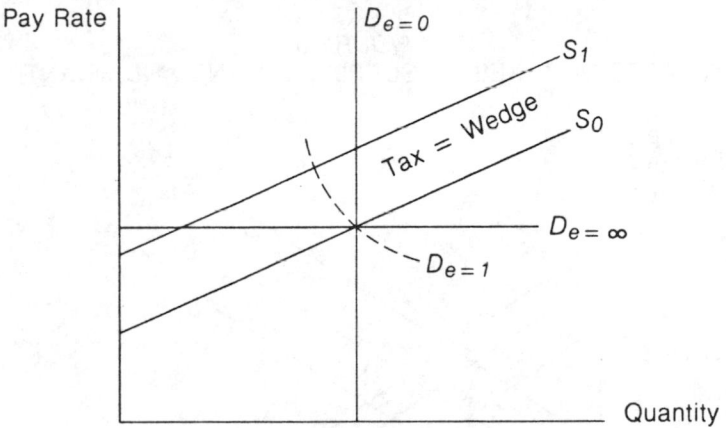

As the elasticity of demand increases, the supplier's ability to pass on the tax weakens. The quantity adjustment becomes more important. Eventually the other extreme is reached: Infinite demand elasticity means that the tax cannot alter price; the entire impact of the tax is evidenced by a reduction in the quantity. The disincentive effect of the tax, brought to our attention by Professor Laffer, is clear. At any demand elasticity greater than zero, the tax results in a reduction of economic activity. Similarly, elimination or reduction of the tax increases output.

The household supply curve, however, is not motivated, as is the firm's, by profit objectives. The family has alternative uses for its resources of labor *and* capital. This substitution effect causes the leisure uses of labor and capital to become more valuable, or less costly, in terms of market receipts, as the tax rate rises. This is offset by the income effect: the desire for, and the need of, income to maximize total satisfaction. As the tax rate rises, there is a need to offer greater quantities of resources to maintain the previous standard of satisfaction. The shift of the supply curve in response to a tax rate change then depends on the interaction and the net value of the substitution and income effects.

The magnitudes of these factors, unfortunately, are not at hand. Yet some inferences can be made about their relative size. Assume that taxes were to increase by $10. At the very most, moved by the substitution effect, the supply curve would shift up by $10. However, the chances are that the shift would be less that the full amount of the tax. The income effect would offset this shift. As taxes increase, the need to earn greater gross income increases. The upward shift would then be mitigated as the income effect holds the curve to a shift less than the jump in taxes. This is shown in Figure 5, where the original supply curve, $S_0$, first shifts up to $S_{1s}$, the substitution effect, and then down to its final positon of $S_{1s} + y$ as the income effect is added.

FIGURE 5
IMPACTS OF TAXES ON SUPPLY, DEMAND AND QUANTITY

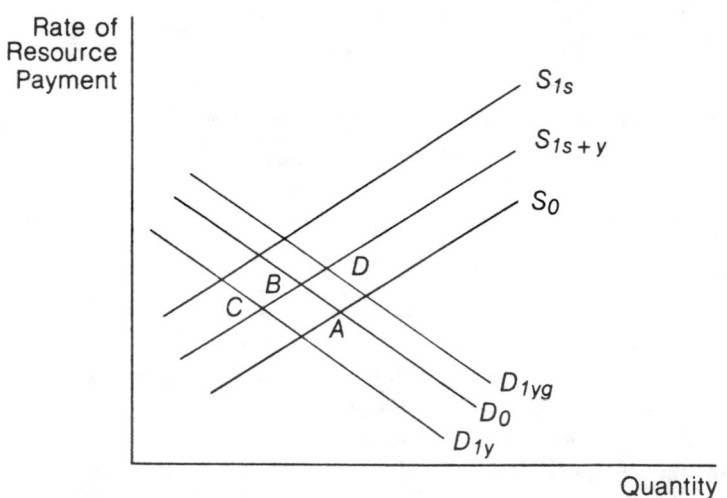

The total work and output impact of the tax increase can now be evaluated. The tax will reduce the incentive to work. This shifts up the supply curve by a wedge no greater than the tax. The income effect now comes into play; greater quantities of resources need to be sold to earn the same take-home income. The supply curve shifts down. The net effect is indeterminate. However, the total shift in the supply curve would be less than the tax increment. With a stable demand curve, total resources used and market output might decline after the tax increase. However, the stronger the desire to maintain standards of satisfaction, the greater will be the tendency for the supply curve shifts to offset each other.

If there is a net decrease in the supply function *and* in the net income of the selling households, the aggregate demand curve will shift down. This decline, however, since the marginal propensity to consume is smaller than one, will be less than the decline in income. The tax receipts of government, on the other hand, will be spent in their entirety, either by the government itself or by those households that receive transfers. Thus the increase in spending will exceed the decrease in spending caused by the tax inducement. The demand for total output, therefore, will shift up. These movements are shown in Figure 5.

On balance, there is no conclusive reason to believe the after-tax position will result in less output than the pre-tax-change equilibrium. Originally, the intersection of $S_0$ and $D_0$ at $A$ describes the pretax position. Considering only the supply shifts, with the substitution effect greater than the income effect, the new position at $B$ as $S_{1sy}$ and $D_0$ cross, indicates that output has declined with tax increases. Once the demand shifts are introduced, the demand curve shifts *up* to $D_{1yg}$ and the new intersection with the $S_{1sy}$ curve is at $D$. This may be to the left or the right of $A$, indicating that less or more factor resources have been hired.

If the income effect of the resource sellers plus the spending effect of the government and the transfer recipients is greater than the substitution and the spending effects of the households that are selling resources, then the posttax output will be greater than the pretax equilibrium. $D$ will be located to the right of $A$. There may exist a paradox of taxation. For if the supply curve shift is less than the tax rate, and the demand curve shift exceeds that, then higher tax rates mean more output—not less—even if the incentive to work and to save has been reduced.[4]

The net impact of the tax change on the quantity of resources hired and the total output depends on the elasticities of demand and of supply. The greater these elasticities, the greater will be the increase in price and the smaller the reduction in output. What values seem reasonable? Over the near and the intermediate terms, the demand for labor and for machinery is free of substantial responsiveness to price change; substitution is limited by the embedded production process. Major shifts in factor use would seem almost impossible despite managements' desires to minimize costs.

The supply of labor, even in the short run, is probably more responsive to price opportunities in *specific* industries, occupations, and locations than it is in the aggregate. While some price elasticity in the total supply of labor exists, it would not seem reasonable to expect it to be large. Though the supply of labor is not static, its movements are likely to be the result of, and restrained by, institutional and technological shifts. The current recession-inflation can provide some insights into the responsiveness of labor to changes in the real wage. The last two years have seen a continuous decline in the real wage. There is little indication that the labor force participation rate—the indicator of the supply of labor—has declined. Surely no one should be suffering from a money illusion, since the acceleration of prices has received ample publicity. Workers are evidently not very responsive to changes in the real wage. Since it is unlikely that households are not aware of the rate of inflation, it also seems that the income effect is substantially stronger than the substitution effect.

Consider the rise in the labor force participation rate of women. Over the past sixty years this has occurred against a background of increasing social welfare programs and a rising effective tax rate. Both these factors decrease the relative price of remunerative work relative to leisure. It is hard to accept the hypothesis of substantial elasticity even in the long run in the supply curve of labor given the persistent increase in the number of women in the labor force. Moreover, since 1965, the rise in the effective tax rate has been accompanied by a decline in the rate of growth of real wages. This can be seen in Table 1. The effective tax rate on earned personal income—that is, personal income minus transfers—has increased over the entire period covered (see line 5 in the table). In 1979 it was almost half again as large as in 1965. Moreover, the effective tax rate is an average; thus it tends to understate systematically the marginal tax rate as the average rate rises. Since most married women are not the prime earners in their household, then with progressive income taxes, the appropriate tax rates allocated to their incomes are much larger than for their male counterparts. Even if the women were to earn much more, given the chronology of family formation and the resultant entry into the labor force, their incomes would still be charged the marginal rate of the higher tax bracket. Yet the entry rate of women into the labor force has continued unabated. In fact, it increased in the very years that the tax rate was reaching new highs. In the nine years between 1965 and 1973, the growth rate of female labor force participation exceeded 2 percent only twice. In the five years since then, the growth rate was greater than that five times. The growth rate in the real weekly wage (line 9) was greater in the early period, when the female entry rate was not as large, than in the last five years. Yet this latter period shows the labor force participation rate growing more rapidly. None of these associations of data can be used to substantiate the contention that there is a substantial elasticity of labor supply with respect to effective tax rates nor with respect to real wages.

The trend of men's participation rates is down over the entire

## TABLE 1
### SELECTED INCOME, TAX, SPENDING, AND LABOR FORCE DATA

| | 1965 | 1966 | 1967 | 1968 | 1969 | 1970 | 1971 | 1972 | 1973 | 1974 | 1975 | 1976 | 1977 | 1978 | 1979 |
|---|---|---|---|---|---|---|---|---|---|---|---|---|---|---|---|
| 1. Personal Income | 537 | 585 | 627 | 685 | 746 | 801 | 859 | 943 | 1,052 | 1,155 | 1,256 | 1,382 | 1,532 | 1,717 | 1,924 |
| 2. Transfers | 40 | 45 | 53 | 60 | 67 | 80 | 94 | 104 | 119 | 141 | 178 | 194 | 208 | 224 | 252 |
| 3a. Earned Personal Income[1] | 497 | 540 | 574 | 625 | 679 | 721 | 765 | 839 | 933 | 1,014 | 1,078 | 1,188 | 1,324 | 1,493 | 1,672 |
| 3b. Personal Taxes[2] | 65 | 75 | 82 | 97 | 115 | 115 | 116 | 141 | 151 | 170 | 169 | 197 | 226 | 259 | 300 |
| 4. Disposable Earned Income | 432 | 465 | 492 | 528 | 564 | 606 | 649 | 697 | 782 | 844 | 909 | 991 | 1,098 | 1,234 | 1,372 |
| 5. Effective Tax Rate | 13.1 | 13.9 | 14.3 | 15.5 | 16.9 | 16.0 | 15.2 | 16.8 | 16.2 | 16.8 | 15.7 | 16.6 | 17.7 | 17.3 | 17.9 |
| 6. Consumption Less Transfers | 390 | 420 | 437 | 476 | 513 | 539 | 574 | 629 | 691 | 749 | 801 | 896 | 1,002 | 1,127 | 1,258 |
| 7. Earned Propensity to Consume[3] | 90.3 | 90.3 | 88.8 | 90.2 | 91.0 | 88.9 | 88.4 | 90.2 | 88.4 | 88.7 | 88.1 | 90.4 | 91.3 | 91.3 | 91.7 |
| 8. Real Weekly Wage All Industries | 139 | 147 | 151 | 155 | 158 | 160 | 163 | 168 | 172 | 168 | 167 | 171 | 176 | 177 | |
| 9. Growth Rate (%) | 3.1 | 5.8 | 2.7 | 2.6 | 1.9 | 1.3 | 1.9 | 3.1 | 2.4 | -2.3 | -0.1 | 2.4 | 2.9 | 0.6 | |
| Labor Force Participation Rates (%) | | | | | | | | | | | | | | | |
| 10. Total | 58.9 | 59.2 | 59.6 | 59.6 | 60.1 | 60.4 | 60.2 | 60.4 | 60.8 | 61.3 | 61.2 | 61.6 | 62.3 | 63.2 | 63.7 |
| 11. Male | 80.7 | 80.4 | 80.4 | 80.1 | 79.9 | 79.7 | 79.1 | 79.0 | 78.9 | 78.7 | 77.9 | 77.5 | 77.7 | 77.9 | 77.9 |
| 12. Female | 39.2 | 40.3 | 41.1 | 41.6 | 42.8 | 43.3 | 43.3 | 43.9 | 44.7 | 45.6 | 46.3 | 47.3 | 48.5 | 50.0 | 51.0 |
| 13. Growth Rate | 1.3 | 2.8 | 1.2 | 1.2 | 2.9 | 1.2 | — | 1.4 | 1.8 | 2.0 | 1.5 | 2.2 | 2.5 | 3.1 | 2.0 |

Source: Wharton Econometric Associates Data Bank

1. Wages and salaries, interest, rent, dividends, and proprietor income.
2. Federal, state, and local government tax and nontax payments.
3. Assumes that the propensity to consume of transfers equal to 1.0.

period. Most of this reflects a shift in the age brackets of male workers. The older groups' participation rates have declined while those of the two youngest groups have increased. One might argue that the mature workers have a greater opportunity to shift out since the income effect is not as urgent, given the accumulation of pension rights and other assets over their lifetimes. Yet it would be possible to sustain the claim that the younger groups have fewer resources and that therefore their responsiveness to the economic choices is smaller. The data, then, for male participation are inconclusive. There seems to be little evidence that the supply of labor is elastic. This means that the quantity effect of a tax rate change would be small.

Even if the substitution effect is greater than the income effects and if the supply curve shifts up in response to higher taxes, the decline in output need not lead to lower government tax receipts. If the demand for resources is inelastic, then, at the higher supply price and with fewer units hired, the total wage bill and income earned will be greater. After taxes have risen, total labor income will also rise. Since government tax collections are related to resource income, tax receipts, too, will increase. This result, based on the inelasticity of the demand curve, will occur despite the disincentive effect of the higher tax burden. Thus the Laffer Curve forecast would not prove to be correct.[5]

The demand for investment capital, the other resource in the labor-capital production function, is not very responsive to price. The long literature on monetary policy[6] and the ineffectiveness of reducing interest rates indicate this. The supply side is more difficult to characterize. One complicating factor is the role of corporate savings and the way that individuals use this vehicle to increase their personal asset balance. The past two years have seen a drastic change in the level of nominal interest rates and in the personal savings ratio. Given the decline in the savings ratio and in the real rate of interest, it would be appropriate to infer that the personal savings function is quite interest-elastic. Yet the falloff might be attributable to the strengthening of inflationary expectations, the shift into commodities, and the decline in real income.

Even if the supply of savings were interest-elastic, reductions in taxes would increase only the quantity saved, and with an inelastic demand for investment, would not lead to an increase in government revenue. It seems unproductive to explore the income tax rate elasticity of the personal savings function when Congress has created, and permits the continuation of, substantial imperfections for the bulk of savers. These small savers are faced with 6 percent ceilings on passbook savings, minimum requirements on longer certificates, and Treasury issues in astronomical denominations. Just recently, new restrictions were placed on money market funds. Yet these have done more to evade the arbitrary legal restrictions on the money market, and encourage saving, than any other measure that comes to mind. It is ill advised to consider whether tax cuts, or exemptions of interest income, would call forth greater personal saving. Government could achieve this goal easily by constraining its extravagant growth, which prevents most households from entering the money market and earning the going rate of return on their savings.

It is clear that the tax imposes a wedge between the marginal revenue product of the resource and its market remuneration. It is questionable, though, whether it is appropriate to construct this wedge as a constant as is done by Laffer. His Figures 1 and 2 in "The Output and Employment Effects of Fiscal Policy in a Classical Model" show constant shifts even though the text treats the tax as proportional. The diagram is reproduced here as Figure 6. It shows a lump-sum tax, rather than a tax related to the level of income. The lump-sum tax shifts up the supply curve without changing its slope. Thus the magnitude of the disincentive effect is the same regardless of the wage rate. This causes the relative burden of the tax, and its associated discouraging effect, to decrease as income rises. Moreover, the income tax structure in the United States is progressive: It yields a greater effective tax rate as income rises. This means that the wedge becomes larger as the wage rate increases. This is shown in Figure 7. The supply curve shifts up to $S_c$ since the tax is unchanged at all income levels. The supply curve that reflects the progressive tax structures is $S_p$. At a minimum its relative burden and monetary disincentive is equal for all wage rates. The wedge is relatively greater for the high-income earner than for those at the lower end of the wage gamut.

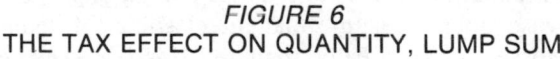

## FIGURE 6
### THE TAX EFFECT ON QUANTITY, LUMP SUM

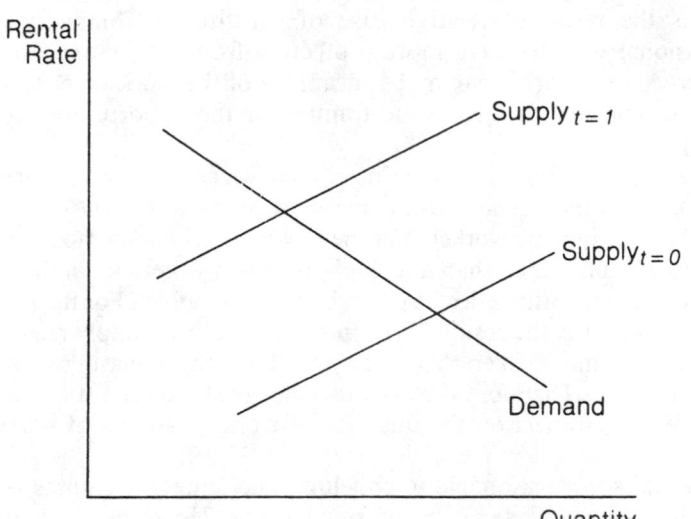

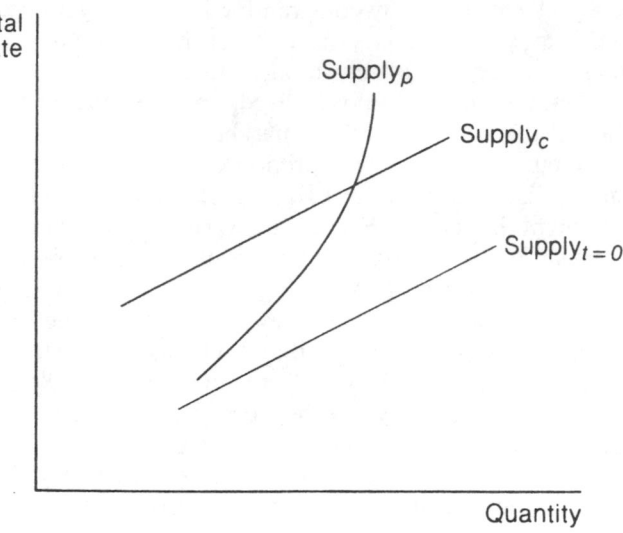

*FIGURE 7*
THE TAX EFFECT ON SUPPLY, LUMP SUM AND PROGRESSIVE

For any demand curve, a tax cut will lead to a much greater response in the quantity when the shift is from the proportional or progressive tax, $S_p$, than when it is from the lump-sum tax, $S_c$. Yet to assess the economic and the revenue impact of a tax change, the elasticity of demand for the resource must be considered. If the wage rate structure reflects the occupational distribution and the scarcity of skills, then it would be reasonable to assume that the elasticity of demand for the low-wage workers is far greater than that for high-wage employees. This is the result of relative ease of substitution. Managers and professional workers have more protection from alternative production processes; machines may be incapable of the work managers do. Other people may not have the training or the opportunities to fill these jobs.

On the supply side, given the differential wedge, the elasticity falls as the wage rate rises. The low-income worker has a less elastic supply than the high-income worker. Yet the low-income worker faces a more elastic demand curve than the high-income worker. In both cases, therefore, the quantity effect is offset by the price effect. For the low-income worker it is the result of the inelasticity of the supply curve; for the high-income worker this is achieved by the inelasticity of the demand curve. Therefore the tax rate change would seem to have the same relative impact on the quantity of work regardless of the wage rate.

It would seem reasonable to conclude that supply responses to tax rate changes are likely to be of small order. However, even if the elasticity of supply were substantial, it is doubtful that the institutional rigidities of the labor market would permit the realization of the additional desire for work. While allocative efficiency and Pareto optimality are useful devices, unfortunately the real world offers restricted, noncontinuous choices. Nowhere is this imperfection more in evidence than in the labor market. The number of hours in a workday and the length of vacations cannot be negotiated by individuals. Either one works the regular shift in its entirety or one does not get, or keep, the job. Overtime cannot be had at will and must be worked when offered. Moonlighting is discouraged; even this name for a second job suggests cheating at worst and inability to meet bills at best. Every so often one reads of a professor, with two or even three teaching appointments, who turns in astounding performances at each institution, has tenure and all . . . and who, when found out, is forced to quit the other jobs. It is difficult to imagine executives holding similar jobs in two different firms. Moreover, given the primary eight-to-five business day, second jobs mean less desirable hours; besides, the duties of some managers and professionals are limited to the prime shift. It would require substantial tax rate changes to shift the supply curve enough to make more people want to work a full eight-hour shift at a less desirable time.

The Laffer Curve cannot be justified by claiming that the rigidities and distortions from optimality exist now as well. Substantial incentives would be required to move individuals over the discontinuities. "Reasonable" tax cuts would not be capable of achieving this result. Alternatively, restructuring the workday and removing obstacles to free flows of labor and capital in response to small price changes would yield far greater results—more output and more government revenues—at a much smaller cost.

## The Macro Aspects

The essence of Laffer's supply-side economics is that rewards are required to entice work effort. Increasing the rewards encourages production. Since taxes reduce the effective pay, all government actions reduce output. The traditional theory holds that it is impossible to know a priori whether a cut in rates will reduce or increase the desire to work.[7] The income effect, indicative of the need to work more at lower recompense, may or may not outweigh the substitution effect, now that the cost of leisure, relative to work, has fallen. Laffer[8] aggregates over all taxpayers and transfer recipients. Since the former's loss becomes the latter's gain, he claims that their combined income effects add up to zero. All that is left is the negative substitution effect of *both* parties. This causes income and output decline.

There is no reason to believe that the two income effects are equal in absolute terms. This depends on the taste structure of each member of the society. It is unlikely, in fact, that these would be uniform over people selected at random. Here the requirement is much more stringent. They need to be the same for individuals separated by wide gulfs in earnings, occuptions, education, and social positions. Indeed, the burden of proof of this assertion rests with Professor Laffer.

It is true, of course, that a dollar taken away by government yields a dollar of income to the transfer recipient. With taxes on income, the taxpayer, however, needs to earn more than a dollar to return to the previous net income position. With the progressivity of income taxes, redistributions from those in the upper levels must lead to a greater positive income effect than the negative impacts felt by the receivers of these funds, who are clustered in much lower, if any, marginal tax brackets.

The structure that Laffer envisions is of resource owners, highly responsive to net-of-tax rewards, moving in and out of the market-place. It is cost-biased. Work offers decline as the tax rate rises. The employer will hire fewer workers as the tax wedge increases. Nowhere in this analysis is there a recognition of the role of the sales, price, and profit expectations of business firms. Surely output is produced only in anticipation of final demand, regardless of the cheapness of the resource inputs. Neglecting this factor, Laffer can claim that "counter-cyclical government spending increases the economy's cyclicality."[9] This result occurs because less real output remains for those who work to support the unemployed. In this formulation, transfers result in less incentive to work. Even during recession, those who are still employed, while the unemployed mill around them, will quit or work fewer hours, because the rewards, in real terms, have declined. It is doubtful that the substitution effect is so great. This sequence, however, overlooks the role of aggregate demand. Unemployment compensation and other transfers that are triggered by the business cycle may have welfare dimensions; for the macroeconomist, however, they are automatic stabilizers. They dampen the cut in employment and output—and in income, and other, tax receipts—by maintaining total demand. This leads to an enhancement of the business climate that encourages production by increasing profitability; it is reasonable to assume that this will outweigh the substitution effect.

The hypothesis that tax increases discourage work has an implicit corollary. Occupations and professions that permit tax evasion would experience an influx of workers when taxes increase; these industries would be expected to expand. Underreporting of tips by waitresses, waiters, and taxi drivers are especially difficult to police. As shown in Table 1, the effective tax rate since 1965 has an upward trend. We would anticipate on the tax account an increase in the number of well-served restaurants and available taxis. Yet, during this time, the traditional restaurant has given way to the fast-food operation. Taxis have become increasingly difficult to find. These results are contrary to the theoretical presumption that tax rates are of significant importance in motivating the supply of resources.

The Internal Revenue Service's study on tax evasion[10] estimates that between 6 percent and 8 percent of total personal income in 1976 went unreported. The largest part of this shortfall—almost $100 billion—was attributed to individuals who were self-employed in proprietorships or partnerships. Casual empiricism would not uphold the contention that rising effective tax rates have led to an expansion of small businesses and proprietorships in recent times. To the contrary, there has been an upsurge in franchising. This method of operation has accounting procedures that are oriented to audit schemes that maximize the franchisor's profits; this reduces the ability of the individual businessperson to underreport income to the IRS. Regardless of the reasons for the expansion of franchising, these tax-related features cast doubt on the hypothesis that changes in effective tax rates are important considerations in determining the supply of total output.

Congress has sponsored much research in its attempt to evaluate the advisability of legislating the massive tax cuts specified in the Kemp-Roth bill. Walter Heller, for example, sheds light on the claim that the 1964 Kennedy-Johnson tax cut worked through supply-side, rather than demand-side, stimulation. Heller testified[11] that the success of the tax cut was the result of increased desires and abilities to spend. He notes that if the recovery in output were the result of policy-oriented shifts in supply, substantial jumps in productivity and capacity should have occurred after the tax cut. Yet no significant changes in these measures were discovered. He therefore dismisses the supply-side argument.

The econometric model studies and simulations are inconclusive. The mainline models—such as Wharton and DRI—do not have structural equations that can be used to test the econometric effects of tax cuts. They initiate these changes by arbitrary assignment of values to tax-related variables and then let the model run. Professor Laffer and Michael Evans, individually, have developed models whose simulations, it is claimed, uphold the supply-side thesis. They are said to show that substantial output and tax gains are possible by reducing tax rates. Since there have been few, if any, peacetime tax cuts that were supply-side in nature, it is difficult to perceive what data points were used to estimate the parameters of these supply-side models. Accordingly, it is wiser to reserve judgment on the econometrics of supply-side economics.

One thing is certain, though. For the supply effects of the Laffer Curve to work, for the tax rate cuts to cause an increase large enough in output to recoup the loss from reducing the rate of taxation, the multiplier effect has to be large. For example, federal income taxes of $224 billion represented 15.6 percent of the 1979 real GNP of $1432 billion. A tax cut to an effective average rate of 10 percent would require a jump in real output to $2240 billion just to make the tax receipts at the new, lower rate equal to last year's actual collections. The required increase in real output is $808 billion; the dollar value of this tax cut is $81 billion (the tax collections of 1979 less the 1979 GNP taxed at 10 percent). This yields a multiplier requirement as large as 10 —$808 divided by $81. In contrast, the working econometric models have tax multipliers no greater than 2, and most lie in the range of 1¼ to 2. Surely such divergence in the multiplier is not realistic. It is not consistent with the record of the major models over the past twenty-five years.

## Conclusions

The contribution of the Laffer Curve is significant. It reminds us that supply-side impacts are important and must be included in economic policy decisions. Surely if the incentive effect has been underestimated, the work of Professor Laffer will help demonstrate its importance. The ability of tax rate cuts from present levels to increase tax receipts, however, remains doubtful. Increases in output that follow tax cuts are principally demand- and multiplier-related. Until substantial productivity changes and capacity increments from tax cuts can be demonstrated, supply-side stimulation will play a secondary role in macro policy. Indeed, the current drive to deregulation, if it were extended to the labor and the small savers' money market, would probably show greater output and tax returns than tax cuts. Moreover, such dismantling of government interferences would be consistent with our traditions of limiting government roles. Their effects and marginal impacts would be more manageable and measurable than a tax cut as huge as that recommended by Professor Laffer and the Kemp-Roth bill.

# Notes

1. Jude Wanniski, "Taxes, Revenues and the Laffer Curve," *Public Interest*, Winter 1978.

2. Peter M. Gutmann, "Taxes and the Supply of National Output," *Financial Analysts Journal*, November/December 1979.

3. V. A. Canto, A. B. Laffer, and O. Odogwu, "The Output and Employment Effects of Fiscal Policy in a Classical Model," mimeographed (Los Angeles: University of Southern California, 1977).

4. There may be a tax illusion at work. This would mean that harder and longer work for more pretax income but less net-of-tax income is preferred to less work and lower gross pay but greater net pay.

5. If the production function is Cobb-Douglas, the elasticity of demand for resources is unitary. Income will be uniform regardless of the tax rate.

6. *See*, for example, Michael K. Evans, *Macroeconomic Activity* (New York: Harper & Row, 1969).

7. Richard A. Musgrave and Peggy B. Musgrave, *Public Finance in Theory and Practice*, 2nd ed. (New York: McGraw-Hill, 1973), p. 407.

8. Arthur B. Laffer, "An Equilibrium Rational Macroeconomic Framework," in *Economic Issues of the Eighties*, ed. Nake M. Kamrani and Richard Day (Baltimore, Md.: Johns Hopkins University Press, 1980).

9. Ibid.

10. Department of the Treasury, Internal Revenue Service, *Estimates of Income Unreported on Individual Income Tax Returns* (Washington, D.C.: Government Printing Office, September 1977).

11. Walter W. Heller, "Tax Cuts, the Kemp-Roth Bill and the Laffer Curve," statement before the Midyear Review Hearing, Joint Economic Committee, June 28, 1978. This and other viewpoints, can be found in Donald W. Kiefer, "An Economic Analysis of the Kemp-Roth Tax Cut Bill . . ." (Washington, D.C.: Congressional Research Service, Library of Congress, July 31, 1978).

# Limitations of the Laffer Curve as a Justification for Tax Cuts

David Henderson

Professor Laffer's paper[1] leads me to ask four questions, which I shall address in turn:

1. Is the Laffer Curve an accurate depiction of economic reality?

2. Are we in a prohibitive region of the Laffer Curve, that is, a region in which a tax rate cut would increase tax revenues?

3. If we are not in a prohibitive region, could we cut income tax rates and get the positive output effects without also cutting government spending?

4. Should we let our answer to the second and third questions determine our position on cutting taxes?

We know that both a zero tax rate and an extremely high tax rate would yield zero revenues and that tax rates in between yield positive revenues, and therefore the Laffer Curve may be said to approximate reality. But the curve may not be as simple as the one Laffer is said to have drawn on a napkin in a Washington restaurant in 1974 (see Figure 1). It should look instead like Figure 2, because a tax rate cut would not necessarily cause people to work more. If people use the higher take-home pay that they get as the result of a tax rate cut (from point A to point B in Figure 2) to "buy" more leisure by working less (in economists' jargon, if the income effect of a cut in tax rates outweighs the substitution effect), then the tax base would actually decrease and tax revenues could fall proportionately more than tax rates. Laffer excludes this possibility, arguing that the decrease in government services induced by the tax cut lowers people's real income and thus lowers their demand for leisure exactly as much as the increase in real income raises their demand for leisure. But to make his claim, he must assume, as he admits, that people spend their increased real income on goods that they value neither more nor less than the goods that the government would have bought with their money. I find this implausible. It is much more likely that people value goods they can choose themselves more highly than goods that the government would have chosen for them, in which case a tax rate cut would

*FIGURE 1*
**THE SIMPLE LAFFER CURVE**

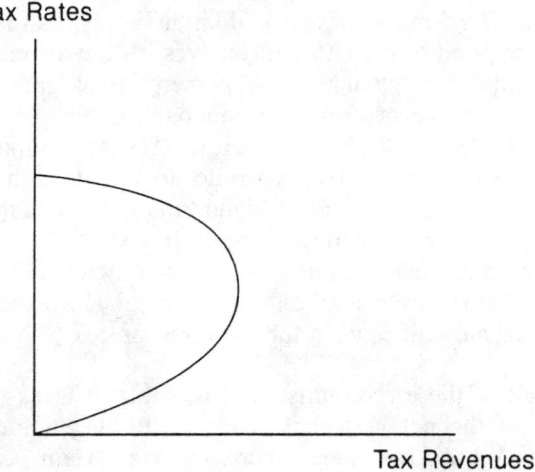

Tax Rates

Tax Revenues

*FIGURE 2*
**A MORE COMPLEX LAFFER CURVE**

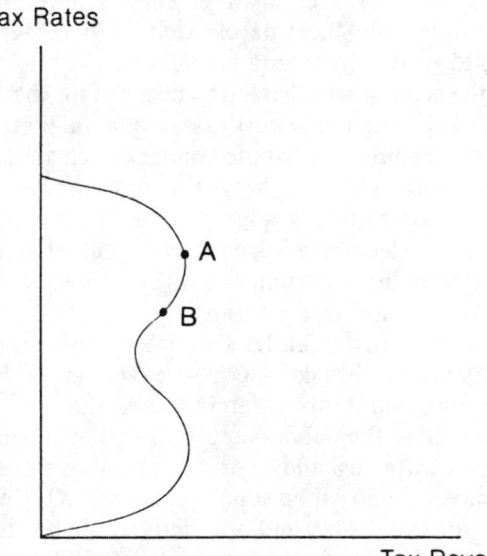

Tax Rates

Tax Revenues

increase both their real income and their demand for leisure. We cannot, therefore, exclude the possibility of a more complicated shape to the Laffer Curve.

Whether a decrease in tax rates would increase tax revenues depends to a large extent on the elasticity of labor supply, that is, on how much workers respond to increased incentives.[2] If the average tax rate is 30 percent and the marginal rate is 40 percent,[3] then for a 10 percent cut in tax rates to leave tax revenues unchanged, people would have to respond by working 8.33 percent more. (See Appendix, Part A, for the derivation of this result.) They would do so only if their labor supply elasticity were 1.25, which is higher than the average labor supply elasticity found by virtually all economists who have studied the issue. Most economists have found a zero elasticity for men[4] and a positive elasticity between 0.6 and 2.1 for women.[5] However, their findings must be taken with caution for these reasons:

1. Most of these economists fail to subtract taxes from income in arriving at the net wage, and as a result they understate the true elasticity. When gross wages increase by a certain percentage in our progressive tax system, people move into higher tax brackets, and after-tax wages increase by a lower percentage. Dividing the percentage change in hours worked by the percentage change in gross wages gives too low an estimate of elasticity. The correct method would be to divide the percentage change in hours worked by the percentage change in *after-tax* wages.

2. None of the economists takes account of the *intensity* of work effort, their measure of labor supply being simply hours worked. If labor supply elasticities are positive, then failure to account for intensity will understate the true elasticity, since higher wages will induce people to work harder in a given hour.

3. Most of the economists also fail to account for the fact that many people decide how much to work as part of a lifetime plan, and therefore it is misleading to attribute changes in current hours of work only to current wage changes. Workers may have changed current hours in anticipation of future wage changes. However, this may not cause problems since a current wage increase generally indicates higher wages in the future, and a current tax rate cut means higher after-tax wages both currently and in the future.

It would appear, then, that Laffer's argument is stronger than current elasticity estimates would indicate. Moreover, as Laffer points out, using one elasticity and one marginal tax rate for the economy probably understates the labor supply effect of a cut in tax rates because women whose husbands work face an above-average marginal tax rate and have a high labor supply elasticity. On the other hand, since married women's wages and productivity are less than men's, the additional output from their working more would not be as high as otherwise. There is still a good chance that not enough new labor will be supplied to prevent tax revenues from falling.[6]

However, even if labor supply elasticities are too low to make up for lost tax revenues, labor supply is not the only factor that would increase the tax base. As Laffer notes, a decrease in tax rates would also increase saving and capital formation and would reduce the incentive to acquire tax shelters. And as Professor Moszer notes, decreases in tax rates shift production from the "underground" to the "above-ground" sector.[7]

Is there any other way of determining whether a cut in tax rates would increase revenues? We could examine the effects of past tax rate cuts and increases. If tax rate cuts led to revenue increases and if tax rate increases caused revenues to decrease, then a cut in tax rates today would probably increase tax revenues because tax rates are higher now than in all but a few earlier years.

Professor Laffer looks at past tax cuts, quoting evidence from a paper by Canto, Joines, and Webb on the effect of the Kennedy-Johnson tax rate cuts.[8] These three scholars concluded that the 1962 and 1964 cuts in tax rates caused only a small decrease in tax revenues, but they did not correct for any of the other factors that would have expanded the tax base at the same time, such as tariff cuts and the coming of age of the baby-boom generation. Laffer justifies this procedure by citing Charles Nelson's finding that a simple empirical method using only knowledge of the history of a variable usually forecasts as well as or better than a model that takes account of other factors.[9] I hesitate to criticize Laffer on this point because Professor Nelson is a capable and respected time-series analyst, and I know only the rudiments of time-series analysis. But should not Canto, Joines, and Webb or Laffer demonstrate that their method is appropriate in *this* case and not just in most cases? I suspect that if they had corrected for the expansion of U.S. trade with other countries and the U.S. labor force expansion, they would have found a large drop in tax revenues due to the early sixties' tax cuts. If so, one would be inclined to believe that a tax rate cut today would also decrease tax revenues.[10]

What if a cut in tax rates does cause tax revenues to fall? Professor Laffer claims that even if a 10 percent cut in tax rates is not completely self-financing immediately, the economic growth it would generate would make up for lost tax revenues in less than two years. But what happens meanwhile? If the government does not decrease spending to match the decrease in revenues, then the Treasury has to increase the deficit, selling bonds to the public or to the Federal Reserve Bank. If it sells bonds to the public, it must at some future date increase taxes to redeem those bonds. Selling bonds to the Federal Reserve Bank will increase inflation, which is also a tax, and thus although the income tax cut would change the tax *structure* it would not necessarily reduce total taxation. Then Laffer's whole argument would collapse. True, the lower income tax rate would encourage production, but the higher anticipated future taxes or the inflationary tax would discourage production. The net effect on production could be positive, negative, or zero.[11]

If we want to argue for a tax cut, we cannot depend on Laffer's claim that the government would not have to cut spending. Nor do we need to. There are many other good reasons for cutting taxes. Taxation takes from us what is ours and denies our freedom to use our income in any peaceful way we see fit. It denies our civil liberties[12] and reduces our material well-being.[13] Taxation has made it easier for the government to wage war abroad.[14] These are reasons enough for a tax cut.

In addition, to say that one must call for spending cuts as well as tax cuts is not to say that spending cuts must come first. In fact, if we wait for spending cuts, we may never get tax cuts. A better strategy for reducing taxation would be and has been to cut taxes first and let the legislators and special interests bicker over who gets what. This strategy has been easier to accomplish at the state level[15] (because most states facing debt limits cannot respond to a tax cut by increasing their deficit), but it would be at least partly effective at the federal level also. Presumably the federal government's ability to run deficits would be somewhat constrained, although a constitutional amendment requiring the federal government to balance its budget would certainly help. But the argument for tax cuts on the basis of the Laffer Curve is a castle made of sand.

## APPENDIX

### Part A

Assume that "the" marginal tax rate, that is, the weighed average of all individuals' marginal rates, is 40 percent and the average tax rate is 30 percent. Assume that national income is $1,000. Therefore tax revenues are $300.

A 10 percent tax rate cut reduces the marginal tax rate to 30 percent and the average to 27 percent. If national income remained constant, tax revenues would decrease by 10 percent, from $300 to $270. Laffer refers to this as the "arithmetic" effect. But the added incentive to work would increase the tax base. The new income generated would be taxed at the marginal rate of 36 percent. Thirty dollars in new tax revenues must be forthcoming to keep tax revenues constant. Therefore national income must increase by $30/.36 or $83.33, or 8.33 percent.

The after-tax wage from each additional dollar earned increases from 60 cents to 64 cents, or by 6.67 percent. For income to increase by 8.33 percent, the elasticity of labor supply (which equals the percentage change in labor supplied divided by the percentage change in wage) must be 1.25.

## Part B

Assume that all women are married and women's average work time per week is twenty hours. Assume all men work forty hours. Assume that men's labor supply elasticity is zero and women's is 2. Assume that working women's wages are 60 percent of men's. Assume that national income is $1,000.

When the marginal and average rates fall from 40 and 30 percent respectively, men work the same amount but women work more. Women's after-tax wage increases by 6.67 percent (as in Part A), and they respond by working 13.34 percent more (since their elasticity is 2), or 2.67 hours more per week. Weekly income in the economy increases by $(2.67 \times .6) \div [(20 \times .6) + 40]$, or 3.1 percent.

Tax revenues were $300 before the tax cut (30 percent of $1,000) and would have fallen to $270 had the tax cut not increased the tax base. Since income increases by $31 (3.1 percent of $1,000), new tax revenues of $11.16 (equal to $.36 \times $31$) are generated, so that tax revenues end up at $281.20. The net effect is still a substantial reduction in tax revenues.

# Notes

1. Arthur B. Laffer, "Government Exactions and Revenue Deficiencies," *Cato Journal*, 1 (Spring 1981): 1.

2. Professor Moszer (Max Moszer, "A Comment on the Laffer Model," *Cato Journal*, 1 [Spring 1981]: 23) challenges the idea that people can choose their hours of work, referring to "arbitrary, institutional restraints on both the maximum and minimum number of hours and/or days that can, or need, be marketed." He correctly points out that a person has some difficulty in choosing his hours, but it does not follow that the constraints on hours are arbitrary. Such constraints, where they are not imposed by law, probably represent the preferences of the average or median worker. If most workers' preferences about hours shift, as they would with a general income tax cut, then so would the institutional constraint since entrepreneurs would compete with each other in choosing working hours that fit their employees' preferences. Even if the constraints are legally imposed, lowering tax rates would increase the incentive to get around them. Moreover, the fact that men's and women's hours of work vary and that their labor supply elasticities are often found to be nonzero is evidence that they can choose their hours.

3. The marginal tax rate is purposely set high in order to bias the case in Laffer's favor. The higher the marginal rate, the larger the percentage of increase in after-tax wages as a result of a tax cut, and the bigger the incentive effect. To take two extreme cases, a 10 percent cut in the marginal rate from 90 percent to 81 percent raises the after-tax wage from 10 percent to 19 percent of the gross wage, or by 90 percent. A 10 percent cut in a 10 percent marginal rate from 10 percent to 9 percent raises the after-tax wage from 90 percent to 91 percent of the gross wage, or by only 1.1 percent.

4. *See* Glen G. Cain and Harold W. Watts, "Toward a Summary and Synthesis of the Evidence," in Cain and Watts, eds., *Income Maintenance and Labor Supply*, Institute for Research on Poverty Monograph Series (Chicago: Rand McNally, 1973), pp. 332-35.

5. *See* James P. Smith, ed., *Female Labor Supply: Theory and Estimation* (Princeton, N.J.: Princeton University Press, 1980).

6. *See* Appendix, Part B, for a sample calculation using a women's labor supply elasticity of 2.

7. Moszer, "A Comment on the Laffer Model," p. 25.

8. V. A. Canto, D. H. Joines, and R. I. Webb, "Empirical Evidence on the Effects of

Tax Rates on Economic Activity," *Proceedings of the Business and Economics Statistics Section: 1979* (Washington, D.C.: American Statistical Association, 1979).

9. Charles A. Nelson, *Applied Time Series Analysis for Managerial Forecasting* (San Francisco: Holden Day, 1973); and "The Predictive Performance of the FRB-MIT-PENN Model of the U.S. Economy," *American Economic Review* 62 (October 1972): 902-17.

10. I am pleased to note that in the transition from his oral presentation to his written paper, Laffer has dropped his use of evidence of revenue increases following tax rate cuts in Puerto Rico and California. As I stated in Chicago during my discussion of his oral presentation and as he now points out, because of high labor mobility within a country and low labor mobility between countries (due largely, although he does not mention it, to immigration barriers), the elasticity of factor supply to a locality is much higher than to the country as a whole. Therefore a tax cut within, say, a state, would lead to a greater relative inflow of labor and a greater relative increase in the tax base than a tax cut for the whole nation.

11. Milton Friedman also makes this argument in "The Kemp-Roth Free Lunch," *Newsweek*, August 7, 1978, p. 59.

12. *See* Ronald Hamowy, "The IRS and Civil Liberties: Powers of Search and Seizure," *Cato Journal*, 1 (Spring 1981): 225.

13. *See* Jude Wanniski, *The Way the World Works* (New York: Simon and Schuster, 1978).

14. *See* Lloyd Dumas, "Taxes and Militarism," *Cato Journal*, 1 (Spring 1981): 277.

15. For instance, when tax indexing reduced projected 1981 revenue in Minnesota, the governor pushed an 8 percent spending cut (*Wall Street Journal*, January 14, 1981).

# Chapter 5:
# Supply-Side Factors in Macroeconomic Models

## A Time for Supply Economics

### Otto Eckstein

The current recession poses an extraordinary opportunity to put the U.S. economy on a better development path for the 1980s. The severity of the decline makes fiscal stimulus inevitable, particularly given the $73 billion two-year swing in the full-employment budget (Table 1), with new energy taxes raising $25 billion by 1981, payroll taxes up an extra $23 billion, and inflation boosting personal taxes by $28 billion, the economy would be sustaining the most severe tax increases attempted since the outbreak of World War II. We need a balanced budget badly, but the program of tax increases now on the books cannot be implemented fully in the midst of a severe recession.

How should the fiscal plan be modified? We have learned the bitter lesson that aggressive policies against recession have been among the principal causes of the present economic impasse. Policies of successful stimulus ended with the tax cut of 1964. The major moves since then, whether they were the New Economic Program of 1971 or the hastily conceived antirecession spending programs of 1975-78, precipitated excess demand which worsened core inflation and ultimately necessitated credit crunches and painful recessions. If history is any guide, the traditional approach of rushing to fight recession with across-the-board tax reductions and abandonment of budget discipline can only lead to a repeat of the cycle: quicker recovery of 1981-82, to be followed by higher core inflation, another boom, a third round of OPEC prices increases, and another credit crunch and recession.

I believe that virtually every responsible observer of the economic scene, whether economist, businessman or political leader, understands this basic situation and is not at all anxious to continue to pursue the pattern of policies that has worked so badly in the last 15 years. But what should be done? Here, too, I believe there is a general agreement among serious people covering a broad range of the political spectrum: the next set of economic policies must deal with our fundamental problems, namely, the lack of productivity growth, worsening core inflation, decline in our international competitive position, absence of progress in family living standards, and a weakened leadership role for the United States.

*TABLE 1*

RECENT BUDGET ACTIONS: A DETAILED VIEW OF CURRENT POLICY

[Calendar years, billions of dollars]

|  | 1978 | 1979 | 1980 | 1981 |
|---|---|---|---|---|
| Full-employment[1] budget surplus or deficit (—) | −29.9 | −12.4 | 1.2 | 51.0 |
| Change from previous year . . . . . . . . . . . . . . . . | 4.5 | 17.5 | 13.6 | 49.8 |
| Due to: |  |  |  |  |
| Expenditure cuts[2] (— indicates cut) . . . . . . | 1.2 | 6.0 | −7.0 | 12.1 |
| Inflation-induced personal[3] tax increases . . | 5.7 | 8.7 | 12.4 | 12.9 |
| Social insurance tax rise . . . . . . . . . . . . . . . | 8.0 | 10.1 | 5.6 | 17.1 |
| Windfall profits tax (net) . . . . . . . . . . . . . . |  |  | 6.1 | 8.9 |
| Oil import levy, gas tax . . . . . . . . . . . . . . . |  |  | 7.1 | 2.8 |
| Other . . . . . . . . . . . . . . . . . . . . . . . . . . . . . . | −1.4 | 1.4 | 2.5 | −4.0 |
| Tax cuts (—)[4] . . . . . . . . . . . . . . . . . . . . . . . | −9.0 | −8.7 | −13.1 | 0 |

1. Assumes 6.1 percent full-employment unemployment rate.
2. Dollar magnitude of the change in the full-employment expenditure-to-GNP ratio.
3. Assumes an elasticity of personal taxes with respect to taxable income of 1.5.
4. This item also includes the impact of the Revenue Act of 1978 and the 1977 tax cut.

## The New Supply Economics

The intellectual capital available to deal with long-term problems is (a body of knowledge) known as "supply economics." While supply antedates demand in the history of economic thought starting with the work of Adam Smith (1776) and stretching to John Stuart Mill (1848), and always retained at least an equal share with demand in the field of microeconomics, it must be acknowledged that demand overshadowed supply in macroeconomic analysis since the Great Depression and the rise of Keynesian national income analysis (1936). In the serious academic literature, however, supply theory regained prominence rather quickly: the path-breaking growth model of R. F. Harrod (1939) analyzed, at least in a primitive way, the need to match the growth of aggregate supply and aggregate demand, and the model of Domar (1946) introduced Harrod's ideas into the American literature. The modern theory of growth initiated by Solow (1956) revived the aggregate production function of Cobb-Douglas, showed its central role in the economy, and launched a search for better aggregate production functions. Even in the Keynesian years, the input-output analysis of Wassily Leontief (1939) offered theoretical and empirical models which had a production and supply focus. Kuznets's studies on economic development, Kendrick's and Denison's analyses of growth and productivity, Schultz's and Becker's work on human capital, and a large body of writings by Griliches, Jorgenson and many other scholars made the 1950s and 1960s the most fertile decades for the scientific study of the supply-side of the economy.

However, this body of work had little impact on the macroeconomics used for policy. Aggregate demand seemed to be the determining factor of output and the price level in the postwar decades. The growth of aggregate supply could be modeled adequately by the simplest productivity calculations, multiplying labor supply by a productivity trend derived by historical extrapolation. Okun's Law, which was based at least implicitly on these productivity projections, seemed perfectly adequate to identify the gap between aggregate demand and aggregate supply, to estimate the unemployment rate and to help set the gauges for fiscal policy. The great tax cut of 1964 was derived from Okun's Law estimates of the "gap" divided by accepted estimates of the multiplier on personal tax cuts. Even in the immediate years after 1965, when demand became excessive and highly sophisticated methods for estimating aggregate production functions were available, the simpler methods seemed to suffice: taxes should have been higher, but it was not a shortcoming of economic analysis that made policy wrong.

The large-scale econometric models which began to take over the tasks of policy analysis in the early 1970s did contain some supply-side elements: aggregate production functions, sophisticated equations for investment and capital stocks, detailed measures of industrial production and capacity, and equations for the availability of finance. But the production functions used were still relatively simple and unresponsive, following the Cobb-Douglas tradition in which the link of investment to potential output is relatively weak and slow, and the technology residual is exogenous and impervious to policy. Energy was not in the picture, of course.

The decade of the 1970s posed different and increasingly serious challenges to macroeconomic analysis. The worldwide boom of 1971-73 produced acute shortages of capacity in the materials-producing industries even though aggregate measures did not signal shortages. The OPEC revolution of 1973 and the subsequent surges of world oil prices had devastating effects on the economic performance of the entire industrial world. The end of productivity growth in 1973 and the resultant explosion of employment repealed Okun's Law or any simple calculation of the productivity trend.

These changes posed a challenge to economic policy which has produced several disparate responses. The first was a call for economic planning, to assure that specific shortages of individual commodities would never again abort general economic growth. The Humphrey-Hawkins movement sought analyses, reports, and policy commitments which would have enlarged the degee of government responsibility for the assurance of supplies in the private economy. The culmination of this movement was the passage of a watered down Humphrey-Hawkins Act, whose main product so far has been the embarrassment of defining unattainable goals.

A more recent strand of supply-oriented economic policy owes its origin to Colin Clark, the distinguished Australian econometrician who first advanced the thesis in the late 1940s that a tax burden in excess of 25 percent would lead to inflation. He argued that higher tax burdens would discourage saving and work, reduce the supply of output, and nullify the Keynesian effects of demand restraint. The Clark thesis fell on deaf ears, perhaps because many western countries pushed past the 25 percent tax limit without apparent damage to economic performance. The important set of studies conducted in the early 1950s by the Harvard Business School on the effects of taxation on work and investment also induced complacency by finding those effects to be small and of uncertain direction. However, a series of theoretical and econometric studies by Feldstein and others began to find more important tax and transfer disincentive effects. By 1975 the Clark idea was revived by Laffer, Wanniski, and Roberts, who emphasized the disincentive effects of excessively high marginal tax rates. In the more extreme form embodied in the "Laffer Curve" the thesis became the basis of the Kemp-Roth movement, which would cut taxes without any restraining offset such as lower government spending or tighter money on the theory that the benefits to aggregate supply would outweigh the boost to demand.

### Supply-Side Economics in the Data Resources, Inc. Model

The supply features in the Data Resources, Inc. model are described in the report recently prepared for the Joint Economic Committee, "Tax Policy and Core Inflation."[1] The idea of supply is so pervasive in economics that over half of the 800 equations in the model could be characterized as supply-oriented. However, the supply issues that pertain to policy are far more limited. Table 2 describes the critical supply policy features in the current Data Resources, Inc. model. Some features have always been part of the model, while others have been developed in the last year. The effects of corporate tax changes on investment have long been established in the scientific literature and are fully modeled, using Data Resources, Inc.'s modification of the neoclassical Jorgenson theory of investment which adds more explicit financial effects and a more elaborate output expectations mechanism. Data Resources, Inc.'s inclusion of the effects of personal tax levy is relatively new. Previous econometric models made little allowance for the effects emphasized by Clark, Feldstein, Laffer and others because the literature was still very limited. Data Resources, Inc. chose its current parameters after extensive exploration over various historial periods of estimation and alternate specifications. The parameters chosen were representative, not outliers in the statistical experiments.

The table also shows that the modeling of supply economics is far from complete. There is little in the model at this stage to represent the effects of taxes and social security on personal saving. Research on the effects of the tax system on the valuation of common stocks and the resultant impact on portfolio choices and corporate finance is at too

TABLE 2

Summary of Tax Effects on Supply in the DRI Model

| Tax | Equations | Results of statistical testing | Description of tax effects on DRI model |
|---|---|---|---|
| Corporate income tax rate. | Investment, macro and industries, R. & D. | Well-established effect using Jorgenson theory | Affects rental price of capital and cash flow. Elasticity of investment with respect to revenue is −0.28 over the 1982-85 period. |
| Depreciation lives | Investment, R. & D. | Same | Same. Elasticity is −1.13. |
| Investment tax credit | Investment on equipment, R.&D. | Same | Same. Elasticity is −0.90. |
| Personal taxes | Labor supply | Significant at 5 percent level, using average effective rate of personal income and personal payroll taxes. Transfer payments affect supply of workers over 65 and of women aged 25 to 44. Period of fit affects parameter. Value in model is typical. | Elasticity of labor with respect to tax burden is −0.04. Elasticity of labor with respect to tax-induced change in real wages is −0.20. |
|  | Potential output | Average effective burden of personal and payroll taxes is significant at significance level of 5 percent. Choice of period affects parameter, DRI model uses typical value obtained over various intervals and various specifications. | Elasticity of potential output with respect to personal tax rate is −0.05. Extra potential raises productivity and lowers inflation. |
|  | Savings deposits and bond holdings of households. | Savings flows affected by disposable income and by after tax interest return. | Principally affects mortgage market and residential construction. |
|  | Wages | Payroll tax burden has impact on compensation per hour. | Higher compensation affects prices and core inflation. |

early a stage to identify reliable equations. In addition, investment in human resources is not yet modeled explicitly. The remaining residuals time trends in the potential output and productivity equations are a measure of the analytical tasks still to be fulfilled.

## Illustrative Simulations of Supply-Oriented Tax Policies

In order to use the new analytical tools in the current policy context, it is first necessary to define the basic supply multipliers or elasticities which show the effects of the policies on the critical dimensions of the economy. A series of model simulations has been run to illustrate these tools.

In running these exercises, it is important to distinguish simulations in which supply measures are analyzed on the "different incidence" basis long established in the public finance literature from simulations in which both supply and demand effects are allowed to occur. The differential incidence method requires that an offset be defined which neutralizes the Keynesian aggregate demand effects. Pure supply multipliers can only be demonstrated if the total levy of activity is held constant by an offsetting policy of restraint.

### Broad personal tax reduction without offset under different economic circumstances

A typical Kemp-Roth-type proposal, representing a 30 percent reduction of the personal income tax staged over three years, has been simulated without any offsetting measure of restraint. The real level of government purchases is left unchanged, and a neutral monetary policy is represented by an expansion of bank reserves which leaves real interest rates unchanged.

The first simulation applies the policy in an economy which is experiencing full resource utilization. Unemployment averages 6 percent in the base case. Other economic conditions are drawn from the actual situation of today, including an assumption of OPEC price increases of $6 in 1981 and $8 in 1982. Legislated domestic oil and gas decontrol will add to further energy increases. Social security tax hikes are another significant shock. The total shock inflation is estimated to average 2 percent for the next three years. The results of this simulation are summarized in Table 2.[2] As is to be expected, the increase in consumer purchasing power created by the tax cuts drives the economy into a state of excess demand and worsened inflation. Low unemployment drives up wages by an extra 1 percent a year; high utilization of industrial capacity hurts delivery conditions and raises wholesale prices 1.6 percent a year. The GNP deflator is up by 1.8 percent by 1985. The Federal Reserve, under the rule of constant real interest rates, accommodates the inflation by providing the reserves for the higher rate of money growth.

There are important supply effects, to be sure. Potential GNP is up by 1.9 percent by 1985, and productivity is boosted by a similar amount. The labor supply increases by 300,000 people by 1985 because of the eased tax burden, a contributing factor to the better advance of potential. The capital stock also grows more rapidly despite the reduction focused on the personal tax side. Higher activity creates more profits and higher output expectations, thereby boosting investment by 3.3 percent a year. Higher demand and supply effects raise real GNP by 2.6 percent by 1985, compared to an increase in the price level of 5.0 percent, or an average of 0.5 percent a year for growth and 1.0 percent a year for inflation. Core inflation is worse by 1.1 percent in 1985.

While there is a net benefit to potential and actual output, the major effect of this particular package for boosting both supply and demand is to make inflation worse. The actual inflation rate is driven up over a few years because of the high level of demand. The core inflation rate worsens later because of the slow process by which the price expectations underlying the core are focused. However, if the basic goal of new policies is to escape from the current 9+ percent core inflation rate, the deterioration created in this critical measure of economic performance would make this particular policy option unattractive in the circumstances analyzed.

When this type of tax proposal is viewed in the context of a deep recession, the trade-offs become somewhat more favorable, though inflation is still worsened to an unacceptable degree (Table 3). To analyze this case, a deep recession scenario was used as the baseline, and the above exercise was repeated. In an economy with slack, the tax cut creates less inflation and a larger boost in output. The increase in the inflation is 0.7 percent a year, and real output growth is also boosted by 0.7 percent a year. The supply effects are a little better in the slacker economy; the 5-year rise in the level of potential output is an extra 2.2 percent compared to the 1.9 percent boost in the base case.

These simulation experiments show that very large tax cuts without offset even in a recession economy have a serious unfavorable effect on prices. The effect of tax cuts without an offsetting decline in government purchases is initially the stimulation the "recession" economy needs. Unfortunately, these "stimulative effects" outlast the need for stimulation and aggravate inflation.

### Personal tax reduction with full government spending offset

A simulation exercise based on the "differential incidence" method incorporating an offset to neutralize demand effects shows much safer results. A simulation was run in which a Kemp-Roth-type personal tax reduction was offset by reductions in federal nonmilitary purchases of goods and services of sufficient magnitude to keep the unemployment rate unchanged. Since the demand multiplier of government purchases is inevitably somewhat higher than for personal tax reduction, such a

TABLE 3
Personal Tax Reduction Without Offset

|  | 1981 | 1982 | 1983 | 1984 | 1985 |
|---|---|---|---|---|---|
| Policy change (change in billions of dollars): | | | | | |
| Personal tax revenues ........ | −29.9 | −66.7 | −115.5 | −127.1 | −137.1 |
| Federal deficit (NIA) ......... | −24.7 | −53.2 | −97.3 | −118.3 | −146.8 |
| Effects (percent difference in levels): | | | | | |
| Real GNP ................. | 0.7 | 1.8 | 2.8 | 2.6 | 2.6 |
| Real potential GNP .......... | .1 | .5 | 1.1 | 1.6 | 1.9 |
| Labor supply ............... | .1 | .3 | .4 | .4 | .3 |
| Productivity ............... | .2 | .6 | 1.4 | 1.8 | 1.9 |
| Difference in rates: | | | | | |
| Unemployment ............. | −.5 | −1.1 | −1.3 | −.9 | −.8 |
| Inflation rates: | | | | | |
| GNP deflator ............ | .1 | .5 | 1.2 | 1.8 | 1.8 |
| Core inflation ............ | .1 | .1 | 0 | .5 | 1.1 |
| Wages ................. | .1 | .7 | 1.4 | 1.7 | 2.0 |

TABLE 4
Personal Tax Reduction with no Offsetting Government Spending Reduction
[Lower base scenario]

|  | 1981 | 1982 | 1983 | 1984 | 1985 |
|---|---|---|---|---|---|
| Policy change (change in billions of dollars): | | | | | |
| Personal tax revenues ........ | −30.7 | −67.2 | −116.5 | −126.4 | −134.2 |
| Federal deficit (NIA) ......... | −25.3 | −52.9 | −93.6 | −105.1 | −121.6 |
| Effects (percent difference in levels): | | | | | |
| Real GNP ................. | 0.7 | 1.9 | 3.1 | 3.5 | 3.8 |
| Real potential GNP .......... | .1 | .5 | 1.1 | 1.7 | 2.2 |
| Labor supply ............... | .1 | .2 | .4 | .3 | .2 |
| Productivity ............... | .3 | .8 | 1.8 | 2.6 | 2.6 |
| Difference in rates: | | | | | |
| Unemployment ............. | −.3 | −1.0 | −1.3 | −.9 | −1.3 |
| Inflation rates: | | | | | |
| GNP deflator ............ | 0 | .3 | .7 | 1.3 | 1.2 |
| Core inflation ............ | −.1 | −.1 | −.1 | .2 | .6 |
| Wages ................. | .1 | .4 | .9 | 1.0 | 1.4 |

TABLE 5
*Personal Tax Reduction with Offsetting Government Spending Reduction*

|  | 1981 | 1982 | 1983 | 1984 | 1985 |
|---|---|---|---|---|---|
| Policy change (change in billions of dollars): |  |  |  |  |  |
| Personal tax revenues . . . . . . . | −32.9 | −75.5 | −131.8 | −154.4 | −178.1 |
| Federal deficit (NIA) . . . . . . . . | −20.3 | −41.0 | −65.7 | −65.6 | −68.6 |
| Government spending . . . . . . . | −11.6 | −31.2 | −59.6 | −79.8 | −99.6 |
| Effects (percent difference in levels): |  |  |  |  |  |
| Real GNP . . . . . . . . . . . . . . . | 0.1 | 0.4 | 0.9 | 1.3 | 1.6 |
| Real potential GNP . . . . . . . . . | .1 | .4 | .9 | 1.3 | 1.6 |
| Labor supply . . . . . . . . . . . . . | .1 | .1 | .2 | .2 | .2 |
| Productivity . . . . . . . . . . . . . | .1 | .3 | .7 | 1.2 | 1.6 |
| Difference in rates: |  |  |  |  |  |
| Unemployment . . . . . . . . . . . . | −0 | −0 | −0 | −.1 | −0 |
| Inflation rates: |  |  |  |  |  |
| GNP deflator . . . . . . . . . . . | −0 | −0 | −.2 | −.4 | −.2 |
| Core inflation . . . . . . . . . . . | −.1 | −.2 | −.4 | −.5 | −.5 |
| Wages . . . . . . . . . . . . . . . | −0 | −0 | −.1 | −.2 | −.2 |

package increases the government deficit somewhat. The simulation is summarized in Table 4.

The supply effects of personal tax reduction are important, and are little affected by the government spending cuts. The rate of growth of potential GNP is boosted by 0.3 percentage points, bringing it to a level of 1.6 percentage points higher by 1985. The labor force is enlarged by 200,000 individuals because of the lower tax burdens, and the annual rate of productivity growth is boosted by 0.3 percentage points. Both the actual inflation and the core rates are improved by an average of 0.2 percent, principally because of the better productivity performance.

## Personal tax reduction with monetary policy offset

If a large personal tax cut is combined with the monetarist approach to Federal Reserve policy, the beneficial supply effects are allowed to occur, though there are some offsetting reductions in the supply of capital, particularly the housing stock.

A simulation was run in which the Kemp-Roth type of personal tax cut was offset by monetary policy designed to neutralize the aggregate demand effects. To do this, the supply of bank reserves is reduced substantially, thus leading to severe tightness in credit markets. This simulation is summarized in Table 6.

The gain in potential GNP of this supply-oriented package is 0.25 percent a year, or 1.3 percent in the fifth year. Productivity is up by similar percentages. The demand for credit is stronger and interest rates are markedly higher. With the higher rates, a greater velocity is inevitable, and therefore the Federal Reserve has to lower its monetary target in response to the tax cut. Inflation is lowered, with the core rate cut by 0.2 percent.

The government deficit produced by this package is also quite worrisome. The higher interest rates neutralize the feedback revenues, so that the increase in the deficit is not much smaller than the size of the tax cuts themselves. In the third year, after the final step of the tax reductions has occurred, the deficit exceeds a hundred billion dollars and is mounting rapidly.

The composition of output is also affected. The housing industry suffers from the high interest rates, and so the average number of starts is reduced by 20 percent. On the other hand, real consumption is larger by 2.2 percent in 1985. Business fixed investment receives a small boost of 0.4 percent, which, along with the labor supply gain and the better productivity, combines to produce 0.25 percent a year pick-up in the growth of potential GNP.

### Corporate tax cuts of three kinds

The analysis of corporate tax cuts, whether in terms of rates, depreciation reform, or investment tax credits is well-established terrain in which the Data Resources, Inc. model reproduces the consensus results. Table 6 summarizes three exercises, all of them conducted on the differential incidence basis using a combination of personal tax increases and reduced government spending as the fiscal offsets. Real interest rates are left unchanged.

It can be seen that, in the neoclassical investment theory under which decisions are made on the basis of present value calculations, corporate rate cuts are less effective than investment tax credits or liberalized depreciation. The impact of incentives on the rate of return on investments is substantially greater, per dollar of tax relief, than across-the-board rate reductions which are largely paid out on the profits earned on investments of the past. The cash flow effects are similar for the three measures in the model, although in actuality the incentive measures focus the augmented cash flow more accurately on those companies that have the strongest investment opportunities.

Rate reduction has the most favorable effect on the equity cost of capital for investment. The model reflects the apparent reality of stock valuation by investors in which publicly reported after-tax earnings are the valuation basis. Investment tax credits and depreciation allowances tend not to be fully flowed through to reported earnings, and consequently give a lesser boost to stock prices. It should be recognized, however, that this is an assumed bit of irrationality on the part of the investors, in which they fail to perceive that the gap between

## TABLE 6
### Personal Tax Cut Accommodated By Monetary Policy That Keeps the Unemployment Rate Unaffected

|  | 1981 | 1982 | 1983 | 1984 | 1985 |
|---|---|---|---|---|---|
| Policy change (change in billions of dollars): |  |  |  |  |  |
| Personal tax revenues ........ | −32.6 | −74.8 | −130.6 | −152.5 | −174.7 |
| Federal deficit (NIA) ......... | −33.6 | −77.1 | −134.9 | −160.3 | −189.8 |
| Effects (percent difference in levels): |  |  |  |  |  |
| Real GNP .................. | 0.1 | 0.4 | 0.8 | 1.2 | 1.3 |
| Real potential GNP .......... | .1 | .4 | .8 | 1.2 | 1.3 |
| Labor supply................ | .1 | .1 | .2 | .2 | .2 |
| Productivity ................ | 0 | .3 | .7 | 1.1 | 1.3 |
| Difference in rates: |  |  |  |  |  |
| Unemployment.............. | −0 | −0 | −0 | −0 | −0 |
| Inflation rates: |  |  |  |  |  |
| GNP deflator ............. | −0 | −.1 | −.3 | −.5 | −.5 |
| Core inflation ............. | −.1 | −.2 | −.3 | −.4 | −.3 |
| Wages .................. | −0 | −0 | −.1 | −.2 | −.3 |

the taxes paid and taxes accrued is increased by the incentive measures.

In the report I prepared recently for this committee, a policy of sizable tax incentives in the form of depreciation reform and larger investment tax credits, was presented in some detail.[3] The conclusions showed that a set of measures which would reduce corporate tax accruals by 18 percent after three years would accomplish a reduction in the core inflation rate of 1 percent by the fifth year; other inflation rates would be similarly reduced. Since this tax package represents a much smaller revenue loss than the large personal tax reductions

## TABLE 7
### Effects of Various Corporate Income Tax Reductions

|  | Policy | | |
|---|---|---|---|
|  | Corporate tax rate | Investment tax rate | Depreciation reform |
| Percent change in levels (billions of 1972 dollars—1985): |  |  |  |
| Investment in producers' durable equipment | 2.6 | 9.4 | 12.0 |
| Stock of producers' durables ............. | 1.4 | 4.3 | 5.0 |
| Potential GNP ....................... | .2 | .6 | .7 |
| Percent change in rates—1985: |  |  |  |
| Implicit GNP deflator .................. | .2 | .2 | .2 |
| Core inflation ....................... | .2 | .4 | .7 |

analyzed above, it can be seen that corporate tax incentives are a much more efficient means to reduce the core inflation rate and boost the growth of potential GNP.

The reasons are several. Whereas personal tax reduction relies mainly on relatively modest increases of the supply of labor and improvements of productivity, the corporate tax incentives create sizable boosts in the capital stock and therefore in productivity and potential GNP. The scarce tax resources therefore seem to be used more effectively in the corporate area. Further, the U.S. economy is currently not suffering from a shortage of labor, but it is suffering from a shortage of industrial capacity. The long period of regulation since the 1960s and the several decades of an over-valued exchange rate which eroded the competitive position of our primary processing industries have produced a major imbalance in the economy's productive structure: essentially, there is too much labor for the existing industrial capital stock. Therefore, as the economy reaches prosperity, the utilization rate of industry is in the inflationary range event while unemployment remains over 6 percent. Personal tax reduction does not lead to significant relief from these industrial bottlenecks, whereas investment credits and depreciation reform directly focus the tax resources where they are needed, in industrial investment.

The relative efficiency of the various measures in augmenting potential GNP and in reducing inflation is shown in Table 8. This table shows the percentage reductions in the core inflation rate and the percentage increases in the level of potential GNP which can be achieved for every $1 billion of revenue reduction through personal tax cuts, depreciation reform, investment tax credits, and lower corporate rates. While the resultant ranking, which makes the corporate measures appear as far more efficient supply measures than personal tax reductions, is subject to the specifics of the parameters embodied in the Data Resources, Inc. model, it would take very drastic changes in these parameters to upset the conclusions. If we are serious

## TABLE 8
### Relative Efficiency of Supply-Side Tax Cuts[1]

| | Effect on potential GNP[2] | Effect on core inflation[3] |
|---|---|---|
| Personal tax cut | 0.16 | −0.003 |
| Cut in corporate tax rate | .38 | −.021 |
| Increase in investment tax credit | 1.60 | −.061 |
| Depreciation reform | 1.16 | −.070 |

1. Assumes government purchase offset.
2. Refined as increase in level of potential GNP or decrease in core inflation rate both per dollar loss of total revenue, for the year 1985.
3. Change in core inflation rate per billion of tax cut for the year 1985.

about getting productivity going again, enhancing our international competitiveness and returning the economy to a normal growth path, major changes in taxation of industry must be the initial step.

This is not to argue that the tax reduction which will surely occur during this recession should be entirely focused on the corporate side. The personal tax burden has risen so rapidly, by over 50 percent on the typical worker in the last 15 years, that equity considerations alone would more than justify early personal tax reductions. Further, there is not much doubt left that a tax burden is discouraging participation in the labor force and affecting productivity adversely. Even if the measured efficiency and augmenting supply is less for the personal tax reduction than for the corporate cuts, a mix of the two is still justified. The 50-50 split between personal and corporate tax reduction recommended in this committee's 1980 report (p. 44) is a sound combination. This leaves room for major tax incentives for investment, as well as providing some meaningful relief for workers. I urge you to focus the personal cuts on the middle brackets of workers, in the $10,000-$25,000 income range, rather than to provide additional relief to the upper-income brackets that gained under the tax reform act of 1978, or the low-income brackets where the burden has been cut very sharply over the last decade.

### Concluding comments

The interplay of new ideas with new problems is an exciting undertaking for the economists, legislators, and officials responsible for the development and conduct of economic policy. We are at one of those great moments where the opportunity to reverse the steady slide of our economic system exists, and where new ideas are being offered to accomplish the turnaround. So far, the administration has firmly applied the good old ideas of demand restraint and credit scarcity to create the recession and unemployment necessary to take the immediate inflationary steam out of the economy. Having paid the political price of starting the recession, and making the society pay the human price, the administration and the Congress now have the opportunity to reap the benefits of the recession and apply new ideas to get a solid start on the solution of our long-term problems.

Unfortunately, we must recognize the uncertainty which attaches to the supply-side ideas. It would be a gamble with our economic system to go all out with massive supply-side tax cuts which can succeed in accomplishing their goals only if the most extreme values are assumed for the critical supply multipliers.

Under the parameters built into the Data Resources, Inc. model, based on a careful but limited research of the historical record, the contribution of supply-side measures is fundamental, but not sufficient to permit disregard of the demand side of the problems. On average, we need a greater degree of demand restraint than we have seen in the last 15 years. Despite the recession, a shift toward fiscal restraint, as measured by the full-employment budget, is still needed.

The scheduled tax increases in a recession environment create the necessity for some stimulative fiscal move. Supply economics dictates that the actions be focused on the tax side. Incentives for industrial capital formation should be at the top of the agenda.

If we provide greater incentives for business to invest and greater incentives for individuals to work, we can make a good start toward making the 1980s a decade of improvement.

## Notes

1. Otto Eckstein, "Tax Policy and Core Inflation," a study prepared for the U.S. Congress, Joint Economic Committee, April 1980.

2. Appendices elaborating the data in Tables 2-6 may be found in Otto Eckstein, "A Time for Supply Economics," in *Forecasting the Supply Side of the Economy*, hearings before the U.S. Congress, Joint Economic Committee, May 21, 1980.

3. Eckstein, "Tax Policy and Core Inflation."

# The Supply-Side of the Economy: A View From the Perspective of the Wharton Model

Lawrence R. Klein

It is no coincidence that I entitled my presidential address to the American Economic Association (December, 1977) "The Supply Side."[1] That presentation was motivated by the large effort that had been in place all during the 1970s in building a full supply side to the Wharton model. Nothing could be further from the truth than the charges that mainstream, large scale econometric models neglect the supply-side of the economy.

The reason the Wharton forecast fully anticipated the recessionary impact of the 1973 oil embargo and subsequent price escalation in energy markets is that supply limitations were imposed on the projections from the Wharton model in October, 1973. These constraints were fully explained in a paper entitled "Supply Constraints in Demand Oriented Systems: An Interpretation of the Oil Crisis" delivered in Vienna (January, 1974).[2]

Another reason why Wharton Econometric Forecasting Associates have emphasized supply-side modelling for such a long time is that we recognize the inability of aggregative demand management policies to deal fully with the economic problems of our times. This is not to deny the importance of demand-side policies. They are necessary but not sufficient. After they have been put in place in an appropriate way, we must turn attention to policies for the thorny issues of achieving better energy balance between supply and demand, protecting the environment, achieving an equitable distribution of income, increasing productivity, stemming inflation, and stabilizing the dollar. To achieve these multiple goals, we must look far beyond demand management. That is an accepted point of view among many econometricians and finds its place in the opening statement of the final version of the Humphrey-Hawkins Bill.

## Supply-Side Content in the Wharton Model

There are two Wharton models dedicated to explanation of U.S. economic activity. One model is quarterly and focuses on short run business cycle analysis. The other is annual and emphasizes trend analysis, for decades or longer periods, in yearly steps. It is the latter model that has the principal supply-side emphasis in the Wharton group, but both the short and long run models have a great deal of supply-side content.

The centerpiece of the Wharton annual model is an input-output sector with some 56 sectors in a square array, showing inputs in up and down columns and outputs across rows. Input-output systems by themselves contain large amounts of supply-side information from the point of view of technology and capacity limitations on the economy but are used in the Wharton model in a way that contributes particularly to supply-side phenomena. The coefficients in the table are not fixed, as in conventional input-output analyses, but are variables. They vary according to shifts in relative prices. This feature has been especially important for interpreting technical changes from the supply-side as a result of large shifts in relative prices of energy products. By using the input-output system in this way, the Wharton model was able to predict a decline in the national ratio of energy use to GNP, a crucial development that has been going on at a significiant pace since the embargo of 1973.

Not only has the Wharton model made projections of shifting patterns of energy use since 1973, but it has also studied the impact of energy on the economy by relating energy import prices to domestic inflation with slower real growth. What has been true of energy has also been the case for other basic material markets including agricultural products. Energy, materials, capital, and labor costs all impact on domestic prices in the model. These impacts are moderated by productivity gains or accentuated by productivity losses. Factor productivities are also important variables in the Wharton model, generated by technical production function relationships.

The supply of goods, whether as inputs or as outputs, reflects the forces operating on the supply-side of the economy. The supply of factors of production also contributes to the supply-side analyses. In this respect, the Wharton model goes far in developing equations for labor supply. Population, labor force participation, and unemployment are all generated by (1) age and (2) sex groupings. Fundamental demographic processes of birth and death are partly responsible for population and labor force estimates, but real wages, disposable income, and unemployment rates are important economic variables in these relationships. These three variables are used for the labor supply function of the Wharton quarterly model. The annual model uses only the unemployment rate, in a lag distribution, at the present time.

A great deal of attention attaches these days to the effect of taxation on economic incentive. Indeed, the proper meaning of supply-side economics is often distorted by being interpreted solely as a reflection of tax-related incentives. In its proper place, the Wharton model relates tax rates to labor supply. The equations of labor force participation show that supply of effort responds inversely to indirect taxation because such imports lower the real wage incentive (by raising the denominator). In general, indirect tax increases (other things unchanged) lead to lower real output and employment. This is why OPEC increases of crude oil prices restrain output and spur inflation. This is a perfectly natural model result and has been a feature of our analysis for the past seven years.

Direct taxes also enter the equations of labor supply. As real disposable income per capita rises, labor supply tends to fall. This is a classical economic phenomenon known as the "backward bending supply curve of labor." Disposable income subtracts taxes from gross personal receipts; therefore, as taxes fall, disposable income rises and (with a distributed time lag) labor supply slackens.

Special tax incentives—investment tax credit, accelerated depreciation charges, and employment tax credits—all work in the same direction. As the incentives are increased, production and employment rise. There will be cyclical gains in productivity and consequently tendencies to restrain inflationary pressures. In the case of investment incentives, there will be additional gains in the form of trend increases in productivity. In the medium term this enhances real growth and restrains inflation.

The Wharton Index of Capacity Utilization has been in use for almost twenty years as an indicator of supply-side economic restraint. On many occasions, we in the Wharton group have disputed other index measurements that gave misleading impressions about abundance of spare capacity in the economy. The Wharton index has served well in providing early warnings about inflationary pressures associated with escalation of the military effort in Vietnam, the commodity price explosion of 1973, and the expansion of 1977-79. By its very construction, the Wharton index is more sensitive to supply limitations than are other indexes because it is indirectly associated with general equilibrium throughout all the sectors of the economy as a whole. In the Wharton quarterly model, capacity output is endogenously generated by the production functions of the system; therefore, capacity output and the degree of capacity utilization are integral parts of the system, feeding into productivity and investment. This methodology is fully documented and explained in an article "Direct Estimates of Unemployment Rate and Capacity Utilization in Macroeconometric Models."[3] This indicates that capacity constraint problems have long been recognized as important in the structure of the Wharton model and have contributed much to inflation analysis. It is simply incorrect to state that the supply-side has been neglected.

## Some Supply-Side Sensitivities of the Wharton Model

To illustrate how supply-side effects work their way through the Wharton model, let us consider changes in assumptions about oil prices. In a baseline forecast over the period 1981-1989 (prepared in November, 1979) the world oil price was assumed to increase on average by 9.0 percent. In an alternative projection, we increased this price trajectory to the average rate of 12.3 percent.

TABLE 1
Effects of Alternative Oil Prices
[In percent]

|  | 1980 | 1981 | 1982 | 1983 | 1984 | 1985 | 1986 | 1987 | 1988 | 1989 |
|---|---|---|---|---|---|---|---|---|---|---|
| Baseline price .. | 24.9 | 13.8 | 9.0 | 9.0 | 9.0 | 9.0 | 9.0 | 9.0 | 9.0 | 9.0 |
| Higher price alternative ...... | 24.9 | 14.7 | 10.3 | 11.9 | 14.3 | 13.7 | 12.5 | 12.0 | 12.0 | 12.0 |
| Baseline GNP .. | 0 | 3.4 | 3.1 | 2.8 | 3.3 | 2.9 | 3.0 | 2.7 | 2.8 | 2.7 |
| Alternative GNP | 0 | 3.3 | 2.9 | 2.7 | 3.0 | 2.4 | 2.8 | 2.5 | 2.5 | 2.6 |
| Baseline inflation | 9.1 | 8.2 | 8.1 | 7.5 | 7.0 | 6.5 | 6.5 | 6.4 | 6.3 | 6.3 |
| Alternative inflation .......... | 9.1 | 8.2 | 8.3 | 7.7 | 7.4 | 7.0 | 7.1 | 7.1 | 7.0 | 7.0 |

On average, the real growth rate drops from 2.9 percent to 2.66 percent and the GNP deflator, as a measure of overall inflation, rises from an average of 7.33 percent versus 6.84 percent in the base case. Thus, the model produces quantitative estimates of the extent to which foreign oil price changes induce higher inflation and lower growth. Towards the end of the decade, the unemployment rate is a full point higher under the high price alternative and the productivity improvement factor runs about 0.1 to 2.0 percentage points lower. The all important energy/GNP ratio falls in both projections, but in the base case it reaches 46.8 (thousand BTU/GNP, 1972$) by 1989, while in the alternative it falls to a point as low as 45.55 (thousand BTU/GNP, 1972$). In terms of millions of BTU consumed per person the respective figures for 1989 are 359.4 versus 343.1, a saving of 4.5 percent.

A popular policy proposition depending on supply-side effects on the economy is the proposal to deal with the productivity slow down through investment expansion. The resulting investment outlays will simultaneously stimulate the economy (through the demand-side) and contribute to lesser inflationary pressures (through the supply-side—productivity gains) and work towards coping with stagflation.

Wharton model inputs were changed to reflect an increase in the investment tax credit from 10 to 20 percent and its extension to structures investment as well as equipment. The end result is an improved real growth rate, a lower inflation rate, and better yearly increments to productivity. The relevant figures are set out in Table 2, where the investment tax credit alternative is set beside the baseline solution of December, 1979. The investment tax credit policy was chosen for simplicity of application in the present exercise, but similar improvements could have been achieved through accelerated depreciation or other kinds of investment incentives.

According to Table 2, the increase in the investment tax credit raises the real growth rate by just under one-half percentage point for the first half of the decade, but the growth patterns of the two projections approximately converge after 1985. The improvements to productivity growth and inflation rate are more persistent and prevail for the whole decade.

### TABLE 2
### Effects of Investment Tax Credit

|  | 1980 | 1981 | 1982 | 1983 | 1984 | 1985 | 1986 | 1987 | 1988 | 1989 |
|---|---|---|---|---|---|---|---|---|---|---|
| Baseline GNP . . | −0.3 | 2.5 | 2.3 | 2.5 | 2.7 | 3.0 | 3.0 | 3.1 | 3.0 | 3.2 |
| Tax credit alternative . . . . . . . . | −.1 | 3.1 | 2.7 | 2.7 | 3.1 | 3.1 | 3.0 | 3.0 | 3.1 | 3.0 |
| Baseline inflation | 9.3 | 7.7 | 7.7 | 6.8 | 6.8 | 6.5 | 6.5 | 6.2 | 6.0 | 5.7 |
| Tax credit alternative . . . . . . . . | 9.3 | 7.5 | 7.5 | 6.6 | 6.5 | 6.1 | 6.2 | 5.9 | 5.6 | 5.3 |
| Baseline productivity . . . . . . . . . | −.5 | 1.9 | 1.2 | 1.2 | 1.3 | 1.5 | 1.4 | 1.5 | 1.4 | 1.6 |
| Tax credit alternative . . . . . . . . | −.4 | 2.2 | 1.4 | 1.4 | 1.6 | 1.6 | 1.5 | 1.6 | 1.7 | 1.6 |

### Taxes and Economic Incentives

Targeted reductions in taxes through investment credits, employment credits, or depreciation allowances all work, in the Wharton model, in the expected direction of increasing capital formation or employment. Also, cuts in indirect taxes hold down price indexes and stimulate final demand. These are well established tax effects and play important roles in the Wharton models—whether quarterly (short run) or annual (medium term). But to some economists and to many interested citizens, supply-side economics is, as we already noted, closely identified with general cuts in direct taxes.

Tax cuts stimulate the economy through expenditure increases on the demand side. This effect shows up clearly in demand-oriented models as a typical fiscal policy exercise. They contribute, in the very short run, to budget deficits (or lower surplus) and to general inflationary pressure. A new element has been injected into the ongoing economics debate through supply-side arguments that claim that lower tax rates will spur work incentives, raise productivity, increase public revenues, and, ultimately, restrain inflation.

Work incentives are subjective. While it is not impossible to establish their relationship to taxation, it is a very difficult process that cannot be validated by mere assertion. Some real evidence, beyond personal hunches, will have to be brought to bear on the argument in order to make the case convincing.

The assertion that lower rates of taxation induce more work effort has about the same status of scientific validation as the assertions, during 1978, that lower capital gains rates induce more funds for venture capital. It was not proven, on the former occasion, that subjective investment decisions respond inversely to capital gains rates. There is some plausibility to the hypothesis, but deep research would have to be undertaken to establish the relationship on a footing that equals our confidence in the relationships between investment and the targeted tax incentives mentioned earlier. There is a fair history of changes in investment tax incentives on which to base an estimate of the effects on capital formation. There is no comparable data base for changes in investment and changes in capital gains rates or for changes in work effort and changes in personal income tax rates.

Personal interviews of workers and examination of work place records would be needed, on a systematic sampling basis, in order to establish the kind of relationship that proponents of tax cutting think exists. If there were an independent increase in productivity as a result of tax reductions, the inflation factor could be reduced or held in restraint, but we do not know that this effect is well based in fact. There is some evidence for the "backward bending supply curve of labor," and this effect works in the opposite direction. It would be misleading to claim that this effect necessarily outweighs the effect that would increase productivity, but there is good evidence that the work-leisure trade-off is a real phenomenon.

## Some Tentative Responses

In calling these hearings, Senator Bentsen asked some searching questions.

BENTSEN: Do taxes, inflation, and government regulation have effects on the supply of labor, capital, and production which have not been adequately captured in recent years by demand-oriented econometric models?

KLEIN: Some of the better known econometric models have a great deal of supply-side content and are not as heavily demand-oriented as many people think. The effects of taxes, inflation, and government regulation are well understood in the investment process. Government regulation effects worker productivity and this is well shown in some models. The principal issue that remains to be settled in whether the rate of direct taxation has an effect one way or the other. The effects of indirect taxation are already included in some models.

BENTSEN: What areas on the supply-side offer the most intriguing prospects for investigation and research?

KLEIN: Econometric models are approximations to reality and can obviously be improved in the estimation of the supply-side effects that are already present. Much work needs to be done to improve and extend the treatment of government regulation for protection of the environment, maintaining competition, protection of health and safety. More of these regulations and their associated costs should be explicitly included. Supply limitations of energy and other resources should be given separate display in models. A number of these limitations have already been modeled, but there is room for a great deal of improvement, especially on the side of opening up new supplies. Definitive research projects for investigating effects of capital gains taxation, value added taxation, and the general levels of income taxation should be initiated.

The supply of savings, by type of asset/liability instrument and sector should be introduced into econometric models. This can be done most effectively by fully integrating a flow-of-funds system with a large supply/demand model.

BENTSEN: What traditional policy tools, approaches, or rules of thumb should be reassessed, modified or even scrapped in view of new understanding of supply-side factors?

KLEIN: There should be a recognition that the traditional inflation-unemployment trade-off is not a unique relation. An appropriate supply-side model, like the Wharton model, can produce a positive association between inflation and unemployment if price rises occur as a result of supply-side shocks. There should also be full recognition of the fact that demand management must be supplemented with supply-side policies dealing with structural changes if economic stability is to be achieved in the face of the kinds of problems that confront us at the present time.

BENTSEN: Can the government use the economics of incentives more skillfully in the future to deal with problems of productivity, inflation, and employment simultaneously instead of on an either-or basis?

KLEIN: In the first place, government should have multiple targets. It is possible to improve the prospects for productivity, inflation, and employment simultaneously. One of the most promising routes would be to introduce well-balanced investment incentives in the tax system, to establish youth differentials in the minimum wage, to roll back social security payroll tax increases, to streamline government regulation of the economy, to induce more energy conservation, and to enhance energy supplies. These are not comprehensive, but are main policy lines that could lead us far along the path to better stability of the economy.

# Notes

1. Lawrence R. Klein, "The Supply Side," *American Economic Review*, 68 (March 1978): 1-7.

2. Lawrence R. Klein, "Supply Constraints in Demand Oriented Systems: An Interpretation of the Oil Crisis," *Zeitschrift für Nationalökonomie*, 34 (March 1974): 45-56.

3. Lawrence R. Klein and Vincent Su, "Direct Estimates of Unemployment Rate and Capacity Utilization in Macroeconometric Models," *International Economic Review*, 20 (October 1979): 725-740.

# New Developments in Econometric Modeling: Supply-Side Economics

Michael K. Evans

For the past fifteen years the economic situation in the United States has been worsening. The average rate of inflation for the period from 1948 to 1965 was 2 percent; today it is close to 10 percent. Productivity increased at an average rate of 3 percent over that period; today it is stagnant or declining. Unemployment is far higher than it was during the 1950s and 1960s, while the maximum potential growth rate of the economy has slowed from 3.5 percent to 2.7 percent. The dollar, once the foundation of international commerce, has been chronically weak for over a decade.

The underlying cause of these problems has been a shift in resource allocation from investment to consumption, both private and public. For the past fifteen years, fiscal and monetary policies have tilted in the direction of subsidizing consumption and penalizing investment. We have had tax cuts, rebates, and a huge increase in the proportion of national resources devoted to transfer payments. When these pump-priming policies lead to excess demand, monetary policy is then invoked to reduce investment and cause a recession. This vicious cycle has led to an ever-increasing rate of inflation since 1965, with the end nowhere in sight.

To a certain extent, this cycle has been fueled by political consider-ations. Tax cuts for lower income individuals are easier to defend than tax cuts for businesses. Rebates are more "equitable" than tax cuts for upper income taxpayers, particularly those who save enough that they do not "need" further tax reduction. Increased social welfare benefits can be defended on the grounds that they reduce the suffering of the poor, the ill, and the aged. Furthermore, personal income tax cuts and transfers affect the economy with a shorter lag than do business tax cuts.

However, another reasoned that demand oriented policies have been used almost exclusively in the past 15 years is that all of the current large scale econometric models have indicated that these policies will have a more beneficial effect on the economy than will supply-side cuts. Embedded in these models is the implicit assumption that an increase in demand will automatically "trickle down" to increase aggregate supply, thus insuring balanced, noninflationary growth.

However, there is nothing magical about the balance between aggregate demand and supply. If incentives are lacking for investment, capital formation will stagnate. If incentives are lacking for labor, labor force participation will decline, the amount of labor offered by those already in the labor force will be reduced, and productivity will diminish. As a result, total productive capacity of the economy will grow more slowly than total demand, and bottlenecks, shortages and higher inflation will eventually result.

According to Keynesian demand economics, this higher inflation must then be fought by causing a recession and reducing aggregate demand. It is true the the gap between aggregate demand and supply must be widened in order to diminish inflationary pressures. However, surely there are two ways to accomplish the same aim. One is indeed to diminish demand, thereby causing higher unemployment. The other is to increase aggregate suppply, thereby raising the production possibility curve of the economy and increasing jobs and output at the same time that inflation is being lowered. This is the fundamental hypothesis underlying our supply-side modeling.

As already noted, most fiscal policy analysis of the past 15 years has been based on the belief that an increase in government spending will lead to a larger rise in demand and output than an equivalent reduction in taxes. The reasoning which leads to this conclusion is straightforward if inaccurate. If the government increases its spending, the entire dollar is used to raise aggregate demand. If taxes are cut, however, some of each dollar is used for saving. Since existing Keynesian models do not incorporate the links between saving and investment, demand does not rise as much.

Furthermore, these models also state that a personal income tax cut has a larger effect than a corporate income tax cut, and for much the same reason. Individuals spend a larger proportion of the extra money they receive from reduced taxes than do corporations, and that leftover saving does not contribute to economic growth or prosperity.

The supply-side model which we have built gives exactly the opposite result: an income tax cut has a larger effect on the economy than an increase in government spending. The supply-side mechanisms which support this conclusion can be qualitatively summarized as follows. In particular, a reduction in personal and corporate income taxes will set in motion the following chain of events.

1. An increase in the aftertax rate of return on personal saving occasioned by a reduction in personal income tax rates raises the incentives of individuals to save. This increase in saving leads to lower interest rates and higher investment.

2. A reduction in the effective corporate income tax rate, either through lower tax rates, a higher investment tax credit, or more liberal

depreciation allowances, improves capital spending directly by increasing the average rate of return.

3. An increase in both personal and corporate savings leads to greater liquidity and less loan demand, thereby lowering interest rates. These effects help both capital spending and residential investment.

4. A rise in the ratio of investment to GNP leads to higher productivity, which means that more goods and services can be produced per unit of input. As a result, unit costs do not rise as fast and inflation grows more slowly.

5. A reduction in personal income tax rates leads to a rise in labor force participation and work effort, thereby increasing the supply of labor necessary to produce more goods and services.

6. Thus labor supply, capital stock, and productivity are all increased by lower tax rates, thereby expanding the maximum productive capacity of the U.S. economy.

7. As a result of higher maximum capacity the inflationary pressures of shortages and bottlenecks diminish, thereby reducing the rate of inflation.

8. An increase in maximum capacity also permits the production of more goods and services for export markets. This improves our net foreign balance and strengthens the dollar, thus leading to lower inflation because imported goods decline rather than advance in price.

9. Lower personal income tax rates lead to smaller wage gains, since wage bargaining is based at least in part of the level of aftertax income. This in turn reduces inflation further.

10. Thus lower tax rates cause a reduction in inflation through several channels. Inflationary pressures decline as the gap between actual and maximum potential GNP rises; productivity increases, thereby lowering unit labor costs; the dollar strengthens, causing less imported inflation; and wage rates rise more slowly.

11. Lower inflation leads to higher real disposable income, since bracket inflation is mitigated. The rise in income leads to an increase in consumption, output and employment.

12. Lower inflation leads to lower interest rates, stimulating investment in both plant and equipment and in housing.

13. The increased demand for goods and services stemming from lower inflation is matched by the rise in the maximum potential capacity of the economy to produce these goods and services, thereby resulting in balanced, noninflationary growth.

We now comment briefly on the empirical evidence contained in the supply-side model for each one of these links.

The vast majority of previous empirical work on the consumption function implies that the interest rate has no significant effect on the proportion of disposable income which is consumed or saved. It is true that a simple correlation between the saving rate and the interest rate reveals no relationship. However, we have found a very strong link between the real aftertax rate of return and personal saving. After substantial testing, we have determined that this rate can best be represented by the long-term bond yield multiplied by (1—average tax rate on personal income) minus the average rate of inflation over the past four years. Thus defined, this rate of return is found to have an important effect on consumption and saving. Specifically, a 1 percent increase in the rate of return—e.g., from 3 percent to 4 percent—would raise saving by $12 billion. Furthermore, we find that the importance of the aftertax rate of return on saving has been increasing in recent years as interest rates and inflation move to higher levels.

An across-the-board $10 billion personal income tax cut from, say, 30 percent to 29 percent would have relatively little effect on saving over and above the increase stemming from higher income, although as we note later it would have a much larger effect on labor market behavior. However, the increase in saving from this tax cut due to the increased rate of return would be only about $1 billion. On the other hand, a tax cut of the same size which was targeted only to increase saving through a higher rate of return would result in a rise in saving of some $13 billion. Thus the form of the tax cut is all-important in determining the effect on consumption and saving.

Unlike the results of personal saving, existing econometric models already incorporate some positive relationship between increases in the rate of return on investment and capital spending. These increases can occur either through a decline in interest rates, a rise in stock prices, a reduction in the corporate income tax, an increase in the investment tax credit, more favorable treatment of depreciation allowances, or other tax benefits not specifically incorporated in our supply-side model. Where existing models have been deficient is in their inability to link changes in saving and investment, and changes in investment to productivity and economic growth.

Our results indicate that a $1 billion increase in aftertax profits, whether this occurs from a cut in income tax rates, an increase in the investment tax credit, or a reduction in depreciation lives, will raise fixed business investment by about $0.7 billion. We also found that a decline in interest rates by 1 percentage point—e.g., from 9 percent to 8 percent—would raise investment by $1.4 billion, while the increase in stock prices resulting from lower interest rates would raise investment by an additional $2.1 billion.

One of the most important sets of linkages in the supply-side model is the relationship between saving and investment. For if saving rises but these funds are just used to increase idle cash balances, investment may not expand. However, these links are well documented in our model.

A $10 billion increase in personal saving raises time deposits by $3.0 billion and thrift institution deposits by $1.6 billion. In addition, it reduces loan demand by $3.6 billion.

As a result of these changes in the balance sheet of commercial banks, demand for U.S. Government securities by the banks increases by $11.5 billion. This results in approximately 1 percent decline in interest rates and a 3.2 percent increase in stock market prices.

These changes have two related effects on investment. First, lower interest rates and higher stock prices stimulate fixed business investment. Second, easier credit increases housing starts and mobile homes and, to a lesser extent, producers' durable equipment.

As would be expected, nonresidential construction is more sensitive to changes in interest rates and stock prices than is equipment. Thus we find a $2.5 billion increase in structures, compared to a $1.3 billion rise in producers' durable equipment from a $10 billion increase in personal swing. Residential construction rises $1.5 billion because of credit easing and $1.2 billion because of lower interest rates. These are, of course, only first-round effects which do not take into account the increase in investment stemming from higher income and output. However, these results do document the strong linkages between savings and investment which exist in the supply-side model. For if these linkages are not strong, the second-round effect will not be observable either.

Another important breakthrough in our supply-side model is the endogenous explanation of productivity, which has heretofore been treated exogenously. In addition to the changes in productivity which occur because of fluctuations in GNP and levels of capacity utilization, we have been able to identify four major factors responsible for the decline in the long-term growth rate of productivity from 3 percent per year during the first twenty years of the postwar period to its present level of approximately 0 percent. Productivity growth is closely tied to the investment ratio, but also depends on several other factors which are enumerated below.

*Reduction*
*caused in*
*annual rate*
*of productivity*
*growth (percent)*

1. Decline in the ratio of productive fixed business investment less cars and small trucks to GNP . . . . . . . . . . . . . . . . . . . . . . . . . . . . . . . .    1
2. Costs of government regulation for pollution abatement, occupational safety and health, consumer product safety, toxic substances control act, and other federally mandated standards . . . . . .    1
3. Increase in the proportion of secondary workers in the labor force; the average level of training and education of these workers is initially less than for primary workers . . . . . . . . . . . . . . . . . . . . . . . . . . . . . .    ½
4. Increase in the relative price of energy . . . . . . . . . . . . . . . . . . . . . . . .    ½

We now turn to the effect of changes in tax rates on labor market variables. In addition to the beneficial aspects of tax cuts on saving and investment, we have also found significant relationships between changes in personal income taxes and labor market conditions. These can be subdivided into three areas: labor force participation, amount and quality of work offered, and increase in wage rates.

The results for labor force participation are best divided into primary and secondary members of the work force. The effects on primary workers, defined here as males aged 25 to 54, are significant but small. A one percentage point (p.p.) reduction in the marginal personal income tax would result in only a 0.05 percent increase in the primary labor force. But it would result in a 0.37 percent increase in the secondary labor force. However, total increase in the labor caused by a 1 p.p. reduction in the tax rate would be 0.25 percent, or approximately 270,000 workers at the present size of the labor force.

The labor force participation equations also indicate that a 1 percent increase in the real minimum wage (adjusted for inflation) would decrease labor force participation for those aged 16-25 by 0.2 percent. At the other end of the age scale, a 1 percent increase in real per capita social security benefits would diminish labor force participation of those 55 and over by 0.4 percent.

The equations relating the amount of utilized labor to output capital stock and productivity are usually known as inverted production functions or labor demand functions. However, they are actually a reduced form of labor demand and supply equations, since the amount of labor used depends both on the demand for labor by business and the degree of willingness to offer that labor.

These combined effects are very significant. We find that a 1 percent increase in the average personal income tax rate including social security taxes will reduce the amount of labor utilized by 0.5 percent. This decline is caused by several factors. First, an increase in the cost of labor through higher social security taxes will reduce the demand. Second, an increase in tax rates will reduce hours worked per week; we find that this effect accounts for slightly over half of the total reduction in labor offered. Third, higher taxes lead to a rise in vacation time, absenteeism, and unwillingness even to work at all by some members of the labor force.

The results we have found on the effect of changes in taxes on work effort are quite striking. Yet they are corroborated by some cross-section studies which we performed for the years 1962 and 1966. These years were chosen because they bracketed the major 1964 tax cut. We used the IRS tapes and stratified the income tax returns by income classification in order to determine what happened to work effort when taxes were reduced.

Basically the approach we have taken is the following. We know that tax rates were reduced significantly between 1962 and 1966. For any given level of adjusted gross income (AGI), we examined what happened to the proportion of income accounted for by the sum of wages and salaries and business and professional income—in other words, income earned from current work effort. If this proportion remained unchanged we could conclude that the reduction in tax rates had no significant influence on work effort. If it increased, however, we could conclude that the tax reduction heightened work effort. Note that by holding AGI constant in the regressions we have automatically excluded any increase in work effort which might have accrued from the overall growth in the economy or rise in productivity. Our analysis is strictly a marginal one for any given level of income.

We found the following results for a 1 percent reduction in tax rates. For lower income workers, such a reduction would raise work effort by about 0.1 percent. For middle and upper-middle workers, the reduction was about 0.25 percent. For upper income workers—those with taxable income of $120,000 or more—we found that the elasticities were in excess of 2.0. The upper income elasticities are probably overstated for the following reason. When the top marginal tax rate dropped from 91 percent to 70 percent, many individuals simply shifted some of their compensation from capital gains and stock options back into earned income. As a result, tax revenues in the top bracket more than doubled from 1964 to 1966 after accounting for growth in the economy even though the top bracket rates dropped drastically.

Even if the upper income elasticities are overstated, these combined cross section and time series show conclusively that work effort is negatively related to the level of taxation. Furthermore, this result is not confined to the lower end of the income spectrum, but is significant at all levels of income and increases as the marginal tax bracket rises.

Hence an increase in tax rates diminishes labor force participation and use of labor by businesses. However, that is not the end of the story. In addition, it raises the cost of labor by increasing wage rates. We find that a 1 percent increase in tax rates will result in a 0.4 percent increase in wage rates directly and a 0.7 percent increase after including the secondary effects of higher wage rates and unit labor costs on prices. Conversely, a 1 percent decline in tax rates will eventually reduce prices by 0.7 percent because of lower unit labor costs, and even more if we consider the beneficial effects of lower interest rates and other factor prices.

The structure of the supply-side model thus ties major factors of production—labor, capital, and productivity growth—directly to maximum potential GNP of the U.S. economy. Hence the model does not have to depend on exogenous assumptions about how fast potential GNP will grow in future years; this growth rate is directly related to labor input, capital stock, and productivity.

A 1 percent increase in the amount of labor supplied, assuming no offsetting decline in productivity, will raise potential GNP by 2/3 percent. An increase in investment sufficient to raise the capital stock by 1 percent will raise potential GNP by 1/3 percent; at present levels, this would be about a 10 percent increase in fixed business investment. Such an increase would also raise the investment by 1 percent, which would increase productivity by a further 0.6 percent.

A 1 percent increase in productivity will not only expand maximum potential GNP by that amount; it will initially lower prices by 2/3 percent, since labor costs consist of 2/3 of total factor costs. This is only the first-round effect, since lower prices will lead to lower wages and further declines in unit labor costs and prices. The total effect of a 1 percent increase in productivity is to reduce prices by about 2 percent.

We are also able to introduce other innovations into the supply-side model because of the endogenous treatment of maximum capacity. In particular, the model introduces the concept of the cumulative gap, which we define as the cumulative difference between 99 percent of maximum GNP and the actual level of GNP when this gap is negative. When it is positive—i.e., actual GNP is below maximum potential output—inflationary pressures do not build because of bottlenecks and shortages. However, when it is negative, prices start to rise faster than would be indicated by the cost of factor inputs alone.

So far this term does not sound greatly different than an index of capacity utilization, although it is much more inclusive in that it covers all sectors of the economy. However, we have cumulated this gap for all periods when the gap is negative. This term therefore indicates that inflationary pressures build up over many years and do not disappear every time a mild recession occurs. The inefficiences and distortions which occur when the economy is operating near full capacity are not reversed overnight, and remain as a legacy until the cumulative gap once again returns to zero. This term may also represent the gradual buildup of inflationary expectations.

The final area of the model in which supply-side economics has been incorporated is the integration of the international sector with the U.S. economy. Again, this is an area where theoretical economists have long posited strong links, but they have never been empirically documented within the context of a macroeconomic model.

Supply-side effects are important in two specific areas. First, an increase in the gap between actual and maximum potential GNP raises exports, since the greater capacity of the U.S. economy permits the production of more goods and services for export markets as well. A 1 percent increase in this gap raises net exports by about $0.7 billion per year; since the gap is cumulative, this figure continues to increase linearly and is, for example, $2.1 billion after three years.

The second major effect is the link between the trade-weighted average of the dollar, which is itself closely tied to the size of the net foreign balance, and the overall rate of inflation. We find that a 10 percent decline in the value of the dollar relative to a trade-weighted average of the Deutschemark, French franc, Belgian franc, Dutch guilder, and Japanese yen raises the producer price index 1.3 percent and the consumer price index about half that much after a period of two years.

Thus we can document several supply-side relationships that have a significant effect on inflation as well as the rate of growth. All these figures refer to the change in the CPI and are impact estimates only. First, a 1 percentage point decline in the personal income tax rate will lower wage rates and thus prices by about 0.5 percent. Second, a 1 percent increase in productivity will lower prices by 2/3 percent. Third, a 10 percent improvement in the trade-weighted average of the dollar will reduce inflation by about 0.6 percent. Fourth, after a three-year period, a 1 percent increase in the gap between actual and maximum GNP will lower prices by 0.4 percent. It is worth repeating that all of these figures are impact estimates only and do not take into account the interaction between wages, prices, productivity, and other factors of production. Indeed, the final changes in prices are between two and three times the initial impacts, depending on cyclical conditions at the time.

Thus we find that the nemesis of demand-side economics, namely that output must be reduced and unemployment increased in order to dampen the rate of inflation, is only one of several alternatives. Inflation can also be reduced by increasing productivity, reducing personal and corporate tax rates, and strengthening the value of the dollar. We would not quarrel with the statement that the size of the gap between actual and maximum potential GNP is one of the factors determining the rate of inflation, but do believe that other factors must be considered as well.

We now use a preliminary version of the supply-side model which we have recently constructed to examine the effects of a 30 percent across-the-board personal income tax cut spread over three years. We consider the following three cases:

1. Baseline case: No further tax cuts. Federal government receipts rise 15 percent per year whereas expenditures rise 12 percent per year, assuming a 9 percent inflation rate and 3 percent average increase in real growth. Under this set of assumptions, the budget first reaches balance in the fiscal year 1983 and the surplus grows rapidly thereafter.

2. A 10 percent across-the-board personal income tax cut for each three consecutive years and no offsetting decline in government spending. The Federal budget reaches a peak of −$62 billion in fiscal year 1983 and remains in deficit throughout the 1980-85 period.

3. The same 10 percent across-the-board personal income tax cut for three years, but no increase in government spending in real terms until the budget is balanced, which first occurs in 1984. After that, spending and taxes increase at the same amount. The results are summarized in Table 1.

## TABLE I

| Fiscal year | Case A | | | Case B | | | | Case C | | | | Memo — GNP, unemployment for Case A | |
|---|---|---|---|---|---|---|---|---|---|---|---|---|---|
| | Receipts | Expenditures | Surplus or deficit | Change in receipts due to tax cut | Less: Reflows | Equals: Total receipts | Surplus or deficit | Change in receipts due to expenditure cut | Total receipts | Total expenditure | Surplus or deficit | Amount | Percent |
| 1979 | 466 | 494 | −28 | ...... | ...... | | | ...... | | | | 2,314 | 5.8 |
| 1980 | 532 | 569 | −37 | ...... | ...... | | | ...... | | | | 2,527 | 6.8 |
| 1981 | 618 | 638 | −20 | −29 | 6 | 595 | −43 | −5 | 590 | 620 | −30 | 2,783 | 7.9 |
| 1982 | 711 | 715 | −4 | −66 | 16 | 661 | −54 | −11 | 650 | 676 | −26 | 3,118 | 7.3 |
| 1983 | 817 | 800 | 17 | −115 | 36 | 738 | −62 | −19 | 719 | 737 | −18 | 3,492 | 6.9 |
| 1984 | 940 | 896 | 44 | −132 | 48 | 856 | −40 | −19 | 837 | 837 | 0 | 3,911 | 6.5 |
| 1985 | 1,081 | 1,004 | 77 | −152 | 65 | 994 | −10 | −22 | 972 | 972 | 0 | 4,380 | 6.1 |

Case A: No further tax cuts, receipts grow 12 percent, expenditures 12 percent per year.
Case B: 10 percent personal income tax cut for 3 years, expenditures grow 12 percent per year.

Case C: Same tax cut, but expenditures grow 9 percent per year until budget is balanced. Underlying economic assumptions after 1980: real growth 3 percent per year, inflation (GNP deflator) 9 percent per year.

## Effect on Unemployment and Inflation

### Case B

| | Reduction in unemployment | New unemployment rate | Effect on inflation | | |
|---|---|---|---|---|---|
| | | | Demand side | Supply side | Total |
| 1981 | 0.3 | 7.6 | 0 | 0 | 0 |
| 1982 | .9 | 6.4 | +.6 | −.3 | .3 |
| 1983 | 1.6 | 5.3 | +1.2 | −.9 | .3 |
| 1984 | 2.0 | 4.5 | +3.5 | −2.7 | .8 |
| 1985 | 2.4 | 3.7 | +6.6 | −4.8 | 1.8 |

### Case C

| | Reduction in unemployment | New unemployment rate | Effect on inflation: Demand side/supply side | | | |
|---|---|---|---|---|---|---|
| | | | Less unemployment | Less G | Less T | Total |
| 1981 | 0.1 | 7.8 | 0 | 0 | 0 | 0 |
| 1982 | .3 | 7.5 | .1 | −.2 | −.3 | −.4 |
| 1983 | .7 | 6.2 | .4 | −.8 | −.9 | −1.3 |
| 1984 | 1.3 | 5.2 | 1.3 | −1.6 | −2.7 | −3.0 |
| 1985 | 1.8 | 4.3 | 2.3 | −2.6 | −4.8 | −5.1 |

Even Case B, which is akin to the old Kemp-Roth bill, does not materially worsen the economic situation. While the deficit reaches a peak of $62 billion in fiscal year 1983, the supply-side effects of lower tax rates are substantial. The inflation rate increases only about 1 percent per year faster, although this rate would accelerate were inflation to remain below 4 percent indefinitely. By 1985 the unemployment rate registers only 3.7 percent instead of 6.1 percent as projected in the base line solution.

Case C, which is similar to the recent Roth-Armstrong bill, appears to be far superior. The unemployment rate declines to 4.3 percent by 1985, but the rate of inflation is reduced by about 2 percent per year in 1984 and 1985. Here the effects of higher inflation through lower employment are offset not only by the supply-side effects of lower tax rates, but the salutory effects of lower government spending as well, which increases productivity by shifting resources from the private to the public sector.

In conclusion, a fiscal policy program which incorporates a 10 percent personal income tax cut for three years in a row and keeps the level of government spending increasing about 3 percent per year in real terms would raise the inflation rate about 1 percent from its current underlying rate of 9 percent to 10 percent per year and would reduce the rate of unemployment by slightly more than 2 percent by 1985. A program which incorporated the same 10 percent tax cut but also limited government spending to the rate of inflation until the federal budget were balanced would not only reduce the unemployment rate almost 2 percent by 1985 but would also reduce the rate of inflation by approximately 2 percent per year.

# Evidence Relating to Supply-Side Tax Policy

Robert E. Keleher

## Introduction

This essay briefly summarizes the evidence relating to "supply-side" tax policy, and is organized as follows. First, since supply-side aspects of fiscal policy have come to mean different things to different people, I briefly describe the criteria which distinguish supply-side tax policies from other tax policies. Secondly, I summarize some of the empirical evidence relating to various tax-cutting policies. In particular, the effects of tax cuts on the supply of labor, as well as on saving and investment, are briefly reviewed; so is evidence relating to the effects of tax cuts (especially of the Kemp-Roth variety) on aggregate supply or output and on tax revenues. The third part of the essay adduces reasons why the existing evidence and conventional views on tax policy may be misleading. As a result of the analysis in part three, I suggest in part four evidence drawn from historical experience which seems more relevant to tax-cut policy.

## Supply-Side Tax Cuts

Supply-side fiscal policies have come to mean different things to different economists. It is often asserted, for example, that any tax policy which affects aggregate supply is a supply-side tax policy. Several vendors of large econometric models contend that their models encompass supply-side economics because they include variables measuring aggregate supply or production and tax variables which, when changed, affect aggregate supply.

Early proponents of supply-side economics, however, contend that supply-side tax policies constitute more than a mere recognition that tax changes affect aggregate supply. Rather, what is important and what distinguishes supply-side policies from other policies is the manner in which tax changes affect factors of production and, hence, aggregate supply. In particular, these economists emphasize that tax changes which are especially relevant to aggregate supply are changes in tax *rates*—more specifically, changes in *marginal tax rates* (the rate at which the additional increment of activity is taxed)—that is, it is tax rates at the margin (not average tax levels) which affect behavior and incentives. Consequently, these economists make an important distinction between tax rates and tax revenues. Moreover, they contend that changes in tax rates are changes in *relative prices* and thus affect choice, the allocation of resources, and hence, real economic activity. According to this view, then, tax rate changes should be thought of as relative price changes and not as revenue or income changes; it is the change in relative prices and not the change in income or spending that matters for aggregate supply. Thus, tax cuts are *not* seen as injections of purchasing power or spending by the early proponents of supply-side economics.

Keynesian tax policies, on the other hand, emphasize the importance of spending levels as a determinant of economic activity. Since spending increases are considered necessary to increase production, the deficit itself is the spur to expansion. Whereas tax rebates and larger tax exemptions would be seen as conducive tax cuts by Keynesian economists, for example, supply-side advocates recognize that such tax changes have little or no effect on tax rates and, hence, have little effect on incentives and aggregate supply.

## A Brief Review of Some Empirical Evidence

### Tax Cuts and the Supply of Labor

Several empirical studies have examined the effects of tax cuts on the supply of labor. The consensus view or the bulk of the evidence tends to indicate that income tax reductions have some limited effect on the overall supply of labor (usually measured by hours of work). That is, hours of work are mildly related to after-tax wage rates (i.e., the elasticity of aggregate labor with respect to wages has been found to be low or somewhat inelastic). Elasticities of labor with respect to tax changes, for example, have been estimated anywhere from about 0.1 to about 1.0 (i.e., a 10-percent income tax reduction would increase hours of work by 1 percent to 10 percent).[1]

These elasticities are especially low (about 0.1) for prime age male workers. A 10-percent income tax reduction, for example, might increase labor supplied by such workers by only 1 percent.[2] That is, tax cuts are seen as having little or no effect on hours worked by prime age males. Secondary workers, as well as younger and older workers (which, in total, make up about one-half of the total work force), have been found to be much more responsive to changes in after-tax wage rates (elasticities for married women workers, for example, have been estimated to be about 1.0).[3] Moreover, some evidence shows that workers in high wage brackets are very sensitive to changes in tax rates. In sum, then, the evidence tends to indicate that tax cuts will have some small effect on the labor supplied by prime age males, whereas the effect on other workers tends to be greater.

## Tax Cuts and Savings

Although few studies have carefully examined this issue, most of those that do address the issue argue that saving is not responsive to changes in interest rates. For example, as Michael Boskin stated, "The notion that saving is perfectly interest inelastic has received wide-spread acceptance among empirical and policy-oriented macroeconomists."[4] This conventional view holds that tax cuts which would increase the after-tax rate of return on saving would have little or no effect on increasing the supply of saving. Because of this, some large econometric models overlook the effect of taxes on personal savings.

However, recent evidence contradicts this accepted doctrine. Employing more relevant measurements of interest rates, Boskin found a substantial interest elasticity of saving of about 0.4.[5] While this is not an enormous elasticity by conventional standards, it is substantially larger than virtually all previous estimates and conventional wisdom. Results indicating a substantial interest elasticity of saving have also recently been found by Evans, Turé, and especially King, Summers, and Boskin and Lau.[6] This recent evidence tends to indicate that the interest elasticity of saving is larger than conventionally believed—some of these recent estimates have been as high as 2.0 and 2.5! This implies that tax cuts which increase the real after-tax return to saving would work to induce an important increase in saving.[7]

## Tax Cuts and Investment

Whereas the accepted, conventional doctrine holds that tax cuts have relatively small effects on the supply of saving, as well as on the supply of labor, the consensus indicates that tax changes can significantly affect investment. The evidence suggests that tax cuts directed at investment may be the most potent area to stimulate aggregate supply via their effect in increasing the capital stock. Data Resources, Inc. (which epitomizes the consensus view), for example, suggests that tax cuts for investment are the best way to boost real GNP. Most large econometric models have incorporated various mechanisms by which tax cuts can stimulate investment. These include changes in depreciation allowances, investment tax credits, and corporate income tax rates. The ultimate effect on investment and the capital stock, of course, depends on the size and type of the tax cut. Data Resources, Inc. indicates that the elasticities of investment with respect to taxes (over the 1982-85 period) for various tax policies are the following: (a) corporate income tax rate, -0.3; (b) depreciation lives, -1.1; and (c) investment tax credit, -0.9.[8]

As an illustration of the potency of depreciation allowances, Data

Resources, Inc. did a study of the so-called 10-5-3 proposal and concluded that if this proposal had been enacted in 1980, real business fixed investment would have been $20.9 billion higher in 1984 (moreover, during the phase-in period before 1984, additional investment would have averaged $10 billion a year).[9] Several authors contend that if judiciously chosen, tax cuts in the investment area could lead to a substantial increase in investment without any large revenue loss to the government; it is possible for certain of these tax cuts to be self-financing.[10]

## Tax Cuts and Aggregate Supply

What does all this mean for aggregate supply? In view of the foregoing discussion, the conventional view holds that tax cuts do—to some extent—increase the supply of labor, saving, investment, and hence, aggregate supply. However, in view of the conventional perception of the elasticities of various factor supplies (with respect to taxes), the conventional view holds that the effect of tax cuts on aggregate supply will not be very large.

Eckstein, for example, simulated Kemp-Roth-type income tax cuts which were run by Data Resources, Inc.[11] Data Resources, Inc. concludes that the elasticity of potential output with respect to personal income taxes is small—i.e., -0.05. If Kemp-Roth had been introduced in 1980, real GNP would have increased by 2.6 percent and potential GNP would have increased by 1.9 percent by 1985. Thus, according to Data Resources, Inc., personal income tax cuts have little effect on aggregate supply. (Data Resources, Inc. indicates that the 50 percent increase in the personal income tax rate over the last fifteen years has reduced potential GNP by only 2.5 percent.) Of course, the consensus view of Kemp-Roth is premised on the assumption of little or no response of either labor or capital to a reduction in personal income tax rates. The Data Resources, Inc. model, it should be remembered, is essentially a demand-oriented, income-expenditure model with little or no supply-side effects built into it.

Supply-side models, on the other hand, have been built by Laffer, Evans, Turé, and others. The Evans model, for example, includes a more elastic response of savings and labor to a cut in taxes. Evans indicates that you get important supply-side effects in three to five years with a Kemp-Roth-type tax cut. He argues that unemployment will be reduced by 2.4 percent by 1985 if the tax cuts are not offset by government spending decreases and by 1.8 percent if they are offset. (Inflation is slightly worsened—up by 1.8 percent in 1985—with these tax cuts if they are not offset by government spending cuts, but is is substantially improved—down by 5 percent—if these tax cuts are accompanied by spending limits.)[12]

## Tax Cuts and Tax Revenues

There is little empirical evidence bearing on the so-called Laffer Curve. Conventional opinion often tends to equate tax rate cuts with tax revenue cuts so that both tax rates and tax revenue are often presumed to fall in the same proportion. However, since the conventional view concedes that Kemp-Roth-type tax cuts induce some small increases in aggregate supply, they are forced to admit that feedback effects do exist and, consequently, tax revenues will fall proportionally by less than will tax rates. Hausman, for example, estimates that a 10 percent cut in tax rates will result in a fall of tax revenue by 6.1 percent.[13] However, this conventional view emphasizes that Kemp-Roth-type tax cuts are not self-financing (especially in the short run).

Some evidence exists indicating that tax cuts aimed at specific sectors (i.e., investment), aimed at specific groups (i.e., high income groups), or tax cuts aimed at specific localities may be self-financing. That is, the Laffer effect (of self-financing tax cuts) is more likely to exist for narrowly based taxes than for broadly based taxes. The only empirical study of the Laffer curve (for labor) at the macro level—by Fullerton—indicates that the U.S. could conceivably be operating in the prohibitive area, but for this to be the case, labor supply elasticity with respect to tax rates would have to be higher than most estimates now suggest.[14]

The supply-side models of both Evans and Laffer indicate that Kemp-Roth tax cuts are self-financing in a long-run time frame. The Evans model, for example, indicates that such tax cuts would bring about a surplus of $78 billion by 1985, even if government spending continued to grow at a 10 percent rate. The Laffer model indicates that Kemp-Roth would increase total aggregate tax revenue by the fifth year after passage above what it would have been in the absence of a tax cut.[15]

## Some Criticisms of the Evidence

Why hasn't the supply-side theory received more empirical support? Is the theory wrong? Are the appropriate data not available? Is the theory difficult to test? This section will review some arguments indicating that a good deal of the above evidence may be misleading.

## Measurement Problems

One problem with much of the evidence relating to supply-side tax policy concerns measurement. As shown above, the critical tax variable for supply-side economists is the marginal tax rate. Marginal tax rates, however, differ among individuals and across sectors of the economy. Moreover, because of inflation and economic growth, they change over time, as well. Hence, there are many difficulties in measuring an aggregate marginal tax rate. Consequently, "average tax rates" and even "levels of tax revenue" are often employed as proxies for "marginal tax rates" in various empirical studies. (In testimony before the Joint Economic Committee, for example, Otto Eckstein admitted that in their simulations relating to Kemp-Roth, Data Resources, Inc. employed changes in the levels of tax revenues as a proxy for marginal tax rates!)[16] The use of such variables can surely obscure the effects that rising marginal tax rates may have on economic activity. Thus, many of the studies purporting to test supply-side propositions have employed the wrong tax variable.

The problem with most of the labor-supply evidence relates to the use of "hours worked" as a proxy for "labor supply." Because of the institution of a 40-hour workweek, this variable would not be expected to be responsive to tax changes for much of the labor force. However, other variables relating to the supply of labor may still respond to tax incentives. Although difficult to measure, for example, variables such as motivation, entrepreneurship, work intensity, the quality of work, innovation, managerial skills, and ambition may respond to tax incentives and be very important for the supply of labor. Moreover, tax cuts may result in less absenteeism, more part-time work, later retirement, and shorter periods of unemployment. In addition, they might encourage people to assume more responsibility and accumulate more human capital. These effects are not measured in the conventional empirical work. It they were, the elasticity of the supply of labor with respect to tax changes would undoubtedly be greater than is normally believed to be the case.

Finally, the effect of the so-called underground economy is not recognized in any of these studies. The supply of labor to the market may be more elastic with respect to tax changes if this could be measured. In this regard, virtually all economists recognize that the Laffer Curve works better for narrowly based taxes than for broadly based taxes. The existence of the underground economy (not to mention various tax loopholes) implies that personal income tax is much more narrowly based (and is becoming more so) than is commonly believed. Laffer effects, then, may be more plausible than is conventionally believed.

### Some Criticisms of the Large Econometric Models

The large macroeconometric models which are often used to simulate tax policies such as Kemp-Roth are deficient for several reasons. *In general*, these models are demand-oriented, income-expenditure models in which the supply-side simply is not well developed. Being income-expenditure models, they emphasize spending flows rather than relative prices. Consequently, they are unable to detect the supply-side effects that may be induced by changes in marginal tax rates. (In the Data Resources, Inc. model, for example, changes in taxes have no noticeable impact on saving or on the supply of labor. Indeed, as of June 1980, Data Resources, Inc. did not even have taxes in their wage equation.) Since they cannot detect the ways in which tax cuts affect aggregate supply—the only feedback effects are often through aggregate demand—they exaggerate revenue losses.

Secondly, saving is not properly specified in most models. That is, taxation is often assumed to have no independent effect on saving in these models. Eckstein has admitted, for example, that "there is little in the model at this stage to represent the effects of taxes and social security on personal saving."[17] Moreover, as Evans has shown, changes in saving do not translate into changes in investment in these models. Instead, saving is construed to retard demand whereas investment increases it.

Thirdly, many *general effects* of tax rate reductions are not captured in these models and studies. For example, the common notion implicit in many studies of Kemp-Roth, that taxes on individuals only affect labor income, is simply not correct. The individual income tax affects small businesses as well as income from interest, dividends, and capital gains. Personal income taxation, then, is hardly irrelevant to capital formation.[18] Indeed, a reduction in income tax rates affects at least *four* relative prices at the same time. Specifically, it affects: (1) The price of leisure vis-à-vis work. That is, leisure is now more expensive in terms of the income given up. (At the margin, then, a tax rate reduction lessens the attractiveness of tax-free unemployment and welfare benefits relative to work.) (2) The price of current consumption vis-à-vis future consumption—i.e., saving and investment. Current consumption is now more expensive in terms of future income foregone by not saving or investing. (3) The return to work in the market economy vis-à-vis work in the nonmarket (underground) economy. (4) The return on investment in the taxable sector vis-à-vis the return on investment in the tax shelters. Consequently, at the margin, resources will shift from leisure to work, from consumption to saving and investing, from the underground economy to the market economy, and from investments in tax shelters to more productive taxable investment.

*None of the studies of Kemp-Roth or econometric models contain all of these relative price changes and capture all of these resource shifts into saving and investment as well as into market labor.* If they did, the response of aggregate supply to reduction in tax rates would undoubtedly be larger than is commonly supposed.

### Time Frames

Finally, supply-side economics relates to the *long run*. Many of the studies, as well as the large macroeconometric models, focus on a relatively short-term time frame. Alice Rivlin, in her testimony before the Joint Economic Committee on supply-side economics, for example, admitted the inadequacies of macroeconometric models in dealing with issues relating to long-run economic growth.[19] Economists *all* recognize that elasticities become larger the longer the time frame under consideration. Hence, supply-side economics becomes more relevant the longer the time frame. Supply-side economics, then, has nothing to do with stabilization policy; it has everything to do with long-run economic growth.

### Some Broader Historical Evidence

Because much of the econometric evidence cited above may be inadequate, other sources of information about supply-side tax policy should be considered. One source is the careful examination of specific historical episodes during which supply-side tax policies were implemented. There is a great deal of "casual evidence" whereby tax rate cuts have been associated with tax revenue increases—particularly for narrowly based taxes (such as tariffs). The classical economists, for example, often described such situations.[20] In nineteenth century Britain, under Gladstone's government, tax rates were reduced and economic growth and tax revenues increased.[21] Historical examples of cuts in income taxes are not as numerous. The recent experience in Puerto Rico, however, provides one example. There has been a series of 5 percent income tax cuts each year from 1977 through 1979 in Puerto Rico. The apparent results have been faster economic growth and greater tax revenues.[22]

The U.S. has had very little historical experience with significant reductions in federal income tax rates. The Mellon tax cuts in the 1920s and the Kennedy tax cuts in the early 1960s provide probably the only good examples. Although no rigorous empirical work has been done on the Mellon tax cuts, the casual evidence seems to support the supply-side position. Specifically, the tax cuts—which lowered *marginal* rates of taxation—were associated with both rapid economic growth and increases in tax revenues.

Marginal income tax rates were also reduced in the early 1960s. Although there are always important differences between historical periods, the Kennedy tax cuts provide a useful example of the type of impact that a Kemp-Roth tax cut might have. In 1964, marginal tax rates were cut across the board from 91 percent to 70 percent at the top and from 20 percent to 14 percent at the bottom. These cuts were phased in over two years. Business taxes were also cut. The total tax cut came to 12 billion—in 1964 dollars it should be emphasized.

Evidence provided from several sources indicates that the Kennedy tax cuts worked, but not for the reasons the Keynesians who designed them have stated. Specifically, Denison's estimate of the gap between actual and potential GNP for 1962 and 1963 indicates that this gap was too small for demand-side policies to have created the growth in real GNP that actually ensued.[23] Something else had to have caused aggregate supply (potential GNP) to increase. What happened appears to be fully consistent with an increase in aggregate supply in response to the various tax incentives which were created. This is fully supported by two recent extensive empirical studies by Canto, Joines, and Webb.[24]

The evidence with respect to tax revenues also seems to support the supply-side view. The work of Canto, Joines, and Webb indicates that the Kennedy tax cuts caused only a small loss of revenues from the individual income tax by 1966—a loss which was largely offset by gains in corporate and other tax receipts from the increased real economic growth. Walter Heller, one of the architects of this tax package, supported these conclusions before the Joint Economic Committee in 1977:

> The tax cut . . . was the major factor that led to our running a $3 billion surplus by the middle of 1965 before escalation in Vietnam. . . . It was a $12 billion tax cut . . . and within one year the revenues into the Federal Treasury were already above what they had been before the tax cut.[25]

(Heller, of course, believed that tax revenues had been generated from Keynesian demand-side multipliers.)

## Conclusions

In my view, the foregoing analysis leads to these conclusions: A supply-side cut in income and business taxes will probably result in some increase in the supply of labor, saving, investment, and hence, in aggregate supply. Because of this additional real growth, the tax base will increase and, hence, revenues will not fall in proportion to tax rates. In short, the deficit will not be as large as many have predicted because of these feedback effects. Moreover, with real economic growth, some government spending (such as transfers) may decline, further minimizing the deficit. Despite the increase in aggregate supply, the tax cuts will produce an increase in the deficit, at least in the short run. However, to the extent that the tax cuts create an increase in saving, the deficit may be, in part, financed without increasing the money supply. In the long run, the supply-side effects should be more potent. Consequently, in a long-run time frame, the deficit should be less worrisome. Supply-side economics has to do with long-run economic growth policy rather than short-run stabilization policy. If lower tax rates increase deficits for two to three years but result in a stronger economy after that, in the long run, future taxpayers may inherit both a stronger economy and smaller deficits. Given these conclusions, should tax cuts be made? Several factors should be considered regarding such a policy: Tax rates for individuals, as well as for businesses, have increased substantially in recent years. As classical economists argued repeatedly and forcefully, when people spend a significant amount of time and resources in order to circumvent or avoid taxes, tax rates probably are too high. (The underground economy may be telling us something.) In addition to being too high, tax rates on labor, saving, and investment are increasing every day due to inflation. In addition to increases due to inflation, Social Security tax increases, as well as increases in windfall oil profits taxes, are already scheduled. In short, tax rates are not only too high but are increasing every day and scheduled to increase even further. *Thus, to some extent, a Kemp-Roth-type tax cut will simply be offsetting these past, present, and future increases in tax rates.* Although a few supply-side zealots still contend that tax cuts can be made without regard to government spending, many supply-side economists have indicated a need to restrain and reduce government spending (as a proportion of GNP). It is a common assertion among these economists that government spending restraints should accompany the tax cuts wherever possible. If such restraints do accompany tax cuts, the deficit will be smaller and less worrisome.

### Finally, what does all this mean for monetary policy?

Virtually all supply-side economists recognize that monetary control is critical to supply-side tax cut policies. That is, these economists recognize that these tax policies must be accompanied by stable monetary growth. This concern for monetary control is epitomized by some of President Reagan's supply-side advisors who have advocated implementing a new "monetary accord" with the Federal Reserve. As a consequence of this concern, Federal Reserve efforts at monetary control should receive strong support from the Reagan administration. Since supply-side tax policies imply that the Federal deficit will increase in the short run, adherence to monetary targets is critical over the next several years. Increases in the deficit, however, do not necessarily lead to monetary expansion. One problem with interest rate targeting was that increases in credit demand (from either the public or private sectors) increased interest rates, and the federal Reserve—in employing interest targets—worked to accommodate these demands. A principal reason for the Fed's shift to reserves targeting procedures was to minimize this accommodation of credit demand. In other words, *reserves targeting implies that we are less likely to monetize the deficit.* All of this implies that we should focus on efforts to improve both monetary control as well as our reserves targeting procedures and, by all means, should not revert to focusing on interest rates.

## Notes

1. *See,* for example, Harvey Rosen, "What is Labor Supply and Do Taxes Affect It?" *American Economic Review* 70 (May 1980): 171-76; Don Fullerton, "On the Possibility of an Inverse Relationship between Taxes and Government Revenues," Working Paper Series, National Bureau of Economic Research, Inc., (April 1980); and Jerry Hausman, "Income and Payroll Tax Policy and Labor Supply," paper prepared for a conference on "The Supply-Side Effects of Economic Policy," Washington University

and the Federal Reserve Bank of St. Louis, October 24-26, 1980. The labor studies referred to here are cross-section studies and, hence, are not associated with a time dimension. Consequently, they provide no information as to the timing of the response.

2. Hausman, "Income and Payroll Tax Policy," p. 25.

3. Rosen, "What is Labor Supply?" p. 171. (Elasticities for married women workers, for example, have been estimated to be as high as 1.0).

4. Michael J. Boskin, "Taxation, Saving, and the Rate of Interest," *Journal of Political Economy* 86, no. 2, pt. 2 (April 1978): 54. Boskin's study employs annual time series data. His results, then, imply that a 10 percent increase in the after-tax rate of return would increase saving by 4 percent per year. The other studies mentioned can be interpreted similarly.

5. Ibid.

6. Michael K. Evans, "An Econometric Model Incorporating the Supply-Side Effects of Economic Policy," paper prepared for a conference on "Supply-Side Effects of Economic Policy," Washington University and Federal Reserve Bank of St. Louis, October 24-26, 1980; Norman B. Turé, testimony before U.S. Congress, Joint Economic Committee, *Forecasting the Supply Side of the Economy: Hearings*, Ninety-sixth Congress, Second Session, May 21, 1980; M. King, "Savings and Taxation," in G. A. Hughes and G. M. Heal, eds., *Essays in Public Policy* (London: Allen Unwin, Ltd., 1980); Lawrence H. Summers, "Tax Policy in a Life Cycle Model," Working Paper Series, National Bureau of Economic Research, Inc., 1978; and Michael Boskin and L. J. Lau, "Taxation, Social Security, and Aggregate Factor Supply in the United States," in *Compendium of Tax Research*, U.S. Treasury, Office of Tax Analysis (Washington, D.C., 1978).

7. King, "Savings and Taxation;" Summers, "Tax Policy in a Life Cycle Model;" and idem, "Tax Policy and Corporate Investment," paper prepared for a conference on "The Supply-Side Effects of Economic Policy," Washington University and Federal Reserve Bank of St. Louis, October 24-26, 1980, p. 32.

8. Otto Eckstein, "A Time for Supply Economics," prepared statement submitted to U.S. Congress, Joint Economic Committee, Ninety-sixth Congress, Second Session, May 21, 1980.

9. Otto Eckstein, "Tax Policy and Core Inflation," a study prepared for the U.S. Congress, Joint Economic Committee, Ninety-sixth Congress, Second Session, April 10, 1980.

10. Summers, "Tax Policy and Corporate Investment."

11. Eckstein, "A Time for Supply Economics."

12. Evans, "An Econometric Model."

13. Hausman, "Income and Payroll Tax Policy and Labor Supply." This study is based on cross-section data. *See* note 1.

14. Fullerton's research, for example, indicates that high elasticities of labor supply with respect to tax rates—elasticities at least as high as 1.7 (together with a tax rate of at least 30 percent)—would make the Laffer effect plausible. It should be remembered that Fullerton's paper applies only to labor, whereas the Laffer Curve applies to all factors of production.

15. Evans, "An Econometric Model;" and Arthur B. Laffer and David Ranson, "The Prototype Wedge Model: A Tool for Supply-Side Economics," (Boston: H.C. Wainwright & Co., Economics) September 14, 1979.

16. King, "Savings and Taxation;" Summers, "Tax Policy in a Life Cycle Model;" idem, "Tax Policy and Corporate Investment."

17. Eckstein, "A Time for Supply Economics," p. 26.

18. Alan Reynolds, "Individuals and the Tax Question," *Wall Street Journal*, October 24, 1980; *see also* "World Report," First Chicago Corporation, July-August 1980.

19. Alice Rivlin, Statement before U.S. Congress, Joint Economic Committee, *Forecasting the Supply-Side of the Economy: Hearings* Ninety-sixth Congress, Second Session, May 21, 1980.

20. Robert Keleher and William P. Orzechowski, "Supply-Side Fiscal Policy: An Historical Analysis of a Rejuvenated Idea." Ch. herein. (Unpublished paper. See Chapter 3.)

21. Ibid.

22. Ibid.; also, Andrew W. Mellon, *Taxation: The People's Business* (New York: MacMillan & Co., 1924); Jude Wanniski, *The Way the World Works* (New York: Basic Books, 1978): and Rep. Jack Kemp, "Kemp on Stein: Are We All Supply-Siders Now?" letter to the *Wall Street Journal*, April 4, 1980.

23. E. F. Denison, *Accounting for Slower Economic Growth* (Washington, D.C.: Brookings, 1979); Paul Craig Roberts, "The Economic Case for Kemp-Roth," in Arthur B. Laffer and Jan P. Seymour, eds., *The Economics of the Tax Revolt* (New York: Harcourt Brace Jovanovich, 1979) p. 61.

24. Victor A. Canto, Douglas H. Joines, and Robert I. Webb, "Empirical Evidence on the Effects of Tax Returns on Economic Activity," *Proceedings of the Business and Economic Statistics Section of the American Statistical Association* (Washington, D.C., 1979); idem, "The Revenue Effects of the Kennedy Tax Cuts," unpublished manuscript, University of Southern California, November 1980.

25.Walter W. Heller, Statement before U.S. Congress, Joint Economic Committee, February 7, 1977.

# Chapter 6:
# Policy Lessons:
# Kennedy and Thatcher

## The Kennedy Tax Cuts

Bruce R. Bartlett

When President John F. Kennedy took office in January 1961 the economy was still recovering from a recession. During the last three quarters of 1960 real gross national product "grew" at a negative rate and unemployment rose. Although GNP rebounded in 1961 the unemployment rate remained high, averaging 6.7 percent for the year. By mid-1962, Kennedy and his economic advisors had decided on the need for an across-the-board tax cut. He first mentioned this possibility at a press conference on June 7, but he did not fully elaborate his plans until later in the year. In a speech before the Economic Club of New York on December 14, 1962, Kennedy outlined his thinking:

> The most direct and significant kind of federal action aiding economic growth is to make possible an increase in private consumption and investment demand—to cut the fetters which hold back private spending. In the past, this could be done in part by the increased use of credit and monetary tools—but our balance of payments situation today places limits on our use of those tools for expansion. It could also be done by increasing federal expenditures more rapidly than necessary—but such a course would soon demoralize both the government and the economy. If government is to retain the confidence of the people, it must not spend a penny more than can be justified on grounds of national need and spent with maximum efficiency.

> The final and best means of strengthening demand among consumers and business is to reduce the burden on private income and the deterrents to private initiative which are imposed by our present tax system—and this administration pledged itself last summer to an across-the-board, top-to-bottom cut in personal and corporate income taxes to be enacted and become effective in 1963.[1]

Kennedy seemed to be saying that although Keynesian economics held that aggregate demand could be just as easily stimulated by increasing government spending or by increasing the quantity of money, because of the U.S. balance of trade deficit and resistance to increased expenditures solely for macroeconomic reasons, a tax cut was the only viable option. A tax cut also had special political appeal. As Walter Heller, chairman of the Council of Economic Advisors, put it,

"The use of tax reduction made it possible to induce a coalition of conservative and liberal forces to endorse and work for an expansionary fiscal policy even in the face of an existing deficit, an expanding economy, and rising government expenditures."[2]

Nevertheless, although conservatives generally favored tax reduction, they were even more concerned about deficit spending. Thus Kennedy made clear from the very beginning his belief that high tax rates were reducing revenues and that lower tax rates would increase revenue. Again from his Economic Club of New York speech:

> Our true choice is not between tax reduction, on the one hand, and the avoidance of large federal deficits on the other. It is increasingly clear that no matter what party is in power, so long as our national security needs keep rising, an economy hampered by restrictive tax rates will never produce enough revenue to balance the budget—just as it will never produce enough jobs or enough profits. Surely the lesson of the last decade is that budget deficits are not caused by wild-eyed spenders but by slow economic growth and periodic recessions—and any new recession would break all deficit records. In short, it is a paradoxical truth that tax rates are too high today and tax revenues are too low—and the soundest way to raise revenues in the long run is to cut rates now. . . . I repeat: our practical choice is not between a tax-cut deficit and budgetary surplus. It is between two kinds of deficits—a chronic deficit of inertia, as the unwanted result of inadequate revenues and a restricted economy—or a temporary deficit of transition, resulting from a tax cut designed to boost the economy, increase tax revenue and achieve a future budget surplus. The first type of deficit is a sign of waste and weakness—the second reflects an investment in the future.[3]

In his economic report, issued on January 21, 1963, Kennedy continued his tax cut theme. As he put it, "The main block to full employment is an unrealistically heavy burden of taxation. The time has come to remove it."[4] Three days later, on January 24, Kennedy sent his tax cut message to Congress, outlining the specifics of his proposal:

(1) A reduction in all individual income tax rates. Rates would be lowered from a range of 20 percent at the bottom and 91 percent at the top—rates essentially the same as those during World War II—to 14 percent at the bottom and 65 percent at the top. The reductions would average 20 percent in every bracket and be phased in over three years.

(2) The corporate tax rate would be reduced from 52 percent to 47 percent, with special reductions for small businesses.

In addition, Kennedy proposed numerous tax "reforms" designed to raise $3.4 billion and offset some of the revenue loss from rate reductions.[5]

The House Ways and Means Committee deliberated on the tax bill, H.R. 8363, most of the summer, not completing action until September 13, 1963. Interestingly, Section One of the bill declared that it was the sense of Congress that the tax reduction provided by the bill, through stimulation of the economy, would, after a brief transitional period, raise (rather than lower) revenues. The committee report elaborated this point:

> It is recognized that to many it may seem inconsistent to think of cutting taxes as a way of increasing revenues. Nevertheless, past experience demonstrates that this can happen; in fact, given today's conditions it can be expected to happen. The events of the period 1954-56 demonstrate how this can occur. In 1954 Congress allowed the individual income tax increases imposed during the Korean War to expire, made certain excise tax reductions, allowed the excess profits tax to expire and made certain other tax reductions as well. The total of these reductions amounted to about $7.4 billion. Yet, only 2 years later, in 1956, receipts were $3.2 billion above the level existing before the reductions were made.[6]

The Republicans on the Ways and Means Committee, however, opposed the Kennedy tax reduction as fiscally irresponsible, because taxes were being reduced while expenditures were not. In other words, they believed that it was more important to balance the budget by raising taxes than to suffer a temporary deficit.[7] They seem not to have understood (as many today do not) that tax rates are not fixed; as inflation or real income growth occurs people are pushed up into higher tax brackets. Kennedy and his advisors referred to this as "fiscal drag" which must be offset by "fiscal dividends," such as tax cuts or expanded federal programs.[8]

On the floor of the House, Wilbur Mills, chairman of the Ways and Means Committee, attempted to refute the view that the proposed tax reductions would lead to larger deficits, as charged by the Republicans:

> The idea . . . that tax reductions will provide the rate of growth we need in this country to solve the problems I have listed for you, and that the tax reductions, after a brief transition period, will actually increase revenues above the levels that would have been achieved in the absence of tax reductions are not new or novel ideas as some would suggest. . . . It is on the basis of this type of reasoning, Mr. Chairman, that I have reached the conclusion that this bill will provide a sufficient increase in the gross national product so that the larger revenues derived from this additional income will result in the federal budget being balanced sooner than would be the case in the absence of this tax cut.

> Mr. Chairman, there is no doubt in my mind that this tax reduction bill, in and of itself, can bring about an increase in the gross national product of approximately $50 billion in the next few years. If it does, these lower rates of taxation will bring in at least $12 billion in additional revenue.[9]

Similar statements were made during Senate debate by Senate Majority Leader Mike Mansfield and Sen. Russell Long, later to become chairman of the Senate Finance Committee.[10]

What did the tax cut actually do for the economy? Virtually all of the econometric studies of the Kennedy tax cut agree that it was highly stimulative to the economy. Arthur Okun, chairman of the Council of Economic Advisors under President Johnson, has stated that "the tax cuts of 1964 are credited with a $25 billion contribution to our GNP by mid-1965, a $30 billion effect by the end of 1965, and an ultimate $36 billion increment."[11] Similar estimates have been made by Lawrence Klein, Data Resources, Inc., Wharton Econometric Forecasting Associates, Inc., and the Congressional Budget Office.[12]

The effects of the tax cut can probably be seen most dramatically, however, in the unemployment rate. As shown in Table 1, the unemployment rate for all workers dropped almost by half between 1961 and 1969. In terms of adult black males the drop was phenomenal, going from 11.7 percent unemployment in 1961 to a mere 3.7 percent in 1969. In no other time in recent history have minorities fared so well.

*Table 1*
Unemployment Rates (1961-69)
(Percent)

| Year | Whites | | | | Females Over 20 |
| | Total | Males | Males Over 20 | Females | |
|------|-------|-------|---------------|---------|----------------|
| 1961 | 6.0 | 5.7 | 5.1 | 6.5 | 5.7 |
| 1962 | 4.9 | 4.6 | 4.0 | 5.5 | 4.7 |
| 1963 | 5.0 | 4.7 | 3.9 | 5.8 | 4.8 |
| 1964 | 4.6 | 4.1 | 3.4 | 5.5 | 4.6 |
| 1965 | 4.1 | 3.6 | 2.9 | 5.0 | 4.0 |
| 1966 | 3.3 | 2.8 | 2.2 | 4.3 | 3.3 |
| 1967 | 3.4 | 2.7 | 2.1 | 4.6 | 3.8 |
| 1968 | 3.2 | 2.6 | 2.0 | 4.3 | 3.4 |
| 1969 | 3.1 | 2.5 | 1.9 | 4.2 | 3.4 |
| Blacks and Others | | | | | |
| 1961 | 12.4 | 12.8 | 11.7 | 11.9 | 10.6 |
| 1962 | 10.9 | 10.9 | 10.0 | 11.0 | 9.6 |
| 1963 | 10.8 | 10.5 | 9.2 | 11.2 | 9.4 |
| 1964 | 9.6 | 8.9 | 7.7 | 10.7 | 9.0 |
| 1965 | 8.1 | 7.4 | 6.0 | 9.2 | 7.5 |
| 1966 | 7.3 | 6.3 | 4.9 | 8.7 | 6.6 |
| 1967 | 7.4 | 6.1 | 4.3 | 9.1 | 7.1 |
| 1968 | 6.7 | 5.6 | 3.9 | 8.3 | 6.3 |
| 1969 | 6.4 | 5.3 | 3.7 | 7.8 | 5.8 |

Source: Department of Labor, Bureau of Labor Statistics.

## TABLE 2
## Comparison of Estimated Revenue Loss and Actual Revenue Gain, 1965

| Adjusted Gross Income Class ($ in Thousands) | Millions of Dollars | | | | Difference As % of Estimate |
|---|---|---|---|---|---|
| | Estimated Revenue Loss | Estimated 1965 Tax | Actual 1965 Tax | Difference | |
| 0-5 | $1,656 | $4,374 | $4,337 | −$37 | −0.8 |
| 5-10 | 3,411 | 13,213 | 15,434 | +2,221 | +16.8 |
| 10-15 | 1,412 | 6,845 | 10,711 | +3,866 | +56.5 |
| 15-20 | 467 | 2,474 | 4,188 | +1,714 | +69.3 |
| 20-50 | 914 | 5,104 | 7,440 | +2,336 | +45.8 |
| 50-100 | 342 | 2,311 | 3,654 | +1,343 | +58.1 |
| 100+ | 204 | 2,086 | 3,764 | +1,678 | +80.4 |
| Total | 8,406 | 36,407 | 49,530 | +13,123 | +36.0 |

Source: Internal Revenue Service, *Statistics of Income—1965, Individual Income Tax Returns*; Joseph A. Pechman, "Evaluation of Recent Tax Legislation: Individual Income Tax Provisions of the Revenue Act of 1964," *Journal of Finance* (May 1965), p. 268.

While there may be little debate about the overal economic effects of the tax cut there is still considerable debate about the revenue impact. Congressman Jack Kemp has argued, based on a study by the Congressional Research Service, that the tax cut increased revenues substantially.[13] The Treasury Department strongly disagrees with this view, citing the closeness of revenue estimates contained in the President's budgets during the early 1960s with actual receipts.[14] This obviously proves nothing, for the estimates themselves took into consideration the feedback effects. Interestingly, Ohio's Democratic Congressman Charles Vanik, who serves on the House Ways and Means Committee, recently charged that the revenue was never recovered; that the government is still losing revenue because of the Kennedy tax cut. As he told the House:

> Yes, government spending and government waste have contributed to our debt and deficit. However, the major impact on our debt and our deficit has resulted 10 times more from tax cuts which have taken place over the last 15 years. . . . The 1962 tax cut has had a cumulative cost to the Treasury of $10 billion; the 1964 tax cut, $228 billion; the 1971 tax cut, $73.6 billion; and the 1975 tax cut, $56 billion.[15]

This is clearly absurd. It is just the old trick of holding everything else constant while breaking all the rules. In other words, Vanik is assuming that even without all those tax cuts we still would have gotten the same amount of economic growth. Such an assumption is obviously invalid.

Nevertheless, data does exist to suggest that revenues increased fairly quickly to above where they otherwise would have been. For example, a 1965 study of the tax cut done by Joseph Pechman forecasts a revenue loss of $8.4 billion in 1965. But a study of actual receipts showed revenues to be $13.1 billion above the forecast (see Table 2).

Another study, by Dr. Michael K. Evans, showed that there was substantial revenue growth in upper tax brackets (see Table 3). The percent of total income tax revenues paid by those with incomes over $100,000 increased from 5.1 percent in 1963 to 6.3 percent in 1964, 7.6 percent in 1965, 8.5 percent in 1967, and 9.2 percent in 1968. As Evans notes, these data strongly rebut the view that tax cuts for the wealthy are a "raid on the Treasury."[16]

It is for this reason that many people argue today, as Andrew Mellon did in the 1920s, that the best way to get more tax revenue from the rich is to lower their tax rates. As the *Wall Street Journal* recently put it:

> It stands to reason, and we thoroughly believe, that the U.S. economy would benefit enormously if the rich paid more taxes. We have been arguing this, at least implicitly, for years. What we have not been able to get the politicians to understand, though, is that you can't get rich people to pay more in tax *revenues* by raising their tax *rates*. If you raise the rates, it becomes even more

profitable for them to hire lawyers and accountants to find them loopholes, and the cost of this misdirected effort is a dead loss to the economy. Or they stop working entirely and dissipate their capital drinking champagne and sailing yachts, which is also a dead loss to the economy. Either way, they contribute less in tax revenues, and the burden of supporting government expenditures falls on the middle class and the poor.[17]

TABLE 3
The Kennedy Tax Cut and the Rich

| Year | Maximum Tax Rate | Taxes ($ in Millions) Collected From Adjusted Gross Income Classes of: | | |
|---|---|---|---|---|
| | | Over $1,000,000 | $500,000 to $1,000,000 | $100,000 to $500,000 |
| 1961 | 91% | 342 | 297 | 1,970 |
| 1962 | 91 | 311 | 243 | 1,740 |
| 1963 | 91 | 326 | 243 | 1,890 |
| 1964 | 77 | 427 | 306 | 2,220 |
| 1965 | 70 | 603 | 408 | 2,752 |
| 1966 | 70 | 590 | 457 | 3,176 |

Lastly, on the question of whether the Kennedy tax cut increased revenues, one should note that in 1977 Walter Heller testified before the Joint Economic Committee that it did. In response to a question from Sen. Jacob Javits, who cited the same figures used by Congressman Kemp, Heller replied:

> What happened to the tax cut in 1965 is difficult to pin down, but insofar as we are able to isolate it, it did seem to have a tremendously stimulative effect, a multiplied effect on the economy. It was the major factor that led to our running a $3 billion surplus by the middle of 1965 before escalation in Vietnam struck us. It was a $12 billion tax cut which would be about $33 or $34 billion in today's terms, and within one year the revenues into the Federal Treasury were already above what they had been before the tax cut. . . . Did it pay for itself in increased revenues? I think the evidence is very strong that it did.[18]

The reason why the stimulative effects of the Kennedy tax cut did not continue is because the excessive government spending and increases in the quantity of money which took place from 1965 on created inflation that pushed everyone up into higher tax brackets. Considering the magnitude of the tax increase that has taken place over the last fifteen years, it would seem quite in order to have a reduction in tax rates which would put everyone back into the same relative tax position they were in following the Kennedy tax cut.

As Table 4 shows, despite numerous tax cuts since 1964-65, which have tended to keep the aggregate tax burden as a percentage of

*TABLE 4*
Distribution of Taxable Income by Marginal Tax Rate,
Federal Income Tax, 1968, 1972 and 1977

| | Summary Table | | |
| --- | --- | --- | --- |
| | Percent of Taxable Income | | |
| Marginal Rate | 1968 | 1972 | 1977 |
| 14-19% | 72.78 | 65.45 | 49.13 |
| 22-32 | 19.90 | 26.97 | 39.06 |
| 36-48 | 3.52 | 4.00 | 6.65 |
| 50-70 | 4.11 | 3.60 | 5.12 |
| | Distribution by Individual Rate | | |
| | Percent of Taxable Income at Each Marginal Rate | | |
| Marginal Tax Rate | 1968 | 1972 | 1977 |
| 14% | 13.80 | 11.20 | 7.52 |
| 15 | 12.06 | 9.81 | 6.61 |
| 16 | 11.35 | 9.67 | 6.82 |
| 17 | 9.85 | 8.34 | 5.97 |
| 19 | 25.72 | 26.40 | 22.21 |
| 22 | 11.12 | 13.72 | 15.90 |
| 25 | 4.70 | 7.79 | 12.45 |
| 28 | 2.48 | 3.33 | 6.39 |
| 32 | 1.60 | 2.13 | 4.32 |
| 36 | 1.12 | 1.35 | 2.50 |
| 39 | 0.82 | 0.90 | 1.49 |
| 42 | 0.65 | 0.75 | 1.18 |
| 45 | 0.51 | 0.60 | 0.91 |
| 48 | 0.42 | 0.40 | 0.57 |
| 50 | 2.25 | 1.54 | 2.65 |
| 53 | 0.53 | 0.38 | 0.47 |
| 55 | 0.32 | 0.27 | 0.34 |
| 58 | 0.21 | 0.17 | 0.20 |
| 60 | 0.14 | 0.14 | 0.18 |
| 62 | 0.16 | 0.17 | 0.22 |
| 64 | 0.10 | 0.12 | 0.15 |
| 66 | 0.07 | 0.09 | 0.11 |
| 68 | 0.05 | 0.07 | 0.09 |
| 69 | 0.03 | 0.06 | 0.06 |
| 70 | 0.25 | 0.59 | 0.65 |

Source: Internal Revenue Service, *Statistics of Income;* Tax Foundation computations.

personal income from rising, the progressivity of the tax code has greatly increased due to inflation.

As one can see, there has been a significant upward movement in the percentage of taxpayers who are affected by high marginal tax rates—the tax on each additional dollar earned. This translates into a massive erosion of incentive, as year after year people keep less and less of each additional dollar they earn.

It is ironic that the most important reduction in tax rates since the 1920s was accomplished by a liberal Democrat for decidely liberal reasons—to pump up demand. Yet today liberal Democrats are the major opposition to efforts to duplicate the Kennedy tax cut by Sen. William Roth and Congressman Jack Kemp. Similarly, it is ironic that the major opposition to Kennedy came from conservative Republicans concerned about the deficit. Yet today it is conservative Republicans who wish to emulate Kennedy. In any case, the economic record is clear: the period following enactment of the Kennedy program is the best this country has had in the last quarter century. If we want to restore the economic health we had in the mid-1960s, a good way to start would be to put taxpayers back into the same relative tax position they were in in 1965.

# Notes

1. *The Commercial and Financial Chronicle* (December 20, 1962).
2. Walter Heller, *New Dimensions of Political Economy* (Cambridge: Harvard University Press, 1967), p. 113.
3. *The Commercial and Financial Chronicle* (December 20, 1962).
4. *Public Papers of the Presidents of the United States, John F. Kennedy, 1963* (Washington: U.S. Government Printing Office, 1964), p. 60.
5. Ibid., pp. 73-92. Subsequently, the Congress only reduced the top marginal rate to 70 percent and the corporate rate to 48 percent.
6. House Report No. 749, 88th Cong., 1st sess., pp. 6-7.
7. Ibid., pp. C5-C28.
8. Heller, *New Dimensions*, p. 65; Herbert Stein, *The Fiscal Revolution in America* (Chicago: University of Chicago Press, 1969), pp. 399-400.
9. *Congressional Record* (September 24, 1963), p. 17907.
10. Idem (January 23, 1964), p. 1002; idem (February 25, 1964), p. 3397.
11. Arthur M. Okun, "Measuring the Impact of the 1964 Tax Reduction," in Walter Heller, ed., *Perspectives on Economic Growth* (New York: Random House, 1968), p. 47.
12. Lawrence R. Klein, "Econometric Analysis of the Tax Cut of 1964," in James Duesenberry, et al., eds., *The Brookings Model: Some Further Results* (Chicago: Rand McNally & Co., 1969), pp. 459-72; Committee on the Budget, U.S. House of Representatives, *Economic Stabilization Policies: The Historical Record, 1962-76* (Washington: U.S. Government Printing Office, 1978), pp. 11-147; Congressional Budget Office, *Understanding Fiscal Policy* (Washington: Congressional Budget Office, April 1978), pp. 23-25.
13. *Congressional Record* (July 14, 1977), pp. H 7156-57 (daily edition).
14. Committee on the Budget, U.S. House of Representatives, *Leading Economist's Views of Kemp-Roth* (Washington: U.S. Government Printing Office, 1978), pp. 94-96.
15. *Congressional Record* (March 15, 1979), p. H 1376 (daily edition).

16.  Michael K. Evans, "Taxes, Inflation and the Rich," *Wall Street Journal* (August 7, 1978).
17.  Editorial, "Tax the Rich!" *Wall Street Journal* (March 8, 1977).
18.  Statement before the Joint Economic Committee, Congress of the United States, February 7, 1977.

# Kennedy Economics Revisited

Walter W. Heller

What approaches to investment stimulus do the initiatives and experiences of the 1960s seem to validate? What do the 1960s have to offer the 1980s in the formulation and management of fiscal and monetary policy? Does the remarkable price stability of the early 1960s suggest that incomes policies have a logical role to play in trying to bring the inflation of the 1980s under control? Do the tax cuts of the 1960s in fact provide as much aid and comfort for "supply-side tax cuts" as their proponents claim?

The passage of time and the sour economic experience of the seventies have led to new perspectives and some sobering second thoughts. But in order for these new perspectives and second thoughts to be credible, discussion needs to be consistently anchored in a high-fidelity perception of the economic thinking, the economic policies, and the economic record of the 1960s. In sharp contrast, much of the recent discussion of that economic experience—and especially of the 1964 tax cut—seems strangely out of focus. Lessons are being drawn for which the actual experience of the sixties provides little warrant.

The super-supply-siders, feverishly searching for historical reeds on which to lean, reinterpret the 1964 tax-cut experience as an undiluted supply-side success story. Many an anti-Keynesian, who comes not to praise but to bury the 1960s, sees only a total preoccupation with demand management, with fine-tuning, and with "fiscalism."[1] And an occasional aberrant assures us that the expansion of the early 1960s traces almost entirely to a military buildup.

My endeavor is this brief commentary—as objectively as is possible for a direct participant in the process—is to put the experience of the early sixties back into focus. In the process, I will try not to fall prey to the syndrome that, "the past remembers better than it lived." I cannot claim complete objectivity, but I have at every possible point tested my recollection of events and policies and the thinking that lay behind them against not just the data but the public and private statements (as in our *Economic Reports*, speeches, testimony, and memoranda to the President) that we were making at the time. What emerges—or reemerges, since in part this is a repetition of oft-told tales—will, I hope, be useful in evaluating the views of the latter-day revisionists.

## The Main Components

It may be worthwhile to start out by asking: What was not new about the "new economics," as the press quickly dubbed the economics of the New Frontier in 1961? Surely not the theory—much of that went back nearly a quarter of a century to John Maynard Keynes. What *was* new, however, was the translation of modern economics into practice—and into numerical targets—under the leadership of a willing and responsive president. At the very outset, President Kennedy directed his Council of Economic Advisors to "return not just to the letter but to the spirit of the Employment Act of 1946."

The distinctive stamp that the Kennedy administration put on economic policy and policymaking was made up of half a dozen major elements. First, the ambiguous mandate of the Employment Act of 1946 to achieve "maximum employment, production, and purchasing power" was translated into the concrete goals of full employment, price stability, more rapid growth, and external payments equilibrium (under the constraints of maintaining freedom of economic choice and promoting greater equality at economic opportunity).

Second and perhaps more important, the Council converted the key qualitative goal into specific quantitative targets, and the President endorsed those targets. Thus, in place of a general but vague commitment to "full employment, as in the Eisenhower years," the Kennedy administration adopted a specific target of 4 percent unemployment (at a time, by the way, when the 1960 recession had boosted unemployment to 7 percent). The target for economic growth—that is, the growth in the economy's potential to produce—was set at 4 percent per year in place of the 3 percent to 3.5 percent rate of growth in potential GNP in the 1953-60 period (and the 2.5 percent actual rate of expansion of real GNP in that period). As to price stability, the goal was to maintain the very low rate of inflation of just over 1 percent per year that had been left as a welcome legacy of the Eisenhower era (at the heavy cost of three recessions in eight years, high unemployment, and low rates of growth). Once these numerical targets were adopted and accepted throughout government, they exerted a discipline on policy that the more abstract and qualitative goals could not achieve.

The third element was the concomitant shift in policy focus from moderating the swings of the business cycle to achieving the full-employment potential of the economy. It was not enough simply to reverse recession and temper expansions. Success was to be measured in terms of hitting a moving target, namely, the rising full-employment potential of the economy. The point was to close the gap between actual and potential output without triggering inflation. The concepts of full-employment potential and gap-closing were not brand new—they traced back to the bold and innovative Truman Council under the leadership of Leon Keyserling. But until Kennedy came along, the country never had a President who was willing to embrace such seemingly unorthodox doctrines and unabashedly move modern economics to the front burner.

Fourth was the development of a new policy of voluntary wage-price restraint. The Kennedy wage-price guideposts were introduced in January 1962 to induce labor and business to hold wage and price increases within the bounds of productivity advances and thus help ensure that fiscal-monetary stimulus would not run off into higher prices and wages but would instead express itself in higher output, jobs, profits, and investment. Indeed, the 1961-65 record shows that the guideposts played their part—wage increases in manufacturing did stay within the bounds of productivity increases, thus contributing to continued price stability and a sustained advance in real wages and living standards. Corporate profits doubled in those years.

Fifth, less tangible, but no less important, was the orchestration of policy through skilled White House management utilizing such instruments as the "Troika" (the heads of Treasury, Budget, and CEA) and the "Quadriad" (adding in the Federal Reserve Chairman). Economic policy differences were ironed out and presented to Congress and the public as a united and coherent effort. The vital ingredient in this was the leadership by a sagacious President, quick to accept modern economic thinking and to reject the old cliches that had hobbled policy. Banished were the beliefs that deficits in a weak economy were instruments of the devil and that public debt was a "burden on our grandchildren." John F. Kennedy was the first President to set aside these shibboleths, to fix as his target budget-balance not every year but at full employment, and thus to facilitate a more activist economic policy.

A counterpart of the new activism was the President's use of the White House "as a pulpit for public education in economics" (a use he urged on us even before his inauguration). Just as he constantly urged his staff to explain and clarify national economic goals, concepts, and policies to the press, on television, and so on, the President himself provided a sense of direction through this own speeches to business and financial groups, on national television programs, at press conferences, and in the famous Yale speech in June of 1962.

Finally, one should mention the quality of economic thinking that President Kennedy attracted throughout his administration. Outside the CEA, it was typified in the outstanding economic and fiscal leadership of David Bell in the Budget Bureau, Douglas Dillon and Robert Roosa in the Treasury, George Ball in the State Department, and Carl Kaysen in the White House. The CEA had as council members Kermit Gordon, James Tobin, Gardner Ackley, and John Lewis; as staff members, people like Kenneth Arrow, William Capron, Richard Cooper, Arthur Okun, George Perry, Vernon Ruttan, Warren Smith, Robert Solow, Nancy Teeters, and Lloyd Ulman; and as close-in consultants, the likes of Otto Eckstein, John Meyer, Joseph Pechman, Paul Samuelson, and Charles Schultze.

## The First Year: Supply-Side Economics

Except for a quick but mild dose of demand stimulus in an early 1961 antirecession package, the first year was essentially a year of supply-and cost-side measures. We did not use the catch phrase, "supply-side economics," but that's exactly what it was. The actions speak for themselves: (1) Introduction of the investment credit—to this day the backbone of tax incentives for growth through business capital formation. Proposed in 1961, it was not enacted until 1962, largely because of misgivings and often hostility from both the business and labor communities. (Either because of its novelty or because of its form, the investment tax credit was at first opposed by many business leaders. Secretary Douglas Dillon was fond of telling the story of a man who asked him to explain it, step by step, and at the end added, "One last question: Why am I against it?"). (2) Liberalization of tax depreciation guidelines, also put into effect in 1962. (3) The "monetary twist," designed to reduce long-term interest rates and make more funds available for long-term investment while holding up short-term rates to cut outflows of funds overseas. (4) Stepped-up investment in human capital through worker training and retraining programs. (5) The use of wage-price guideposts to help ensure that stimulative measures would not run off into wage and price inflation. (6) Perhaps least well recognized, the decision in late 1961 to go for the "Cambridge-New Haven Growth School" formula of tilting the fiscal-monetary mix to favor capital formation relative to consumption. How? By holding off on tax cuts in the hope that the economy could struggle up to full employment under the then-existing burden of taxation and thus produce a full-employment surplus. This would increase saving and facilitate investment.

Let me pause here to note two oft-misunderstood points. The first is that while the supply-side effects of tax cuts on work effort and on saving are murky at best, there's no doubt that running a surplus at full employment would have positive supply-side effects. To be more specific:

True, the bulk of the evidence does show a significant investment response to sharply targeted measures like investment tax credits and more liberal depreciation. But on work response, the evidence is ambiguous. Countless studies show that existing workers' responses to tax cuts are an amalgam of (a) added work by some—the "eager beavers"—as they keep a larger proportion of their rewards for work effort and thus see the cost of leisure going up; (b) no change by those who are locked into a pattern of fixed hours; and (c) reduced work by those "laid-back" members of the labor force who ease off because they can now achieve their income-after-tax targets with fewer hours of work. Contrary to loose—but ever-confident—assertions by some supply-side economists, painstaking research has not yet established for sure even the sign—plus or minus—of workers' net response, let alone the magnitude. (Studies do show that increases in take-home pay elicit significant positive responses of labor effort by spouses and other second earners.)

Similarly, on savings, we are not quite sure which response dominates: to save *more* in the light of lower taxes on savings or to save less since lower taxes enable the saver to achieve a given target living standard with less saving. Most economists would agree that, on net balance, there is a modest positive response of saving to tax cuts. We do know that when governments cut their deficits or run surpluses, *that* constitutes net saving (i.e., either reduced dissaving or positive saving) and releases funds for business investment and housing, provided that the economy is not operating at low ebb and that the monetary authorities do not offset the effect by single-minded pursuit of the wrong target.

The second point is that although President Kennedy sought some significant expenditure increases from Congress, both for social programs and defense, his success ratio on civilian programs was not high, and total defense spending as a percentage of GNP declined steadily during his administration. I underscore the latter point because the idea that he got the economy moving again through a defense buildup is a canard that dies mighty hard. Recently, a *New York Times* guest columnist confidently asserted that "the higher growth rates of the 1960s were achieved only after President Kennedy succeeded in persuading Congress that, in light of the Berlin crisis, defense spending should be increased by 50 percent." In *absolute* terms, national defense expenditures rose less than 10 percent in the early sixties, from $46 billion in 1960 to $50 billion by 1965. More important, in *relative* terms, defense outlays actually fell as a percentage of GNP, from 9 percent in 1960 to about 7.5 percent in 1965, just before escalation in Vietnam. So much for the notion that defense powered the 1961-65 expansion.

## The Demand-Side Follow-Through: The 1964 Tax Cut

The shift to demand-side economics came in 1962 when it became painfully apparent that the overburden of taxes was so heavy that the economy could not achieve prosperity under its yoke. Alas, the Cambridge-New Haven hope for big full-employment surpluses had to go by the boards. With economic expansion faltering in 1962, with Congress in no mood to provide economic stimulus from the budget-spending side, and with top individual income tax rates still at 91 percent—far too high—we launched the offensive for a big tax cut in

March of 1962. Its main purpose was to step up the pace of expansion and bring the economy up to its full-employment potential.

From March 1962 on, the Council campaigned for a $10 billion—later a $12 billion—tax cut. The Treasury was initially willing to go along with $3 or $4 billion of it, mainly to facilitate tax reform. But it was not until we hammered out an agreement in the Cabinet Committe on Growth late in 1962 that the President adopted the $12 billion tax-cut goal. The tax cut's nine-month White House gestation period was then followed by 15 months of labor in Congress. To be pushing a large tax cut in the face of a sizable deficit and a rising economy was unprecedented. It was a rocky road.

Fairly early in the game, the President had to drop much of his reform package in order to clear the track for the cut itself. And much of the Kennedy Cabinet voiced only lukewarm support (and some, privately, opposition or apprehension) lest the tax cut deprive them of revenues needed for their programs. That it would stimulate the economy and provide a sounder basis for later increased appropriations was not an easy case to sell.

That calls for another word about the bizarre notion that a tax cut will pay for itself by so stimulating *supply*—by unleashing such torrents of work effort, savings, and investment—that the reflow of tax revenues will match the initial tax loss. When an economy is operating far below its potential, as in the early 1960s, a tax cut's *demand*-side effect boosts purchasing power and puts both idle machines and factories and idle workers back to work and thus broadens the tax base—not enough fully to pay for itself, but enough to cut the revenue loss significantly.[2] The notion that a tax cut's prompt demand stimulus—let alone its long-delayed supply stimulus—could generate enough revenue to pay for itself is unfortunately not supported by the statistical evidence and analysis.[3] (One time, in an exuberant response to a leading question by the late Sen. Hubert Humphrey, then chairman of the Joint Economic Committee, I suggested that the tax cut had paid for itself—but on careful inspection of the evidence, I publicly recanted later in a letter to the *Wall Street Journal*.)

In any event, the tax cut—20 percent for individuals and, in combination with the earlier tax breaks for business, 20 percent for corporations—became law after President Kennedy's death. To a remarkable degree, it "delivered the goods" until it was overtaken by Vietnam events.

Enacted in March 1964, the cut stimulated a more vigorous expansion of the economy and reduction of unemployment without agitating inflation. The specific numbers: by July of 1965 (just before escalation of the war in Vietnam), the unemployment rate had dropped to 4.4 percent, while the consumer price index was rising at a rate of only 1.5 percent per year. Given the noninflationary environment, it was possible to put expansionary fiscal policy in harness with an accommodative monetary policy rather than having them pull in opposite directions. Dropping top individual tax rates from 91 percent to 70 percent helped to weaken somewhat the incentives for tax avoidance and strengthen the incentives for investment, while easing of low-bracket rates and tightening of the capital gains tax helped improve the equity of the tax structure. In two-track policy, emphasizing both demand and supply stimulus, the tax cuts provided a powerful boost to demand while at the same time providing incentives to increase risk taking and enlarge the flow of investment funds. In point of fact, the ratio of private investment to GNP reached a new postwar peak in 1965. (Yet, one cannot simply equate added investment with faster productivity growth, as demonstrated by the simultaneous slowdown of productivity growth and step-up of capital accumulation after the 1964 tax cut).

As later events proved, the surest path to more adequate financing for government programs was, paradoxically, through tax reduction. With the acceleration of expansion through the tax cut, the economy soon returned to full prosperity. Both the atmosphere thus created and the resulting generous flows of federal, state, and local revenues led the country to a more sympathetic attitude toward expansion of government social programs. As President Kennedy put it in a conversation just eleven days before his death, "First we'll get your tax cut, and then we'll get my expenditure programs." And on November 19, he assured me that a direct attack on poverty would be part of his 1964 program. The 17 percent rise in GNP in the two years after the tax cut—between the first quarters of 1964 and 1966—made possible a 13.5 percent rise in government spending at lower average tax rates.

The tax cut proved the flip side of the Kennedy dictum that success has a thousand fathers, but failure is an orphan. In a perverse way, I treasure an April 1964 release by the American Taxpayers Union of New Jersey assuring one and all that it had "planned, initiated, and spearheaded the crusade that resulted in the recent [federal] tax cut." Showing a nice sense of proportion, it went on to note its support of legalized off-track betting.

Successful as the tax cut was, one has to add one disappointing postscript. When, with Vietnam, the time came for President Johnson and the Congress to turn the "new economics" around—to use tax increases to cut aggregate demand and subdue inflation—the political process was found wanting. It was not until mid-1968 that a tax increase was finally enacted. Meanwhile, the superimposing of some $25 billion per year of Vietnam expenditures on an economy already programmed for full employment had done its malevolent work, overheating the economy and letting the inflationary tiger out of its cage. Against the great human and political tragedy of Vietman, the economic cost may not loom so large. But without that tragic war, I doubt very much that we would have been blown so far off the course of economic-growth-with-price-stability on which President Kennedy set us in his exhilarating thousand days.

# Notes

1. This position, in extreme form, is typified by Irving Kristol: "The Keynesian assumption was that, so long as total demand is adequate to achieve full employment, one need pay no attention to the incentives to save, invest, or engage in entrepreneurial risk-taking. Indeed, one could safely frustrate those incentives through taxation and regulation, just so long as our clever economists on the Council of Economic Advisors 'fine-tuned' economic demand to the proper level." (*Wall Street Journal*, December 19, 1980).

2. Arthur Okun, "The 1964 Tax Cut," in Walter W. Heller, ed., *Perspectives on Economic Growth* (New York: Random House, 1968).

3. Office of Management and Budget, *Midsession Review of the 1982 Budget*, July 15, 1981.

# The Thatcher Experiment: A Requiem?

John Burton

## The Thatcher Experiment—An Overview

### Margaret Thatcher and the Social-Democratic Background

The coming to power to Margaret Thatcher in May 1979 was initially heralded, both in Britain and overseas, as a watershed event in the governance of Britain and the direction of British economic policy.

Throughout the previous three decades British governments—of whatever political color (Labor, Conservative, or Liberal-Labor coalition)—had operated on so-called mixed economy lines. There was a tacit acceptance of this general program and of the political-economic philosophy that underpinned it among politicians of all parties, the civil service mandarinate, most media commentators, and the public generally.

In the fifties this consensus political package of economic policies had been labelled in Britain as "Butskellism," after two of its most noted practitioners—the Conservative R. A. Butler and the Labor party leader Hugh Gaitskell. That term has now generally fallen out of use, and I shall here call the consensus view the *social democratic program*. It was a "philosophy" of pragmatism in economic policy, a "philosophy" of overt avoidance of ideological (or other) principles, a "philosophy" of *ad hoc* tinkering with the economy in response to short-run political pressures or economic problems, a "philosophy" of avoiding basic questions or issues.

Specifically, the social democratic program of all post-war governments in Britain from the beginning of the fifties until 1979 was for an admixture of Keynesian aggregate demand management, to stabilize the economy and provide full employment; an extensive "welfare state," conducted by the provision of "free" (i.e., zero-price but tax-financed) welfare services by government bureaucracies; income redistribution conducted by the provision of social security benefits to the poor, financed supposedly by high marginal rates of taxation at the other end of the income scale; the persistence (no great change either way) of the extensive volume of state ownership of industry in Britain; perennial attempts to cure inflaton via incomes policies; ragged attempts to improve economic coordination by planning the economy *à la Francais* (i.e., corporatist/indicative planning); acceptance and accommodation of the trade union movement as one of the "great economic interests;" and extensive government financial intervention in "private" industry via subsidies and government-sponsored mergers, to promote industrial efficiency and to solve "regional" (often marginal constituency) problems.

## The Roots of the Thatcher Experiment

By 1979 there had arisen in Britain an extensive (although uneasy and not always clear) public perception that this social democratic consensus program had not worked as promised. The nature and sources of that failure have been extensively analyzed elsewhere,[1] and will not detain us much further here. Suffice it to say that, by the latter years of the seventies, there was a widespread public appreciation that something was going badly wrong in the general drift of things. There was a feeling that the pragmatism of the social-democratic program had produced, not a balanced mixture in the economy, but rather a badly mixed-up economy, exhibiting ever-present tendencies towards the growth of government expenditure and taxation as government after government rushed in with further doses of yet more interventionist medicine in order (temporarily) to cover up the failure of disagreeable consequences of previous doses. Furthermore, Keynesianism had failed to deliver the goal of full employment at zero or acceptable inflation. The reality of the Keynesian era in Britain was that there had been a secular increase in the level of unemployment, accompanied by a secular increase in the rate of inflation. Again, inefficiency in the welfare bureaucracies and in the departments of central and local government was increasingly becoming a naked and commonplace fact of everday life. Nor was it "the rich" who were paying for the extension of bureaucracy in the name of social welfare. Inexorably, the level of direct taxation had risen in Britain, the brunt of finance for the welfare state falling upon the broad mass of voters. It was also recognized that the sheer progressivity of the tax system in Britain, most especially as it affected those in the lowest and upper income groups—some in the lower stretches facing marginal tax rates of over 100 percent—was creating a disinclination to work. Finally, despite experiment after experiment with income policies, none had succeeded in containing inflation. The last of these, the "social contract" between the Labor government and the Trades Union Congress during the period 1974-79, had been bought at great cost from the unions by the government of the day—and for little long-run benefits to the quelling of wage and price inflation. Under the social contract, the government bought trade union compliance with incomes policy at the price of massive changes in the labor law, which greatly reinforced trade union powers.[2]

In the winter of 1978/79, the "Contract"—which was not a legally enforceable agreement in any way—broke down. Public sector unions in particular used their muscle to prosecute large wage claims. In the ensuing strike wave, public patience with the trade unions was greatly exhausted. Much had been given to the unions (more than most people had understood) to buy their support for incomes policy. All this remained on the statute book. Union support for incomes policy had subsequently melted away. The gains from the legislative revolution in terms of inflation had clearly been temporary. There was an extensive strike in the road haulage (trucking) industry in the winter of 1978/79, which threatened serious disruption to the distribution of food and of supplies of materials to industry. Meanwhile, the public was also subjected to strikes throughout the public sector: in the hospital services, burial services, rubbish disposal services, the state school system, and the water supply system. The spectacle of people with injuries being prevented from entering a hospital by a picket line was a particular focus of public resentment.

This was one of the roots of the Thatcher "revolution": voter perception that the social democratic "pragmatist" program was going badly wrong. As Lord Harris of High Cross points out, "it cannot be doubted that Margaret Thatcher was swept to power in May 1979 by widespread public anxiety about the excesses of trade unions, taxation, bureaucracy and inflation."[3]

The other root of the Thatcher revolution was intellectual. Classical liberal economic thought started to make a strong comeback in Britain near the end of the sixties, and most especially in the seventies. The works of Milton Friedman, Friedrich Hayek, and other classical liberal economists were to become fashionable and influential.

Two politicians clearly so influenced were Sir Keith Joseph, now secretary of state for industry, and Margaret Thatcher, now prime minister. Sir Keith Joseph—a life-long Conservative party member — was to announce that his actual conversion to Conservatism took place in April of 1974. This was to be followed by a large number of "provocative" speeches and pamphlets by the new guru of Conservatism that set out an essentially classical liberal position.[4] Margaret Thatcher, although less "academic" in her presentation, trod the same path.[5] Although both possessed a somewhat austere and thus unattractive "TV personality," they at least offered a "new" alternative to the endless drift of the social democratic program.

Many Britons wanted to see an escape from the creeping "British disease" of stagflation, slow growth, continuously increasing government and bureaucracy, strikes, and the abuse of trade union power. They wanted something different. In the general election of May 1979, they got it. Margaret Thatcher came to power with a clear and decisive 43-seat majority in the House of Commons.

## The Thatcher Preelection Pledges

Whatever the precise balance of forces that brought about Margaret Thatcher's electoral victory, there can be no doubt that she came to power in the spring of 1979 with a clear and decisive electoral mandate to reestablish correspondence with economic realities in the British economy, to reject and reverse measures of government intervention, to cut government expenditure, waste, and taxation, to deal with inflation via control of the money supply, and to reduce trade union power.

This, at least, was what the public expected. A detailed inspection of the preelection Conservative policy document, *The Right Approach to the Economy*[6] which detailed a ten-point series of main commitments, reveals that the image of Thatcherism in people's minds did not correspond entirely to the actual promises. The "hard" commitments in this document were four in number: (1) Provision of a more stable economic climate with as few changes as possible and a firm brake on legislation. (2) Strict control by the government of the rate of growth of the money supply. (3) Firm management of government expenditure. (4) Lower taxation on earnings, capital, and savings. Commitment (1) is the strategy of "gradualism," (2) is the strategy of (Friedmanite) monetarism,[7] while (3) and (4) constitute a commitment to what is known (in the U.S.) as "supply-side economic policy."

Although the wording of these four primary pledges looks straightforward, a little reflection reveals ambiguity. First, there is no specification of *how* the Thatcher administration would institute a "strict control" of the money supply. Second, "firm management" of government spending does not imply anything about how or where it would be cut, or by how much. We shall see, later, how these ambiguities were to prove to be great weaknesses of the Thatcher experiment.

There were two other major weaknesses of the *Right Approach to the Economy*. First, the document was muted to the point of vapidity on the topic of trade union law reform. Item (7) of the strategy, not listed above, refers to the goal of "the encouragement of better methods of collective bargaining"—which could mean anything or nothing. Later in the document there is also talk of introducing a "code of practice" in collective bargaining procedures (i.e., an unspecified set of government "guidelines" for bargainers), and the introduction of another "code of practice" regarding the negotiation of closed and union shop agreements. There is a world of difference, however, between a suggestion and statutory reform.

The second other weakness was the document's lack of precision about industrial policy. Its main positive commitment was that of supply-side economic policy, the purpose being to restimulate economic growth "by the gradual and systematic removal of the deterrants and discouragements that have grown up to hold back Britain's instinctive industrial and commercial vitality."[8]

Apart from this, there was little positive content to the statement on industrial policy. Specifically, little or nothing was said on how the government would deal in actuality with a failing enterprise or industry nor how it would resist the temptation to cave in to trade union (and other) demands for a bail-out operation in such circumstances.

We shall see later how these various weaknesses in the Thatcher economic strategy eventually were to undermine drastically its general viability.

### The International Significance of the Thatcher Experiment

The Thatcher experiment is of general international significance in four main ways. First, the British political system is ordered so that any British government—so long as it retains majority support in the House of Commons—has the power to make massive and radical changes in the economy and polity. Britain has no (or, rather, very little) written Constitution that constrains the executive branch of government. A majority-based British government is thus not beset by the sort of constitutional checks and balances that constrain the actions of American presidents, or the trade-offs in policy necessary in coalition governments (as in Sweden today). This means that, if a truly collectivist party ever came to power in Britain (by no means an impossibility as the Labor party is now very much to the left, its "social democrats" having split off to form a new political party of their own), we may witness a very rapid transmogrification of the British polity and economy into an East European-type situation. On the other hand, the same characteristics of the British political system allow a government that is oriented toward a philosophy of freedom of choice and free enterprise to make very rapid and radical changes in that direction also. In other words, the Thatcher experiment is of international significance because the political-institutional impediments to a rapid "return to the free market" are weak in Britain. If the trick cannot be worked in Britain, then the difficulty of that task in many other countries must be judged greater. This is of particular relevance to the Reagan experiment in America. As Atkinson notes:

> Although the Thatcher policies are extremely unpopular [in Britain], there is as yet little opposition to them within the government. Parliament, except in extraordinary circumstances, carries out the will of the government in power. By contrast, it is hard to imagine Congress going along with the entire Reagan administration program—especially all of the promised slashes in federal spending.[9]

A second factor that makes the Thatcher experiment of international significance is the character of the prime minister herself. *Pravda* dubbed her "the Iron Lady," and there is an element of truth in this characterization. Mrs. Thatcher is (correctly) viewed—both domestically and internationally—as a particularly tenacious prime minister. She also has the firmest of attachments to free society/free market views to be observed among the political leaders of the contemporary West, with the possible exception of President Reagan. Again, if the Iron Lady cannot successully launch a market counterrevolution, we must judge the possibilities of weaker reeds achieving it as the more remote.

There are some *caveats* that must be issued at this point. The governance of Britain is constitutionally in the hands not of the prime minister but of the cabinet. The British system of government is formally one of cabinet government; the prime minister is a minister of the crown, like other cabinet members, but is *primus inter pares*. The cabinet in turn works on the principle of collective responsibility: decisions are made collectively, and the responsibility for such policy decisions is shared collectively. In practice, this difference between a British prime minister and a U.S. president is more apparent than real in the usual case because the prime minister appoints the members of the cabinet and can ask for their resignation at will. However, the difference remains.

In the current context, this point is important because the cabinet of Margaret Thatcher is not fully behind her. The statement quoted above, that there is "little opposition" to Thatcherite policies within the present British government, is quite inaccurate. British journalists describe the situation by dividing the cabinet into a group of "wets" (who are opposed to the pace, if not the direction, of the Thatcher experiment) and "drys" (who are philosophically with Margaret Thatcher). The "wets", the most notable of whom is James Prior (employment secretary), would like to see a "bold" reflationary strategy and a general "softly, softly" approach to reform—most notably trade union reform. The "drys" are for sound finance and for pushing ahead with the general Thatcher program. This division into "wets" and "drys," however, somewhat oversimplifies the situation. A perhaps better assessment was offered by the political scientist Professor Robert McKenzie who estimates that, among the current British cabinet, one-third (at most) are in agreement with Mrs. Thatcher's economic policies, one-third are skeptical, and one-third are actively hostile.[10] This situation within the British cabinet has most certainly impeded the implementation of the Thatcher experiment, particularly as regards cutting the level of public expenditure (which the "wets" have resisted). It has to be presumed that Mrs. Thatcher does not rid herself of at least some of her opponents in the cabinet because she fears this might provoke a split within her own Conservative party ranks within the House of Commons. She would have been wiser to have chosen a predominantly loyal team of cabinet ministers at the beginning of her administration, while public opinion was still in the "honeymoon" period after the election, and her possibilities of political maneuvering and appointment were at their zenith.

A third reason why the Thatcher experiment is of general international significance is that Britain retains (despite—or perhaps because of—its status as the "sick man of Europe") a residual significance for intellectual thought and political developments in other countries that is quite disproportionate to the country's actual population size, economic performance, or military "punch." This influence of British developments upon ideas and practices elsewhere is most prominent in America: it has long been said (by Americans) that political developments in America follow those in Britain—with a long lag. Tyrell notes the point:

> Since—roughly speaking—the first quarter of the nineteenth century, a powerful sense of cultural inferiority has crept into the realms of American leadership. This sense of inferiority (combined with shared customs) has given Europe, specifically England, a powerful influence over American life. The "progressive" ways of the English have been extolled throughout this century by Americans intent on conducting America along the British path, and so successful have these Americans been that today most of our government expenditures go to institutions very similar to England's.[11]

It is not well appreciated today, in Britain or other countries, that if the Thatcher experiment fails, either economically or politically (or both), it could have pervasive ramifications for the directions of political change in other Western countries. Many people in many countries, and notably their politicians, will see in the success or failure of the Thatcher experiment an answer to some of their own general questions. Can we reverse the trend towards collectivism? *Is* there an escape route? Or must we accept that things have now gone too far? Could it—the same sort of political medicine—work here?

This brings us to the fourth major reason for the international significance of the Thatcher experiment: the lessons to be learnt for the Reagan experiment in the U.S.A.

## The Thatcher and Reagan Experiments

The Reagan administration was voted into power on the basis of a package of proposals closely resembling the Thatcher preelection promises. Government spending, the budget deficit, and the rate of growth of the money supply were to be controlled. Taxes—or at least the rate of growth of taxes—were to be cut. Meanwhile, economic growth would be rekindled by a liberal application of supply-side economics.

As the results of the Thatcher experiment have turned from the disappointing to the grim, so Reagan's economic policy lieutenants have sought to emphasize the differences between the Reagan and

Thatcher programs. The message is: "it will work here, because we are doing it all different."

The (supposed) basic differences between the two approaches can be illustrated by means of two equations:

Proposition 1. $\dot{P}=\dot{M}-\dot{Q}$

Proposition 2. $G=T+C+\Delta B+\Delta M^H$

Where: $\dot{P}$ is the rate of price inflation

$\dot{M}$ is the rate of growth of the money supply

$\dot{Q}$ is the rate of growth of real output in the economy

G is the volume of government spending

T is tax revenues (direct and indirect)

C is charges on prices for publicly provided services

$\Delta B$ is the addition to government borrowing (i.e., increase in the national debt)

$\Delta M^H$ is the increase in the money stock used to finance (part of) government spending.

Equation (1) is the (dynamic form) of the quantity theory of money; inflation (it says) is caused by money growth outstripping real output growth. Equation (2) is the government's budget constraint, stating that government spending cannot exceed the sum of its income (T+C), borrowing ($\Delta B$), and issue of new money ($\Delta M^H$).

The supposed differences between Thatcher and Reagan strategies may now be defined. Lewis Lehrman, a "supply-side economist" who has influenced David Stockman (director of the Office of Management and Budget), argues as follows. As we see from equation (1), there are two ways to reduce inflation: by cutting $\dot{M}$ or by raising $\dot{Q}$. Margaret Thatcher has put the emphasis upon the first—monetary control— which has led to recession. The alternative is the approach of supply-side economics: to raise the rate of growth of the economy. Supply-siders do not deny the necessity of containing monetary growth. But they see a major part of the anti-inflation drive as operating through measures to stimulate output, not by Keynesian demand management, but by raising the "natural" rate of growth in the economy. Thus, we have Treasury Secretary Donald T. Regan's statement that "a major reduction in inflation and a resurgence of economic growth are not only compatible but inseparable."[12]

The supply-siders argue that economic growth can be stimulated naturally—and not artificially, à la Keynes—by the freeing of market processes, this involving a reduction in the scale of the public sector (thus releasing resources for private sector expansion) and tax cuts to stimulate greater effort and new enterprise. In other words, they propose that the Reagan experiment be conducted primarily through the G and T variables in equation (2).

The prominent supply-sider, Arthur B. Laffer (director of the Center for the Study of Private Enterprise at the University of Southern

California), thus charges that the Thatcher experiment went wrong because it was not sufficiently free market in orientation:

> Quite simply, the policies put into effect by Margaret Thatcher and the Conservative Party have not been oriented towards free markets. Taxation definitely has not been reduced. Instead, the preponderance of the policies affected by the Conservative government reflect further drift from the basic precepts of private incentives and free markets. . . .
>
> The overall rate of taxation was raised, not lowered, as promised by candidate Margaret Thatcher.[13]

It is also noted that, instead of gradually reducing government expenditure, the Thatcher administration has in fact allowed it to start rising again, to 47 percent of gross domestic product (including transfer and national debt interest payments).[14]

With its emphasis upon supply-side economics, will the Reagan experiment work where the Thatcher experiment failed? Are the supply-siders correct in their analyses and contentions?

There are good grounds for claiming that the supply-siders are in part deluding themselves and the Reagan administration. First, as was noted in the foregoing, the Thatcher preelection pledges *fully incorporated* a commitment to supply-side economics. Mrs. Thatcher and her close colleagues such as Sir Keith Joseph and Sir Geoffrey Howe thus shared the same basic economic philosophy as Laffer, Lehrman, Stockman, and Regan. The basic strategy was the same: what proved so difficult in the Thatcher experiment was the translation of this philosophy into political *practice*. It is easy to talk supply-side economics—cutting government expenditure and taxation, deregulation, the freeing of markets. The difficulty, it appears, is in trying to do it, because of powerful lobbies (who gain from the level/allocation of government spending) virulently oppose any such moves. Here the supply-siders are ignoring vital lessons about the Thatcher experiment. This essay tries to provide some of the missing insights.

Second, the supply-siders are dabbling in unadorned optimism when they argue that inflation can be quelled reasonably quickly by measures to raise the "natural" (i.e., long-run or equilibrium) rate of growth of the economy. The rate of growth of the money supply is (at least in principle, though it did not work that way in the practice of the Thatcher experiment) quickly controllable by government. The long-run rate of growth of the economy is certainly subject to the influence of government, but any such influences appear to take a very long (and indeed unknown) time to work. Furthermore, the natural rate of growth of an economy cannot be varied dramatically (even in the long run) in the same manner as the rate of growth of the money supply: it might possibly be boosted by a few percentage points by the freeing of markets, but we must not expect (according to the available evidence) that the (rather minor) government spending and tax cuts contemplated by the Reagan administration will somehow transform an economy in stagnation into a double-digit growth rate economy. Yet that is the order of magnitude of the growth rate jump that is necessary if an economy (as in the U.S. or the U.K.) with double-digit inflation is to defeat inflation by movement on the supply-side instead of the monetary side. This is the simple implication of the quantity theory of money, exhibited in equation (1).

And the Reagan tax "cuts" *are* of minor significance. As Atkinson notes:

> The [promised] Reagan tax "cuts" are actually from a rising tax burden. In Britain, personal income taxes have been indexed so that they do not rise automatically with inflation. The income tax cuts in Thatcher's first budget left the real income tax burden lower—rather than merely slowing its rise, as would be the case here. But even this real increased "incentive" did not revitalize the British economy as promised.[15]

The simple fact is that the only reasonably quick, and eventually effective, way to cut inflation is to cut the rate of growth of the money supply. And all evidence suggests that changes in the rate of growth of the money supply (at least, those which are unanticipated) have effects on the level of output and employment. The inevitable consequence, as has happened in every monetary stabilization crisis in history, is that the side effect of monetary deceleration is a period of recession.

The general point is that the Reagan experiment will eventually run into the same sort of problems, from one side or another, that have afflicted the Thatcher experiment. Public spending will prove difficult to control, let alone to cut. Economic adjustment problems caused by the attempted cuts will emerge and will result in at least some back sliding of the government. Moreover, many spending cuts will be, sooner or later, opposed by vocal and often economically powerful lobbies and their representatives. These cries will be amplified by the tactics of bureaucrats who seek to contain and reverse the effect of spending cuts on the size of their organizations and who therefore have an incentive to implement cuts in a manner which maximizes public outcry.

Again, the Reagan administration will find that, to contain inflation with any reasonable speed, it will have to cut monetary growth sharply: but to do this, without causing a surge in the level of government borrowing (and thus the level of interest rates—which will damage business, as happened in the Thatcher experiment) or the foregoing of its tax "cuts" program, will take remarkably tough action on the level of federal government spending. And the initial impact of both spending cuts and monetary deceleration will be a rise in unemployment, resulting in a loss of (income and sales) tax revenue, and a rise in government welfare spending on the unemployed.

The Reagan administration faces the same vicious circle of problems as confronted the Thatcher administration. There will be no easy escape through an instantaneous "magic wand" effect of supply-side economics.

None of this is to deny that things may work out differently in the Reagan experiment than in the Thatcher experiment, for a number of reasons. First, the contexts in which the experiments have been conducted are different. Some such differences have already been noted; others are also important. A primary factor is that the dimensions of the public sector differ in the two countries. Approximately one quarter of the employed British work force are direct or indirect employees of government (central or local) or employeyss of state-controlled concerns. Many others are in receipt of government transfer payments of one form or another, thus taking the total in receipt of government disbursements to well over half the population. A very large constituency thus has an interest in maintaining the size of the public sector. The size of this political problem is smaller in the U.S.A. —although still very large.

Second, the degree of unionization is higher in Britain than in the U.S. (roughly over half as against one-fifth of the work force), and evidence indicates that wage adjustments are more sluggish in unionized than nonunionized labor markets. Monetary restraint policies might thus work the quicker, and at lower costs in terms of unemployment and lost output, in the U.S. than in Britain.

Third, the British economy is far more open internationally than the U.S. economy. Over the past few years, the combination of high interest rates (attracting foreign money inflows) and the massive export earnings from North Sea oil have pushed the sterling exchange rate to high levels on foreign exchange markets, with the effect that Britain's (nonoil) export industries have suffered from declining competitiveness on international markets. The relatively closed nature of the U.S. economy would reduce the impact of the effects of monetary restraint compared to Britain (it would not, however, be immune).

Fourth, any incoming U.S. administration has the ability to emplace its "own" men and women to positions not only in the cabinet but way down in the hierarchy of government. In Britain, a government comes to power, the cabinet changes, but "the civil service remains." Cabinet ministers in the U.K. are surrounded by the same set of permanent officials, all with clear vested interests in the maintenance of the size of their present operations. Consequently, in Britain, any "wagon train" of a new government is surrounded by a permanent force of "red Indian" civil servants. Although the latter are (in British constitutional theory) supposed to be politically neutral advisors to, and instruments of, their ministers, these civil servants have an incentive to resist radical change (in either political direction)—to go for a "quiet life" — and most especially so when cost-pruning measures are contemplated.

Fifth, as the Thatcher experiment preceded the Reagan experiment, it has been possible for the incoming Reagan administration and its advisors to learn from experience and to avoid at least some of the potential pitfalls. The most notable instance of such learning at a distance relates to the failure of the Thatcher government to cut government spending sharply and decisively in the early "honeymoon" period after its installation. In February 1981, representatives of the U.S. House Budget Committee visited Britain to examine the Thatcher experiment at close quarters. Before leaving, the committee chairman, Rep. Jim Jones, was to state: "If there is one conclusion we have aimed at here, it is that we should be quick, dramatic and explicit in cutting (government) spending before we do anything else."[16]

President Reagan's announcement, later in the month, of $49.1 billion of proposed spending cuts in the federal government's budget demonstrates that at least one lesson of the Thatcher experiment has already gone home.

Finally, the Thatcher and Reagan experiments are taking place against the background of differently textured sociocultural "climates." In the U.K., the "British disease" is deeper and longer entrenched, resulting in a long swing in the national mood towards pessimism. State control and ownership have become so deeply and extensive embedded in the economy (e.g. the National Health Service, the nationalized industries, the welfare state) for such a long period of time that their continued existence has come to be taken as an incontestable and unalterable fact. Many Britons, including many (if not most) of the highly educated, seem to suffer as if under a "spell" of collectivism. They cannot even conceive of an alternative to existing state institutions. In America, things may be different—at least in degree. There still seems to be a general ethos of individualism, optimism about the future, and a distaste for centralized decision making: the spell of collectivism seems less deeply embedded in the average human psyche. Such factors may make the Reagan experiment the easier to implement.[17]

Thus, a variety of factors may make the problems encountered by Reagan's four-point "Program for Economic Recovery" different in degree from those that have deflected the Thatcher strategy. He may find the ride less rough. But this does not detract from the general point. The Thatcher and Reagan programs are very similar in terms of their general philosophy, and they are being introduced in two societies which have broadly similar economic, political, and social structures, and which, moreover, are closely connected by the ties of history. The Reagan program is thus likely to run into the same sort of *general* problems as the Thatcher strategy, because a very similar politico-economic "experiment" is being tried under very similar environmental conditions. Whatever differentiation President Reagan's supply-side economic advisors may seek to make between the Thatcher and Reagan experiments, this central fact cannot be avoided. Ronald

Reagan, no less than Margaret Thatcher, is eventually likely to face a political Rubicon. The lessons of the Thatcher experiment, described in this essay, may perhaps make the crossing of it the easier.

## II. What Went Wrong? A Diagnosis

### Images and Realities

When Mrs. Thatcher first came to power, the stock market bubbled with enthusiasm. Equity prices swelled in anticipation of higher economic growth and profits.

Even eighteen months later, despite mounting economic and political difficulties in Britain, the Thatcher experiment was continuing to receive a good press, and open admiration in some quarters, in the U.S.A. One American commentator was then to write of Mrs. Thatcher's progress:

> Into the most crucial positions in her administration she has brought leading free market advocates, particularly the new secretaries of industry and of trade, the budget director, and the chancellor of the exchequer.
>
> Together, they have made inroads against the socialistic tide. Thatcher has slashed the income tax, reduced public spending, eliminated the powerful price commission, taken government out of collective bargaining, and made plans to denationalize several key industries. In the works are proposals to break up government monopolies such as the post office.[18]

The reality, as increasingly comprehended in Britain by that time, was more sombre. In the same month as the Castrovinci article appeared, an *Economist* lead article was to comment on Mrs. Thatcher's policies thusly:

> Elected to cut public spending, control inflation through tight monetary control and regenerate industry, she has presided over a rise in the public sector's share of GDP, a 20 percent wage round, a surge in money supply, an over-10 percent drop in manufacturing production and a squeeze on company profits. This week both sterling (higher against the dollar than for seven years) and unemployment (higher than for forty years) soared beyond the limits of her government's nervous expectation of the likely results of its policies. How did it get in such a miserable mess?[19]

This chapter seeks to answer that question.

The image of the Thatcher government among the British public is also wide of the mark. It is generally felt that the government's actual program is radical in its dimensions. This has been sustained by the pronouncements of two political sources: the Thatcher government itself, and its political opponents. The rhetoric of government ministers, and most especially of Mrs. Thatcher herself, has until recently aimed at sustaining the impression that the government is acting radically and toughly to remove the sources of the "British disease."

The rhetoric of the political opponents of the administration has also aimed at conveying the impression that the current government represents the most radically reactionary, ruthless, and procapitalist British government in half a century or more. Tony Benn, leader of the far left "Labor Co-ordinating Committee" of the Labor party, has presented it in the following terms:

> What we are getting is political strategy designed to bring about a fundamental and irreversible shift in the balance of wealth and power in favor of the owners of capital at the expense of working people and their families. . . .

> We are at the receiving end of a comprehensive strategy devised to end full employment, dismantle the Welfare State, widen social inequalities and reduce working people to a state of greatest subservience to their employers. To achieve all that, trade unionism as it has grown in Britain has got to be driven back and neutralized as a serious force in industry and politics.

Specifically, four things are commonly charged by the opponents of the Thatcher government:

(1) It is pursuing a "hardline" monetarist policy, involving a strict control of the money supply, which is responsible for the current recession.

(2) It has inflicted "savage" cuts in the level of public spending.

(3) It is dismantling the nationalized industries and pursuing, full speed ahead, a return to the market economy.

(4) It is undermining the basic legal "rights" (i.e., immunities) of the trade unions and seriously challenging their power.

None of this stands up to scrutiny. The rhetoric of neither the government nor its opponents has corresponded very much with reality. It is true that some elements of that Thatcher cabinet would have liked to take a firm grip on the money supply and public spending; it is true that an even smaller component of the cabinet would have wished to cut down government involvement in industry and to end some of the immunities of the unions. But this has not, in reality, been done. This chapter seeks to analyze the causes and consequences of these policy failures of the Thatcher experiment. We address three central topics: monetary and financial policy, fiscal policy, and supply-side policies.

## The Failure of Monetary and Financial Policy

The Thatcher government's detailed plans for monetary and financial control were announced as its "medium term financial strategy" and published in March 1980. Target ranges for the growth of the money supply—specifically, a monetary aggregate known officially as sterling M3—were announced for the four forthcoming years. Sterling M3 was targeted to grow in the range of 7-11 percent in 1980/81, 6-10 percent in 1981/82, 5-9 percent in 1982/83, and 4-5 percent in 1983/84.[20] The purpose of the financial strategy was to reduce inflation to single figures over a number of years, at minimum cost to output and employment, by a gradual, steady, and predictable reduction in the growth rate of the money supply.

Despite the detailed commitments, and the importance which the government attached to monetary control as a vital element in its strategy against inflation, things did not work out very much as planned. Some calculations suggest that the measured growth of sterling M3 was roughly double its target over the period February-October 1980: 20 percent at a per annum rate, as against a target of 7-11 percent. As we shall see below, this could partly have been caused by a distortion of the figures. However, as a prestigious monetary review was to comment: "What is certain is that monetary growth has not decelerated steadily or predictably; it has probably accelerated, but to an extent which is not precisely known."[21] The bulge in the measured rate of money stock growth in the latter part of 1980 was probably partly caused by the removal (in the summer of 1980) of a central bank-imposed quantitative constraint on the volume of interest-bearing deposits of the commercial banks, a constraint which had been in operation since December of 1973. This control was known as the "corset" and had originally been imposed to stop the commercial banks competing for funds by offering higher interest rates to depositors. In the latter part of the last decade, it was also to be used as a supposed means of containing monetary growth, so as to attain certain monetary targets.

As with any price control scheme (in this case, regarding the price of a certain type of loanable fund), there were incentives to circumvent the regulation—and circumvention occurred. One device was by means of bankers' acceptances, whereby the commercial banks in effect lent to borrowers without this appearing on their balance sheets. The primary effect of the corset was thus to convert overt trading between willing buyers and sellers into a concealed activity. In other words, the effect of the corset was to conceal the true rate of money stock growth, and not to suppress it. When the corset was removed, this hitherto concealed component of monetary growth moved back into its normal posture—and became visible in both banks' balance sheets and the money growth figures.

However, even when the money growth statistics are adjusted to take out this effect, the underlying rate of monetary growth seems to have been well above its target range in 1979 and 1980.[22]

Why was this? The main answer is that the U.K. monetary authority had chosen an inadequate means for controlling the (true or undistorted) rate of growth of the money supply—certainly an inadequate technique as many monetarists would see it. Such monetarists as Professor Milton Friedman in the U.S., and Professor Brian Griffiths and his colleagues at the Center for Banking and International Finance in the U.K., tend to favor controlling the money supply by control of the "monetary base," or the "high-powered money supply." This magnitude—$\Delta M^H$ in equation (2) of the previous chapter—is thusly termed because commercial banks need to hold a certain proportion of their assets in this form. It is therefore a means of controlling the volume of commercial bank deposits, the primary component of the total supply of money.

The Bank of England—the equivalent of the Federal Reserve Board in the U.S.—prefers, on the contrary, to seek to control the money supply by controlling the level of interest rates. For the past several decades the bank has seen one of its primary objectives as being the control (in particular, the stabilization) of the level of interest rates, rather than the rate of growth of the money supply. When asked by government, in the latter part of the seventies, to control the stock of money, the response was simply to adapt traditionally-favored techniques to the new request. The money supply would be controlled via the control of the level of interest rates. The idea is to choose an interest rate level that will generate a volume of demand and supply for commercial bank loans that is consistent with the specified monetary growth target. That interest rate level can in turn be achieved by choosing the right price at which to sell new issues of government stock (or so the argument went).

In a world of perfect certainty in which, furthermore, political constraints on the manipulation of interest rates for the purpose of monetary control never appeared, such a technique of monetary policy would be sufficient for the task. But we do not live in a world like that at all.

Firstly, we live in a world of always-changing and highly complex conditions. No one can predict the demand for bank loans or the demand for gilt-edged (i.e., government) stock with certainty. For example, the British treasury's forecasting equation for the sale of gilt-edged has a standard error in explaining past behavior of (plus or minus) over 3 percent of sterling M3. Second, there is often political interference in the setting of interest rates, particularly in response to the house-owning and business lobbies. Politicians are eager to see interest rates fall to get these groups "off their backs."

The current practices of the Bank of England are consequently not a very efficient or predictable means of controlling the supply of money. Furthermore, the erratic movements in the money supply produced by the present techniques generate uncertainty about monetary growth and inflation in the future, thus enhancing the economic problems of the supply-side of the economy.

A further problem of the medium term financial strategy is that, even if the monetary growth targets were to be achieved by the present techniques and not overshot, they would not likely produce a single-figure inflation rate before 1983-84, due to the long lags that operate in the connection between money growth and inflation. But 1983-84 is the likely eve of the next British general election. As the Center for Banking and International Finance has pointed out, "the [present] monetary targets seem too high even to deliver with any certainty a single figure inflation rate which could be paraded in the election year as a symbol of the success of the Government's policy."[23] Mrs. Thatcher will then be faced with the charge that she has created enormous economic waste via unemployment and lost output—unemployment is likely still to be high by that time—for little result in terms of reducing inflation, as a result of supposedly "hardline" monetarist policies. The basic problem is that these policies have not been hardline at all. The gradualism of the Thatcher experiment would seem to have been far too gradual.

## Monetarism and Unemployment

Have, however, the actually "softline" and erratic monetary control policies of the Thatcher government been responsible for the high level of unemployment? This is what many critics of the current situation claim—that monetarism is responsible for rising unemployment, which currently stands at over 10 percent of the work force. In April 1981, some 350 British economists wrote a collective letter to the London *Times*, blaming the unemployment situation upon the pursuit of monetarist policies, and calling for their abandonment.

There are a number of points to note about this contention. First, the underlying rate of unemployment has been rising in Britain since at least the mid-sixties, as has also happened in most other western economies. Numerous factors have been put forward to account for this, including structural changes in the world economy; variable inflation; legislation (such as that relating to redundancy payments and equal pay for women) which has raised the cost of labor; increased benefits provided by government which have the effect of extending the duration (and thus level) of unemployment; and the growth of the "black" (or "underground") economy. The precise balance of importance among these various factors is beyond our present knowledge. All we do know is that the "natural" (or equilibrium) unemployment rate appears to have been rising for a long time.

However, it is also likely that the current rate of unemployment is above the underlying natural rate, which has been estimated by some studies to be in the range of 4.5 percent to 6 percent of the work force for the year 1977.[24] The Liverpool Research Group in Macroeconomics has recently estimated that the natural rate of unemployment had risen by 1981 to 8 percent of the labor force. A main factor behind this apparent deviation between the current and natural rates of unemployment would appear to be that the ratio of wage earnings to the money supply rose sharply in 1979 and 1980. There is a close (and positive) correlation between the level of unemployment and this ratio.[25] When the ratio of wage earnings to the money supply rises, so apparently does unemployment. This is what happened in the U.K. in 1979 and 1980; in the latter year earnings rose by 23 percent.

The mechanism behind this connection would appear to be the standard one of economic analysis: when wages rise relative to prices and the money supply, firms are given an incentive to reduce the volume of their labor inputs. The question that thus arises is why earnings jumped so high in 1979 and 1980 in the U.K. There would appear to be two main reasons. First, workers' expectations of continuing price inflation were apparently still high. Second, the rise in the general level of wage earnings in 1980 was heavily conditioned by the very high level of pay settlements in the public sector. As the Center for Banking and International Finance argues:

> The 23 percent inflation in earnings in 1980 consisted of a 17 1/2 percent rise in private sector pay and a massive 30 percent rise in public sector pay. In effect, public sector pay settlements squeezed private sector workers out of jobs.

Many economists (mainly those in public sector employment, e.g., in the universities) ignore the foregoing matters. The high level of unemployment is blamed by them simply on monetarism; they call for reflation to "cure" unemployment.[27]

To conclude: the monetary policies of the Thatcher government have exhibited serious weaknesses. Meanwhile naive economists and politicians in Britain have succeeded to some extent in their intention to give "monetarism" a bad public image. We have also seen that part of the present monetary/unemployment problem in Britain traces back to a failure to contain public sector pay expenditures. This leads us on to our next item.

### The Failure of Budgetary Policy

The Tories entered office with promises to cut both public spending and the level of taxation. We shall examine their actual performance on these two fronts separately.

### The Public Spending "Cuts" Farce

Leftist and trade union (usually public sector) critics of the Thatcher government have been successful in conveying the image to the public in Britain that Thatcher policies have led to "savage" cuts in public spending. A "fight the cuts" campaign, run by a medley of left-wing and trade union organizers, exists throughout the country.

It is indeed true that the government has conducted what it likes to term as four "rounds of public spending cuts" since it came to power (in June and November 1979, March and November 1980). The newspapers in Britain have, meanwhile, been almost continuously filled with stories about the much proclaimed "cuts": where they are occurring, the infighting that is going on in and out of cabinet over them, and their consequences.

The most curious aspect of all this ballyhoo is that, to date, the Thatcher government has not cut the level of public spending one iota. To the contrary, it has presided over a considerable rise in the level of government spending. There has undoubtedly been reallocation among the various spending programs, with home (e.g., overseas aid) being pruned while others (e.g., defense) have gained in budget size. But there can be no question that the overall level of public spending —both in volume terms and as percentage of GDP—has risen considerably, and well above that undertaken by the previous Labor administration in the years 1978 and 1979.

The ironic aspect of this is that the previous Labor government actually *did* achieve a considerable cut in public spending—some 6 percent in volume terms—over the years 1975/76 to 1977/78, against a background of extremely muted trade union opposition. Yet both the Labor party and the (especially, public sector) unions are now screaming blue murder about Mrs. Thatcher's "cuts" in the level of public spending.[27]

To separate reality from fantasy, we need to examine two questions. First, what were the public spending plans of the Thatcher administration upon entering office and, secondly, what actually happened—and why?

Spending plans were set out by the government in its medium-term financial strategy and in a public expenditure white saper published in March 1980. These set out clearly a number of specific intentions. First, *planned* public expenditures were to be reduced by four percent in volume terms over the period 1979/80 to 1983/84 (Mrs. Thatcher's term of office). Second, stricter cash limit methods were to be adopted in controlling public spending: if costs rose more than the cash provided, volume would have to be pruned back. Third, the government intended that the first real cut in volume of public spending would occur in 1981/82. All the "cutting" up until now has therefore consisted in the lopping back of the previous government's plans for *even higher* levels of public spending over the period 1979/81. Thus, in general, the government planned for some eventual and moderate (amounting to perhaps 2 percent of GDP) cut in the level of its own spending. There was clearly no intention to "dismantle the welfare state" or to "destroy the public sector," as claimed by numerous leftist critics of the government. The sorry reality is that the government planned to do remarkably little about the bloated level of public sector spending in the U.K.

The story of "what actually happened" is also instructive. The reality is that the actual outturn in both public spending and the public sector borrowing requirement (PSBR, otherwise known as the budget deficit) has been *consistently above* the levels planned by the government. Why has this been so? A number of factors are worthy of mention.

First, the Thatcher administration had, by a preelection pledge, signed an open cheque to the unions on many public sector pay settlements. The background, in 1979, was that there had been, over the winter of 1978/79, a long series of public-sector strikes that seemed gravely to undermine that previous public feeling that "only a Labor government can handle (or buy off) the unions." To quell these electorally damaging strikes, the Labor administration of James Callaghan tried to buy its way out. First, it conceded immediate wage increases of above 10 percent in the public sector. Second, it set up a comparability commission, chaired by Professor Hugh Clegg, to award further unspecified (but presumed to be large) pay increases to the striking unions in central and local government—*after* the election. Mrs. Thatcher entered this politics of open-ended auction and promised to honor the recommendations of the Clegg Commission, if and when she got to power.

Although supposedly based on "scientific" comparisons with compensation in the private sector, the recommendations of the Clegg Commission were based, in reality, on thin (mostly hot) air. There is *no* way known to labor economists or industrial relations analysts of diagnosing the appropriate wage for any type of labor, apart from the test of the market: are job applicants fewer in number than job vacancies or not? The basic problem is that there is no way of scientifically deciding upon the values of non-wage aspects of different jobs. Civil servants in Britain are almost of tenured job status and have fully inflation-proof pension schemes. How much are these worth, in subjective terms, vis-à-vis current wages? There is no way of knowing in the absence of markets. And in the publicly financed sector of employment, the test of market demand has, by definition, been abolished.

Nevertheless, the Clegg recommendations went ahead—and were honored. The civil servants were given a 25 percent salary rise, doctors and dentists obtained a 30 percent rise, and the average rise in public-sector pay in 1980 was 30 percent. The Clegg Commission has now been abolished, and the Thatcher government has issued a 6 percent increase "guideline" on public-sector pay settlements in current wage negotiations. Specifically, the civil servants have been offered a rise of 7 percent by the government. At the time of writing, Britain is once again embroiled in a rash of civil service strikes—including attempts to paralyze the tax collection system, to bring air traffic to a halt, to delay the issue of passports (thus wrecking the holiday plans of vast numbers of people), and to prevent the operation of Britain's nuclear deterrent submarines.

A second reason for the buoyancy of public spending over its planned levels has been that certain programs have overshot their targets and cash limits—and these excesses have been allowed through by the government. Defense overspent by £600 million in 1979/80. Local government spending (much of which is funded by central government in Britain) also greatly exceeded its agreed current spending target in 1980. Finally, the nationalized industries (most specifically the "big loser" concerns such as British Steel, the National Coal Board, British Rail, and British Shipbuilders) all were to overshoot their cash limits. This latter matter will be taken up with more detail in the next section of this chapter.

Third, the social security part of the budget has been much larger than expected, due to a volume of unemployment (predominantly in the private sector) much larger than that which the government had anticipated. Each extra unemployed British worker costs an average of £5,000 a year to the government—or, rather, the taxpayers.

There have been three serious consequences of this public expenditure overshooting. First, the effect of huge public sector pay settlements, set in an environment of cash limits generally laying down no more than 13-14 percent public spending increases in 1980, meant that there had to be volume reductions in public spending programs.

Second, instead of cutting their inputs—specifically, their labor inputs—bureaucrats typically reacted by cutting the *outputs* of their bureaus. A report presented in February 1981 by the Engineering Employers' Federation, as a budget submission to the government, notes pointedly that, since the Thatcher government came to power, only 2,977 government employees had been made redundant. This compares with a figure of 665,707 redundancies for the labor market as a whole over the same period.[29] Meanwhile, there have been significant, and genuine, reductions in the output of many bureaus in Britain:

> [T]he way in which the [volume] cuts have been effected have had little effect on public sector employment but a great dislocation of public sector services—old people's homes, adult education centers, hospital wards, nursery facilities. Part of the problem here is that civil servants have been given considerable discretion over where the cuts take place and the strategy which they have developed seems to be to cut vital services first, then cut capital expenditure, then conceivably agree to a wages bill on their area of public sector but [to] avoid at all costs reducing public sector employment.[30]

In this sense, there have undoubtedly been cuts in the public sector since the Thatcher government came to power, but these reductions have taken the form of lower real outputs from, and less capital spending by, public bureaus in Britain. The bureaus of central and local government have responded to the combination of hugely increased pay bills and tighter cash limits by cutting their labor productivity (the ratio of output to labor input) and their capital inputs. What they have *not* done is precisely what was needed: to cut into organizational slack, to improve their efficiency, and to shed excessive labor inputs. All this, of course, was only to be expected.

Ultimately, it reflects the power of two important interest groups in Britain to resist, indeed to overturn, the desires of a government elected by a majority vote of the people to cut down on public-sector waste: bureaucrats and the public-sector unions.

A third consequence of public sector out-turn expenditure being above planned levels has been that the public-sector borrowing requirement has had to be much larger than planned. As we can see from equation (2) in the foregoing chapter, governments have only four ways of financing their spending, be it planned or unplanned: by taxes, by charges, by borrowing, or by creating money. The present Thatcher government has generally eschewed a policy of increased charging for public services. That leaves only three routes open. It has also sought to keep to its commitments on taxation (but see below) and on monetary growth (but see below). That left only one route open: increased public spending had to be financed out of increased borrowing from the non-bank public. The size of the PSBR is given by the equation:

Proposition 3. PSBR = G-T-C-$\pi$+N
where: G is total government spending
T is total tax revenue
C is the revenue from charges for public services
$\pi$ is the net profits of the nationalized industries
N is the net acquisition of financial assets by the public sector

The government has sought to ameliorate the rise in the PSBR by a number of devices. Some charges (e.g., for school meals and medical prescription charges) have been raised; these increases account for relatively miniscule amounts of public money. Secondly, the government has attempted to make the N term in equation (3) negative, by the sale to private persons of some public sector assets. The government's Expenditure Plan, 1980-81 (Command 7746), revealed the intention to raise £1 billion from the sale of public-sector assets. This was not nearly enough. For the financial year 1980/81, the official estimated PSBR was to rise from £8.5 billion to £11.5 billion, as the result of the "unexpected" surge in government spending. The problem is that, if government borrows more, the price of borrowing from the nonbank public is caused to rise, i.e., the level of interest rates goes up. Private enterprises, many of which have been in the grips of a profitability crunch and liquidity crisis, thus find it more expensive to tide themselves over difficulty by borrowing from the banks. Consequently, the number of bankruptcies and redundancies in private-sector British industry has risen. In other words, the failure of the public sector to adjust has ultimately heaped further problems onto the back of the private sector in the U.K.

## The Tax Cuts Fiasco

The Conservatives promised to restore personal incentives by slashing income taxation. In his first budget presentation to Parliament, Sir Geoffrey Howe (the chancellor of the exchequer) did precisely this. The standard rate of income taxation was reduced from 33 percent to 30 percent. There was also a reduction in the top rate of income taxation from 83 percent to 60 percent on incomes over £25,000. *However*, to cover (partially) the "cost" of this move (in terms of tax revenue foregone) excise taxes were raised. The theory was that a switch-over from direct to indirect taxation would release greater work effort and entrepreneurial endeavor.

The theory is, in fact, deeply flawed. The basic problem with such a strategy has been expressed neatly by Arthur B. Laffer:

> On formal economic grounds, there always exists a constellation of taxes on incomes that corresponds precisely to any given constellation of taxes on products. Therefore, in the abstract, there is no analytic difference whatsoever between indirect [product] taxes and direct [income] taxes. Thus, there is no presumption that merely switching the source of government revenues from inland revenues [direct taxes] towards customs and excises will have a beneficial impact on the United Kingdom economy. . . . People work to acquire goods and services and don't care how their spending power is reduced; they care only how much it is reduced.[31]

In the spring budget of 1981, furthermore, the chancellor introduced sharp increases in taxes on gasoline, cigarettes, and alcohol. The commitment to the monetary targets of the medium-term financial strategy, combined with the soaring level of public expenditure, were the causes of this.

## The "Failure" of Supply-Side Policies

As earlier seen, a central component of the Thatcher strategy was the rejuvenation of the British economy via steps to free the economic system. Sir Keith Joseph stated that strategy forthrightly:

> Monetarism is not enough. . . . [I]t is not enough unless there is also the essential reduction of the state sector and the essential encouragement of enterprise. We are over-governed, over-spent, over-taxed, over-borrowed and over-manned. . . . [W]e must also have substantial cuts in tax and public spending and bold incentives and encouragements to the wealth creators. . . .[32]

We have already seen, in the foregoing, how the commitment to "substantial cuts in tax and public spending" worked out in reality. In this section, the supposed failure of other supply-side policies of the Thatcher administration are noted. We examine two in particular: industrial policy and the reform of industrial relations.

The *intention* to do something about the supply-side problems was, at least in the beginning, certainly clear. Indeed, as Lord Harris of High

Cross argues, "It would not be difficult to parade an impressive list of the measures already taken to shift economic policy in the right direction."[33] He lists some of them: (1) repeal of statutory control over prices and profits, and the ending of formal incomes policy; (2) outright abolition of foreign exchange control; (3) sale of council houses (public housing units) to tenants at discounts of 33 to 50 percent; (4) first breach in 60 years of rent control by introducing "short-hold" leases of up to five years for new rentals; (5) weakening of so-called employment protection guarantees; (6) suspending full indexation of (untaxed) unemployment benefits; (7) creating "enterprise zones" in run-down city centers; (8) deregulation of long-distance coaches and some local buses; and (9) ending the post office monopoly for priority mail and charity deliveries. However, while there has been "some" progress in the right direction, major failures have occurred as well—notably in the two central (and, as we shall see, related) areas of industrial policy and labor relations policy.

### The U-Turn on Industrial Policy

In the seventies, Sir Keith Joseph emerged as a stern critic of the then-incumbent (1974-79) Labor government's industrial strategy. The essence of that strategy was the attempt to regenerate British industry by large injections of taxpayers' money, British Leyland being the paradigm example of the approach. Sir Keith castigated this industrial policy remorselessly:

> For every job preserved in British Leyland, Chrysler, and other foci of highly-paid outdoor relief, several jobs are destroyed up and down the country. If Ministers and union leaders were genuinely concerned to prevent unemployment and to safeguard productive employment, they would not have acted as they have done. On the contrary, they would have helped slim down these costly giants so greedy of resources, and done everything possible to improve the economic climate in which the small and medium firms live.[34]

The Center for Policy Studies, set up by Sir Keith and Margaret Thatcher in 1974, published a series of studies exposing the fallacies in the theory and practice of trying to cure industrial problems by bailing out and subsidization; a study by the present writer was among them.[35]

In the early days of the Thatcher government, Sir Keith (appointed as secretary of state for industry) announced that there would be cuts in regional aid programs and that criteria for selective industrial grants would be applied more "toughly."

By the winter of 1980/81, this initial resolve began to disappear. First, a covert sea-change in industrial policy became evident—the criteria were not, it now appeared, to be applied so "toughly" after all. Second, there appeared a series of spectacular bail-outs of such bankrupt nationalized concerns as British Leyland and British Steel. A *Daily Telegraph* columnist, James Wightman, observed:

Ministers have found it much more difficult to be ruthless about State funding of loss-making nationalized industries than they imagined before returning to office nearly two years ago.

Mrs. Thatcher's resolve not to prop up lame ducks has had to be subdued under the Cabinet's majority view against action which would bring heavy redundancies and perhaps mean the closure of the public car and steel firms. . . . Sir Keith Joseph's performance as Industry Secretary over [British] Leyland and British Steel has shown that his hard attitude before taking office has lost some of its edge.[36]

Sir Keith was led to make various massive advances of public money to a series of public-sector concerns—British Steel, British Leyland, Rolls Royce, British Shipbuilders, and British Airways, in particular—adding something like £4-5 billion to current public expenditure. A new grant of £1.14 billion for British Leyland was announced in January 1981, and £200 million for the computer firm, ICL, in March 1981; but the largest single bail-out came with the decision to fund the losses of the nationalized steel concern, British Steel. In January 1981, new "funding arrangements" were announced, involving the writing off of some £2.7 billion in loans and debts, the provision of up to £750 million in new loans, and the promise of £1 billion more over the next two years.

The most humiliating reversal on industrial policy for the government, however, was to occur in the face of the miners' strike in February 1981. The background was that the government had published in 1980 a coal industry bill which announced the phasing out of operating subsidies over the next three years. In the following February the National Coal Board announced a plan to accelerate its rate of pit closures. Some twenty-three pits, which were uneconomic or worked out, were to be closed by March of 1982 (a number of which had already been agreed to by the National Union of Mineworkers). Although the total manpower involved in these closures was 20,000 men, it was estimated that the majority of these potential redundancies could be avoided by relocation of the workers to new, more profitable, and expanding coal pits. A total volume of redundancies of around 2,500 to 3,000 men, per year, for two years, was envisaged. In the light of the size of the industry, and compared to the scale of redundancies now going on in the private sector of British industry, this redundancy program was comparatively miniscule.

The national executive of the National Union of Mineworkers (NUM) gave the government and the National Coal Board an ultimatum of seven days to "change their minds" over the closure program; otherwise, they would ballot their members with a recommendation to undertake a national strike. Memories of the miners' strikes of 1972 and 1974—the latter of which precipitated the electoral defeat of the Conservative government of Edward Heath—were in the air. Arthur Scargill, the Marxist president of the Yorkshire area of the NUM, declared to a crowd of 500 mineworkers: "We are creating the conditions to bring about an early General Election to get rid of this Tory government once and for all."[37]

Mrs. Thatcher and the government initially showed resolve over this challenge: "The Government will not intervene to stop a reduction in coal production, and possible pit closures, Mrs. Thatcher made clear in the Commons. . ."[38] The cash limit of £882 million of "external" (i.e., public) finance was to hold: "we shall stand by this arrangement," Mrs. Thatcher stated firmly.

Yorkshire miners' leaders announced their intention to take industrial action within the next ten days, because of the threatened closure of the 130-year-old Orgreave colliery (near Sheffield). It was also made clear that they would seek to maximize disruption by the use of "flying pickets" sent to other coal fields, despite the fact that this picketing technique had become unlawful under the 1980 Employment Act (see later). The colliery officials and staff area of the NUM also announced that its members would not provide vital emergency cover in the event of a strike, not check ventilation systems or roofing supports, not pump out flooded mines.[39]

The government started to show signs of worry. A plan to buy off the threatened disruption and strike by extremely generous redundancy payments was to surface. Under this mooted scheme, redundant miners were to receive payments of up to "£20,000 per man (tax free) —many times the size of payments typically made in the private sector of British industry."[40]

A rash of unofficial (wildcat) strikes, in advance of the balloting of NUM miners on strike action, broke out and the entirety of Welsh coal production was brought to a halt. In the midst of this, Mrs. Thatcher decided to capitulate to the NUM. A senior coal board official was later to say (privately): "we had backed ourselves up against the wall— ready to take a strike—and the wall collapsed." The Iron Lady, who had thundered a week before in the Commons that "I am not *forced* to do anything," had apparently been cowed. James Prior, the leading cabinet "wet," was given free rein to negotiate the government's capitulation. Denis Howell, secretary of state for energy, delivered the notice of surrender to the mineworkers' leaders on February 18. Joe Gormley, president of the NUM announced: "My executive which meets tomorrow will have no need to take a ballot for a national strike. The closure programme no longer exists and there is no need to take strike action."[41] The capitulation promised three changes of policy within the general U-turn. First, the government was now to "pressure" the National Coal Board to "reconsider" (i.e., drop) the pits closure program. Second, there was an agreement to "review" the NCB's external financial limits for 1981/82: in other words, the government promised to plug in the necessary subsidies to keep uneconomic pits open. Third, there was some (unclear) agreement to limit lower-cost coal imports from America and elsewhere. It has subsequently been announced that, instead of phasing out public subsidies to the coal industry, the government will *more than double* its subsidies to the industry.

The effect of this capitulation on the morale in the private industry in Britain was stunning. A city editor noted the general resultant mood:

> All those companies in the private sector, going through the agonies of reconstruction and demanning, fighting the unions and cutting their wage claims, must now feel a great wave of disillusion. Why should they suffer in the cause, while the public sector gets all it asks for?[42]

The fear has been expressed that this particular surrender of the government to the interests of the unions will make forthcoming and current public-sector pay disputes in Britain harder and more expensive to settle—witness the obduracy of the civil servants in the current dispute. It is further feared that the miners will put in a substantially higher pay claim than they might otherwise have done. They are now used to the taste of Danegeld.

Why did Mrs. Thatcher cause such difficulties for herself? The suggestions in the press are that she did not want to go into a confrontation with the miners on ground that was not of her own choosing. A more likely and revealing explanation was given a few days later after the capitulation in a TV interview. John Biffen, a cabinet minister who is one of Mrs. Thatcher closet colleagues, admitted: "The spectre that frightened the government was that there would be massive industrial action on the issue. . . ."[43] *The Financial Times*, in a leading article (Feb. 20, 1981), commented "in Tory Britain the miners rule."

Another motive behind the government's surrender was probably that it feared the massive use of secondary picketing techniques, as well as public exposure of the fact that its legislative reform of industrial relations (contained in the 1980 Employment Act) would not resolve the problem. This leads us on to our next topic.

### (White-)Papering Over the Union Problem

A major public concern that had brought Mrs. Thatcher to power was the dismay and indignation occasioned by the "winter of discontent" strike wave of 1978/79. The Tories promised to grasp the nettle of trade union power.

Upon election, Mrs. Thatcher entrusted James Prior with this task, as secretary of state for employment. It is worth noting that Prior is a known advocate of the "softly, softly" approach to the union problem in Britain. His privately expressed view, it is rumored, is that things have simply gone too far in Britain to hope to do much about the question of trade union power. The very best that a government may now do is to hold the line in the hope things will not get too much worse.

It is with such an attitude that the government's promised reform of industrial relations, embodied in the 1980 Employment Act, was approached.

The act is composed of two separate parts, one of which deals with an individual's rights at work while the other deals with the legal environment of collective labor relations. Here, we shall be concerned only with the latter aspect.

Spokesmen of the union movement in Britain have sought to portray the 1980 Employment Act as an attempt to outlaw union action.[44] It is no such thing. The truth is that the act is a measure designed to give the impression that the government has "done something" about union power—while doing very little at all about anything at all. It is a papering-over exercise.

The provisions of the act, insofar as they affect trade unions and collective labor relations, concern four main matters: union ballots, the closed shop, picketing, and secondary action.

On union ballots (e.g., strike decisions), the Employment Act entitles trade unions to cover from public funds the cost of conducting postal ballots. The idea is that full postal balloting would allow moderate views to prevail over extremist ones in union decision-making. However, this provision of the act is most likely to be a dead letter, as the TUC has advised all its affiliated unions not to apply for funds. Nor have any yet done so.

As regards the closed shop, the grounds for an objection to union membership are somewhat expanded by the act, and those victimized by closed-shop arrangements may complain to an industrial tribunal. The tribunal, in turn, may order compensation for unfair dismissal. However, the permissible grounds for objection to the closed shop are widened only a little, from the previous standard of an objection based on religion to an objection on "grounds of conscience of other deeply-held personal conviction." All existing closed shops are permitted to continue in Britain. A code of practice, specifying that closed shops should be subject to "periodic review," has been published but this does not have the force of law. However, it will be a bit more difficult to introduce a *new* closed shop as the legislation requires that a ballot must be held in which "not less than 80 percent of those entitled to vote" are in favor of its introduction. In effect, the law means that the pattern of compulsory unionization is likely to be frozen at its present level (affecting about one-quarter of the work force in Britain).

The Employment Act bans the use of flying pickets (i.e., mobile picket squads); pickets may congregate only "at or near" their place of work. There is also a code of practice regarding picketing which gives a "guidance" that the number of pickets should not exceed six at any entrance to a work place. Once again, this does not have the force of law behind it.

The provisions of the act relating to secondary picketing (i.e., industrial action taken by workers against an employer who is not a party to the original dispute) are complicated. Under the new act, secondary action becomes unlawful if it interferes with commercial contracts by interfering with the employment contracts of people working for any employer who is not a party to the dispute. However, a major exception is made to this: secondary action may lawfully be undertaken in respect of *direct* suppliers and customers, with the purpose of disrupting supply. Secondary action taken against a direct supplier is therefore permissible; that taken against a supplier's supplier is not. It will still be quite lawful for the miners to picket the power stations, as they did in 1974.

Thus, the 1980 Employment Act simply removes the previous blanket protection given to secondary action. It also throws a considerable burden of evaluation upon the judges, as they are left with the task of determining what the purpose of any secondary action was and whether it was *likely to achieve* disruption (which is the permissible ground for industrial action against a direct supplier or customer).

All in all, the 1980 Employment Act hardly constitutes a revolutionary change in British law on collective labor relations. It will, perhaps, give some little annoyance to the trade union, an increased income to labor lawyers, and some headaches to the judiciary. It may, in the long run, hamper further growth of the closed shop. But what it will not do is remove the manacles of union-imposed rigidities from the torpid body of the British economy. The large increases in trade union power produced by the previous Labor government's legislation on collective labor relations in the period 1974-76 will be only marginally affected by the 1980 act.

### The Underlying Malaise

We have seen how, in her main strategic thrusts, Mrs. Thatcher has been forced back in the space of two years. Some of these failures (as in monetary policy) are of a technical nature, the result of bad advice or of incompetence in the application of policy. Others (such as the preelection pledge to honor the Clegg recommendations) represent electoral pragmatism which may or may not have been justified. But the central failures of the Thatcher experiment all relate to a deeper, underlying problem.

The British disease is a complex malady involving the triune features of raging inflation, economic sluggishness, and union power. The basic one is sluggishness—the fact that the British economy itself has become very sick. Indeed, the inflation problem is properly seen as a symptom, and not a basic cause, of the British disease. It is the consequence of the underlying malaise of economic sclerosis. This is so because successive British governments have sought to cover up the problem of economic arthritis—unemployment, low productivity and faltering growth—by repeated application of a supposed wonder drug of public expenditure growth and monetary stimulation. Events in Britain indicate clearly that such a prescription provides only temporary relief from the pangs of economic sluggishness, and it leads to unremitting inflation.

Underlying this sluggishness are a number of rigidities which have been introduced, extended, and protected by British unions—acting not only in their natural capacity as a monopolizer of the labor market but also in their capacity, developed over the past six decades, as a principal operator in the political market. It is certainly unfair to charge the unions with *sole* responsibility for having produced this sickness; it should nonetheless be noted that all too often other parties who must share the blame (e.g., employers, politicians, bureaucrats, etc.) have been overwhelmed and/or overawed by the degree of power overall which British unions have acquired.

Mrs. Thatcher has attempted to cure this disease by tackling the symptom—inflation. The monetary stimulant which kept the patient going has been removed—somewhat erratically, but a least the nurse had the right intention and has tried to move in the right direction. Tackling a symptom is not the same thing, however, as tackling the disease. To take away the monetary drug is only to reveal the underlying racking pain in its true intensity. What the Thatcher team failed to do is to tackle, head on, the disease itself.

This underlying malaise relates to the fact that powerful interest groups (notably those who work in and run Britain's innumerable bureaucratic empires) and the trade unions (particularly the public-sector unions) have a vested interest in the maintenance of the present, inefficient allocation of resources. And many of these interest groups have the power to make things go their way. The bureaucrats (most of whom are union organized) have the informational advantages over the government, to conduct their instructions regarding the containment of public spending in such a way as to minimize the effect upon them and to maximize the embarrassment to the government. They also have great political power through their partisanly active, voting memberships. The trade unions in the public sector do not necessarily have much economic power—coal and steel could often be imported more cheaply from abroad—but they do have "military" power in their ability to block ports and power stations. Again, they represent large numbers of voters (e.g., the NUM alone has 230,000 members).

The government had the clear preelection intention of reforming the supply-side of the economy; of tackling this underlying malaise. Indeed, in the very year the government was elected in which he later became a leading figure, Sir Keith Joseph penned a widely reported pamphlet titled *Solving the Union Problem is the Key to Britain's*

*Recovery*.[47] But the actual behavior of Mrs. Thatcher's government has demonstrated that its leaders are (as yet?) afraid, or unable, firmly to grasp the nettle of reform on the supply-side. The chancellor of the exchequer has privately admitted that public expenditure is "out of control"; great streams of public money continue to be poured into bankrupt state-run concerns. The leader who "was not for turning" fled with her petticoats gathered around her knees at the first signs of a confrontation with the miners—over what was a relatively trivial issue of redundancy (compared to the massive redundancies in the private sector of the British economy). The underlying problem, of trade union power, has been hardly touched by the legislation of the current government. Meanwhile, the total level of spending has had to be raised, to cover the soaring costs of public outputs, while holding to the shadow of the monetary targets outlined in the medium term financial strategy. What we now have in Britain is supply-side economics of a peculiar mirror or reversed-image sort. Or, as Christopher Story has put it, "we [in Britain] have a stabilization crisis but no stabilization."[48]

The tendency in much of the literature has been to visualize the British disease as primarily an economic phenomenon with economic origins. Certainly there are economic aspects to the British disease, e.g., the rigidity of the British labor market. Reflection on recent experience, however, suggests that the more dangerous (because more insidious) aspects of the disease are political. While undoubtedly important, the economic problems directly attributable to extensive unionism are less significant than are the political implications of this power: these implications may be seen in the unions' ability to frustrate or to frighten off attempts at reform, and to convince many people (including many current government ministers) that reformist medicine is ineffective. No one should doubt that the propaganda barrage to the Thatcher government's policies has successfully misdirected public attention in Britain and has blocked implementation of those economic reforms which have been attempted. "If the medicine really works, why is the patient still so sick?" This is the repeated question from persons whose motives in posing this argument must be suspect. Unfortunately, the question has been raised so often and insistently that many others have begun to take up the refrain.

The truth, as this essay has sought to express, lies elsewhere. The facts are that the prescription has largely not been written correctly, even in terms of Mrs. Thatcher's own philosophy; that, where written correctly, it has yet to be administered to the patient; and that, where delivered, it has been withdrawn too soon, or applied too timidly, for healing to begin.

## III: Conclusions—A Requiem on the Thatcher Experiment?

### The Consequences

The failure of the Thatcher administration to tackle swiftly and decisively the underlying malaise of the British economy, a malaise that lies embedded primarily in the public sector, has meant that an even greater burden of adjustment has had to be thrown on the back of private industry. Already faced with a high exchange rate and world recession, industry has had to put up with higher taxation (particularly in the form of increased national insurance contributions) and higher interest rates than might otherwise have been the case.

The government has consequently come under great pressure from industry. The director-general of the Confederation of British Industry (CBI), Sir Terence Beckett, went on the attack in the CBI conference of October 1980 and publicly declared the need for a "bare-knuckle fight" with the government. Later, in the run-up to the spring budget of 1981, the CBI mounted pressure for large-scale aid to industry in the form of tax cuts, reductions in interest rates, and intervention in the foreign exchange market, in order to lower the pound.[49] Although the word "reflation" was not used, this is what the proposals would amount to. The Trades Union Congress has weighed in with its own call for reflation—although it wants to see this come through the medium of higher public spending, as well as lower tax rates.[50] Thus, from both sides of industry, the government is under increasing pressure to give up its surviving commitment to monetary deceleration. Both sides are crying to be put back on the drug of monetary growth and fiscal expansionism. Numerous ex-prime ministers—Harold Macmillan, Edward Heath, James Callaghan, and Sir Harold Wilson—have all spoken in a similar vein. As earlier noted, a large group of British academic economists have exerted pressure in the same direction, via the signing of a collective letter to *The Times*.

Whether the Thatcher government will be able to resist the siren cry for reflationism is an open question. It has changed course, as we have seen, on some of its strategies already. In February 1981, Mr. Pym, a senior cabinet minister, made a speech admitting that the government's general strategy had had to be "adjusted" in the face of worse economic circumstances that had been expected upon entering office.[51] Perhaps there is one more "adjustment" yet to come. There has already been talk, in the corridors of Whitehall and Westminster, of "getting Maggie out" and replacing her with somebody who is more "amenable."

Nor is the economic outlook in Britain very hopeful. While econometric forecasts disagree as to precise timing, few now see any economic turnaround before the end of 1981.[51] Most foresee unemployment as remaining high thereafter, even if there is some business upturn, and inflation edging downwards. Of course, no firm prophecies (in the absence of Divine inspiration) can be made. It is entirely possible that Mrs. Thatcher may yet bring about an economic turnaround in Britain's situation within the time-scale of the next general election. But, at the time of writing, the prospects of this eventuality are not exactly bright. It is to be conceded that it is *possible* that the Thatcher strategy could work out—*provided* that the government returned to its original plans. But it shows no political will to do this. As Batchelor states:

> In the first two years of the Thatcher Government, half of the policy prescription—the micro-economic [or supply] side—has not been implemented at all, and the macro-economic strategy has run into a political swamp.[52]

It will be difficult, politically, to pull out of this nose-dive —to do a U-turn in the U-turn, as it were. But that is the only hope there now is for the Thatcher experiment—that it is given a real try.

### Are There Any Silver Linings?

Governments often claim, when things do not work out as intended, that they have been "blown off course" by factors beyond their control. But sometimes they have good luck, too. There are two main sources of such "luck" for the Thatcher experiment.

(1) *Adjustment in the Private Sector.* The sharpness of the recession has provoked major changes in private British industry. There has been, for the first time in decades, a real shake-out of overmanning, and the elimination of many makework practices. Attitudes of private-sector union bargainers have softened remarkably, and the very low wage settlements—many on the order of 6 percent increase or less—have become the order of the day. As some would argue;

> We are now experiencing the long-overdue and much-needed shake-out that British industry should have gone through 30 years ago, as structural change which is as important as the Second World War was to Germany or Japan and which will result in a permanently higher level of productivity, improved industrial relations practices, and export competitiveness.[53]

There is some evidence for this view. The latest analysis of the Liverpool Research Group in Macroeconomics suggests that the underlying growth in productivity in British manufacturing during 1980 may have been as high as 6 percent. Again, interview studies with British management attest to an entirely "new mood" in private British industry. Turner reports:

> I have never felt such briskness, such urgency among the [British] managerial classes. . . . They are actually working as if their jobs depended on it. Some have even spoken to their workers without trade union permission.[54]

Another of his reports indicates this new atmosphere in collective bargaining. Ray Ashworth, a British manager, is quoted as saying:

> In the past, we knew it cost us . . . [£100,000] if this place stopped,
> so why not take the easy way out and give in? . . . You wouldn't be-
> lieve some of our old manning agreements, people being paid
> overtime for doing nothing. Now, everything has changed . . . it's
> simply a matter of survival.[55]

Thus, organizational slack is being eliminated fast in private industry in Britain. Perhaps the forecasts, then, are wrong: there has been a
"structural break" in British economic performance. However, organizational slack is *not* being eliminated, or at least at not a fast enough
pace, in the public sector of the British economy. This remains the
Achilles heel of the Thatcher experiment.

(2) *The Tax Revenue Bonus of North Sea Oil.* Estimates of the size of
tax revenue generated by North Sea oil vary enormously: the government's own estimates incline to the pessimistic end of the range of
forecasts. Others are the more optimistic. For example, Beenstock
argues:

> Thanks to North Sea oil the Medium Term Financial Strategy
> does not imply any major cutbacks in public expenditure. . . on the
> contrary, by maintaining public expenditure at its 1970s volume
> . . . the Government could most probably fulfill its hope to reduce
> the standard rate [of income tax] to 25 percent by 1984.[56]

Perhaps this optimistic assessment is right; perhaps Mrs. Thatcher will
be able to slash other taxes *while* maintaining public expenditure and
monetary control according to target. But, if this is so, it will mean that
the Thatcher experiment has been "saved" only because of fortuitous
circumstances, i.e., the accidents of geology and the consequences of
the Middle East situation for world oil prices.

### Some Final Reflections

For the foregoing reasons, and others, it is too early to write an
obituary notice on the Thatcher experiment. However, in the first two
years of the experiment, things have gone badly wrong on many fronts.

There would appear to be three major lessons to be learned from all
this. First, the basic difficulty in carrying out a Thatcher/Reagan-type
experiment lies not in the private sector of industry but in the public
sector. Here, powerful pressure groups seek to thwart reform. Second,
the problems that the Thatcher experiment has run into are not
unconnected. They all trace back to a failure to tackle the deep-seated
problems of the supply-side, specifically in the public sector, and a
failure to confront decisively the entrenched interest groups able to
frustrate the policies needed.

Third, and most importantly, if such an experiment is to be worked,
it must be done swiftly and decisively—before pressure groups have
time to organize and thwart the strategy. The only stabilization crises
that succeed are those that are done in this manner. Drawn-out
scenarios end in failure. Here, President Reagan—with his plans to

slash federal spending—may have got things more right than Margaret Thatcher. But it is likely that the Reagan experiment will face the same sort of problems sooner or later—and Ronald Reagan has no North Sea oil card to play.

Furthermore, at least in Britain there is the growing recognition (if not, apparently, the will to do something effective about it) that trade union power creates many opportunities to frustrate a stabilization strategy; yet very little can be found in the run-up to Reagan's election, or in the months since, to indicate any similar recognition within his administration that the special privileges and immunities of the U.S. unions are a hidden source of potentially powerful opposition to the Reagan experiment. This particular difference may in fact turn out to be the undoing both of Mr. Reagan and of the accomplishment in the U.S. of what Mrs. Thatcher has tried, but so far failed, to do in Britain.

# Notes

1. R. Emmett Tyrell, ed., *The Future That Doesn't Work: Social Democracy's Failures in Britain* (New York: Doubleday, 1977).

2. John Burton, *The Trojan Horse: Union Power in British Politics* (London: Adam Smith Institute, 1979).

3. Lord Harris of High Cross, "Promises, Progress, and Prospects . . . How Goes the Thatcher Revolution?" *Guilt-Edged Review* (London: Montague Stanley and Co., 1980).

4. Keith Joseph, *Reversing the Trend* (Chichester: Barry Rose, 1975); idem, *Monetarism Is Not Enough* (London: Center for Policy Studies, 1976).

5. Margaret Thatcher, *Let Our Children Grow Tall: Selected Speeches 1975-1977* (London: Center for Policy Studies, 1977).

6. Agnus Maude, et al., *The Right Approach to the Economy* (London: Conservative Central Office, 1977).

7. Although Milton Friedman is publicly viewed as the "leader" of monetarism, his brand of monetarist thought is in fact only one variety thereof.

8. Maude, et al., *The Right Approach to the Economy*, p. 43.

9. Caroline Atkinson, "Thatcher and Reagan," *The Washington Post* (Outlook), February 1, 1981, p. C1.

10. Stated on a TV discussion program.

11. Tyrell, *The Future That Doesn't Work*, p. 1.

12. Atkinson, "Thatcher and Reagan."

13. Arthur B. Laffer, "Thatcherism Isn't Free Market," *Competition*, February 1981, p. 5.

14. The figure for government expenditures depends on the precise measure chosen, but all indicators show a rise.

15. Atkinson, "Thatcher and Reagan."

16. Quoted in "Reagan's Bold Experiment," (London) *Daily Telegraph*, February 2, 1981, p. 19.

17. However, national "mood" is a fickle thing. Mrs. Thatcher initially entered office against the seeming background of a new national acceptance of economic realities and the necessity of painful adjustments. Two years later, public opinion has turned sharply against her. The British columnist, Auberon Waugh, has noted that ". . . the new President faces many of the same problems as Mrs. Thatcher, and I am afraid that he may come up against the same insurmountable difficulty, a collapse of national resolve." ("Hail to the Chief," *The Spectator*, November 15, 1980, p. 6.)

18. Joseph Castrovinci, "Thinking Out Realistic Solutions to America's Economic Problems," *San Francisco Business*, October 1980, p. 25-26.

19. "In Thatcherland," *The Economist*, October 25, 1980, p. 13.

20. Tony Benn, "Towards a New Constitutional Settlement," in James Prior, et al.,

*The Role of the Trade Unions* (London: Granada, 1980).

21. Center for Banking and International Finance, *Annual Monetary Review* no. 2 (London: The City University, 1980) p. 5.

22. G. Wood, "Failure of Monetary Control—Another Whitehall Farce?" *Journal of Economic Affairs* 1 (1981): 79-84.

23. Center for Banking and International Finance, *Annual Monetary Review* 1980, p. 5.

24. J. T. Addison, "What Price Unemployment?" *Journal of Economic Affairs* 1 (1981): 89-94.

25. Center for Banking and International Finance, *Annual Monetary Review* 1980, p. 13.

26. Ibid., p. 14.

27. I have detailed the delusion of such arguments in John Burton, "Reflation Will Not Cure Unemployment," *Journal of Economic Affairs* 1 (1981): 84-88.

28. The term "volume" here refers to the physical quantity of inputs—teachers, navy ships, civil servants, etc.—valued at some chosen index year's prevailing price structure.

29. "Employers Protest at Low Level of State Job Cuts," (London) *Daily Telegraph*, February 14, 1981, p. 8.

30. Center for Banking and International Finance, *Annual Monetary Review* 1980, p. 7.

31. Laffer, "Thatcherism Isn't Free Market," p. 5.

32. Joseph, *Monetarism Is Not Enough*, p. 199.

33. Lord Harris of High Cross, "Promises, Progress—and Prospects . . . How Goes the Thatcher Revolution?", p. iii.

34. Joseph, *Monetarism Is Not Enough*, p. 14.

35. John Burton, *The Job Support Machine: A Critique of the Subsidy Mess* (London: Center for Policy Studies, 1979).

36. James Wightman, "Resolve on Lame Duck Firms Subdued by Cabinet," (London) *Daily Telegraph*, February 2, 1981, p. 2.

37. Quoted in D. Harding and P. Simmonds, "Who Is to Blame for the Pits Fiasco?" (London) *Sunday Telegraph*, February 22, 1981, p. 17.

38. P. Pryke, "No Intervention on Mining Cuts or Closures," (London) *Daily Telegraph*, February 11, 1981, p. 10.

39. P. Routledge, "Yorkshire Miners Prepare for Disruption within Ten Days in Attempt to Save Threatened Pit," (London) *The Times*, February 10, 1981.

40. C. Leake, "20,000 Cash Lure for Miners: 'Handshake' Plan to Avert Strike," (London) *Daily Telegraph*, February 16, 1981, p. 1.

41. Quoted in R. Bedlow, "Pit Closures Abandoned," (London) *Daily Telegraph*, February 19, 1981, p. 1.

42. Ian Fallon, "Out of the Jaws of the Miners' Defeat," (London) *Sunday Telegraph*, February 22, 1981.

43. Statement made on the *Weekend World* TV program, February 22, 1981.

44. Jeremy McMullen, *Employment Law Under the Tories* (London: Pluto Press, 1981).

45. As described in Burton, *The Trojan Horse*.

46. Sudha B. Shenoy, "Why Monetarism Is Not Enough," *World Money Analyst*, August 1980.

47. Keith Joseph, *Solving the Union Problem is the Key to Britain's Recovery* (London:Center for Policy Studies, 1979).

48. Christopher Storey, "Inflationary Road to Higher Unemployment," (London) *Daily Telegraph*, January 30, 1981, p. 16.

49. Confederation.

50. Trades Union Congress, *Plan for Growth: The Economic Alternative* (London: Trades Union Congress, 1981).

51. Business Brief, "Can the Government Win?", *The Economist*, June 21, 1981, pp. 108-109.

52. R. Batchelor, "Thatcherism Could Succeed," *Journal of Economic Affairs* 1 (1981): 137-145.

53. Ian Fallon, "The Medicine and the Cure," *Sunday Telegraph*, November 30, 1981, (London) p. 20.

54. G. Turner, "The Grindstone Gets Familiar with the Manager's Nose," *London Daily Telegraph*, February 13, 1981a, p. 18.
55. G. Turner, "What About the Workers?" *London Daily Telegraph*, February 16, 1981b, p. 16.
56. M. Beenstock, "Taxation, Public Expenditure and Oil Tax Revenue," *Journal of Economic Affairs* 1 (1981): 73-77.

# References

Addison, J.T. "What Price Unemployment?" *Journal of Economic Affairs* 1 (1981): 89-94.
Atkinson, C. "Thatcher and Reagan." *Washington Post*, February 1, 1981, p. C1.
Batchelor, R. "Thatcherism Could Succeed." *Journal of Economic Affairs* 1 (1981): 137-145.
Beenstock, M. "Taxation, Public Expenditure and Oil Tax Revenue." *Journal of Economic Affairs* 1 (1981): 73-77.
Been, T. "Towards a New Constitutional Settlement." In J. Prior et al., *The Role of the Trade Unions.* London: Granada, 1980, pp. 34-60.
Burton, J. *The Trojan Horse: Union Power in British Politics.* London: Adam Smith Institute, 1979a.
Burton, J. *The Job Support Machine: A Critique of the Subsidy Morass.* London: Center for Policy Studies, 1979b.
Burton, J. "An Economy in the Grip of the Pressure Groups." *Daily Telegraph*, March 30, 1980a, p. 18.
Burton, J. "The Return to the Market: Will the 'Thatcher Experiment' Succeed?" *Svensklinje*, no. 4, 1980b.
Burton, J. "Reflation Will Not Cure Unemployment." *Journal of Economic Affairs* 1 (1981): 84-88.
"Can the Government Win?" *The Economist*, June 21-27, 1980, pp. 108-109.
Castrovinci, J. "Thinking Out Realistic Solutions to America's Economic Problems." *San Francisco Business*, October 1980, pp. 25-26.
Center for Banking and International Finance. *Annual Monetary Review.* No. 1. London: The City University, 1979.
Center for Banking and International Finance. *Annual Monetary Review.* No. 2. London: The City University, 1980.
Confederation of British Industry. *Budget Representations to the Chancellor, January 1981.* London: CBI Productions, 1981a.
Confederation of British Industry. *Economic Situation Report.* London: CBI Publications, 1981b.
Crawford, M. "If the Medicine is Working, Mrs. Thatcher, Why is the Patient So Sick?" *Sunday Times Business News*, February 15, 1981, p. 53.
Economic Forecasting Center *The Economic Outlook 1980-1984*, vol. 5, no. 5. London: London Business School Center for Economic Forecasting, 1981.
Fallon, I. "The Medicine and the Cure." *Sunday Telegraph*, November 30, 1980, p. 20.
Joseph, K. *Reversing the Trend.* Chichester: Barry Rose, 1975.
Joseph, K. *Monetarism is Not Enough.* London: Center for Policy Studies, 1976.
Joseph, K. *Solving the Union Problem is the Key to Britain's Recovery.* London: Center for Policy Studies, 1979.
Laffer, A.B. "Thatcherism Isn't Free Market." *Competition*, February 1981, p. 5.
Liverpool Research Group in Macroeconomics. *The Economic Outlook 1981.* No. 1. University of Liverpool: Liverpool Occasional Papers, 1981.
Lord Harris of High Cross. "Promises, Progress—and Prospects . . . How Goes the Thatcher Revolution?" *Guilt-Edged Review.* London: Montague Loebl Stanley and Co., 1980.
Lord Roberthall. "Are the Unions Usurping Parliament?" *Journal of Economic Affairs* 1 (1981): 149-155.
Melloan, G. "The Cost of Good Intentions in the U.K." *Wall Street Journal*, February 19, 1981.
McMullen, J. *Employment Law Under the Tories.* London: Pluto Press, 1981.

Minford, P., et al. *The Economic Outlook 1980*. No. 4. University of Liverpool: Liverpool Occasional Papers, 1980.

Shenoy, S. "Why Monetarism Is Not Enough." *World Money Analyst*, August 1980, p. 12.

Stein, H. "Britain and the Ordeal of Margaret Thatcher." *Wall Street Journal*, February 25, 1981.

Story, C. "Inflationary Road to Higher Unemployment." *Daily Telegraph*, January 30, 1981, p. 16.

Thatcher, M. *Let Our Children Grow Tall: Selected Speeches 1975-1977*. London: Center for Policy Studies, 1977.

Trades Union Congress. *Plan for Growth: The Economic Alternative*. London: Trades Union Congress, 1981.

Turner, G. "The Grindstone Gets Familiar with the Manager's Nose." *Daily Telegraph*, February 13, 1981a, p. 18.

Turner, G. "What About the Workers?" *Daily Telegraph*, February 16, 1981b, p. 16.

Tyrell, R. E., Jr. ed. *The Future that Doesn't Work: Social Democracy's Failures in Britain*. New York: Doubleday, 1977.

Wood, G. "Failure of Monetary Control—Another Whitehall Farce?" *Journal of Economic Affairs* 1 (1981): 79-84.

# Chapter 7:
# The Reagan Phenomenon:
# Policy Assessment

## The Reagan Economic Plan:
## Supply-Side, Budget and Inflation

James Tobin

A speaker who casts doubts on President Reagan's economic recovery program is likely to be as unwelcome as a ghost at a wedding feast. After viewing the euphoria of the joint session of Congress when the President displayed his resilience and his oratorical magic, I hate to be a wet blanket. I wish that his was a cause to which I too could rally. I would like to be enthusiastic about the dawn of the New Beginning.

There are several ways in which we might view the program. We could examine its microeconomics, how it reorders the nation's priorities, reallocates the country's resources, and redistributes income, wealth and power among individuals, groups, and regions. These may be the most important issues, the most fundamental new directions. The Reagan counterrevolution proposes to shift resources from public sector to private sector, from civilian government to national defense, from the federal government to state and local governments, from beneficiaries of social programs to the taxpayers, from the poor and the near-poor to the affluent and the very rich. These proposals deserve to be considered in detail, item by item, and evaluated in terms of their economic efficiency and equity.

However, the administration bills and sells its program primarily as a macroeconomic policy. The President and his spokesmen appeal for support of their counterrevolutionary reallocations and redistributions not on their intrinsic merits, but on the grounds that they are necessary and sufficient to solve the problem of stagflation. Here, we are told, is the remedy, the only remedy, for high unemployment, high inflation, low growth, and lagging productivity. We are asked to swallow the microeconomic medicine not because it tastes good but because it is good for what ails us. So far, it appears, Congress, press, and public readily accept the program as the necessary remedy for our macroeconomic ills.

It is the macro aspect of the program that I propose to discuss. I'll begin by reminding you that there is precious little evidence in international experience that successful macroeconomic management is inversely correlated with size of government, tax burdens, public debt, and social transfers. Some countries whose macroeconomic performance we envy have much larger public sectors, more generous social welfare programs, greater tax burdens, and higher budget deficits.

The Reagan recovery program, viewed as macro policy, has a fiscal side and a monetary side. Together they are projected to accomplish the disinflation and the real economic growth shown in columns four and five of my Table 1 and columns one and three of my Table 2.

## A Neutral Fiscal Package

The fiscal policy, viewed from the standpoint of conventional aggregate demand analysis, does not seem to be a significant factor of either stimulus or contraction over the five years for which it is projected. It is important to judge the impact of fiscal policy against what is and has been going on, last year and this year, and not to use as a hypothetical reference path President Carter's January budget. The Carter budget, since it eschewed tax cuts to offset fiscal drag, would have tightened fiscal policy dramatically over the next few years. The Congressional Budget Office (CBO) compares the Reagan budget program with a more realistic baseline, the Carter budget modified for

### Table 1
## Monetary Growth Targets vs. Reagan Projections of Inflation and Real Growth Implications for Monetary Velocity
### (percent per year, yearly averages)

| Year | (1)<br>Monetary<br>(M-1B)<br>Growth<br>$\left(\dfrac{\Delta M}{M}\right)$ | + | (2)<br>Velocity<br>Growth<br>$\left(\dfrac{\Delta V}{V}\right)$ | = | (3)<br>Nominal<br>GNP<br>Growth<br>$\left(\dfrac{\Delta\$GNP}{\$GNP}\right)$ | = | (4)<br>Price<br>Inflation<br>$\left(\dfrac{\Delta P}{P}\right)$ | + | (5)<br>Real GNP<br>Growth<br>$\left(\dfrac{\Delta Q}{Q}\right)$ |
|---|---|---|---|---|---|---|---|---|---|
| 1980 actual | 6.7 | | 2.2 | | 8.9 | | 9.0 | | −0.1 |

| | Announced Policy Implied by<br>Other Columns | | Reagan Administration Projections* | |
|---|---|---|---|---|
| 1981 | 3.5-6 | 7.6-5.1 | 11.1 | 9.9 | 1.1 |
| 1982 | 3  -5.5 | 9.8-7.3 | 12.8 | 8.3 | 4.2 |
| 1983 | 2.5-5 | 9.9-7.4 | 12.4 | 7.0 | 5.0 |
| 1984 | 2  -4.5 | 8.8-6.3 | 10.8 | 6.0 | 4.5 |
| 1985 | 1.5-4 | 8.3-5.8 | 9.8 | 5.4 | 4.2 |
| 1986 | 1  -3.5 | 8.3-5.8 | 9.3 | 4.9 | 4.2 |

*Office of Management and Budget, *Fiscal Year 1982 Budget Revisions,* March 1981, Table 6, p. 13.

Discrepancies between (3) and (4) + (5) are in original sources, and are due to second-order effects $\left(\dfrac{\Delta P}{P} \cdot \dfrac{\Delta Q}{Q}\right)$ quarterly compounding, and rounding.

*TABLE 2*
### Real Gross National Product and Unemployment, 1980-86
### Reagan Scenario compared to Conventional Estimates

| | (1) | (2) | (3) | (4) | (5) | (6) |
|---|---|---|---|---|---|---|
| | GNP (1980 $billion) | | Unemployment (%) | | GNP (1980 $billion) | Reagan Scenario GNP Relative to |
| | Reagan Scenario | Estimated Potential at 6% Unempl. | Reagan Scenario | CBO Alternative | Conventional Estimate for Reagan Unempl. | Conventional Estimate |
| 1980 | 2629 | 2746 | 7.2 | 7.2 | — | — |
| 1981 | 2658 | 2815 | 7.8 | 7.8 | 2663 | .998 |
| 1982 | 2769 | 2886 | 7.2 | 7.9 | 2802 | .988 |
| 1983 | 2908 | 2958 | 6.6 | 7.8 | 2914 | .998 |
| 1984 | 3039 | 3032 | 6.4 | 7.7 | 3001 | 1.013 |
| 1985 | 3167 | 3108 | 6.0 | 7.5 | 3108 | 1.019 |
| 1986 | 3300 | 3185 | 5.6 | 7.2 | 3217 | 1.026 |

(1) and (3) Office of Management and Budget, *Fiscal Year 1982 Budget Revisions,* March 1981, Table 6, p. 13. GNP converted to 1980 dollars by deflator projections given in same scenario.

(2) and (5) Author's estimates, assuming (a) Potential GNP grows at 2.5% per year, (b) $Y^* - Y = Y[.025(U-6.0)]$ where $Y^*$ is potential GNP (2), U is unemployment percentage (3), .025 is the assumed Okun's Law coefficient, and the equation is solved to give Y, "actual" GNP (5).

(6) -(1)/(5) For 1986, the Reagan scenario gives real GNP 2.6% higher than its unemployment projection would indicate in a conventional Okun's Law calculation.

(4) Congressional Budget Office estimate of unemployment conditional on Reagan budget with less optimistic economic forecast. Congressional Budget Office, *An Analysis of President Reagan's Budget Revisions for Fiscal Year 1982.* Staff Working paper, March 1981. Summary Table 3, p. xviii.

1982 and 1983 by some business tax reductions and by a 10 percent personal income tax reduction and by unspecified tax cuts to maintain effective tax rates constant after 1983. The CBO projections show little difference between the Reagan budget and this baseline in macro impacts. If anything, the Reagan program is a little tighter than the assumed baseline. Reagan spends less and taxes less, and the net effect is close to neutral.

Actually the high employment budget deficit (calculated for, say, 6 percent unemployment) declines slightly over the next few years under the Reagan proposals, even when the administration's optimistic inflation scenario is replaced by the more pessimistic price forecasts of the CBO and private model-builders (see Table 3). These are conventional Keynesian calculations, without supply side optimism. (Neither do they apply to the federal government the inflation accounting we recommend to private businesses, which would of course tell us that even the actual budget is already balanced.)

The composition of the budget, as well as its totals and its balance, affects its macroeconomic impact. Under the Reagan program, federal

Table 3
### THE FEDERAL BUDGET, 1980-84
### OUTLAYS, REVENUES, DEFICIT, HIGH EMPLOYMENT DEFICIT

| | (1) | (2) | (3) | (4) | (5) | (6) |
|---|---|---|---|---|---|---|
| | | | | | | CBO Alternative Inflation Scenario |
| | Budget Outlays ($billion) | | | Budget Revenues ($billion) | | |
| | Reagan Estimates | CBO Estimates for Reagan Scenario | Estimates for 6% Unempl. and CBO Inflation | Reagan Estimates | Estimates for 6% Unempl. and CBO Inflation | % increase in GNP Deflator |
| 1980 | 580 | 580 | 577 | 520 | 554 | |
| 1981 | 655 | 660 | 657 | 600 | 662 | 10.3 |
| 1982 | 695 | 708 | 716 | 650 | 710 | 9.2 |
| 1983 | 732 | 740 | 761 | 709 | 765 | 8.6 |
| 1984 | 770 | 782 | 812 | 771 | 827 | 8.1 |

| | (7) | (8) | (9) |
|---|---|---|---|
| | Deficit ($billion) | | High Employment Deficit ($billion) |
| | Reagan Estimates | CBO Estimates for Reagan Scenario | Estimates for 6% Unempl. and CBO Inflation |
| 1980 | 60 | 60 | 23 |
| 1981 | 55 | 60 | -5 |
| 1982 | 45 | 58 | 6 |
| 1983 | 23 | 31 | -4 |
| 1984 | -1 | 11 | -15 |

(1), (4), (7) Congressional Budget Office, *An Analysis of President Reagan's Budget Revisions for Fiscal Year 1982.* Staff Working Paper, March 1981, Summary Table 1, p. xiii.

(2), (8) Reagan estimates plus subtotal for Alternative Programmatic Assumptions, Spending Rates, and Other Factors, CBO, *op. cit.,* Summary Table 4, p. xxi.

(6) CBO alternative inflation forecast conditional on Reagan program, *op. cit.* Summary Table 3, p. xviii. Compare Reagan scenario column (4) of Table 1.

(3) Column (1) plus Total Reestimates from CBO Summary Table 4, *loc. cit.,* less author's estimate of reduction in outlays due to difference between CBO unemployment projections in Summary Table 2 and 6%. In principle, column (3) differs from (1) by adding outlays due to higher CBO estimates of inflation and interest rates and by subtracting outlays, mainly unemployment compensation, due to projected unemployment rates above 6%.

(5) Column (4) multiplied by $(1 + 1.5(x -1))$ where x is the ratio of column (2) Table 2 to column (1) Table 2, i.e., potential GNP to projected actual GNP. The elasticity of revenues with respect to GNP is assumed to be 1.5.

(9) = (3) – (5) Negative figures are surpluses.

purchases of goods and services rise because of the defense buildup. Transfers and taxes fall. The changes in composition are large, but I think they don't change the macro story just told. For the same budget totals, the shift to defense purchases is expansionary. On the other hand, the shift of purchasing power from liquidity-constrained transferees with high marginal propensities to consume to higher income taxpayers is moderately contractionary. Some economists believe that defense is intrinsically highly inflationary and cite with foreboding the fact that Reagan's projected buildup is comparable percentage-wise to Johnson's Vietnam spending binge. The analogy is far from perfect. This defense buildup starts in an economy with a much larger amount of slack than there was in January 1966. And it lacks the compulsion to disregard costs and budget constraints that an actual war provides.

No observer of the current political scene can forebear comment on the ironies of the political parties' reversals of roles. Now the Republicans defend planned deficits against Democratic attack, advocate tax cuts not just to arrest recession but to sustain incipient recovery, and resist Democratic proposals to tilt tax reduction further toward businesses at the expense of individuals. It was a Democratic president who deliberately declined, ever since 1977, to recommend tax cuts to compensate for fiscal drag and bracket drift, and who sanctimoniously foreswore countercyclical fiscal measures to overcome the recent recession. It is the Democrats in Congress who now issue dire warnings of the inflationary effect of stimulating the economy by three years of tax reduction even when the unemployment rate is 7.5 percent and capacity utilization is barely 80 percent. It is the Republicans—some of them, it is true, without full conviction in their new religion—who say that it is idle and self-defeating to try to balance the budget by higher and higher effective tax rates. The final irony is that it is a Republican budget, proposed by a president who is a free enterprise hero, to which the securities markets are currently registering a vote of no confidence.

The budget is taking a bad rap from those, whether liberal Democrats or conservative investment bankers, who say it is a reckless gamble to reduce taxes so much. To say this is not to agree with extravagant administration claims that their package increases the national propensity to save, but only to say that it doesn't decrease it; clearly the tax cuts by themselves, without the expenditure cuts, would diminish saving relative to GNP. Nor is it to agree with Lafferite views that the tax cuts will actually maintain or increase revenues. That is most improbable, as I shall explain below.

In judging the fiscal package to be more or less innocuous in its macroeconomic impact, I am not endorsing it. I have serious microeconomic and distributional objections, but I will confine myself here to two macroeconomic reservations. First, I regret that once again opportunities are being lost to use tax reduction to gain ground on inflation. We could cut taxes that directly boost labor costs and prices, e.g., by reducing payroll levies. We could go further and offer tax inducements for disinflationary wage and price behavior. Second, we could aim for a different fiscal-monetary mix, one better designed to foster capital formation and growth. In my opinion, that would involve a tighter budget policy compensated by a monetary policy that would give us lower real interest rates.

### Monetary Policy: Disinflation the Fed's Job

I turn now to monetary policy, where the greatest inconsistencies in the Reagan recovery program occur. The President and his administration have assigned the Federal Reserve responsibility for inflation.

You take care of prices, they say in effect, and we'll get the economy moving again. Criticizing imperfect marksmanship of the past, the President and his economic policymakers order the Fed to cut the rate of monetary growth in half over the next five years. This was already the Fed's policy, as anyone who listens to Paul Volcker knows. Now he has Beryl Sprinkel and other monetarists looking over his shoulder, if not waiting in the wings.

The monetary targets of the Fed and the administration are shown in the first column of Table 1. The idea that money and prices can be detached and delegated to central bankers while Congress and the executive independently take care of budget, taxes, employment, and output is the kind of fallacy that makes exam questions for freshman economics, a fallacy now elevated to presidential doctrine. If Amtrak hitches engines at both ends of a train of cars in New Haven station— we still do have a railroad there—one engine heading west to New York, the other east to Boston, and advertises that the train is going simultaneously to both destinations, most people would be skeptical. Reagan is hitching a Volcker engine at one end and a Stockman-Kemp locomotive to the other and telling us the economic train will carry us to full employment and disinflation at the same time.

This inconsistency is shown in Table 1. The third column is the official administration projection of nominal GNP, equal to the totals of columns four and five, the Reagan scenarios for inflation and real output growth. Subtracting the monetary targets of column 1 from the dollar-GNP projections of column 3 gives the implied growth rates of velocity of M1B, column 2. The two numbers correspond to the two limits of the M1B target brackets.

There has never been a two-year period over which the average growth of M1B velocity has exceeded 5 percent. It would have to beat that in each of the next five years, hitting 7, 8, almost 9 percent to make the Reagan scenario come true. These increases in velocity are beyond historical experience, even in the recent decade of unprecedented financial innovation. Finance is one sector where American technology remains the best in the world, and the possibility of even faster progress in economizing cash can't be completely ruled out. But if policymakers were to accept rescue from velocity miracles, or *a fortiori* from further regulatory changes, they would be substituting shadow for substance, appearance for reality. Although the Fed might be tempted by any escape route from the credibility impasse they have painted themselves into, I assume the Fed really means to do literally no more than what their targets say, and to do less if the spirit of the policy so dictates.

This translates, whether the administration realizes it or not, into significantly lower rates of growth of dollar spending on GNP than the official projections (column 3). Of course, another way to achieve high velocity growth is to engineer even higher nominal and real interest rates than those we're now suffering. But they would surely be inconsistent with the substantial recovery of real and nominal GNP promised by the President (columns 3 and 5). On the other hand, if the inflation and interest rate projections of the administration were realized, velocity would slow down.

## Missing: A Strategy for Disinflation

As devastating as this inconsistency is to the credibility of the President's program, the scenario contains a more fatal flaw. This is the division of nominal GNP, column 3, between inflation, column 4, and real output growth, column 5. It defies historical experience to expect price inflation to subside as rapidly as shown in column 4 while output recovers as vigorously as projected in column 5. Experience tells us the combination is a most unlikely one, given the stubborn inertia of existing patterns of inflation. Experience tells us that disinflation requires recessions, prolonged slack, and high unemployment. What entitles this administration to expect to cut inflation in half while output is growing faster than its sustainable potential for five years?

The only answer that has trickled out of Washington is an appeal to self-fulfilling expectations. The public will read column 5. Observing the decisive budgetary moves of the new administration, believing them to be the proper medicine for inflation as advertised, the public will act to make the predictions come true. That means they will negotiate lower wage bargains and slow down price increases. Previous optimistic inflation forecasts from the White House have not been self-fulfilling or otherwise fulfilled, but maybe this time will be different.

This is an expectations argument, but certainly not a rational expectations theory. Rational expectations require a model that makes sense, one that truly connects policy actions to results. Rational expectations not only generate but are generated from such a model. In this case no such model exists, and Robert Lucas and Robert Hall are as unlikely as Lane Kirkland and Sam Church to believe and act upon the advertised disinflation.

The two major English-speaking democracies are in conservative economic hands, but the policies and public stance of Margaret Thatcher in Great Britain are very different from those of Ronald Reagan in the United States. Their prime ministers threatens workers, managers, and plain citizens like an authoritarian schoolmaster disciplining an unruly class. You won't have jobs, profits or prosperity until you stop inflating your wages and prices. Our President promises disinflation without tears, indeed with prosperity. He encourages unions and managements to carry on business as usual. After all, inflation is only the government's fault, and all we citizens are asked to do is to accept tax goodies and stop indulging the poor. The Federal

Reserve, it is true, has been following a Thatcher-like policy but in whispers. I am one of the thousand or so Americans who hear and read Paul Volcker and know that M1B is not an army rifle. I pay attention to Henry Wallich too. I believe they will do what they say they will do, and I am duly scared. If *I* were Lane Kirkland, I would take the monetary threats seriously and tell my constituent unions to take it easy.

The Fed's muted threat is quite different from Her Majesty's first minister's standing up in Parliament and throughout her country to say that she doesn't care how much unemployment there is for how long, or what is the real rate of growth or decline; she will stick it through whatever the pain, however long it takes to eliminate inflation. Reagan has said nothing like that, and Volcker isn't well known in Peoria or Spokane, in the shops and offices where wages and prices are made. Federal Reserve threats are heard in financial circles all right, but the bond market does not seem to be impressed. In summary, if the Reagan antiinflation strategy depends on expectations, the administration has done and said nothing to make expectations work in its favor.

Let there be no illusion. There is no way to reduce inflation in this country so long as wage increases proceed at 10 percent a year. There is no possible miracle of productivity that can validate such a trend in money wages. Our lost 2 percent per year productivity trend may reappear as mysteriously as it vanished. If we are very, very lucky, policy to speed investment and research and development might add another half point or full point, not this year or next but some years down the road. But with the best of good fortune we would be left with domestic core inflation of 7-8 percent unless the money wage pattern is broken—and it may be more difficult to break it when workers can claim to have earned more via improved productivity. We must also expect an adverse trend in the terms of trade between American labor and resource-based commodities imported from abroad or produced within the country. This may be equivalent on average to a half point or full point of decline in worker productivity.

I emphasize the persistent inertial trend of money wages in the central nonagricultural "fixprice" sector of our economy, because no lasting solution of our inflation is possible unless it is brought much closer to the sustainable trend of productivity. In short runs, especially month to month and quarter to quarter, popular price indexes can vary widely around this core inflation rate, from the weight of flexible prices loosely tied to U.S. wages. In the next eighteen months, for example, the volatile elements in the Consumer Price Index might be favorable, and the administration might be able to point to some apparent successes in its battle against inflation. If mortgage interests rates stay put or fall, the housing component will contribute less to CPI inflation news than in 1979-80. Perhaps we have purchased a respite on the oil front by selling AWACS to Saudi Arabia, as well as by slowing down our economy and swallowing the decontrol of domestic prices in one gulp early this year. Our tight monetary policy, if it does nothing else, is appreciating the dollar against other currencies; this may be bad for the U.S. export-import position but it lowers dollar prices of some imports and world-traded commodities. Food price prospects, always uncertain, are not so favorable, given the end of the grain embargo and the low level of world stocks. My purpose is not to predict prices but to warn that transient luck in the volatile elements of price indexes does not signify final victory, any more than transient misfortune justified panic about runaway inflation acceleration in 1979-80.

At the beginning of my talk, I pointed out that countries with enviable inflation records in recent years are not invariably those with Reagan-like fiscal policies. If the successful countries have a common characteristic, it is that they have some kind of handle on money wage decisions.

Here in the United States whoever was the victor in the November 1980 election had, I thought, the rare opportunity to use the window of good feeling that Americans open at the start of a new presidential term to gain control over our wage-price spiral. To engineer disinflation without a protracted dose of recession and economic stagnation, I believe it is necessary to give everybody assurance that everybody else is going to disinflate. Otherwise the fear and suspicion of each group that it will lose real and relative income lead it to stick to the existing inflationary pattern. This makes tough going for a Thatcher policy, and even tougher going for a contractionary policy without a clear and credible threat.

For this reason, I have favored a preannounced schedule of gradually declining standards for wage increases over a five-year transitional period. Inducements to obey the guideposts would be provided by payroll tax rebates for employees in complying firms, and for employers too if their percentage markups do not rise. The guidepost schedule would be consistent with a macroeconomic disinflationary policy to which the administration, Congress, and Federal Reserve would be solemnly and visibly committed. Since nominal GNP growth and wage-cost inflation would decline in concert, there would be neither suppressed demand-pull inflation nor the damage to real economic performance caused by cutting monetary demand growth while money cost inflation proceeds unabated.

Such a policy clearly requires a consensus among labor, business, and government, and such a consensus clearly requires strong and persuasive leadership by a popular president. We lost that opportunity this year, just as we lost the chance to follow a "cold turkey" policy with some chance that inflation would melt faster than previous statistical evidence leads us to believe it will.

## Supply-Side Economics: No Free Lunch

But can't we take hope from the recent discovery that the economy has a supply side? This remarkable revelation plays a big role in the rhetoric that rationalizes the Reagan program, although, as I argued above, the fiscal program as macro strategy does not really depend on Laffer-Kemp calculus. The official macroeconomic scenario does contain a small bit of supply-side magic. Real GNP five years out is somewhat larger, relative to the projected unemployment rates, than received "Okun's Law" wisdom would allow (Table 3, column 6). There appears to be on average an extra half percent per year of real growth, beyond what would normally accompany the unemployment reductions shown. It is not clear from what source these gains are supposed to come.

From labor supply? Supply-side wisdom is that the upward drift of marginal personal tax rates is drying up the supply of productive labor. That there has been such a drift, particularly since 1977, is undeniable, though it is not as great as often alleged. The Brookings Institution tax file permits calculation of the federal marginal rate of personal income tax, averaged over all brackets, faced by a breadwinner with spouse and two children: 1960, 18.8 percent; 1965, 15.9 percent; 1970, 18.2 percent; 1975, 18 percent; 1980, 21.6 percent. Yet it is hard to find evidence of a weakened propensity to supply labor in recent experience. Labor force participation, overtime hours of work, multiple job holding, weekly hours of work corrected for changes in industry mix—none of these indicators seem out of line with trends and cyclical effects dating from the 1950s and 1960s. Believe it or not, most of our seven million unemployed fellow citizens really do want work, and there are many "not in labor force" who do also. Finally, I observe that although the administration's tax bill reduces marginal rates for taxpayers, especially those in high brackets, its budget cuts will seriously impair work incentives for low-income families and individuals dependent on welfare, food stamps, and other transfers.

In the belief that a curve deserves a theory, I have derived rigorously a Laffer Curve based on labor supply response to after-tax real wages. Indeed, I have derived two Laffer Curves, one for tax revenues and one for national saving (more precisely for tax revenues plus private savings, which exceeds national saving by the amount of government purchases, assumed constant). These are pictured in Figure 1, which also contains a rather cryptic, but I hope sufficient, explanation of their derivation. The important parameters are the Cobb-Douglas elasticity of output with respect to capital, $\alpha$, and with respect to labor, $1-\alpha$, and the elasticity of labor supply $1/\beta$. In the numerical example, I took both $\alpha$ and $1/\beta$ to be $1/3$. That is a generous estimate of labor supply response; the consensus guess is no higher than $1/6$. With these values my Laffer Curve peaks at a wage tax rate of $5/6$. The National Saving

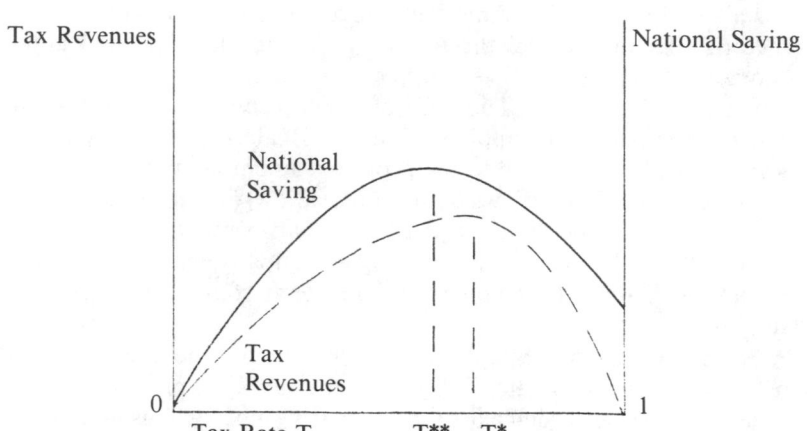

*Figure 1*
Laffer Curves

$\alpha$ = capital share of output

$\dfrac{1}{\beta}$ = labor supply elasticity

$C_k$ = marginal propensity to consume capital income

$C_w$ = marginal propensity to consume labor income

$$T^* = \frac{\alpha + \beta}{1 + \beta} \qquad T^{**} = 1 - \frac{1 - \alpha}{(1 + \beta)\,(C_w\,(1 - \alpha) + C_k\,\alpha)}$$

Curve involves also the marginal propensity to consume, which I took in the exercise to be .4 for capital income and .8 for after-tax labor income. The peak of this second, and more economically significant, Laffer Curve is at a tax rate of 3/4. I doubt that we are on the wrong slope of either Laffer Curve now, and I hope we don't go there.

A more credible supply-oriented policy is to stimulate nonresidential fixed investment, in the hope that accelerating the growth of capital relative to output and labor supply will raise productivity. As one of the Kennedy team that originated the investment tax credit in 1962, I have some sympathy with this goal. Clearly I do not have time to discuss adequately the Reagan administration's investment stimuli, so I will confine myself to four short remarks.

First, as I stated earlier, I regret that we cannot adopt a mix of macroeconomic policies, fiscal and monetary, that would shift the composition of output toward capital formation. Why can't we? The main reason is simply the monetarist dogma embraced by the administration, to which the Federal Reserve is hostage. This locks us into a particular path of a particular monetary aggregate, invariant to fiscal policy and other macroeconomic circumstances.

Second, there are ways to provide investment incentives in the taxation of business that do not make a shambles of economic efficiency and tax equity, as the present proposals for accelerated depreciation do. If the intention is to make amends for the overstatement of taxable profits due to historical cost depreciation, there are straightforward ways of doing so without freezing into the tax code a depreciation system that will still be there if and when inflation abates. Anyway, this investment disincentive is offset, partially or fully, by another inflation distortion in the tax code, the deductibility of nominal interest.

Third, whatever investment incentive is enacted now should be effective immediately. Its impact is diluted by a gradual phase-in such as the administration proposes, because this gives an inducement to delay investment projects.

*Figure 2*
**Derivation of Laffer Curves**

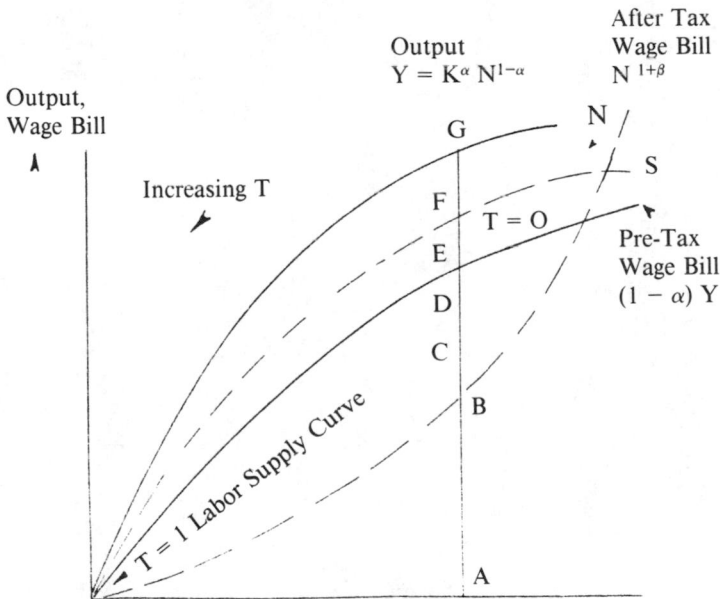

N ➤     Labor Supply and Employment
AB: Workers' Consumption          BC: Workers' Saving
CD: Workers' Taxes                DE: Capitalist Taxes
EF: Capitalist Saving             FG: Capitalist Consumption
BF: Taxes and saving available for government purchases and private investment $(G + I)$
CE: Tax Revenues

Fourth, plant and equipment is not the only social capital. If we wish as a society to make better provision for the future, we should also be concerned with the preservation and improvement of human capital, natural resources, and public sector facilities and infrastructure, all of which are sacrificed in the Reagan budget, pervaded as it is by the ideology that only private business capital is productive.

The outlook, I am afraid, is for continued stagflation, with disappointing results on all fronts—inflation, unemployment, real output, interest rates, and capital formation. We will unwind the Great Society, redistribute income regressively, withdraw the federal commitment to the environment, and we will have little or no macroeconomic progress to show. The program will not fulfill the promises that have led the country to support it. I wish I knew what will happen when the administration, Congress, and public confront this reality.

# The Reagan Economic Plan

Robert Hall

Let me start by saying that in no sense am I a spokesman for the President's program. The closest I came to participating in the formulation of the policy was serving as a member of the task force on inflation, which made its report last November. Since then, I have been an academic on the sidelines.

What do economists and the public think is wrong with the American economy today? In the first place, the economy suffers from disappointing real growth. The disappointment dates back to 1973 in its worst form, but actually real growth as we knew it in the 1960s came to an end in 1969. Since then, periods of growth have alternated with severe recessions, and, over the whole period, net growth has been weak. The past few years have been especially bad. And the prospect for the economy today is for continuing disappointments in real incomes and real growth. As I understand it, the administration is very, very concerned with the growth issue.

The second problem, first on the public's list but second on mine, is inflation. People are very tired of struggling with a dollar that loses some 10 percent of its value every year. The public has been clear about its desire to end inflation. There is a very strong political commitment to end inflation. We as economists have an obligation to say, how can we do it?

The third item on my list is excess government control over the use of resources in the economy. There is simply too much intervention in various forms—regulation, taxing, and spending. A particular form of excess government intervention is the heavy taxation of the return to savings. There is virtually a crisis in the taxation of one of the most critical channels of savings and investment, equity-financed purchases of plant and equipment by corporations. Those transactions are taxed in the U.S. economy today at rates of something like 60 or 70 precent, which is simply excessive. On the other hand, as Professor Tobin points out, we have another problem today, that the tax system subsidizes tax shelters, because of the deductibility of interest. The tax system is completely out of kilter as a result of inflation, and we need to do something about it.

That's my short list of things that are wrong with the economy. Let me turn now to what we shouldn't do about it, and here you will find me in agreement with what Professor Tobin just said. The leading example of what not to do with the economy today is what the British are doing. Let me review the elements of the British macro policy as I see them. In the first place, the British have brought about a sharp reduction in money growth. And that has brought with it the usual symptoms of a financial crisis, including high interest rates, over-valued currency, and the like. Second, government expenditures are continuing to rise. That, I think, is the central problem they are facing. They simply do not have a handle on the budget in Britain. Part of the budget problem takes the form of direct government purchases of goods and services, including the continuing sad story of deepening government involvement in operating government enterprises, in spite of Margaret Thatcher's commitment to free enterprise. Another important source of budget strain comes from transfers, which have risen because of the reduction in real activity and employment. Finally, under the influence of, I think, a very basically incorrect interpretation of supply-side arguments, the British have sharply raised commodity taxes and sharply cut income taxes at the same time. The net effect on the budget from these two moves was not large but it brought about a sharp increase in inflation. There is a large amount of feedback from the cost of living index to wages and transfers in the British economy. And the worsening of inflation has not been offset by any supply-side response, either in theory or in fact. A fundamental supply-side analysis says that the incentive to work depends on the ratio of take-home wages to prices. That's not affected by a move which increases take-home wages but also increases prices.

Let's not do what the British are doing. I'm happy to see that, by and large, the Reagan administration is not moving in the British direction. None of the three elements that I've listed in the British example exist in the proposed policy of the administration. So what should we do? Again, I have a list, and it differs from the administration's policy only in one of its elements.

In the first place, we need to limit government expenditures. Here, I think, is probably the largest disagreement with what Professor Tobin has said. There are a great many federal spending programs, transfer programs, and regulations which the people don't want, which have an unfavorable effect on the public's spendable real incomes. We should make a list of all the rat holes that the government is pouring money into today, and we should eliminate them. If you go through the budget proposals of the Reagan administration, you will find that the character of the expenditure reductions is largely, though not exclusively, elimination of rat holes. One can give countless examples. One which has been quite prominent is the Export-Import Bank—a good example of a program which simply does not have a proper role in a well-run economy. It certainly does not benefit the poor, and is something which should be dispensed with. Well, there are many, many things in the budget that should be dispensed with. My personal list would be considerably longer than the one the administration has come up with. Furthermore, my cuts would be larger in those cases where the administration has successfully identified a rat hole and then said, our way of dealing with the problem is to cut the budget by twenty percent. Having found a rat hole, I think we should simply stop pouring anything down it. Whole segments of the budget—like the Energy Department—are just collections of rat holes. Together, they consume a nontrivial fraction of real GNP.

Let me be very clear that I do not include in this category the types of expenditure which have virtually eliminated poverty in the United States over the past twenty years. I am very happy to see that antipoverty programs like AFDC, supplemental security income, and food stamps have not been gutted. Though these programs are not completely satisfactory, they represent a very important step forward in improving the distribution of income in the most important way, by helping those at the very bottom. The President has been very clear on the need to retain antipoverty expenditures. I think it's very unfortunate that a large number of opponents of the package have described it incorrectly as aimed primarily at eliminating expenditures on behalf of the poor. That's simply not correct. There are, of course, some attempts to improve the performance of transfer programs, but it seems to me that one can correctly characterize most of the expenditure cuts as eliminating rat holes.

President Reagan has also proposed large increases in military spending. I don't feel qualified to judge the desirability of this move, but I think that economists do have one very important thing to say with respect to military expenditures—macro policy is capable of delivering full employment and price stability for virtually any level of expenditures. Here I agree completely with what Professor Tobin said. There are good examples of economies which have much larger public sectors than ours, and have full employment and price stability. If necessary, we could support a much larger military establishment than we have now without automatically creating any significant macroeconomic problems. Of course, resources available to the private sector for investment and consumption would necessarily be less in an economy that was devoting a large amount of its output to military or other government purposes. Within that limitation, the total level of output and the behavior of prices are things that policy can control. An increase in government spending is not by itself a threat to the performance of the overall economy. Nor is a decrease in spending. We ought to be able to design macro policies that handle any of these contingencies.

One of the most controversial features of the President's program is substantial reduction in tax rates. I emphasize that what's being proposed are rate reductions, and not necessarily revenue reductions. One does not have to accept the labor supply rationale of the Laffer Curve to entertain the proposition that a tax rate reduction could increase revenue. A very good example of that is the reduction in capital gains tax rates that went into effect in 1978. In a recent study, the Treasury concluded that revenue remained about the same as a result of a large reduction in tax rates. Rate reductions can stimulate revenue because people have a good deal of discretion about how they arrange their affairs and how they fill out their tax returns. When tax rates go down, the incentives to shelter income are dramatically reduced; certainly that was the case with the capital gains reduction. And a fairly small fraction of total income actually flows through people's income tax returns. In spite of high apparent marginal rates, it's a curious fact of the U.S. economy that only 11 percent of personal income is paid to the federal government as personal income tax. I agree completely that the evidence that people work harder when they are taxed less is not nearly strong enough to support the notion that revenue would respond favorably to a tax cut. What the reduction in capital gains rates suggests is that people's incentive to avoid taxes would be dramatically reduced by cutting top marginal rates, and that would mean that revenue at least would not fall nearly as much as a simple calculation might suggest.

Although I am skeptical about the strength of the supply response to reduced tax rates, I endorse tax cuts as a way to restore real growth. Perfectly standard macro analysis, in which labor supply is exactly inelastic with respect to real wages, will tell you that tax cuts are expansionary. The idea that was pushed very hard and successfully in 1961 through 1964 is correct today. And it seems to me that it should be pushed today. One doesn't have to believe in an exotic labor supply function to take the view that the time has come for tax cuts.

I also favor tax cuts as by far the best way to keep expenditures under control. It seems to me that the reason that government expenditures haven't swollen worse than they have is Congressional fear of deficits. If we don't have a tax cut, there will be that much more room for pouring money down rat holes, which is not something I'd like to see happen.

The last topic on the fiscal side is investment incentives. As I said at the outset, heavy taxation of some kinds of investment income is one of our worst current problems. The President's proposal for accelerated depreciation—the 10-5-3 plan—is very much a stimulus to investment through reduced taxation of its return. I don't think it is the best way to cut taxes on investment, however. I would far prefer to see the following combination of changes: On the one hand, allow an immediate write-off of all corporate investment—this would be the ultimate extension of accelerated depreciation. On the other hand, we should deny all interest deductions under the corporate income tax. That combination of proposals would provide even more stimulus than 10-5-3, and it would eliminate the inefficient subsidy we now pay to leveraged investment as well. In the long run, such a tax has a zero effective rate on a corporation that has no monopoly earnings. In a sense, it amounts to a proposal to abolish the corporate income tax, which I don't think would be a bad idea. Even with 10-5-3, the corporate income tax would become a very small part of the federal revenue picture. The big engine of revenue in the U.S. economy in the future will be the payroll tax—not the corporate income tax and not the personal income tax.

With respect to monetary discipline, what is needed is the establishment of a long-run framework for monetary policy. We need to be able to promise a move toward monetary stability, and therefore to price stability, over the next half decade or decade. We need a convincing way to express that policy. It's not a matter of adopting a harsh reduction in money growth over the next 12 months. Rather, we need a way to promise the American public that we will not push the economy too hard at any one time, but we will push it to long-run price stability. So far, the administration's proposals have not been in the form I would like to see—there has not been a strong announcement of a long-run monetary framework. Partly this is a recognition of the independence of the Federal Reserve System, and a reluctance for the President to appear to be trying to dictate to an independent branch of government what it should be doing.

What should the Fed be doing? The type of announcement I would like to see would state the target of monetary policy in terms of a path of nominal GNP. Take column 3 in Table 1 in Professor Tobin's article and say, this is what monetary policy will achieve. We would love to accomplish what is shown in columns 4 and 5. We'd love to get inflation down that rapidly; we'd love to raise real growth to these exceptional rates year after year. We can't promise either. What we can promise through the use of a sensible long-run monetary policy is column 3. We can promise to use monetary instruments to keep nominal GNP growth at a reasonably high level, that is, not undergo sharp recession, and yet, reduce this growth gradually to a non-inflationary level. What I don't want to see, and what I am afraid I am hearing more and more from the administration, is that money growth will stick, come hell or high water, to the predetermined target of column 1. We can see from the table that column 1 does not mesh with column 3. I couldn't agree more strongly with Professor Tobin's comments on this contradiction. There's simply nothing in the economy that's going to give velocity growth as high as is suggested by column 2. Furthermore, to the extent that a policy is successful in bringing inflation to an end, it will also gradually reduce interest rates.

Lower interest rates should cause velocity to fall, so the problem is even compounded relative to Professor Tobin's discussion.

One of the things I like most about the new administration is its commitment to strong real growth. To the extent that policy is successful in bringing growth, the economy will need more money. We shouldn't be afraid of money growth, if the reason we need it is growth in real GNP. The strict target of low money growth of column 1 just doesn't make sense in a rapidly growing economy. We can get out of the box by announcing a nominal GNP target instead of a money growth target. So far, the administration's position has been incomplete in this area.

Taken together, the policy of reduced federal command over resources, lower tax rates, and investment stimulus adopted by the administration promises progress in solving economic problems. If coupled with a good long-run framework for monetary and price stability, it would be a very large step forward in economic policymaking.

# Chapter 8:
# Economic Growth:
# Alternative Views

## Slow Economic Growth

### Lester C. Thurow

Interest in accelerating economic growth has gone in and out of fashion. Along with the missile gap, it was one of the key campaign issues in 1960. The Russian growth rate exceeded that of the United States, and Nikita Krushchev was threatening to bury us economically and militarily. Faced with shortages of key materials and a sharp decline in America's productivity growth, accelerating economic growth has once again become an important issue.

The heart of the issue is productivity—output per man-hour. Our ability to consume ultimately depends upon our ability to produce. If we produce more per hour, each of us can have more purchasing power to buy the things we want. If productivity does not rise, our money incomes can rise, but it is not possible to have more real purchasing power. Often the issue is referred to as *supply-side economics*. How can we increase the supply of goods available for private consumption, corporate investment, and government expenditures? To find an answer we must find a way to accelerate the growth of productivity.

To stop inflation recent administrations have chosen to tighten monetary and fiscal policies to produce idle capacity. Whatever the merits of idle capacity in the fight against inflation, it exacts a stiff price in slower productivity growth. With idle capital, incentives to invest diminish. There is little need for new, more productive facilities. Knowing that they do not need to expand, firms often cut back on research and development for new production processes. With high unemployment workers fear that technical progress will cost them their jobs and that alternative work will be hard to find. Consequently they push for more restrictive work rules to stop technical progress. The end result is a stagnant economy with a productivity slowdown on top of a basic productivity growth rate that already puts us at the bottom of the industrial league—with about one-third the productivity growth of Japan.[1]

Unless this decline can be reversed, and unless productivity can be accelerated to the levels being achieved by West Germany and Japan, it is only a question of time until we slip into relative backwardness. Few major countries have been brought down by foreign enemies;

many have disappeared because of their internal failures. How are we to eliminate our failures and make our economy more dynamic that it ever has been?

Here again the problem is not in finding policies that would significantly accelerate economic growth (there are many), but in adopting policies that would inevitably cause significant income reductions for someone. To increase investment someone's share of the national product must decline. Whose? Even more difficult is the process of disinvestment. We tend to think of economic growth in terms of investment and new products, but disinvestment is a necessary precondition. To have the labor and capital to move into new areas we must be able to withdraw labor and capital from old, low-productivity areas. But every disinvestment represents a threat to someone.

Disinvestment is what our economy does worst. Instead of adopting public policies to speed up the process of disinvestment, we act to slow it down with protection and subsidies for the inefficient. If our steel industry cannot compete, we protect it. If our television industry lags behind, we negotiate "orderly" marketing arrangements to keep out foreign-made sets. If textiles are a low-productivity industry that should be located abroad, we adopt stiff tariffs to preserve a local industry. Our shipbuilding industry is an industry completely dependent upon subsidies. All of these actions are designed to provide economic security for someone, yet each of them imprisons us in a low productivity area. If we cannot learn to disinvest, we cannot compete in the modern growth race.

### The Process of Economic Growth

The process of economic growth can be compared to a complicated road-building operation. The first step is to scout the landscape and survey the terrain to see where you want to go and find the best possible routes for reaching desirable objectives. This is the role of scientific research. Generally scientific research proceeds far ahead of the rest of the road-building operation. We knew theoretically that an atomic bomb could be built four decades before we actually did it. At the moment, we know that fusion energy is theoretically possible (we can explode a hydrogen bomb), but several decades will have elapsed before we harness fusion reactions to generate electricity.

Well behind the frontiers of scientific research lies the domain of engineering research. The direction to go and the basic principles of how to get there are known, but a practical road must be designed. When engineering research has been completed, products and processes move from the domain of the theoretically possible into the domain of those processes that have been mastered and can actually be done. Using rockets for space travel was an idea whose origin is lost in the mists of history, but it passed the frontier of engineering knowledge when we were able to put a man on the moon and get him back.

While scientific explorations and engineering designs both are important, neither affects economic growth directly. The landscape may be known, the road can be built, but the road won't be built unless the economic benefits from having the road are greater than the costs of building it. Space travel is clearly feasible, but it costs so much that there is no economic demand for regular space travel to the moon. New knowledge only becomes relevant to our economy when costs have been reduced to the point that the information can produce goods and services, which we want, at a price we can afford to pay.

Further scientific and engineering research and development is necessary before a road will actually be built. Economic feasibility must be achieved. It is at this point that new knowledge starts to impact productivity. We build the road and start to use the new processes that produce better or cheaper products than we previously had. Our standard of living rises.

But an economy is not composed solely of new products and processes. It takes time and resources to shift to the new, so that any economy is a mixture of new, high-productivity activities and old, low-productivity activities. Some plants produce the newest products with the newest technologies while other plants produce old products with old techniques. The average level of productivity depends upon the relative weights in this mixture.

Our economy encompasses a wide range of productivities. Between broad industrial categories we had a productivity gap of almost five to one in 1977. Typically within each industry there is a range of productivities on the order of four to one. The result is a very wide distribution of productivities; but there comes a point when any product or process is so obsolete that it is no longer used. New products and processes drive old products and processes out of the economy. The old roads are torn up and abandoned.

This means that there are three factors that control the growth of productivity. First, how rapidly is the frontier of economic feasibility leading to higher-productivity activities. Second, how rapidly is the economy discarding low-productivity activities. And third, what is the distribution of activities between these extremes. Are most of our economic activities concentrated toward the high-productivity end of the spectrum or toward the low-productivity end of the spectrum? The frontiers of scientific and engineering knowledge are only relevant in that they are a distant road-building operation whose speed limits the long-run speed of movement toward higher-productive techniques and processes.

Already we are in a position to see some of the reasons why productivity has grown faster in countries such as Japan and West Germany. If a country is rebuilding from wartime devastation it will rebuild with new plants. Even if its best practice plants are no better than those in other countries, a larger proportion of the plants will actually be located near the best practice frontier. This will give them faster productivity growth, even if they have no advantage in terms of their best practice plants.

Often people talk of this phenomenon as if it were better to lose a war and have your country blown up than to win a war and escape destruction. This is simply silly. To recover, the West Germans and the Japanese must devote a large fraction of their GNP to investment. The result is a much lower standard of living during the recovery period. Productivity grows rapidly but only at the sacrifice of real standards of living. If it were an advantage to have your country blown up, the winners could do likewise. They could junk their old plants (bomb them if you like) and build new plants. They don't because to do so is to reduce their standard of living. Consumption would have to fall both because production is down and because investment would have to rise.

Rebuilding countries do, however, have an advantage. Often countries find it difficult to get out of low-productivity industries and products even when economic analysis would call for it. Individuals lose their jobs and firms go bankrupt. Workers and firms lobby for government protection, subsidies, and regulations. If they are successful, the economy is locked into low-productivity operations much longer than economic circumstances would warrant. In the devastations of a postwar period, there is nothing to protect or subsidize, and no one could afford to do so even if there were. The economic losses that have been suffered can be blamed on someone else's army. The net result is that obsolete industries are not rebuilt. Disinvestment in low-productivity industries occurs at a much faster rate than it usually does.

### Disinvestment

While there are many voices calling for more investment, the process of disinvestment is even more important. Eliminating a low-productivity plant raises productivity just as much as opening a high-productivity plant. But doing so takes fewer resources. Large investments are not necessary. To close a low-productivity plant also makes it possible to move the workers and capital that have been tied up in this activity into new, high-productivity activities. With more men and investment funds, new activities can grow more rapidly. Paradoxically the essence of investment is disinvestment.

While we may have problems with research and development and with investment, our main failure lies in the area of disinvestment. We simply are not very good at accomplishing it. This is one of the places where the mixed economy has not worked. Capitalism is, after all, a doctrine of failure. The inefficient (the majority) are to be driven out of business by the efficient (the minority), and in the process productivity rises. Yet we are extremely reluctant to practice this part of our economic religion. This reluctance has a real moral basis at the level of the individual (a failing individual is a starving individual), but it has no moral basis when it comes to firms. Yet if anything, we have more programs to protect institutions (all of course justified in the name of protecting individuals) than we do individuals.

Low-productivity firms are often located in industries where the demand is stagnant or falling. This is partly due to the fact that new plants do not need to be built to meet new demands, but it is also due to a human problem. Dying industries simply cannot be managed as efficiently as growing industries. Growing industries attract bright aggressive managers who want to advance rapidly with their companies. In dying industries promotions are few and far between. Smart young managers know that they should be avoided. Who wants a job where the basic problem is to decide who to fire each day and where new, exciting investments are not happening? In a dying industry everyone is out to protect what they have rather than to build something better. They know that any gains in efficiency will simply result in more layoffs.

The result is a set of attitudes and actions on the part of both managers and workers that makes it virtually impossible to have rapid productivity growth in an industry where output is not growing or falling. The phenomenon can be seen all across America from railroads to schools. Efficiency falls as output drops. In the Boston area, where school enrollments are now rapidly falling, I know of no school system anywhere that has managed to reduce personnel nearly as fast as enrollments have fallen.

The basic problem in disinvestment is the desire each of us has to avoid the economic pains that are endemic whenever disinvestment occurs. Someone is worse off because of those disinvestments, and he or she has every incentive to appeal for government aid to stop or slow down the process of disinvestment. Regulations are adopted to stop railroads from abandoning noneconomic lines. Subsidies are used to keep an inefficient shipbuilding industry in business. Instead of shrinking with declining enrollments, schools discover special education and the need for more teachers. While it is easy to say that such things should not occur, each of us would be demanding the same protection if we were in the affected industries or communities.

### Process Innovations

Often the productivity problem is portrayed as if it were a simple problem of too little investment. If we just cut consumption and invested a larger fraction of our GNP, our productivity would be higher. One of the problems with this analysis is that more investment would now be occurring if it were profitable to do so. In most of the post-World War II period our economy has had the problem of wanting to save more than it wanted to invest. The result has been a series of recessions where demand (consumption plus investment) was below what the economy could produce. If anyone had wanted to invest more, there was no shortage of savings or production facilities, yet the investment did not occur. Taxes are often blamed, but our business taxes are no higher than those abroad. For some reason we just do not seem to have as many profitable investments.

Part of the explanation for this lack of investment can be seen in the context of what economists call *learning curves*. The learning curve phenomenon first came into focus in the production of Liberty ships and airplanes during World War II. After the plants were built and in operation, the number of man-hours of work necessary to build a ship or airplane fell rapidly as more and more ships or airplanes were built. The capital equipment did not change appreciably, but productivity rose dramatically.

This same phenomenon has been widely observed in civilian production. Following the introduction of a new product or the start-up of a new plant, labor costs typically drop sharply for a few years and then more slowly, even though the labor force is working with the same capital equipment. Investments ultimately prove to be profitable or unprofitable depending upon the steepness of the learning curve and the pace of productivity advancement after the plant has been built. Based on engineering data, it is not easy to predict production costs since production costs are not constant over time. Multinational firms find that they can build the same plant in different countries or different regions and yet have very different productivity results.

The learning curve is related to the process of informal, on-the-job acquisition of skills and team productivity.[2] In the process of production workers learn and improve their individual job skills and learn to work together as a team. New workers are inferior to those who have been working on the job for some period of time, even though their formal education and skills may be identical. As a product is being built, new and better ways of building it are found with experience. Each innovation in the production process may be small, but the cumulative effect of many small improvements is often large.

The net result is a sharp rise in productivity as a plant goes down its learning curve. Labor costs of production at the bottom of the learning curve are often a mere fraction of those at the top. But the process is not automatic. It depends upon high quality management and a cooperative work force. If the work force is unhappy, it can stifle the learning process. If managers are incompetent, opportunities for new labor-saving procedures are missed. An early adoption of rigid work rules can freeze the plant into its initial productivity level and prevent it from proceeding down the learning curve. (This is an important factor in Britain where rigid work rules are usually negotiated before a plant goes into producton.) The problem is to descend as far as possible and as quickly as possible down the learning curve. The firm that does so will have the lowest costs of production and the most profits.

This creates an interdependence between capital and labor that is not recognized in the simple cry to raise investment. If the Japanese are able to generate a steeper learning curve than Americans, the same steel mill may be a good investment in Japan and a poor investment in the United States. To raise investment it is necessary to improve the characteristics of the labor market. New skills and higher earning depend upon new investments, but new investments also depend upon a cooperative work force. Simply raising the income of capitalists, with tax cuts that must be paid for with tax increases for workers, is unlikely to achieve either more investment or a higher growth of productivity. In generating more profitable investment opportunities, skill acquisition and a cooperative work force are as important as more funds to buy new equipment. Starting a class war is hardly the way to proceed. Imagine what those who believe that all work effort is dependent upon large income differences would predict about an economy where large firms give lifetime jobs, where relative wages are almost completely dependent upon seniority rather than personal skills and merit, and where income differentials are 50 percent smaller than in the United States. Yet the Japanese have the world's highest rate of productivity growth. *Why?*

The answer is found in the incentives this system provides for going down the learning curve. With lifetime employment and seniority wages, technical progress is not threatening. Whatever is invented, it is not going to threaten either employment or wages. With the typical worker getting about 50 percent of his or her wages in twice yearly bonuses that depend upon profits, a steep learning curve is of direct concern to each worker. Every worker has an incentive to maximize productivity by welcoming technical change, learning new skills, and contributing to industrial teamwork in a way that makes U.S. employers envious. Often this phenomenon is dismissed as a cultural one impossible to duplicate in the United States, but it probably has more to do with the economic incentive system than it has to do with culture. Faced with the same incentives, U.S. workers would respond in the same way. In any case, we need to find some system that achieves the same results.

### Recent Declines in Productivity

While we need to do much more than simply reverse our recent slowdown in productivity, the slowdown is interesting since it sheds some light on what might be done to accelerate productivity. But more importantly, it vividly illustrates the complexity of the problem and the irrelevance of simple one-factor solutions such as more investment.

There is no doubt that the rate of introduction of new products and new processes has fallen. Productivity in the private business economy was growing at 3.2 percent per year from 1948 to 1965, at 2.3 percent per year from 1965 to 1975, and at 1.1 percent from 1972 to 1978.[3]

A wide variety of possible causes has been suggested for the lack of performance. Research and development expenditures are lower now than they were in the 1960s. It is often said that investment has fallen. We invest a smaller fraction of our GNP in plant and equipment than most of our industrialized neighbors. Government health, safety, and environmental regulations may have made growth more difficult. The age-sex mix of the labor force has been shifting toward inexperienced (low productivity?) workers—women and the young. Stop-go economic policies and inflation have made investors reluctant to invest. Uncertainty has risen. Workers are alienated and less cooperative in producing productivity gains. With high unemployment and more fears about job security, work rules have become more restrictive. The list of possibilities is almost endless.

Two of the commonly suggested causes simply do not fit the facts. Research and development expenditures are down from 3 percent of the GNP at the beginning of the 1970s to slightly more than 2 percent at the end of the 1970s, but productivity started to fall in 1965 well before the downturn in R&D expenditures.[4] In addition, as we have seen there is a long-time lag between R&D and productivity. A lack of R&D in the 1970s may cause productivity problems in the 1980s, but it does not explain productivity problems in the 1970s much less than in the 1960s. Our industrial neighbors have also consistently invested less in R&D than we.

Plant and equipment investment cannot explain the decline because it is up, not down. When our productivity was growing most rapidly (1948-65), plant and equipment investment averaged 9.5 percent of the GNP. Productivity growth fell after 1965, but investment rose to 10.2 percent of the GNP from 1966 to 1972. Productivity growth took another fall after 1972, but investment stayed up at 10.1 percent of the GNP from 1973 through 1978, despite the sharpest post-World War II recession.[5] Perhaps we should invest more, but declining investment is not the source of our problems.

If you analyze the pattern of productivity growth, it is clear that large productivity gains are associated with any surge to full employment. Conversely productivity growth falls as the economy moves away from the full utilization of men and machines. This occurs because we have a large proportion of overhead labor and plants designed to operate most efficiently at capacity. Managers, research departments, salesmen, maintenance workers, and the like either cannot be or are not cut back proportionally when output falls. The result is a drop in productivity since more man-hours are now necessary to produce a unit of output. Conversely when output rises toward capacity, we do not have to expand the overhead labor force. Output goes up, but overhead man-hours do not go up, and the result is a rapid gain in productivity.

About 30 percent of our productivity slowdown can be attributed to idle capacity. In our efforts to fight inflation, we have deliberately chosen to hold the demand for goods and services below what the economy could produce. Whatever benefits this may create in terms of less inflation, one of the costs is a slower rate of productivity growth. This part of the productivity problem will be cured only when we solve the inflation problem or decide to fight inflation with some other technique.

About 40 percent of the decline can be traced to a shift in the mix of goods and services being demanded and produced. If there are substantial differences in productivity among industries, as there are, the mix of output demanded by consumers, business, and government can have a substantial effect on the rate of growth of productivity. If demands are shifting toward high-productivity industries, the economy's productivity will grow rapidly. If demands are shifting toward low-productivity industries, the economy's productivity will grow slowly.

In the United States there are large differences in productivity among industries. In 1977 a man-hour of work produced $4.92 (1972 $) worth of output in services and $23.59 worth of output in finance. This is a range of almost five to one.[6] Despite what is often believed, manufacturing productivity ($8.44 per hour in nondurables and $8.42 in durables) is not much above that of the economy as a whole ($8.09). High productivity industries are finance, wholesale trade, utilities, communications, and mining. Low productivity industries include services, retail trade, construction, and agriculture.

With such wide differences in productivity, the mix of goods and services demanded can have a large effect on productivity. For a substantial period of time after World War II, the mix effect was enhancing productivity. We were leaving low-productivity industries, mainly agriculture, and entering high-productivity areas. But this process ended around 1972. The mix of goods and services demanded started to decelerate the rate of growth productivity rather than accelerate it. The sharp movements out of agriculture ended, and services (another low-productivity industry) started to grow much more rapidly.

From 1948 to 1972 agriculture, an industry whose productivity was 60 percent below the national average in 1948, reduced its demand for labor by 500 million man-hours per year. Every worker leaving agriculture and entering the urban economy meant a sharp rise in productivity, and there were millions of such workers. But by 1972 this process had essentially ended. Productivity was still rising rapidly in agriculture, but agriculture had become so small that it no longer was releasing millions of workers. After 1972 annual reductions were down to 50 million man-hours per year. Large amounts of labor were no longer being released from a low-productivity industry.

Quite the reverse was now occurring. Another low-productivity industry, services, started to grow much more rapidly. While less than 30 percent of the additional man-hours added to the economy from 1965 to 1972 had been in services, 47 percent of all man-hours added to the private economy after 1972 were in services. Since service productivity is 40 percent below the national average, every worker moving into services represented a sharp cut in average productivity. What had been a sharp shift toward higher productivity became a sharp shift toward lower productivity.

Almost half of those extra services workers went into health care. If we want health care, that is what we want—but one of the inevitable consequences is a lower growth of productivity. The essence of the problem can be seen in the 300,000 security guards added to our economy since 1972. Since security guards protect old goods and do not produce new goods they add nothing to output, but they increase man-hours of work. The same number of passengers are flying from Boston to Los Angeles, but now it takes more hours of work to get them there since their luggage must be checked. The net result is a decline in productivity even though our sense of well-being may be up.

The remaining 30 percent of the decline can be traced to particular problems in three industries—mining, construction, and utilites. Mining and construction have even experienced negative productivity growth. Output per man-hour is less now than it was a decade ago. Utility productivity growth is down sharply.

The decline in productivity growth in electrical, gas, and sanitary utilities is the easiest to explain. This is a clear case where productivity growth is highly dependent upon the growth of output. Additional output is produced in new efficient plants, and a very large fraction of the labor force is overhead labor needed to maintain the distribution systems. When more energy is consumed, output goes up very rapidly relative to employment. Conversely when output stabilizes or goes down, productivity stabilizes or goes down. With the much higher prices of energy, output growth has slowed and some years even fallen, with a sharp fall in productivity growth from over 6 percent per year to 1 percent per year. The obvious cure is a return to rapidly growing consumption, but this is not likely given what is expected to happen to energy prices.

Mining productivity has fallen 23 percent since 1971. This is the one place where it is possible to lay part of the blame at the door of new health, safety, and environmental regulations imposed by government. But much of the problem is due to geology. Less oil is being produced from many more wells, and this shows up as a decline in productivity.

This is not to say that the regulations are either unwise or unwarranted. Greater health, safety, and environmental protection simply imposes large costs in mining. If we want safe mines and a clean environment, we are going to have a slower growth of productivity in mining, at least for a while, than if we do not want those things.

Construction is another industry with negative productivity—down 19 percent since 1968. Here the problem is partly a measurement problem and partly a real problem. How do you measure output in an industry that does not produce a standardized product? The standard technique is to use inputs (the volume of construction materials) to measure output, and this may underestimate real output if progress is being made in using materials more efficiently. We may also be demanding more variety in our construction—fewer large housing projects, fewer massive road projects—than in the past. And as a result, the construction industry does not get to take advantage of its learning curve or economies of scale.

As the decline in productivity is examined more closely, simplicity disappears. Even when the causes are clear, the solution is not. We have elected to fight inflation with idle capacity, and this explains 30 percent of our productivity decline. If agriculture were still disgorging massive amounts of labor, our productivity would be higher, but that phase of our industrial life is now over. Productivity would be higher if we did not want so many services, but the demand for services is only a problem if we were in some sense buying more services than we really want. One can argue, for example, that medical insurance leads us to buy more health care than we would buy if insurance were not available and every bill had to be paid in cash. But who wants to go without health insurance? Our real standard of living would grow more rapidly if we happened to want goods made in high-productivity industries, but we don't. To buy a high-productivity good that you do not want is not to raise your real standard of living, although it would accelerate the growth of productivity.

Productivity growth would be higher if energy prices were falling and consumption rising, if it were easy to make mines safe and environmentally sound, and if we all wanted to live in identical homes, work in identical factories, and shop in identical stores. But none of these things is possible. Simply raising investment might lower productivity growth since it would allocate more resources to an industry with below-average productivity—construction.

Just as the causes of our productivity slowdown are complex and varied, so will be the cures. In light of the fact that productivity has been growing at about 3 percent per year for as long as we have been measuring productivity growth (well back into the nineteenth century), and that our neighbors have achieved growth rates double or triple this in the last few decades, it is very unlikely that there will be a simple cure. Current productivity growth rates are deeply embedded in the structure of our economy, and major changes will be necessary before we see major improvements.

## Productivity and International Competition

While advance in productivity in any sector contributes to our overall standard of living, our international competitiveness is primarily dependent upon what happens to productivity in two industries—agriculture and manufacturing. In this we differ from most other industrial powers in that over 20 percent of our exports are agricultural commodities. While we lag in manufacturing, in agriculture we continue to lead the productivity race with more than a 6 percent annual gain.

In agriculture the problem is not productivity but opening foreign markets to our producers. Agriculture is the industry that everyone, including ourselves, protects the most. For all practical purposes, the United States is a residual supplier to the rest of the world. Each country buys only what it cannot produce itself. Operating behind high price supports, Common Market farmers produce whatever they can. If crops are bad, the Common Market is a massive agricultural importer. If crops are normal, the Common Market is a large importer. If crops are very good, the Common Market subsidizes exports. Other countries do the same. This leaves us subject to large demand shocks and sudden price changes, but it also deprives us of one of our major export markets. As a consequence, we become more dependent upon our relatively weak sector—manufacturing.

To survive in today's international competition we must push for freer trade in agricultural products. It is our area of greatest comparative advantage. But it is also an area that illustrates our basic problem. While we have a large comparative advantage in the production of most agricultural commodities, we are not in a position to push for free trade since we protect weak agricultural areas (sugar, cheese, and processed meats) as much, or more, than the rest of the world protects its farmers. We need free trade in agricultural commodities if our economy is to compete, but we cannot demand it because we do not practice it. Overall, farmers would make large income gains, but particular farmers in some regions of the United States would lose. Here again, we cannot play an economic game with a substantial zero-sum element.

To keep pace economically we are going to have to give up our own protection in some areas and demand access for our products in other areas. We no longer can afford to accept a world where our agricultural commodities are excluded. Basically this is going to mean getting tough with our allies. West Germany and the rest of the Common Market have got to stop preaching free trade in manufacturing while practicing protection in agriculture. If Japan wants to export cars it has to be willing to import food.

Very limited progress was made in the recent Tokyo round of trade negotiations, but it was so limited as to not even constitute the first step in a very long march. Future trade negotiations must make progress on agricultural commodities. If necessary, we should begin limiting others' manufacturing access to our markets if they do not give us agricultural access to their markets.

In manufacturing there is no evidence of a slowdown in productivity once a correction is made for idle capacity, but this is the area where our productivity growth rates are the poorest relative to the rest of the world. Often these problems are blamed on American multinational corporations. As is true in most cases, the worries are greatest when the problems have passed their peak. In the past, United States multinationals undoubtedly moved production abroad faster than would have happened if they could not have owned those foreign facilities. But this activity is clearly on the decline.

Multinationals need low wages, stable governments, and educated labor forces to establish facilities that can compete with those in the United States. In Europe low wages are already gone. And they are rapidly disappearing in those parts of Asia (Korea, Taiwan, Hong Kong, Singapore) that have stable governments and an educated labor force. There are, of course, many countries with low wages that will be attractive for low-productivity industries, but these are precisely the activities where we should be disinvesting. If anything, foreign multinationals should contribute to manufacturing productivity in the future. Since wages are lower there, they are now starting to enter the United States. In the past we had little to gain, but now a company like Michelin brings us knowledge about producing radial tires that we do not seem to possess. When foreign multinationals enter the United States they speed up the transmission of industrial knowledge from high-productivity areas abroad to low-productivity areas in the United States.

## Accelerating Productivity

Outside of agriculture, our basic problem is accelerating the growth of productivity. Our research and development expenditures may be too small (the right proportion of GNP to devote to R&D is one of those imponderables), but the real problem is a substantial bias toward developing new products rather than new processes for producing old products. This bias exists for two reasons.

First, new products are always more glamorous than new processes for producing old products. Scientists and engineers would rather have government R&D money go into new products. Second and more importantly, we have great difficulty in publicly funding process R&D in an economy where production is almost always in the private sector. When government funds are used to finance the development of new products in universities, no one can predict the chief economic beneficiary if success is achieved. Government officials cannot be accused of deliberately raising the income of some particular firm. In process R&D, however, the potential gainer is clearly identifiable—the firms that now make the product in question. In the case of defense or space we are willing to provide public R&D funds for process improvements since government is the ultimate buyer of the products that will be more efficiently produced. But when it comes to civilian production, we are reluctant to provide public funds for process R&D, since the question arises as to why the taxpayer should have to contribute to make some stockholder richer. To engage in process R&D, tax money must be taken from one private individual and given to another. But this is what we cannot do.

Yet as we have seen, the heart of the productivity problem lies in quickly advancing down the learning curve. Process R&D expenditures are needed to generate a steep learning curve, but the learning curve lies in the private sector. One could argue that the private sector should finance its own learning curves, but there are good reasons why R&D is financed by government both here and abroad.

R&D expenditures are financed by government for the simple reason that no private firm can hope to appropriate all of the benefits that might occur. A new product may be developed, but it may not be of use to the firm financing the work. The firm does not have the expertise or complementary products necessary to take advantage of the breakthrough. If the product is developed with public funds, the research lies in the public domain, and the firms that can use the product can gain access to the knowledge necessary to exploit it. Governments pay for R&D since what may be a good investment for the whole society may be so risky for any one firm that it will not undertake the expenditure.

The same inability to appropriate all of the benefits exists with process R&D. Suppose a new product has been developed—solar cells that directly transform sunlight into electricity for our existing space satellites. Given current volumes and production techniques, they are too expensive for earthly electricity generation. You are a manufacturer thinking about civilian production. You know that large process R&D expenditures and large initial investments would be necessary to go into production. If the learning curve is very steep your investment will be profitable, but a shallow learning curve could exist which would make your investment unprofitable.

If you were certain that you and only you could reap the benefits of success, you might take the risk, but you know that this is very unlikely. If you succeed and the learning curve is very steep, you may get your product to market first, but other firms now know that success is possible. They can start production knowing that a steep learning curve exists. Eventually they will find the path you found and gain some of the benefits you were counting on.

In essence the problem is similar to that of a book on chess end games. If you are told that the game can be won in four moves, it is almost always possible to find the four moves, but in a real game not knowing that victory is within your grasp you do not look hard enough and never find the four moves. The first person down the learning curve paves the way for the followers. He demonstrates that success is possible. But not being able to get all of the benefits, no one may be willing to be first. And even if someone is willing to be first, we have an inefficient process where different firms must essentially reinvent the wheel—the desired process.

To speed up productivity we must find an acceptable technique for involving government in process R&D. There are probably three essential ingredients. First, we all have to accept the fact that any government program is going to help someone. The fact that the winners can be identified ahead of time does not make a program wrong. As long as we have a private profit system of enterprise, any public efforts to raise productivity will make more profits for someone. Second, there is nothing wrong with profits and making someone rich if we have a fair system of taxation. Tax reform, and having what is perceived as a fair system, is an important ingredient in stimulating productivity since it allows us politically to shift R&D to areas where it can have a large productivity payoff. Third, process innovations paid for with government funds should be available to everyone in an industry. Other firms should be able to study how it was done at the first firm so that they can get the same productivity gains without having to make duplicating R&D expenditures.

This is essentially what we now do in agricultural R&D where new processes are tried out on experimental farms and then offered to all farmers. In this case the experimental farms are owned by government, but this is not possible in most industrial operations where production units may be very large. But however we do it, we must restructure the economy so that we can engage in more process R&D and gain more of the potential benefits of steep learning curves. New products are important, but at any point in time most of the economy is composed of old products. Making these products more efficiently is the heart of the productivity problem.

While foreign analogies should be treated with caution, it is instructive to think about Japan's success with process innovations. They have not been a leader in new products, but they have been a leader in better processes for producing old products. This springs from the absence of a sharp dividing line between public and private, and a willingness to engage in process R&D. But to do this the Japanese must take revenue away from some Japanese and give it to other Japanese. We are reluctant to do this when it comes to private corporations because we cannot justify a transfer of resources from one American to another.[7]

Accelerating disinvestment is the second ingredient in speeding productivity growth. Ending subsidies, protection, and favorable regulations will help, but we are not going to be able to do so until we find a way to provide economic security for individuals without providing economic security for failing institutions. At the same time we also need to go beyond a free market policy that promotes disinvestment and encourages reinvestment in high-productivity areas.

We do not need central economic planning in the sense of an agency that tries to make all economic decisions, but we do need the national equivalent of a corporate investment committee to redirect investment flows from our "sunset" industries to our "sunrise" industries. Such committees play an important role in the investment decisions of large corporations, and they could play an equally important role in national investment and disinvestment decisions.

With our current system of internal finance, growth in high-productivity areas is often limited by the funds that can be internally generated. This often lowers their growth and our national growth below what it should be. Similarly with internal financing, "sunset" industries often have access to plentiful funds for new investment. They can reinvest their internal savings, but their steady cash flows also let them borrow in the capital markets. Often these investments should not occur. A national investment committee could help make sure they did not occur.

For most of our industrial competitors the central bank plays an important role in allocating investment funds. In addition to worrying about the money supply and the rate of interest, it attempts to direct funds toward areas of major national interest. The system is probably most heavily developed in Japan but exists to some extent in Italy, France, and West Germany. In the past our Reconstruction Finance Corporation played a similar role. It could and did provide major funding for large projects in new areas.

A national investment bank could be regarded as a competitor with private banks or it could work through private banks as it does in Japan. It certainly represents more government in the mixed economy, but the time has come to recognize that if we are going to compete with some of our more successful industrial neighbors, we are going to have to change the way we have been doing things in the past. Simply retreating into the past and calling for the end of government involvement won't solve the problems. We have to do much better than we have ever done pre-or post-New Deal if we are to compete in the productivity race of the 1980s.

While there is much to be gained by taking our foot off the current economic brakes on economic change, we must also learn to put our foot on the economic accelerator. If others have learned how to more quickly reorientate their economy to new growth areas, so must we. We do not have to reinvent the wheel, we merely have to adopt and adapt what others have learned to our culture and institutions.

While a decline in investments did not cause our current productivity problems, an increase in investment is probably one of the ingredients in a cure. Those who are doing better than we invest a substantially larger fraction of their GNP. But to invest more, we have to do two things. We have to create incentives to increase investment, and we have to accumulate the necessary funds for this investment.

The simplest part of the problem is increasing the incentives to invest. The easiest solutions would be to abolish the corporate income tax and integrate corporate and personal taxation. With full integration, there would be no corporate income tax but each individual shareholder would be liable to pay personal taxes on all income (retained or paid out) earned on his or her behalf. At the end of the year, shareholders would get the equivalent of a W-2 form telling them how much income to add to their other sources of income and how much income tax had been withheld on their behalf.

Since corporate after-tax rates of return would approximately double, corporate managers would have a strong incentive to increase investments. At the same time, we would increase both the equity and progressivity of the personal income tax. Each shareholder, rich or poor, would now pay taxes at a rate commensurate with his own income position rather than at some common rate. Taxes would go down for some, up for others.

The corporate income tax should be abolished regardless of whether you are a conservative or a liberal. Based on our principles of taxation, the corporate income tax is both unfair and inefficient. In a country with a progressive personal income tax, every taxpayer with the same income should pay the same tax (horizontal equity), and the effective tax rate should rise in accordance with whatever degree of progressivity has been established by the political process (vertical equity). The corporate income tax violates both of these canons of equity. Consider the earnings that are retained in the corporation on behalf of the individual stockholder. Low-income shareholders with personal tax rates below the corporate rate of 46 percent are being taxed too much on their share of corporate income. To the low-income shareholder the corporate income tax is unjustly high. Conversely, high-income shareholders with personal tax rates above 46 percent are being taxed too little on their share of corporate income. To the high-income shareholder the corporate income tax is a tax shelter or tax loophole. As a consequence, vertical equity is being violated. Horizontal equity is also being violated, since two individuals with exactly the same income will pay different taxes, depending upon the extent to which their income comes from corporate sources.

It is important to notice, however, that to eliminate the horizontal and vertical inequity of the corporate income tax, the tax must be eliminated on both dividends and retained earnings. Simply eliminating the corporate income tax on dividends increases the tax shelter aspect of the tax without achieving equity.

While corporations are legal entities that write checks to government, they do not pay taxes. They simply collect money from someone —their shareholders, their customers, or their employees—and transfer it to government. There is no such thing as taxing corporations as opposed to individuals. This immediately raises the issue of who ultimately pays the corporate income tax. The incidence of the corporate income tax is an area of economics with a large literature and little or no argument. Depending upon the exact assumptions used, the definition of incidence, and the time periods under consideration, it could be a tax on shareholders, a sales tax on consumers, or a tax on employees. (Personally, I believe that it is a tax on shareholders in the short run and a sales tax in the long run, but my advocacy of its elimination does not hang on that belief.) While there may be certain perverse political virtue in collecting a tax where no one is sure whether he pays it, simple economic efficiency and equity would seem to call for the elimination of taxes where incidence is uncertain. Only if we do so can we establish a tax system that is fair and has the economic consequences we intend.

Since interest payments are deductible business expenses while dividends are not, the corporate income tax also biases the structure of capital toward debt capital and away from equity capital. Debt capital becomes cheaper than equity capital, not because that is true in the market, but because the tax laws make it so. From the point of view of the efficient allocation of capital and an efficient capital structure, there is no reason why government should be intervening to bias business choices in the direction of debt capital and away from equity capital. From the point of view of having a healthy, vital capitalistic economy, government should, if anything, be doing the opposite. Eliminating the corporate income tax would eliminate this bias in capital structure and hence improve the efficiency of the capital market.

But the capital market would also be improved in another way. Since the maximum personal tax rate (70 percent) on property income is substantially above the corporate income tax rate (46 percent), and most corporate shares are held by high-income individuals, there is a strong incentive for firms to retain earnings, reinvest them, and provide benefits to their high-income shareholders in the form of a larger capital stock and higher stock prices. As long as the stock is held, no personal income tax will be paid, and when it is sold, only the lower capital gains tax need be paid. While there is nothing wrong with retained earnings, it once again should be up to the market rather than the tax laws to determine how much income should be retained rather than paid out to the shareholders. Eliminating the corporate income tax would remove the tax incentive to retain earnings. As a result, both the supply and demand for funds in the capital market would increase, once again leading to greater efficiency.

To the extent that the corporate income tax is in fact a sales tax collected from the buyers of corporate products, a number of benefits would accrue from its elimination. The prices of corporate products would gradually fall with favorable effects on the rate of inflation. Because of lower prices, our competitiveness in international markets would also increase, and this would be especially true vis-à-vis countries that can rebate their value-added taxes on exports. The net result would be more goods sold and more Americans employed.

If all of these advantages exist, why do we have the corporate income tax, and why is it still defended? Many people, including the man on the street, think that it is a way to tax the rich. As I have shown, this is simply a mistaken perception. To the extent that the corporate income tax is a sales tax or a tax on employees, it is not a tax on the rich. Even if it is ultimately paid by the shareholder, it is not a very good tax on the rich. To tax the moderately rich we must tax the poor at very high rates and provide a tax shelter to the very rich. If we want to tax the rich, the personal income tax is the right way to do it.

Some liberals oppose the elimination of the corporate income tax on the grounds that low-income stockholders would not have enough cash income to pay the taxes owed on the earnings retained on their behalf. This is not a problem, since corporations could be required to withhold taxes for shareholders just as they now do for employees. Every year shareholders would receive the equivalent of a W-2 form that would list their corporate earnings and the taxes that had been withheld on their behalf. Those overwithheld would receive a refund, and those underwithheld would have to pay the additional taxes owed just as they now do on their wage and salary earnings.

Some business managers support the corporate income tax on the grounds that it encourages retained earnings, and it gives them more funds not subject to the competitive bidding of other managers in the capital market. To some extent this perception is undoubtedly true, but I suspect that shareholders would still be willing to tolerate some substantial amount of retained earnings in a system where the tax system was neutral with respect to whether earnings were or were not paid out.

Those who manage government often oppose the taxation of corporate income as personal income on the pragmatic grounds that less revenue would be collected and thus some other tax would have to be raised. Depending on exactly which estimate of the distribution of stock ownership by income class is used, Treasury losses range from $4 to $10 billion or from 2 to 5 percent of the revenue now collected from personal and corporate income taxes. To put this amount in perspective, simple elimination of the corporate income tax on dividends would cost the Treasury $13 billion. The revenue shortfall arises not so much because individual shareholders would pay less than they now do (some would pay more, some would pay less, and the balance depends upon the distribution of stock ownership by income class), but because a substantial amount of stock is owned by institutions (charities, pension funds, and so forth) that do not pay personal income taxes.

In the long run much of this shortfall would be recouped, and that which is not recouped would yield substantial benefits. To the extent that pension funds have higher incomes, they are either going to reduce contributions (leading to higher taxable incomes) or increase the pensions paid (leading to higher taxable incomes). If nonprofit charities have higher incomes, the public will, to some extent, give less to charities (leading to higher taxable incomes). To the extent that the higher earnings of charities are not offset by lower annual giving, they will be doing more good works. And this is, after all, why we made them tax exempt in the first place. If we really want to tax them, we can easily pass a law doing so in any case. At the moment we are simply being inconsistent and taxing their corporate, but not other, sources of income.

When you review the arguments, there isn't any case for the retention of the corporate income tax. It is both unfair and inefficient. It ought to be eliminated. And all corporate incomes—retained or paid out as dividends—ought to be taxed at personal income tax rates appropriate to the shareholders who own them. In doing so we will increase the fairness of the tax system, improve the allocation of investment funds, and create a powerful incentive for more investment.

Increasing the incentives to invest is relatively simple, but raising the necessary funds for investment is difficult—not economically but politically. We are confronted with the question that I posed to the Harvard alumni reunion. If we were to raise investment from 10 percent of the GNP to the 15 percent level of West Germany or to the 20 percent level of Japan, who would be willing to give up 5 or 10 percent of the GNP? Conservatives say that we should generate the extra savings by lowering taxes on savers and raising taxes on consumers. Basically this means shifting the tax burden from rich to poor since savings propensities are naturally much higher for the rich than for the poor.

There is no doubt that the extra savings could be raised in such a manner if the shift in the distribution of income were sharp enough. Suppose that households with incomes below $16,000 per year (the bottom 60 percent of the population in 1977) saved nothing, and that households with incomes above $38,000 (the top 5 percent of the population) saved 50 percent of their extra income.[8] To raise savings by 5 percent of the GNP you would have to transfer $188 billion from the bottom 60 percent of the population to the top 5 percent of the population. This would lower the real standard of living of the bottom 60 percent of the population by 25 percent. The income of the top 5 percent would rise by 46 percent. (In fact the transfers would probably have to be larger than this since the bottom 60 percent do some saving and the top 5 percent may not have a 50 percent marginal savings rate.) To accomplish the necessary objective—more savings—a majority of the population would have to endure a sharp reduction in their current consumption. Not surprisingly they are reluctant to do so. Yet more savings are necessary if more investments are to be made.

The direct way to solve the problem in an equitable manner is simply to run a surplus in the government budget of the appropriate magnitude. Taxes are raised by the necessary amount, and each of our incomes is reduced in accordance with a tax system. If we have an equitable tax system we have an equitable spreading of the burdens. But this directly poses the question of what is an equitable tax system and an equitable distribution of after-tax income.

More investment, speedier disinvestment, more process R&D— they all pose the fundamental zero-sum distributional question. Someone's income will have to go down and these losses are going to be substantial. For those that lose, the existence of even larger social gains are irrelevant. They are only interested in preventing their losses.

## Notes

1. Joint Economic Committee, *Manufacturing Productivity Growth, 1960–77* 5, no. 7, p. 1.
2. Lester C. Thurow, *The Zero-Sum Society: Distribution and the Possibilities for Economic Change* (New York: Basic Books, Inc., 1980). See Chapter 3.
3. Council of Economic Advisers, *Economic Report of the President,* January 1979, p. 226.
4. U.S. Department of Commerce, *Statistical Abstract of the United States* (Washington, D.C.: U.S. Government Printing Office, 1978), p. 622.
5. U.S. Department of Commerce, *Survey of Current Business* 59, no. 7 (July 1979): 26.
6. Ibid., pp. 52, 56.
7. Thurow, *The Zero-Sum Society.* See Chapter 8.
8. U.S. Bureau of the Census, *Current Population Reports, Consumer Income 1977,* Series P-60, no. 117 (December 1978), p. 19.

# Economic Growth and Market Processes

Richard H. Fink

## I. Introduction

The aim of this essay is to provide an alternative view of economic growth in a market economy through what is known as a market-process perspective—so called because of its emphasis on disequilibrium, uncertainty, evolutionary change, and the paramount importance of the subjective perceptions of market participants. Since all economic phenomena are the result of the actions of individuals, the market-process economist traces the intended and unintended consequences of individual interaction in alternative institutional settings. Since success of any one individual's plans depends upon the actions of other market participants, the coordination of plans among economic actors is critically important for successful economic growth. The market-process economist views the market as an evolving institution that primarily serves to generate the information and the incentives to facilitate this necessary plan coordination. Market signals such as prices, profits, and interest rates are important coordinating phenomena that have spontaneously evolved in the market system. Since uncertainty and imperfect information pervade the world, these sensitive signals provide vital information to market participants and greatly facilitate the plan coordination of producers and consumers, complementary and competing firms, and the intertemporal activities of all economic actors. Given this view of the market as an institution that not only disseminates critical market-coordinating information, but also *generates* this information, the market-process economist is especially concerned with economic policies that unintentionally distort these market signals and therefore interfere with plan coordination.

Only with a coherent theory of economic growth can one understand the causes of the signficant productivity problems facing America and not be misled by the scores of plausible but ultimately erroneous explanations of prosperity and stagnation. Section II, Economic Growth—A Market-Process Perspective, offers the rudiments of such a theory. Since this essay is intended to explain an alternative view of economic growth and not to explore the fine points of theory, the model is intentionally simplistic and therefore passes over many of the rich theoretical refinements and controversies surrounding some of its assumptions. Section II endeavors to establish the connection between individual decision making and economic growth, as well as the need to think beyond the concepts of aggregate savings and investment. Instead, I suggest focusing analysis on the way in which individuals' plans to save and invest must interlock with the plans of other economic actors to be successful. The functions of prices, profits, and interest rates in the overall process of market coordination are given special attention.

Section III, The Effects of Government Policies on Economic Growth, builds on the basic model presented in Section II and demonstrates how recent economic policies have disrupted the conditions necessary for sustained economic growth. These policies have not only reduced the level of savings and investment but have consistently frustrated market coordination. The key point in this section is not only that government policies reduce the available resources for investment activities, but that these policies unintentionally distort the market signals necessary for individuals to successfully carry out plans in the face of the uncertainties and complexities of an industrialized economy. One example, monetary disruptions of the coordinating function of the interest rate, is developed in some depth. Although any of a number of possible examples would serve to illustrate the importance of plan coordinaton in successful economic performance, the example of the interest rate was chosen because most economists, including supply-side advocates, either completely ignore or explicitly dispute this particular coordination problem.

Section IV, Keynesian, Neoclassical, Supply-Side and Market-Process Approaches, explains why the conventional Keynesian and neoclassical tools are ill-equipped to deal with some of the critical problems connected with economic growth in a dynamic economy. By contrast, a market-process framework readily enables one to see that a key to understanding many of our present day economic problems lies in the examination of economic policies affecting market coordination within and across industrial sectors, rather than just focusing on the aggregate size of these sectors. Coordination problems are lost in the level of aggregation employed in Keynesian macromodels and they are assumed away in neoclassical growth models. Supply-side economists in general ignore coordination problems for both of these reasons. Section IV also explains how supply-siders confuse the coordinating functions of various market signals when they analyze the impact of government policies.

Part V, Policy Recommendations, welcomes the attention on tax cuts by supply-side economists and the Reagan administration, but not without serious reservations. While taxes are a significant factor affecting economic growth, they are neither the only factor nor necessarily the most important factor. Concerns about productivity must address the significant consequences of policies other than taxes that affect economic growth. The most important challenge to supply-side economists will be to address the problems of market coordination which are almost totally ignored in the current literature. Reindustrialization, industrial welfare, and varied depreciation schedule changes advocated by some supply-siders have significant implications for market coordination which are presently ignored and can result in severe disruptions to sustained economic growth. These disruptions can be readily appreciated in a market-process framework that examines the market mechanisms that tend to coordinate intrasector as well as intersector economic activity.

## II. Economic Growth—A Market-Process Perspective

The amount of attention currently being given to taxation, productivity, and economic growth is largely due to the inability of the American economy to maintain a satisfactory track record. As a result we have seen many competing explanations of our economy's woes and even more recommendations of how to alleviate these problems. This section of my analysis will attempt to present a market-process theory of productivity and economic growth, which will provide the reader with at least one foil with which to evaluate current economic policies.

No final and all-encompassing definition of economic growth exists among economists. Economic growth has been associated with a number of different phenomena including technological progress, "lengthening" of the structure of production, and an increasing stock of capital. I prefer to view the quest for economic growth as simply an attempt to raise future living standards relative to present living standards.[1]

As a science, economics has nothing to say about the *desirability* of economic growth. As along as scarcity exists, men must choose between competing ends, and a choice of one of these ends implies the sacrifice of other ends. Like any end, economic growth has its opportunity costs, for it must compete with other goals such as more present consumption or more leisure. The advocate of an increase in economic growth rates is implicitly making the claim that future benefits from growth outweigh the current sacrifices necessary to achieve this growth. Which end is most important is a value judgment and such judgments are outside the realm of the value-free science of economics. However, what an economist can do is contrast the consequences of, and possibilities for, economic growth in various institutional settings.

One such institutional setting is an unhampered market economy. This proves to be an especially fruitful setting for examining productivity and economic growth because by initially factoring out existing government policies we can obtain a clearer picture of the cumulative consequences of these policies. We can then examine previous government policies which helped determine our present productivity as well as the proposed policy measures intended to improve our situation.

A variety of factors are relevant for determining how much an economy will grow and what sort of growth will be achieved. The most important of these factors are time preference (savings-consumption decisions), the ability of the price system to allocate resources to their most highly valued uses, intertemporal coordination of plans, and the degree to which new investment projects are successfully integrated into the existing capital structure.

To illustrate these points, assume that on one of your frequent trips to the French Riviera your plane crashed into the ocean and because of your superior swimming skills you become the sole survivor on a deserted island. After waking up from a deep sleep that allowed your body to recover from the trials of the crash and your struggle to reach the shore, you find that you have to search eight hours a day for food just to survive. Assume that you prefer fish (as opposed to coconuts or other culinary delights that the island has to offer)—so you fish eight hours a day and engage in leisure (rest) the remainder of the day. You soon become unhappy with your present standard of living and want to increase it in the future. Therefore, you decide to fish twelve hours a day and after two days you have accumulated enough fish to sustain you for a third day without fishing. Now you are facing at least two choices: one of consumption, e.g., sunbathing the third day, or investing—building a net to increase your future production possibilities. By saving or accumulating fish for two days and abstaining from the present consumption of leisure, i.e., sunbathing, you have been able, through the construction of the net, to realize economic growth, i.e., have raised your future living standards. Now you can catch your daily subsistence of fish in four hours instead of eight. Your act of savings allowed you to engage in economic growth. The foregoing of present consumption allowed you to produce a capital good (the net) and to develop a longer and more productive structure of production. This has traditionally been called "lengthening the structure of production" and is illustrated below by the additional step in the production process.

Man $\overset{1}{\rightarrow}$    fish $\overset{2}{\rightarrow}$    consumption.

Man $\overset{1}{\rightarrow}$    net $\overset{2}{\rightarrow}$    fish $\overset{3}{\rightarrow}$    consumption.

(capital good)

In this primitive society savings directly determined the level of investment, for the number of fish you caught directly determined how many days you could devote to investment (building the net). This direct relationship between savings and investment is altered in a complex monetary economy, as the existence of money creates an "intercession" between savings and investment. Acts of saving and investment will usually be performed by different groups of individuals (or individuals acting in different roles) who will most likely have different purposes. Such complexity poses serious problems involving the coordination of all these various plans—a problem of economic coordination that all economic systems must solve.

In a complex industrial society such as the United States, the price system is a critical mechanism for discovering and disseminating information about the thousands of economic resources and almost limitless possible combinations of these resources. Prices are the reflection of the value that the millions of individual actors within the economy place on specific economic goods. Information on consumers' valuation is of necessity scattered, vague, and incomplete. Market prices synthesize this value information and convert it to a usable form. Buyers, by bidding for goods, are attempting to establish the case that particular goods are most urgently demanded and most valuable to them because they are willing to bid the highest in order to purchase them. Suppliers, guided by the bids of demanders, are alerted to where scarce resources should be channeled to reach their most useful employment. This familiar tale of the interacton of suppliers and demanders illustrates the critical coordinating function of prices in allocating scarce resources to their most highly valued uses. Since prices are the direct result of bidding by economic actors, expressing the value of resources in their plans, and because they convey the most accurate and timely information, then external interference with market-generated prices will cause people to act on distorted information. And, an individual's economic plans based on distorted information disrupts not only his activities but the plans of others because of the extensive interdependence of economic activity in a complex economy.

Profits, on the other hand, provide the incentive for effectively utilitizing the information disseminated by prices. In addition to rewarding successful entrepreneurial behavior and penalizing entrepreneurial errors, profits act to redirect the command of scarce resources away from entrepreneurs who either are inept at reading price signals or have acted on incorrect information (and thus suffer losses) toward entrepreneurs with a demonstrated record of success (i.e., profit makers). Profits put money—and therefore the command of scarce resources—in the hands of entrepreneurs who have demonstrated good judgment. Thus, profits and losses play at least two key roles in a market economy: they provide incentives to produce the goods that consumers must urgently want and direct resources into the hands of those most competent in bringing the goods to market.

The interest rate is another important market signal. It aids in redirecting resources *across time*, by reflecting individuals' preference for economic growth as well as their commitment to make the necessary sacrifice of present consumption to realize this growth. Interest rates are, therefore, a critical information-generating signal for allocating savings and investment and hence the prospects for realized economic growth. To the extent that the rate of interest tends toward its market clearing level, it will serve to coordinate *ex ante* the plans of savers and investors by disseminating information about the terms on which economic opportunities will be offered.

The very act of saving on the part of an individual implies that his demand for present consumer goods has gone down and that his demand for future consumer goods has increased. After all, few people save indefinitely for no reason—most people save to provide for enhanced future consumption in a few years, for their old age, or for their heirs. How much an individual saves depends on his time preference in conjunction with the constraints he faces in the market. Time preference is the subjective evaluation of future command in relation to present command over scarce resources. The decision to save $100 today in order to be able to purchase $110 worth of goods next year indicates a time preference reflected by the 10 percent return. You prefer $110 a year from today over spending the $100 today. If you prefer the $100 today you would have a higher time preference — something higher than $110, perhaps $120, would be required to induce you to save the $100 today for the opportunity to spend it a year from now.

As can be seen from this example, time preference is merely the trade-off we all have between present goods and future goods. We save today in the expectation of being able to exercise an increased ability to demand goods in the future (future goods). This is what the demand for economic growth is: the preference for a rise in future living standards at the expense of present living standards (consumption). To realize this increased preference for growth requires increased saving —the present sacrifice for future gain.

How does the market respond to this decline in present demand for consumption goods and the increase in future demand that results from the decision to increase savings? It responds in the same way that is does whenever the relative demand between any other two goods changes—it provides the incentive and the information for entrepreneurs to decrease the supply of present goods to match the decreased demand and to increase the supply of future goods to match the increased future demand. (See Figure 1.)

When people decrease their present demand for goods, the funds generated by this saving increases the amount of money in the loan

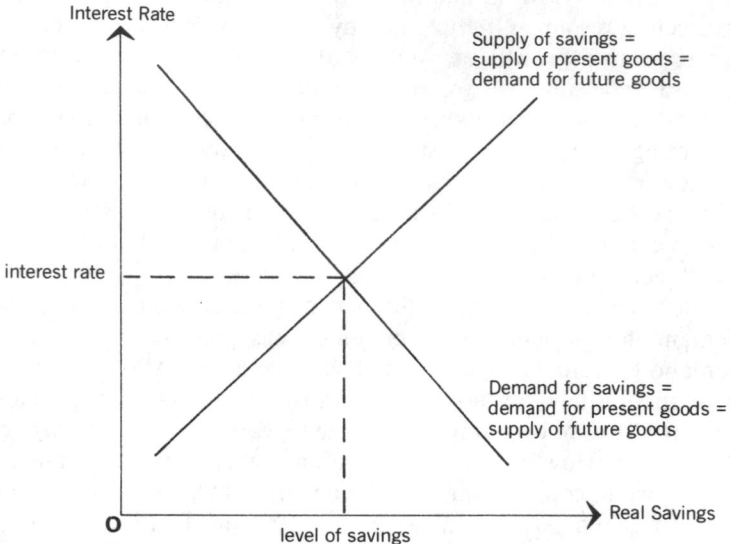

## FIGURE 1
## INTEREST RATE DETERMINATION

Interest Rate

Supply of savings =
supply of present goods =
demand for future goods

interest rate

Demand for savings =
demand for present goods =
supply of future goods

O

level of savings

Real Savings

market which in turn decreases the interest rate (assuming that people don't put all of this "excess money" under their pillow). The lowered interest rate allows entrepreneurs to borrow these funds for new investment projects that will eventually bring an increased supply of goods to the market, just as the net in our desert island example increased the future supply of fish. (See Figure 2.)

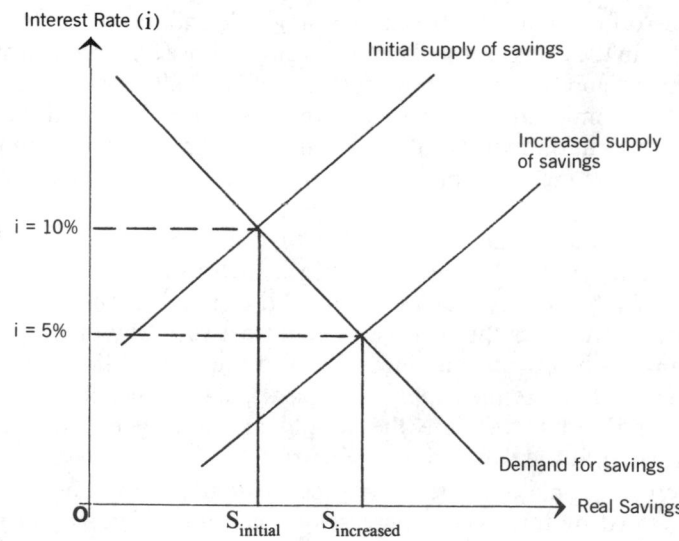

## FIGURE 2
## DECREASE IN TIME PREFERENCE

Interest Rate (i)

Initial supply of savings

Increased supply
of savings

i = 10%

i = 5%

Demand for savings

O

$S_{initial}$    $S_{increased}$

Real Savings

The previous discussion should help clarify the importance of prices, profits, and the interest rate for the intertemporal plan coordination of economic actors in any discussion of economic growth. Intertemporal plan coordination is necessary for savings to be converted into the most highly valued investments, and the price mechanism is the primary means through which this process is accomplished.

Perhaps the least understood feature of economic growth is the necessity of creating new capital goods which will perform a complementary function with other capital goods. The importance of this particular sort of coordination is often forgotten in neoclassical models which treat capital as a homogenous aggregate rather than as a complex heterogeneous structure. Yet different sorts of new investments should not be treated as equivalents because each investment will effectively "interlock" with the existing capital structure in a different way and to a different degree. An example of this point is given by Western aid to underdeveloped nations. While agencies such as the World Bank may advance the capital which allows the lesser developed countries to purchase such technologically advanced ventures as steel mills, hydroelectric plants, and mechanized agriculture, these projects are rarely integrated into the structure of production of the underdeveloped nation. More often than not, these countries will have little or no support industry to produce spare parts, to train the necessary high-skilled labor, or even to use the products of the new industry. The amount of capital will have increased in the lesser developed countries if we view capital as a homogeneous aggregate. Therefore the addition of the steel mill to the capital stock will appear as equally valuable as any other investment of comparable magnitude. But if one views capital as a heterogeneous structure, the steel mill is a misallocation because it is not integrated into the existing capital structure.

The extent to which an economy manages to coordinate its capital structure is due primarily to the degree to which its key market signals —prices, profits, and interest rates—are not impeded in performing their coordinating functions.

## III. The Effect of Government Economic Policies on Economic Growth

When the problems of economic growth and the effects of macroeconomic policy are examined within a microeconomic market-process framework, the implications are that government policies critically lower the level of savings as well as distort market activities that affect virtually every economic decision made in the economy: interest rates, the incentive to invest (profits), the relative profitability of investing in particular economic sectors (opportunity costs), and the coordination both of plans among entrepreneurs and with the consumption plans of consumers (prices). These implications are not adequately addressed in either aggregate demand models or aggregate supply models.

## A. Savings

Using a market-process framework, some interesting questions arise concerning the level of savings and the low rate of economic growth in the United States during the past twenty years. What factors affected individuals' proclivity to save—to finance economic growth? One important factor is the income taxes people have to pay on the money they earn from productive activity. Much of what remains after their income tax is paid is used to purchase present consumption goods on which, more often than not, one must pay a sales tax. If a person owns property, he pays additional property taxes. If you wish to provide for your family when you die, you pay inheritance taxes. If an individual wants to provide for other people while they are living, they pay gift taxes. Whatever is left to save and generate interest income is also taxed. When all taxes, visible and hidden, are taken into account, nearly half of a person's income can go to taxes. After that, a major part of the remaining half will probably not be available for savings. No doubt the largest portion of the remaining income will usually be spent to provide subsistence in the present—housing, food, clothing, etc.—leaving very little for savings.

In addition to the burden imposed by taxes, the American consumer is able to extract far fewer products out of his remaining income because there are fewer goods available and the prices they command are higher as a result of thousands of government regulations and edicts. Controls raising prices, such as minimum wage laws, interest rate regulations, milk price supports, natural gas price regulations, rent controls, and subsidies ranging from Chrysler to tobacco growers to beekeepers all result in a drain on the consumer's pocketbook.

Exacerbating the strain on savers and further distorting the production structure is inflation, which has destroyed traditional avenues of saving and therefore pushed people to search for alternative places to sink their money needed to provide for the future. Precious metals, jewelry, and art objects have been favorite sinkholes. Regulations on the maximum interest rates that financial institutions can offer have also tended to discourage saving and rechannel savings into alternative institutions. Inflation has helped cause a dollar invested in tax avoidance and/or tax evasion bring a much larger return than a dollar devoted to saving as evidenced by the tremendous growth in the number of accountants and the underground economy. Lastly, what saving *is* encouraged is usually channeled into consumer durables, such as housing, because of tax laws, inflation, and subsidies. Any thorough treatment of economic growth since World War II needs to investigate these phenomena.

## B. Production

The problem is twofold. The first difficulty is that government economic policies substantially diminish the stock of goods available for future consumption. However, even more significant than the effect on total output is how government policies influence the structure of production, once the crimped pool of saving is invested. Prices that normally direct resources into those channels of industry that satisfy the most urgent demands of consumers are artificially altered. Marginal producers exit the industry and nonspecific factors of producton are shifted into other industries. Specific factors may lie idle instead of being utilized to produce the goods that consumers most readily demand. Resources shift out of overregulated and price-controlled sectors into less urgent uses, such as subsidized industries. Effort and expenditure, normally devoted to production, is diverted into avoiding the wealth losses from unfavorable regulations and clamoring for subsidies and favorable regulation. All of these distortions have serious consequences both for the quantity of savings and for the uses to which these savings are put. A more thorough study than is warranted here would examine further distortions to productivity caused by labor laws, tariffs, licensing laws, etc. which alter relative prices and therefore distort resource allocation devoted to the provision of such services as medical, legal, plumbing, electrical, carpentry and imported as well as domestically produced goods.

Government policy also affects economic growth through its impact on investment decisions made by the producers of the actual capital equipment, such as the steel mills, and the research and development necessary to supply the goods that will help generate a rising standard of living. A brief run-through of several pertinent facts is revealing. The corporate sector of the United States has been taxed at a nominal rate between 40 and 50 percent. However, after taking inflation into account, the real tax burden is sometimes over 100 percent. The impact of such a high rate of taxation on the profitability of investment is staggering. According to Martin Feldstein of Harvard University and the National Bureau of Economic Research, the average rate of return on investment is around 4 percent.[2] A 4 percent return on capital invested is generally not an adequate incentive for the risks and efforts of many entrepreneurs. Other reasons for this low return on capital invested include the hidden tax of regulation that has been estimated by various economists to cost from $20 billion to $200 billion a year.

Another factor harmful to economic growth is the tremendous consumption of our national resources by government itself, a process which drives up the prices of the remaining resources and distorts the relative prices of all resources. Government absorption of resources that would ordinarily go to fuel economic growth is nowhere so evident as in American land and labor markets. "The U.S. land area is 2,271,343,000 acres. The federal government owns, manages or controls slightly over one-third, approximately 760,532,000 acres. Most of the public domain is located in the West, with about 63 percent of all the land in the thirteen western states owned by the federal government. Additional holdings by state and local governments bring the total government land ownership of the U.S. to about 40 percent."[3] Not only does government control of land raise the price of various land parcels but it also distorts the prices of privately owned land, strategic minerals, and various other natural resources. In terms of the supply of labor available for building a foundation of growth, employment of one out of every five workers is directly related to government. And an even greater number is indirectly diverted from production because of government-mandated paperwork studies, impact reports, etc. These two primary factors of production, land and labor, therefore require a greater expenditure to be utilized in many production processes than might occur in an economy with a smaller government sector. The market signals determining their allocation have been significantly altered by government policies.

Government bail-outs and subsidies to inefficient firms are another factor that not only wastes valuable resources but also impinges on the normal incentive structure of the unhampered market. Major industries such as automobiles, television, and steel are now clamoring for protection from foreign competition in order to lessen the market forces of competition that weed out inefficient producers. Corporate America, like the individual citizen, finds that it is extremely profitable to devote scarce resources not to produce but to discover ways to reduce their tax and regulatory burden. Firms find that a dollar spent lobbying in Washington for special favors brings a greater return than a dollar spent in production. Rather than outcompete a rival, it is cheaper to lobby for selective regulations to drive him out of business.

Unemployment insurance, minimum wages, immigration laws, affirmative action quotas, welfare, CETA, and government intrusions into the labor market tremendously raise certain costs of production as well as redirect resources away from their most highly valued uses. Union activity, normally part of the market mechanism, has been distorted by government interference which allows unions to prevent lower income people from bidding jobs away from higher paid workers in industries with union-induced wage scales. Strikes and the threat of strikes can cause a tremendous amount of resources, normally devoted to enhanced production, to be diverted to stockpiling inventories in order to allow a firm to survive a strike. These factors all affect economic growth and should be incorporated into any analysis.

Inflation is another factor that has received a tremendous amount of attention, but it has not been fully integrated into the microeconomics of economic growth. Most analyses of inflation ignore the fact that relative prices are distorted as new money is pumped into the economy. These distortions occur because the new money created by the government enters the economy in specific ways and therefore raises specific prices in a certain pattern. As these artificially induced prices continue to rise, entrepreneurs respond as they do to all relative price changes—they redirect resources into the newly (seemingly) profitable areas. But this flow is exposed as a malinvestment when the government stops pumping new money into the economy (or more often, slows the rate of increase). So there is good reason to suspect that the boom induced by government policies affecting the money supply is causally related to recessions (where the malinvestments are revealed). The economist studying economic growth must address these business cycles where vast amounts of resources are wasted because, for some reason, *most* entrepreneurs in whole sectors of the economy are in error (when in normal times only some entrepreneurs make critical errors). Why do these highly skilled profesionals systematically err at one particular point in time and generate a recession? The creation of false price signals generated by government-induced monetary expansion provides some interesting clues.

While many analysts recognize the income redistribution effects of inflation, most are either unaware of or deny the serious redistribution of *resources* caused by inflation. The most important example of this redistribution of resources can be seen operating through the "time market." The critical link between economic growth, the quantity of savings, and the interest rate was explained earlier. We saw that when individuals lower their time preference (decreasing their present consumption and increasing their savings), they are effectively exercising an increased demand for economic growth. Suppliers react to these future demands when the increased saving lowers the interest rate and therefore makes investment less costly than before because interest outlay is a significant aspect in the investment decision. Not only are most investment projects stimulated, but they are stimulated to different degrees. The relative profitability of longer-run projects increases relative to shorter projects. A short example will illustrate the point:

Assume that you are faced with two investment projects that have the same net present value after you take into consideration outlays, expected income, and subjective preferences.

*Where $N$ = number of years project lasts, $i$ = the interest rate, and $R$ = net anticipated revenues generated by the investment project.

$$NPV_1 = \frac{RN}{(1+i)} = \frac{1100}{1.1} = \$1,000$$

$$\text{where} \quad N = 1 \text{ year}$$
$$i = .10$$
$$R = \$1100$$

$$NPV_2 = \frac{R}{N} = \frac{100}{.10} = \$1,000$$

$$\text{where} \quad N = \infty$$
$$i = .10$$
$$R = \$100$$

Investment project 1 returns $1,100 in income in one year and no revenue thereafter. Assuming the interest rate to be 10 percent, the net present value of this project is $1,000.

Investment project 2 returns $100 in revenue every year in perpetuity. Assuming that the interest rate is 10 percent, the net present value of this investment project is $1,000. Assuming that you have incorporated all your subjective preferences into the outlay and revenue figures, you should be indifferent between these two projects.

Let's suppose that the interest rate declines to 5 percent because of the increases in the supply of savings (see Figure 2). The net present values of these two projects will increase but to different degrees.

$$PV1 = \frac{R}{(1+i)} = \frac{1100}{1+.05} = \$1,050 =)\uparrow 5\%$$

$$PV2 = \frac{R}{i} = \frac{100}{.05} = \$2,000 =)\uparrow 100\%$$

While the net present value of investment project 1 will increase 5 percent, the net present value of investment project 2 will increase 100 percent, making the longer-run project a much more attractive investment.

This example illustrates the crucial signaling role played by interest rates. Just as distorted prices cause a misallocation of resources in various markets, distorted interest rates cause a misallocation of resources over time. Past monetary policies have affected interest rates in a systematic fashion and therefore have had systematic effects in the capital goods markets. As government pumps money into the economy through the commerical banking system, the banks find that they have more money to lend out. In order to lend out this increased quantity of money, they lower the interest rate—generating an increased quantity demanded of funds and, as shown above, altering the relative attractiveness of various investment projects, by making longer run projects relatively more profitable. To the extent that entrepreneurs base their plans on the lower interest rate, they are responding as if consumers demanded more economic growth when in fact they do not. In this way monetary policy generates false signals inducing entrepreneurs to supply an increased quantity of future goods to consumers who have not expressed this preference. If the government doesn't continue pumping money into the economy at an increasing rate, firms will find themselves short of funds available to complete their investment projects. But in the meantime, capital resources are being misallocated on long-term business ventures throughout the economy.

Neither have the consequences of credit expansion by a monetary authority been widely recognized. Nor have some of the secondary consequences of the monetary authorities' decision to slow down, stop, or actually decrease the money supply been fully appreciated by economic analysts.

A decrease in the money supply (or a decrease in the rate of increase of the money supply) will cause interest rates to rise. (See Figure 3.) The unexpected shortage of funds will lead people to scramble for money and credit in order to minimize the disruption of their ongoing plans. The shortage of money will send producers to the loanable funds markets to bid for the reduced supply of bank credit and this will result in higher interest rates. What has been surprising to many analysts during periods where the monetary authority reverses its expansionist policy is not the fact that interest rates rise but the degree to which they rise and the length of time they stay "high" before they approach "normal" levels.

### FIGURE 3
### INTEREST RATE LOWERED
### BY CREDIT EXPANSION

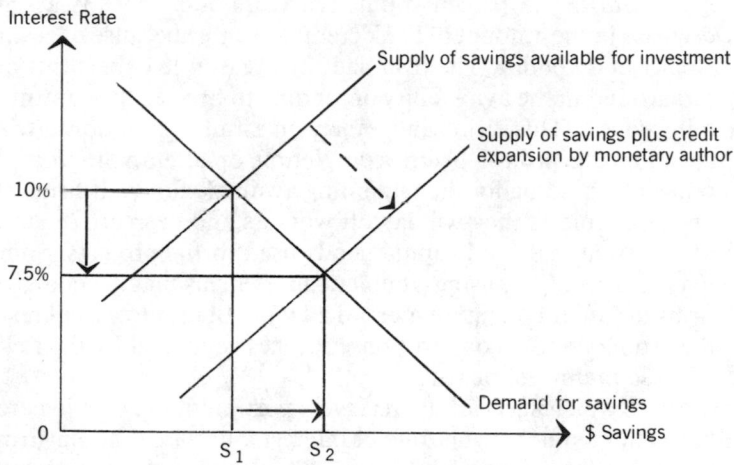

### INTEREST RATE RAISED BY CREDIT CONTRACTION

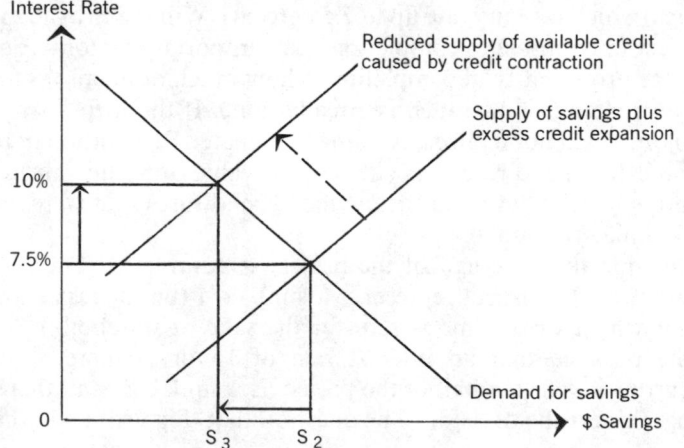

Inflationary expectations are often the catchall used to explain high interest rates during such periods, despite the fact that one would expect a decreasing rate of price inflation. However, there is another possible explanation that helps to explain the interest rate pattern associated with the retraction of an expansionist monetary policy.

An example is perhaps the simplest method of illustrating the point. Let us assume that a firm starts a long-term investment project that is expected to take ten years to complete. The project is thought to be profitable if the outlays, including financing costs, are constant or will increase at a moderate rate. Assume that the project is expected to generate $10 million in revenue when it is completed ten years later, and that the expected profitability is based on interest rates of around 7.5 percent (either that interest rates are currently 7.5 percent and will continue to be so or that they are lower and are expected to rise to a maximum of 7.5 percent). But five years later there is a significant decrease in the amount of bank credit available because of contractionist monetary policy. The firm had little reason to expect this dramatic turnaround in the availability of funding to finance the continuation of this project. This firm, and others in similar situations, will either abandon the project before completion or attempt to complete the project by bidding for the remaining available funds. If firms abandon ongoing projects they will lay off workers and decrease or stop orders for raw materials and capital goods used in the projects. Some firms may go bankrupt causing complementary firms that depended on these firms to suffer. Unemployment of all types of resources will result from the primary and secondary consequences generated by the revelations of these malinvestments.

Firms which successfully receive a portion of the existing credit will have paid a much higher rate of interest. Suppose that our firm is able to acquire the existing funds to complete the investment project, but it must pay an interest rate of 15 percent. The 15 percent interest rate is much higher than what was originally considered to be a profitable range (which was any rate up to 7.5 percent). Will the firm abandon the project or continue to completion? One important factor in determining the profitability of completion is how much of the project remains to be done and how much is already done. If the firm abandons the project, it will not realize any of the anticipated $10 million in revenue. All it can hope to recoup is either scrap value or resale value of its resources which is often far below the expenditures that were necessary to produce the goods.

Assume that one-half of the project is completed. The completed portion of the project represents a sunk cost (net of resale and scrap value which we assume is zero for the sake of simplicity). Now it is quite possible that an interest rate of 15 or 20 percent is worth incurring given that half of the project is a sunk cost and therefore no longer enters the decision. The question that this firm and others with ongoing projects face is: given the substantial wealth loss they have incurred because of the jump in the interest rate, given the fact they would never have started the project if they could undo their decision, will the $10 million of revenue warrant paying a 15 percent interest rate for the next five years? Even though the project represents a substantial loss from the perspective of the start of the project, it may still be worth completing. Bygone costs are of course bygone; all that needs to be determined is whether or not the additional costs required to complete the project, including 15 percent financing costs, are less than the expected $10 million in revenue.

*Ceteris paribus*, the closer the project is to completion, the lower the interest elasticity of the demand for funds. The further the project is from completion, the higher the interest elasticity of demand for funds. The demand for credit depends not so much on the demand to finance new investment projects, which represent only a small portion of investment activity, but on the credit needed to finance the completion of existing projects that were started at various points in the past. Only new investment projects will immediately be abandoned because of the much higher elasticity of demand for credit in these projects.[4]

The example presented above assumes away many complications as any example must, but the introduction of such complications as the effect of interest rates on replacement costs, of inflationary expectations raising the costs of completing the project, and of the degree of specificity in the component parts of the project, would alter the numbers and the empirical applications, yet the basic point would not change. Moreover anything which leads entrepreneurs to expect that there will be more funds available and therefore a lower interest rate than actually occurs will eventually generate higher interest rates.

During the period of unusually high interest in 1981, some economic analysts argued that investment activity was healthy despite the fact that the interest rate had risen to over 20 percent. One of the reasons given in support of this view was that producers were borrowing at such high rates and that therefore they must feel that the investment projects will generate a greater than 20 percent return. Thus, profitable investment activity had not dried up, and entrepreneurs must be very optimistic because of their strong demand for funds. Of course, what is true in this argument is that only people who anticipate that the benefits outweigh the opportunity costs will borrow funds at 20 percent. One doubts, however, whether the borrower of funds at a 20 percent interest rate, who expected to be able to borrow funds at 10 percent and has lost millions of dollars because of the higher interest rates, will view the investment climate as healthy. Surely he will prefer to borrow than not, given his desperate straits—but with such a notion of health one can only wonder what ill-health would be like.

The real question that must be examined is why there have been so many errors in anticipating the profitability of investment projects and the level of interest rates. Why, during the normal course of affairs, do we see some people making errors, but most making correct decisions with little disruption to economic growth? Why, at other times, do we observe that the majority of entrepreneurs are induced into making poor investment decisions?

The success of entrepreneurs is almost wholly dependent on their ability to deal with the uncertainty of the future. The signals that entrepreneurs rely upon (prices and interest rates, et al.) are geared to capture information about future events. An explanation of business cycles must examine the reasons why these entrepreneurial tools fail at certain periods of time. One candidate involves the methods used to administer monetary policy. Expansionary monetary policy that increases the availability of funds for investment through open-market operations initially lowers the interest rate below what it would have otherwise been. The expansionist monetary policy causes price inflation, which after a time induces the monetary authorities to reverse the policy. Because the monetary authorities have a history of trying to affect peoples' expectations by pronouncements, one can rarely base his plans on what the monetary authorities say they will do. But the reversal of the inflationary policies is inevitable—usually before the inflation causes the destruction of so much of the industrial structure, as in Germany in the early 1920s. After having induced lower interest rates by increasing the money supply, the monetary authorities induce higher interest rates by reversing this policy.

The major point being stressed here is that at least one key market signal for allocating resources over time—the interest rate—is distorted by government monetary policy and therefore generates serious coordination problems. Changing incentives by altering tax policy will not remove these distortions to the capital structure any more than it will address the problems of distortions to market prices caused by regulatory policies. Stimulating the aggregate or macroeconomic levels of savings and investment will not solve the uncoordination generated by monetary policy which channels these funds into malinvestments.

## IV. Keynesian, Neoclassical, Supply-Side, and Market-Process Approaches

An interesting way to illustrate some of the critical differences among Keynesian, neoclassical, supply-side, and market-process views of economic growth is provided by an analytical tool called "the production possibilities frontier," which portrays the locus of all technologically efficient, full-employment opportunities that the economy can reach. (See Figure 4.) Areas to the right of the curve represent nonachievable output because the technical apparatus of the country is not sufficient to produce such high levels of output even when the economy is fully coordinated and operating at "full capacity." Areas within the curve denote production possibilities that are associated with higher than technically efficient unemployment levels—unemployment of all factors of production including land, capital goods, and labor. Although, in reality, one would want to consider all goods and the nearly infinite number of possible combinations among these goods, for expository purposes we will let the graph demonstrate the production of only two goods. This simple graph examines the traditional split among neoclassical, Keynesian, supply-side, and the market-process approaches.

Standard neoclassical microeconomic theory adopts assumptions and models that are basically concerned with the desirability of point B relative to point C from the perspective of the consumer. If one adopts the neoclassical view of the world and follows its basic assumptions, one will reach the conclusion that the economy will always tend to a full employment situation and that the economy will automatically jump from point B to C or from point C to B as consumers desire. The Keynesian challenge to neoclassical economics addressed points such as A where it appeared that the economy had stagnated at a state of high levels of unemployment and showed little tendency to move to a full employment situation, such as B or C, as neoclassical economics would lead one to believe. Economists were essentially left with two contrary theories to explain one world. One postulated an automatic market mechanism able to bring the economy to full employment, and the other postulated a market mechanism more likely to stagnate at intolerable levels of unemployment.

*FIGURE 4*

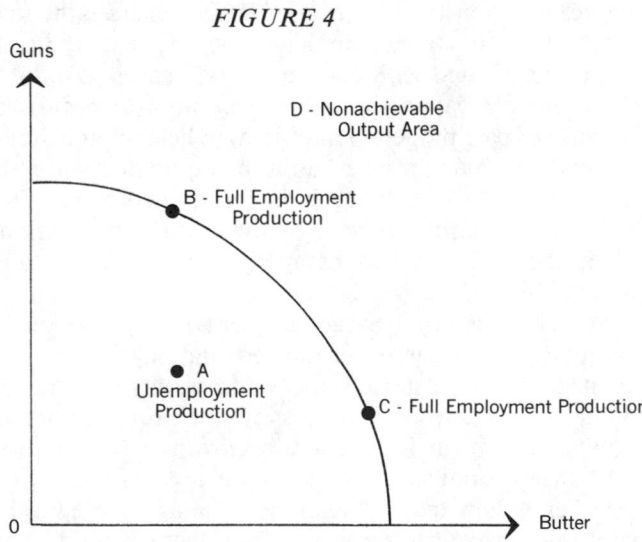

In an attempt to reconcile these two theories, Paul Samuelson developed what has been called the "neoclassical synthesis," which essentially maintained that aggregate demand policies were necessary to push the economy toward the production possibility frontier—but once the economy reached any point on the frontier the neoclassical notion of market adjustment took over and shifted resources to areas where consumers most readily demanded them. The idea was that government is needed to assure that the economy hovered around the production possibilities frontier. If the economy deviated significantly from the frontier, unemployment, low national product, and low national income generated negative expectations which rippled through the economy (i.e., the multiplier) and resulted in an inadequate level of aggregate demand. However, once government monetary and fiscal policies assured a reasonable level of aggregate demand then the market could perform reasonably well.[5]

Market-process economists point out that construing the jump from A (recession or a depression) to B or C (full employment) in terms of aggregates ignores a number of important considerations, for the economy is not a piece of clay easily molded by aggregate policies. Whether the economy moves along a path of A→B or A→C is critically important. Machinery, trained laborers, resource requirements, etc., geared to produce B cannot be switched to produce C without a disruption to the economy. If government monetary and fiscal policies distort prices, profits, and the interest rate and therefore push the economy toward B while voluntary exchange and consumer preference would have led to market signals that geared the economy toward C, then retooling of the economy from A to C will lead to significant economic problems. The boom caused by government policy employing resources in the direction of B will generate the bust or recession when the productive equipment, laborers, etc., are inevitably retooled to be coordinated with consumer preferences at point C. The reason the economy was in the range of point A to begin with is precisely because of past monetary and fiscal policies channeling resources into malinvestments that later had to be liquidated and retooled.

The value of these insights is exemplified by the fact that market-process economists warned of the coming depression of the 1930s while the economy was booming in the 1920s. They were able to determine that market signals—prices, profits, and interest rates—were being distorted by government policy and that the scarce resources were being mischanneled and malinvestments were being created because distorted prices and profits were misdirecting entrepreneurs into sending resources into the wrong sectors of the economy.

What is critical for economic growth in a market-process economist's view is not so much the overall level of activity in the economy, nor merely how many resources are being devoted to investment and consumption, nor some aggregate measure of productivity or percentage increase of GNP. Rather, it is whether or not the plans of entrepreneurs who are allocating particular new materials, capital goods, labor, and consumer goods are coordinated with the plans of other members of the economy. The problem of coordination, far from being minimized by current monetary and fiscal policy, has been greatly aggravated by it in the market-process view. Merely stimulating aggregate demand or aggregate supply doesn't address the real requirements for sustained economic growth. The critical aspects missed by Keynesian and neoclassical economists when dealing with growth are the need for coordinated economic activity, the effects of institutional changes on individual action, and the effects of government economic policies on market coordinating information generated by such market signals as prices, profits, and the constellation of interest rates.

Supply-side economists on the other hand confuse the roles played by different market signals. They especially misconstrue the nature of *prices*. For example, these economists have discussed the need to change the relative prices of consumption and savings and of leisure and work in order to encourage investment and enhance productivity.[6] However, no such "prices" exist because "consumption," "leisure," and the like are summary categories of particular types of behavior and not economic goods. Prices, as generated by the market, express the exchange value of *specific* goods and services—not general classifications of human activity. Prices are the result of a valuation process that attempts to capture the interplay between the utility that a good offers to consumers and the opportunity costs of the producers who supply the good. Prices aid market participants in making the benefit-opportunity cost comparisons that are necessary to channel resources into the production of goods most urgently demanded by consumers.

Nor is the distinction between relative prices and profitability only a theoretical refinement. For if supply-siders feel that in addressing incentives, they are also addressing the coordination problems inherent in pricing, their policies will end up being woefully short-sighted. In their conceptual confusion, they run the risk of overlooking coordination problems altogether. If relative price information is distorted, then the most urgently demanded goods are not produced.

Accurate price information helps ensure that the "right" things will be produced. Profitability, on the other hand, does not provide the information of what specific goods and services to produce. Rather it provides the incentive for producers to use price information effectively. The decision to produce and the choice of what to consume are made at different times. The producer or entrepreneur is always dueling with uncertainty as he tries to guess consumer demands, and prices are an important calculating tool. But distorted prices will tend to generate distorted plans which result in market coordination problems, regardless of either incentives or profitability.

Thus supply-side economics does address the market role of incentives, but it has not addressed the informational problems associated with economic coordination. Supply-siders have correctly focused on the disincentives toward harder and longer work when marginal tax rates are high. However, even if supply-side tax policies are instituted and the level of savings and investment increases dramatically, the informational problems associated with distorted prices and interest rates that guide the channeling of this investment remain. For example, tax cuts do not address the problem of determining which specific capital goods should be bought, where should new plant and equipment be located, how capital-intensive should any given production process be, and how do these investment plans dovetail with the plans of other producers and with consumers. These problems can be solved only by removing the distorting influences on prices and other market signals. Despite their claims to the contrary, supply-siders are still dealing in the realm of macroeconomics in much the same way as aggregate demand theorists. By confusing relative profitability with relative prices, supply-side economics has missed the crucial issue of microeconomic coordination.

Assuming away critical informational problems has a well-established tradition in economics. It is not widely known that Karl Marx had a keen awareness of the coordination problems that must be solved in a market economy. However, Marx ignored the key informational problems inherent in a centrally planned economy.[7] As soon as Marx discovered a possible market coordination problem, he immediately assumes that a centrally planned economy would have no such problems. Neoclassical economists, many of whom insightfully focused on the informational problems associated with resource allocation in a socialist or centrally planned economy, assumed away crucial information problems when they drew their isoquants and their indifference curves. The neoclassical notions of perfect competition and monopoly are further evidence of the lack of understanding of the market's function of generating, as well as disseminating, information. Somehow, some way, all the critical information is assumed to be known. Consumer preferences and consumer demand, technical transformations and marginal cost curves are all obvious to everyone, and coordination is automatically achieved simply by following neoclassical optimality rules. Who would need a market if we had all of this information—all we would really need is a very large computer.

Now the supply-side economists assume away another set of informational problems. One can only guess at the reason that market coordination problems have not been addressed. One possible reason is the use of conventional neoclassical tools which assume that the information needed to solve coordination problems is readily available and therefore coordination is automatically achieved if neoclassical optimality rules are followed. In this view, the market economy becomes a giant "computer" (perfect or flawed depending upon the economist) that assures the efficient allocation of resources and maximizes output.

The market-process economist sees the market in a fundamentally different role. In his view, the value of the market lies in its institutional role for discovering and disseminating information, information that is not available in other institutional settings and that is then effectively distributed to economic agents who can utilize it to coordinate their plans with the plans of others.

An alternative explanation is that supply-side economists believe that an unhampered market tends to solve the problems of economic coordination. If this is true, then an unhampered market also effectively deals with the problems of incentives. While supply-side economists have recognized the distortions to the market-incentive system they have simply overlooked the fact that these same economic policies also distort market information. This puts supply-side economists in a somewhat ironic position. If they continue to focus exclusively on incentives, then the supply-side approach is inadequate. If they expand their theoretical and policy horizons to deal with problems of information and plan coordination, there will be little to distinguish supply-side from market-process economists who, for decades, have recognized and analyzed the incentive problems caused by taxation as well as the distortions of market information caused by monetary and regulatory policies.

## V. Policy Recommendations

If one were to accept the goal that government policy should be primarily concerned with increasing productivity and stimulating economic growth, then the market-process perspective would suggest that the government should systematically eliminate policies that distort market signals—particularly relative prices, profits, and the interest rates. One would first attempt to eliminate those policies that cause the most distortion. This is hardly an easy task, but certainly monetary policies would have to be considered as critical as the realigning of incentives through tax policy. Supply-side tax policies designed to alter incentives to increase the level of savings and investment are of questionable value if this encouragement results in the production of malinvestments. Supply-side tax policy must be accompanied by an equally important focus on coordination problems caused by other distorting economic policies in so far as the ultimate aim is economic growth.

While it would be best to repeal first those policies that have the most distortive effects on the economy, if political reality dictates beginning with a program of marginal tax-rate cuts, critics of supply-side policies would be wrong to oppose such a move. But insofar as these critics are alerting supply-siders to unaddressed or under-emphasized problems associated with other government policies that may thwart supply-side goals, their advice is invaluable. Supply-siders must understand that the lack of incentives is only part of the productivity problem and that there must be a systematic effort to repeal distorting economic policies. The level of savings and investment is important, but problems of market coordination may be even more significant.

On the other hand, government interventions on the supply-side—"reindustrialization," new taxes on consumption instead of investment, business subsidies, and the like—would damage long-run prospects for economic growth in the same way that past demand-management policies did. Like the earlier policies, they would distort market signals and misallocate resources.

## Notes

1. Therefore, an individual's "economic growth" decision involves the attempt to create a future circumstance where he or she will be able to command more scarce resources in the future than he or she would otherwise be able to do.

2. Martin Feldstein, "Inflation, Taxes, and the Rate of Savings" (Lecture delivered at a conference on "Inflation: The Consequences for the Economy," sponsored by the Institute of Humane Studies and the Austrian Economics Program, Rutgers University, Newark, N.J., April 28-29, 1979).

3. Robert J. Smith, "Preserving the Earth—The Property Rights Approach," *Policy Report* 4 (Washington, D.C.: Cato Institute, February 1982): 1.

4. F. A. Hayek, "Investment that Raises the Demand for Capital," in idem, *Profits, Interest, and Investment* (Clifton, N.J.: Augustus M. Kelley, 1975), pp. 74-76.

5. William H. Branson, *Macroeconomic Theory and Policy* (New York: Harper and Row, 1972), pp. 3-4.

6. The confusion over the role of relative prices and relative profitability is evident in even the most prominent supply-side economists. For example, see Paul Craig Roberts, "The Breakdown of the Keynesian Model," *The Public Interest*, no. 52, (Summer 1978); and Norman Turé, "The Economic Effects of Tax Changes: A Neoclassical Analysis," in U.S. Congress, Joint Economic Committee, *Special Study on Economic Change* 4, *Stagflation: The Causes, Effects and Solutions* (December 17, 1980): 316.

7. David Lavoie, "Rivalry and Central Planning: A Reexamination of the Debate over Economic Calculation under Socialism" (Ph.D. diss., New York University, 1981), pp. 165-169.

# Savings Is the Key to Supply-Side Economics: A Proposal

Stanley Kaish

The term *supply-side economics* has been broadened to cover so much ground that for a while it appeared that we were all supply-siders. A similar thing happened a generation ago when a new body of thought named after Lord Keynes acquired sufficient breadth to encourage Milton Friedman to write a *Theory of the Consumption Function* and Richard Nixon to declare himself also a Keynesian in 1971. Supply-side economics appeared to have reached that same happy state where all but the most iconoclastic become co-opted in name, if not entirely in fact.

Still, it was never quite right to label everyone who is concerned with increasing output a supply-sider. Even though Walter Heller came to insist that his 1962 tax and capital consumption programs were supply-oriented, they were still very different from the Jude Wanniski-Jack Kemp proposals. There are many ways to increase output: improve education, reduce regulation, raise aggregate demand, improve manpower mobility, etc. If the term *supply-side economics* referred only to the achievement of increased supply, all of these could be included. It doesn't, of course. Supply-side economics is as much concerned with *process* as outcome, and the process it is concerned with is the enhancement of people's incentives to work, invest, and trade as a result of being assessed lower taxes. Those who want to increase supply by means other than lower taxes, or who want to lower taxes for reasons other than increased output fall outside the narrow bounds of this criterion.

While the goal is to increase output through a tax cut, there is, of course, more. Supply-siders also contend that they will lower inflation rates as well. Since inflation is a condition where too many dollars are chasing too few goods, an increase in the supply of goods, they argue, will reduce the root cause of inflation. It is hard for anyone who has ever shifted a pair of curves on the blackboard of a microeconomics class to argue against this point. The difficulty arises among those who teach *macroeconomics*. They know that tax cutting doesn't only give an incentive to work. It also gives increased disposable personal income and a resultant rise in demand for consumer goods. During the 1960s the rationale for tax cutting at a time when federal deficits were high and demand was sluggish was that demand would be stimulated and this would put people back to work. Today we are asked to suspend disbelief and accept the proposition that cutting taxes at a time when deficits are high is good for us precisely because demand will not be stimulated. Instead the increased disposable income will go into saving and be available for investment.

I am reminded of the 1952 Terence Rattigan movie called *Breaking the Sound Barrier*. The plot hinged on efforts of a test pilot to fly a plane in a power dive at speeds exceeding the speed of sound. The difficulty was that each time the pilot pulled back on the stick to get the plane out of the dive the craft broke up and crashed. Finally, in a moment of desperation the plane's designer suggested that the pilot push forward on the stick instead. It worked like a charm. Contrary to all precedent, the plane rose smoothly out of the dive as a result of this unorthodox treatment and history was made. Those accustomed to the idea that the way to combat inflation is through a holding down of demand may well feel that the Kemp-Roth prescription is akin to pushing forward on the stick while the plane is breaking up.

### Will The Tax Cut Be Saved?

It all comes down to whether or not people will save the tax cut. If they do save it, a redistribution of income out of current consumption use and into investment is possible. If they don't, nothing will have happened from the supply-side point of view. Consumption will be shifted from government to households, but it will still represent spending that is intended to satisfy current desires rather than to provide for future wants. If the consumption is added on in addition to the government spending—rather than instead of it—the country will have a severe inflationary situation on its hands.

Supply-siders appeal both to logic and history to convince us that lowering taxes will increase savings. One approach is to argue that lower taxes increase the net return on investments. Hence the opportunity cost of current consumption rises relative to the future satisfactions that are possible if one only saved for a while at the higher rates. At the old maximum 70 percent tax rate on unearned, (that is, *interest* income) it is a good deal more rational for rich people to buy luxury goods than it is to save. The alternative to purchasing a $50,000 Rolls Royce is to save the $50,000 and invest it. Perhaps the investment will yield 10 percent, or $5,000, annually. In the top tax bracket an investor would get to keep only $1,500 of that after taxes. Thus, a rich man buys a Rolls Royce at an opportunity cost of $125 per month— less than the cost of renting a Pinto. To clinch the deal, we note that if the savings are invested, inflation will depreciate the value of both income and principal over time. On the other hand, it is highly likely that the Rolls will appreciate in value under these circumstances. Evans sums up the theoretical argument with the simple assertion that "a reduction in tax rates increases the incentive of individuals to save by raising the rate of return on assets held by individuals. This higher savings leads to lower interest rates and higher investment."[1]

To back up this assertion Paul Craig Roberts calls our attention to the increase in personal saving and investment that followed the 1964 tax cut in the U.S. Although advertised as a demand-side program, he points out that the actual result was a higher rate of saving and capital formation over the next three years. Roberts adds, "Keynesians sometimes claim that the investment boom resulted from the investment tax credit, but the sharp rise in investment could not have taken place if consumers had not released resources from consumption by saving a larger share of their income."[2]

What are we to make of these logical and historical arguments? It seems safe to admit that they may be valid, but on the other hand, a strong possibility exists that they are not. The opportunity-cost argument depends on the substitution effect between saving and consumption. Raising the price of consumption through lower taxes will reduce its desirability. We should, however, include the income effect in our considerations as well. By lowering taxes we raise the level of net income that will occur with any given amount of savings, and this tends to encourage more consumption as well. Indeed, the Brookings Institution's Robert Z. Lawrence, after reviewing the pros and cons, concludes, "Economic theory is agnostic on the relation between saving and the interest rate. When the rate of return on saving rises there is a substitution effect and an income effect and the sum of these effects may be either positive or negative."[3]

If we turn to Paul Craig Roberts's "evidence" taken from the 1964 experience, we find we are on equally ambiguous ground. Remember, in order for the tax cut to be noninflationary it is necessary that the bulk of the increased disposable personal income accruing to individuals be saved. This is not the same thing as seeing savings occur over the next three years. Just because savings eventually rose, it doesn't follow that the tax cut was saved. Indeed, Keynesian theory posits a chain of events that sees saving rise as a result of the increase in income that occurs if the tax cut were consumed. The simple multiplier process would produce the income rise and a positive marginal propensity to save will yield up the saving.

When we look at the figures, the best we can say is that they are ambiguous on this matter. Certainly savings went up in the 1960s. Over the three years following the 1964 tax cut we can measure a $12 billion increase in personal saving. However consumption during the same period rose by $93 billion. It seems just as reasonable to claim from this evidence that personal saving rose because of the increase in income as it is to suggest that income rose because of the rise in saving.

Furthermore, the representation that the substantial increase in investment could only have occurred if there had been an equally substantial release of funds from personal saving must also be questioned. True, national income accounting requires that saving must equal investment. But personal saving comprises only about a quarter of the annual gross saving generated by the domestic economy. The balance comes from capital consumption allowance, retained earnings, and net government surplus. Most private investment is financed out of internal business savings which in the year following the tax cut rose $7.5 billion against an increase of less than $2 billion for personal saving. The investment tax-credit may very well be more responsible for higher investment in the 1960s than the cut in personal taxes.

Two additional considerations cast shadows over the likelihood that a 1981 tax cut will be saved. The first is the different impact that a cut in tax rates had on savings in the inflation-free 1960s as contrasted to the inflation-ridden 1980s. In 1964 a cut in nominal tax rates was also a cut in real rates. Since then we have become all too aware of the phenomenon of bracket creep. Inflation is continually pushing people into higher income brackets and, due to our progressive tax system, into higher marginal rates. When a 10 percent reduction in tax rates is accompanied by a 10 percent increase in nominal income, it is not long before one is right back where he started from in the tax table. Under these circumstances it is hard to mount a compelling substitution-effect argument. So, even if we concede that a rise in savings occurred in 1964, conditions in 1981 may differ critically.

The second difficulty arises from the administration's insistence on a three-year tax cut. While there are sound political reasons for striking while the iron is hot, there is also a great deal of economic theory and evidence that shows that permanent changes in people's income tend primarily to affect their consumption, while temporary changes mostly affect their savings. For example, the 1968 temporary tax surcharge levied in the hope that consumer demand would be diminished, thereby facilitating the allocation of resources to the Vietnam war effort, failed entirely. Between April of 1968 when the tax became effective and April 1969 personal saving fell by $12 billion. Evidently people kept right on consuming and paid their added tax levy out of savings. A similar experience occurred in 1975 when a one-time tax rebate was passed in an effort to raise consumption and stimulate the economy. The record shows that the next year a $37 billion fall in personal tax revenue was matched by a $34 billion rise in personal saving. Here was an instance where the Carter administration was trying to induce consumption and instead raised saving.

It would seem that if any lesson is to be learned from these fiscal experiments it would be reaffirmation of the permanent income hypothesis: people plan their consumption in terms of their expected long-run personal income. Temporary changes are saved. The three-year advance tax cut is exactly the wrong way to go to gain an increase in saving. It allows long-run planning of the use of the new disposable income, and the odds are that it will be used pretty much like the old —basically for consumption. If a supply-side event is to be induced by tax cutting, the tax cut should be one that engenders a sense of uncertainty in the minds of consumers and of certainty in the minds of businessmen. That is, personal tax cuts should ostensibly be temporary, but business tax cuts permanent.

## An Old Proposal

Since a favorable inflationary outcome of the tax reduction program depends so heavily on individuals saving rather than consuming their tax cuts, and since there is little historical and theoretical reason to be assured that they will, it is quite surprising that the program has found the wide support it has. Undoubtedly it is due to the absence of viable alternatives. Kemp-Roth advocates have successfully exploited the political truism that "you can't beat somebody with nobody." When challenged, supply-siders simply and effectively answer, "We've tried Keynesian programs for the past twenty years, and they have produced deficits, inflation, and unemployment. What else do you suggest?" So far, no credible alternative has been offered by the other side.

It was within this context that early in 1981 I proposed that a variation of Keynes's compulsory saving plan be adopted to accompany the Kemp-Roth tax bill. [4] Published in 1940, Keynes's book *How to Pay for the War* offered an antiinflation program for Great Britain's financing of World War II. [5] He recognized that it would be impossible to fund the total cost of the war through taxation, and that it was highly inflationary to finance it through debt unless purchasing power of consumers was deflected. Keynes thus called for a temporary compulsory saving plan whereby each earner would be required to set aside part of his current income for later consumption. The funds would be invested by a private portfolio manager selected from an approved list. As in today's Keogh plans, dividends and interest would accrue and the total would be returned to each individual at a time of the government's choosing. Keynes proposed returning the funds at the end of the war to boost an anticipated sag in the economy.

The proposal received near universal praise in the academic community at the time of its publication. Some flavor of this can be gathered from a review written by F. A. Hayek, no ardent Keynesian then or now. Hayek wrote, "The outstanding topic in financial circles in the past week has been the ingenious proposal we owe to the most fertile mind among living economists. This is not surprising for if the proposal were adopted, it would go far to solve one of the most difficult and pressing problems of the war and immediately affect the position of a great majority of the population."[6] What supply-sider wouldn't be pleased to receive such a glowing review from a traditional adversary?

I suggested that since the long-term supply benefits of tax reduction were ardently desired, but the short-run inflationary pressure that will follow such a cut held the potential for disaster, compulsory saving was an idea whose time had come. Linked to the Kemp-Roth tax cut, it would give both the incentive-minded supply-siders and the inflation-wary Keynesians an opportunity for accommodation. Some portion of the tax refund would be diverted to a Keogh-like investment fund for professional management, and these funds and their earnings would accumulate in an account that is owned but not possessed by the taxpayer. I departed from the Keynesian plan when it came to choosing a time to return the principal and accrued interest. Rather than use it as a countercyclical measure, which requires that we be able to forecast recessions well enough to head them off, I suggested a form of universal pension. As with the Keogh and IRA accounts, the funds would be held until retirement, taking some of the financial pressure off our burdened Social Security program.

Since I made that proposal, two important events have taken place. (1) The Kemp-Roth tax cut has become a reality, at least to the extent of a 25 percent reduction spread over three years, and (2) a general awareness of problems in the Social Security system has been thrust on the public. This juxtaposition of events has created a unique political opportunity for Congress to do something really important from the supply-side point of view. In one stroke it can minimize the inflation-ary impact of the tax cut, eliminate the solvency question hanging over Social Security, and substantially encourage capital formation. It can do this by using part of the Kemp-Roth fiscal dividend to convert Social Security from a pay-as-you-go to a funded retirement system.

While the focus in this paper is on enhancement of capital forma-tion, Social Security's bleak financial outlook is certainly a compelling reason for change in and of itself. When Congress established the system on a pay-as-you-go transfer basis instead of as an actuarially funded program back in the 1930s it launched a vessel that sooner or later had to end up on the rocks. In 1945 there were 50 workers to sup-port every retiree and as recently as 1955 there were 8.3. Today, changing birth rates, earlier retirement—in large measure encouraged by Social Security regulations—and greater longevity have reduced the worker-to-retiree ratio to just over 3-to-1 with some pessimistic projections suggesting a decline to 1.15-to-1 by the year 2055.[7] Where in the past rising benefits could be paid by new groups joining the system, today the only substantial cohort still outside the system is the federal government's employees, and they steadfastly resist being co-opted. In fact, several of those state and local governments whose employees have a choice have chosen to leave the system. A more sophisticated public is aware that the money it contributes today is not held in trust for it, but rather is going out as rapidly as it comes in. Young workers are increasingly skeptical about whether the promises being made to them today will be kept by a generation of workers still unborn.

Both Congress and the administration have suggested steps to improve the fiscal situation including an increase of retirement age to sixty-eight, a reduction of benefits to those retiring at age sixty-two, and a change in cost-of-living indexing formulas. The substantial constituencies of those retired and about to retire made no bones about their rejection of these proposals. Considerable political peril awaits anyone who tampers with the benefits side of the Social Security equation. Yet during the next seventy years the President's Commission on Pension Plans has projected an average shortfall of between 1.52 and 6.17 percent in payroll tax rates depending on one's degrees of pessimism.[8] It appears that some kind of Social Secuity tax rise will be inevitable, and this is obviously contrary to the direction today's supply-siders want to go.

While these financial difficulties have focused our attention on the need to "do something" about Social Security, they are, as suggested earlier, only part of the story. Less appreciated than Social Security's financial problems—but in the long run more important—is the extent to which pay-as-you-go funding has reduced our national rate of saving and hence our national rate of capital formation. If we are really intent on reindustrialization and supply-side enhancement, we should take steps to change our Social Security from a transfer to a funded system regardless of financial exigency. Let us see why.

Most contempoary economic models incorporate some form of life-cycle hypothesis of consumer behavior. In essence this theory suggests that people apportion their income between consumption and savings in a manner designed to even out the level of consumption they can enjoy over their lives. This requires that they accumulate financial assets during the productive working years in order to provide for retirement. In calculating the assets they intend to use during the retirement years, people include savings accounts, stocks, pensions, property and, of course, Social Security. Recent estimates show that the annuity value of Social Security benefits to the American people is in excess of $5.5 trillion.[9] Controversial though the idea may be, it seems clear that without these benefits to rely on working people would save more for their retirement.

Of course, the Social Security drag on capital formation occurs because there is no actual asset to represent that annuity claim. Contributions made by today's workers go directly to retired people who (according to the life-cycle hypothesis) spend the money almost immediately. Social Security is a program for consumption, not saving. As far as individual behavior is concerned it makes relatively little difference if there is a fund or not. In fact, many citizens are probably unaware of the peculiar nature of this funding. Milton Friedman has made much of what he terms "Orwellian doublethink" by the Social Security Administration (SSA) in its dealing with the public, charging that SSA literature intentionally misleads the public on the nature of their contribution.[10] Because the individual until recently neither knew nor cared how his Social Security was financed, he behaved as if savings were in the bank waiting for him when in fact they weren't.

Martin Feldstein has been the most important force in pushing an awareness of the economic growth implications of this phenomenon.[11] He has estimated that the economy loses one dollar of personal savings for every two dollars of Social Security benefits. While controversy swirls around Feldstein's figures and the method he uses to estimate them, the basic thrust of his argument seems irresistible. Social Security is the single most important source of retirement income in the U.S. by far. Even if the saving loss is one dollar for every five dollars of Social Security, instead of two dollars as Feldstein asserts, we find a shortfall of $1 trillion in capital formation due to this. No supply-sider can be oblivious to magnitudes of this order.

## A New Proposal

Given the current set of circumstances: (1) a constituency ready to accept something called supply-side economics, (2) the recently enacted Kemp-Roth tax cut, (3) the need to increase national savings to reduce the inflationary impact of the tax cut, (4) the public's concern over the Social Security system's solvency, and (5) the adverse impact of pay-as-you-go Social Security on capital formation, the time is opportune for implementation of a Social Security Investment Fund.

• Beginning in 1984, half of the personal income tax reduction scheduled to go back to individuals should instead be earmarked for a Social Security Investment Fund (SSIF).

• The SSIF should be used as a complement to the existing payroll tax. The two sources combined will sustain the current level of scheduled benefits.

• A network of private portfolio managers should be contracted to invest and manage the SSIF as fiduciaries. This will avoid socializing the investment decisions that must be made in managing this vast pool of wealth.

• The payroll tax rate should be gradually reduced and eventually the tax eliminated as the assets of the SSIF build up.

The ability of a Social Security Investment Fund to reduce the amount of payments needed to provide a given level of benefits is impressive. The existing transfer payment financing should be considered as equivalent to compelling people to engage in interest-free lending to the government. The money enters a revolving door, and even though the contributor sacrifices the short-run use of his money, he or she doesn't get the customary interest income reward for doing so. Under the SSIF, he or she does, and every dollar the fund can accumulate in interest earnings is a dollar less that taxpayers must eventually contribute.

A look at the annuity tables must impress us anew with the power of compounding. One dollar per year contributed over a working life of forty-five years and invested at 5 percent compounds to $159.70. Under the present—no interest—transfer system, of course, one dollar paid in each year for forty-five years brings only $45 worth of Social Security benefits. The other side of this coin is to consider what type of retirement income each can provide. The accumulation of $159.70 can finance an expected life retirement of sixteen years at $14.50 per year. Without interest, one dollar per year buys an annual retirement income of $2.80. To provide a more realistic retirement benefit level of $600 per month, it would be necessary to contribute $500 per year for forty-five years if it is permitted to accumulate at 5 percent annual interest. Under today's transfer program, with 3.2 workers supporting each retiree, annual payments of $2,250 per worker are required to support one pensioner at $600 per month. As the ratio of workers to retirees falls this figure will grow prohibitively.

This transition from pay-as-you-go to funded Social Security would occur gradually. As each worker retires, the fund will provide part of the benefits that would otherwise have to be paid through payroll tax transfers. The immediate offset to payroll taxes would be slight for older workers soon to retire. However, by the time the youngest in today's work force are ready to call it quits, they will have accumulated enough to supplant virtually all of the payroll tax that others would be called upon to pay for them.

## Conclusions

It is clear that the nation is embarked on an experiment called supply-side economics premised on increased savings, investment, and effort coming forth in response to reduced taxation. There is substantial risk to be found here. This paper suggests that both logic and history give us reason to doubt that savings will respond as hoped. A proposal is made to establish a Social Security Investment Fund that will work to reduce the inflationary risk inherent in the tax cut and at the same time address some of the vexing anomalies of our Social Security system—the drag on capital formation and the difficult solvency situation that is developing. If this measure is added to the revolutionary changes that have occurred in U.S. fiscal policy recently, chances will substantially improve for supply-side economics to affect a permanent cure to the ailment of stagflation without bringing on the iatrogenic side effects of worsened inflation.

It is interesting that the germ of the idea proposed here comes from Keynes, an economist blamed by the supply-siders for our current economic difficulties. Keynes would appreciate the irony of this, for he wrote in *The General Theory* . . ., "Practical men, who believe themselves to be quite exempt from any intellectual influences are usually the slaves of some defunct economist . . . some academic scribbler of a few years back."[12] Elsewhere, he observed, perhaps still more relevantly, "On the economic front we lack not material resources, but lucidity and courage."[13] Hopefully, it will turn out that we showed a rare combination of both in the 1980s.

# Notes

1. Michael K. Evans, "The Bankruptcy of Keynesian Econometric Models," *Challenge* 22 (January-February 1980): 19.

2. Paul Craig Roberts, "Reagan's Tax-Cut Program: The Evidence," *Wall Street Journal*, May 21, 1982, p. 24.

3. Robert Z. Lawrence, "Comments," in Joseph A. Pechman, ed. *What Should Be Taxed: Income or Expenditures?* (Washington, D.C.: Brookings, 1980), p. 31.

4. Stanley Kaish, "Cutting Taxes Without Inflation," *New York Times*, February 6, 1981, p. A: 23.

5. John Maynard Keynes, *How to Pay for the War* (London: MacMillan & Co., 1940).

6. F. A. Hayek, "Review of *How to Pay for the War*," *Economic Journal* 50 (June 1940): 321.

7. President's Commission on Pension Policy, *Toward a National Retirement Income Policy* (Washington, D.C., 1981) p. 23.

8. Ibid., p. 24.

9. "The Crisis in Social Security," *Newsweek* (June 1981), pp. 25-27.

10. Wilbur J. Cohen, Jr. and Milton Friedman, *Social Security: Universal or Selective?* (Washington, D.C.: American Enterprise Institute, 1972).

11. Martin Feldstein, "Social Security Hobbles Our Capital Formation," *Harvard Business Review* 57 (July 1979): 6-8.

12. John Maynard Keynes, *The General Theory of Employment, Interest, and Money* (London: MacMillan & Co., 1936), p. 383.

13. Keynes, *How to Pay for the War*, p. 1.

# Chapter 9:
# Monetary Policy, The Deficit, and the Gold Standard

## Are Monetarism and Supply-Side Economics Compatible?

### Manuel H. Johnson

Comparing two schools of economic thought is a common intellectual exercise among academic economists. However, aside from usefulness as an exercise, a comparative analysis of monetarist and supply-side theories has important policy implications. The degree of harmony between these two schools of thought is a critical issue because the current government has adopted economic policy prescriptions based on the theories of both schools. The President's top economic advisors belong to monetarist and supply-side camps. Obviously, if there are significant inconsistencies between the two theories, the government's economic policy could create serious problems for the economy. Therefore, it is helpful to trace briefly the events that led to the acceptance of monetarist and supply-side principles by policymakers and to determine the extent to which these two views can be reconciled.

### The Retreat from Keynesianism and the Rise of Supply-Side Economics and Monetarism

For the past two decades, Keynesian demand-management policies have been the primary means for macroeconomic stabilization and growth in the U.S. economy. Unfortunately, the historical record has not proved favorable for the Keynesian policymakers. The empirical evidence documents progressively worsening economic performance with rising rates of inflation and unemployment. Demand-management put monetary policy on a roller coaster that required ever larger gyrations in the money supply. Under Keynesianism, government pursued its full employment goals through the stimulation of aggregate demand using the budget as its tool. In theory unemployment required a budget deficit to increase total demand or spending in the economy, while the relief of inflation required a budget surplus to reduce total demand in order to relieve pressures on the price level. In practice, this approach produced deficits in nineteen out of the last twenty years.[1]

During periods of persistent unemployment, government economists would calculate the magnitude of government spending required to shift aggregate demand to the full employment level. Deficit spending was deemed necessary in order to have a real expansionary effect. In addition, for the deficit to actually add to spending, the Federal Reserve was obliged to accomodate it with an increase in the money supply. In effect, Keynesian theory became translated into a policy fighting unemployment by printing money.

Expansion of the money supply would eventually drive up the price level so that the Federal Reserve would then have to yield to pressures for tightening money and raising interest rates in order to slow spending. As recession set in, unemployment claims and government interest payments would rise—keeping spending high while revenues declined and the budget deficit would unintentionally swell. With unemployment higher, the government would once again pursue its deficit spending policy and the business cycle would begin all over again. Each cycle left in its wake a higher level of unemployment at the peak and a higher inflation rate at the trough. Figure 1 illustrates this phenomenon showing the higher inflation rates corresponding to ever higher natural rates of unemployment. During the relatively prosperous mid 1960s, the minimum level of unemployment averaged less than 4 percent and the inflation rate hovered around 3 percent. By the late 1970s, however, minimum unemployment had climbed to almost 6 percent and was associated with an inflation rate of about 10 percent annually. The Keynesian policymakers did not realize it, but their problems were created by stimulating demand through a monetary expansion that resulted in serious supply disincentives. The inflation, created by too much money, pushed individuals into higher marginal tax brackets and eroded the value of business depreciation allowances.

These facts were pointed out by the traditional school of monetarists and a new generation of classical economists called "supply-siders." Monetarists had argued for years that expansions in the money supply were almost directly translated into a higher general price level and that any economic stabilization policy should contain provisions for a low and steady rate of growth in the monetary aggregates.[2] Supply-side economists on the other hand contend that Keynesian analysis was faulty because it failed to recognize the supply disincentives caused by the changing relative prices that resulted from excessive government spending.[3]

Both the monetarist and supply-side critiques of Keynesianism were incorporated in the platform of the new Republican government under President Ronald Reagan and provided the basis for his sweeping victory over the Democratic Party in the November 1980 elections. The combination of monetarist and supply-side policies called for a deceleration of the money supply and a simultaneous reduction in marginal tax rates and government spending. The decline in inflation and inflationary expectations resulting from less money would restore confidence in the economy and reduce the inflationary component of interest rates. Lower marginal tax rates along with accelerated depreciation allowances would reduce the relative price of work effort, saving, and investment causing an increased supply of productive factors in the economy and, therefore, would lead to greater real output and income. In addition, the greater aggregate saving due to the supply-side incentives would contribute to a reduction in real interest rates by increasing the supply of loanable funds.[4]

Overall, the new government's economic policy is a bold attempt to reverse the policy mistakes of the past. Rather than stimulate demand through money-financed deficit spending that discourages supply, the new policy is designed to increase supply relative to demand in a noninflationary manner. Reductions in government spending are intended to offset any private spending that might follow from the tax cuts so that aggregate demand remains relatively unchanged. A nonaccomodating monetary policy is expected to resist pressures to monetize any portion of the federal budget deficit that might result from the tax cuts. The tax cuts themselves are intended to increase the real rate of return on labor and capital so that aggregate supply will rise, creating higher real incomes and lower unemployment.

The expected outcome from these combined policies is ambitious but plausible. However, the likelihood of their success depends on how compatible the two theories are regarding control and stability of the money supply and the relationship between money and real output.

### The Money Supply and Prices: Conflicting Views?

Agreement among monetarist and supply-siders regarding the effect of changes in the money supply on the general price level is somewhat mixed. A number of influential supply-siders hold views similar to those of the monetarists while others maintain more conflicting opinions.

According to the monetarist school, a change in the money supply will translate into an almost equal change in the price level anywhere from six to eighteen months later. The initial effect of, say, an increase in the money supply produces an excess supply of money balances that individuals will attempt to reduce through spending for goods and services. This increase in aggregate demand will temporarily cause firms to expand their output by hiring additional labor or requiring overtime hours. However, after firms realize that demand is permanently higher and that they cannot sustain the higher level of output, prices will rise across-the-board and inflation will result.[5] The inflationary process is described in the following equation of exchange:

$$MV = PQ$$

where M is the money stock, V is the income velocity or number of times a dollar is turned over annually, $P$ is the price level, and $Q$ is real output. In terms of rates, the equation becomes:

$$\%\Delta M + \%\Delta V = \%\Delta P + \%\Delta Q.$$

Solving for the inflation rate gives
$$\%\Delta P = \%\Delta M + \%\Delta V - \%\Delta Q,$$
which says that the percentage change in the general price level is a positive function of the growth rates of money and velocity and a negative function of the growth rate of real output. Monetarists argued that, historically, the long-run growth rate in velocity has remained relatively stable, so that after a temporary period of real output growth, the inflation rate is determined almost solely by the growth rate of the money supply. Monetarists consider the long-run trend rate of growth of velocity to be stable because they believe that a primary determinant —demand for money—is also stable.

The policy implications arising out of monetarism are rather obvious: By controlling the supply of money to the economy, the monetary authority (Federal Reserve) can stabilize the price level and insure a steady rate of growth in real output. In an economy already suffering from the effects of high inflation, a deceleration in the rate of growth in the money supply is necessary to bring down prices, inflationary expectations, and nominal interest rates. Economic policy at the Federal Reserve has taken the form of primarily controlling the monetary aggregate M1-B. Federal Reserve monetarists are pursuing a quantity rule that is intended to reduce the growth in M1-B from an actual rate of 7.3 percent in 1980 to 4.3 percent by 1986.[6]

Among supply-siders, there are two different views concerning the efficacy of a quantity rule for stabilizing prices. Supply-side economists such as Paul Craig Roberts and Norman Turé at the Treasury Department basically agree with monetarists that a slow and steady rate of growth in the money supply is necessary to control inflation. However, they are somewhat skeptical of the degree of stability associated with income velocity and the demand for money because they believe that dramatic changes in incentives can produce substantial variation in these variables. Therefore, they do not attribute as much effectiveness to money supply changes as do monetarists. In addition, the supply-siders voice concern as to whether the monetary aggregates can actually be controlled so that they grow at a steady pace rather than generating uncertainty by oscillating widely from period to period. Beryl Sprinkel, the Reagan administration's leading monetarist, has also expressed concern about the Federal Reserve's ability to smooth out the trend in the money supply. He and other government monetarists have pressed the Fed to focus on control of the monetary base rather than on M1-B, and to concentrate instead on managing the discount window since it is a major source of unexpected additions to the base. Overall, Treasury supply-siders agree that if the Federal Reserve can establish credibility by demonstrating that it will not waver from its tight monetary policy and if it can stabilize the monetary aggregates, confidence in the dollar can be restored, and inflation and inflationary expectations should subside. If, however, a quantity rule cannot be enforced, Treasury supply-siders would be willing to consider a more disciplined approach to monetary policy such as the adoption of a price rule.

Another strain among supply-siders, represented by Arthur Laffer, Jude Wanniski, and Lewis Lehrman, favors almost immediate return to a gold standard in order to instill confidence in the dollar. Laffer argues that the tight money policy pursued by the Fed will have profound effects on the demand for money so that prices will rise rather than fall. Accordingly, Fed actions such as charging a higher discount rate and raising the reserve requirement to member banks are equivalent to imposing a tax on the activities of these banks. A higher rate of taxation on the production of bank services will cause banks to raise their prices on loans. Since the demand curve for loanable funds from member banks is elastic due to the large variety of substitutes, banks' profits will decline and both the supply of and the demand for member bank assets will ultimately be reduced. Laffer, therefore, concludes that:

> Both demanders and suppliers of credit will substitute out of dollars held in member banks into Eurodollar accounts, foreign currency denominated balances, indexed accounts, and gold. In short, the Fed's actions have reduced the viability and attractiveness of the dollar, and especially of dollars produced by member banks. As such, the Fed's actions per se have increased the prospects for inflation, in spite of the fact that their actions clearly will result in a slower growth in measured quantity of money.[7]

This view is not totally out of line with Treasury supply-siders; however, they are reluctant to agree that the demand for money could decline to the extent that the increase in the rate of velocity would more than offset the impact of a reduction in the growth rate of the money supply. Laffer, Wanniski, and associates regard monetarism as incompatible with supply-side economics because prices and interest rates will rise not fall as a result of tight money and will choke off the economic expansion that would occur through tax rate reductions. The difference between Treasury and Laffer-type supply-siders is that the former think in terms of "if" the quantity rule fails, while the latter think in terms of "when" it fails. Doubts about monetarism among supply-siders influenced Congress to authorize the Gold Commission in 1980 to study the advantages and disadvantages of converting our monetary system back to a gold standard.

## Monetary Restraint and Economic Growth

While Treasury supply-side have shown a willingness to give monetarists a chance to prove that their policies for achieving stable prices will work, they have been unwilling to compromise regarding the effectiveness of tax rate reductions and other incentive measures on real economic growth. Administration monetarists contend that the process of wringing inflation out of the economy via deceleration of the money supply will necessarily constrain the growth in real output. This, in the view of the monetarists, is because the long-term trend in income velocity has remained stable at an annual growth rate of approximately 3.2 percent.[8] They concede that on a quarterly basis or even over the course of a year, velocity can vary substantially from its trend rate but insist that it will return to trend at the end of these short fluctuations. Temporary fluctuations from trend can be explained by relating them to monetary disturbances and other real variables, and by taking account of the time lags in the effects of money on output and prices. The reason monetarists attribute such stability to velocity is that the demand for money is also believed to be stable over time. As with velocity, variations in the demand for money can be explained by changes in real variables, monetary policy, and time lags. In fact, the reciprocal of velocity is often used as a proxy for the demand for money in econometric studies.[9]

Most of the supply-side-monetarist controversy over velocity centers around the Reagan administration's projections of economic performance which is, in turn, based on policies incorporating both theories. Table 1 contains the official administration scenario which shows that between 1980 and 1986, a tight monetary policy is expected to reduce the inflation rate from 9 percent to 4.9 percent while supply-side fiscal policy simultaneously increases real output growth from -0.1 percent to 4.2 percent. Monetarists argue that, given the planned reduction in money supply growth from 6.4 percent to 3.4 percent, the trend growth in velocity required to produce the anticipated growth rates in real output is unrealistic. Annual growth in velocity would have to average 6.1 percent over the six-year period from 1981 to 1986 as opposed to the historical trend of 3.2 percent. Administration monetarists are not prepared to accept the supply-side assumption that velocity can be sustained well above trend for such a lengthy period. Therefore, they have continuously pushed for a revision in the economic forecast that would include real output growth estimates consistent with the historical trend in velocity. Treasury supply-siders have strongly resisted any such revision on the basis that the demand for money and velocity are not nearly as stable as monetarists claim and, more importantly, that the incentives created by supply-side fiscal policies are unprecedented in U.S. history, so that the historical trend in velocity does not capture these effects.

With respect to the demand for money, supply-siders point to recent empirical work by several economists that demonstrates that the demand for M1 money balances has been unstable since 1972 when a sharp downward shift was detected.[10] As for the stability of velocity, studies have shown that the stochastic structure of the velocity of M1-B is characterized by large and purely random fluctuations about the trend.[11] Some of these studies indicate a random walk with no particular direction of drift in the velocity series. Other work points to a random walk in velocity about an upward trend. If the growth of velocity is purely random and uncorrelated with past random fluctuations, as these results suggest, it is impossible to predict velocity with precision at any time. The situation is exacerbated if the random noise has a large variance, since then the effects of money on income will be dominated by a purely random fluctuation which cannot be ascertained on the basis of prior experience. The variance of the random fluctuation seems to be high enough to raise issues of this sort. One way to characterize the magnitude of this variance, and of the fluctuations it induces around trend, is to compute a confidence interval for the change in velocity. For quarterly variations in velocity this interval is very large—equivalent to annual growth rates of from −4.1 percent to 10.3 percent in any quarter. For the annual change in velocity it is somewhat smaller, 0.4 percent to 5.8 percent.[12]

Attempts have been made with varying degrees of success to correlate fluctuations in velocity with movements in other variables such as the money supply and interest rates. However, these attempts have not provided a completely satisfactory explanation of the trend component of velocity change. One approach to explaining velocity trends is to correlate them with real output trends. Support for this approach is provided by the argument that since people demand money to protect themselves against uncertainties in their income streams—both wage income and the return to investments—a faster growing economy will increase velocity by providing assurance of a sufficiently high level of steady and predictable income. With faster and more predictable growth, people will be more inclined to get rid of unproductive money and buy new capital for the return it yields. Econometric estimates show that about 68 percent of trend velocity growth can be explained by the increase in trend output growth.[13] With a real output growth of 3.3 percent, which is the average annual rate of growth since 1955, empirical results show an average annual rate of velocity growth of 3.2 percent, which is what it actually was over this period. For a trend output growth of 4.5 percent, the predicted trend velocity growth is 4 percent, and for real output growth of 5 percent, 4.3 percent in velocity trend growth is predicted. This evidence suggests that significantly higher output trends expected in coming years may well accelerate velocity trends. Rather than being constrained by velocity as monetarists predict, real output growth may well induce proportionate increases in velocity.

In addition to real output, velocity trends also depend upon other factors such as government regulation, the structure of payments, and technological advance. In order to isolate the influence on velocity of these other factors, the effects of real output can be "controlled for" by including real output growth in a time-trend analysis of velocity. A statistical examination of velocity over the last 100 quarters—1956-III to 1981-II—shows that M1-B velocity grew 3.4 percent from 1956-III to 1966-IV, decelerated to 1.7 percent from 1966-IV to 1972-IV, then increased to 3.6 percent from 1972-IV to 1981-II. These subperiods represent significant structural shifts in the trend over the last twenty-five years.[14]

Such findings call into question the belief of monetarists that trend velocity growth since the mid-1950s has been about 3.2 percent, and that it will continue to average around 3.2 percent for the next several years. Results show that there have been at least three shifts in the trend growth rate over the previous quarter century. Moreover, trend growth since the early 1970s has been considerably above 3 percent at about 3.6 percent. This growth rate would have been even higher if real output had not grown at a relatively slow 2.6 percent over that subperiod. Statistics show that if real Gross National Product (GNP) had grown at 3.3 percent from 1972 to the present—its average rate of growth since the mid-1950s—trend velocity would have grown at a 4 percent annual rate. If the next several years follow the recent past, velocity should grow on average in the 3.6 to 4 percent range. Supply-siders would argue, however, that there are reasons to believe that the velocity trend will accelerate beyond 4 percent.

The Economic Recovery Tax Act of 1981, which was proposed by the Reagan administration and passed by the Congress, provides a number of incentives related to capital formation and productivity that should, according to the supply-siders, dramatically increase real output. For example, marginal tax rates will be reduced 25 percent by 1983, and starting in 1984 individual income tax brackets will be indexed to mitigate the effect of pushing taxpayers into higher tax brackets. Both of these changes should have a significant impact on productivity. Productivity should rise because total output in the private sector will go up by more than the increase in labor hours—reflecting the incentives for increased work effort, less absenteeism, the induced higher rate of saving and capital formation, and the associated higher level of economic activity.

Four other provisions of the 1981 tax bill are important for their positive effects on real output: (1) The acceleration of capital cost recovery allowance will reduce the cost of capital services and lead to an increase in investment and more rapid growth in the capital-labor ratio, more rapid replacement of old plant and equipment, and possibly an additional boost from the increased scale of operations. More rapid replacement of plant and equipment will make it possible for firms to incorporate the latest advances in technology that are important for accelerating productivity improvement. (2) Enhancement of the investment tax-credit will further reduce the cost of capital services. (3) Liberalization of leasing provisions in the tax code will help firms with little or no taxable income to better utilize the increased tax write-offs provided in the tax bill. (4) The tax credit for certain research and development expenditures should stimulate a more rapid rate of innovation.

If, in fact, supply-side tax incentives produce real output growth of approximately 5 percent, econometric estimates indicate a corresponding velocity trend growth of 5.6 percent in 1982-IV and 6 percent in 1984-IV.

Monetarists might still argue that the predicted downward movement in interest rates induced by the administration's restrictive monetary policy will have a depressing effect on velocity. Theory suggests that high interest rates attract individuals and businesses away from holding money and into securities and other real assets, causing the demand for money to fall and velocity to rise. Alternatively, a decline in interest rates should lead to an increase in the demand for money and lower velocity. Therefore, as the government's restrictive monetary policy is expected to reduce inflation from 9 percent to 4.9 percent by 1986, the inflationary component of nominal interest rates is expected to decline and thus produce an increase in the demand for money that will lower velocity.

Supply-siders respond to this argument by pointing out that insofar as money demand is a function of the interest rate, the appropriate rate to use is the interest rate after tax. This is because the decision to allocate wealth between money and assets that yield a return depends upon the return actually received from those assets; that is, the return after tax. Moreover, the appropriate tax rate is the marginal rate, since the marginal after-tax return will determine whether the marginal dollar is held or used to buy assets. Statistical studies verify the relative importance of after-tax interest rates for explaining changes in velocity.[15] The significance of after-tax interest rates is that because the supply-side economic policy calls for a reduction of marginal income tax rates, the after-tax interest rate may rise rather than fall and velocity will not be subject to downward pressure.

Therefore, there is a considerable amount of empirical evidence that lends support to the supply-side view that a restrictive monetary policy need not constrain economic growth. For, a strong case can be made that the current trend rate of growth in velocity is significantly greater than the 3.2 percent subscribed to by the monetarists and that velocity is influenced positively by real output growth and after-tax interest rates.

## A Reconciliation?

Monetarism and supply-side economics do not contain irreconcilable differences. Both schools of thought believe that money matters, especially in determining the price level. They agree that monetary discipline is the proper policy for restoring price stability to the marketplace. Treasury supply-siders and monetarists are in accord with the concept that Federal Reserve management of the monetary aggregates (use of a quantity rule) is the most feasible means of maintaining the stability of prices. A gradual deceleration of the growth rate in the money supply to a rate consistent with productivity growth is believed to be the correct approach.

While other supply-siders also agree that monetary discipline is the key to a stable economy, they seek return to a gold standard as the means to regulate the money supply. The dollar would be defined in terms of a fixed quantity of gold that would in turn be determined by gold's market value at some specific date. Such a policy would establish an automatic rule requiring the quantity of money to be tied to the country's gold supply. Gold standard supply-siders see a major conflict between their views and those held by monetarists. They assert that monetarism is destabilizing because the policy tools employed by monetarists cause prices to move in the opposite direction from the quantity of money. But this position falls outside the mainstream of economic thought and is not shared by supply-siders holding policy-making positions in the government.

Supply-siders and monetarists do not disagree over the theoretical structure of the macroeconomy. They agree that the demand for money is influenced by the same independent variables, and they agree on the directional influence of these variables. Those differences that do arise between the two schools are empirical in nature. In fact, at the center of attention among supply-siders and monetarists in the Reagan administration is the issue of velocity of money. As pointed out above, monetarists insist that the long-run trend in velocity is highly stable and that its growth rate is about 3.2 percent annually. Therefore, any growth in real output that results from greater supply incentives is ultimately constrained by the quantity of money and the almost constant rate at which it turns over. Supply-siders emphasize the basic consistencies between their views and those of monetarists and believe that the empirical evidence solidly supports a theory of flexible velocity growth.

## Notes

1. A thorough discussion of the weaknesses in Keynesian macroeconomic policy can be found in Paul Craig Roberts, "The Breakdown of the Keynesian Model," *The Public Interest* no. 52 (Summer 1978): 20-33; Martin Feldstein, "The Retreat from Keynesian Economics," *The Public Interest* no. 64 (Summer 1981): 92-105; and Paul Craig Roberts, "For Supply-Siders, the Focus is Incentives," *The Washington Post*, April 13, 1981.

2. The most often cited article on the design of monetarists' economic policy is Milton Friedman, "The Role of Monetary Policy," *American Economic Review* 58 (March 1968): 1-21.

3. A comparison of supply-side and Keynesian analysis of the effects of tax changes is available in Norman B. Turé, "The Economic Effects of Tax Changes: A Neoclassical Analysis," in U.S. Congress, Joint Economic Committee, *Special Study on Economic Change, Vol. 4: Stagflation: The Causes, Effects, and Solutions*, December 17, 1980, pp. 316-347.

4. For a statement of the Reagan administration's economic assumptions and objectives, see *America's New Beginning: A Program for Economic Recovery*, The

White House, Office of the Press Secretary, February 18, 1981.

5. A discussion of lags in the effect of money supply changes on prices and output can be found in Milton Friedman and Anna Schwartz, *A Monetary History of the United States, 1867-1960* (Princeton, N.J.: Princeton University Press, 1963); and Milton Friedman, *The Optimum Quantity of Money and Other Essays* (Chicago: Aldine Publishing Co., 1969).

6. Reagan administration money growth targets are not published; however, accurate estimates can be obtained from the testimony of David Stockman before U.S. Congress, House Committee on the Budget, March 26, 1981, p. 9: ". . . during the past four years, the growth of M1-B, the basic money supply measure, has averaged nearly 8 percent. Over the next five years, however, the administration expects the rate of money growth to decline by approximately one-half."

7. Arthur B. Laffer, *The Monetary Crisis: A Classical Perspective.* (Rolling Hills Estates, Calif: A.B. Laffer Associates, 1980), p. 6.

8. A memorandum prepared for Beryl Sprinkel, undersecretary of the treasury for monetary affairs, on the velocity of money dated September 16, 1981, states that, "Despite . . . substantial changes in the structure of the economy and the monetary system, the trend of velocity has been quite stable. Since 1951, velocity has increased at a trend rate of about 3.2 percent per year."

9. Much of the literature dealing with the stability of the demand for money is summarized in David E. Laidler, *The Demand for Money: Theories and Evidence,* 2nd ed. (Scranton, Pa: International Textbook Co., 1977).

10. Empirical studies of the demand of money that show instability since the early 1970s are: J. Enzler, L. Johnson, and J. Paulus, "Some Problems of Money Demand," *Brookings Papers on Economic Activity,* no. 1 (1976); S.M. Goldfeld, "The Case of the Missing Money," *Brookings Papers on Economic Activity,* no. 3 (1976); and David Laidler, "The Demand for Money in the United States—Yet Again," *Carnegie-Rochester Series on Public Policy* (Spring 1980), pp. 219-271.

11. *See* for example J.P. Gould and C.R. Nelson, "The Stochastic Structure of the Velocity of Money," *American Economic Review* 64 (June 1974): 405-18.

12. Ninety-five percent confidence intervals for variations in velocity were determined using both quarterly and annual data on M1-B velocity over the period 1956 to 1981. M1 velocity data were used to complete the time series prior to 1959. Time trend regressions were computed using log differences of M1-B velocity.

13. The regression reported below was an attempt to capture the relationship between velocity and output:

$$V = 0.935 + 0.680 \text{ GNP} \qquad R^2 = 0.50$$
$$\quad (2.15) \quad (9.58) \qquad\qquad \text{D-W} = 1.91$$

The dependent and independent variables, V and GNP, are the annualized quarterly changes in the logs of M1-B velocity and real GNP, respectively, for the period 1956-I to 1981-I (annualized quarterly log changes closely approximate quarterly percent changes at an annual rate). T-statistics are in parenthesis below each coefficient. The equation proceeds on the assumption that a simple regression of velocity on GNP will average out random fluctuations in velocity and the influences of other variables on velocity, and hence should pick up the influence of GNP trends on velocity trends.

14. The following two regressions were performed to estimate the stability of trend velocity over the period 1956 to 1981:

(1) $V = 1.498 + 0.613 \text{ GNP} - 1.863 D1, \qquad R^2 = 0.51$
$\quad\quad (4.09) \quad (9.56) \qquad\qquad (-3.02) \qquad\quad \text{D-W} = 1.68$

(2) $V = 1.041 + 0.625 \text{ GNP} - 1.447 D1 + 0.931 D2, \qquad R^2 = 0.52$
$\quad\quad (2.21) \quad (9.75) \qquad (-2.16) \qquad (1.63) \qquad\quad \text{D-W} = 1.71$

where,

V = percent change in M1-B velocity, that is, percent change in GNP divided by M1-B. M1-B is spliced with old M1 before 1959.

GNP = percent change in real GNP.

D1 = dummy variable, 1 in 1967-I to 1972-IV, 0 otherwise.

D2 = dummy variable, 1 in 1973-I to 1981-II, 0 otherwise.

Equation 1 shows M1-B velocity growth regressed upon real GNP growth and a dummy for a second subperiod 1967-1972. The dummy is clearly significant, showing a marked difference in trend growth apart from the influences of real GNP between the middle subperiod and the first and third subperiods.

Equation 2 adds a separate dummy for the third subperiod. The dummy for the second subperiod is still significant, although less so than before. The dummy for the last subperiod has a low t-ratio, but it is significant at the 10 percent level in a test against the alternative that the coefficient is strictly positive. It is of course difficult to measure shifts in trends over relatively short time periods, since so many factors affect velocity. Therefore the high standard error on this dummy probably indicates not that there is no shift, but rather that there is so much noise in the data that the shift cannot be measured very precisely. It should be noted that a test of the hypothesis that both dummies have zero coefficients based on this regression leads to rejection of the hypotheses at the 1 percent level.

15. *See* for example Vito Tanzi, "Demand for Money, Interest Rates and Income Taxation," *Banca Nazionale Del Lavoro* (December 1974), pp. 3-12.

## FIGURE 1
## INFLATION AND UNEMPLOMENT RATES

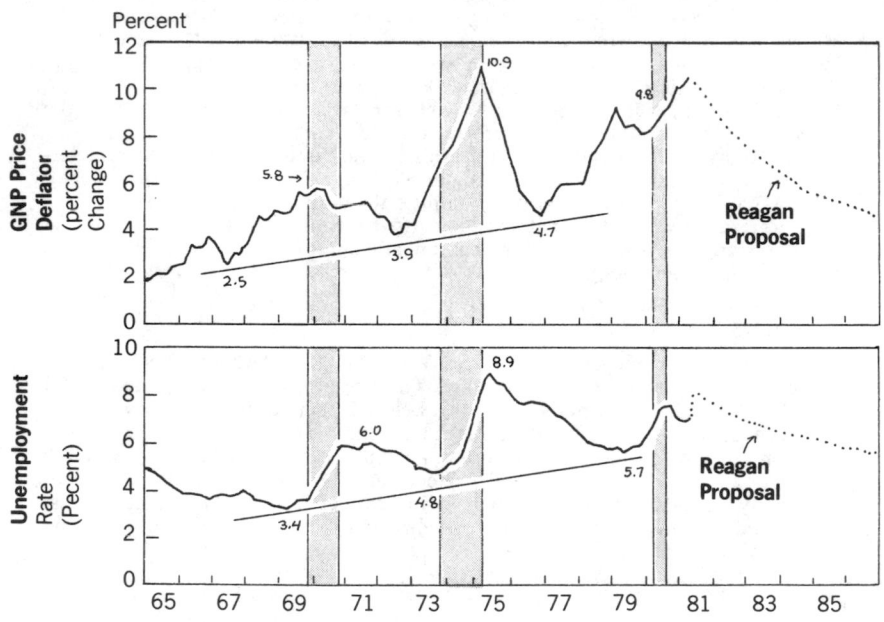

Source: U.S. Department of Treasury, Office of Economic Policy

## TABLE I
### ACTUAL AND FORECASTED GROWTH RATES IN SELECTED ECO-NOMIC VARIABLES
### 1980 -1986
(Percent change, year over year)

| | Administration's Forecast | | | |
| --- | --- | --- | --- | --- |
| Year | %ΔM (money supply M1-B) | %ΔV (velocity) | %ΔP (GNP deflator) | %ΔQ (Real Gross National product) |
| 1980 | 6.4 | 2.5 | 9.0 | -0.1 |
| 1981 | 5.9 | 6.3 | 9.6 | 2.6 |
| 1982 | 5.4 | 6.0 | 8.0 | 3.4 |
| 1983 | 4.9 | 7.1 | 7.0 | 5.0 |
| 1984 | 4.4 | 6.1 | 6.0 | 4.5 |
| 1985 | 3.9 | 5.7 | 5.4 | 4.2 |
| 1986 | 3.4 | 5.7 | 4.9 | 4.2 |

NOTE: The money growth rate figures are based upon the administration's economic scenario which "assumes that the growth rates of money and credit are steadily reduced from the 1980 levels to one-half of those levels by 1986." (See *A Program for Economic Recovery,* February 18, 1981, p. II-23.) All other figures come from the *Mid-Session Review of the 1982 Budget,* Office of Management and Budget.

# Monetary Aspects of Supply-Side Economics

## William P. Orzechowski

Proponents of supply-side economics suggest that the reduction of both tax rates and inefficient government expenditures will have a positive effect upon the operation of economic incentive. However, the incentive effects of supply-side policy are inextricably related to monetary policy as well. In what follows, an attempt is made to explain the interaction of monetary and fiscal policy from a supply-side perspective. The first section discusses the importance of a relatively tight monetary policy for supply-side economics. The remaining sections focus upon the issue of supply-side tax cuts and budget deficits.[1]

### A. Monetary Policy and Relative Price

Monetary policy is important for the development of supply-side policy because of the relationship between inflation and the money supply. In this regard, most supply-side theorists accept the major principles of the monetarist approach to aggregate demand. Consequently, changes in the absolute price level are, generally, considered to be caused by monetary factors. The problem of inflation is thus related to the political system's ability to control the money supply.

An inflationary or unstable monetary policy is unfavorable to the implementation of supply-side policies because of adverse effects upon relative prices and incentives. There are three major reasons for this.

First, an inflationary monetary policy will ultimately entail higher effective tax rates. This can happen in a number of ways. The most notable cases are, "bracket creep"—which is caused by the interaction of the progressive personal income tax code and inflation—improper evaluation of depreciation allowances due to historical cost accounting procedures, and overstatement of capital gains, which is due to the reporting of illusory profits. All of these effects tend to counteract the tendency for tax cuts to create incentives for work, savings, and investments. Secondly, an inflationary monetary policy can affect relative prices through the creation of inflationary expectations among the public at large. This occurs because unanticipated inflation reduces the returns from saving, for example, below what individuals had expected. Individuals then develop unfavorable expectations about future returns from saving, which causes the substitution of present consumption for saving, thereby reducing the funds available for investment. Third, the instability of monetary policy can bring on price and interest rate volatility, causing greater uncertainty in the marketplace and increasing the risk of relying on relative price signals for accurate information on the value and use of various economic resources.

Because of the adverse effects inflation has upon the reliability of relative prices, most proponents of supply-side economics advocate monetary restraint and stability. Yet, the advocacy of relatively tight monetary policies in conjunction with tax cuts inevitably turns attention to the interaction of monetary and fiscal policy. Especially at issue is the creation of deficits and their impact upon interest rates. An analysis of this problem is not only important in itself but also aids in distinguishing the supply-side position from standard macroeconomic treatments of this issue.

## B. Monetary Restraint and Tax Cuts

A deficit can emerge because of an asymmetrical trim of the budget, which can in turn occur if legislated tax cuts exceed the amount of expenditure reduction. Since monetary restraint is part of a consistent supply-side strategy, supply-siders shrink from "monetizing" deficits, and any deficit emerging from an asymmetrical budget trim would therefore lead to an increase in the government's demand for new credit—an action which may "crowd out" private investment in the competition for funds in capital markets. A critical question emerges: Will the incentive stimulus provided by tax reduction be offset by interest rate pressures in the bond markets? In order to resolve this issue, a brief review of some conventional views is in order. This will help to distinguish the supply-side approach to the problem.

In some of the earlier Keynesian models, capital markets did not impose constraints upon aggregate demand. This is because of assumptions regarding the elasticity or availability of financial resources.[2] The argument was framed in terms of the so-called liquidity preference schedule. Under certain conditions, an extremely elastic source of idle balances is presumed to exist, which would accommodate any increase in the demand for credit. Consequently, an unmonetized expansion of the budget deficit entailed little, if any, "crowding out" of private investment. The real interest rate would remain the same, and the expenditure multiplier would generate its full impact upon the economy. In this view, a budget deficit was perceived as a useful means to stimulate the economy.

The short-run monetarist approach to aggregate demand severely criticized this argument. The monetarists held that the principle of elastic finance was an unrealistic assumption, and they substituted a sort of "constant-sum" view of financial resources. Any attempt to draw upon a part of this financial pool would necessarily eliminate— "crowd out"—an equivalent amount of alternative investment. In this case, an unbalanced tax cut would increase the government's demand for credit by the amount not covered by additional savings. Since, by assumption, there are few "idle" balances available, the interest rate will rise to a point that chokes off an equivalent amount of private investment. For example, if taxes are reduced by $10 billion and the marginal propensity to consume is 80 percent, then $2 billion of new savings is available to finance the newly emerging deficit of $10 billion. This means that the government must raise $8 billion in capital markets, an action which "crowds out" an equivalent amount of investment through rising interest rates.

Between these two extremes is an intermediate or "partial crowding-out" model. Here it is assumed that the elasticity of liquidity preference is neither as much as in the earlier Keynesian models nor as little as in the extreme monetarist version. In this case, the government's demand for credit in excess of new savings can be met, in part, by the activation of "idle" balances. Consequently the interest rises, but not as much as in the previous case (zero liquid balances). Therefore, a smaller portion of private investment is "crowded out."

Each of these models attempts to assess the effects of an unmonetized budget deficit through its short-run impact on savings and investment. In their evaluation of supply-side policy, many critics have relied upon the "crowding-out" models to discredit supply-side economics. These models assume that savings is primarily determined by *income* and that investment is mostly a function of the *interest rate*. Consequently, an unbalanced tax cut could not possibly generate enough savings to finance the emerging deficit. Instead, the interest rate will rise and investment will fall.

## C. Deficits, Tax Cuts, and Supply-Side Economics

### Relative Price

A supply-side analysis treats the problem in a different context. The first order effect of a tax cut and monetary restraint is related to relative prices as opposed to income and aggregate demand effects. This constitutes an important shift of emphasis because the volume of real credit is thereby related to decisions which involve long-run expectations and the economic trade-off between future and present consumption.

Crucial to this analysis is the analytical distinction between credit, money, and savings. In supply-side economics, the ultimate basis for real credit is savings—savings being defined as the amount of current income set aside for the ultimate purpose of producing future goods. Therefore, real credit is, generally, synonymous with the willingness of individuals to refrain from current consumption. This decision process involves the calculation of a rate of return in a long-run planning horizon—an assessment which is favorably affected by both lower tax rates and reduced inflationary expectations.

By contrast, the crowding-out models make it appear as if real credit is synonymous with income and money flows. It does not view the credit problem from the relative price perspective. Therefore, a policy that reduces short-run liquidity must ultimately doom credit markets. This occurs in spite of the fact that such a policy (tax reduction) creates an incentive structure compatible with a rising secular savings rate. The weakness of the crowding-out argument is even more apparent when it is used by those who often abuse it as a rationale to justify money expansion as a means to increase credit. In this case, the resultant inflation reduces real returns to savings through anticipated inflation and "bracket creep." As a consequence, the secular savings rate falls, diminishing long-run investment.

Because of its emphasis upon relative price, supply-side analysis accents the beneficial effects of monetary stability and tax cuts on the secular behavior of savings and investment. It argues that a reversal of our stagnating investment and savings rates can only be accomplished by increasing the returns to both. Therefore, crowding out is seen as an unavoidable adjustment problem within a more favorable long-run perspective.

In the case of savings, a supply-side analysis argues that a tax reduction not only increases disposable income but, more importantly, that it changes the composition of total spending toward saving. Tax reduction raises the price of current consumption relative to future income, thereby generating greater savings making it possible for growth in real investment. Monetary stability has the same effect by reducing unanticipated inflation and increasing the real return to saving. Because the conventional approach does not emphasize these effects, it seriously underestimates the long-run influence of monetary restraint and tax cuts upon savings.

The conventional approach is also likely to overestimate the negative repercussions of budget deficits upon investments. This is because the most widely used models assume that investment is strongly related to the interest rate but weakly related to tax rates. Consequently, short-run conditions in financial markets dominate the investment decision. For example, two of the large-scale econometric models show declines of GNP as a result of reduction in corporate tax rates.[3] In these models the interest rate rises as the Treasury increases its borrowing to finance the deficit resulting from the tax cut. Consequently, investment falls in spite of the fact that tax reduction increased the overall profitability of investment.

In contrast, a supply-side analysis accents the favorable consequences of tax reduction upon profit opportunities. This occurs for three reasons. First, a major part of investment behavior is conjectured to be contingent upon the development of new enterprise, invention and other entrepreneurial elements—decisions which are mostly determined by long-run payoffs. Therefore, while initial interest rate pressure may have a negative influence upon investment decisions in the short run, it will have increasingly less importance in the long run. Second, interest rate pressures on investment are likely to be of less significance in the long run as the secular savings rate begins to accelerate. Third, the relative marginal intensities associated with tax cuts and crowding out, in the net, are likely to be favorable to investment because current tax rates are at historically high levels but *real* borrowing costs, over the past decade, have been relatively low. As a consequence, the marginal relief provided to business by tax cuts will be greater than the marginal damage to profit caused by crowding out.

These analytical distinctions can be seen in light of contemporary events. Over the past decade, aggregate demand and nominal disposable income have increased substantially. According to conventional analysis, which accents the dependency of savings upon income, savings should have risen in tandem with these trends. However, the savings rate actually fell over this period. In fact, the savings rate was substantially below the postwar rate by as much as 30 percent.[4]

Over this same period real borrowing costs had fallen largely because of unanticipated inflation. In fact, there is evidence that real after tax borrowing costs have been negative by as much as 3 percent at times in recent years.[5] According to conventional analysis, investment should have boomed because of the dependence of investment on the real interest rate. Yet, investment in plant and equipment fell by almost 40 percent.[6]

The apparent paradox of falling savings and investment rates in spite of rising income and falling real interest rates is puzzling within the expenditures-income framework. However, it is easily explained by the supply-side hypothesis which focuses upon relative prices. Savings rates fell because the return to savings was seriously eroded by "bracket creep," reporting of fictitious capital gains, and unanticipated inflation. The actual damage inflicted upon the returns to savings is shown in Table 1.[7] Those statistics indicate that for income brackets above $20,000, rates of return have been negative and will likely remain negative in spite of the recent tax changes.

On the investment side, even though real borrowing costs fell, active investors (principals) were detered because of rising tax rates. In this regard, the National Bureau of Economic Research estimates that the effective business tax rate over this period rose by almost 25 percent.

This sharp rise in the effective tax rate is the principal reason why the real after-tax return from corporate investment dropped from 5.3 percent in the late 1960s to 2.6 percent in recent years, in spite of a falling real interest rate.[8]

In summary, supply-side economics hypothesizes that tax cuts and monetary stability will elicit a much greater savings and investment response in the long run than do conventional models. This occurs because the secular behavior of savings and investment is directly related to relative prices. In this context savings is not merely limited to changes in disposable income, nor is investment constrained by changes in the interest rate. As a consequence, "crowding out" is seen as part of a short-run adjustment process that will eventually diminish.

## TABLE 1
Real, After-Tax Return on Savings with 8.5% Inflation, 12% Interest Rates, and the Proposed Tax Changes

| Taxable Income Bracket (1) | Present (2) | 1981 (3) | 1982 (4) | 1983 (5) | 1984 (6) |
|---|---|---|---|---|---|
| $ 0    -3,400 | 0% | 0% | 0% | 0% | 0% |
| 3,400 -5,500 | 1.8 | 1.9 | 2.1 | 2.1 | 2.2 |
| 5,500 -7,600 | 1.6 | 1.7 | 1.7 | 1.8 | 1.9 |
| 7,600 -11,900 | 1.3 | 1.5 | 1.7 | 1.6 | 1.7 |
| 11,900 -16,000 | 1.0 | 1.1 | 1.0 | 1.2 | 1.3 |
| 16,000 -20,200 | 0.6 | 0.7 | 0.6 | 0.9 | 0.7 |
| 20,200 -24,600 | 0.1 | 0.3 | 0.3 | 0.6 | 0.3 |
| 24,600 -29,900 | -0.3 | -0.1 | -0.2 | 0.1 | -0.3 |
| 29,900 -35,200 | -0.9 | -1.4 | 0.0 | -0.5 | -0.3 |
| 35,200 -45,800 | -1.7 | -1.4 | -1.5 | -1.1 | -0.8 |
| 45,800 -60,000 | -2.4 | -2.1 | -2.1 | -1.5 | -1.3 |
| 60,000 -85,600 | -3.0 | -2.6 | -2.5 | -1.9 | -1.7 |
| 85,600 -109,400 | -3.6 | -3.2 | -3.1 | -2.4 | -2.1 |
| 109,400 -162,400 | -4.2 | -3.8 | -3.1 | -2.7 | -2.4 |
| 162,400 -215,400 | -4.7 | -4.3 | -3.7 | -2.9 | -2.5 |
| 215,400 and over | -4.9 | -4.4 | -3.7 | -2.9 | -2.5 |

Source: Gary M. Wenglowski and Susanne M. Cahn, "Will the Reagan Economic Program Work?" *Chartroom* (New York: Goldman Sachs Economics, 1980).

### The Adjustment Process
The foregoing analysis shows that much of the controversy surrounding the financial implications of tax cuts hinges on time period assumptions. Since the relative price effects of policy are of a long-run nature, the supply-side scenario of greater investment and economic growth becomes stronger only with the passage of time.

In the short run a variety of lags can indeed delay the supply-side effects of monetary restraint and tax cuts. Some of these lags are well known especially with monetary policy. These lags are associated with the delay of tight monetary policy in reducing actual inflation and reducing inflationary expectations. They can postpone the downward adjustment of nominal interest rates if, for example, individuals feel that the Federal Reserve will re accelerate monetary growth. Consequently, nominal interest rates may not fall in the presence of monetary restraint until individuals can be assured of a long-run commitment to an anti inflation policy.

Lags can also exist in the interpretation and transmission of tax policy. First, there are difficulties of interpretation due to technical complexities. This is especially true for the business tax cut which can involve elaborate sales-leaseback arrangements. Secondly, many of the tax cuts are phased-in over a span of three years. As a consequence, both savers and investors may postpone their actions until they can take full advantage of the complete tax cut. Third, although relative price changes are expected to alter individual behavior, it is reasonable to expect that individuals will not suddenly become thrifty and develop sanguine expectations in the span of a few business quarters. This is especially true in view of the political system's inability to resist a change in policy in the face of short-run adversity, a prime example of this being the contemporary movement for a repeal of the Reagan tax cut through "revenue enhancement." Consequently, a credibility lag will exist until individuals are assured of a commitment to the original policy.

Because of these lags, savings and investment responses are not likely to be overwhelming in the immediate short run. This, coupled with the increased demand for credit by the government, can create short-run "crowding out" with the attendant uncertainty in financial markets. It is in this critical phase that serious doubts can arise about supply-side policy. However, this does not imply that the theory is flawed but may rather indicate that further application of supply-side policy is in order. There are two reasons why this may be the case.

First, the bottleneck in financial markets could be interpreted as part of the short-run adjustment problem outlined above, in which case maintenance of the original policy of tax cuts and monetary stability will eventually be transmitted to the economy and supply-side effects will begin to take hold. Once again, the time period is crucial as policymakers must come to realize that raising supply is a much more difficult process than increasing demand. The former depends on a long-run adjustment of the incentive system while the latter can be accomplished with a mere turn of the "printing press."

Second, if the financial bottleneck continues to stem supply-side effects, this in itself does not imply that tax cuts do not affect incentive but instead may indicate that the continuing high level of government expenditures is the ultimate source of the problem. In order to make a supply-side tax cut more effective, in this second case, government expenditures would have to be reduced. In this regard it must be recalled that the original supply-side proposition was that tax cuts could stimulate incentive *even though* government expenditures remained constant. In fact, the Reagan economic program combines an initially weak tax cut with a substantial increase in the absolute volume of government expenditure. The tax cut is initially weak because it is phased in over a number of years and therefore subject to "bracket creep" and lagged economic response. More importantly, the Reagan administration has only halted the growth rate of government expenditure: it has not reduced the absolute growth. Consequently the effects of the program may be muffled—not due to the failure of supply-side economics—but because of an inability to effectively apply the theory in its initial stage.

### Financial Markets and the Efficiency of Saving

The analysis above has focused upon the total volume of savings and investment. The thrust of the argument has been that supply-side policy will eventually reverse the falling secular trend of savings and investment. However, an equally important concern is not only the growth of savings and investment but their efficient allocation. Viewed from this perspective, a large part of the financial market's problems can be related to the present misallocation of financial resources along the market spectrum. Once this problem is recognized, it becomes evident that there exists a substantial source of funds available to generate growth providing the causes of misallocation are removed. Thus, deficits may not necessarily mean less funds for investment after all.

The allocation or efficiency of savings is directly related to the flexibility of financial markets—that is, to the ability of lenders and borrowers to shift along a time spectrum of credit instruments in times of inflation and uncertainty. This spectrum enables individuals to hedge against monetary instability by trading in the short-term end of the financial spectrum, thereby making it possible for lenders to minimize the effects of unanticipated inflation and "bracket creep." This explains why money-market certificates are now favored by savers. They no longer want to lock themselves into stocks and bonds which are quite sensitive to asset depreciation through inflation and "bracket-creep." It is obvious that at present a relative shift of savings toward the short end of the financial spectrum has occurred.

The shift into short-term credit instruments, however, has negative repercussions for economic growth because active investors (principals) are forced to borrow "short." Thus it becomes more difficult for firms to issue long-term credit in the form of stocks and bonds. They are, in effect, forced to use relatively large amounts of short-term credit such as commerical paper. This especially creates problems in the development plans of newer firms because initial outlays are largely dependent upon equity and bonded capital. Thus, inflation shifts both the quality and nature of investment. It disrupts newer, more dynamic entrepreneurial investment and confines funding to the maintenance of the status quo.

Aside from its negative impact on younger firms, the short-term credit phenomena biases the entire societal capital structure against private sector industrial ventures. For example, some $160 billion is now invested in money market funds, implying that the economy is fairly liquid. This means that there are ample financial resources available for investment in stocks and bonds but that they are being diverted elsewhere. The problem is not a lack of liquidity but more accurately a misallocation of financial resources in short-term finance.

The shift of capital away from stocks and bonds as a result of inflationary fears and uncertainties can also occur with tangible assets such as houses, land, or gold. A sharp increase of the inflation rate means an increase in the yield of tangible assets relative to paper assets.[9] As a consequence of the tax laws and the rapid inflation of the seventies many individuals allocated a larger percentage of their savings for the purchase of tangible assets—stock and bond markets crumbled in the midst of a housing boom. These effects are shown in Table 2 which illustrates the sensitivity of tangible assets to the financial asset ratio in response to greater inflation. However, lower inflation implies the opposite. In fact, some analyses have suggested that each percentage point drop in the inflation rate eventually sends $100 billion in tangible assets people hold back into the financial markets as increased credit supplies.[10]

## TABLE 2

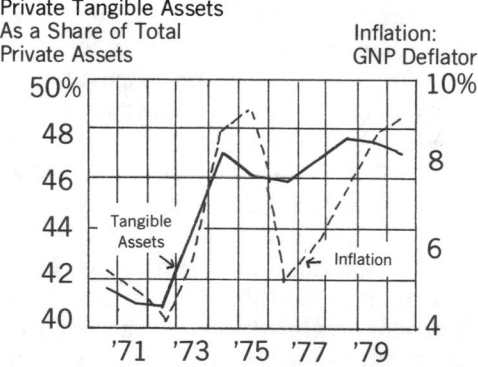

Source: Federal Reserve Flow of Funds Accounts

In order to correct the imbalance that exists in credit markets, confidence and favorable long-run expectations have to be restored. This seems to be a likely outcome of a policy of monetary restraint and decreasing taxes. Monetary stability means less unanticipated inflation and tax cuts mean improved long-run profit conditions. As these policies materialize, the shift from tangible and liquid assets to stocks and bonds should accelerate. Consequently, a supply-side tax cut need not entail a long-run "crowding out" of financial resources for private investment. It is, rather, the main catalyst for the eventual shift of a relatively large pool of capital into stocks and bonds.

From this perspective, policies such as money creation and tax increases in the hope of increasing liquidity and balancing the budget would have negative consequences for growth. By accelerating inflation the former would lead to both a reduction in the volume and efficiency of saving. Similarly, increased taxation would decrease the return from saving relative to consumption and simply aggravate the disinclination to save. The implication is clear: an inability on the part of policymakers to maintain monetary restraint as well as tax cuts will doom "Reagonomics."[11]

## D. Budget Deficits: Conservatives, Monetarists and Supply-Siders

Supply-side economics is seen as an unorthodox approach to economic policy by those who consider balanced budgets a prerequisite for sound economic policy. In order to illustrate the role of balanced budget philosophy for economic policy, a comparison of alternative viewpoints is in order. Toward this end, we will examine the "fiscal conservative" and monetarist positions.

The fiscal conservatives or, "budget balancers," generally direct attention to the alarming growth rate and size of government expenditures. They contend that reducing government expenditures is of primary importance for a healthy economy and that a balanced budget contains curative powers for the economy. As a consequence, they argue that tax reduction must never exceed expenditure reduction, or the imminent budget deficit will lead to higher interest rates, less investment, and lower growth. Ironically, this approach is also trumpeted by former "budget busters" or easy-spending liberals. Their endorsement emerges for other reasons, however. They advocate budget balancing because they fear that tax reduction will eventually entail reductions in government expenditure through loss of tax revenues. They support a balanced budget as a means to preserve the growth and size of government expenditures. So the new "budget balancers" are a curious blend of both conservatives and liberals. Both Bob Dole and Tip O'Neill find themselves part of the same tenuous alliance.

Monetarists object to supply-side tax cuts because they fear that a significant lag will exist before the policy induces economic growth and that initial budget deficits will cause policymakers to demand easier credit conditions, giving rise to monetary excess and inflation.

The supply-side position contains elements of both positions. It agrees with the "real" fiscal conservatives that most any cut in the size of government expenditures will be beneficial to economic growth. It likewise endorses the relatively tight money policies of the monetarists as the basic corrective for inflation and its attendant ills. The basic disagreement between supply-side economics and these approaches is that supply-side economics does not portray budget deficits as inconsistent with economic growth and low inflation.

It differs from the fiscal conservative position because it sees beneficial results not only from cuts in government expenditure but also from reduced taxation. Tax reduction increases the volume and efficiency of savings, thereby providing the funds for investment. Supply-siders fear that an adherence to a balanced budget rule will effectively block any kind of meaningful tax reform because, then, tax reduction would be based on previous government expenditures. But it is often politically unpopular to cut government expenditures, so supply-siders argue that tax reform would be stymied. In essence, a balanced budget philosophy would play into the hands of the liberal spenders who want to preserve or expand the role of the federal government in economic affairs. Worse yet, tax increases would give politicians a false sense of fiscal responsibility, prompting them to reduce their efforts at controlling the budget.

On the other hand, most supply-siders differ from the monetarist position in that they do not see a necessary connection between budget deficits and inflation. Inflation is considered to be a monetary phenomenon that can be controlled through adherence to responsible monetary policy. However, it should be mentioned that certain supply-side economists, including Arthur Laffer, are sympathetic with some of the fears shared by monetarists with respect to the ability of the political system to control monetary growth. As a consequence, they argue for a return to the gold standard, a policy which they feel will ensure monetary restraint and quickly drop the interest premiums associated with inflationary expectations which tend to retard the adjustment of nominal interest rates downward.

Unlike some of the monetarists, however, supply-siders do not endorse tax increases to close the deficit. This would threaten economic growth and make it extremely difficult to balance the budget over the long run.

Although it is difficult to reconcile these diverse positions using empirical evidence, Table 3 provides data that suggest that the "unorthodox" supply-side approach is consistent with recent experience. These data suggest that budget deficits are compatible with economic growth and low inflation—that there is no obvious link between budget deficits and inflation. During the period covered (1977-1979) average deficits and inflation were *not* positively correlated.[12] Inflation was high, for example, in countries with small deficits (Brazil, France, Yugoslavia). Yet it was low in countries in each of the higher deficit categories (Singapore, Switzerland and Austria).

In stark contrast, monetary growth explains relative inflation rates reasonably well. And yet, it does not appear even roughly related to budget deficits. Consequently, monetary policy can be separated from fiscal policy. That is, budget deficits need not necessarily lead to money creation and inflation.

Likewise, budget deficits and slow monetary growth do not necessarily mean crowding out of private investment as the "fiscal conservatives" allege.

### TABLE 3
#### Government Budgets, Money, and Inflation

|  | 1977-79 Budget Deficit (-) or Surplus as % of Outlays: | 1977-80 Annual Growth of Money Supply (M1) | 1977-80 Annual Consumer Price Inflation |
|---|---|---|---|
| Kuwait | 84.7% | 20.0% | 7.5% |
| Colombia | 5.5 | 28.5 | 25.5 |
| Singapore | 3.9 | 11.7 | 5.2 |
| Switzerland | -2.1 | 5.0 | 2.5 |
| Brazil | -3.2 | 50.9 | 54.5 |
| France | -3.3 | 9.8 | 10.6 |
| Yugoslavia | -4.1 | 23.4 | 19.9 |
| Netherlands | -6.9 | 6.7 | 5.3 |
| Germany | -7.0 | 4.0 | 4.0 |
| Austria | -10.4 | 3.5 | 4.8 |
| U.S. | -10.8 | 7.4 | 9.7 |
| U.K. | -11.7 | 12.6 | 13.9 |
| Belgium | -14.3 | 4.6 | 5.7 |
| Japan | -32.0 | 7.1 | 5.9 |

Source: International Monetary Fund

This has been the policy mix of countries toward the bottom of the table, such as Austria, Germany, and Japan. These countries have had relatively large deficits, tight money, and moderate taxation. Most importantly, they have had relatively large growth rates.

In summary, supply-side analysis suggests that a balanced budget rule is not a cure-all for a defective economy. Its most suitable applications would be for a health economy as a safeguard against a wasteful explosion of public expenditures. To the extent that it is used to raise taxes on an already beleaguered economy, the results of budget balancing could be devastating. As one analyst has remarked, it would be possible to initially balance the budget by doubling the corporate tax rate or by confiscating all yearly income above $50,000. In practice, either of these actions would probably destroy the economy.[13] The implication is clear—to the extent that the balanced budget criterion is used to block tax reform—poor economic growth will inevitably persist.

## Notes

1. This discussion treats the issue of budget deficits in the context of problems that arise in the financial markets. Some supply-siders tend to minimize the deficit problem with assumptions of rapid economic growth. The problem with such assumptions is that they ignore all of the important short-run adjustment problems.

2. This is not to imply that supply-siders also use this argument to minimize the problem of "crowding out."

3. *See* Paul Craig Roberts, "The Breakdown of the Keynesian Model," *The Public Interest* no. 52 (Summer 1978).

4. Owen F. Humpage, "Why Government Budgets Ballooned," *Economic Impact*, no. 36 (U.S. International Communication Agency, 1981/4).

5. "Interesting Interest Rates," *Wall Street Journal*, October 18, 1981, Editorial.

6. Martin Feldstein, "Reviving the Business Investment," *Wall Street Journal*, June 19, 1981.

7. Gary M. Wenglowski and Susanne M. Cahn, "Will the Reagan Economic Program Work?" *Chartroom* (New York: Goldman Sachs Economics, 1980).

8. Feldstein, "Reviving Business Investment."

9. This is because the prices of these assets often rise as fast or faster than the consumer price index and individuals often borrow to purchase these assets at interest rates that do not reflect the actual inflation rate.

10. John Rutledge, "Why Interest Rates Will Fall in 1982," *Wall Street Journal*, December 14, 1981.

11. It is because of these initial misallocations in the capital markets that risk of an unbalanced tax cut is reduced.

12. Alan Reynolds, "Do Deficits Matter?" *Wall Street Journal*, December 14, 1981.

13. Ibid.

# The Case for a Return to the Gold Standard: An Interview with Lewis Lehrman

### James C. Roberts

ROBERTS: Mr. Lehrman, my reading of the Republican platform tells me that, at least by implication, the Republican party embraced a return to the gold standard in principle—at least a return to some sort of commodity standard. Do you find a great deal of support for that in the Republican Party?

LEHRMAN: I think there is a great deal of support for the Republican platform in its entirety. There is substantial support for a stable monetary *standard*, and President Reagan himself said that he intends to uphold the Republican platform. He took it very seriously. The Republican platform calls for a monetary standard. Since the optimum commodity monetary standard is the gold standard. I also take the view that eventually the Republican Party will restore the gold standard.

ROBERTS: Was there any significant objection to that plank when it was put in the platform?

LEHRMAN: I was not there, but I understand there was a considerable amount of discussion, debate, and analysis. All concluded that we need a stable dollar. We need a stable dollar over the long run that people can count on. Otherwise, they will never save.

Let me read the relevant paragraph from the official Republican platform of July 14, 1980:

"Ultimately, inflation is a decline in the value of the dollar, the monetary standard, in terms of the goods it can buy. Until the decade of the 1970s monetary policy was automatically linked to the overriding objective of maintaining a stable dollar value.

"The severing of the dollar's link with real commodities in the 1960s and 1970s, in order to pursue economic goals other than dollar stability, has unleashed hyper-inflationary forces at home and monetary disorder abroad, without bringing any of the desired economic benefits. *One of the most urgent tasks in the period ahead will be the restoration of a dependable monetary standard—that is, an end to inflation."*

President Reagan campaigned on this platform and won. In recent years we have not had stable money. But we did have it throughout American history when we had a monetary standard—the gold standard. You can have a nominal money, a paper dollar; or you can have a real dollar, defined by its gold weight. Let us resume the historic American monetary standard, a gold dollar, in order to end inflation. I think that's what the platform means.

ROBERTS: I see on your wall some pictures of Jacques Rueff, who was instrumental in stabilizing the French franc in 1959. What is that story? That, obviously by my reading, buttresses your point of view on the gold standard.

LEHRMAN: Twice in his lifetime, Jacques Rueff saved the French currency. Once during the 1920s—between 1926 and 1928—after the catastrophe of World War I. The second time, in the midst of the collapse of the Fourth Republic, President de Gaulle called Rueff to power to end inflation, reform the French currency, balance the budget, and renovate French economic institutions. Both times he was successful. *The key elements of both French financial reforms was the restoration of convertibility of French currency into gold and the establishment of budgetary equilibrium.*

The economic consequences of Jacques Rueff in 1959 were very simple and very dramatic. They are part of living memory. The Fourth Republic was collapsing; the economy of France was uncertain; inflation raged; French foreign exchange reserves equaled about forty-five days of foreign payments. The currency was declining. The government was virtually bankrupt and immobilized. De Gaulle had been called to power from his home in Colombey-les-deux-Eglises. Rueff was summoned by him to restore financial order.

De Gaulle created the Fifth Republic, the constitution and the presidential system that went along with it, a fact which was not unrelated to his admiration for the American Republic. But it was Jacques Rueff who created the financial conditions which led to the restoration of the France economy.

His plan was very simple: (1) Analyze the causes of financial disorder—which were unbalanced budgets, central bank expansionism through open market securities purchases, and an inconvertible currency; (2) Organize economic policy so as to balance the budget promptly, reestablish convertibility, and deregulate the over-planned French economy.

If you study the development of the French economy since 1959 and the effect of the Rueff financial reforms, you will see that it has been one of the most rapidly expanding economies in the world. Its real tax burden is much lower that our own. Indeed, the average rate of growth in France since 1959 has been the equal of Germany, not the least because of the Rueff-de Gaulle financial plan of currency and budgetary stabilization.

ROBERTS: Was there anything distinctive in the way he reintroduced the gold standard?

LEHRMAN: You will remember that in 1959 Rueff had a considerable advantage. The reform of the French currency occurred under an international monetary system determined by the nominal gold convertibility of the dollar—the Bretton Woods System. You see, Rueff did not have the same problem that we have. Then, under the so-called gold-exchange standard, his target was an existing monetary standard —the gold dollar.

In 1971, as the free world leader, we abandoned the last vestige of the historic gold currency to which all other countries had previously been linked. *The United States broke the monetary link of international financial order. As a result, the weakening chain around inflation collapsed.* Thus, through depreciation of our currency, we forfeited leadership of the free world in monetary matters, as we had already in military matters.

Rueff often despaired that he was never in a position to help create a true gold standard for the whole Western world, as he desired. For that reason, among others, Rueff always looked to the United States for world monetary leadership. He was profoundly disappointed that we did not exercise it. By the way, he loved America, was a believer in her unique destiny.

In any event, then as now, it was up to the United States to restore the monetary standard. We alone can lead the free world. When the agreed-upon leader takes charge, either on the field of sport, battle, or politics, all of the smaller and lesser participants tend to emulate the leader. They will emulate particularly the leader's financial and intellectual conduct. I have no doubt that when we restore the gold standard in the United States during the next decade, the entire world will repair to our monetary standard—even the Soviets.

ROBERTS: What about the battle over the President's program?

LEHRMAN: The battle rages over the boldness and comprehensiveness of the economic program, not to mention the coherence of the different elements.

For example, some supply-siders tend to emphasize the crucial reduction in marginal tax rates. That is very important. It is necessary, but it is not sufficient.

It is true that rising tax rates in a certain way cause rising deficits by shrinking the private economy. But a reduction in marginal tax rates is not a sufficient remedy for the defects of our present economic policy. I place a great deal of emphasis on the condition of the budget and the size of the deficit and federal credit demands, a point on which I argue with many of my monetarist and supply-side friends. I believe *we must balance the budget at the current level of tax receipts*—promptly.

ROBERTS: But some of you monetarist friends don't agree with you on the importance of a balanced budget.

LEHRMAN: You are right. In fact, a curious irony is the agreement of some monetarists and some supply-siders on this point. They are somewhat indifferent to the effects of an unbalanced budget. I think that is a serious error, and I think the consequences of indifference to the public sector deficit have been demonstrated in England under Prime Minister Margaret Thatcher.

The Tory monetarists have been unable to get the budget under control because, in general, at the beginning and even now, in the most recent budget of March 1981, they put too much emphasis on monetarist central bank credit policy and insufficient emphasis on the growth of public spending. They are concerned too little with the size of the government deficit which must be financed by the limited pool of savings.

The deficit has almost doubled in two years under Thatcher—from 7.5 billion sterling to 13.5 billion—5-6 percent of GNP. *The deficit absorbs too much of the savings which English enterprise needs for new investment.* That is why the U.K. economy is foundering as badly as at any time since the beginning of the industrial revolution. Manufacturing output in England during the past year and one-half has fallen almost as precipitously as during the Great Depression of 1929-31.

But the current Reagan program also fails to provide for a true and effective reform of our monetary institutions, domestically and internationally. Such a lasting reform must be based on the gold standard and a balanced budget.

For two decades we have been listening to dedicated Presidents, experienced Federal Reserve Board chairmen, and honest secretaries of the treasury give speeches every month. The speeches always state that our goal is gradually to end the balance-of-payments deficit or gradually end inflation.

Dramatic examples occur in 1961, 1965, 1968, 1971, 1974, recently in the November 1978 Miller measures and the October 1979 Volcker message. They were all going to reduce the rate of inflation. Somehow they have all failed. *The Keynesians have failed. The self-described practical or pragmatic monetarists have failed. Their policy—gradually to reduce the rate of growth of the money supply—has failed thus far.* They have failed, not because they chose the wrong goal—an end to inflation—but because they chose the wrong means. To desire a goal without the effective means to attain the goal is to court political disaster.

ROBERTS: Does the Federal Reserve regulate interest rates even when various chairmen have stated that their desire is not to do that but to get a grip on the money supply?

LEHRMAN: Well, the view of most central bankers at the Federal Reserve System, until about 1979, was to fine-tune the federal funds rate, which is the interest rate at which banks loan excess funds among themselves.

By buying and selling government securities, so-called open market operations, the Federal Reserve tried to maintain a reasonably stable federal funds rate. Such a Fed funds rate was held to be consistent with a certain rate of growth of the money supply.

In October 1979, Chairman Paul Volcker gave several speeches and testified to the Congress that monetary control by interest rate manipulation had been reformulated. Now the Federal Reserve would pay less attention to the federal funds rate and money market conditions. Interest rates would be permitted to fluctuate in a much wider band and the Fed would now focus on manipulating the quantity of commercial bank reserves held at the Fed.

So, instead of targeting interest rates and, in particular, the federal funds rate, the Fed would target a specific quantity of bank reserves, held to be consistent with a certain rate of growth of the quantity of money in circulation, say M-1B. *The trouble is, the Fed cannot successfully implement this abstract formula* in a stable fashion in the real world of money markets, as previous and subsequent Fed performance has demonstrated.

An enormous amount of research is said to have moved the Fed from an interest rate control policy to a bank reserve control policy. So far they have failed to attain the goal of reducing inflation with the new policy. Inflation is still at peak levels, and so are interest rates, even if at times the Fed hits a defined money stock target.

My view is that *the central bank cannot fix the quantity of money in circulation.* Nor, over the long run, can it fix interest rates, the monetary base, and the specific level of bank reserves. Nor should it try, because the effort to do these things is wrecking the money and capital markets.

Ever since the early 1920s, but particularly in the last decade and a half, the great error of central banking has been a lingering belief that the Federal Reserve System is able to fix the quantity of money in circulation in order to "stabilize the business cycle."

I do agree with the monetarists that the Federal Reserve System *influences* financial conditions by the buying and selling of government securities. Also, the Federal Reserve System, through open market operations, can directly affect bank reserves and therefore the supply conditions for credit at the commercial banks. But no matter what the supply conditions, you and I alone decide how much credit or money we will demand or hold.

If the Fed supplies more money than consumers and businessmen desire to hold, then the supply will exceed demand, and the value of money will decline. Thus, the attempt by the Fed to *increase* the supply of money at a fixed rate almost always tends to cause its value to decline—because the desire to hold money over the long run is stable, as decades of research on the subject has shown. Inflation is a decline in the value of money, or a rise of the general price level, caused by the tendency of the Fed to supply more money than the market actually desires to hold.

Each participant in the market, every consumer, every businessman, decides exactly how much money he will demand for whatever purpose he has in mind. All of their purposes cannot be known by the Federal Reserve System, no matter how farseeing or well-intentioned or how systematic and careful its research.

*The goal of the Federal Reserve System should be the stability of the purchasing power of the dollar* or, saying it another way, reasonable stability of the price level—an end to inflation. In the absence of success on this point, what use is the Fed?

The means by which to hit *the correct target of Fed policy— equalization in the market of the supply of money with the amount of money actually desired*—is not the existing technique of open market operations. I will not dwell here on Fed targets, open market operations and the discount rate, because I have written at length on this elsewhere. Briefly, *the most efficient method of monetary control is to remobilize the Fed discount rate and join this reform of central bank procedures to a more general monetary reform—the establishment of a true gold standard.*

ROBERTS: I gather from your response, then, that you don't fully agree with Milton Friedman's idea that it is the responsibility of the Federal Reserve to set the growth of the money supply within fixed parameters?

LEHRMAN: I think that such a *goal* has some merit. The question arises over the appropriate means by which to reach the goal and whether or not the Fed can attain it.

I believe the Federal Reserve System does not have it within its power to create a fixed rate of growth of money, as Professor Friedman argues. I have learned so much from Professor Friedman's work that I hesitate to dispute him. I endorse his general view on free market institutions. But I deny his assumption that, in an open economy, the central bank can determine the rate of growth of the quantity of money in circulation. In order to do that, the central bank must control both the supply of dollars and the demand for dollars in the U.S. market and throughout the world. But the users of dollars throughout the world determine their demand. Market participants, and their demands for dollars, are beyond the precise control of the Fed.

Professor Friedman advocates a monetary rule—namely, that the money supply should grow at a 3 or 4 percent steady rate each year. The monetary goal may be sensible; the goal of 4 percent steady economic growth each year is also sensible. But *what is the best means to attain this end? Honestly to desire a goal is to desire the effective means to attain it.*

Professor Friedman noted in his monumental work on the monetary history of the United States that the gold standard period in the U.S. was generally accompanied by a stable rate of growth in the money supply over the long run. During most of U.S. history, the monetary constitution of the U.S. was the gold standard. The money growth rule, now advocated by Professor Friedman, was largely rendered throughout our history by the rule of the gold dollar.

In the past, the steady rate of growth of the U.S. money supply came to an end only during periods of trade wars and floating exchange rates. Such periods occurred during and immediately after the Civil War, the Depression and at present.

So, if we truly seek an effective monetary constitution and a steady rate of growth of the money supply, consistent with the rate of growth for real economic output, I believe that the optimum means to achieve the goal is the prompt restoration of the gold standard. This is the classical monetary policy.

To desire the gold standard is to desire a peaceful and open world trading system. The gold standard is nothing more than a classical political institution, a measured means to a sensible end. It is not a magical enterprise. It should be stripped of the arcane mystery associated with it in the minds of some. It is strictly a political institution in an imperfect world, though *the gold standard is the least imperfect institution ever evolved to prohibit inflation and produce stable money.*

ROBERTS: It's not really a medium of exchange?

LEHRMAN: It may be. There is no reason why one cannot have gold coins in circulation if people—free people—choose to use or save gold coins as money. Indeed, what I am getting at is that *the gold standard*—i.e., gold, coined as money—*reconstitutes a real money into which all nominal paper and credit money must be convertible.* Also, to restore the gold standard is the only sure way to restore the future value of money and therefore the only certain technique by which to restore the incentive to save and to invest for future returns.

ROBERTS: But Professor Friedman is opposed to that, the restoration of any kind of gold standard. He says that in the second half of the nineteenth century the business cycle psychology produced pressure which caused the eventual establishment of the Federal Reserve System. The gold standard was not satisfactory, he says. It was not satisfactory to the business community, government, anybody. The pressure for the creation of the Federal Reserve was a virtual demand.

LEHRMAN: It is true that the period 1879-1913 has produced much historical debate. It is also true that the business cycle *had* its ups and downs. Then as now, there were Utopians of the right and left who believed they could banish the business cycle. Some of these people favored the establishment of a government monopoly over the currency issue and government regulation of money.

Oversimplified, that is how the Fed came to be in 1913. It was just one more regulatory agency, not unlike the ICC, the Interstate Commerce Commission (1888), which came along during the regulatory craze which swept up the Populist-Progressive movement at the turn of the century. But *it is also a fact that, in the absence of the Federal Reserve, and because of the operations of the international gold standard from 1879-1913, the general price level in 1879 was almost the same in 1913.*

For almost two generations, the purchasing power of the dollar was stable. There was neither inflation nor deflation over the full period. From 1879 to 1895 the price level gradually declined. From 1895 to 1913 the price level gradually rose. During the whole period we had substantial real economic growth.

Professor Friedman has had several views on the gold standard. Thanks to him, we have a lucid article that he wrote in 1961. (I believe it appeared in the *Journal of Law and Economics.*) Professor Friedman stated in this article that he understood and approved a *true gold standard.* So do I. I wish I could quote the article verbatim. All monetarists should read it. Professor Friedman has since suggested that a true gold standard is impractical. It may be politically impossible, he has argued, to reformulate the existing monetary system according to the rules of the true gold standard.

Now I know that Professor Friedman is a great economist, but is he a great politician? And a good political scientist? It seems to me that the proper role of the economist is to analyze what is the very best policy to achieve a certain goal, and then allow the competition for leadership in a free society to determine whether or not a policy is practical and desirable.

I happen to believe that a reformulation of the present monetary system, according to the rule of the true gold standard, is not only the optimum monetary policy, but also practical. I believe that it can be done during President Reagan's administration.

A lack of will, a fear of the unknown, the propaganda against the gold standard by Socialists, liberals, some free market men—by elitists from many philosophical points of view—have tended to intimidate practical men and working people. It is not easy to go against the fashionable and established wisdom of the ruling academic and political elites.

ROBERTS: Should President Reagan choose to take your advice on the gold standard, would it not cause massive dislocations in the American and international economies?

LEHRMAN: We are experiencing right now a massive dislocation in the world economy and in the domestic economy because, during the past two generations, we abandoned the discipline of the gold standard.

We abandoned low taxes and we abandoned balanced budgets. That fact should cause us to reexamine the history and theory of the gold standard as a way by which to end dislocations caused by manipulated currencies and managed floating exchange rates. Floating exchange rates and excessively discretionary central banking policies have caused the present financial disorder. *One should look to the restoration of the gold standard and balanced budgets as the means to end the worldwide financial disequilibrium.*

ROBERTS: What are some of the economic arguments that go along with a true gold standard?

LEHRMAN: First, we must have the determination and the courage to do what the American people voted for in electing President Reagan. They want to balance the budget at the current level of tax receipts, deregulate American life and reduce the level of tax rates. If we can do these things, then I can assure you that the same leadership can and will restore *the gold standard, which is a unique international political institution designed by man to maintain the free market order we desire to uphold throughout the world.* Moreover, it will preserve the value of the dollar over the long run, which is the only way honestly to encourage people to save and to invest again in the future.

I am making the point that if we do not have the political will to achieve the other elements of President Reagan's vision, it is equally true that we cannot achieve monetary reform. Conversely, I do not think it's too much to say that we must do all of these things together or else we may fail to achieve President Reagan's goals of sustained economic growth and an end to inflation.

*The virtue of the gold standard is its ineffable simplicity.* In fact, that is a prime reason why many sophisticated economists and intellectuals deny and reject the gold standard. It is too straightforward. They want something more complex to manipulate.

Mathematicians and economists are taught in graduate school that economics is very complex. Statistics or the manipulation of statistics, we are told, is a very complex science. Therefore, economic theories and policies must be very complex and so must the bureaucracies which create the complex policies. Well, I reject that conclusion. I don't believe that laws, constitutions, or economic institutions must be intricate and complex just because the world economy is beyond the mind of a single man, or group of men, to grasp. If complexity were a virtue, the good Lord would have given us a thousand commandments instead of ten.

ROBERTS: This notion of complexity and elite manipulation is one of the pillars of Keynesian econcomics, is it not? Keynesian macroeconomics?

LEHRMAN: Yes, of course. Every false priesthood is opaque. It invents abstruse and mysterious dogmas and doctrines which cannot be understood by plain people. True priesthoods are accessible, open and simple. *One of the marvels of the gold standard is that,* in the absence of world war and trade wars, *it has actually worked* reasonably well in the past—the best simple test for any political or economic institution. But also, gold money can be understood and its quantity controlled by working people—who do not have sophisticated accountants, economists, lawyers, and investment bankers to talk to the Fed and to work out their financial affairs and their taxes for them.

Thus, we return to your original question. It is for reasons of equity, utility and simplicity that the gold standard was properly a part of the Republican platform. *A gold-based currency is democratic money.* It is money which free people and not the Fed would control.

President Reagan has set the agenda in his speeches for such a new monetary policy. Remember it is he who wants to keep things clear and simple, he who said that we must return authority in economic matters to the people. He also said that we must balance the budget, reduce marginal tax rates, deregulate American life and produce a stable dollar—all together. So, I don't believe that there's anything original in what I am saying. It is the economic policy of the President. In my opinion, *the centerpiece of economic policy is the monetary standard.*

ROBERTS: I think that seems to be one of his great talents that he has been able to take a diverse number of theories and combine them, whereas in the conservative economics profession you have a lot of squabbling going on. Reagan seems to have transcended this and picked up from each one what he wishes, and the whole that he has come up with seems to be pretty much in line with what you are talking about.

LEHRMAN: Yes. He certainly understands—indeed, he is the leader of this idea—that *you must have a comprehensive economic policy and you must try to do it all together;* you cannot do it piece-meal. In the policy speeches of 1980, he made it clear that the Kemp-Roth bill was very important; but it was not a sufficient remedy. He also made it very clear that a balanced budget was important, but even the old-time Republican religion of balanced budgets was insufficient. He understands, unlike some Thatcherites, that monetary policy by itself cannot do the job.

The monetarist prescription of a monetary rule, whereby the central bank tries to create a specified rate of growth of the money supply over the long run, may be a important idea. But even if it could work, it would not be sufficient.

In other words, President Reagan has said that the monetarists have a pretty good idea, the Kemp-Roth advocates have a good idea, the balanced budget advocates—the National Taxpayers' Union and Sen. Strom Thurmond—have a good idea. But the point is that only working together can the policies be sufficient. That was the burden of an article I wrote for the *Wall Street Journal* in June 1980.

ROBERTS: Some of the supply-side types have tended to pooh-pooh the necessity for spending cuts at the federal level. Is this a matter of principle or just a political tactic?

LEHRMAN: I think it is both. There are a few well-known economists, supply-siders and monetarists, who are relatively indifferent to the size and trend of the budget deficit. There are monetary economists who ignore the deficit, who believe that monetary policy can, if conducted properly, conquer inflation alone. There are some supply-siders who believe that attempting to reduce the level of federal spending is "impolitic"; it is bad politics, they say, and it can't be done.

ROBERTS: You don't go along with that?

LEHRMAN: Positively not.

ROBERTS: How about Friedman's point that it's not the deficit itself that's important, but the size of the federal spending relative to gross national product that's important?

LEHRMAN: I think that he is partially correct. The size of the federal spending relative to gross national product is very important. It represents the real tax burden. *Equally important is the size of direct and guaranteed federal borrowing requirements compared to the size of national savings.* But I also believe the scale of the federal deficit and federal credit demands, per se, is very important. Above all, it is the way in which the federal deficit tends to be financed which makes it absolutely crucial.

ROBERTS: You seem to be wedded in principle to the idea of a balanced budget.

LEHRMAN: I am. Undisciplined and inordinate financial conduct of the executive and the legislature cause unbalanced budgets. *I endorse in principle the discipline of a balanced budget at the current level of tax receipts because the economic effects of an unbalanced budget, despite pretenses of theory, are almost always destructive* over the long run. Government deficits consume and dissipate private savings. Without increasing private savings available for investment in business enterprise, the economy must falter.

ROBERTS: But don't you think that were Friedman here, he would say that if you have an economy of a trillion dollars and a federal deficit of a billion dollars it's of no consequence?

LEHRMAN: On that precise example, I would agree. A deficit of a billion dollars in a trillion-dollar economy is insignificant. The problem is that we have a $2.75 trillion economy and a $60 billion deficit, plus off-budget, federal credit, guarantee programs and state and local government borrowing which, all together, are approximately $150 billion of government borrowing this year. This is the true deficit!— about 5-6 percent of GNP—comparable to Thatcher's England. But personal savings are running at only about $100 billion. No one talks about this.

Economists say our deficit is only a small percent of GNP. They are wrong. Often they incorrectly compare our "small" deficit to the "large" deficits of Germany and other countries. But properly calculated, the true deficits, plus federal credit demands, are comparable to those of Germany and England.

And by the way, the corporate sector is now in deficit, too. The reason why a substantial budget deficit and huge and growing federal credit demands are positively destructive under almost all circumstances is very straightforward. The government goes into the capital markets and sells government securities and removes from the capital markets the savings equal to the government deficit and other federal credit programs.

The government *must* have the money to pay its contractual bills and fulfill statutory commitments. Given the scale of the spending problem, *I recommended to Dave Stockman in early November 1980 a national economic emergency statement only in order to make use of the legislative techniques of budgetary recission and deferral to balance the budget.* For the purpose of promptly balancing the budget, deferral and recission are the appropriate lawful means available to Congress and the President.

Now, if government spending were reduced to the level of current tax receipts, current and capital accounts could never be in deficit. Savings would remain in the capital markets for businesses to borrow at lower interest rates. Business would invest these savings in new capital; new machine tools, new plants, new equipment, new technology, new research and development, new products and, most important, new jobs. We could then leave the Japanese and Germans in the dust.

One of the reasons we are no longer competitive with Japan and Germany in some areas is that we have not been able to generate sufficient savings with which to modernize our industrial plants and to finance our voracious government.

In the case of Germany and Japan, they have generated enough savings to finance both big government deficits and new plants and equipment for three reasons: *(1)* they have *a more stable currency; (2)* they permit *higher real after-tax rewards for savings*; and *(3) the U.S. subsidizes their national defense.* We must promptly develop the first two if we want to increase savings rapidly. We are losing markets all over the world to nations which are generating huge savings in order to keep their industries modern and forward-looking.

Our federal government has starved American industry.

One statistic I find most impressive throughout the history of the Industrial Revolution is the correlation between the amount of capital (saving) invested per worker and the average standard of living of the country. It's clear to me that the rate of gain of the standard of living in every advanced industrial economy is directly related to the amount of capital (saving) invested behind each worker. But the amount of capital invested is directly proportional to the quantity of savings available to back up the labor force. The Japanese and the Germans have been investing more capital per worker. And their savings are greater because the real after-tax returns for savings are comparatively better than ours.

ROBERTS: Speaking of Japan and West Germany, I gather from your talk about returning to the gold standard that you are by definition opposed to the floating exchange rates that exist. In addition to that, what other redesign would you propose for U.S. monetary and financial dealings in the international economy?

LEHRMAN: First, *there is only one economy, and that is an integrated world economy.* The distinction between microeconomics and macroeconomics and the distinction between national economic policy and international economic policy is absurd.

Economic policymakers in Washington, Paris, London, Bonn, Tokyo, very often live in a world where they imagine they are making a self-contained policy for their national economies. There is no such thing. *Through the mechanism of arbitrage, the prices in one national economy are linked indissolubly to the prices in every other national economy.* There is a single world economy and it is, to a very great extent, fully integrated. But I believe such openness is a good thing. It leads not only to the maximum amount of liberty for the individual, but also to the maximum production of goods and services—especially for the less well-off at home and the underdeveloped countries abroad.

*You cannot conduct a monetary policy in the national interest, no matter how coherent or comprehensive, unless it is consistent with the stability of the international monetary system to which it is inextricably linked.* For this reason, history and analysis show us that the very best political institution—the optimum international coordinating mechanism, the gyroscope for establishing reasonable price-level stability over the long run throughout the world economy—is the true international gold standard. A convertible gold currency established by law, unlike a paper reserve currency, cannot be easily manipulated by governments to achieve certain types of unfair trading opportunities through currency depreciation and appreciation.

A gold currency is an impartial common currency. But unlike government paper currency, gold is an asset outside the control of national monetary authorities. Unlike paper dollars, it cannot be produced at the discretion of politicians and central bankers. A good currency requires real effort, capital and intelligence to produce. In the past, it produced a reasonably stable price level over the long run throughout the world.

Instead of workers, investors and businessmen speculating on fluctuating paper currency values at home and abroad—constantly confused as to the "real" cost of investment in Germany as opposed to France or the U.S.—there was confidence that the value of gold currencies, linked to one another across national borders, would be stable over the long term. Thus, long-term investment and trading commitments across national borders could be confidently undertaken, leading to an increase in the efficiency and wealth of the integrated world economy.

What's more, the purchasing power of gold has been stable for centuries, as Professor Jastram of the University of California has demonstrated beyond the shadow of a doubt. Professor Jastram's book, *The Golden Constant*, proved what traders and merchants knew from time immemorial.

*Over the long run, the purchasing power of gold is more constant than that of any single commodity or product which could be used as a monetary standard.* Which raises another interesting point.

One often hears today that gold was a good monetary standard in the past, but that today the price of gold fluctuates too rapidly and too violently to be a stable monetary standard. The truth is that it's not the value of the gold which is unstable. Over the long run, history shows that the purchasing power of gold, in terms of real goods and services, is stable. The volatility lies with the fluctuating value of the manipulated paper and credit dollar.

In fact, the very meaning of inflation is that the paper dollar is declining in value while the prices of real goods and services, in terms of that paper currency, are rising. Paper currency, unlinked to a commodity standard, has become an unstable political football in the hands of the politicians and bureaucrats.

ROBERTS: In advocating a return to the gold standard, are you not troubled by those who point out that the two leading producers of gold today are the Soviet Union, a hostile power, and South Africa, which faces a very parlous future? That doesn't bother you at all?

LEHRMAN: Remember that I said the gold standard is a political institution. *The gold standard, being a human institution, is imperfect. Its utility lies in the fact that it is the least imperfect, free political institution which can give reasonable stability to the value of a currency over the long run.* The fact that South Africa and Russia are large gold producers introduces a degree of uncertainty, but not very much, for the following reasons. First, during the history of the gold standard, there were always gold-producing countries which at one time or another were ill-disposed toward the gold standard. Nevertheless, it endured their hostility and served its economic purpose better that contemporary monetary institutions. In fact, *the gold standard, throughout history, has failed only because of world war, excessive protectionism, or self-centered currency manipulation.* Few free economic institutions can survive these xenophobic conditions. In fact, I would suggest that the gold standard signifies the desire for an end to such autarky, and a desire for economic harmony among nations.

Before World War I, huge discoveries of gold in South Africa were insufficient to disturb the stability of the convertible currency regimes throughout the Western World. At that time, the price level rose about 2 or 3 percent a year, and can you believe that our grandfathers called this gradual rise inflation?

The transition in Germany, during the 1870s, from a silver standard to a gold standard was insufficient, even given the enormous weight of the German economy, to destabilize the world currency regime based on the true gold standard. During and after the Civil War, the paper dollar, the "Greenbacks," were not convertible, at par, to gold—from 1862 to 1879.

Even given the weight and the importance of the United States in the world economy at that time, the U.S. Civil War was insufficient to disturb the stability of the gold-based monetary system of Western civilization. So, in each gold standard era, you will always have nations which are not fully integrated into the monetary system of the most advanced industrial parts of the world economy—either morally, which is what some critics of South Africa say, or morally, economically and politically, which is what I would say of the Soviet Union.

ROBERTS: Do you expect the gold standard to be implemented in the future? And what happens if there is a war, or a panic?

LEHRMAN: I'll take the second part of your question first. *The gold standard in no way constrains the freedom of Congress and the President to meet the real threat of war.* In fact, it helps them.

By insuring the future value of the dollar, the gold standard increases savings. In order to rebuild the national defense, or prepare for war, the government must sell defense or war bonds to the people in exchange for their savings. A gold dollar encourages people to save and, with security, to lend them to the government in a national emergency.

I believe that the European governments made a fatal error in 1914 when they abandoned their gold currencies, because the people saved less and the war effort had to be financed through the government printing presses and inflation. This inflationary war finance destroyed Czarist Russia, Imperial Germany, and almost wrecked France in 1926.

Under the gold standard, prudent levels of gold reserves must always be maintained and, under panic conditions, anyone who wished to redeem their paper currency should be satisfied. If they could be satisfied, of course, the panic would quickly subside. Under conditions of all-out war or intense global trade warfare, no monetary system can survive. That, however, is not a defect of the gold standard. It is a defect of human nature which causes the prospect of total war.

ROBERTS: What happens if the Soviets all of a sudden dump a massive quantity of gold on the market?

LEHRMAN: Under conditions characterized by a true gold standard, current gold production is so small, relative to stocks on hand, that the Soviet Union, or even South Africa, which is a much bigger producer, could not affect the stability of the gold standard. The Soviets produce about eight to ten million ounces of new gold per year. Total official and private holdings are over two billion ounces. Approximately one billion ounces of gold are held by official monetary institutions. Now, as you can see, if the Soviets decided to dump their entire annual production on the world market, it could be easily absorbed.

*Soviet gold is like salt in the ocean.* It is but a fraction of 1 percent of total official gold reserves. It is less than one-half of 1 percent of the total volume of gold stocks in the world. This fact elucidates one of the reasons why gold is the optimum monetary standard: *The total amount of new gold production in any single year is only a very minor fraction of the total supply of gold in existence.* Thus, the value of the new production of gold money cannot substantially depress the total value of all existing supplies, given the steady demand conditions for gold in general and in particular under the gold standard.

These conditions in the gold market are unique. That is why other proposed monetary standards are less satisfactory. In any one year the new supply of any other commodity, or "baskets" of commodities, relative to existing stocks in existence, is very substantial. That fact is true for oil, silver, copper, aluminum, lumber, wampum, pork bellies and cinderblocks.

Even were the South Africans to dump an entire year's production of gold on the world market, that would only be about 20-24 million ounces of gold. That is only about 1 percent of the total of public and private world gold stocks. And it is about 2 percent of official government-owned gold stocks. A mere drop in the bucket!

*The technical meaning of the gold standard is that the countries that belong to it are prepared to buy and sell at the official rate all the gold offered or all the gold demanded.* If the U.S. and its allies were determined to uphold the new monetary system, then even South Africans could withhold all their production, a relatively small amount, which is equal to only a very small percentage of total world gold stocks. Conversely, the gold standard countries could absorb easily all sales of the relatively insignificant new output.

ROBERTS: Assuming President Reagan follows your advice and attempts to implement a return to the gold standard, how can he go about doing this in a way that causes the least dislocation and helps his remaining program?

LEHRMAN: Above all, he must reform the domestic monetary system, as part of his overall economic plan, and link the monetary reform to the tax, budget and regulatory program which we talked about. The monetary reform could happen shortly after the rest of the program; but it should be linked in time and policy to the other aspects of the plan.

For example, one can imagine that President Reagan will soon observe the successful progress of his economic reform program in Congress. Let us call it the conservative reform program. It includes the elements that he laid out carefully in his speeches of September 1980 and February 1981. *The goal of the President's economic program is to restore conditions of sustained growth and price level stability.*

In order to end inflation, the most important monetary reform to be introduced would establish the dollar as a weight unit of gold. The reestablishment of a gold dollar would be historic. President Reagan would point out that, since the founding of the Republic, a gold currency has been the traditional base money of Americans. I think he knows this history because, very often in the past, he's thought about and discussed the possibility of the gold standard, though he has never, to my knowledge, committed himself officially to such a program.

How could he implement such a program now? First, he would lay out the history of the gold standard in the United States and in the industrialized world. Then he would lay out the important reasons for creating a stable dollar, a dollar which has a reliable future purchasing power. He would emphasize that a stable dollar is the crucial incentive, a necessary precondition by which to develop sufficient private savings in order to rebuild a competitive national economy. Money savings dry up when the future value of money is in doubt.

Then there would be an analysis of the failed alternatives to a stable convertible currency—Keynesian credit policy and monetarism. *One concludes that only the classical monetary policy—a dollar defined as a weight unit of gold—has given the American currency reasonable stability of purchasing power in the past.* A gold-based currency will do so in the future, he could confidently forecast.

I think a knowledge of history is important. The history of the development of the Western world and of America from a tiny nation of thirteen disparate colonies to a great world power, the greatest nation on earth, is associated with the history of the gold dollar and the international gold standard.

Remember that the thirteen colonies, before the Constitution, had a depreciating inconvertible paper currency—the "continental." That is where the phrase, "Not worth a continental," came from. I do not think it a mere coincidence that in the 1790s, at the beginning of the constitutional period—and also in the 1950s, at the peak of our prestige as a republican world power—we had a hard currency, a sound dollar, a dollar as good as gold.

In any event, the President would announce his intention to restore convertibility, i.e., a gold dollar. The transition period, from the present inconvertible paper dollar regime to a gold standard, would be defined perhaps by a two-year interval. If such a commitment were made, let us say in January 1982, one could initiate the transition and effect the resumption of convertibility in January 1984.

January 1984 would be the date on which the government and the banks would be prepared to redeem paper dollars or bank deposits dollars for a specific weight of gold. During this transition, in addition to establishing an unequivocal trend toward a balanced budget, the credit policy of the Federal Reserve System would have to be cautious and steady. It could not be volatile and it could not be excessively expansionist. The total value of Federal Reserve Bank credit (or the monetary base which is its counterpart) would have to grow at a predictable and steady pace, not inconsistent with the pace that Professor Friedman himself has recommended for the growth of the money supply.

ROBERTS: You are asking the Fed to do something here it has never done before though, right?

LEHRMAN: On the contrary. But for the interruption of war, the Fed operated under the discipline of the international gold standard during the first fifty-eight years of its existence—from 1913 to 1971. When the government and the Federal Reserve conducted a credit policy reasonably consistent with maintaining an open economy and the convertibility of the dollar, the value of the dollar was fairly stable and so was the price level. There was little inflation.

When in 1929, the government defied the rules of the international gold standard by imposing quotas and tariffs on trade, we got deflation in the 1930s; and when the Fed and the government became excessively expansionist, we got inflation in the 1960s and 1970s. *Our big inflation begins in 1972, right after the August 1971 suspension of dollar convertibility.* Look at the commodity charts and the exponential curve of rising inflation immediately thereafter. The fact is undeniable.

ROBERTS: You are talking about *reestablishing* the gold standard though?

LEHRMAN: What I am saying is that the Federal Reserve System, in the past, has conducted its monetary policy in a framework dictated by the fact that, according to law, the dollar was convertible into a weight of gold—and must be maintained at that stipulated value.

So, the central bank, our Federal Reserve System, knew that if it over-expanded the money supply, the so-called dollar/gold convertibility ratio could not be maintained and the value of the dollar would fall. Moreover, if the Fed did not supply the quantity of credit and money actually desired in the market, then it also knew that the price level would fall and the value of money would rise.

So all I meant to say was that the Federal Reserve has in the past conducted a credit policy within the framework of a gold standard. The present government should accept the discipline of the gold standard and do it again.

ROBERTS: But the dollar/gold link between the end of the war and 1971 was much more tenuous than the one you are talking about restoring.

LEHRMAN: That's correct. And that tenuousness was due to a profound defect of the so-called gold-exchange standard, or the dollar reserve currency system. The gold/dollar link after World War II was determined by the Bretton Woods Agreement of 1944 which allowed foreigners to base their currencies on the paper dollar rather than on gold. It was not a true gold standard. It was a defective fixed-exchange rate regime based on reserve currency. It was doomed to failure. *The reserve currency* status of the dollar must be ended. It is both a burden which hobbles us, and an improper privilege, to which our trading partners often object.

In addition, Americans could not get gold for their paper dollars. Only foreigners could. In a true international gold standard the monetary standard for us, as for other countries, could not be the paper dollar. And there would be no restrictions on gold sales and purchases. *Not the paper dollar, but a weight of gold would be the reserve currency.* Gold, unlike domestic paper monies, cannot be manufactured at the printing presses, or created through central bank credit market operations. Nor can a gold currency be quickly depreciated or manipulated by sovereign national authorities.

ROBERTS: Very frankly, are there any other commodities that you could think of that would serve the purpose, the same purpose as well as gold?

LEHRMAN: Throughout history many different commodities have served as monetary standards. But each of these monetary standards quickly failed. They failed quite dramatically, except for silver. We have the case of wampum. We have the case of tobacco in colonial Virginia. We have the case of stones in certain island cultures. And we have the case of mixed standards, bimetallic standards.

The interesting thing is that throughout Western history, as a result of free decisions of free people in the world market, gold has generally emerged as the prevailing optimum monetary standard. *People, who are free to choose their money, decide for gold.* Historians, economists, and economic theorists have often believed that the choice of gold as a monetary standard was adventitious, that there was really no underlying economic reality that brought this about. That's why John Maynard Keynes, one of the greatest economists of our time, referred to the gold standard as a barbarous relic. He did not understand what was unique about gold. The uniqueness of gold has also escaped famous contemporary economists as well. Now is the time to demythologize the gold standard.

Actually, the reason why gold was the historic modern monetary standard is twofold. First, in free markets, free people determine what is money. Not the authorities, but *free people determine what is trustworthy and acceptable as money.* And over the centuries, merchants, consumers, traders, producers gradually selected gold coins, i.e., gold money, as the most desirable money. They didn't have fancy theories to justify it. It was just that over time gold exhibited certain stable characteristics that no other medium of exchange exhibited.

Only when government prohibits gold money, through legal tender laws, does gold take a back seat.

Now *when you examine the underlying economic reasons for the natural selection of gold as money, you find that gold exhibits special monetary properties, characteristics unmatched by any other commodity in the market.*

Let me simplify the issue. The economics of production, for most commodities and products, are often characterized by economies of scale, i.e., declining costs of production per unit of output over time. Now, when you adopt a commodity currency in a modern economy, the authorities and the banks stand ready to give every working man and woman a specified quantity of the commodity money for an equal quantity of the paper (or deposit) money in circulation.

Now if the monetary standard were pork bellies, as Professor Friedman himself has facetiously suggested, or if it were cinderblocks, as the pathbreaking political economist, Jude Wanniski, has humorously suggested, then the monetary authority and the banks would be required to exchange a specific quantity of paper currency and credit money for a specific quantity of pork bellies or cinderblocks.

Now, pork belly output is susceptible to economies of scale characteristic of mass production. Entrepreneurs and innovators will constantly refine the techniques of pork belly production such that their costs of pork belly production will fall to the very minimum under existing market conditions. Cinderblocks are manufactured goods whose production is even more susceptible to economies of scale.

Imagine now that the monetary authority is subject to a statutory rate at which paper currency is convertible into the monetary standard —cinderblocks and pork bellies (or all other commodities or products which we know are more or less susceptible to scale production techniques and declining marginal costs).

Entrepreneurs will constantly discover techniques to lower the production costs of these commodity standards. They would rapidly overproduce these monetary standards at declining unit costs and exchange them for more currency with the monetary authority at the fixed convertible rate. And of course, there would be inflation, i.e., a vast overexpansion and depreciation of the currency.

*Scale production techniques, or potentially rapid exploration and discovery rates, are characteristic of virtually all commodities on the market.* That's why Milton Friedman's pork bellies, or aluminum, or oil, or lumber, or a basket of commodities, and other proposed standards are not good as monetary standards. Their supply can be expanded too rapidly. *But gold is not very susceptible to production economies of scale.*

Throughout history, gold production has *not* been characterized by rapidly declining marginal costs of production per ounce of new gold produced. The marginal cost of producing another unit of gold is generally above or close to its average cost—over long periods of time.

It once took centuries, and now it takes about a generation, for the technology of gold production to improve appreciably. Increasing the production of gold through special mining techniques—leeching, open pit mining, vast amounts of capital equipment, new inventions for finding and extracting—has led neither to rapid discovery nor to economies of scale production. Declining costs of production or quicker supply increases, more typical of other metals such as copper or silver, do not typify good production.

Discovery and innovation in gold production have occurred, but at a pace which never caused, under the gold standard, a sustained rise of more than 3 percent in the price level—very modest inflation compared to the floating dollar of the present.

The average increase in the quantity of gold production over hundreds of years has been limited to one and a half to 2 percent a year—because of the unique conditions of slow discovery and difficult production economics. In a work, gold has a very inelastic supply curve, an ideal characteristic for a monetary standard.

Here I might make an observation about the 3-5 percent monetary growth rule of my monetarist friends. *The monetary rule Professor Friedman would invent, and leave to the discretion of central bankers to carry out, the gold standard provides by virtue of the very nature of underlying economic reality itself.*

You can see that the quantity of gold in circulation expands over the long run at a steady rate. Indeed, that explains why gold has been instinctively and wisely chosen as a monetary standard by free people from all walks of life for over hundreds of years—because the supply conditions of gold tend to parallel the rate of population and economic growth over long periods of time, thus preserving the purchasing power of gold.

Among all potential commodity standards, gold exhibits best another unique characteristic of money—it is an excellent standard of measurement for economic value. *Over the long run, it takes a relatively constant rate of application of a certain quantity of capital and human labor to produce a constant quantity of gold. Gold production is like a metering device which gauges the relative productivity, over time, of capital and labor. For this reason, gold money is the best measuring rod of the value of other economic products desired in the market,* all of which require capital and labor to be produced.

ROBERTS: But there have been periods of inflation in countries with a gold standard?

LEHRMAN: If you mean that during gold standard periods the price level has exhibited tendencies to rise or fall very gently, yes. But under the gold standard, there have been no periods of sustained high, long-term inflation like the 1970s—nothing comparable to the sustained double-digit inflations of pure paper and credit money systems of past and present.

Even during earlier epochs of commodity standards this was true. For example, even during the great "price revolution" of the sixteenth century, when Europe plundered the gold and silver mines of the New World, there was modest inflation compared to the present.

ROBERTS: What about the U.S. in the late 1960s?

LEHRMAN: Don't forget we abandoned the gold standard domestically in 1934, and "de facto" internationally in March 1968.

ROBERTS: I thought it was still in effect to some degree until 1971.

LEHRMAN: Only formally. In March 1968, the U.S. decided to abandon the London gold pool which supplied gold at the fixed rate to the world market on demand. In March 1968 Lyndon Johnson abandoned the gold pool which had maintained the Bretton Woods monetary agreement until that time. In August 1971, President Nixon formally and legally repudiated the last vestige of the international gold standard.

In any case, in the early 1960s, the rate of inflation averaged less than 2 percent. After the onset of the Vietnam War, the rate of inflation rose steadily above 3 percent. But it was not until after 1968 and 1971, when we finally repudiated convertibility entirely, that the rate of inflation rose consistently above 5 percent and then higher. Now for two years in a row, we have averaged 12 percent.

*If historians refer to the "price revolution" of the sixteenth century, when the rate of inflation averaged approximately 3 percent a year over a century, I wonder what historians are going to call the last ten years in the U.S.!*

My point is, of course, that if you establish a monetary standard based upon a real commodity, and that real commodity is gold, there can be no long-term inflation, properly speaking. And depending on business cycle conditions, there will be tendencies for the price level to decline gently during other periods. A true gold standard exhibits a "retrieval phenomenon," always bringing the price level toward stability and unity. Periods of gently falling prices under the gold standard (1875-1895) have led to periods of modest reflation (1895-1914). And by the way, both were periods of economic growth in the U.S.

ROBERTS: I think you were in the midst of describing your method for getting us onto a gold standard when I interrupted you. Could you pick up where you left off?

LEHRMAN: Sure. Since I hope that the Reagan administration has the will to reduce marginal tax rates, balance the budget and deregulate American life, I have no doubt that with the same kind of leadership, the gold standard could be restored within two years. a balanced budget at the current level of tax receipts, reduced tax rates and the gold standard would lead to sustained economic growth with a reasonably stable price level.

If he desired, the President could announce that within two years he would propose to Congress a statute which would establish a dollar convertible into gold. *In fact, there would be no "price" for gold. Properly speaking, the dollar would be redefined as a weight of gold.* The "price," or weight, at which that would be determined would be influenced largely by market conditions preceding the date of resumption. The price of gold in paper dollars right now is about $500 (March 1981). Two years hence, the value of gold in paper dollars would naturally reflect the supply and demand of gold, relative to supply and demand conditions for all other goods, during that particular period.

But because of the President's announcement, the price would be substantially devoid of the inflationary expectations that are included in the paper price of gold now. All the market participants would realize that, with the resumption of convertibility, the fluctuation in the value of paper dollars, and therefore of gold prices expressed in paper dollars, would end.

*The gold standard may be seen, in general, as the way to end the mindless speculation in currencies and, in particular, as the end to speculation in gold.* That's why the gold standard is a very different enterprise from what some people confuse it with—namely, the activities of the "gold bugs." Gold bugs are people who know that paper and credit monies are overproduced. Gold bugs are, therefore, speculators in gold, and they're speculating for the fall in paper monies.

One of the virtues of the gold standard is that it suppresses unproductive speculation and sends the speculators back to producing real goods and services for the market. To want the gold standard is to want an end to such unproductive speculation in the value of currency. The monetary standard of a great nation must be, to the extent possible, like the unvarying thirty-six inch standard of the yardstick. *True money must be a reasonably reliable measuring rod and honest store of economic value.* It must not be a floating vessel in the sea of politics, subject to wave after wave of manipulation and therefore speculation. Imagine changing the length of a yardstick, without warning, every day.

If we truly desire to restore the future of America by reviving the will to save and invest, and if we genuinely desire to renew the spirit of capitalism around the world, then we shall have to give the world a real money, a true and reliable measuring rod of economic value. That's why I believe no economic program in this country will ever yield the American renaissance we hope for unless we restore the international gold standard. It is the unique monetary institution and sovereign symbol of a peaceful, open and growing world market order. Only the United States, as the leader of the West, has the power to establish and maintain a capitalist world market order. Let us get on with our destiny.

# The 100 Percent Gold Standard:
# A Proposal for Monetary Reform

Joseph T. Salerno

## Introduction: The Current Debate on Gold

On October 26, 1981, the Federal Gold Commission held its third meeting since its formation on June 22, 1981 under the aegis of the U.S. Treasury Department.[1] The commission, which consists of seventeen prominent economists, legislators, businessmen, and Reagan administration officials, is charged with studying and reporting upon the feasibility of according a larger role to gold in the monetary system of the U.S. Professor Paul McCracken, one of the commission's leading members and an adviser to three previous Republican Presidents, observed at its first meeting on July 16 that the commission is conducting the first serious governmental monetary study in over seventy-five years. Much more significant, of course, is the fact that the subject of the commission's study is the gold standard.[2]

As recently as the early 1970s, the prospect of a governmental body seriously deliberating the merits of reinstituting the gold standard would have been considered unthinkable. In the years following World War II, the overwhelming majority of economists and economic policymakers as well as the population at large came increasingly to consider gold as a relic of a barbarous and bygone age, unfit to perform the functions of money in a modern industrial economy. The tiny handful of gold standard advocates, both inside and outside the economics profession, were then regarded as hopelessly benighted economic Neanderthals or thralls to a peculiar fetish.

Recent developments in the world economy, however, have conspired to effect a profound rethinking of the prevailing view on gold. In particular, there was the cold reality of the chronic stagflation which began to engulf the market-oriented economies of North America, Western Europe, and Japan in the early 1970s and which has since proved intractable to the orthodox Keynesian demand-management policies of fiscal and monetary fine-tuning. Moreover, the unprecedented and agonizing combination of double-digit inflation and recession-level unemployment which characterizes stagflation could not be explained within the theoretical framework of textbook Keynesianism. Not surprisingly, there has recently emerged a thoroughgoing disenchantment with the Keynesian approach to macroeconomic stabilization policy and a search for alternatives.

One such alternative is offered by Milton Friedman and the "monetarists" who argue that the monetary authority should adopt "a stable and predictable monetary growth rule." However, in Great Britain, Margaret Thatcher's much ballyhooed attempt to implement the monetarist program has produced wildly erratic monetary growth accompanied by a continued and relentless upward spiral in prices and an unemployment rate which has not been exceeded since the Great Depression. For example, during 1980, money supply growth underwent spectacular swings, with the quantity of money growing at annual rates of 10 percent in the first quarter, -4.1 percent in the second quarter, 11 percent in the third quarter, and 17.8 percent in the last quarter, to yield an average growth rate of 8.4 percent for the year.[3] The effect of this monetary inflation was a 12.7 percent increase in consumer prices and a 10.9 percent rise in industrial wholesale prices.[4] In the meanwhile, the British economy was plunged deeper into recession as real gross domestic product and employment declined at annual rates of 3.4 percent and 4.1 percent respectively during the first three quarters of 1980.[5]

The story has been much the same in the U.S. where, in October 1979, the Federal Reserve publicly proclaimed its intention of eschewing all further attempts to control interest rates in favor of implementing the monetarist prescription of maintaining a steady rate of growth of the money supply. While its efforts in this direction have not led to a significant abatement of the symptoms of stagflation, the Fed has found its task impossibly complicated of late by the divergent signals being conveyed by alternative gauges of money supply growth. For example, while both M1-A and M1-B indicated that monetary growth was grossly deficient and, in fact, negative during the four months beginning April 1, 1981, M2 was growing at an annual rate of 7.2 percent over the same period—well within the Federal Reserve's target range of growth for this monetary aggregate.[6] In fact, during July and August, when the growth rate of M1-B (shift adjusted) was below its target range, the rate of growth of M2 actually exceeded its target range.[7] Consequently, while monetarists such as Milton Friedman, who focus on M2 have urged the Federal Reserve to hold the line or even pull the reins in on money supply growth, others such as Undersecretary of the Treasury Beryl Sprinkel have pointed to M1-B and chided the Fed for an overly stringent monetary policy which threatens to precipitate a recession.[8]

It is this perceived failure of both the Keynesian and monetarist alternatives to provide any relief from our current economic malaise that accounts for the growing wave of support for gold and the sympathetic hearing it is being accorded in the renewed debate over macroeconomic stabilization policy.

Although the new advocates of the gold standard are by no means a unified school of thought, the most prominent among them tend to be associated with "supply-side economics." These include Arthur Laffer, Jude Wanniski, George Gilder, Irving Kristol, Representatives Jack Kemp and Ron Paul, Senators Jesse Helms and Roger W. Jepsen, and even President Reagan himself in the early stages of his presidential campaign. Others who have been involved, though less intimately, with the supply-side movement are the eminent monetary economist Robert Mundell and Lewis Lehrman, a businessman and writer.

Support for the gold standard, however, has not been confined to the adherents of supply-side economics. A gold-based monetary standard has also elicited favorable comments from a number of "mainstream" academic economists. For example, the respected monetary theorist, Robert J. Barro, in a recent study, concluded that:

> In relation to a fiat currency regime, the key element of a commodity standard is its potential for automaticity and consequent absence of political control over the quantity of money and the absolute price level. . . . The choice among different monetary constitutions—such as the gold standard, a commodity reserve standard, or a fiat standard with fixed rules for setting the quantity of money—may be less important than the decision to adopt *some* monetary constitution. On the other hand, the gold standard actually prevailed for a substantial period (even if from an "historical accident," rather than a constitutional choice process), whereas the world has yet to see a fiat currency system that has obvious "stability" properties.[9]

Another noteworthy contribution is an historical study of the gold standard by Professor Roy W. Jastram.[10] Quite recently, Jastram summarized the findings of this study for the *Wall Street Journal*:

> From 1792 into the 1930s Britain was on a gold standard and the United States was on either a bimetallic standard or one of gold alone. During all those years, in both countries, price inflations and subsequent deflations average sensibly to zero. The result: for both the U.K. and the U.S. the wholesale price index numbers at the end of the gold standard were at just the level of 1800.[11]

Jastram goes on to suggest that this is "not unpredictable because the gold standard discipline was at work." Thus he concludes that "With the money supply showing ominous signs of being out of control, serious thought must be given to a new form of monetary discipline, one which might be suggested by age-old experience."[12]

A further indication that proposals for a restoration of the gold standard are not being taken lightly can be seen in the growing number of prominent opponents of gold that have been induced to break their silence and join the controversy. For example, under the aegis of the prestigious and neo-Keynesian-oriented Brookings Institution, Edward M. Bernstein, a leading authority on the international monetary system, has taken up his pen against the gold standard.[13] Recently, an historical study of the classical gold standard appeared in the monthly review of the St. Louis Federal Reserve Bank,[14] a widely recognized bastion of monetarism. A critical analysis of the gold standard was contributed by William Fellner to the latest survey of contemporary economic problems published annually by the influential American Enterprise Institute,[15] an institution generally sympathetic to monetarist policy prescriptions. Finally, some former and current high-ranking economic policymakers including Herbert Stein,[16] William Nordhaus,[17] and Henry Wallich[18] have made their cases against gold in the popular press.

Despite its newfound respectability, however, the gold standard remains shrouded in an almost impenetrable fog of myths, which were concocted during the Keynesian revolution and the era of the "new economics" that it ushered in. For the most part, these myths have gone unchallenged to this day. As a consequence, the gold standard still remains for most people—and especially for most economists schooled in the current orthodoxy—beyond the pale of rational discussion. Indeed, if questioned on the issue, many laymen as well as economists are capable of reciting a seemingly formidable litany of objections to the gold standard. The result is that gold is usually peremptorily dismissed at the outset of any discussion of monetary policy. This places the gold standard advocate at a severe disadvantage since he must undertake to demythologize an institution before a rational consideration of his policy prescriptions can even begin.

The monetary reformer intent upon presenting the case for the gold standard confronts another problem created by the very ambiguity attaching to the term *gold standard*. This stems from the fact that the term has been used very loosely to denote a number of diverse historical monetary systems and monetary reform proposals in which gold is a key element. Since these gold-based monetary systems differ in much more than minor details, it behooves the monetary reformer —in order to avoid misinterpretation and misplaced criticism—to carefully specify the precise nature of the "gold standard" he is proposing.

In what follows, I shall present the main argument for the private market-chosen, pure-commodity-money standard as represented by the 100 percent gold standard. After briefly delineating its nature and operation, I shall address the most common objections to such a standard and to the gold standard in general. The paper will conclude with a survey and critique of a number of recent proposals for monetary reform in which gold plays a key role.

## Why a Commodity Money

The case for a free market commodity money such as gold was trenchantly and succinctly stated by Ludwig von Mises nearly sixty years ago:

> The reason for using a *commodity* money is precisely to prevent political influence from affecting directly the value of the monetary unit. . . . Gold is the standard money primarily because an increase or decrease in the available quantity is independent of the orders issued by political authorities. The distinctive feature of the gold standard is that it makes changes in the quantity of money dependent on the profitability of gold production.[19]

Almost one-half century later, with the government-manipulated, pseudogold standard of the Bretton Woods system racked by inflationary spasms and on the verge of collapse, von Mises eloquently restated his argument:

> The quantity of money is the decisive problem. The quality that makes gold fit for service as money is precisely the fact that the quantity of gold cannot be manipulated by governments. The gold standard has one quality, one virtue. It is that the quantity of gold cannot be increased in the way that paper notes can be increased. The usefulness of the gold standard consists in the fact that it makes the supply of money depend on the profitability of mining gold, and thus checks large-scale inflationary ventures on the part of governments.

> Gold cannot be produced in a cheaper way by any governmental bureau, committee, institution, office, international agency, or so on. This is the only justification of the gold standard. One has tried again and again to find some method to substitute these qualities of gold in some other way. But all these methods have failed. . . .

> The eminence of the gold standard is to be seen in the fact that the gold standard alone makes determination of the monetary unit's purchasing power independent of the ambitions and activities of dictators, political parties, and pressure groups.[20]

In short, the case for a commodity money rests on the fact that it furnishes the only effective bulwark against inflation.

## The 100 Percent Gold Standard

Under a pure commodity standard, the monetary unit would be a unit of weight of the commodity chosen by the market as the general medium of exchange. Assuming that the market chose gold—and this need not be the case—the monetary unit would be, e.g., an ounce or a gram of gold. The transformation of the money-commodity into those shapes such as coins which are deemed most useful by buyers and sellers for mediating their exchanges would be performed by private mints competing for profits in a free market. Whatever the various forms in which market participants might prefer to hold gold in their money balances, the total quantity of money in the economy would be rigidly fixed at any moment by the total weight of gold owned by all individuals in the economy. This is true despite the likely development under a pure commodity standard of money substitutes, i.e., claims to money which are tendered and accepted in monetary exchanges in place of the actual money-commodity.

Such claims to money arise when people choose to store a portion of their money holdings in private money warehouses or "banks," receiving in exchange warehouse receipts, whether in the form of paper tickets or deposits subject to draft by check, entitling them to redeem their gold upon demand. If the money warehouses are generally viewed as reputable firms, then the notes and demand deposits which they issue would begin to function as money substitutes because, under certain circumstances, individual transactors would find it less costly to consummate exchanges without the money-commodity being physically present. The use of money substitutes would, however, have no effect on the quantity of money since, as actual warehouse receipts, they are and legally must be fully "covered" by the gold to which they are instantly redeemable claims. Rather than being a net addition to the money supply, the money substitutes would literally substitute for an equal amount of gold in circulation, with the gold so displaced now locked away in the vaults of the various money warehouses. In less apt but more familiar terminology, the banks would be legally required to maintain 100 percent reserves against all demand liabilities.[21]

The fundamental reason for preferring the 100 percent gold standard to other gold-based proposals for monetary reform is that it is the only monetary system which effects the *complete* separation of the government from the supply of money. Under this system, the money supply process is totally privatized: the mining, minting, certification, and storage of the money-commodity as well as the issuance of fully covered notes and deposits are carried out by private firms operating in a free market. In thus removing all vestiges of the government monopoly over money, the pure commodity standard provides a practically inflation-proof currency. This becomes clearer once it is realized that inflation occurs for no other reason than that it benefits that group or institution—in almost every case the national government—which succeeds in arrogating to itself the legal monopoly over money creation. This requires a few words of explanation.

In a money economy, an individual or organization can obtain a money income in one of two ideal typical ways: via the "economic means" or the "political means." The economic means refers to the voluntary production and exchange of useful goods on the market. The political means, on the other hand, denotes the expropriation of income from the producers—that is, those individuals who have obtained their incomes through the economic means.[22] Taxation, a levy on the incomes of the producers, is an example of the political means and is the method regularly employed by all governments to secure the bulk of their revenues. However, whatever the moral or practical justification of taxation, by virtue of the fact that it is essentially coercive, tax increases have historically found little favor with the citizenry. Fearful of arousing political unrest, governments through the ages have cast about for alternative methods of augmenting their revenues. Having secured the legal monopoly of the supply of money precisely for this reason, it is no wonder that almost all governments have resorted to inflation. For inflation provides its practitioners with a relatively simple, costless, and secure "political" avenue to amassing money assets, one which circumvents both the unpopularity connected with the imposition of higher taxes. In substance, all government need do to increase its real income is slap some ink on paper and spend the proceeds on commodities and services produced by the private market. Actually, in the world of modern banking, inflation becomes a much more arcane process little understood by the population at large. This fact serves well to obscure the true cause of inflation and permits the government to shift the blame for the shrinking purchasing power of the monetary unit and the other undesirable consequences of inflation from itself to other groups, e.g., OPEC, monopolistic corporations, powerful nations, spendthrift consumers, etc.

It should be no cause for surprise then that all government-monopolized paper fiat currencies exhibit symptoms of inflationary disorder—just as it is no surprise when other groups in the economy exploit political means to augment their money incomes, e.g., via tariffs, occupational licensure, exclusive public franchises, etc. Indeed, it is a frequent observation of sociology as well as a rule of common sense that an individual or group endowed with a legal monopoly over *any* area of the economy will use it to its own best advantage. To put it rather bluntly, government is an inherently inflationary institution and will ever remain so until it is dispossessed of its monopoly of the supply of money.

Indeed, F. A. Hayek, Nobel Laureate in economics, has recently and forcefully argued that the recurring bouts of macroeconomic instability which have always afflicted market economies are "a consequence of the age-old government monopoly of the issue of money."[23] According to Hayek, furthermore:

> There is no justification in history for the existing position of a government monopoly of issuing money. It has never been proposed on the ground that government will give us better money than anybody else could. It has always, since the privilege of issuing money was first explicitly represented as a Royal prerogative, been advocated because the power to issue money was essential for the finance of government—not in order to give us good money, but in order to give to government access to the tap where it can draw money it needs by manufacturing it. That, ladies and gentlemen, is not a method by which we can hope ever to get good money. To put it into the hands of an institution which is protected against competiton, which can force us to accept the money, which is subject to incessant political pressure, such an authority will not ever again give us good money.[24]

Certainly, Hayek's insight is amply illustrated in the history of government involvement with money which is, for all practical purposes, the history of inflation. Even a staunch proponent of fiat money and government monetary policy, such as William Fellner, has been reluctantly forced to admit recently that there is a "substantial element of truth involved in the assertion that fiat money has been misused in *all* history—has *always* led to the corruption of the currency."[25] (Emphases are mine.)

And therein lies the fatal flaw in the monetarist program. Aside from any theoretical objections to monetarism, its policy prescriptions completely fail to address the radical (in the etymological sense of "root") cause of inflation in the modern world, viz., the governmental monopolies of the money-supply process which exist in every nation. The monetarist "quantity rule" is not an antiinflation *policy* at all, but merely the enunciation of a request that the political authorities exercise restraint in exploiting their monopoly, which, under the monetarist program, would remain virtually intact. Such a request, I might add, is incredibly naive in the light of theory and history.

The virtue of the 100 percent gold standard, in contrast, is precisely that it establishes a free market in the supply of money and, in the event, brings about a complete abolition of the governmental monopoly in this most sensitive and vital area of the market economy. Indeed, although he regards a pure commodity standard as ultimately undesirable because of its high resource cost, Milton Friedman is essentially in agreement with this point. According to Friedman:

> If money consisted wholly of a physical commodity . . . in principle there would be no need for control by the government at all. . . .

> If an automatic commodity standard were feasible, it would provide an excellent solution to the liberal dilemma of how to get a stable monetary framework without the danger of irresponsible exercise of monetary powers. A full commodity standard, for example, an honest-to-goodness gold standard in which 100 percent of the money consisted literally of gold, widely supported by a public imbued with the mythology of a gold standard and the belief that it is immoral and improper for government to interfere with its operation, would provide an effective control against government tinkering with the currency and against irresponsible monetary action. Under such a standard, any monetary powers of government would be very minor in scope.[26]

It should be emphasized that, while almost any type of a gold standard will yield a far less inflationary monetary system than the present regime of national fiat currencies, all but the 100 percent gold standard ascribe a greater or lesser role to the political authorities in their operation. As I shall argue in greater detail below, these watered-down versions of the gold standard are, as a consequence, dynamically unstable because the government can be expected to take every opportunity to use its predominant position in the system to further water down and undermine the barriers to its inevitably inflationary predilections. Historically, this is borne out by the key role played by the governments of the Western nations in the step-by-step transformation of the relatively noninflationary classical gold standard into the nominally gold-based and highly inflationary Bretton Woods system. This almost unrecognizable caricature of the gold standard was adminstered a merciful death in 1971 and, shortly thereafter, a regime of fluctuating national fiat currencies was foisted upon the world economy. It is no coincidence that inflation in most capitalist nations began to accelerate significantly at about the same time.

Although it is, of course, *possible* for the government to engineer an inflationary transformation of the 100 percent gold standard, it is much more difficult than in the case of other gold-based systems. The reason is that under a pure commodity standard every stage of the money-supply process from mining to banking is in private hands. Any steps taken by the state to achieve an initial position of power in this process could not be camouflaged as merely innocuous tinkering with the "rules of the game." Such actions would be easily recognized for what they in fact were—a self-serving assault on private property rights by the government which would more than likely provoke stiff resistance on the part of the populace.

Having made my case for the desirability of the 100 percent gold standard, I shall now attempt to briefly delineate its workings. This will aid in detecting and dispelling the myths underlying a number of the more pervasive and persistent objections to the gold standard.

In order to grasp the functioning of a free market in money, all that is required is a basic understanding of the operation of the venerable supply-and-demand mechanism supplemented by insight into the unique position occupied by money in the sphere of economic goods. To begin with, the function of money is, by definition, to mediate the exchanges of all other goods. People acquire money in exchange for the goods and services which they themselves produce with a view to reexchanging it for more desired goods and services at some time in the future. The performance of this medium-of-exchange function does not necessitate the physical destruction of the money-commodity. This fact differentiates money from consumers' goods and producers' goods —i.e., capital goods and natural resources, since the latter two are used up in performing their respective functions.

On the other hand, money, like other scarce goods, has a price which at any moment is determined by its supply and demand. Money's price is its purchasing power or command over all other goods for which it exchanges on the market. For example, if the demand for money increases while the supply of money remains unchanged, the purchasing power of money will rise. That is to say, the alternative quantities of other goods for which a given unit of money, such as a gold ounce, exchanges on the market will increase as money prices in the economy undergo a general fall. A rise in the purchasing power of money will also result from a decrease in the supply of money in the face of an unchanged monetary demand. Conversely, a decline in the demand for money or an augmentation of its supply, other things remaining equal, will bring about a decrease in the purchasing power of the monetary unit manifested in a general rise of money prices in the economy.

This brings us to the fundamental respect in which money differs from other economic goods. While increases in the supplies of the various nonmonetary goods in the economy augment the satisfaction of human wants—directly in the case of consumers' goods and indirectly in the case of producers' goods—the same cannot be said of an increase in the supply of money. An addition to the physical number of units of money in the economy will not permit money to discharge its medium-of-exchange function any more fully or expeditously. The existing quantity of money is always sufficient to yield society the full utility of a medium of exchange. The sole effect of an increase in the supply of money will be a dilution of the purchasing power of the monetary unit or, what is the same thing, a general increase of money prices.

The foregoing analysis equips us to address some of the more common objections to the gold standard and to bare the myths upon which they stand.

One of the charges most frequently brought against the gold standard is that it cannot provide for the monetary needs of a growing economy. Increases in the supply of money, it is said, are necessary to finance the purchases of the increasing quantities of goods and services resulting from economic growth. The gold standard cannot be depended upon to produce the required additions to the money supply at the right times or in the right proportions. The consequence of such monetary deficiency is a stunting of economic growth or possibly even a precipitous depression. It is this reasoning which underlies a popular explanation of the Great Depression as stemming from a worldwide shortage of gold. It has also served as the rationale of governments for their implementation of policies which led to the progressive debilitation and eventual collapse of the classical gold standard in the 1930s. The view that the relative insufficiency of gold constitutes a barrier to economic growth was summed up in the oft-quoted statement of Keynes that, "at periods when gold is available at suitable depths experience shows that the real wealth of the world increases rapidly; and when but little of it is so available, our wealth suffers stagnation or decline."[27]

However plausible, this line of reasoning is untenable because it ignores the supply-and-demand mechanism operative in a free market for money. The market insures that any quantity of money is capable of performing all the work required of a medium of exchange by adjusting its purchasing power to the underlying conditions of supply and demand. The increasing stocks of goods which sellers seek to exchange for money in a growing economy represent an overall increase in the demand for money. Thus, if the quantity of money remains unchanged in the face of a growth in real output, the result will be a general bidding down of prices in the economy and, *pari passu*, an increase in the purchasing power of money. With each unit of money now capable of doing more work in exchange, the same quantity of money will suffice to finance the increased volume of transactions.

It might be added that it is precisely through falling prices that the fruits of increased productivity and economic growth are spread throughout the market economy. For example, if prices in general fall due to a growth in real output—all other things equal—all individuals in the economy will experience a growth in their real incomes despite the fact that their money incomes remain unchanged. If the government—acting under the false belief that a growth in real output necessitates an increase in the money supply—injects new money into the economy, it will counteract the free-market forces leading to a fall in prices and, consequently, frustrate the natural market process by which productivity gains are distributed throughout society. The result will be that some groups, especially those who receive the new money first, such as stockholders and workers in defense firms working on government contracts, will appropriate a disproportionate share of the gains at the expense of other groups—pensioners, annuitants, and others whose money incomes are fixed.

The same considerations apply to the objection that the gold standard is not flexible enough to withstand the bouts of hoarding which, it is alleged, may spontaneously take hold among consumers and investors in the economy. If not offset by timely injections of new money in the economy, it is argued, such hoarding threatens a shrinkage of expenditure, income, and output which may plummet the economy into a downward spiral of deflation and depression. These fears are groundless, however, because the term "hoarding" denotes nothing more nor less than the voluntary decisions of individuals in the economy to reduce their rate of spending in order to increase their money holdings. The result of these decisions is an increase in the aggregate demand for money on the market. If the supply of money is fixed, the increased demand for money will effect a general fall in money prices. Lower prices will translate into a greater purchasing power of the monetary unit, a development which allows the same quantity of money to fulfill people's desires for increased money holdings. Thus "hoarding"—or more properly, an increase in the social demand for money—far from being economically disruptive, is in fact a boon to society. It is the means by which the free market adjusts the purchasing power of individuals' money balances to suit their voluntarily expressed preferences. Once again, any government intervention designed to offset the effects of hoarding merely hampers this market adjustment process and frustrates the desires of money-holders.

This brings us to the criticism that, under the gold standard, the "price level" is unstable. Among other things, this allegedly reduces money's effectiveness as a "measure of value," introducing widespread inefficiency and instability into the economy. For example, unforeseen changes in money's value or purchasing power cause businessmen to err in their anticipations of future costs and prices and in their subsequent allocation of scarce resources. Moreover, such changes effect an unforeseen redistribution of wealth between debtors and creditors.

Unfortunately, this objection rests on a basic confusion regarding the nature of money. Simply put, money is not some sort of measuring device whose value is or should be eternally fixed. Money is, in fact, a commodity chosen by the market as a medium of exchange. Like other goods on the market it has a price which fluctuates according to changes in its supply and demand. There is no more justification for government to take steps to render the free market supply-and-demand mechanism inoperative in the case of money than there is in the case of other commodities. In fact, changes in the purchasing power of money have important functions on the market. As we saw above, these include the distribution of the fruits of a growing economy to all the public and the satisfaction of people's desires for changes in their money balances. If the government were to succeed in freezing the purchasing power of money—i.e., in "stabilizing the price level"—money would be rendered incapable of performing these vital functions. In practice, of course, the attempts of modern governments to achieve a stable price level through manipulations of the money supply have succeeded only in seriously destabilizing the economy (witness our present stagflation) while, at the same time, rendering the purchasing power of money much more volatile than it ever was under the classical gold standard.

Furthermore, the desire for a stable "price level" betrays a fundamental misconception of the value of money. As noted above, the value or purchasing power of the monetary unit, say an ounce of gold, is a vast array of alternative quantities of goods and services for which a gold ounce exchanges on the market, e.g., one color televison set or four men's suits or one-twentieth of a new automobile, etc. Since the array consists of specific and heterogeneous quantities, it cannot be mathematically manipulated to yield a unitary value such as a "price level." In other words, the value of money is embedded in the specific prices of particular goods and services—e.g., 1 oz. per color television, 1/4 oz. per men's suit, 20 oz. per automobile, etc.

If the value of money cannot be expressed apart from the reality of specific prices paid in specific market transactions, then stabilizing the value of money logically implies freezing all market prices both absolutely and in relation to one another. For it is precisely through the interaction of the supplies and demands for particular goods as expressed in sales and purchases for money that there emerges, at one and the same time and as part of the same process, the exchange-value of each good in terms of every other—"relative prices"—and of each good in terms of money—the so-called price level or purchasing power of money. As a result, the "value of money" is inextricably intertwined with *particular money prices* and the two cannot be even conceptually separated. It is, therefore, meaningless to advocate, as proponents of price level stabilization do, that on the one hand, the value of money or the general level of prices be held constant while, on the other hand, particular prices be left free to vary in relation to one another according to supply and demand.

Of course, those who favor stabilizing the value of money have no desire to see the price of every single good eternally fixed. Instead, they advocate that some arbitrarily chosen statistical index of the prices of selected goods—the consumer price index, the GNP deflator, etc.—be maintained constant through political manipulation of the money supply. Unfortunately, this presents yet another problem. For even if the government possessed the inclination and the ability to implement such a monetary policy, their success in doing so would not suppress fluctuations in the value of money; it would merely alter and distort the structure of particular prices which emerges on the market and through which is reflected the purchasing power of the monetary unit. These distortions in relative prices, furthermore, effect an allocation of investments and resources which is not in accord with the true preferences of consumers and savers in the economy. The result of the continued pursuit of this monetary policy is the piling up of unsustainable malinvestments and resource misallocations which will eventually precipitate a painful but necessary period of liquidation and readjustment for the economy. In sum, every attempt to "stabilize the price level" through governmental monetary policy *inevitably distorts* the free-market pattern of relative prices and *leads to a destabilization* of the entire economy, through business cycles or, in more modern parlance, fluctuations in macroeconomic activity.

Finally, under a free market commodity-money standard, if debtors and creditors truly wished to rid themselves of the uncertainty born of unanticipated changes in the value of money, they could voluntarily avail themselves of the indexing techniques provided by a tabular standard. Under the voluntary tabular standard, the money payments called for in a credit or loan contract would be adjusted according to an agreed-upon index number registering changes in the prices of a selected group of commodities and services. The fact that these voluntary indexing schemes have never been widely resorted to (except, perhaps, during hyperinflation) should indicate to the stabilizationists that, in Murray Rothbard's words:

> Businessmen apparently prefer to take their chances in a specula-
> tive world rather than agree on some sort of arbitrary hedging
> device. Stock exchange speculators and commodity speculators
> are continually attempting to forecast future prices, and, indeed all
> entrepreneurs are engaged in anticipating the uncertain conditions
> of the market. Apparently, businessmen are willing to be entrepre-
> neurs in anticipating future changes in purchasing power as well as
> other changes.[28]

Another oft-repeated criticism of the gold standard is that the supply
of gold and, therefore, of money is determined "arbitrarily," depending
as it does on such fortuitous factors as discoveries of new mines and
technological improvemnts in the methods of extraction. This is surely
a curious, if not vacuous, use of the term "arbitrary," however, since
the supplies of oil and of apples and, for that matter, of every good produced on the market are influenced by changes in the availability of resources specific to their production and by improvements in technology. In truth, what these critics are really objecting to is precisely the
greatest virtue of the gold standard: the determination of the supply of
money solely by market forces and independently of political considerations. In this context, an examination of the money-supply process
operative under a pure commodity standard will serve to illustrate
further the superiority of the gold standard over a government-
monopolized fiat money.

Under the gold standard, the supply of the money-commodity
depends entirely upon the demand for it in monetary and nonmonetary uses and the money costs involved in its production. A change in
either factor brings about a change in the supply of money in the
economy. To delineate the process involved, let us begin from a
position of equilibrium in which the supply of and demand for money
and, hence, its purchasing power are constant. In this situation, gold
mining firms maximize monetary profits by producing a quantity of
gold per year just equal to the annual amount allocated to nonmonetary uses plus the amount used up or destroyed in monetary employment during the course of a year as a result of wear and tear.

An improvement in the technology of mining gold or the discovery
of new, more accessible sources of gold destroys this initial equilibrium
by lowering the costs and, thereby, increasing the profitability of gold
production, resulting in an increased annual supply of gold on the
market. With an unchanged demand for money, the larger supply of
the money-commodity exerts an upward pressure on prices which
reduces the purchasing power of money, as each gold ounce now
purchases fewer goods and services on the market. Happily, the
dilution of the purchasing power of the monetary unit is not the only
effect of the augmentation of the supply of gold. A fall in the monetary
value of gold also reduces the opportunity costs of employing it in
alternative nonmonetary uses like jewelry, dental filling, raw material
in industrial processes, etc. As a result, a portion of the additional

supply of gold is employed in expanding the supplies of producers' and consumers' goods on the market, thus facilitating an increased satisfaction of human wants.

While an increase of the supply of the money-commodity under the gold standard yields net benefits to society (for as long as a nonmonetary demand for gold exists), the same is not true of an increase in the supply of government fiat currency which, by definition, has no alternative nonmonetary uses. In the latter case, as in the case of counterfeiting, an increase in the supply of money benefits primarily those who create the new money as well as the initial recipients of their largesse or expenditures at the expense of the rest of society. Most importantly, however, even in the case in which gold has completely lost its value in nonmonetary uses—certainly a theoretical possibility, if not an empirical likelihood—the production of the money-commodity would still involve the use of scarce and, therefore, costly resources. As a result, the 100 percent gold standard provides a natural, market brake on the supply of money which is practically immune to tampering by the political authorities.

Furthermore, since gold is an extremely scarce as well as highly durable commodity, its annual production tends to be a tiny proportion of the existing stock. Consequently, even relatively large reductions or increases in its costs of production will not cause great fluctuations in the annual supply of money. The significance of the scarcity and durability of gold for the stability of the money supply has been vividly expressed by the monetary theorist, Edwin Kemmerer:

> Largely by reason of its beauty, gold very early in the history of the human race became an object of keen and widespread demand for ornament. The fact, however, that, although gold is found almost everywhere throughout the world, both on land and sea, it usually can be obtained in substantial quantity only by much effort and that nature is very niggardly in her offering of gold to man, except in a few limited parts of the world, makes gold a very scarce commodity. The entire twelve billion dollars of monetary gold in the world today [1935] would represent a cube only about 42.1 feet on a side. A universal demand for gold for ornament and a widespread demand for gold for monetary uses, coupled with this very limited supply, spell scarcity and high values.
>
> Gold is a very durable metal, especially when alloyed with a baser metal like copper, as it usually is. There is gold in the world today that men extracted from nature thousands of years before Christ. Ancient gold ornaments and coins may be seen in almost any of the world's leading museums. Gold in one form is continually being melted down to reappear in another form. Doubtless there are modern gold coins and gold watches in the world today that contain gold that was dug out of the earth thousands of years ago. Although the permanent losses of gold through abrasion, shipwreck and similar causes, are substantial, it should be remembered that, because of their high value, one's gold possessions are usually guarded carefully. The world's present total known supply of gold, therefore, is the accumulation of the ages. Gold being such a

durable object and the world's present stock being the accumulation of the ages, the production of any one year is a small percentage of the total stock. Furthermore, since a large part of the world's known stock of gold—much more than half—is in relatively unspecialized forms, such as coins and bars, forms into which very little labor has been wrought, the major part of the world's accumulated gold at any time is a potential supply on the market. It therefore takes a relatively long time for changes in the amount of gold produced annually to affect materially the market supply.[29]

Under a pure commodity standard, the supply of money also responds to forces operating on the demand side. For instance, an increase in the demand for money, *ceteris paribus*, effects a general lowering of prices in the economy, including lower prices for the resources employed in mining gold. As a result, the production of gold is rendered more profitable relative to the production of other goods and services. Entrepreneurs respond by increasing the rate of production from currently operational mines, by reopening old mines, and by exploiting for the first time previously known but submarginal sources of gold. They also increase investment in the search for new sources of gold and in the development of new and less costly methods of extraction. In addition, the higher monetary value of gold gives individuals an incentive to shift additional amounts of existing gold from nonmonetary to monetary employments. Thus, an increase in the market demand for money, which is initially satisfied by an increases in the purchasing power of the monetary unit, calls forth a gradual expansion of the supply of money that tends, in the long run, to offset the initial decline in prices and to restore the purchasing power of money to its original level.

Conversely, a fall in the demand for money causes a general rise in prices and, in the process, drives up the costs associated with digging up gold. As higher costs reduce the profit margins of gold-mining firms, the production of the metal tends to fall off. Additionally, the lower monetary value of gold induces people to shift some units out of their money balances and into nonmonetary uses, the products of which are now, in effect, purchased more cheaply. The operation of these actors results eventually in a contraction of the supply of money on the market which tends to reverse the initial rise of prices and re establish the original purchasing power of the monetary unit.

In summary, under a gold standard, the supply of money does not change arbitrarily but varies directly with monetary demand, resulting in a tendency to long-run stability in the purchasing power of gold. Moreover, in the short term, large fluctuations in the supply of money are precluded by the natural scarcity and durability of gold. Of course, this is not to argue that the gold standard would, or even should, insure perfect stability in the value of money. In fact, as I have argued above, such a goal is chimerical, and all attempts to achieve it in the real world will only create widespread maladjustments and instability in the economy. The point to be made, however, is that the market, when left to its own devices, has chosen and will choose a commodity money whose qualities render its purchasing power sufficiently stable over time to permit market participants to realize the tremendous benefits of indirect exchange and economic calculation which accrue in the form of a tremendously broadened scope for division of labor and specialization and for capital accumulation. As von Mises has noted in this regard:

> The free market has succeeded in developing a currency system which well served all the requirements both of indirect exchange and of economic calculation. The aims of monetary calculation are such that they cannot be frustrated by the inaccuracies which stem from slow and comparatively slight movements in purchasing power. Cash-induced changes in purchasing power of the extent to which they occurred in the last two centuries with metallic money, especially with gold money, cannot influence the result of the businessmen's economic calculations so considerably as to render such calculations useless. Historical experience shows that one could, for all practical purposes of the conduct of business, manage very well with these methods of calculation.[30]

Indeed, the historical record clearly shows that a gold money, even when adulterated with elements of fiduciary media—uncovered bank notes and deposits and government fiat currency—and subject to a variety of government interventions, has maintained great stability in its purchasing power over the long run.[31] Furthermore, it must be realized that any attempt to improve upon the money which emerges spontaneously on the market involves the enormous presumption that the myriad of individual transactors, whose decisions and actions ultimately conditioned the market's choice of a money over the ages, had consistently and repeatedly erred in assessing the relative benefits and costs of alternative media of exchange. In fact, it is much more likely that the age old political interference with money, far from improving it, has severely hindered the evolution and improvement of money and monetary institutions which would have occurred naturally on the free market. We cannot even presume to know the direction which such improvement would have taken precisely because, like the institution of money itself, it is the unintended result of a free and spontaneous process of interaction among a multitude of human minds. In Hayek's words:

> The monopoly of government of issuing money has not only deprived us of good money but has also deprived us of the only process by which we can find out what would be good money. We do not even quite know what exact qualities we want because in the two thousand years in which we have used coins and other money, we have never been allowed to experiment with it, we have never been given a chance to find out what the best kind of money would be.[32]

This brings us to the most serious objection to the gold standard. Milton Friedman, among others, has argued that the gold standard "is not desirable because it would involve a large cost in the form of resources used to produce the monetary commodity."[33] Surprisingly, many staunch defenders of the gold standard, from Adam Smith to Ludwig von Mises, have conceded the point to their opponents that the scarce resources expended in the provision of a commodity money represent a pure economic loss to society because these resources are diverted from the satisfaction of human wants. Advocates of the gold standard like von Mises go on to contend, however, that "if one looks at the catastrophic consequences of the great paper money inflations, one must admit that the expensiveness of gold production is the minor evil."[34] On the other hand, opponents of gold urge that the substitution of a "practically costless" and "well-managed" paper fiat currency would yield substantial benefits to society because the productive resources previously tied up in gold mining as well as the monetary stock of gold itself could now be allocated to the production of producers' and consumers' goods, leading to a net increase in human want-satisfaction.

The foregoing is a most persuasive argument which has seduced many good economists out of sound habits of thought. Setting aside for the moment the sociological insight that a legal monopoly of money is inherently inflationary and will never be "well-managed," the flaw in the argument is that it proves too much. Thus, it could be argued, *per analogiam*, that the enormous diversity in clothing styles and colors on the free market involves a wasteful expenditure of scarce resources which curtails human want satisfaction in other areas. If only a more "rational," i.e., government-monopolized, production and distribution system for clothing could be organized, the cost of providing the populace with clothing would be drastically cut. And no doubt the outfitting of the whole population with, say, gray Mao pajamas, would diminish the physical amount of resources devoted to producing clothing in the economy. But any economist worth his salt would reject this preposterous proposal out of hand as hardly optimal from an economic standpoint. Why so? Because he understands that, from the point of view of consumers, gray pajamas are a lower *quality* clothing than the clothing array available on the market. In other words, the higher level of resource expenditure associated with clothing diversity is economically justified because the increased quality of clothing which results is more highly valued by consumers than the products yielded by alternative employments of the extra resources.

But the same chain of reasoning holds, link for link, in the case of money, which is itself a tangible economic good necessarily possessing qualitative dimensions. The choice of gold by the market, therefore, was not arbitrary but crucially dependent upon its possession of certain qualities, e.g., general acceptability, natural scarcity, durability, portability, etc., which well suit it to function as the general medium of exchange. On the other hand, since the market has never deemed inconvertible paper tickets issued by one agency fit for monetary use, we are forced to conclude that a paper currency is not more efficient than a gold currency in discharging the functions of money *in the relevant economic sense which must necessarily take into account quality considerations.* As a consequence, the substitution of government-monopolized paper money for a free market commodity money must bring about a misallocation of resources which, ipso facto, raises costs in the economy—and this apart from the misallocations caused by the inflation which will almost inevitably follow.

Although the objection to the gold standard on the grounds of its high resource cost was probably first introduced into economics by Adam Smith, it holds a particular allure for modern economists, who tend to theorize in a general equilibrium framework. Since general equilibrium involves the conceptualization of an economy in which the interrelated phenomena of time and economic change are assumed absent, it in effect assumes away the basic reason why people desire to hold money—the uncertainty of the future bred by ceaseless and unforeseen economic change. Needless to say, what is called "money" in this system "is not a medium of exchange; it is not money at all; it is merely a *numeraire,* an ethereal and undetermined unit of accounting of . . . vague and undefinable character. . . ."[35] For someone who conceives of money in this way, as an insubstantial accounting fiction, it is quite easy to downplay or altogether ignore the qualitative aspects of the tangible economic good which constitutes the general medium of exchange in the real world.[36] The resource-cost argument against a commodity money thus only has validity in the context of a highly unrealistic theoretical construct where the very conditions of money's existence have been assumed away!

There is one other criticism of the gold standard which, because of its apparently wide acceptance by free-market-oriented economists, also warrants brief mention and response. This criticism, generally levelled by proponents of freely floating exchange rates between national fiat currencies, invokes the prestige of the free market against the international gold standard. Thus, it is alleged by these critics that the gold standard is a fixed-exchange-rate system which requires governments to intervene in the market to "fix" the prices of gold and foreign currencies in terms of the domestic currency. Such governmental price fixing, it is said, disrupts the smooth and efficient operation of the free market in foreign exchange and inevitably results in surpluses and shortages of the various national currencies. Government policies, such as tariffs, quotas, exchange controls, etc., designed to suppress the symptoms of these foreign-exchange disequilibria only breed further distortions and inefficiencies in international trade and investment.

While superficially quite plausible, this argument is based on a fundamental conceptual confusion. For, under a genuine gold standard, national currencies do not exist as separate and distinct entities apart from gold. For example, during the era of the classical gold standard prior to 1914, governments did not "fix" the price of gold in terms of their national currencies; the national currency units, such as the "dollar," "pound," "franc," etc., were themselves merely names for a specific weight of the money-commodity, gold. Thus the dollar was *defined* as 1/20 ounces of gold, the pound as slightly less than 1/4 ounces of gold, and so forth. The "rate of exchange" between dollars and pounds was therefore five to one, not as a consequence of government "price fixing," but simply because, by the rules of arithmetic, 5/20 ounces of gold (five dollars) equals 1/4 ounces of gold (one pound). In fact, strictly speaking, it is inappropriate to use the concept of an exchange rate when describing the relationship of equivalence between dollars and pounds. The reason is that an exchange rate or price designates a ratio of quantities of two different goods, whereas pounds and dollars denote different weights of the same good, i.e., gold.

Thus, the argument that the international gold standard involves fixed exchange rates between different national currencies is akin to arguing that the present U.S. monetary system involves fixed exchange rates between, say, nickels, dimes, and dollars. That this is not immediately apparent is the unfortunate result of certain peculiarities of the classical gold standard. Under this system, as already noted, the gold currency unit came to bear different names in different nations rather than being denominated by standard weight units such as the gram or ounce, a development which was actively fostered by governments who stood to benefit thereby.[37] Furthermore, monopolization of the note issue and the centralization of gold reserves were achieved by government-controlled central banks. These developments gave rise to the fiction that the notes issued by the central bank and the deposits of private banks denominated in these notes were not merely claims to the actual money-commodity—gold—but were themselves money. As a result, gold came to be viewed as "reserves" or "backing" for the nation's money supply which was "bought" and "sold" by the central bank at a "fixed price" in terms of the national currency unit.

It should be noted that such confusion could not have arisen under a fully private 100 percent gold standard because, in this case, standard names of weight are used to designate the currency unit, with the consequence that the absurdity of speaking of an "exchange rate" between a gram of gold and an ounce of gold becomes immediately apparent. Furthermore, since bank notes and deposits are issued solely by private, profit-making institutions, which are not invested with the high authority and prestige of a government central bank, there is little likelihood that people will confuse these warehouse receipts for gold with a money that is separate and distinct from gold.

### A Note on Alternative Plans to Establish a Gold-Dollar Link

Recently, a number of plans have been proposed which aim at giving gold a role in the U.S. monetary system once again. Although these plans vary significantly in basic conception as well as in institutional details, all but one suffer, to a greater or lesser degree, from the same fundamental flaw: they leave intact the current government monopoly of money. For purposes of discussion, these monetary reform proposals may be grouped under four headings: (1) the gold certificate reserve, (2) the gold "price rule," (3) the classical gold standard, (4) the *de facto* gold standard.

### (1) *The Gold-Certificate Reserve*

Robert E. Weintraub, senior economist of the Congressional Joint Committee, has proposed the reinstatement of the gold certificate reserve requirement for Federal Reserve notes.[38] Under Weintraub's plan, the Fed would be legally required, as it was prior to 1968, to maintain a reserve of gold certificates the value of which, at a stipulated legal price of gold, would be a fixed proportion of its outstanding note liabilities. Before 1968, when the legal or "par" value of gold was $35 per ounce, the reserve requirement was twenty-five percent and so, in effect, each dollar of currency in circulation was "backed" by 25 cents in gold. Weintraub's plan "would require that the Federal Reserve banks hold at least nine cents in gold certificates at their legal value ($42.22 per ounce since 1973) behind each dollar of note liabilities in perpetuity."[39] The 9 percent reserve requirement reflects the ratio of par value gold certificates held by the Fed to its note liabilities prevailing at the end of 1980. According to Weintraub:

> Legislation to keep the percent of legal value gold certificates behind Federal Reserve notes what it was at the end of 1980 in perpetuity would prevent any future currency growth. And, unless the public wanted to hold an increasing part of its total transactions balances (currency plus checking deposits in depository institutions) in the form of checking deposits, preventing currency growth would prevent any future growth in the transactions or exchange media measure of money.[40]

However, Weintraub finds such a result undesirable because, he opines, some growth in the money supply is necessary "to accommodate our economy's long-term growth potential."[41] His proposal, therefore, includes a provision for increasing the legal value of gold, which would initially be set at the current $42.22 per ounce, at a stipulated monthly rate. This would bring about an effective expansion in the Fed's reserve of gold certificates and permit a corresponding increase in currency in circulation and, hence, in the overall money supply. Weintraub favors an annual rate of increase in the par value of gold which would ultimately facilitate a 3 percent per annum rate of growth in the supply of money. Weintraub expresses the belief, moreover, that "the plan should prove attractive to both monetarists and gold standard advocates."[42] In fact, it should appeal to neither group and for good reason.

To begin with, Weintraub's plan is essentially an attempt to realize through legislation the monetarist goal of a steady and predictable rate of growth of the money supply within the existing monetary framework. Its main drawback, from the monetarist perspective, is that it involves a needlessly complicated and cumbersome technique to achieve the desired goal. Why not simply legally mandate the Fed to pursue a straightforward "quantity rule," as the monetarists have always argued? Weintraub does not provide an answer to this question, if he has one at all.

Advocates of a gold standard, on the other hand, also should find little to be pleased about in this proposal because a gold certificate reserve requirement is not a genuine gold standard at all. Under the gold standard, the monetary unit *is* a weight unit of gold; under Weintraub's plan, gold is not money but a reserve commodity which is supposed to restrain the creation of government fiat money. Furthermore, since Weintraub's proposal leaves untouched the inherently inflationary government monopoly of the money supply, it is unreasonable to expect that the gold certificate reserve requirement, even if enacted, would long serve as a bulwark against inflation. The most likely prospect is that it would be gradually reduced and finally eliminated altogether, no doubt in the wake of a series of "crises." Indeed, Weintraub fully recognizes and is prepared for such a prospect, arguing that his plan "could be amended if the constraint proved to be harmful, and probably it could be changed or repealed in a day or two in such an unlikely case."[43]

Moreover, past experience with the gold certificate reserve also leads to the expectation that it would provide a weak and easily manipulated restraint on inflation. Thus, up until World War II, the Fed was legally required to hold a 35 percent gold certificate reserve for its deposit liabilities and a 40 percent reserve for its note liabilities. To facilitate the wartime inflation, the reserve requirement was reduced to 25 percent for both the Fed's note and deposit liabilities. As a result of persistent, inflation-reduced balance-of-payments deficits, the gold certificate reserve requirement for the Fed's deposit liabilities was abolished in 1965 while the reserve requirement for its note liabilities was finally eliminated in 1968. In conclusion, what Weintraub proposes is not a gold standard but an unwieldly and historically ineffective expedient designed to mitigate the inflationary tendencies of a government fiat money.

## (2) The Gold "Price Rule"

The gold "price rule" denotes the monetary reform proposal put forth in various forms by a number of supply-siders including Arthur Laffer,[44] Robert Mundell,[45] and Jude Wanniski.[46] Laffer's detailed formulation of the proposal has also served as the basis of the Gold Reserve Act of 1980, a bill introduced in Congress by Senator Jesse Helms.[47] According to Laffer's blueprint, at the end of a previously announced transition period of three months, the Federal Reserve would establish an official dollar price of gold "at that day's average transaction price in the London gold market."[48] From that date onward, the Fed would stand ready to convert dollars freely into gold and gold into dollars at the official price. In addition, "when valued at the official price, the Federal Reserve will attempt over time to establish an average dollar value of gold reserves equal to 40 percent of the dollar value of its liabilities."[49] This level of gold reserves Laffer designates as the "target reserve quantity."

Once Laffer's plan was fully operational, the Fed would have full discretion in conducting monetary policy through discounting, open market operations, etc., provided that: (1) the dollar remains fully convertible into gold at the official price; and (2) the quantity of actual gold reserves does not deviate from the target reserve quantity by more than 25 percent in either direction, i.e., actual gold reserves do not fall below 30 percent or rise above 50 percent of the Fed's liabilities, which are also known as the "monetary base." However, should gold reserves decline to a level between 20 percent and 30 percent of its liabilities, the Fed would lose all discretion in determining the monetary base which, as a result, would be completely frozen at the existing level. If, in spite of this, gold reserves continued to decline to between 10 percent and 20 percent of the Fed's liabilities, the Fed would be legally constrained to reduce the monetary base at the rate of one percent per month.

Should these measures prove incapable of arresting the decline of the dollar value of gold reserves before it reaches less than 10 percent of Fed liabilities:

> The dollar's convertibility will be temporarily suspended and the dollar price of gold will be set free for a three month adjustment period.
>
> During this temporary period of inconvertibility, the monetary authorities will be required to suspend all actions that would affect the monetary base. Again, the price of gold would be reset as before and convertibility would be reinstated.[50]

Laffer's plan also includes "a symmetric set of policy dicta" which are to be implemented in the case in which actual gold reserves exceed the target reserve quantity.

The first point which must be made regarding Laffer's monetary reform proposal is that, whatever its merits or drawbacks, it is *not* a blueprint for a gold standard. Rather, it is an outline of an elaborate scheme for legally constraining the monetary authority to adhere to a "price rule" in determining the supply of fiat money in the economy. In fact, as Laffer himself made clear recently, gold has no necessary role in the implementation of such a price rule. According to Laffer and Miles:

> The Fed would institute its dollar "price rule" by stabilizing the value of the dollar in terms of an external standard. This standard would be a single commodity or a basket of commodities (a price index). . . .
> Regardless of precisely which external standard is chosen, there are two basic rules of Fed behavior under the price rule. First, if the dollar price of the standards starts to rise (the dollar starts to fall in value), the Fed must reduce the quantity of dollars through open market sales of bonds, foreign exchange, gold, or other commodities. Second, if the dollar price starts to fall (the dollar rises in value), the Fed must increase the quantity of dollars through open market purchases of bonds, foreign exchange, gold or other commodities. The Fed is charged with keeping the value or price of the dollar stable in terms of the external standard.[51]

Even if gold is chosen as the "external standard" in the price rule regime, it is not itself money, as in the case of a genuine gold standard, but merely "the intervention asset" or "the item for which dollars are exchanged."[52]

Thus stripped of its gold standard terminology, Laffer's price rule appears as a technique designed to control inflation under the current fiat-money standard. It is thus very similar in nature, if not in technical detail, to the quantity rule advocated by the monetarists. This is clearly evident in Laffer and Miles's admission that "in an unchanging world where all information is freely available, there of course would be a 'quantity rule' which would correspond to a given 'price rule.' "[53] In fact, Miles and Laffer prefer a price rule to a quantity rule because they believe that, *under the current monetary system*, the former is technically superior to the latter in "restraining the supply of dollars."[54]

Thus, under close examination, Laffer's plan turns out to be, in essence, a kind of price rule monetarism, the references to gold notwithstanding. As such, it is vulnerable to criticism on precisely the same grounds as the more conventional quantity rule monetarism. The most serious criticism of both varieties of monetarism is that they fail to come to grips with the root cause of inflation, namely, the government monopoly of the supply of money. This is true of Laffer's plan despite the elaborate set of legal sanctions which would be invoked against the monetary authorities for their violations of the price rule. For, in the end, such sanctions, even if rigorously applied, do not prevent inflation but merely respond to a fait accompli. This point is implicitly recognized by Laffer who includes in his plan a provision for "temporary periods" of dollar inconvertibility for the purpose of readjusting the official gold price following sustained violations of the price rule.

Furthermore, as in the case of the gold certificate reserve, we may appeal to history for evidence regarding the success of the gold price rule in stanching the flow of government fiat currency. We need look no further than the late, unlamented Bretton Woods system (1946-1971). Under this "fixed exchange rate" system, the U.S. monetary authority followed a gold price rule, buying and selling gold at an officially fixed price of $35 per ounce. Foreign monetary authorities, on the other hand, pursued a dollar price rule, maintaining their respective national currencies convertible into dollars at a fixed price. According to Laffer and Miles, "as long as the rules of the system were being followed, the supplies of all currencies were constricted to a strict price relationship among one another and to gold."[55] Unfortunately, "the rules of the system" were subjected to numerous and repeated government violations and evasions, including frequent outright "readjustment" of the price rules—exchange rate devaluations—when they became inconvenient restraints on the inflationary policies pursued by particular governments.[56] Needless to say, the Bretton Woods system did not prevent the development of a worldwide inflation which brought the system to its knees in 1968 and led to its final collapse in 1971.

After duly noting the political manipulations involved in the destruction of the Bretton Woods system,[57] Laffer and Miles clearly delineate the reasons why governments prefer and benefit from the removal of any and all checks on their power to inflate the money supply:

> Why should governments be biased toward increasing the money supply at a faster rate? There are essentially two incentives—a political incentive and a financial one. The political incentive is political survival. Many politicians, especially those up for reelection, are familiar with the theory that increases in the money supply promote expenditure, increase GNP, and reduce unemployment. These changes in turn are assumed to make the citizen of the country look more kindly upon the incumbent government. While there may be some validity in this theory, unfortunately it is often implemented under the notion that if a little money creation is good, a lot must be even better.
>
> The financial motive for printing money is the fact that while money is practically costless to produce, it can be used for purchasing goods and services. The resulting seigniorage represents revenue to the government. Revenue gathered in this way means less revenue must be gathered in another way, say, through direct taxation.
>
> Given these incentives to print money, it can be seen why removal of the monetary constraints on governments tends to create inflation rather than deflation.[58]

Given his recognition of the powerful inflationary bias built into the political process and of the historical failure of monetary price rules to hold such a bias in check, Laffer's advocacy of a renewed gold price rule is something of a mystery.

### (3) The "Classical" Gold Standard

Over the past few years, the case for reinstituting the "classical" gold standard has been propounded with great vigor and insight by Lewis Lehrman, a businessman and scholar whose views were influential in formulating the economic policy agenda of the Reagan administration.[59] Lehrman's writings in turn are heavily influenced by the ideas of his former teacher, the late French economist and long-time gold standard advocate, Jacques Rueff.[60] Like his mentor, Lehrman advocates a genuine gold standard which "would establish the dollar as a weight unit of gold."[61] As Lehrman explains:

> Under the gold standard there is no price for gold. The dollar is the monetary standard, set by law equal to a weight of gold. The price of gold does not exist. . . Under the gold standard, the paper dollar is a promissory note. It is a claim to a real article of wealth defined by law as the standard.[62]

In Lehrman's proposal, Federal Reserve notes as well as dollar-denominated demand deposits at commercial banks and other depository institutions would once more become (as they were prior to 1933) warehouse receipts to gold, instantly redeemable for gold dollars at face value upon the demand of the bearer or depositor. Legal reserve requirements for bank deposits would be superfluous since "the failure to redeem . . . excess dollars for gold would, under convertibility rules, threaten the bankruptcy and dissolution of a commercial bank."[63] The monetary authority, for its part, would be "constrained . . . by law to redeem excess dollars with specified weight units of gold. . . ."[64] Or, in other words, it must stand ready "to buy and sell at the official rate all the gold offered or all the gold demanded."[65] The Fed would furthermore be restrained from carrying out any open market operations, although it would be permitted to lend reserves to commercial banks at an "unsubsidized" discount rate, i.e., at a rate at or slightly above the market rate.

Without going into further detail, it is clear that Lehrman proposes a monetary system which very closely approximates the classical gold standard with all its strengths and weaknesses. The most serious weakness of the classical gold standard and of Lehrman's proposal is the predominant role played by what Lehrman himself calls "a monopoly central bank."[66] Lehrman is willing to countenance the existence of such an institution and, indeed, to cede significant powers to it so long as it adopts "reasonable self-denying ordinances."[67] Thus, for example, the Fed would be expected to abstain from manipulating the gold content of the dollar or from directly purchasing assets on the open market. On the other hand, under Lehrman's plan, it would still retain its monopoly of the note issue and its position as the central warehouse and clearinghouse for commerical bank reserves. Moreover, its discretion with regard to discount rate policy would still permit it to function as a "lender of last resort."

With so much power over the monetary system thus concentrated in the hands of a government institution, it is no wonder that Lehrman repeatedly refers to the gold standard as a "political institution"[68] and not once as a "free market institution." In fact, at one point, Lehrman comes perilously close to conceiving the gold standard as price rule monetarism, that is, as merely an efficient political technique for controlling the government monopoly of the money supply. Thus, he writes:

> To be sure, Monetarists would claim to fix the total quantity of money, through a specified money stock rule, in order to regulate the government monopoly (the Federal Reserve Board) which supplies cash balances to the market. Yet the simpler, market-related technique would be to make the value of a unit of money equal to a weight unit of gold, in order to regulate the same monopoly.[69]

In any case, since government is an inherently inflationary instituton, it can be expected to be an implacable enemy of the gold standard. Under these circumstances, to grant to a government institution, such as a central bank, a powerful influence over the operation of the gold standard is not unlike offering the fox an invitation to guard the chicken coop. This is surely the lesson taught by the broad sweep of monetary history, especially in more recent times when we have the spectacle of Western governments employing every means at their disposal to progressively transmogrify the classical gold standard into our current, highly inflationary system of fluctuating national fiat currencies. Von Mises does not exaggerate when he states that:

> The gold standard did not collapse. Governments abolished it in order to pave the way for inflation. The whole grim apparatus of oppression and coercion—policemen, customs guards, penal courts, prisons, in some countries even executioners—had to be put into action in order to destroy the gold standard. Solemn pledges were broken, retroactive laws were promulgated, provisions of constitutions and bills of rights were openly defied.[70]

Von Mises proceeds to demolish the deeply entrenched myth, one Lehrman appears to accept, which likens the gold standard to a political "game" wherein the government players must adhere to some vaguely specified "rules of the game." Writes von Mises:

> But the gold standard is not a game; it is a market phenomenon, and as such a social institution. Its preservation does not depend on the observation of some specific rules. It requires nothing else than that the government abstain from deliberately sabotaging it. To refer to this condition as a rule of an alleged game is no more reasonable than to declare that the preservation of Paul's life

> depends on compliance with the rules of Paul's life game because
> Paul must die if somebody stabs him to death.[71]

In summary, there is no compelling reason to believe—and one searches Lehrman's writings in vain to find any argument to the contrary—that the classical gold standard will prove to be a more durable barrier to political manipulation of the money supply the second time around than it was the first time.

Aside from its overriding political flaw, Lehrman's proposal is characterized by serious economic shortcomings. These are ultimately related to the fact that the type of gold standard that Lehrman proposes is what Hayek has termed a "national reserve system."[72] The essential feature of such a system is fractional reserve banking combined with the concentration of the ultimate cash reserves of all banks within the nation in the nation's financial center or, more likely, in the government central bank.

An historical example of the operation of the national reserve system is provided by the classical gold standard. Under this system, the central bank generally holds the ultimate cash reserve, in this case, gold, for the entire national banking system. The gold reserve serves as immediate backing for the central bank's note and deposit liabilities which, in turn, constitute the reserve base for the notes and deposits of commercial banks. The latter are held, along with central bank notes and gold itself, in the money balances of the public. Since both the central bank and the commercial banks hold fractional reserves against their liabilities, the money and credit structure of the economy resembles an inverted pyramid, with a relatively narrow base of gold reserves supporting a much larger superstructure of bank notes and deposits ultimately convertible into gold.

The result is that the classical gold standard was and is extremely vulnerable to monetary deflations and inflations due to balance of payments disequilibria, changes in the public's preferences for holding gold vis-à-vis bank notes and deposits, financial crises, etc. The reason for this is that any loss or gain of gold reserves by the banking system causes a multiple expansion or contraction of bank notes and deposits which constitute a large proportion of the money supply. These frequent bouts of monetary inflation and deflation, moreover, are likely to be aggravated by the fact that the very mechanism by which the banking system adjusts to changes in the gold reserve base involves an artificial alteration in the entire structure of interest rates in the economy which necessarily leads to a distortion in productive activity.

A brief example will suffice to illustrate this point. Suppose that the central bank is faced with an outflow of gold reserves due to a balance of payments deficit. In order to arrest and reverse this outflow, it will raise the discount rate and thus contract its loans to commercial banks. Commercial bank reserves will, as a result, decline, and, in order to maintain their accustomed or legally required ratio between reserves and liabilities, the banks will be forced to reduce their loans by raising the interest rate they charge. Since the bulk of these loans are taken up for investment purposes, investment spending in the economy will decline relative to consumption spending. This will naturally induce a shift in productive resources and monetary investment away from the production of capital goods and toward the production of consumers' goods.

Unfortunately, this outcome, the rise of interest rates and the decline of investment relative to consumption, does not reflect a genuine and voluntary shift in the time preferences of the public—that is, deliberate choices to save less of their income and spend more on consumption. Consequently, the expansion of consumers' goods industries at the expense of capital goods industries will eventually prove to be unsustainable, resulting in widespread economic losses when economic activity is finally readjusted to more faithfully reflect the time preferences of consumer-savers in the economy. As a matter of fact, the day of reckoning will come when the monetary deflation engineered by the central bank has lowered prices and incomes in the country sufficiently so that the balance of payments deficit is transformed into a surplus and gold reserves flow back into the banking system permitting a "reflation" of the money supply.

On the other hand, an initial influx of gold reserves into the banking system from abroad will set off a monetary inflation, accompanied by declining interest rates and a concomitant boom in investment spending. In this case, productive resources will be bid out of the production of consumers' goods into the production of capital goods. When the inflation comes to a halt, however, interest rates and the allocation of income to consumpton and saving will once again conform to the true time preferences of market participants, and the numerous malinvestments and resource misallocations will be revealed and corrected amidst widespread unemployment and business failures.

In light of the foregoing analysis, it is my belief that Lehrman's plan for restoring the classical gold standard, while it will undeniably provide greater long-run stability in the value of money than the present fiat money regime, will not rid us of the recurring fluctuations in macroeconomic activity which have plagued the market economy for the past two centuries. I hasten to stress that this is not a defect of the gold standard itself but of its organization along the lines of the national reserve system described above. In fact, most of the oft-noted defects of the classical gold standard lie in precisely those areas where its operation diverges from that of a fully free market, 100 percent gold standard. This point has been cogently argued by Leland Yeager:

> National fractional reserve systems are the real source of most of the difficulties blamed on the gold standard. . . . The difficulties arise because the mixed national currencies—currencies which are largely paper, only partly gold—are insufficiently international. The main defect of the historical gold standard is a necessity of

'protecting' national gold reserves. . . . In short, whether a Central Bank amplifies the effects of gold flows, remains passive in the face of gold flows, or 'offsets' gold flows, its behavior is incompatible with the principles of the full-fledged gold standard. . . . Indeed, any kind of monetary management runs counter to the principles of the pure gold standard.[73]

On the other hand, notes Yeager:

> Under a 100 percent hard-money international gold standard, the currency of each country would consist exclusively of gold (or of gold plus fully backed warehouse receipts for gold in the form of paper money and token coins). The government and its agencies would not have to worry about any drain on their reserves. The gold warehouses would never be embarrassed by requests to redeem paper money in gold, since each dollar of paper money in circulation would represent a dollar of gold actually in a warehouse. There would be no such thing as independent national monetary policies; the volume of money in each country would be determined by market forces. The world's gold supply would be distributed among the various countries according to the demands for cash balances of the individuals in the various countries. There would be no danger of gold deserting some countries and piling up excessively in others, for each individual would take care not to let his cash balance shrink or expand to a size which he considered inappropriate in view of his own income and wealth.

> Under a 100 percent gold standard . . . the various countries would have a common monetary system, just as the various states of the United States now have a common monetary system. There would be no more reason to worry about disequilibrium in the balance of payments of any particular country than there is now reason to worry about disequilibrium in the balance of payments in New York City. If each individual (and institution) took care to avoid persistent disequilibrium in his personal balance of payments, that would be enough. . . . The actions of individuals in maintaining their cash balances at appropriate levels would 'automatically' take care of the adequacy of each country's money supply.[74]

### (4) The de facto Gold Standard

The most innovative plan for achieving a gold money is that proposed by Professor R. H. Timberlake. Timberlake's plan holds forth great promise because, unlike the preceding three plans that have been examined, it is predicated on the recognition that inflation "will be stopped only by fundamental changes in the Fed."[75] Thus, Timberlake's plan "would begin with the abolition of the Federal Reserve System as a policy-making central bank."[76] Timberlake foresees no technically insurmountable barriers to such a course of action. He argues that the regulatory functions of the Fed can easily be dispensed with since "banks have no more reason to be regulated than grocery stores" and "should be left alone to justify their existence in a free market system."[77] Regarding the check clearing services provided by the Fed to its member banks, Timberlake points to privatization as the simple and sensible solution. Writes Timberlake:

> The technical check clearing operations of the Federal Reserve
> Bank could still be handled by the existing physical facilities.
> Federal Reserve Banks could be reorganized as regional bank
> clearing houses. Since the Fed banks are already legally owned by
> commercial banks that exercise no control or ownership, the
> solution is simple: Turn the Federal Reserve Banks over to the
> legitimate owners and let the member banks operate them. This
> change would probably result in many interesting innovations and
> economies in bank management and checking facilities.[78]

This brings us to the Fed's functions relating to the execution of
monetary policy. According to Timberlake, these are at best superfluous and at worst highly inflationary. In the case of reserve requirements, Timberlake contends that "banks can manage their own reserve
necessities," noting that "no other system in the world employs reserve
requirement laws to regulate commercial banks."[79] The discounting
function Timberlake holds to be "both unnecessary and undesirable."
Not only does it play a minor role in the Fed's execution of monetary
policy, but commercial banks are able to fulfill their needs for reserves
by borrowing from one another on the well organized and private
federal funds market. "Ending Federal Reserve discounting," writes
Timberlake, "therefore, would simply be ending something that is
largely an advertising gimmick for promoting the image of the Fed as a
banker's welfare agency."[80]

But what of open market operations, "the process that keeps the
money stock growing at inflationary rates?" It is in answering this
question that Timberlake introduces his proposal for a *de facto* gold
standard. First, the U.S. Treasury would sell its entire gold stock (260
million ounces) or distribute a pro rata share to every U.S. citizen
either in coin or in redeemable certificates. Second, the "policymaking
structure of the Federal Reserve System" would be abolished. Finally,
the outstanding note liabilities of the Fed, the currency in circulation,
would be frozen and the member bank reserve accounts converted into
Federal Reserve notes. The commercial banks would have the option
of holding the latter in their own vaults or leaving them on deposit in
the "new" regional clearing houses. Timberlake expects that the gold,
once in private hands, would soon find its way into private depository
institutions, thus giving rise to gold-based demand deposits and notes
redeemable upon demand in gold or Federal Reserve notes at the
option of the depositor. According to Timberlake:

> This new system would not be a gold *standard* because the
> government would not declare gold or anything else legal tender. . ..
>
> Gold-based deposits and currency would circulate side by side
> with the frozen stock of existing federal reserve notes. Prices of
> gold in terms of other moneys would be quickly determined by
> market factors.[81]

Timberlake's proposal includes the two elements that are absolutely
essential to the establishment of a free market commodity money: (1)

the complete liquidation of the government monopoly of money, and (2) the return of the gold stock to private hands. As a result, it is far superior to the first three proposals which I have analyzed because all of them leave the existing structure of the Federal Reserve System, for the most part, untouched. Moreover, under the plans of Laffer and Lehrman, even though the public can convert dollars into gold, the Fed still retains strategic control over the nation's gold stock by virtue of its position as a monopoly "banker's bank."

From the standpoint of the advocate of the 100 percent gold standard, Timberlake's proposal does involve one drawback. By stipulating only that depository institutions are legally required to redeem their notes and demand deposits for gold upon demand, Timberlake is opening the door to a system of "free banking" based on fractional reserves. Although this system would, in fact, produce a much sounder and "harder" money than even the classical gold standard, there would still be potential, albeit severely limited, for inflation.[82] More important than the direct economic effects of such inflation, however, there looms the distinct possibility that the political authority may use the occasional, but highly visible, financial crises and bank failures which follow in the wake of the inflationary boom as a pretext for regulation of the banks "in the public interest." Having thus regained its first crucial foothold, the government would be well on its way to reimposing its monopoly over money.

# Notes

1. *See* "Return to an International Gold Standard Opposed by U.S. Panel Majority at Debate," *Wall Street Journal*, October 27, 1981, p. 16.

2. McCracken's remarks are reported in Rowland Evans and Robert Novak, "Gold Standard Rears Its Head Again," *New York Post*, August 5, 1981, p. 29.

3. Federal Reserve Bank of St. Louis, *International Economic Conditions* (August 15, 1981), p. 50.

4. Ibid., p. 51.

5. Ibid., pp. 52, 53.

6. Federal Reserve Bank of St. Louis, *Monetary Trends* (September 25, 1981), pp. 2, 5.

7. Editorial, "Blaming Volcker," *Wall Street Journal*, October 14, 1981, p. 28.

8. Ibid.

9. Robert J. Barro, "Money and the Price Level under the Gold Standard," *Economic Journal* 89 (March 1979): 31.

10. Roy W. Jastram, *The Golden Constant: The English and American Experience 1560-1976* (New York: John Wiley & Sons, 1976).

11. Idem, "The Gold Standard: You Can't Trust Politics," *Wall Street Journal*, May 15, 1981, p.32.

12. Ibid.

13. Edward M. Bernstein, "Back to the Gold Standard?" *Brookings Bulletin* 17 (Fall 1980): 8-12.

14. Michael David Bordo, "The Classical Gold Standard: Some Lessons for Today," *Review of the Federal Reserve Bank of St. Louis* 63 (May 1981): 2-17.

15. William Fellner, "Gold and the Uneasy Case for Responsibly Managed Fiat Money" in idem, ed., *Essays in Contemporary Economic Problems: Demand, Productivity, and Population* (Washington, D.C.: American Enterprise Institute for Public Policy Research, 1981), pp. 97-121.

16. Herbert Stein, "Professor Knight's Law of Talk," *Wall Street Journal*, October 14, 1981, p. 28.

17. William Nordhaus, "Gold in the Year of the Quack," *New York Times*, October 4, 1981, section F, p. 3.

18. Henry C. Wallich, "Should We (and Could We) Return to the Gold Standard?" *New York Times*, September 6, 1981, section E, p. 4.

19. Ludwig von Mises, *On the Manipulation of Money and Credit*, ed. Percy L. Greaves, Jr. and trans. Bettina Bien Greaves (Dobbs Ferry, N.Y.: Free Market Books, 1978), p. 22.

20. Idem, *On Current Monetary Problems* (Lansing, Mich.: Constitutional Alliance, Inc., 1969), pp. 29-30.

21. For works detailing the nature and operation of a pure commodity money, *see* Murray N. Rothbard, *The Case for a 100 Per Cent Gold Dollar* (Washington, D.C.: Libertarian Review Press, 1974) reprinted from idem, "The Case for a 100 Per Cent Gold Dollar," in Leland Yeager, ed., *In Search of a Monetary Constitution* (Cambridge, Mass.: Harvard University Press, 1962), pp. 94-136; Murray N. Rothbard, *What Has Government Done to Our Money?* (Novato, Cal.: Libertarian Publishers, 1978); Milton Friedman, *Essays in Positive Economics* (Chicago: The University of Chicago Press, 1970), pp. 206-10; idem, *A Program for Monetary Stability* (New York: Fordham University Press, 1959), p. 4-8; idem, "Should There Be an Independent Monetary Authority," in Yeager, *In Search of a Monetary Constitution*, pp. 220-24; Jacques Rueff, "The Fallacies of Lord Keynes's General Theory," in Henry Hazlitt, ed., *The Critics of Keynesian Economics* (Princeton, N.J.: D. Van Nostrand Company, Inc., 1960), pp. 242-46; Mark Skousen, *The 100 Percent Gold Standard: Economics of a Pure Money Commodity* (Lanham, Md.: University Press of America, Inc., 1980).

22. This important distinction between the "economic means" and the "political means" of acquiring income was drawn by the German sociologist and economist, Franz Oppenheimer. *See* Franz Oppenheimer, *The State*, trans. John Gitterman (New York: Free Life Editions, Inc., 1975).

23. F.A. Hayek, *Denationalization of Money—The Argument Refined: An Analysis of the Theory and Practice of Concurrent Currencies*, 2nd enl. ed. (London: The Institute of Economic Affairs, 1978).

24. F.A. Hayek, "Toward a Free Market Monetary System," *Journal of Libertarian Studies* 3, no. 1 (1979): 7.

25. Fellner, "Gold and the Uneasy Case for Responsibly Managed Fiat Money," p. 99.

26. Friedman, "Should There Be an Independent Monetary Authority," pp. 220-22.

27. John Maynard Keynes, *The General Theory of Employment, Interest, and Money* (New York: Harcourt, Brace & World, Inc., 1964), p. 132.

28. Murray N. Rothbard, *Man, Economy, and State: A Treatise on Economic Principles*, 2 vols. (Los Angeles: Nash Publishing, 1970), 2: 742. For a description and critique of the tabular standard, *see also* Edwin W. Kemmerer, *Money: The Principles of Money and Their Exemplification in Outstanding Chapters of Monetary History* (New York: The Macmillan Company, 1937), pp. 103-107.

29. Kemmerer, *Money*, pp. 76-77.

30. Ludwig von Mises, *Human Action: A Treatise on Economics*, 3rd rev. ed. (Chicago: Henry Regnery Company, 1966), p. 425.

31. For abundant evidence of the long-run stability of the purchasing power of gold in English and American monetary experience, *see* Jastram, *The Golden Constant*.

32. Hayek, "Toward a Free Market Monetary System," p. 5.

33. Friedman, "Should There Be an Independent Monetary Authority," pp. 223-24.

34. Mises, von, *Human Action*, p. 422.

35. Ibid., p. 249.

36. Very few economists have taken issue with the resource-cost argument against a commodity money. Two who have come to my attention are the nineteenth-century American monetary economist and 100 percent gold standard advocate, Francis Amasa Walker, and the eminent French monetary theorist, Charles Rist. Both explicitly attacked the argument on the grounds that it ignores the qualitative aspects of money. *See* Francis Amasa Walker, *Money* (New York: August M. Kelley Publishers, 1968), pp. 521-528; and Charles Rist, *History of Monetary and Credit*

*Theory: From John Law to the Present Day*, trans. Jane Degras (New York: Augustus M. Kelley Publishers, 1966), pp. 80-90.

37. On government actions which helped foster the supercession of standard units of weight by national currency names, *see* Rothbard, *The 100 Percent Gold Dollar*, pp. 12-19.

38. U.S., Congress, Joint Economic Committee, *The Gold Standard: Its History and Record Against Inflation*, by Roy W. Jastram, with an Appendix on "Restoring the Gold Certificate Reserve," by Robert E. Weintraub (Washington, D.C.: Government Printing Office, 1981), pp. 21-24. Weintraub's plan is also described in Lindley H. Clark, Jr., "What Kind of a Gold Standard Is Needed?" *Wall Street Journal*, August 19, 1981, p. 33.

39. Weintraub, "Restoring the Gold Certificate Reserve," p. 21.

40. Ibid., p. 22.

41. Ibid.

42. Ibid., p. 24.

43. Quoted in Clark, "What Kind of a Gold Standard Is Needed?" p. 33.

44. Arthur Laffer, *Reinstatement of the Dollar: The Blueprint* (Rolling Hill Estates, Cal.: A.B. Laffer Associates, 1980). *See also* Arthur B. Laffer and Charles W. Kadlec, "The Point of Linking the Dollar to Gold," *Wall Street Journal*, October 13, 1981, p. 32.

45. Robert A. Mundell, "Gold Would Serve into the 21st Century," *Wall Street Journal*, September 30, 1981, p. 33.

46. Jude Wanniski, *The Way the World Works* (New York: Simon and Schuster, 1978), especially pp. 161-67. *See also* Jude Wanniski, "A Job Only Gold Can Do," *New York Times*, August 27, 1981, p. A31.

47. The text of Helms's bill is reproduced in Ernest P. Welker, *Plans to Revive the Gold Standard*, Economic Education Bulletin, vol. 20, no. 10 (Great Barrington, Mass.: American Institute for Economic Research, 1980), pp. 7-9.

48. Laffer, *Reinstatement of the Dollar*, p. 4.

49. Ibid.

50. Ibid., p. 5.

51. Arthur B. Laffer and Marc A. Miles, *International Economics in an Integrated World* (Glenview, Ill.: Scott Foresman and Company, 1982), p. 399-400.

52. Ibid., p. 400.

53. Ibid., p. 401.

54. Ibid.

55. Ibid., p. 260.

56. For accounts of the breakdown of the Bretton Woods System, *see* Jacques Rueff, *The Monetary Sin of the West*, trans. Roger Glemet (New York: The Macmillan Company, 1972); and Guillaume Guindey, *The International Monetary Tangle: Myths and Realities*, trans. Michael L. Hoffman (White Plains, N.Y.: M.E. Sharpe, Inc., 1977).

57. Laffer and Miles, *International Economics*, pp. 259-62.

58. Ibid., pp. 397-98.

59. Lehrman has stated his views on the gold standard in a number of publications, including: Lewis E. Lehrman, *The Case for the Gold Standard: Reflections on the Struggle for Financial Order* (New York: Morgan Stanley & Co., Inc., 1981); idem, *Monetary Policy, the Federal Reserve, and Gold* (New York: Morgan Stanley & Co., Inc., 1980); idem, "The Case for the Gold Standard," *Wall Street Journal*, July 30, 1981, p. 33; idem, "Should We (and Could We) Return to the Gold Standard?" *New York Times*, September 6, 1981, p. E4.

60. For Rueff's views on the gold standard, *see* Jacques Rueff, *The Age of Inflation*, trans. A.H. Meeus and F.G. Clarke (Chicago: Henry Regnery Company, 1964); and idem, *Balance of Payments: Proposals for the Resolution of the Most Pressing World Economic Problem of Our Time*, trans. Jean Clement (New York: The Macmillan Company, 1967).

61. Lehrman, *The Case for the Gold Standard*, p. 21.

62. Idem, "Should We (and Could We) Return to the Gold Standard?" p. E4.

63. Idem, *Monetary Policy, the Federal Reserve System, and Gold*, p. 41.

64. Ibid.

65. Lehrman, *The Case for the Gold Standard*, p. 20.

66. Ibid., p. 6.

67. Ibid.

68. Ibid., pp. 8, 10, 17, 18.

69. Lehrman, *Monetary Policy, the Federal Reserve System, and Gold*, p. 40.

70. Ludwig von Mises, *The Theory of Money and Credit*, trans. H.E. Batson, new enl. ed. (Irvington-on-Hudson, N.Y.: The Foundation for Economic Education, Inc., 1971), p. 420.

71. Ibid.

72. For a discussion of the nature and operation of the national reserve system, *see* F. A. Hayek, *Monetary Nationalism and International Stability*, (New York: Augustus M. Kelley Publishers, 1971), pp. 1-34 passim.

73. Leland B. Yeager, "An Evaluation of Freely-Fluctuating Exchange Rates," (Ph.D. diss. Columbia University, 1952), pp. 11-17.

74. Ibid., pp. 9-10.

75. R.H. Timberlake, Jr., "Solving the Monetary Crisis," *Policy Report* 3 (October 1981): 9.

76. Ibid.

77. Ibid.

78. Ibid.

79. Ibid., p. 10.

80. Ibid.

81. Ibid.

82. For the definitive discussion and defense of the "free banking" system, *see* von Mises, *The Theory of Money and Credit*; also idem, *Human Action*, pp. 434-448.